MATHEMATICAL THEORY OF DOMAINS

Cambridge Tracts in Theoretical Computer Science

Titles in the series

1. G. Chaitin *Algorithmic Information Theory*
2. L.C. Paulson *Logic and Computation*
3. M. Spivey *Understanding Z*
4. G. Revesz *Lambda Calculus, Combinators and Functional Programming*
5. A. Ramsay *Formal Methods in Artificial Intelligence*
6. S. Vickers *Topology via Logic*
7. J-Y. Girard, Y. Lafont & P. Taylor *Proofs and Types*
8. J. Clifford *Formal Semantics & Pragmatics for Natural Language Processing*
9. M. Winslett *Updating Logical Databases*
10. K. McEvoy & J.V. Tucker (eds) *Theoretical Foundations of VLSI Design*
11. T.H. Tse *A Unifying Framework for Stuctured Analysis and Design Models*
12. G. Brewka *Nonmonotonic Reasoning*
14. S.G. Hoggar *Mathematics for Computer Graphics*
15. S. Dasgupta *Design Theory and Computer Science*
17. J.C.M. Baeten (ed) *Applications of Process Algebra*
18. J.C.M. Baeten & W. P. Weijland *Process Algebra*
21. D.A. Wolfram *The Clausal Theory of Types*
22. V. Stoltenberg-Hansen, I. Lindström & E. Griffor *Mathematical Theory of Domains*
23. E.-R. Olderog *Nets, Terms and Formulas*
26. P.D. Mosses *Action Semantics*
27. W.H. Hesselink *Programs, Recursion and Unbounded Choice*
29. P. Gärdenfors (ed) *Belief Revision*
30. M. Anthony & N. Biggs *Computational Learning Theory*
31. T.F. Melham *Higher Order Logic and Hardware Verification*
32. R.L. Carpenter *The Logic of Typed Feature Structures*
33. E.G. Manes *Predicate Transformer Semantics*
34. F. Nielson & H.R. Nielson *Two Level Functional Languages*
35. L. Feijs & H. Jonkers *Formal Specification and Design*
36. S. Mauw & G.J. Veltink (eds) *Algebraic Specification of Communication Protocols*
37. V. Stavridou *Formal Methods in Circuit Design*

MATHEMATICAL THEORY OF DOMAINS

Viggo Stoltenberg-Hansen
Ingrid Lindström and Edward R. Griffor
University of Uppsala

CAMBRIDGE
UNIVERSITY PRESS

CAMBRIDGE UNIVERSITY PRESS
Cambridge, New York, Melbourne, Madrid, Cape Town, Singapore, São Paulo

Cambridge University Press
The Edinburgh Building, Cambridge CB2 8RU, UK

Published in the United States of America by Cambridge University Press, New York

www.cambridge.org
Information on this title: www.cambridge.org/9780521383448

First published 1994
This digitally printed version 2008

A catalogue record for this publication is available from the British Library

ISBN 978-0-521-38344-8 hardback
ISBN 978-0-521-06479-8 paperback

CONTENTS

PREFACE

A domain is a structure modelling the notion of approximation and of computation. A computation performed using an algorithm proceeds in discrete steps. After each step there is more information available about the result of the computation. In this way the result obtained after each step can be seen as an approximation of the final result. This final result may be reached after finitely many steps as, for example, when computing the greatest common divisor of two positive integers using the Euclidean algorithm. However, it may also be the case that a computation never stops, in which case the final result *is* the sequence of approximations obtained from each step in the computation. The latter situation occurs by necessity when computing on infinite objects such as real numbers. Thus an appropriate model of approximation can provide a good model of computation.

To be somewhat more technically precise, a domain is a structure having one binary relation $\sqsubseteq$, a partial order, with the intended meaning that $x \sqsubseteq y$ just in case x is an approximation of y or y contains at least as much information as x. We also require that a domain should include a least element modelling no information. This is not necessary, but is useful for establishing the existence of fixed points. To model infinite computations we require a domain to be complete in the sense that each increasing sequence of approximations should be represented by an element in the domain, that is, should have a supremum. These requirements suffice for obtaining fixed points of continuous functions and also to build function spaces.

An actual computation is performed on concrete objects. For example, a computation on real numbers consists of computations on concrete approximations to real numbers, often the rational numbers. The result of a computation is also given by a sequence of concrete elements. Thus, in order to model computations, we need to abstract the notion of being a concrete element. This abstraction is called a compact element. We require that each element of a domain is represented by all its compact approximations. The structures we have described thus far are called algebraic complete partial orders (cpo's). This class of structures seems to have the computability properties we want, but it lacks one property important for computer science and also for parts of computability theory. The class of algebraic cpo's is not closed under the function space construction! Thus we consider a subclass of the algebraic cpo's, namely those which are consistently complete. These structures, which we call domains, are the main objects of our study.

Domain theory is by now an established and much used part of theoretical computer science. Introductory texts on the *use* of domain theory in giving semantics of programming languages, such as Stoy [1977] and Gordon [1979], appeared at a rather early stage. However, there seemed to be no real attempt to make the *theory* of domains, that is its mathematics, easily accessible in, say, text book form. The only available introduction to the mathematical part of domain theory has until recently been G. Plotkin's "Pisa notes" (Plotkin [1981]), which unfortunately are more cited than generally available. Our book is an attempt to fill this gap by being an introductory text presenting domain theory as a piece of mathematics. We believe that in order to be able to use domain theory properly in computer science it is absolutely necessary to have a proper mathematical understanding of the subject. For this reason we hope that our book will be a significant contribution to the theoretical computer science literature. In addition, we think that domain theory is an interesting subject in itself as a theory of computability. In fact, the initial contributions to the subject were made by mathematical logicians. Hence the subject should be of interest not only to students of computer science but also to mathematicians and logicians.

We have not made any attempt to give an explicit account of the history of the subject. In fact, for the basic parts of the theory we have not included many references, which perhaps is a sign of a maturing subject. Let us therefore record, once and for all, that the creation of and the initial and fundamental contributions to the subject are due to D. S. Scott and Y. L. Ershov, in that order. For the later parts we have been more generous with references in order for the reader to be able to further pursue certain directions, but we make no claims of being complete. Only a very small part of the results in the text and the problems is due to the authors.

This book has its origin in a seminar series held in Uppsala by two of the authors (Stoltenberg-Hansen and Lindström) in the year 1984–1985. The manuscript reached its embryonic state as handwritten notes for a course on the mathematical theory of domains given jointly by all three authors in Uppsala in the spring of 1986. That course, which incorporated (with permission) some notes by Stan Wainer from a course on the mathematical theory of computation in Leeds, was too ambitious in that it covered subjects from each chapter but one of the final manuscript. However, the course did decide the shape of this book.

The book consists of two parts. The first part contains the basic material on the mathematical theory of domains whereas the second part contains more special topics such as representability of structures using domains, effective domains, power domains and models of the λ-calculus. It has not been possible to cover all topics of domain theory and all the various types of domains existing in the literature. For example, we have not included a discussion of continuous domains nor of stability. Our omissions by no means imply that we regard these topics as unimportant. We hope that the original papers describing such topics are easily accessible to readers having mastered the basic material of our book. If this is true and if some readers acquire sufficient interest in the subject to pursue further topics then we will be well pleased with the result of our effort.

Early versions of parts of the manuscript have been used in courses taught at Uppsala, Göteborg, Passau and Swansea. The courses given in Uppsala have had as core material Chapters 1 through 4 and parts of Chapters 5 and 6. In addition, some topics from the remaining chapters have been included depending on the taste of the instructor and the interest of the students.

Due to possible (and actual) confusion we need to say a few words about the numbering system used. Each chapter is divided into a number of sections. Each section is given a two digit number, the first indicating the chapter and the second indicating the section within the chapter. Thus Section 4.2 denotes the second section of the fourth chapter. Each numbered statement, that is definition, theorem, proposition, lemma, example or remark, is given a two digit number, the first indicating the section (within the chapter) and the second the statement. Thus Definition 2.1 in Chapter 4 is the first numbered statement of Section 4.2. When referring to this definition within Chapter 4 we simply say Definition 2.1, while we say Definition 4.2.1 when referring to the same definition outside of Chapter 4.

Each author is responsible for a part of the manuscript as follows:

V. Stoltenberg-Hansen: Chapters 1, 2, 3, 5, 8, 9 and 10.
I. Lindström: Chapters 4, 7 and 11.
E. R. Griffor: Chapters 0, 6 and 12.

However, much of the material has been discussed, criticised and amended by the authors.

A number of people have read parts of early drafts of the manuscript and have provided (sometimes extensive) lists of corrections and suggestions and also much encouragement. In particular, we thank Jirí Adámek, Ulrich Berger, Jens Blanck, Karl Meinke, Erik Palmgren, Helmut Schwichtenberg, Inger Sigstam, Gunnar Sjödin and John V. Tucker. We thank Stan S. Wainer for his kind permission to use his lecture notes, which have strongly influenced Sections 1.1 and 9.3. We also thank David Tranah of Cambridge University Press for his patience and encouragement.

Finally we would like to thank students of domain theory in Uppsala and Göteborg who suffered early exposure to our manuscript. Not only did they provide constructive criticisms of the contents and presentation but they also generated enthusiasm making it very enjoyable to teach the subject, in fact so enjoyable that we fell for the temptation to write this book.

Uppsala
October 1993

Viggo Stoltenberg-Hansen
Ingrid Lindström
Edward R. Griffor

CHAPTER 0

PRELIMINARIES

Some concepts and elementary results from the theory of sets, the theory of ordered sets and category theory will be assumed in the chapters that follow. In this chapter we will review these for the sake of completeness. We shall make use of the symbols $\neg$, $\wedge$ (or &), $\vee$, $\rightarrow$ (or $\Rightarrow$) and $\leftrightarrow$ (or $\Leftrightarrow$) to denote the propositional logical connectives *not*, *and*, *or*, *implies* and *logical equivalence*. In addition we use the notation $\forall x$ and $\exists x$ for the quantifiers *for all* x and *there exists* x.

Section 0.1 Some Basic Notions of Set Theory

We shall work within *naive set theory*. The terms set or collection of objects will be used to refer to the same thing. The statement a *is an element of the set* X will be abbreviated by $a \in X$. A set is determined by its elements in the sense that two sets having the same elements are the *same* set. The simplest set is the *empty set*, denoted by $\varnothing$, that is the set having no elements. Less trivial examples are the set of real numbers, $\mathbb{R}$, the set of natural numbers, $\mathbb{N}$, and the set of rational numbers, $\mathbb{Q}$. A set A is a *subset* of another set B, denoted by $A \subseteq B$, if all elements of A are also elements of B. The collection of all subsets of a set B is called the *power set* of B and is denoted by $\wp(B)$. Often we are only concerned with the *finite* subsets of a set B and use instead $\wp_f(B)$ to denote the collection of all finite subsets of B. A is a *proper subset* of B, denoted by $A \subset B$, if A is a subset of B but A is not equal to B. The *complement* of a set $A \subseteq X$ in X, denoted by $X - A$, is the set of all elements of X which are not elements of A. If X is understood then we write instead A^c for the complement of A in X.

Sets are often referred to by giving a property which all of its elements, and no others, have. More precisely, if X is a set and P(x) is a statement about or property of the elements of X, then $\{x \in X : P(x)\}$ (or $\{x \in X \mid P(x)\}$) will denote that *subset* of X consisting of all x for which P(x) is true. This means of referring to sets is useful, since giving a set by explicitly giving all its elements is a method we can only hope to succeed with for rather small finite sets. A *class* is the extension of a property, that is, all objects having that property, and will be denoted in *set notation*: $\{x : P(x)\}$. A class which is not a set is called a *proper class*. The assumption that all classes are sets leads to well-known paradoxes, e.g., Russell's paradox where the assumption that the class $\{x : x \notin x\}$ is a set leads to a contradiction.

Given sets A and B, we denote by $A \cup B$, $A \cap B$, $A \times B$ and $A \uplus B$ the *union, intersection, cartesian product* and *disjoint union* of A and B, respectively. If J is a set and A_j is a set, for each $j \in J$, then we denote by $(A_j)_{j \in J}$ the *family of sets* A_j *indexed by* J. Given a family of sets $(A_j)_{j \in J}$, then $\bigcup_{j \in J} A_j$, $\bigcap_{j \in J} A_j$, $\prod_{j \in J} A_j$ and $\biguplus_{j \in J} A_j$ denote the *union, intersection, cartesian product* and *disjoint union* of the A_j, respectively. Perfectly general representations of the elements of the latter two operations on families are, in the case of a product, as functions or sequences $f : J \to \bigcup_{j \in J} A_j$ satisfying $f(j) \in A_j$ and, in the case of disjoint union, as ordered pairs (j, a) where $a \in A_j$. The former are often written as sequences $(a_j)_{j \in J}$ where a_j is an element of A_j for each j, or simply as (a_j). If $n \in \mathbb{N}$ and A is a set, then the *n-fold cartesian product* of A with itself, denoted A^n, is defined by induction on n:

$$A^1 = A \text{ and } A^{n+1} = A^n \times A.$$

If A and B are sets, then a (*total*) *function* (or a *mapping*) f *from* A *to* B, denoted $f : A \to B$, is an operation which to each $a \in A$ associates an element $f(a)$ of B. We use $\lambda x.(\dots x \dots)$ as shorthand for *the function which takes* x *to* $(\dots x \dots)$. In Chapter 12 this informal notion is replaced by $\boldsymbol{\lambda}$ in order to avoid confusion with the corresponding formal symbol of the λ-calculus. Another notation used to refer to *the function which takes* x *to* $(\dots x \dots)$ is $x \mapsto (\dots x \dots)$. Two functions $f, g : A \to B$ are said to be *equal*, if for all $a \in A$ we have that $f(a) = g(a)$. For $n \in \mathbb{N}$, an *n-ary function from* A *to* B is a function $f : A^n \to B$ and then n is said to be the *arity of* f, that is, the number of arguments f requires. As usual, we write $f(a_1, \dots, a_n)$ instead of $f((a_1, \dots, a_n))$. In case $A = B$ we say that f is an *n-ary operation on* A. Given functions $f : A \to B$ and $g : B \to C$, the *composite function* (the composition of f and g), denoted $g \circ f : A \to C$, is the function defined by:

$$g \circ f(x) = g(f(x)), \text{ for all } x \in A.$$

For $A' \subseteq A$ and $f : A \to B$, the *restriction of* f *to* A', denoted $f|_{A'}$, is given by $f|_{A'}(x) = f(x)$, for all $x \in A'$. On the other hand if $f : A \to B$ and $g : X \to B$ for some X such that $A \subseteq X$, then we say that g is an *extension* of f if, for each $x \in A$, $g(x) = f(x)$. The *image of* A' *under* f is denoted by $f[A']$, that is, $f[A'] = \{f(a) : a \in A'\}$. A function $f : A \to B$ is *injective*, if $f(x) = f(y)$ implies that $x = y$; f is *surjective*, if for all $z \in B$ there is an $x \in A$ such that $f(x) = z$;

and f is *bijective* (or a *one-to-one correspondence*), if f is both injective and surjective. Two sets A and B are said to have the same size or *cardinality*, denoted by $|A|=|B|$, if there exists a bijection $f: A \to B$. A set which can be put in one-to-one correspondence with the natural numbers less than some given one is said to be *finite*. A set A is *infinite* if there is an injective function $f: \mathbb{N} \to A$, and A is *countable* if there is a surjective function $f: \mathbb{N} \to A$. An infinite set is said to be *countably infinite* if it is countable, otherwise it is said to be *uncountable*.

A *partial function* from A to B, $f: A \xrightarrow{p} B$, is an operation which to each element of the set A may or may not associate an element of B; if $a \in A$ and the operation f *does* associate to a an element $f(a) \in B$, then we say that f(a) is *defined at* a and write $f(a)\downarrow$ (otherwise f is *undefined at* a and we denote this by $f(a)\uparrow$). Given $f, g: A \xrightarrow{p} B$ and $a \in A$, we write $f(a) \simeq g(a)$ to denote the fact that if one of f(a) or g(a) is defined, then both are defined and $f(a)=g(a)$ (this notion was introduced by S. C. Kleene, see Kleene [1952], and called *complete* or *strong equality*). Given $f: A \xrightarrow{p} B$, the *domain of* f, denoted by dom(f), is defined by $\mathrm{dom}(f)=\{a \in A : f(a)\downarrow\}$. For any f, total or partial from A to B, we define the *range of* f, denoted rg(f), by $\mathrm{rg}(f)=\{b \in B : (\exists a \in A) f(a) \simeq b\}$. The set of all total functions from A to B is denoted by B^A or simply by $A \to B$, while the set of partial functions is denoted by $A \xrightarrow{p} B$. Clearly, $A \to B \subseteq A \xrightarrow{p} B$. Given $f: A \xrightarrow{p} B$, the *graph of* f, denoted by graph(f), is given by

$$\mathrm{graph}(f)=\{(a,b) \in A \times B : f(a) \simeq b\}.$$

Identifying a function with its graph, it is natural to say that a 0-ary function is just a constant. If A' is a subset of A, then we have the *inclusion mapping* from A' to A, $\iota: A' \to A$ defined by $\iota(a)=a$. If $A=A'$, then the inclusion mapping is denoted by $\mathrm{id}_A: A \to A$.

A *binary relation* from a set A to a set B (a *binary relation on* A, if $A=B$) is a subset of $A \times B$. We often use infix notation and write aRb instead of $(a,b) \in R$ to denote the statement that a *bears the relation* R *to* b. Clearly, any subset of $A \times B$ is a binary relation from A to B. More generally, any subset of $A_1 \times A_2 \times \ldots \times A_n$ is an *n-ary relation* between the sets $A_1, A_2, \ldots, A_n$ (an n-ary relation *on* A if $A=A_1=A_2=\ldots=A_n$). For a relation $R \subseteq A^n$ and $B \subseteq A$, the *restriction of the relation* R *to* B, denoted $R|_B$, is just:

$$R|_B = R \cap B^n.$$

In analogy with the corresponding definition for functions, the relation R in this case is said to be an *extension* of the relation $R|_B$.

The case of a binary relation has an additional interpretation in terms of directed graphs. A *graph* is a triple (N, E, Δ) consisting of a set of *nodes* N, a set of *edges* E and a function Δ from E to sets of nodes having at most two elements. If Δ is taken instead to be a function from E to $N\times N$ then (N,E,Δ) is said to be a *directed graph*.

By a *mathematical structure*, or simply a *structure*, we will mean a tuple:

$$A=(A;R_1,\dots,R_m,f_1,\dots,f_n),$$

where A is a non-empty set, the *underlying set* or *universe* of the structure A, R_i is a t_i-ary relation on A (i.e., $R_i\subseteq A^{t_i}$) and f_j is a k_j-ary operation on A. Notice that we use the same symbol to denote a structure and its underlying set. Note also that some of the f_j may be 0-ary, that is, constants or elements of A. The tuple consisting of the arities of the various relations and functions of a structure, in this case $(t_1,\dots,t_m;k_1,\dots,k_n)$, is called the *similarity type* or simply the *type* of the structure A. A structure $A=(A;R_1,\dots,R_m,f_1,\dots,f_n)$ is said to be a *substructure* of a structure $B=(B;S_1,\dots,S_m,g_1,\dots,g_n)$, if $A\subseteq B$ and for each i and j, $R_i=S_i|_A$ and $f_j=g_j|_A$.

Let $A=(A;R_1,\dots,R_m,f_1,\dots,f_n)$ and $B=(B;S_1,\dots,S_m,g_1,\dots,g_n)$ be two structures with similarity type $(t_1,\dots,t_m;k_1,\dots,k_n)$. A *homomorphism* or simply a *morphism from* A *to* B is a function $\varphi:A\longrightarrow B$ such that, for all i and j and all $(c_1,\dots,c_{t_i})\in A^{t_i}$, $(d_1,\dots,d_{k_j})\in A^{k_j}$:

$$(c_1,\dots,c_{t_i})\in R_i \Leftrightarrow (\varphi(c_1),\dots,\varphi(c_{t_i}))\in S_i$$

and

$$\varphi(f_j(d_1,\dots,d_{k_j}))=g_j(\varphi(d_1),\dots,\varphi(d_{k_j})).$$

The homomorphism $\varphi:A\longrightarrow B$ is said to be an *isomorphism*, if the function φ is a bijection. Two structures A and B are *isomorphic*, denoted by $A\cong B$, if there exists an isomorphism $\varphi:A\longrightarrow B$.

Section 0.2 Ordered Sets

Let A be a set. A binary relation R on A is *reflexive*, if aRa, for all $a\in A$; R is *symmetric* just in case aRb implies bRa, for all $a,b\in A$; R is *transitive*, if, for all $a,b,c\in A$, aRb and bRc imply that aRc; and R is *antisymmetric*, just in case aRb and bRa imply that $a=b$. R is an *equivalence relation*, if R is reflexive, symmetric and transitive, in which case $[a]_R=\{b\in A: aRb\}$ denotes the *equivalence class of* a with respect to the equivalence relation R. The *quotient of* A *by* R, where R is an equivalence relation, is the collection of all equivalence classes and is denoted by A/R. In this case, there is a canonical mapping of

A onto A/R, $\pi_R: A \to A/R$, given by $\pi_R(a) = [a]_R$. We will omit the subscript R in $[a]_R$ and π_R if the equivalence relation is clear from the context.

2.1 Example Let $J' \subseteq J$ be sets and let $(A_j)_{j\in J}$ be a family of sets indexed by J. For $(a_j)_{j\in J}, (b_j)_{j\in J} \in \prod_{j\in J} A_j$, set $(a_j)_{j\in J} \sim (b_j)_{j\in J}$ if $a_j = b_j$ for all $j \in J'$. Then $\sim$ is an equivalence relation on $\prod_{j\in J} A_j$. If $\pi: \prod_{j\in J} A_j \to \prod_{j\in J} A_j/\sim$ is the canonical mapping onto the quotient, then $\pi(f)$ can naturally be interpreted as an element of $\prod_{j\in J'} A_j$ namely $f|_{J'}$.

Some simple examples of mathematical structures are various kinds of *orderings on a set.* Given a set A, a *preorder on* A (often denoted by $\leq$ in analogy with familiar orderings on numbers) is a reflexive and transitive relation on A. A *partial order on* A is a preorder which is also antisymmetric. A *total* or *simple order on* A is a partial order on A which satisfies:

$$a \leq b \text{ or } b \leq a, \text{ for all } a, b \in A.$$

The latter is also frequently called a *linear order* on A. A linearly ordered subset of a partially ordered set is called a *chain.* Preordered sets, partially ordered sets and totally ordered sets are sets with, respectively, a preorder, a partial order or a total order on that set.

Let A be a partially ordered set and $S \subseteq A$. An element $a \in A$ is an *upper bound* for S in A, if $x \leq a$, for all $x \in S$; an upper bound a for S is a *least upper bound* or *supremum* for S (abbreviated by $\sup S$) if for any upper bound a' for S, we have that $a \leq a'$. Analogously, one defines a *lower bound* for S and a *greatest lower bound* or *infimum* for S (denoted by $\inf S$). Note that each $S \subseteq A$ has at most one supremum (infimum). An element $a \in A$ is said to be *maximal* if there are no elements strictly greater than a, that is if $a \leq b \Rightarrow b \leq a$, in which case $a = b$. The following is a useful variant of the axiom of choice.

2.2 Zorn's Lemma A non-empty partially ordered set in which each chain has an upper bound has at least one maximal element.

The definitions in the paragraph preceding the lemma make sense as well for preorders although then suprema and infima need no longer be unique.

A linear ordering $\leq$ on a set A is a *well-ordering*, if each non-empty $S \subseteq A$ has a least element, that is there is $s \in S$ such that $s \leq s'$, for all $s' \in S$. A set X is said to be *transitive*, if $x \in X$ implies $x \subseteq X$. Finally, a set X is an *ordinal* (*number*), if it is transitive and well-ordered by the relation $\in$. Lowercase Greek letters, $\alpha, \beta, \gamma, \ldots$, are used to denote ordinals. **OR** is the class of all ordinals. Define, for each set X, $X+1 = X \cup \{X\}$. Clearly $\varnothing$ is an ordinal and if $\alpha \in \mathbf{OR}$ then $\alpha + 1 \in \mathbf{OR}$ (the reader should verify that $\alpha + 1$ is the least ordinal greater than α). If $\alpha=\beta+1$ for some ordinal β then we say that α is a *successor ordinal*; otherwise α is a *limit ordinal.* The union of a set of ordinals is easily seen to be an ordinal and the least non-empty limit ordinal ω is the union of (or the supremum with respect to $\in$ of) the set of all finite ordinals. Natural numbers are identified with finite ordinals using the following recursive definition on $\mathbb{N}$:

$$\underline{0}=\varnothing$$
$$\underline{n+1}=\underline{n}\cup\{\underline{n}\}=\underline{n}+1.$$

Then $\omega=\{\underline{n}: n\in\mathbb{N}\}$ and we may (and do) identify $\mathbb{N}$ with ω. It is a fact that each well-ordered set is isomorphic to a unique ordinal (as ordered sets). Thus the definition of ordinals is a way of choosing one canonical representative of each isomorphism class of well-orderings. Two important consequences of well-orderings and hence of the notion of an ordinal are the principles of *transfinite induction* and *transfinite recursion,* generalizing the principles of induction and recursion for the natural numbers.

Limits

There are two notions of *limit of a system of sets*, where an essential ingredient comes from the theory of ordered sets. They can be viewed as generalizations of the union and intersection of a family of sets. We say that a partially ordered set I is *directed*, if it is non-empty and if, for all $a,b\in I$, there is a $c\in I$ such that $a\le c$ and $b\le c$. A *directed system of sets* indexed by a directed set I, consists of a set A_a for each $a\in I$ and a collection of functions $f_{a,b}:A_a\to A_b$, for every pair $a,b\in I$ such that $a\le b$, where:

$$f_{a,a}=id_{A_a}:A_a\to A_a,\ \text{for all } a\in I;$$

and

$$f_{a,c}=f_{b,c}\circ f_{a,b}:A_a\to A_c,\ \text{for } a\le b\le c \text{ in } I.$$

We denote the directed system by $(A_a,f_{a,b})$. The *direct limit* of the directed system $(A_a,f_{a,b})$ is defined to be a set $\varinjlim(A_a,f_{a,b})$, together with a family of functions $f_a:A_a\to\varinjlim(A_a,f_{a,b})$ such that, for $a\le b$, $f_a=f_b\circ f_{a,b}$, and satisfying a *universality* condition stating that: if B is a set together with a family of functions $g_a:A_a\to B$ satisfying $g_a=g_b\circ f_{a,b}$, for $a\le b$, then there is a unique function $g:\varinjlim(A_a,f_{a,b})\to B$ such that $g\circ f_a=g_a$, for all $a\in I$.

The standard construction of a solution to this *universal problem* is to take the set in question to be $(\uplus_{a\in I}A_a)/{\sim}$, where $\sim$ is the equivalence relation on the set $\uplus_{a\in I}A_a$ obtained by setting $(a,x)\sim(b,y)$ just in case there is a $c\ge a,b$ such that $f_{a,c}(x)=f_{b,c}(y)$. The functions f_a are then defined by letting $f_a(x)=[(a,x)]$, for $x\in A_a$.

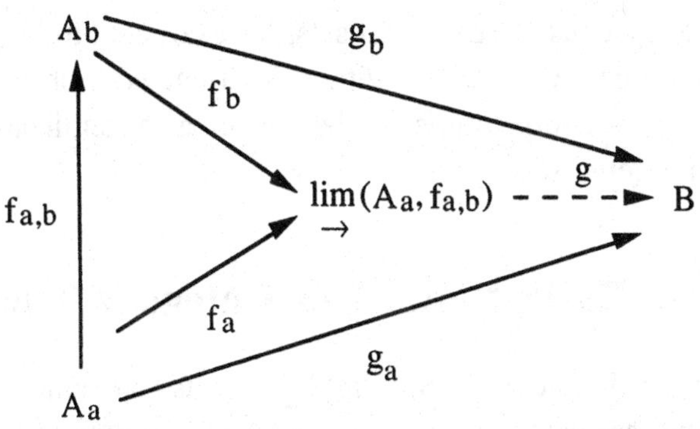

Figure 2.1 A diagram displaying the universality condition in the definition of the direct limit of a directed system of sets.

Dual to the notion of a directed system of sets is an *inverse* or *projective system of sets* $(A_a, f_{a,b})$ which consists of a family of sets A_a indexed by $a \in I$ (I directed), together with a family of functions $f_{a,b}: A_b \longrightarrow A_a$ (notice the direction of this arrow!) for $a \leq b$ such that:

$$f_{a,a} = id_{A_a} \text{ and } f_{a,c} = f_{a,b} \circ f_{b,c}, \text{ for } a \leq b \leq c \text{ in I.}$$

The *inverse limit* of $(A_a, f_{a,b})$, is defined as a set $\underleftarrow{\lim}(A_a, f_{a,b})$, together with functions $f_a: \underleftarrow{\lim}(A_a, f_{a,b}) \longrightarrow A_a$ such that if $a \leq b$, then $f_a = f_{a,b} \circ f_b$, which satisfies the universality condition stating that: given B and $g_a: B \longrightarrow A_a$ such that $g_a = f_{a,b} \circ g_b$, for $a \leq b$, then there is a unique function $g: B \longrightarrow \underleftarrow{\lim}(A_a, f_{a,b})$ such that $g_a = f_a \circ g$, for all $a \in I$. The standard construction of a solution in the case of an inverse limit is to take the set consisting of all sequences $(x_a)_{a \in I} \in \prod_{a \in I} A_a$ such that, if $a \leq b$, then $f_{a,b}(x_b) = x_a$. The functions f_a are then simply the projections given by setting $f_a((x_a)_{a \in I}) = x_a$.

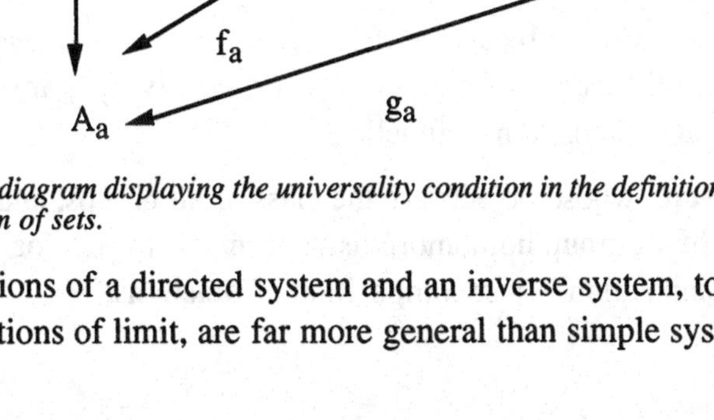

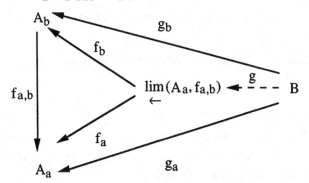

Figure 2.2 A diagram displaying the universality condition in the definition of the inverse limit of an inverse system of sets.

The notions of a directed system and an inverse system, together with their respective notions of limit, are far more general than simple systems of sets. They are equally applicable to systems of structured sets, for example groups, rings, ordered sets, etc.; and are naturally treated within the framework of *category theory*. There the direct and inverse limits can be viewed as generalizations of suprema and infima on ordered sets.

Section 0.3 Some Basic Notions of Category Theory

The direct limit of a directed system of sets $\underrightarrow{\lim}(A_a, f_{a,b})$ is an example of a set where another set, in this case each A_a, can be identified *in a natural way* with a subset, although A_a is not, properly speaking, a subset of $\underrightarrow{\lim}(A_a, f_{a,b})$. The natural representation of $x \in A_a$ in the construction of $\underrightarrow{\lim}(A_a, f_{a,b})$ mentioned in the previous section is $[(a,x)]_\sim$ and, in fact, $f_a(x) = [(a,x)]_\sim$. In a similar fashion, one structured set can often be seen to be a *substructure* of another modulo a "relabelling" of its elements. A systematic way of studying this and related questions is to consider some class of mathematical structures of the same *sort* together with relabellings or functions preserving that structure. The field of mathematics which takes this as its point of departure is known as *category theory*.

A *category* $\mathbf{C}$ consists of a class of *objects*, also denoted by $\mathbf{C}$ (be it sets, mathematical structures or simply "abstract" objects), together with, for each pair of objects $a, b \in \mathbf{C}$, a *set* of *morphisms from* a *to* b denoted by $\mathrm{Hom}_{\mathbf{C}}(a,b)$ (be it functions, homomorphisms or simply abstract *arrows*). When there is no danger of confusion between categories, we shall write simply $\mathrm{Hom}(a,b)$ for the set of morphisms from a to b. For each $a \in \mathbf{C}$, $\mathrm{Hom}_{\mathbf{C}}(a,a)$ contains a distinguished element, denoted by id_a, *the identity morphism of* a. With the sets $\mathrm{Hom}_{\mathbf{C}}(a,b)$ is associated an operation of *composition* satisfying, for all $a,b,c \in \mathbf{C}$:

(i) if $f \in \mathrm{Hom}_{\mathbf{C}}(a,b)$ and $g \in \mathrm{Hom}_{\mathbf{C}}(b,c)$, then $g \circ f \in \mathrm{Hom}_{\mathbf{C}}(a,c)$
(ii) if $f \in \mathrm{Hom}_{\mathbf{C}}(a,b)$, then $f \circ id_a = f$ and $f = id_b \circ f$
(iii) if $f \in \mathrm{Hom}_{\mathbf{C}}(a,b)$, $g \in \mathrm{Hom}_{\mathbf{C}}(b,c)$ and $h \in \mathrm{Hom}_{\mathbf{C}}(c,d)$, then $(h \circ g) \circ f = h \circ (g \circ f)$.

3.1 Examples

(1) The *category* **Set**, whose objects are the class of all sets, and where $\mathrm{Hom}(x,y)$ is the set of all functions from x to y or, simply, y^x, for $x, y \in \mathbf{Set}$. Composition is the usual composition of functions.

(2) The *category* **Grp**, whose objects are the class of all groups, and where $\mathrm{Hom}(G,H)$ is the set of all group homomorphisms from G to H, for $G, H \in \mathbf{Grp}$. Again composition is just composition of functions.

(3) The *category* **Top**, whose objects are the class of all topological spaces, and where $\mathrm{Hom}(X,Y)$ is the set of all continuous functions from X to Y, for $X, Y \in \mathbf{Top}$. Composition is composition of functions.

(4) If V is a collection of sets, then we have the *category* $\mathbf{Set}_V$ whose objects are all the elements of V, and where $\mathrm{Hom}(x,y) = y^x$, for $x, y \in V$. Composition is, as with **Set**, composition of functions.

(5) The *category* **Rng**, whose objects are the class of all rings, and where $\mathrm{Hom}(R,Q)$ is taken to be the set of all ring homomorphisms from R to Q, for $R, Q \in \mathbf{Rng}$. Composition is composition of functions.

(6) Any *set* A *with a preordering* $\leq$ is a category $\mathbf{C}_A$. The class of objects $\mathbf{C}_A$ is A and

$$\mathrm{Hom}(a,b) = \begin{cases} \{i_{a,b}\} & \text{if } a \leq b \\ \varnothing & \text{otherwise} \end{cases}$$

for $a, b \in \mathbf{C}_A$. Finally, we set $i_{b,c} \circ i_{a,b} = i_{a,c}$. Note how the existence of identity morphisms and the definition of composition in a category correspond to the axioms for a preordered set.

An *initial* (*terminal*) *object* in a category $\mathbf{C}$ is an object $c \in \mathbf{C}$ such that, for all objects $d \in \mathbf{C}$, there is exactly one morphism $f \in \mathrm{Hom}_{\mathbf{C}}(c,d)$ ($f \in \mathrm{Hom}_{\mathbf{C}}(d,c)$). In the case of example (6) above of a preorder, an initial or terminal object corresponds to a least or largest element in that preorder.

3.2 Remarks

(a) Other notations for the collections of arrows of a category are, for two objects a and b in a category $\mathbf{C}$, to write $\mathbf{C}(a,b)$ or $\mathrm{Mor}_{\mathbf{C}}(a,b)$ for the collection of morphisms from a to b.

(b) **Rng** and **Grp**, as well as **Set** and $\mathbf{Set}_V$, are examples of pairs of categories where one category is *included* in another in different ways. Every ring is a group under its additive operation and every ring homomorphism can be seen as a corresponding group homomorphism. On the other hand, a group homomorphism need not be a ring homomorphism. In a similar fashion, we have that the objects of $\mathbf{Set}_V$ are all objects of **Set**, but in this case we have that the morphisms between objects common to both categories are the same.

(c) Examples (1)–(5) are called *concrete* categories, since the morphisms are functions (with or without additional preservation properties); instances like example (6) are called *abstract*. We shall, primarily, be concerned with concrete categories. We say that a category $\mathbf{C}$ is *large*, if its objects comprise a proper class (otherwise, **C** is *small*). Thus, examples (4) and (6) are small, while the others are examples of large categories.

Commutative Diagrams

A fundamental tool of category theory is the graphic representation of equalities between compositions of morphisms which are called *commutative diagrams.* A *diagram* is simply a directed graph (equivalently, a two-place relation on a set), whose vertices are objects of a category **C** and whose edges are labelled by morphisms of the same category **C** in such a way that, if an edge labelled with f from a to b occurs in a diagram, then $f \in \mathrm{Hom}_{\mathbf{C}}(a,b)$. Such a diagram is said to be *commutative*, if, for every pair of vertices a and b, any two paths consisting of directed edges leading from a to b in the diagram yield, by the composition of their labels, equal morphisms from a to b.

3.3 Example A simple example is the associativity of a category **C**'s composition operation, which is expressed as the commutativity of a diagram in the category **C** (see Figure 3.1 below).

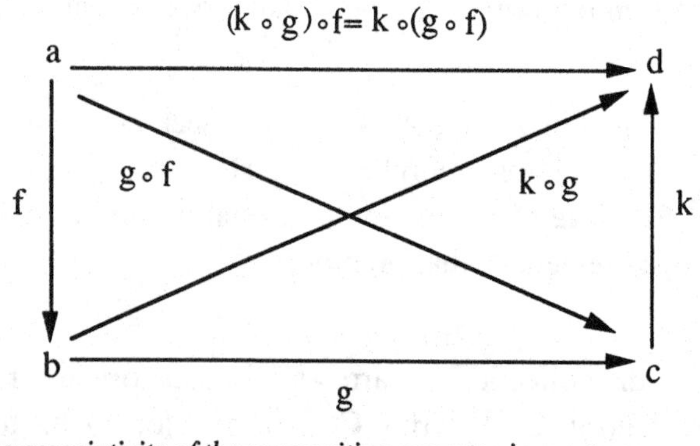

Figure 3.1 The associativity of the composition operator in a category expressed in terms of the commutativity of a diagram.

Many properties of mathematical constructions can be represented by *universal properties of diagrams.* Consider the *cartesian product* of two sets X and Y, $X \times Y = \{(x,y): x \in X \text{ and } y \in Y\}$, where (x, y) is the ordered pair of x and y. The *projections* $(x,y) \mapsto x$ and $(x,y) \mapsto y$ on the *axes* X and Y are functions $\pi_0 : X \times Y \longrightarrow X$ and $\pi_1 : X \times Y \longrightarrow Y$. Any function from a third set W into the set $X \times Y$, $h : W \longrightarrow X \times Y$, is uniquely determined by the two compositions $\pi_0 \circ h$ and $\pi_1 \circ h$. On the other hand, given a set W and two functions $f : W \longrightarrow X$ and $g : W \longrightarrow Y$, then there is a unique $h : W \longrightarrow X \times Y$, namely $h(w) = (f(w), g(w))$, which makes the corresponding diagram commutative (see Figure 3.2).

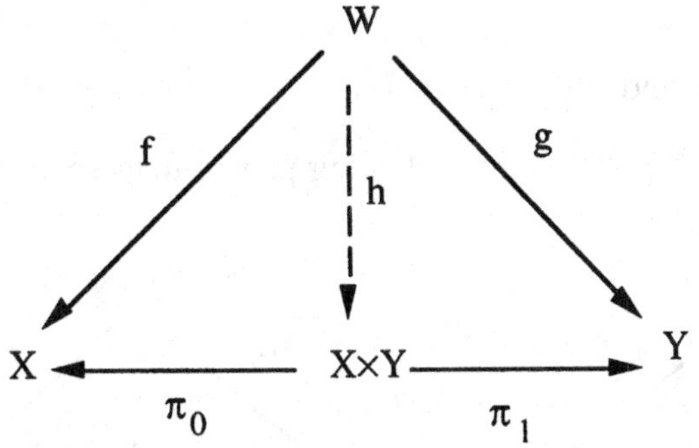

Figure 3.2 The diagram expressing the universality of the standard projection maps π_0 *and* π_1 *for the Cartesian product of two sets.*

Thus given sets X and Y, we say that X×Y together with the pair of mappings (π_0, π_1) is *universal among pairs of functions from some set to* X *and to* Y, *respectively,* since any other such pair (p,q) factors *uniquely* via h through (π_0, π_1) (that is, can be written as a *product,* in the sense of the composition of the category, of π_0, respectively π_1, and some unique h). This property describes, in **Set**, the cartesian product of two sets X×Y uniquely. To facilitate an explanation of the latter claim, let $a, b \in \mathbf{C}$, **C** a category. We say that a *is isomorphic to* b *in* **C**, if there exists $f \in \mathrm{Hom}_{\mathbf{C}}(a, b)$ and $g \in \mathrm{Hom}_{\mathbf{C}}(b, a)$ such that $g \circ f = id_a$ and $f \circ g = id_b$ (we call such a pair, (f,g), an *isomorphism pair*).

Returning to the uniqueness of X×Y in **Set**: suppose that some other set Z and a pair (p,q) had the universal property expressed above for all W and maps (f,g). Applying that property to X×Y and (π_0, π_1), while at the same time applying that same property of X×Y and (π_0, π_1) to Z and (p,q), we obtain the diagram in Figure 3.3.

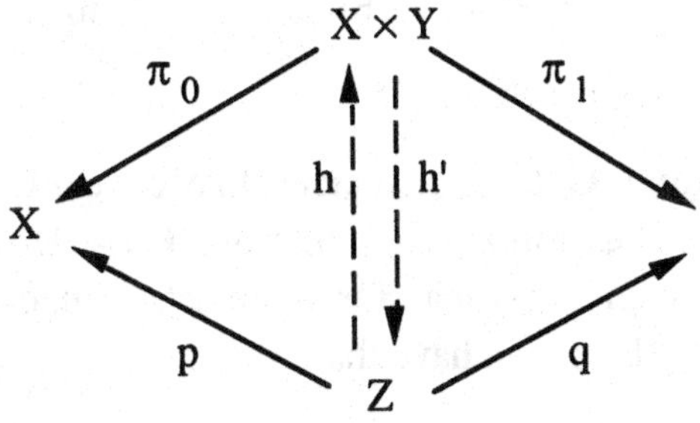

Figure 3.3 The diagram resulting from the assumption that X×Y *with* (π_0, π_1) *and* Z *with* (p,q) *both enjoy the above universal property.*

Its commutativity, together with the associativity of composition, yields the equalities:

$$p = p \circ (h' \circ h) \quad \text{and} \quad q = q \circ (h' \circ h),$$

as well as

$$\pi_0 = \pi_0 \circ (h \circ h') \text{ and } \pi_1 = \pi_1 \circ (h \circ h').$$

These equalities, in turn, imply that the following pair of diagrams are commutative.

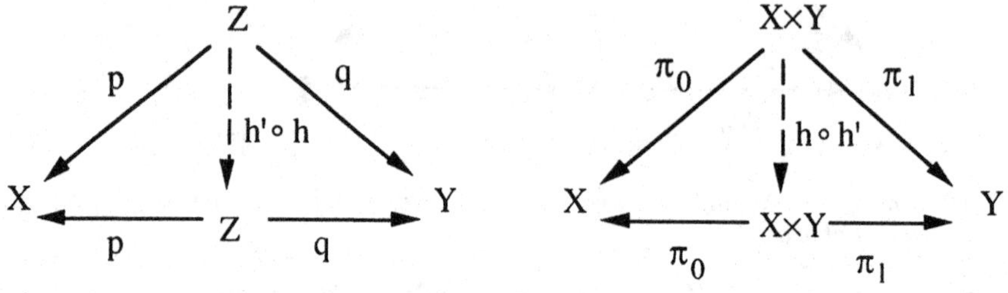

Figure 3.4 The diagrams giving the isomorphism pair witnessing the uniqueness of the Cartesian product in the category of sets.

But id_Z and $id_{X\times Y}$, in place of $h' \circ h$ and $h \circ h'$ respectively, clearly render the diagrams in Fig. 3.4 commutative. In turn, the uniqueness of these maps forces $h' \circ h = id_Z$ and $h \circ h' = id_{X\times Y}$. Thus Z and $X \times Y$ are isomorphic in **Set** and (h, h') is an isomorphism pair.

Functors

A functor is a morphism of categories. Suppose that $\mathbf{C}$ and $\mathbf{B}$ are categories. Then a (covariant) *functor from* $\mathbf{C}$ *to* $\mathbf{B}$, denoted by $\mathbf{F}:\mathbf{C} \longrightarrow \mathbf{B}$, consists of two related functions (both denoted by $\mathbf{F}$): the *object function* assigning to each object $a \in \mathbf{C}$ an object $\mathbf{F}(a) \in \mathbf{B}$ and the *arrow* (or *morphism*) *function* which assigns to each morphism $f \in Hom_{\mathbf{C}}(a, b)$ a morphism $\mathbf{F}(f) \in Hom_{\mathbf{B}}(\mathbf{F}(a), \mathbf{F}(b))$ such that, for all objects a, b, c and for all $f \in Hom_{\mathbf{C}}(a, b)$ and $g \in Hom_{\mathbf{C}}(b, c)$:

$$\mathbf{F}(id_a) = id_{\mathbf{F}(a)} \text{ and } \mathbf{F}(g \circ f) = \mathbf{F}(g) \circ \mathbf{F}(f).$$

A *contravariant* functor $\mathbf{F}$ from $\mathbf{C}$ to $\mathbf{B}$ associates to each $c \in \mathbf{C}$ an object $\mathbf{F}(c)$ of $\mathbf{B}$ and to each arrow $f \in Hom_{\mathbf{C}}(a, b)$ an arrow $\mathbf{F}(f) \in Hom_{\mathbf{B}}(\mathbf{F}(b), \mathbf{F}(a))$ (in the opposite *direction*) in such a way that, for all objects a, b, c and for all $f \in Hom_{\mathbf{C}}(a, b)$ and $g \in Hom_{\mathbf{C}}(b, c)$, we have that:

$$\mathbf{F}(id_c) = id_{\mathbf{F}(c)} \text{ and } \mathbf{F}(g \circ f) = \mathbf{F}(f) \circ \mathbf{F}(g).$$

Two functors can be composed. Given covariant functors $\mathbf{F}:\mathbf{C} \longrightarrow \mathbf{B}$ and $\mathbf{G}:\mathbf{B} \longrightarrow \mathbf{D}$, the composite functions $a \mapsto \mathbf{G}(\mathbf{F}(a))$, for $a \in \mathbf{C}$, and $f \mapsto \mathbf{G}(\mathbf{F}(f))$, for $f \in Hom_{\mathbf{C}}(a, b)$, define a covariant functor $(\mathbf{G} \circ \mathbf{F}):\mathbf{C} \longrightarrow \mathbf{D}$. Composition of contravariant functors is defined analogously. This composition is associative and it also has a *unit*, $\mathbf{id}_{\mathbf{C}}:\mathbf{C} \longrightarrow \mathbf{C}$, the *identity functor* from $\mathbf{C}$ to $\mathbf{C}$, satisfying

$\mathbf{F} \circ \mathbf{id}_{\mathbf{C}} = \mathbf{F}$ and $\mathbf{id}_{\mathbf{B}} \circ \mathbf{F} = \mathbf{F}$, for $\mathbf{F}: \mathbf{C} \longrightarrow \mathbf{B}$. If the categories **C** and **B** are the same, then we call **F** a *functor on* **C**.

3.4 Examples

(1) The *power set functor*, $\wp: \mathbf{Set} \longrightarrow \mathbf{Set}$, has an object function such that, for $x \in \mathbf{Set}$, $\wp(x) = \{z \in \mathbf{Set}: z \subseteq x\}$ (the *power set* of x) and an arrow function taking $f \in \mathrm{Hom}(x, y)$ to $\wp(f): \wp(x) \longrightarrow \wp(y)$, sending $z \subseteq x$ to the *image of* z *under* f, that is, $\wp(f)(z) = \{f(t): t \in z\}$.

(2) A functor which simply "forgets" some or all of the structure of an algebraic object is called a *forgetful functor.* For example, consider $\mathbf{U}: \mathbf{Grp} \longrightarrow \mathbf{Set}$. Given a group G the functor $\mathbf{U}$ yields $\mathbf{U}(G)$ the set of G's elements (forgetting the group structure) and, given $f: G \longrightarrow H$ a morphism of groups, $\mathbf{U}(f)$ is the same function regarded as a function between sets.

To each category **C** we associate the *opposite* category $\mathbf{C}^{op}$. Its objects are the objects of **C**. The arrows of $\mathbf{C}^{op}$ are all f^{op}, where for each arrow f of **C**:

$$f \in \mathrm{Hom}_{\mathbf{C}}(a, b) \text{ iff } f^{op} \in \mathrm{Hom}_{\mathbf{C}^{op}}(b, a)$$

and, for $f \in \mathrm{Hom}_{\mathbf{C}}(a, b)$ and $g \in \mathrm{Hom}_{\mathbf{C}}(b, c)$, we have that:

$$f^{op} \circ g^{op} = (g \circ f)^{op}.$$

We denote by **Cat** the category of all small categories, whose objects are all small categories. $\mathrm{Hom}_{\mathbf{Cat}}(\mathbf{C}, \mathbf{D})$ is then the set of all functors from **C** to **D** and the operation is that of composition of functors. An *isomorphism of categories* $\mathbf{F}: \mathbf{C} \longrightarrow \mathbf{D}$ is a functor whose object and morphism functions are bijections (equivalently, $\mathbf{F}: \mathbf{C} \longrightarrow \mathbf{B}$ is an isomorphism, if there is a functor $\mathbf{G}: \mathbf{B} \longrightarrow \mathbf{C}$ such that $\mathbf{G} \circ \mathbf{F} = \mathbf{id}_{\mathbf{C}}$ and $\mathbf{F} \circ \mathbf{G} = \mathbf{id}_{\mathbf{B}}$). This definition provides a notion of *identity between categories.* However, there are weaker properties than isomorphism. One of these depends on the definition of an *arrow between functors*.

3.5 Definition Let **C** and **D** be categories and let $\mathbf{F}, \mathbf{G}: \mathbf{C} \longrightarrow \mathbf{D}$ be functors. A *natural transformation* τ from **F** to **G**, denoted by $\tau: \mathbf{F} \dot{\rightarrow} \mathbf{G}$, is an assignment, to each $c \in \mathbf{C}$, of a morphism $\tau_c: \mathbf{F}(c) \longrightarrow \mathbf{G}(c)$ in such a way that, when $f \in \mathrm{Hom}(c, c')$, then $\mathbf{G}(f) \circ \tau_c = \tau_{c'} \circ \mathbf{F}(f)$ (see Figure 3.5 below).

For a natural transformation τ one also says that $\tau_c: \mathbf{F}(c) \longrightarrow \mathbf{G}(c)$ is *natural* in c or *defined in the same way* for all $c \in \mathbf{C}$. For objects $c \in \mathbf{C}$, the morphisms τ_c are called the *components* of the natural transformation τ. A natural transformation τ, where every component τ_c is invertible in **C**, is called a *natural* *equivalence* or a *natural isomorphism* and is denoted $\tau: \mathbf{F} \cong \mathbf{G}$ (in which case the inverses $(\tau_c)^{-1}$ are the components of a natural isomorphism $\tau^{-1}: \mathbf{G} \cong \mathbf{F}$). Two categories $\mathbf{C}$ and $\mathbf{D}$ are said to be *equivalent*, if there are functors $\mathbf{F}: \mathbf{C} \to \mathbf{D}$ and $\mathbf{G}: \mathbf{D} \to \mathbf{C}$ together with natural isomorphisms $\mathbf{id}_\mathbf{C} \cong \mathbf{G} \circ \mathbf{F}$ and $\mathbf{id}_\mathbf{D} \cong \mathbf{F} \circ \mathbf{G}$. Note that, if two categories are equivalent, then from a category-theoretic point of view the two categories are essentially the same. As a consequence, a category-theoretic construction on the one passes over, via the appropriate functor, to the same category-theoretic construction on the other.

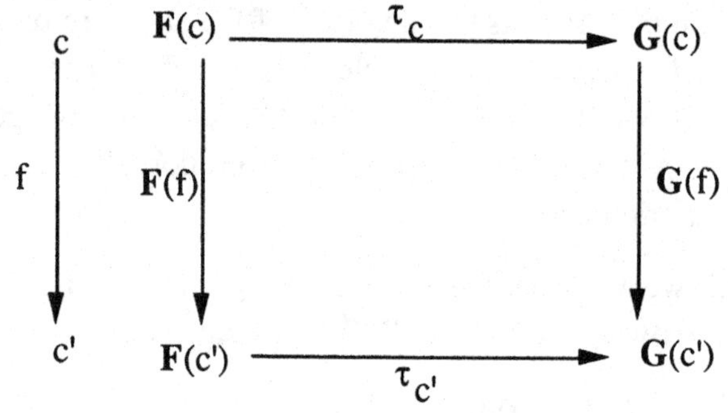

Figure 3.5 The commutative diagram associated with a natural transformation.

Given categories $\mathbf{C}$ and $\mathbf{B}$, $\mathbf{C} \times \mathbf{B}$ denotes the *product category* whose objects are pairs consisting of an object in $\mathbf{C}$ and an object in $\mathbf{B}$ and whose morphisms are pairs of morphisms from $\mathbf{C}$ and $\mathbf{B}$. Composition on the product category is coordinatewise composition. A *bifunctor* is a functor from a product category $\mathbf{C} \times \mathbf{B}$ into some category $\mathbf{D}$. A bifunctor $\mathbf{F}: \mathbf{C} \times \mathbf{B} \to \mathbf{D}$ can be covariant or contravariant in one or both of its arguments. Perhaps the simplest example of a bifunctor that we have seen thus far is the *product functor* on the category of sets which is covariant in both of its arguments and gives the cartesian product of two sets.

A functor $\mathbf{F}: \mathbf{C} \to \mathbf{B}$ is said to be *full*, if, for all $a, b \in \mathbf{C}$ and each $g \in \mathrm{Hom}_\mathbf{C}(\mathbf{F}(a), \mathbf{F}(b))$, there is a $f \in \mathrm{Hom}(a, b)$ such that $\mathbf{F}(f) = g$. $\mathbf{F}$ is *faithful*, if, for all $a, b \in \mathbf{C}$ and all $f, g \in \mathrm{Hom}_\mathbf{C}(a, b)$, $\mathbf{F}(f) = \mathbf{F}(g)$ implies that $f = g$.

3.6 Example The forgetful functor $\mathbf{U}: \mathbf{Grp} \to \mathbf{Set}$ is faithful, but not full and not a bijection on objects.

3.7 Remark Equivalently, given $a, b \in \mathbf{C}$, we have the mapping of morphisms given by a functor $\mathbf{F}: \mathbf{C} \to \mathbf{B}$:

$$(*) \quad \mathbf{F}_{a,b}: \mathrm{Hom}_\mathbf{C}(a, b) \to \mathrm{Hom}_\mathbf{B}(\mathbf{F}(a), \mathbf{F}(b)),$$

given by $f \mapsto \mathbf{F}(f)$. $\mathbf{F}$ is full, when the mappings $\mathbf{F}_{a,b}$, for all $a, b \in \mathbf{C}$, are surjective and $\mathbf{F}$ is faithful when they are injective. Thus, for full and faithful $\mathbf{F}: \mathbf{C} \to \mathbf{B}$, all the mappings $(*)$ are bijections, although $\mathbf{F}$ need not be an isomorphism of categories (many of the objects of $\mathbf{B}$ may not be in the image of the object function of $\mathbf{F}$).

We say that $\mathbf{C}'$ is a subcategory of $\mathbf{C}$, if $\mathbf{C}'$ is a category, $\mathbf{C}' \subseteq \mathbf{C}$ (i.e. each object of $\mathbf{C}'$ is an object of $\mathbf{C}$) and, for all $a, b \in \mathbf{C}'$, $\mathrm{Hom}_{\mathbf{C}'}(a, b) \subseteq \mathrm{Hom}_{\mathbf{C}}(a, b)$. The obvious inclusion $\mathbf{I}_{\mathbf{C}',\mathbf{C}}: \mathbf{C}' \to \mathbf{C}$ is a functor, the inclusion functor. $\mathbf{I}_{\mathbf{C}',\mathbf{C}}$ is faithful. $\mathbf{C}'$ is a full subcategory of $\mathbf{C}$, if the inclusion functor is full.

3.8 Example $\mathbf{Set}_V$ is a full subcategory of $\mathbf{Set}$.

PART I

BASIC THEORY

CHAPTER 1

FIXED POINTS

We take fixed points as an initial motivation for the subject we are about to study. In Section 1.1 we consider a simple but illuminating example of fixed points and then abstract what we need in order to guarantee the existence of least fixed points which are, at least in an intuitive sense, computable. This abstraction leads us immediately to the concept of an ω-cpo, given in Section 1.2.

Section 1.1 An Example

We start by considering three questions about programs and then provide some answers in the light of a simple example. The questions are: What does a program define *explicitly*? What does a program compute *implicitly*? What is the relationship between the explicit definition and the implicit intention?

1.1 Example Consider the following PASCAL program.

```
PROGRAM      gcd  (input, output);
    CONST    m=maxint;
    TYPE     natural=0 .. m;
    VAR      a, b : natural;
    FUNCTION     gcd (x, y : natural): natural;
        VAR z : natural;
        BEGIN
            z := x MOD y;
            IF z=0 THEN gcd := y
            ELSE gcd := gcd(y, z);
        END;
    BEGIN
        read (a, b);
        write ('greatest common divisor is ', gcd(a, b));
    END;
```

The program is a recursive formulation of the Euclidean algorithm. The problem is to give meaning to or interpret gcd:=gcd(y,z). That is, what is the mathematical content or explanation of a function defined in terms of itself?

For simplicity, we give a mathematical formulation of the program:

$$\mathrm{gcd}(a,b)=\begin{cases} b & \text{if } \mathrm{rem}(a,b)=0 \\ \mathrm{gcd}(b,\mathrm{rem}(a,b)) & \text{otherwise} \end{cases}$$

where

rem(a, b) = the unique r for which there is a q such that $a=qb+r$ and $0\le r<b$.

Implicitly, this definition is intended to be interpreted as an iterative method for computing the function gcd. This is, we suspect, rather unproblematic for a programmer. She or he just computes according to the program. This iterative method of computing may be said to be the *operational semantics* of the program.

Explicitly, the mathematical content of the example is a *functional* GCD with three arguments, h, a and b, where h varies over the partial functions from $\mathbb{N}^2$ into $\mathbb{N}$ and a, b vary over $\mathbb{N}$, defined as follows:

$$\mathrm{GCD}(h;a,b)\simeq\begin{cases} b & \text{if } \mathrm{rem}(a,b)=0 \\ h(b,\mathrm{rem}(a,b)) & \text{otherwise.} \end{cases}$$

Note that GCD is, indeed, defined explicitly, that is in terms of previously defined functions, namely in terms of rem, definition by cases and Ap, where Ap is the application operator defined by $\mathrm{Ap}(h;x,y)\simeq h(x,y)$, and $\simeq$ is complete or, as we shall say, strong equality as defined in Chapter 0.

The relationship between the implicit intention and the explicit definition can now be formulated precisely. The function which the program is intended to compute is the *least fixed point of the functional* GCD with respect to the partial order $\subseteq$ between partial functions. In other words, the program should compute the least h, in the sense of inclusion between graphs of partial functions, such that for all $a,b\in\mathbb{N}$,

$$h(a,b)\simeq \mathrm{GCD}(h;a,b)$$

or, in short, the least h such that $h=\mathrm{GCD}(h)$.

Assume for the moment that the least fixed point h exists. Then h satisfies the equation of our example:

$$h(a,b)\simeq\begin{cases} b & \text{if } \mathrm{rem}(a,b)=0 \\ h(b,\mathrm{rem}(a,b)) & \text{otherwise.} \end{cases}$$

It is an easy exercise to show that if h satisfies the above equation and if $a\ge b>0$ then h(a,b) is defined and equal to the greatest common divisor of a and b.

In summary we have that a program gives rise to an explicitly defined *functional* $F(f; a_1, \ldots, a_n)$. The function computed by the program is the least fixed point of the functional F.

Let us now consider the underlying theory. We shall isolate conditions necessary to guarantee the existence of intuitively computable least fixed points. Let A and B be non-empty sets and let $A \xrightarrow{p} B$ denote the set of partial functions from A to B. Let f and g vary over $A \xrightarrow{p} B$, and let a and b vary over A and B respectively. We identify partial functions with their graphs. This provides a natural partial order $\subseteq$ on $A \xrightarrow{p} B$, by saying that $f \subseteq g$ if the graph of f is a subset of the graph of g. A *functional* F is a mapping $F : (A \xrightarrow{p} B) \longrightarrow (A \xrightarrow{p} B)$. Note that a functional is a *total* mapping, that is F(f) is defined for each partial function f. However, F(f) is a partial function. We often use the notation F(f; a) for F(f)(a). Thus F(f; a) is either undefined or an element of B.

1.2 Definition Let $F : (A \xrightarrow{p} B) \longrightarrow (A \xrightarrow{p} B)$ be a functional.

(i) F is *monotone* if $f \subseteq g \Rightarrow F(f) \subseteq F(g)$.

(ii) F is *continuous* if F is monotone and if, for any f and a, F(f; a) depends only on finitely many values of f in the following precise sense: whenever $F(f; a) \simeq b$ then there is a finite $g \subseteq f$ (that is the graph of g is a finite set) such that $F(g; a) \simeq b$.

(iii) A partial function $f \in (A \xrightarrow{p} B)$ is a *fixed point* of F if $F(f) = f$. It is said to be the *least fixed point* of F, if it is a fixed point of F and least with respect to the partial order $\subseteq$ on $A \xrightarrow{p} B$.

Thus f is the least fixed point of the functional F if $F(f) = f$, that is $F(f; a) \simeq f(a)$ for each $a \in A$, and if $F(g) = g$ then $f \subseteq g$.

1.3 First recursion theorem (Kleene) Each continuous functional $F : (A \xrightarrow{p} B) \longrightarrow (A \xrightarrow{p} B)$ has a least fixed point.

In its usual formulation the first recursion theorem also states that the least fixed point f of F is computable whenever F is computable. This will be intuitively clear from our proof below. However we are not in a position to prove it since we have not yet given a mathematical definition of computability. Indeed, it is true that every monotone functional has a least fixed point (see Exercise 2), but that fixed point need not be computable.

Proof: Let $\varnothing$ be the everywhere undefined function (its graph is the empty set) and define recursively

$$\begin{cases} f^0 = \varnothing \\ f^{n+1} = F(f^n). \end{cases}$$

Since $\varnothing$ is the least element in $A \xrightarrow{p} B$ we have $\varnothing = f^0 \subseteq f^1$. By the monotonicity of F we then obtain $F(f^0) \subseteq F(f^1)$, that is $f^1 \subseteq f^2$. Thus, inductively, we obtain a chain

$$(*) \qquad \varnothing = f^0 \subseteq f^1 \subseteq \ldots \subseteq f^n \ldots .$$

Let $f = \bigcup \{f^n : n \in \mathbb{N}\}$, again identifying functions with their graphs. Thus $f(a) \simeq b \Leftrightarrow \exists n\, (f^n(a) \simeq b)$. Note that f is a function by (*), albeit partial, that is f has at most one value, so $f \in (A \xrightarrow{p} B)$. Furthermore, f is the least upper bound of the chain (*) in $A \xrightarrow{p} B$. For suppose $f^n \subseteq g$ for each $n \in \mathbb{N}$ and $f(a) \simeq b$. Then for some m, $f^m(a) \simeq b$ and hence $g(a) \simeq b$. Thus $f \subseteq g$.

To show that $F(f) = f$, note that for each n, $f^n \subseteq f$, and hence we have that $f^{n+1} = F(f^n) \subseteq F(f)$ by the monotonicity of F. But then

$$f = \bigcup \{f^n : n \in \mathbb{N}\} = \bigcup \{f^{n+1} : n \in \mathbb{N}\} \subseteq F(f).$$

For the converse inclusion $f \supseteq F(f)$, suppose $F(f)(a) \simeq b$. We must show that $f(a) \simeq b$. By the continuity of F there is a finite $g \in (A \xrightarrow{p} B)$ such that $g \subseteq f$ and $F(g)(a) \simeq b$. Let $\mathrm{dom}(g) = \{a_1, \ldots, a_k\}$ and choose for each i an $n_i \in \mathbb{N}$ such that $a_i \in \mathrm{dom}(f^{n_i})$. Let $n = \max\{n_1, \ldots, n_k\}$. Then $\mathrm{dom}(g) \subseteq \mathrm{dom}(f^n)$ and hence $g \subseteq f^n$. By the monotonicity of F, $F(g) \subseteq F(f^n) = f^{n+1}$. But $F(g)(a) \simeq b$ and hence $f^{n+1}(a) \simeq b$, so $f(a) \simeq b$.

Finally, to prove that f is the least fixed point of F, assume g is a fixed point, that is $F(g) = g$. Again, $\varnothing = f^0 \subseteq g$ and hence $f^1 = F(f^0) \subseteq F(g) = g$ by the monotonicity of F. Inductively, we obtain $f^{n+1} = F(f^n) \subseteq F(g) = g$ and hence $f = \bigcup \{f^n : n \in \mathbb{N}\} \subseteq g$. □

We gave the above proof in detail, despite its relative simplicity, since it is important that each step be properly understood. Note that the continuity of F was only used to show that $F(f) \subseteq f$. There it was only necessary in order that the inductive definition of the f^n's should close off at level ω. Had we continued into the transfinite, the monotonicity of F would have sufficed to get a least fixed point. However, given that the inductive definition does close off at ω, we obtain an algorithm for computing the least fixed point, provided F is computable. Given $a \in A$, search effectively for some n such that $f^n(a)\downarrow$. If such an n exists, then compute f(a). If no such n exists, then our computation does not terminate.

Let us return to our introductory example of the greatest common divisor. First, to show that the functional GCD is monotone, suppose $h_1 \subseteq h_2$ and $GCD(h_1; a, b) \simeq d$. We must show that $GCD(h_2; a, b) \simeq d$. If $\mathrm{rem}(a, b) = 0$ then this is clear. Suppose therefore that $\mathrm{rem}(a, b) = c > 0$. Then $h_1(b, c) \simeq d$ and hence $h_2(b, c) \simeq d$, that is $GCD(h_2; a, b) \simeq d$. The continuity of GCD is even simpler to establish, since GCD(h; a, b) clearly depends on at most one value of h, namely h(b, rem(a, b)).

Thus the program of Example 1.1 gives rise to the obviously computable functional GCD which we showed to be continuous. By the first recursion theorem it follows that GCD has a least fixed point which, as already observed, computes the greatest common divisor of two positive numbers, as intended.

Section 1.2 ω-complete Partial Orders

In this section we analyse precisely what was needed for the proof of the first recursion theorem, in order to arrive at an abstract class of structures for which the proof yields least fixed points.

Let us first consider which properties of the set $A \xrightarrow{p} B$ were used. First we had a partial order $\subseteq$ with a least element $\emptyset$. For a given functional F we obtained an ω-chain

$$(*) \qquad \emptyset \subseteq f^0 \subseteq f^1 \subseteq \ldots \subseteq f^n \ldots$$

where $f^{n+1} = F(f^n)$, and the least fixed point of F was the supremum of the chain (*) in $A \xrightarrow{p} B$. Thus we used the fact that $A \xrightarrow{p} B$ is ω-complete in the sense that every ω-chain has a supremum in $A \xrightarrow{p} B$. This leads us to the following definition.

2.1 Definition A structure $\mathbf{D} = (D; \sqsubseteq, \bot)$ is an *ω-complete partial order* (*ω-cpo*) if D is a set and $\sqsubseteq$ is a partial order on D with a least element $\bot$ (called *bottom*), such that every ω-chain

$$x_0 \sqsubseteq x_1 \sqsubseteq \ldots \sqsubseteq x_n \sqsubseteq \ldots$$

in D has a supremum in D.

When D is an ω-cpo and $A \subseteq D$, we denote the supremum of A by $\bigsqcup A$, if it exists. In terms of computations, one should think of $x \sqsubseteq y$ in D as stating that y contains at least as much information as x or, perhaps better, that x is an approximation of y. Thus $\bot$ contains no information at all since it approximates every element in D.

Let us now consider what requirements on a function $F: D \longrightarrow D$ seem necessary in order that the proof of the first recursion theorem should go through. Monotonicity is clear since we deal with partially ordered sets. However, to lift the notion of continuity used in the proof to our abstract setting we must first introduce a notion of *finiteness* for elements of D. This will be done when we study algebraic cpo's in Chapter 3. For now we will take the easy route by saying that F is continuous if inductive iterations of F, as in the proof of the first recursion theorem, close off at level ω.

2.2 Definition Let D and E be ω-cpo's and let $F: D \to E$. Then
(i) F is *monotone* if $x \sqsubseteq_D y \Rightarrow F(x) \sqsubseteq_E F(y)$.
(ii) F is *ω-continuous* if F is monotone and if, for each ω-chain

$$x_0 \sqsubseteq_D x_1 \sqsubseteq_D \dots \sqsubseteq_D x_n \sqsubseteq_D \dots$$

in D, we have $F(\bigsqcup_D\{x_i : i \in \mathbb{N}\}) = \bigsqcup_E\{F(x_i) : i \in \mathbb{N}\}$.

In the sequel we write $\sqsubseteq$ and $\bigsqcup$ instead of $\sqsubseteq_D$ and $\bigsqcup_D$ when the partial order in question is clear from the context. Observe that all suprema in part (ii) of the definition exist. Firstly, $\bigsqcup\{x_i : i \in \mathbb{N}\} \in D$ since D is an ω-cpo. Secondly, we get an ω-chain in E by the monotonicity of F,

$$F(x_0) \sqsubseteq F(x_1) \sqsubseteq F(x_2) \sqsubseteq \dots$$

and hence $\bigsqcup\{F(x_i) : i \in \mathbb{N}\}$ exists in E.

2.3 Fixed point theorem Let $D = (D; \sqsubseteq, \perp)$ be an ω-cpo and let $F: D \to D$ be ω-continuous. Then F has a least fixed point in D, that is there is $x \in D$ such that $F(x) = x$, and such that if $F(y) = y$ then $x \sqsubseteq y$.

Proof: Define recursively the sequence

$$\begin{cases} F^0(\perp) = \perp \\ F^{n+1}(\perp) = F(F^n(\perp)). \end{cases}$$

By the monotonicity of F and the fact that $\perp$ is the least element in D we obtain an ω-chain

$$\perp = F^0(\perp) \sqsubseteq F^1(\perp) \sqsubseteq F^2(\perp) \sqsubseteq \dots .$$

Let $x = \bigsqcup\{F^n(\perp) : n \in \mathbb{N}\} \in D$. Then by the ω-continuity of F,

$$\begin{aligned} F(x) &= F(\bigsqcup\{F^n(\perp) : n \in \mathbb{N}\}) \\ &= \bigsqcup\{F(F^n(\perp)) : n \in \mathbb{N}\} \\ &= \bigsqcup\{F^{n+1}(\perp) : n \in \mathbb{N}\} \\ &= x. \end{aligned}$$

Suppose $F(y) = y$ for some $y \in D$. Then $\perp \sqsubseteq y$ and hence, by the monotonicity of F, $F(\perp) \sqsubseteq F(y) = y$. Inductively it follows that $F^n(\perp) \sqsubseteq y$ for each n, and hence $x = \bigsqcup\{F^n(\perp) : n \in \mathbb{N}\} \sqsubseteq y$. □

Let D be an ω-cpo and let $[D \xrightarrow{\omega} D]$ denote the set of ω-continuous functions from D into D. Then the fixed point theorem provides us with a function $\text{fix}: [D \xrightarrow{\omega} D] \longrightarrow D$ defined by

$$\text{fix}(F) = \text{the least fixed point of } F.$$

Some natural questions arise. Can $[D \xrightarrow{\omega} D]$ be considered as an ω-cpo? Can this be done in such a way that the function fix will be continuous? We shall see that the answers in both cases are yes.

1.3 Exercises

1. Suppose h satisfies the equation

$$h(a,b) \simeq \begin{cases} b & \text{if } \text{rem}(a,b)=0 \\ h(b, \text{rem}(a,b)) & \text{otherwise.} \end{cases}$$

Show that if $a \geq b > 0$ then $h(a,b)$ is defined and equal to the greatest common divisor of a and b.

2. Show that every monotone functional has a least fixed point. [Use transfinite induction.]

3. Consider $\mathcal{P} = \mathbb{N} \xrightarrow{p} \mathbb{N}$ as an ω-cpo. Let $F: \mathcal{P} \longrightarrow \mathcal{P}$ be monotone. Show that F is continuous in the sense of Definition 1.2 if and only if F is ω-continuous with respect to $\subseteq$.

4. (The Ackermann function) Consider the functional

$$\text{ACK}(f; x, y) \simeq \begin{cases} y+1 & \text{if } x=0 \\ f(x-1, 1) & \text{if } x \neq 0 \text{ and } y=0 \\ f(x-1, f(x, y-1)) & \text{if } x \neq 0 \text{ and } y \neq 0 \end{cases}$$

where x and y vary over $\mathbb{N}$.

(i) Show that ACK is continuous.

(ii) Let ack be the least fixed point of ACK. Define $\text{ack}_n(y) = \text{ack}(n, y)$ and show that

$$\begin{cases} \text{ack}_0(y) = y+1 \\ \text{ack}_{n+1}(y) = \text{ack}_n^{y+1}(1) \end{cases}$$

where $f^n(z) = f(f(\ldots f(z) \ldots))$, the n-fold application of f to z.

(iii) Show that $\text{ack}_n(y) < \text{ack}_n(y+1)$ and $\text{ack}_n(y+1) \leq \text{ack}_{n+1}(y)$.

(iv) Determine explicitly the functions ack_1 and ack_2. Then show that $2^{y+1} \leq ack_3(y) \leq 3^{y+1}$, for $y \geq 3$.

Note that by (iv), ack_3 grows approximately as an exponential function. The function ack_4 may be viewed as a generalized exponential function. Let $g(n) = ack(n, n)$. One can show that g grows faster than every primitive recursive function (these are defined in Chapter 9). On the other hand, there is an easy algorithm to compute ack, and hence g is recursive. Thus g is an example of a recursive function which is not primitive recursive.

5. Let **ω-Cpo** be the category whose objects are the ω-cpo's and whose morphisms are the ω-continuous functions between ω-cpo's. Verify that **ω-Cpo** is indeed a category.

6. Let D be an ω-cpo and let $F: D \longrightarrow D$ be ω-continuous. Show that $D' = \{x \in D: F(x) = x\}$, with the ordering inherited from D, is an ω-cpo.

7. Let D be an ω-cpo and assume $F: D \longrightarrow D$ is ω-continuous. To say that F has a least fixed point $\sqsupseteq a$ means that the set $\{x \in D: F(x) = x \text{ and } x \sqsupseteq a\}$ has a least element.
(i) Show that it is not always the case that F has a least fixed point $\sqsupseteq a$.
(ii) Give sufficient conditions on $a \in D$ so that F will have a least fixed point $\sqsupseteq a$.

8. (i) Show that $\mathbb{R}^* = (\mathbb{R}^*; \leq, -\infty)$ is an ω-cpo, where $\mathbb{R}^* = \mathbb{R} \cup \{-\infty, \infty\}$ is the set of extended real numbers with the usual ordering $\leq$.
(ii) Show that there is a countable set $A \subseteq \mathbb{R}^*$ such that for each $x \in \mathbb{R}^*$ there is an ω-chain $a_0 \leq a_1 \leq \ldots$, where $a_i \in A$, such that $x = \bigsqcup\{a_n: n \in \mathbb{N}\}$.

9. Consider the extended real numbers $\mathbb{R}^*$ and, for $x \leq y \in \mathbb{R}^*$, let $[x, y] = \{z \in \mathbb{R}^*: x \leq z \leq y\}$. Let $D = \{[x, y]: x \leq y \ \& \ x, y \in \mathbb{R}^*\}$ and define the relation $\sqsubseteq$ on D by

$$[x, y] \sqsubseteq [x', y'] \quad \text{iff} \quad [x', y'] \subseteq [x, y].$$

Show that $\mathbf{D} = (D; \sqsubseteq, [-\infty, \infty])$ is an ω-cpo. (How could one use **D** in order to compute functions on $\mathbb{R}$?)

10. Give an example of an ω-cpo **D** and a monotone $F: D \longrightarrow D$ such that F has *no* fixed point.

11. Let $\mathbf{D} = (D; \sqsubseteq, \bot)$ be a partially ordered set with least element $\bot$. A set $A \subseteq D$ is said to be *directed* if $A \neq \varnothing$ and whenever $x, y \in A$ then there is

$z \in A$ such that $x \sqsubseteq z$ and $y \sqsubseteq z$. (Thus each ω-chain is a directed set.) D is said to be a *complete partial order* (*cpo*) if D has a least element $\bot$, and if $\sqcup A$ exists in D for each directed $A \subseteq D$.

(i) Let D be a cpo. Show that if $f: D \longrightarrow D$ is monotone then f has a least fixed point. (Compare with Exercise 10.)

(ii) Let D and E be cpo's and let $f: D \longrightarrow E$. Suppose that whenever $A \subseteq D$ is directed then $f[A] = \{f(x): x \in A\}$ is a directed set in E and $f(\sqcup_D A) = \sqcup_E f[A]$. Show that f is monotone.

12. Let D and E be ω-cpo's.

(i) Show that every *denumerable* directed subset of D has a least upper bound in D.

(ii) Show that $F: D \longrightarrow E$ is ω-continuous if and only if for every denumerable directed set $A \subseteq D$, $F[A]$ is directed and $F(\sqcup_D A) = \sqcup_E F[A]$.

CHAPTER 2

COMPLETE PARTIAL ORDERS

Complete partial orders, the subject matter of this chapter, are still rather simple structures in that the important notion of finiteness is ignored. Nonetheless these structures suffice for a considerable portion of program semantics. They may also be considered as a minimal model for a computation theory. In the first section, complete partial orders are introduced and the continuous functions which live on them are discussed. Then, in the remaining sections, various important constructions on these structures are treated, such as the cartesian product and the function space construction.

Section 2.1 Complete Partial Orders

We consider now a variant of the ω-complete partial orders introduced in Section 1.2. The difference is that we allow a more general form of increasing sequences, rather than increasing ω-sequences, and require that our partial order be complete with respect to such generalized sequences. This is equivalent to requiring completeness with respect to sequences of arbitrary ordinal length.

1.1 Definition Let $D=(D;\sqsubseteq)$ be a partially ordered set. A set $A\subseteq D$ is *directed* if $A\neq\emptyset$ and whenever $x,y\in A$ then there is $z\in A$ such that $x\sqsubseteq z$ and $y\sqsubseteq z$.

For $A\subseteq D$, where D is a partially ordered set, we denote the supremum or least upper bound of A, if it exists, by $\bigsqcup A$. As usual, we write $x\sqcup y$ for $\bigsqcup\{x,y\}$.

1.2 Definition Let $D=(D;\sqsubseteq,\perp)$ be a partially ordered set with least element $\perp$. Then D is a *complete partial order* (*cpo*) if whenever $A\subseteq D$ is directed then $\bigsqcup A$ exists in D.

Computationally, the partial order $\sqsubseteq$ should be thought of as an approximation relation. Thus $x\sqsubseteq y$ should be interpreted as x is an approximation of y or y contains at least as much information as x. In particular, $\perp$ contains no information since it approximates each element in D. A directed set A is a generalized increasing sequence in the sense that the information in A is consistent and gives increasingly better approximations. This means that for each $x, y \in A$ there is an element in A which they both approximate. In particular, x and y cannot contain contradictory information. A cpo is then complete in the sense that every generalized increasing sequence A in D converges to an element in D, namely $\sqcup A$. Note that each cpo is an ω-cpo but not conversely (Exercise 1).

It is helpful to decide on some notational conventions. Upper case letters, often D and E, will denote cpo's while lower case letters will denote elements of cpo's. Furthermore, we use upper case letters A and B for subsets of cpo's. In the usual fashion we use subscripts and superscripts in order to make our collection of symbols infinite. When considering a particular cpo D, we should perhaps write $\sqsubseteq_D$ for the partial order on D in order to distinguish it from the partial order on, say, E. However, we will hardly ever do so except when the context does leave some room for ambiguity. Similar remarks apply to $\sqcup$ and $\bot$.

First we formulate the notion of continuity for cpo's and observe some basic facts. Note that our definition here is equivalent to that of being ω-continuous for ω-cpo's.

1.3 Definition Let $f: D \longrightarrow E$ where D and E are cpo's.

(i) The function f is *monotone* if, for each $x, y \in D$, $x \sqsubseteq y \Rightarrow f(x) \sqsubseteq f(y)$.

(ii) The function f is *continuous* if whenever $A \subseteq D$ is directed then $f[A]$ is directed and $f(\sqcup A) = \sqcup f[A]$.

We do not want to stipulate that $f(\bot) = \bot$, in order to be able to obtain non-trivial least fixed points. Hence it is important in the definition above that directed sets were required to be non-empty.

1.4 Lemma Let $f: D \longrightarrow E$ where D and E are cpo's.

(i) If f is continuous then f is monotone.

(ii) If f is monotone and $A \subseteq D$ is directed then $f[A] \subseteq E$ is directed and $\sqcup f[A] \sqsubseteq f(\sqcup A)$.

Proof: We prove (i) and leave (ii) as an exercise. Suppose $x \sqsubseteq y$ in D. Then $A = \{x, y\}$ is directed and hence, by continuity, $f[A] = \{f(x), f(y)\}$ is directed. Furthermore, again by continuity,

$$f(y) = f(\sqcup A) = \sqcup f[A],$$

that is $f(x) \sqsubseteq f(y)$. □

In order to prove that a function $f:D\longrightarrow E$ is continuous it is often convenient to first show that f is monotone and then show that $f(\bigsqcup A)\sqsubseteq\bigsqcup f[A]$ whenever $A\subseteq D$ is directed.

1.5 Lemma Let D, E and F be cpo's.
(i) Every constant function from D into E is continuous.
(ii) The identity function $id:D\longrightarrow D$, given by $id(x)=x$, is continuous.
(iii) If $f:D\longrightarrow E$ and $g:E\longrightarrow F$ are continuous then so is $g\circ f:D\longrightarrow F$.

Proof: We prove (iii). Suppose $A\subseteq D$ is directed. Then $f[A]$ is directed and hence $g[f[A]]=(g\circ f)[A]$ is directed, by the continuity of f and g. Similarly,

$$(g\circ f)(\bigsqcup A)=g(f(\bigsqcup A))=g(\bigsqcup f[A])=\bigsqcup g[f[A]]=\bigsqcup(g\circ f)[A]. \qquad \square$$

We say that cpo's D and E are *isomorphic*, denoted $D\cong E$, if there is a bijection $f:D\longrightarrow E$ which is *order-preserving*, that is for each $x,y\in D$ we have $x\sqsubseteq y \Leftrightarrow f(x)\sqsubseteq f(y)$. The function f is said to be an *isomorphism*. It is easily seen that an isomorphism is a continuous function.

The category of complete partial orders, which we denote by **Cpo**, is defined as follows. The objects of **Cpo** are the complete partial orders and the morphisms from D to E are just the continuous functions from D into E, that is

$$Hom(D,E)=\{f\mid f:D\longrightarrow E,\ f \text{ is continuous}\}.$$

It follows from Lemma 1.5 that **Cpo** is a category.

Recall that $D\cong E$ in **Cpo** if there are continuous functions $f:D\longrightarrow E$ and $g:E\longrightarrow D$ such that $g\circ f=id_D$ and $f\circ g=id_E$. The next lemma shows that the two notions of being isomorphic for cpo's coincide.

1.6 Lemma Let D and E be cpo's. Then $D\cong E$ in **Cpo** if and only if there is an order-preserving surjection $f:D\longrightarrow E$ if and only if there is an order preserving bijection $f:D\longrightarrow E$.

Proof: Exercise 2. $\square$

That which distinguishes the class of cpo's from the class of partially ordered sets with a least element, is that $\bigsqcup A$ exists in D whenever $A\subseteq D$ is directed. Thus, when D is seen as a structure, it seems reasonable to consider $\bigsqcup$ as an operation on D taking a subset of D to D. Of course, the operation $\bigsqcup$ differs from the usual kinds of operations we consider in algebra, such as addition for rings, in that it is an infinitary operation taking possibly infinitely many arguments and it is also a partial operation. Nonetheless considering $\bigsqcup$ as an operation serves as a guide in deciding what should be the morphisms between cpo's. Thus a function $f:D\longrightarrow E$ is continuous if it preserves $\sqsubseteq$ and $\bigsqcup$, of course the latter for arguments where the operation is guaranteed to be defined, that is for directed sets. However, contrary to the above discussion, we have *not* required that a continuous function preserve $\perp$.

1.7 Definition A function $f:D \longrightarrow E$ between cpo's is *strict* if $f(\perp)=\perp$.

Thus the strict continuous functions are those which preserve all operations and relations of cpo's. The category of *strict cpo's*, denoted $\mathbf{Cpo}_\perp$, has cpo's as objects and strict continuous functions as morphisms. We write $f:D \longrightarrow_\perp E$ to express the fact that f is a strict continuous function.

There is a very good reason for considering the category **Cpo** and not, exclusively, $\mathbf{Cpo}_\perp$: the least fixed point of a strict continuous function $f:D \longrightarrow_\perp D$ is $\perp$. So in order to get non-trivial least fixed points, a major motivation for our interest, we must consider the larger category **Cpo**.

From our discussion above, we also obtain the following notion of subcpo.

1.8 Definition A cpo $D=(D;\sqsubseteq_D,\perp_D)$ is a *subcpo* of a cpo $E=(E;\sqsubseteq_E,\perp_E)$ if $D \subseteq E$, $\sqsubseteq_D$ is the restriction to D of $\sqsubseteq_E$, $\perp_E=\perp_D$ and whenever $A \subseteq D$ is a directed set then $\bigsqcup_E A = \bigsqcup_D A$.

For the latter two properties it suffices to show that $\perp_E \in D$ and $\bigsqcup_E A \in D$ whenever $A \subseteq D$ is a directed set.

A related and important notion is that of a projection pair.

1.9 Definition A *projection pair* for (D,E) is a pair of continuous functions (f,g), where $f:D \longrightarrow E$ and $g:E \longrightarrow D$, such that $g \circ f = id_D$ and $f \circ g(y) \sqsubseteq y$ for each $y \in E$.

1.10 Proposition If there is a projection pair (f,g) for (D,E) then D is isomorphic to a subcpo of E.

Proof: Let (f,g) be a projection pair for (D,E). Note that f is order preserving. For suppose $f(x) \sqsubseteq f(y)$. Then $g(f(x)) \sqsubseteq g(f(y))$ since g is monotone. But $g \circ f = id$ so $x \sqsubseteq y$. Thus $D \cong f[D]$ by Lemma 1.6. To show that $f[D]$ is a subcpo, note first that $f(g(\perp_E)) \sqsubseteq \perp_E$ and hence $f(\perp_D)=\perp_E$. Furthermore, if $A' \subseteq f[D]$ is directed then $A=f^{-1}[A']$ is directed since f is order-preserving and hence $f(\bigsqcup_D A) = \bigsqcup_E f[A] = \bigsqcup_E A'$ by the continuity of f. □

We close this section by giving a number of examples of complete partial orders.

1.11 Flat cpo's. Let A be a set. Then put $A_\perp = A \cup \{\perp\}$, where $\perp \notin A$ is a distinguished element, and order $A_\perp$ by $x \sqsubseteq y \Leftrightarrow x=\perp$ or $x=y$. Thus the ordering of $A_\bot$ contains as little information as possible, only enough to be a cpo. For example, if $\mathbb{B}=\{tt, ff\}$ is the Boolean set of true and false then $\mathbb{B}_\bot$ is:

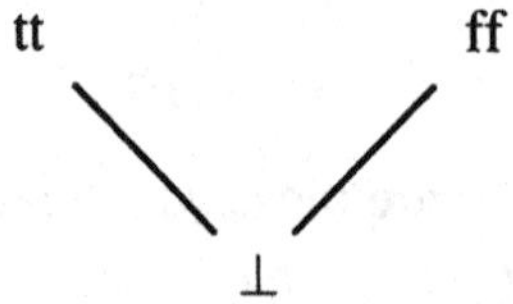

The set of natural numbers $\mathbb{N}$ gives rise to the flat cpo $\mathbb{N}_\bot$:

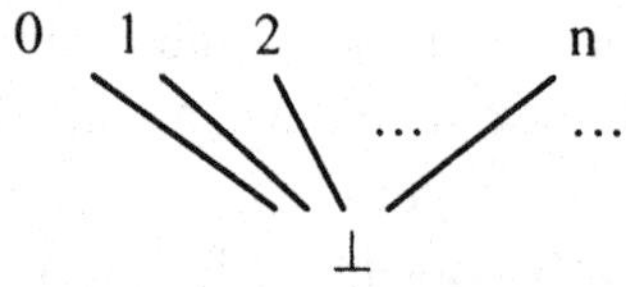

The importance of flat cpo's is that *any* set, structure or datatype can be construed as a cpo. Furthermore, if $f: A \to B$ is an arbitrary function, then there is a continuous *minimal extension* $f_\bot: A_\bot \to B_\bot$ given by $f_\bot(x)=f(x)$ if $x \in A$ and $f_\bot(\bot)=\bot$. Thus our theory is general.

1.12 Cantor space as a cpo. We call the set $2^\omega=\{f \mid f: \mathbb{N} \to \{0,1\}\}$ the *Cantor space*. Equipped with the product topology from the discrete topology on $\{0,1\}$, discussed in Chapter 5, 2^ω is homeomorphic to the usual Cantor space, a subspace of the reals $\mathbb{R}$. We shall make 2^ω into a cpo, reflecting how the elements of 2^ω are approximated by finite sequences, simply by extending 2^ω to include all such. For each $n \in \mathbb{N}$, define

$$SEQ_n = \{\sigma \mid \sigma : \{0,1,\dots,n-1\} \to \{0,1\}\},$$

the set of sequences of length n, and let $SEQ = \bigcup_{n \in \mathbb{N}} SEQ_n$. Finally put $\mathbb{C} = SEQ \cup 2^\omega$. Then $\mathbb{C} = (\mathbb{C}; \sqsubseteq, <>)$ is a cpo, where $<>$ is the empty sequence or function and where the partial order $\sqsubseteq$ is defined by

$$f \sqsubseteq g \Leftrightarrow graph(f) \subseteq graph(g).$$

The original Cantor space 2^ω may be recovered from $\mathbb{C}$ since 2^ω is the set of maximal elements in $\mathbb{C}$ with respect to $\sqsubseteq$. Note that SEQ is countable while 2^ω is uncountable. This gives us the possibility to approximate certain elements in 2^ω, using SEQ, in a computable fashion.

$\mathbb{C}$ may be pictured as a binary tree where each node corresponds to an element of SEQ and each infinite branch corresponds to an element in 2^ω. Denoting elements in SEQ as tuples $<,\ldots,>$ and letting $*$ denote the concatenation operator, the tree is:

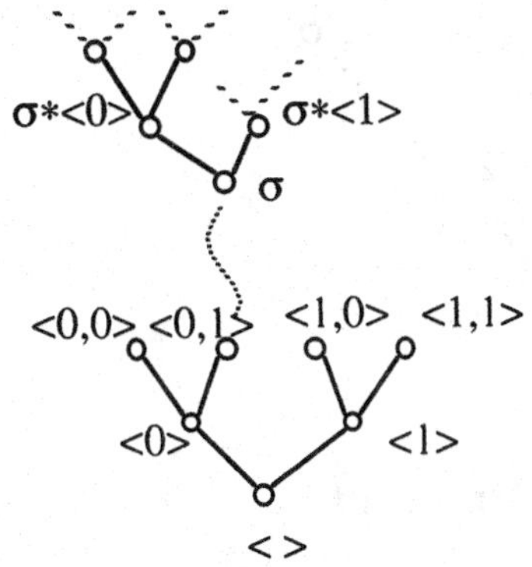

1.13 Baire space as a cpo. The Baire space is the set $\omega^{\omega} = \{f \mid f: \mathbb{N} \to \mathbb{N}\}$. Given the appropriate topology, namely the product topology from the discrete topology on $\mathbb{N}$, ω^{ω} is homeomorphic to the irrational numbers. One way of making the Baire space into a cpo is to proceed as described in 1.12 above. Then we would obtain a tree which is infinitely branching. Let us consider another way, giving a different cpo, which works as well for the Cantor space.

Let $\mathcal{P} = \mathbb{N} \xrightarrow{p} \mathbb{N}$, the set of partial functions from $\mathbb{N}$ into $\mathbb{N}$, and order $\mathcal{P}$ by $f \sqsubseteq g \Leftrightarrow \text{graph}(f) \subseteq \text{graph}(g)$. Then $\mathcal{P} = (\mathcal{P}; \sqsubseteq, \varnothing)$ is a cpo and ω^{ω} can be recovered from $\mathcal{P}$ as the set of maximal elements in $\mathcal{P}$. It is still true that each element in ω^{ω}, in fact in $\mathcal{P}$, can be approximated by finite elements, but there are also infinite elements in $\mathcal{P} - \omega^{\omega}$.

Let $[\mathbb{N}_{\perp} \to \mathbb{N}_{\perp}]$ be the set of continuous functions from $\mathbb{N}_{\perp}$ into $\mathbb{N}_{\perp}$. In Section 2.3 it will be shown that $[\mathbb{N}_{\perp} \to \mathbb{N}_{\perp}]$ is a cpo. We can embed $\mathcal{P}$ into $[\mathbb{N}_{\perp} \to \mathbb{N}_{\perp}]$ by sending f to $\bar{f}$ where, for $n \in \mathbb{N}$,

$$\begin{cases} \bar{f}(n) = f(n) & \text{if } f(n)\downarrow \\ \bar{f}(n) = \perp & \text{if } f(n)\uparrow \\ \bar{f}(\perp) = \perp. & \end{cases}$$

Thus the cpo's $\mathcal{P}$ and $[\mathbb{N}_{\perp} \to \mathbb{N}_{\perp}]$ are essentially the same, but note that the cpo $[\mathbb{N}_{\perp} \to \mathbb{N}_{\perp}]$ contains only total functions in that "undefined" is represented as a value in $\mathbb{N}_{\perp}$, namely $\perp$.

1.14 Ordinals as cpo's. Clearly, if α is a limit ordinal then α with the ordering $\leq$ is not a cpo. For α itself is a directed subset of α and the supremum of α is α (since α is a limit ordinal), while $\alpha \notin \alpha$. However, if α is a successor ordinal, that is $\alpha=\beta+1=\beta\cup\{\beta\}$, then $\alpha=(\alpha;\leq,0)$ is a cpo. In particular, $\omega+1$ is the cpo:

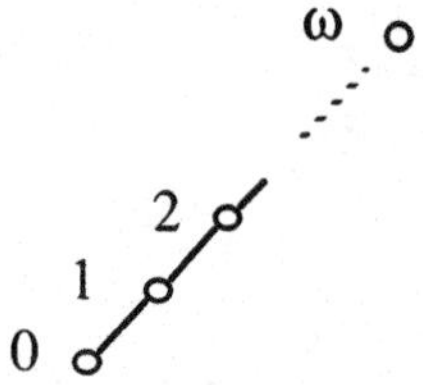

Section 2.2 Cartesian Products

In this section we show how to form finite cartesian products of cpo's and we study some of their properties.

2.1 Definition Let D and E be partially ordered sets with a least element. Then the *cartesian product* of D and E, denoted $D\times E$, is the following partially ordered set.

Universe: $D\times E=\{(x,y): x\in D,\ y\in E\}$.

Ordering: $(x,y)\sqsubseteq(z,w) \Leftrightarrow x\sqsubseteq z \ \&\ y\sqsubseteq w$.

Its associated *projection functions*

$\pi_0: D\times E\longrightarrow D$ and $\pi_1: D\times E\longrightarrow E$

are defined by $\pi_0(x,y)=x$ and $\pi_1(x,y)=y$.

Thus we obtain a partial order on the set-theoretic cartesian product by ordering coordinatewise. It has a least element, namely $(\perp_D,\perp_E)$. Of course, whenever $f: D\times E\longrightarrow F$ then we write in the usual manner $f(x,y)$ for $f((x,y))$ and regard f as a function of two variables.

The following lemma describes the essential features of the cartesian product construction for cpo's.

2.2 Lemma Let D and E be cpo's. If $A\subseteq D\times E$ is a directed set then $\pi_i[A]$ is directed for $i=0,1$ and $\sqcup A=(\sqcup\pi_0[A],\sqcup\pi_1[A])$.

Proof: Suppose $A\subseteq D\times E$ is directed. Each π_i is monotone and hence $\pi_i[A]$ is directed. Let $a=\sqcup\pi_0[A]\in D$ and $b=\sqcup\pi_1[A]\in E$. We must show that $\sqcup A=(a,b)$. Clearly (a,b) is an upper bound for A. Suppose (c,d) is an upper bound for A. Let $x\in\pi_0[A]$ and choose $y\in E$ such that $(x,y)\in A$. Then $(x,y)\sqsubseteq(c,d)$ so in particular $x\sqsubseteq c$. Thus c is an upper bound for $\pi_0[A]$ and hence $a\sqsubseteq c$. Similarly $b\sqsubseteq d$ and hence $(a,b)\sqsubseteq(c,d)$. □

Note that $A \subseteq D \times E$ need *not* be directed even though both $\pi_0[A]$ and $\pi_1[A]$ are directed.

2.3 Theorem Let D and E be cpo's. Then $D \times E$ is a cpo and the projection functions π_0 and π_1 are continuous.

Proof: By Lemma 2.2. □

To say that $f: D_0 \times D_1 \to E$ is *continuous in its first argument* means that for each $b \in D_1$, the function $x \mapsto f(x,b)$ from D_0 into E is continuous. We will often use the λ-notation informally to denote this function. Thus $\lambda x.f(x,y)$ denotes the function from D_0 into E given by f, where y is kept fixed. The definition of f being *continuous in the second argument* is analogous.

The following proposition is often useful.

2.4 Proposition Let D_0, D_1, E and F be cpo's.
(i) A function $f: D_0 \times D_1 \to E$ is continuous if and only if f is continuous in each argument.
(ii) Let $g: D_0 \times D_1 \to E$ be continuous and suppose $h_i: F \to D_i$ is continuous for $i = 0, 1$. Then $f: F \to E$ defined by $f(x) = g(h_0(x), h_1(x))$ is continuous.

Proof: (i) Suppose $f: D_0 \times D_1 \to E$ is continuous. Fix $b \in D_1$ and define $g: D_0 \to E$ by $g(x) = f(x,b)$. The function g is clearly monotone, since if $x \sqsubseteq y$ in D_0 then $(x,b) \sqsubseteq (y,b)$ in $D_0 \times D_1$ and hence $f(x,b) \sqsubseteq f(y,b)$. Suppose $A \subseteq D_0$ is directed. Then

$$\begin{aligned} g(\bigsqcup A) &= f(\bigsqcup A, b) & \\ &= f(\bigsqcup (A \times \{b\})) & \text{(Lemma 2.2)} \\ &= \bigsqcup f[A \times \{b\}] & \text{(f continuous)} \\ &= \bigsqcup g[A]. & \end{aligned}$$

Thus g is continuous.

Conversely, suppose $f: D_0 \times D_1 \to E$ is continuous in each of its arguments. First of all, f is monotone. For suppose $(x,y) \sqsubseteq (z,w)$. Then

$$f(x,y) \sqsubseteq f(z,y) \sqsubseteq f(z,w)$$

by the monotonicity in each argument. Now suppose $A \subseteq D_0 \times D_1$ is a directed set. Let $a = \bigsqcup \pi_0[A]$ and $b = \bigsqcup \pi_1[A]$, so that $\bigsqcup A = (a,b)$ by Lemma 2.2. Then

$$f(\bigsqcup A) = f(a,b) = f(a, \bigsqcup \pi_1[A]) = \bigsqcup_{y \in \pi_1[A]} f(a,y)$$

where the last equality follows from the continuity of f in the second argument. Similarly we obtain for fixed $y \in \pi_1[A]$,

$$f(a, y) = f(\sqcup \pi_0[A], y) = \sqcup_{x \in \pi_0[A]} f(x, y).$$

It follows that

$$f(\sqcup A) = \sqcup_{y \in \pi_1[A]} \sqcup_{x \in \pi_0[A]} f(x, y).$$

Let $x \in \pi_0[A]$ and $y \in \pi_1[A]$ and choose z and w such that $(x, z) \in A$ and $(w, y) \in A$. Since A is directed there is $(u, v) \in A$ such that $(x, z) \sqsubseteq (u, v)$ and $(w, y) \sqsubseteq (u, v)$. But then $(x, y) \sqsubseteq (u, v)$ and hence by the monotonicity of f,

$$f(x, y) \sqsubseteq f(u, v) \sqsubseteq \sqcup f[A].$$

Thus

$$f(\sqcup A) = \sqcup_{y \in \pi_1[A]} \sqcup_{x \in \pi_0[A]} f(x, y) \sqsubseteq \sqcup f[A]$$

and hence f is continuous.

(ii) Follows by a similar argument using Lemma 1.5. The details are left as an exercise. □

In a category **K** the *product* of objects A_0 and A_1 is an object B along with morphisms $p_i \in \mathrm{Hom}(B, A_i)$ which satisfy the following universal property. If C is an object in **K** and $f_i \in \mathrm{Hom}(C, A_i)$ then there is a unique $h \in \mathrm{Hom}(C, B)$ making the diagrams below commute for $i = 0, 1$.

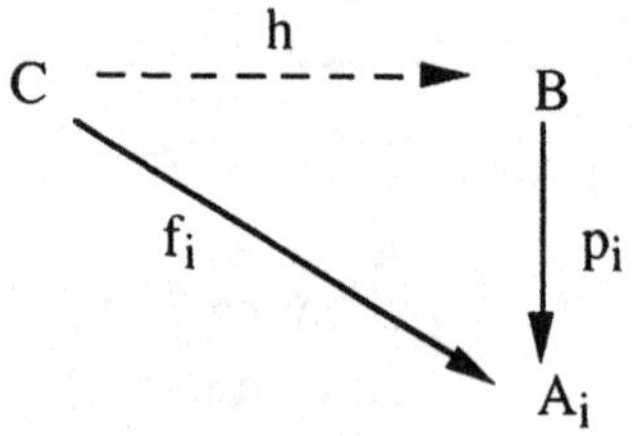

Suppose D_0 and D_1 are cpo's and consider $D_0 \times D_1$ along with its projection functions π_0 and π_1. Suppose further that E is a cpo and let $f_i : E \longrightarrow D_i$ be continuous for $i = 0, 1$. Then there is a unique continuous mapping h making the following diagrams commute.

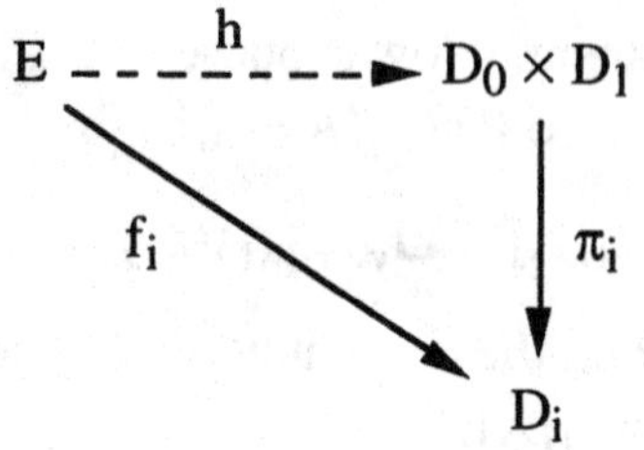

For, let $h: E \to D_0 \times D_1$ be defined by

$$h(x) = (f_0(x), f_1(x)).$$

Clearly h is the unique mapping making the diagrams commute and h is continuous by Proposition 2.4. Thus $D_0 \times D_1$ along with the projections π_0 and π_1 is the product of D_0 and D_1 in the category **Cpo**.

In order to obtain arbitrary finite cartesian products we simply iterate the construction.

2.5 Definition Let $D_0, D_1, \ldots, D_{n-1}$ be cpo's. Then the *cartesian product* of $D_0, D_1, \ldots, D_{n-1}$ is defined inductively by

$$\prod_{i<n} D_i = (\prod_{i<n-1} D_i) \times D_{n-1}$$

where $\prod_{i<2} D_i = D_0 \times D_1$.

Clearly $\prod_{i<n} D_i$ is isomorphic to the set $\{(x_0, \ldots, x_{n-1}) : x_i \in D_i\}$ with the coordinatewise ordering

$$(x_0, \ldots, x_{n-1}) \sqsubseteq (y_0, \ldots, y_{n-1}) \Leftrightarrow (\forall i < n)(x_i \sqsubseteq y_i).$$

Thus we identify $\prod_{i<n} D_i$ with this cpo. The appropriate projection mappings are

$$\pi_i : \prod_{j<n} D_j \to D_i \text{ defined by } \pi_i(x_0, \ldots, x_{n-1}) = x_i.$$

We also write $D_0 \times D_1 \times \ldots \times D_{n-1}$ for $\prod_{i<n} D_i$.

It follows from the iterative definition of $\prod_{i<n} D_i$ that all results of this section extend from the case $n=2$ to arbitrary n. In fact we have already provided both the bases and the inductive steps in the proofs.

2.6 Example Let $A_0, A_1, \ldots, A_{n-1}$ and B be non-empty sets. Then $(A_0)_\perp \times (A_1)_\perp \times \ldots \times (A_{n-1})_\perp$ and $B_\perp$ are cpo's. Note that, unless $n=1$, $(A_0)_\perp \times (A_1)_\perp \times \ldots \times (A_{n-1})_\perp$ is no longer a flat cpo. Suppose we have a function $f: A_0 \times \ldots \times A_{n-1} \to B$. Then $f_\perp : (A_0)_\perp \times (A_1)_\perp \times \ldots \times (A_{n-1})_\perp \to B_\perp$ is an extension of f defined by

$$f_\perp(x_0, \ldots, x_{n-1}) = \begin{cases} \perp & \text{if some } x_i = \perp \\ f(x_0, \ldots, x_{n-1}) & \text{otherwise.} \end{cases}$$

It is immediate that $f_\perp$ is continuous, since it is monotone, and it is also strict. The function $f_\perp$ is called the *minimal extension* of f.

It is often useful, for example when solving domain equations, to consider each construction for cpo's or domains as a functor. This means that we must also decide how a particular construction is to act on continuous functions.

Suppose $f_i : D_i \to E_i$ are continuous functions between cpo's, for $i < n$. Then we define $\prod_{i<n} f_i : \prod_{i<n} D_i \to \prod_{i<n} E_i$ by

$$(\prod_{i<n} f_i)(x_0, \ldots, x_{n-1}) = (f_0(x_0), \ldots, f_{n-1}(x_{n-1})).$$

The function $\prod_{i<n} f_i$ is also written as $f_0 \times \ldots \times f_{n-1}$. When the n is clear from the context we simply write $\prod$ for $\prod_{i<n}$.

2.7 Proposition Let $f_i : D_i \to E_i$ and $g_i : E_i \to F_i$ be continuous for $i<n$.
(i) $\prod f_i : \prod D_i \to \prod E_i$ is continuous.
(ii) $\prod id_{D_i} = id_{\prod D_i}$ where $id_D : D \to D$ is the identity function.
(iii) $\prod (g_i \circ f_i) = (\prod g_i) \circ (\prod f_i)$.

Proof: Exercise. □

The proposition shows that $\prod$ is a *covariant functor* from $\mathbf{Cpo}^n$ into $\mathbf{Cpo}$.

Section 2.3 Function Spaces

The most important and interesting construction on cpo's, and for that matter on domains, is that of the function space. In this section we show that given cpo's D and E we can construe the set of continuous functions from D into E as a cpo. Furthermore we show that this construction is the exponentiation or function space operation in the category **Cpo**. Then, in combination with the results of the previous section, we conclude that **Cpo** is a *cartesian closed category*.

3.1 Definition Let D and E be cpo's. Then the *function space* of D into E, denoted $[D \to E]$, is the following partially ordered set.

Universe: $[D \to E] = \{f \mid f : D \to E,\ f \text{ is continuous}\}$.

Ordering: $f \sqsubseteq g \Leftrightarrow f(x) \sqsubseteq g(x)$ for each $x \in D$.

Its associated *evaluation function* $eval : [D \to E] \times D \to E$ is defined by

$eval(f, x) = f(x)$.

It is easily verified that $[D \to E]$ is a partially ordered set with least element $\lambda x.\bot_E$. If we think of $[D \to E]$ as a subset of a possibly infinite cartesian product with D indexed copies of E, and its elements, therefore, as possibly infinite tuples, then the defined partial order is just an extension of the coordinatewise ordering of finite cartesian products.

3.2 Theorem Let D and E be cpo's. Then $[D \to E]$ is a cpo. Furthermore, if $\mathcal{F} \subseteq [D \to E]$ is directed then $\bigsqcup \mathcal{F}$ is the function defined by

$$(\bigsqcup \mathcal{F})(x) = \bigsqcup \{f(x) : f \in \mathcal{F}\}.$$

Proof: Let $\mathcal{F} \subseteq [D \to E]$ be a directed set and let $\mathcal{F}_x = \{f(x) : f \in \mathcal{F}\}$ for each $x \in D$. Then $\mathcal{F}_x \neq \varnothing$ since $\mathcal{F} \neq \varnothing$. Suppose $f(x), g(x) \in \mathcal{F}_x$. Since $\mathcal{F}$ is directed there is $h \in \mathcal{F}$ such that $f \sqsubseteq h$ and $g \sqsubseteq h$. But this implies that $f(x) \sqsubseteq h(x)$ and $g(x) \sqsubseteq h(x)$ and hence $\mathcal{F}_x$ is a directed set in E. Thus $\bigsqcup \mathcal{F}_x$ exists in E for each $x \in D$. Define $k : D \to E$ by $k(x) = \bigsqcup \mathcal{F}_x$. We show that k is continuous. First suppose $x \sqsubseteq y$ in D. Then, for $f \in \mathcal{F}$,

$$f(x) \sqsubseteq f(y) \sqsubseteq \bigsqcup \mathcal{F}_y = k(y),$$

so

$$k(x) = \bigsqcup \mathcal{F}_x = \bigsqcup \{f(x) : f \in \mathcal{F}\} \sqsubseteq k(y).$$

Thus k is monotone. Now suppose $A \subseteq D$ is directed. Then

$$\begin{aligned} k(\bigsqcup A) &= \bigsqcup_{f \in \mathcal{F}} f(\bigsqcup A) = \bigsqcup_{f \in \mathcal{F}} \bigsqcup_{x \in A} f(x) = \bigsqcup_{x \in A} \bigsqcup_{f \in \mathcal{F}} f(x) \\ &= \bigsqcup_{x \in A} k(x) = \bigsqcup k[A] \end{aligned}$$

showing that k is continuous. Here we used the continuity of $f \in \mathcal{F}$. That the supremum operations could be interchanged is the content of Exercise 3. It is easily verified that k is the least upper bound of $\mathcal{F}$ in $[D \to E]$. □

3.3 Proposition The function $\mathrm{eval} : [D \to E] \times D \to E$ is continuous.

Proof: By Proposition 2.4 it suffices to show that eval is continuous in each argument. This is trivially true of the second argument, since the fixed f in the first argument is continuous. Now fix $x \in D$ and let $h = \lambda f.\mathrm{eval}(f, x) = \lambda f.f(x)$. Clearly, h is monotone. Suppose $\mathcal{F} \subseteq [D \to E]$ is directed. Then

$$h(\bigsqcup \mathcal{F}) = (\bigsqcup \mathcal{F})(x) = \bigsqcup \{f(x) : f \in \mathcal{F}\} = \bigsqcup \{h(f) : f \in \mathcal{F}\} = \bigsqcup h[\mathcal{F}].$$

Thus h is continuous and hence eval is continuous. □

Let **K** be a category with finite products and let A and B be objects in **K**. Then an object C along with a morphism $e \in \mathrm{Hom}(C \times A, B)$ is the *exponentiation* or *function space* of A into B if it is a solution to the following universal problem: if D is an object in **K** and $f \in \mathrm{Hom}(D \times A, B)$ then there is a unique morphism $g \in \mathrm{Hom}(D, C)$ for which the following diagram commutes.

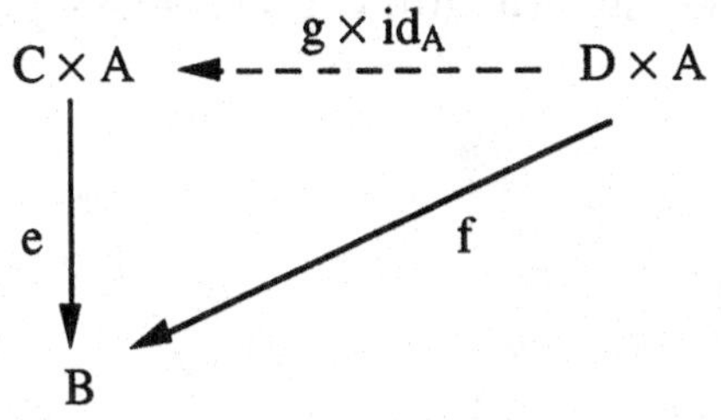

A category **K** is said to be *cartesian closed* if it has a terminal object and is closed under finite products and exponentiation. The trivial cpo $\{\bot\}$ is clearly a terminal object in the category **Cpo**. Thus it follows from the theorem below that **Cpo** is cartesian closed.

3.4 Theorem Let D, E and F be cpo's and suppose $f: F \times D \longrightarrow E$ is continuous. Then there is a unique continuous mapping $g: F \longrightarrow [D \longrightarrow E]$ making the diagram below commute.

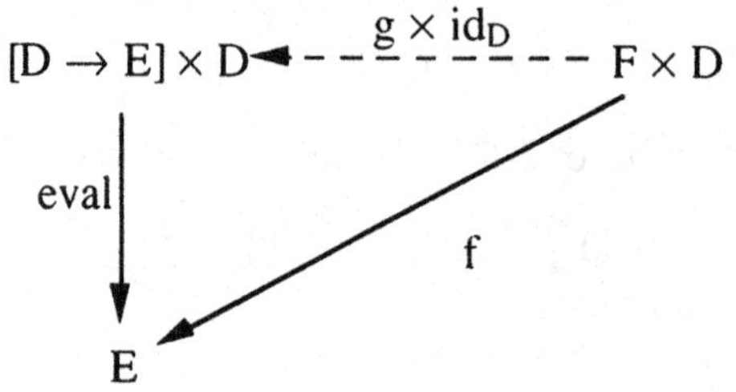

The unique function g of the theorem is denoted by curry(f). In Exercise 6 it is shown that the function $\text{curry}: [F \times D \longrightarrow E] \longrightarrow [F \longrightarrow [D \longrightarrow E]]$ defined by the theorem is itself continuous.

Proof: First we note the uniqueness of g assuming the existence of such a g. Let $x \in D$ and $u \in F$. Then, by the fact that the diagram above commutes,

$$\begin{aligned} g(u)(x) &= \text{eval}(g(u), x) \\ &= \text{eval}((g \times id_D)(u, x)) \\ &= f(u, x). \end{aligned}$$

Thus g is completely determined by f and hence is unique.

To prove existence, define g by $g(u) = \lambda x.f(u, x)$. Thus $g(u)$ is the function from D into E such that $g(u)(x) = f(u, x)$. Note that $g(u) \in [D \longrightarrow E]$ for each $u \in F$, since f is continuous and hence continuous in its second argument. We now show that g is continuous. Suppose $u \sqsubseteq v$ in F. Then for each $x \in D$,

$$g(u)(x) = f(u, x) \sqsubseteq f(v, x) = g(v)(x)$$

by the monotonicity of f, showing that $g(u) \sqsubseteq g(v)$. Now suppose $A \subseteq F$ is directed. Then for each $x \in D$,

$$
\begin{aligned}
g(\bigsqcup A)(x) &= f(\bigsqcup A, x) \\
&= \bigsqcup f[A \times \{x\}] \qquad \text{(f is continuous)} \\
&= \bigsqcup \{f(u,x) : u \in A\} \\
&= \bigsqcup \{g(u)(x) : u \in A\} \\
&= (\bigsqcup g[A])(x).
\end{aligned}
$$

Thus $g(\bigsqcup A) = \bigsqcup g[A]$ so g is continuous. □

The curry function, whose effect is to transform functions in two variables to functions in one variable, is very useful when defining continuous functions. Let D, E and F be cpo's and suppose we want to define a continuous function $h : F \to [D \to E]$. Thus we want $h(u)$ to be continuous for each $u \in F$ and h itself should be continuous. Given $u \in F$ we may define $h(u)$ by how it acts on $x \in D$. If we obtain $h(u)(x) = f(u,x)$ for each $u \in F$ and each $x \in D$, where $f : F \times D \to E$ is continuous, then we know that $h = \text{curry}(f)$ by the above theorem. In particular, we know that $h(u)$ is continuous for each u and that h is continuous. For an application of this, see Example 3.7.

Let us consider exponentiation as a functor. For ease of notation, denote $[D \to E]$ by $H(D,E)$. To make $H : \mathbf{Cpo}^2 \to \mathbf{Cpo}$ into a functor we must decide how H is to act on continuous functions. After some reflection (see the diagram below) it becomes clear that a reasonable choice is to make H contravariant in the first argument and covariant in the second argument. Let $f_0 : E_0 \to D_0$ and $f_1 : D_1 \to E_1$ be continuous. Then define $H(f_0, f_1) : [D_0 \to D_1] \to [E_0 \to E_1]$ by

$$H(f_0, f_1)(h) = f_1 \circ h \circ f_0.$$

Thus we obtain the following diagram.

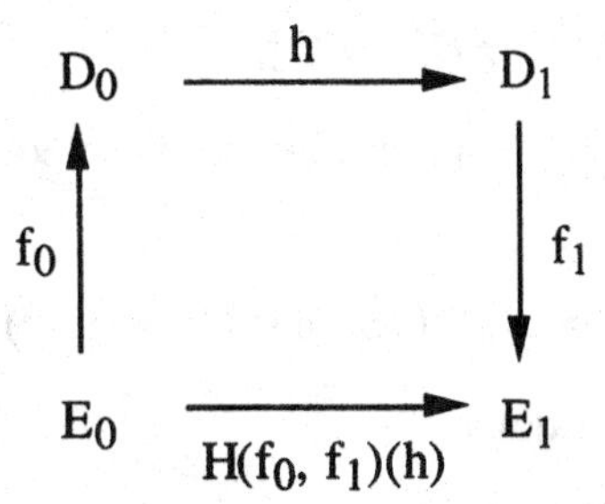

This makes H into a bifunctor, which is contravariant in the first argument and covariant in the second argument, by the following proposition.

3.5 Proposition Let $f_0:E_0\to D_0$, $g_0:F_0\to E_0$, $f_1:D_1\to E_1$ and $g_1:E_1\to F_1$ be continuous. Then
(i) $H(id_D, id_E)=id_{H(D,E)}$, and
(ii) $H(f_0\circ g_0, g_1\circ f_1)=H(g_0,g_1)\circ H(f_0,f_1)$.

Proof: Exercise. □

Now we formulate our fixed point theorem.

3.6 Theorem Let D be a cpo. Then each $f\in[D\to D]$ has a least fixed point in D. Furthermore, the mapping $fix:[D\to D]\to D$ defined by

$$fix(f)=\text{least fixed point of } f$$

is continuous.

Proof: Every cpo is an ω-cpo. Thus each $f\in[D\to D]$ has a least fixed point by Theorem 1.2.3 and this fixed point is $\sqcup\{f^n(\bot): n\in\mathbb{N}\}$. For fixed n, define $h_n:[D\to D]\to D$ by $h_n(f)=f^n(\bot)$. By induction on n we show that each h_n is continuous. First of all, $h_0(f)=\bot$, so h_0 is continuous since it is a constant function. Assuming h_n is continuous we have that

$$h_{n+1}(f)=f^{n+1}(\bot)=f(f^n(\bot))=f(h_n(f))=eval(f,h_n(f))$$

and hence h_{n+1} is continuous by Propositions 2.4 and 3.3. For each $f\in[D\to D]$,

$$\bot\sqsubseteq f(\bot)\sqsubseteq f^2(\bot)\sqsubseteq\ldots\sqsubseteq f^n(\bot)\sqsubseteq\ldots$$

that is

$$h_0(f)\sqsubseteq h_1(f)\sqsubseteq h_2(f)\sqsubseteq\ldots\sqsubseteq h_n(f)\ \ldots\ .$$

But then

$$h_0\sqsubseteq h_1\sqsubseteq h_2\sqsubseteq\ldots \text{ in } [[D\to D]\to D],$$

that is the set $\{h_n: n\in\mathbb{N}\}$ is an ω-chain and hence directed. Now we let $h=\sqcup\{h_n: n\in\mathbb{N}\}$. Then

$$h(f)=\sqcup\{h_n(f): n\in\mathbb{N}\}=\sqcup\{f^n(\bot): n\in\mathbb{N}\}=fix(f),$$

so $fix=h$ and hence fix is continuous. □

3.7 Example Let $sg_\bot:\mathbb{N}_\bot\to\mathbb{B}_\bot$ be defined by

$$sg_\bot(x)=\begin{cases} tt & \text{if } x=0\\ ff & \text{if } x>0,\ x\in\mathbb{N}\\ \bot & \text{if } x=\bot\end{cases}$$

and let $dc:\mathbb{N}_\bot\times\mathbb{N}_\bot\times\mathbb{B}_\bot\to\mathbb{N}_\bot$ be defined by

$$dc(x,y,z) = \begin{cases} x & \text{if } z = tt \\ y & \text{if } z = ff \\ \bot & \text{if } z = \bot. \end{cases}$$

Let P and S be the predecessor and successor functions on the natural numbers $\mathbb{N}$, and let $P_\bot$ and $S_\bot$ be their minimal extensions to $[\mathbb{N}_\bot \to \mathbb{N}_\bot]$. Define $H: [\mathbb{N}_\bot \times \mathbb{N}_\bot \to \mathbb{N}_\bot] \to [\mathbb{N}_\bot \times \mathbb{N}_\bot \to \mathbb{N}_\bot]$ by

$$\begin{aligned} H(f)(x,y) &= dc(x, S_\bot(f(x, P_\bot(y))), sg_\bot(y)) \\ &= dc(x, S_\bot(eval(f, (x, P_\bot(y)))), sg_\bot(y)). \end{aligned}$$

Then H is continuous since H is the curry of a continuous function. Thus H has a least fixed point. It is easy to see, by induction, that this fixed point is addition on $\mathbb{N}$ extended to $[\mathbb{N}_\bot \times \mathbb{N}_\bot \to \mathbb{N}_\bot]$.

We close this section by considering simultaneous fixed points. Often in mathematics, also in the theory of cpo's and domains, one is interested in solving systems of equations. Of course this cannot always be done, for example when the equations in the system are contradictory. For cpo's we have the following positive result.

3.8 Proposition Let $D_0, D_1, \ldots, D_{n-1}$ be cpo's. Suppose that the functions $f_i: D_0 \times D_1 \times \ldots \times D_{n-1} \to D_i$ are continuous for $i = 0, \ldots, n-1$. Then the system of equations

$$(*) \qquad \begin{cases} x_0 = f_0(x_0, x_1, \ldots, x_{n-1}) \\ \quad \vdots \\ x_{n-1} = f_{n-1}(x_0, x_1, \ldots, x_{n-1}) \end{cases}$$

has a solution $(x_0, \ldots, x_{n-1}) \in D_0 \times D_1 \times \ldots \times D_{n-1}$.

Proof: Let $\langle f_0, \ldots, f_{n-1} \rangle : \prod_{i<n} D_i \to \prod_{i<n} D_i$ be defined by

$$\langle f_0, \ldots, f_{n-1} \rangle (x_0, \ldots, x_{n-1}) = (f_0(x_0, \ldots, x_{n-1}), \ldots, f_{n-1}(x_0, \ldots, x_{n-1})).$$

It is easily seen that $\langle f_0, \ldots, f_{n-1} \rangle$ is continuous by Proposition 2.4 (ii). The least fixed point $(x_0, \ldots, x_{n-1})$ of $\langle f_0, \ldots, f_{n-1} \rangle$ is then clearly a solution to the system of equations (*). □

Section 2.4 Further Constructions

In this last section we consider some further constructions on cpo's. These constructions, though important, are mathematically simpler than that of the function space. Therefore, our presentation will be descriptive in the sense that we leave all proofs to the reader. Actually, most of the constructions make sense for partially ordered sets, just as was the case for the cartesian product. For later reference we will formulate the constructions in terms of partially ordered sets when possible.

First we consider a construction corresponding to taking disjoint unions.

4.1 Definition Let D_0 and D_1 be partially ordered sets. Then the *separated sum* of D_0 and D_1, denoted D_0+D_1, is the following partially ordered set.

Universe: $D_0+D_1=\{(0,x): x\in D_0\}\cup\{(1,y): y\in D_1\}\cup\{\bot\}$.

Ordering: $u\sqsubseteq v \Leftrightarrow u=\bot$ or $u=(i,x)$, $v=(i,y)$ and $x\sqsubseteq y$.

Its associated injections $in_i: D_i \longrightarrow D_0+D_1$, for $i=0,1$, are defined by

$in_i(x)=(i,x)$.

Here we assume, of course, that $\bot$ is a distinguished element which does not belong to $\{0\}\times D_0\cup\{1\}\times D_1$. It is easily verified that D_0+D_1 is a cpo if D_0 and D_1 are cpo's. It may be pictured as:

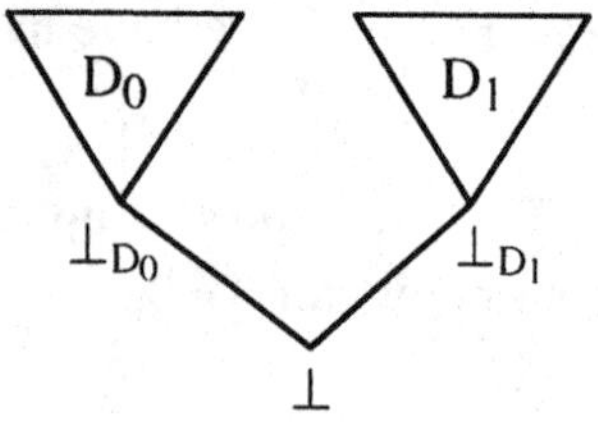

Let D_0 and D_1 be cpo's. Then each in_i is continuous. Suppose in addition that E is a cpo and $f: D_0\longrightarrow E$ and $g: D_1\longrightarrow E$ are continuous functions. Then there is a continuous function $[f,g]$ making the following diagram commute.

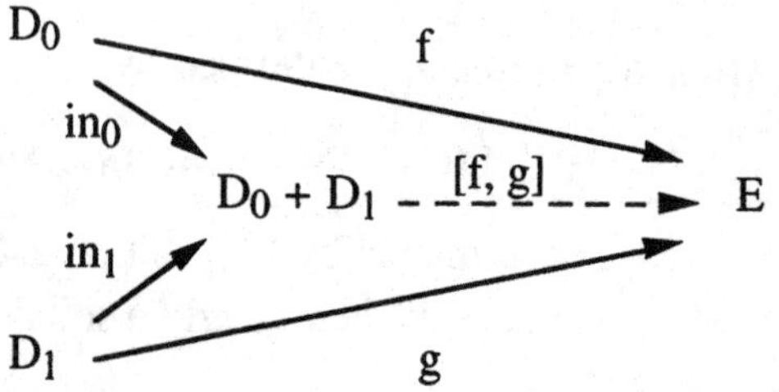

Namely, define $[f,g]: D_0+D_1 \longrightarrow E$ by

$$[f,g](w)=\begin{cases} f(x) & \text{if } w=(0,x) \\ g(y) & \text{if } w=(1,y) \\ \bot_E & \text{if } w=\bot. \end{cases}$$

However, $[f,g]$ need not be the unique continuous function satisfying the diagram, since it is in general easy to find a non-strict continuous function which also makes the diagram commute, by choosing an appropriate value for $\perp$. The notion of a *coproduct* in a category is the dual to that of a product, that is all arrows in the definition of a product are reversed. The lack of uniqueness for $[f,g]$ illustrates why the category **Cpo** does not have coproducts. Also observe that the operation $+$ is not associative, that is

$$(D+E)+F \not\cong D+(E+F)$$

in general.

Computationally, if we identify non-termination with $\perp$, the separated sum corresponds to lazy evaluation. The constructors $in_i(\cdot)$ do not force evaluation of their arguments, since $in_i(\perp) \neq \perp$.

As usual, we want to consider $+$ as a functor from $\mathbf{Cpo}^2$ into **Cpo**. Let $f_i : D_i \longrightarrow E_i$ be continuous, $i=0,1$. Define $(f_0+f_1) : (D_0+D_1) \longrightarrow (E_0+E_1)$ by

$$(f_0+f_1)(w) = \begin{cases} (0, f_0(x)) & \text{if } w=(0,x) \\ (1, f_1(y)) & \text{if } w=(1,y) \\ \perp & \text{if } w=\perp. \end{cases}$$

We leave it as an exercise to show that the separated sum, $+$, defined in this way is a covariant functor.

Now we consider a product which when interpreted computationally corresponds to eager evaluation. Identifying $\perp$ with undefined, this means that a tuple is defined if and only if all components are defined.

4.2 Definition Let D and E be partially ordered sets with a least element. Then the *smash product* or *strict product* of D and E, denoted $D \otimes E$, is the following partially ordered set:

Universe: $D \otimes E = \{(x,y) \in D \times E : x \neq \perp_D \ \&\ y \neq \perp_E \text{ or } x = \perp_D \ \&\ y = \perp_E\}$.

Ordering: $(x,y) \sqsubseteq (z,w) \Leftrightarrow x \sqsubseteq z$ and $y \sqsubseteq w$.

It is easily verified that if D and E are cpo's then $D \otimes E$ is a cpo, in fact a subcpo of $D \times E$. Note that if D and E are flat cpo's then $D \otimes E$ is also flat, while $D \times E$ is not unless both D and E are trivial.

Let $\iota : D \otimes E \longrightarrow D \times E$ be the inclusion mapping and let $\otimes : D \times E \longrightarrow D \otimes E$ be defined by

$$\otimes(x,y) = \begin{cases} (x,y) & \text{if } x \neq \perp \ \&\ y \neq \perp \\ (\perp,\perp) & \text{otherwise.} \end{cases}$$

Then, for cpo's D and E, ι and $\otimes$ are continuous functions and they form a projection pair for $(D \otimes E, D \times E)$.

To define $\otimes$ as a functor from $\mathbf{Cpo}^2$ into $\mathbf{Cpo}$ assume $f_i: D_i \rightarrow E_i$ are continuous for $i=0,1$. Define $(f_0 \otimes f_1): D_0 \otimes D_1 \rightarrow E_0 \otimes E_1$ by

$$(f_0 \otimes f_1)(x,y) = \otimes(f_0(x), f_1(x)).$$

Then $(f_0 \otimes f_1)$ is continuous by Proposition 2.4 and Lemma 1.5. It is easily verified that the properties of a functor hold.

There is also a strict version of the function space.

4.3 Definition Let D and E be cpo's. The *strict function space* of D into E, denoted $[D \rightarrow_{\perp} E]$, is the set

$$[D \rightarrow_{\perp} E] = \{f \mid f: D \rightarrow E, \ f \text{ is strict and continuous}\}$$

with the ordering inherited from $[D \rightarrow E]$.

If $\mathcal{F} \subseteq [D \rightarrow_{\perp} E]$ is a directed set then clearly $\bigsqcup \mathcal{F}$ is a strict function. It follows that $[D \rightarrow_{\perp} E]$ is a subcpo of $[D \rightarrow E]$. Let $\iota: [D \rightarrow_{\perp} E] \rightarrow [D \rightarrow E]$ be the inclusion mapping and define $j: [D \rightarrow E] \rightarrow [D \rightarrow_{\perp} E]$ by

$$j(f)(x) = \begin{cases} \perp & \text{if } x = \perp \\ f(x) & \text{if } x \neq \perp. \end{cases}$$

Then (ι, j) is a projection pair from $[D \rightarrow_{\perp} E]$ to $[D \rightarrow E]$. To see $\rightarrow_{\perp}$ as a functor is completely analogous to the case for $\rightarrow$, since strictness is preserved under composition.

We also consider the strict version of the disjoint union.

4.4 Definition Let D_0 and D_1 be partially ordered sets with a least element. The *smash sum* or *amalgamated sum* of D_0 and D_1, denoted $D_0 \oplus D_1$, is the partially ordered set

$$D_0 \oplus D_1 = \{(0,x): x \in D_0, x \neq \perp_{D_0}\} \cup \{(1,y): y \in D_1, y \neq \perp_{D_1}\} \cup \{\perp\}$$

with the ordering inherited from $D_0 + D_1$.

Thus $D_0 \oplus D_1$ is the the partially ordered set obtained from $D_0 + D_1$ by identifying the bottom elements in D_0 and D_1. We have the following picture.

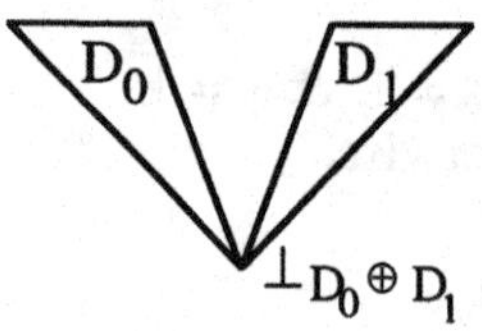

If D_0 and D_1 are cpo's then $D_0 \oplus D_1$ is a cpo. Define $in_i : D_i \to D_0 \oplus D_1$, for $i = 0, 1$, by

$$in_i(x) = \begin{cases} (i, x) & \text{if } x \neq \perp_{D_i} \\ \perp & \text{if } x = \perp_{D_i}. \end{cases}$$

Then, for cpo's D_0 and D_1, the functions in_i are strict and continuous. Recalling our discussion for the separated sum it is clear that $D_0 \oplus D_1$ together with the injections in_i is the coproduct of D_0 and D_1 in the category $\mathbf{Cpo}_\perp$. In contrast with the separated sum, it is easily seen that $\oplus$ is associative, that is $(D \oplus E) \oplus F \cong D \oplus (E \oplus F)$. The construction $\oplus$ becomes a covariant bifunctor by defining its action on morphisms just as in the case of the separated sum $+$. Note that $f_0 \oplus f_1$ is strict.

Finally we consider a construction which transforms continuous functions into strict continuous functions.

4.5 Definition Let D be a partially ordered set and let $\perp \notin D$ be some distinguished element. Then the *lifting* of D, denoted by $D_\perp$, is the set $D_\perp = D \cup \{\perp\}$ ordered by $x \sqsubseteq y \Leftrightarrow x = \perp$ or $x \sqsubseteq_D y$.

Clearly $D_\perp$ is a cpo whenever D is. Its picture is:

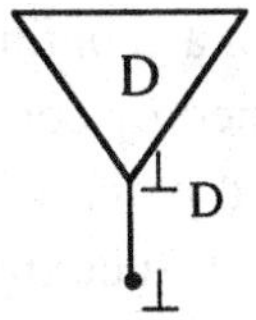

Let $\iota : D \to D_\perp$ be the inclusion mapping. Suppose D and E are cpo's and that $f : D \to E$ is continuous. Then there is a unique strict continuous function $h : D_\perp \to_\perp E$ such that the following diagram commutes.

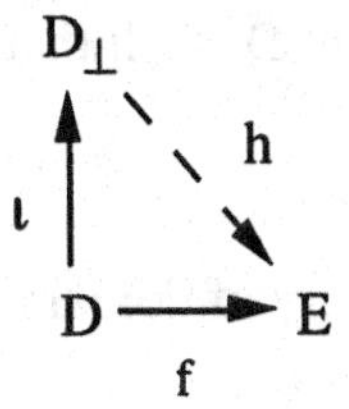

Namely the function h defined by

$$h(x) = \begin{cases} f(x) & \text{if } x \in D \\ \perp_E & \text{if } x = \perp. \end{cases}$$

Let lift(f) denote the unique strict continuous h above. Then it is easily verified that $\text{lift}:[D\to E]\to[D_\perp\to_\perp E]$ is continuous. Thus lift continuously extends a continuous function $f:D\to E$ into a strict continuous function $\text{lift}(f):D_\perp\to_\perp E$. Finally, in order to consider lifting as a covariant functor, suppose $f:D\to E$ is continuous. Then define $f_\perp:D_\perp\to E_\perp$ by

$$f_\perp(x)=\begin{cases} f(x) & \text{if } x\in D \\ \perp & \text{if } x=\perp. \end{cases}$$

Clearly $f_\perp$ is continuous and also strict and the properties of a functor hold.

Starting from simple cpo's, for example flat ones, we are now in a position to construct rather complicated cpo's by the methods described above. However such constructions are finitary in the sense that each such cpo is constructed from basic ones using finitely many applications of these operations. Can this be extended to the transfinite? We have taken care to see each construction as a functor. Thus composing the given constructions we obtain functors from $\mathbf{Cpo}^n$ into **Cpo**. For example, the functor $F:\mathbf{Cpo}\to\mathbf{Cpo}$ defined by

$$F(D)=\mathbb{N}_\perp+[D\to D]$$

is obtained in this way. Suppose we could consider **Cpo** as a "cpo" (ignoring for the moment that the class of objects in **Cpo** is not even a set) and suppose that each of our constructions provided us with a "continuous" functor with respect to the "cpo" **Cpo**. Then each functor obtained by composition of our constructions would have a least fixed point by the fixed point theorem. In particular, from the functor F above we would obtain a cpo D such that

$$D=\mathbb{N}_\perp+[D\to D].$$

Of course, for trivial set-theoretic reasons this is too much to hope for. A function from D into D cannot be an element of D. However, by the reasoning sketched above we will be able to obtain fixed points up to isomorphism. Thus the functor F will give us a cpo and in fact a domain D such that

$$D\cong\mathbb{N}_\perp+[D\to D].$$

These issues belong to the important theory of domain equations which is the subject of Chapter 4.

2.5 Exercises

1. Clearly each cpo is an ω-cpo. Give an example of an ω-cpo which is not a cpo. Is there a countable such ω-cpo?

2. Let D and E be cpo's and suppose $f: D \longrightarrow E$.
(i) Show that f is continuous if f is order-preserving and surjective.
(ii) Show that $D \cong f[D]$ in case f is order-preserving and continuous.
(iii) Is any direction of the following equivalence true: f is continuous if and only if f is order-preserving?

3. Let D be a cpo and suppose $a_{ij} \in D$ for $i \in I$ and $j \in J$. Assume also that $A_i = \{a_{ij} : j \in J\}$ and $B_j = \{a_{ij} : i \in I\}$ are directed sets for each $i \in I$ and $j \in J$ and that $\{\bigsqcup A_i : i \in I\}$ and $\{\bigsqcup B_j : j \in J\}$ are directed. Show that $\bigsqcup_{i \in I}(\bigsqcup_{j \in J} a_{ij}) = \bigsqcup_{j \in J}(\bigsqcup_{i \in I} a_{ij})$.

4. Let D and E be cpo's.
(i) Let $f: D \longrightarrow E$ be continuous. Show, by providing a counterexample, that it is not always the case that $f(\bigsqcup A) = \bigsqcup f[A]$ for each $A \subseteq D$ such that $\bigsqcup A$ exists.
(ii) Suppose (f, g) is a projection pair for (D, E). Is it then true that $f(\bigsqcup A) = \bigsqcup f[A]$ for each $A \subseteq D$ such that $\bigsqcup A$ exists?

5. Let $\mathbf{Cpo_p}$ be the category whose objects are cpo's and whose morphisms are projection pairs.
(i) Show that $\mathbf{Cpo_p}$ is a category.
(ii) State what it means that $D \cong E$ in $\mathbf{Cpo_p}$.
(iii) Let D and E be cpo's. Is it true that $D \cong E$ in $\mathbf{Cpo_p}$ if and only if $D \cong E$ in $\mathbf{Cpo}$? Is either of the two implications true? Investigate this question by providing proofs and/or counterexamples.

6. Let curry: $[D \times E \longrightarrow F] \longrightarrow [D \longrightarrow [E \longrightarrow F]]$ be the function defined by Theorem 3.4. Give an explicit definition of curry and show that curry is continuous. Is curry an isomorphism?

7. Let $\mathbf{K}$ be a cartesian closed category. Show that the exponentiation or the function space of objects A and B is unique in $\mathbf{K}$ up to isomorphism. [You must show that if C and E are objects satisfying the universal problem given before Theorem 3.4 then $C \cong E$ in $\mathbf{K}$.]

8. Let $f:D\times E\to D$ and $g:D\times E\to E$ be continuous functions, where D and E are cpo's. Let $h(y)=\text{fix}(\lambda x.f(x,y))$ and then set $k(y)=g(h(y),y)$. Consider the system of equations

$$(*)\qquad \begin{cases} x=f(x,y) \\ y=g(x,y). \end{cases}$$

(i) Show that h and k are continuous.
(ii) Let $\bar{y}=\text{fix}(k)$ and $\bar{x}=h(\bar{y})$. Show that $(\bar{x},\bar{y})$ is the least simultaneous fixed point of $(*)$.
(iii) Explain what this amounts to when $f(x,y)$ is independent of y. Explain further what happens if g does not depend on x.

9. Let D be a cpo and define D^ω by $D^\omega=\{f \mid f:\mathbb{N}\to D\}$, that is D^ω is the infinite power of D.
(i) Define a partial order on D^ω making D^ω into a cpo such that $D^\omega\cong D\times D^\omega$. (Thus D^ω is the infinite cartesian power of D.) Make the isomorphism $D^\omega\cong D\times D^\omega$ explicit, that is prove that D^ω and $D\times D^\omega$ are isomorphic.
(ii) More generally, let I be a set and suppose D_i is a cpo for each $i\in I$. Let

$$\Pi_{i\in I}D_i=\{f \mid f:I\to \cup_{i\in I}D_i,\ f(i)\in D_i \text{ for each } i\in I\}.$$

Define a partial order on $\Pi_{i\in I}D_i$ such that $\Pi_{i\in I}D_i$ becomes a cpo and such that if I is finite then $\Pi_{i\in I}D_i$ is the usual cartesian product. Is it true that $f:\Pi_{i\in I}D_i\to E$ is continuous if and only if f is continuous in each argument?

10. Let $\mathbb{B}_\perp$ be the flat Boolean cpo and let $\mathbb{C}$ be the Cantor space as a cpo (see Examples 1.11 and 1.12).
(i) Show that there is a projection pair from $\mathbb{C}$ into $\mathbb{B}_\perp^\omega$. (See Exercise 9.)
(ii) Are $\mathbb{C}$ and $\mathbb{B}_\perp^\omega$ isomorphic?

11. Let Σ be a finite alphabet (i.e. a set) and denote by Σ^* the set of all words over Σ and by Σ^ω the set of all ω-words over Σ. (So if $\Sigma=\{a_1,\ldots,a_n\}$ then

$$\Sigma^*=\{a_{i_1}a_{i_2}\ldots a_{i_k}: 0\le k,\ 1\le i_j\le n\},\ \text{and}\ \Sigma^\omega=\{a_{i_1}a_{i_2}\ldots : 1\le i_j\le n\}.)$$

Let $D=\Sigma^*\cup\Sigma^\omega$. For each $w\in\Sigma^*$, define $f_w:D\to D$ by $f_w(x)=wx$, where the operation is concatenation.
(i) Define a partial order on D making D into a cpo such that each f_w is continuous.

(ii) For which $w \in \Sigma^*$ will f_w have unique fixed points?
(iii) Suppose $0, 1 \in \Sigma$ and consider the system of equations

$$\begin{cases} X = 0Y \\ Y = 1X. \end{cases}$$

Solve the system in D.

12. Let D be a cpo, $a \in D$, and define $D_a = \{x \in D : x \sqsubseteq a\}$.
(i) Show that D_a is a cpo.
(ii) Let $f: D \longrightarrow D$ be continuous and suppose $f': D_{fix(f)} \longrightarrow D_{fix(f)}$ is the restriction of f to $D_{fix(f)}$. Explain why $f'(x) \in D_{fix(f)}$ for $x \in D_{fix(f)}$ and why f' is continuous. How many fixed points does f' have?

13. Let D, E and F be cpo's. Define $eval: [D \longrightarrow_\bot E] \otimes D \longrightarrow_\bot E$ by $eval(f, x) = f(x)$. Suppose $f: F \otimes D \longrightarrow_\bot E$ is strict and continuous. Show that there is a unique strict and continuous function $g: F \longrightarrow_\bot [D \longrightarrow_\bot E]$ such that the following diagram commutes:

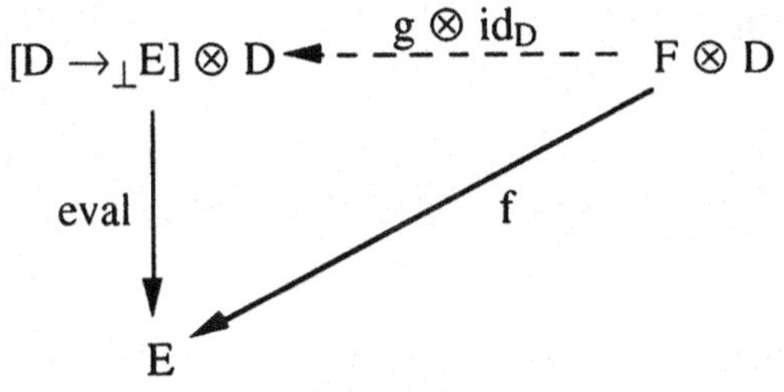

The unique g is denoted $curry_\bot(f)$.

14. Is the category **Cpo**$_\bot$ cartesian closed? If so, what is the product and what is the exponentiation?

15. Let D and E be cpo's.
(i) Show that $D + E \cong D_\bot \oplus E_\bot$. Draw a picture of $D_\bot \oplus E_\bot$.
(ii) Show that $(D \times E)_\bot \cong D_\bot \otimes E_\bot$.

16. Say that a strict continuous mapping $f: D \longrightarrow_\bot E$ is *very strict* if $f(x) = \bot$ if and only if $x = \bot$. Show that $\otimes$ is the product in the subcategory of **Cpo**$_\bot$ whose morphisms are the very strict continuous functions.

17. Show that $(D \times E) \times F \cong D \times (E \times F)$. Is the same true for $\otimes$?

18. Show that a non-empty partial order $D=(D;\sqsubseteq)$ is a cpo if and only if for each chain (that is, linearly ordered set) $C \subseteq D$, $\bigsqcup C$ exists in D.
[Use ordinals.]

19. Let D and E be cpo's and suppose D is finite. Is it then true that $f:D \to E$ is continuous if and only if f is monotone? What about the same question for $g:E \to D$?

CHAPTER 3

DOMAINS

When we abstracted from our introductory example of the partial function spaces $A \xrightarrow{p} B$ in Chapter 1 to complete partial orders, we deferred the consideration of the central notion of finite. In this chapter we enrich our structures by defining an abstract notion of *finite* or, as we shall say, *compact*, which makes sense for any cpo and which is a generalization of finiteness in partial function spaces. Then we restrict our attention to those cpo's which have the desirable computability property that each element is the limit of its compact approximations. A cpo satisfying this requirement is said to be *algebraic*. The compact elements in a cpo are considered to be the concrete elements on which we can compute. We then extend our computations to an arbitrary element, provided that this element is the limit of compact elements, by saying that the result of the computation is the limit of the results of the computation on each finite or compact approximation. For this reason the algebraic cpo's seem satisfactory from a computational point of view. However, the class or category of algebraic cpo's is still not adequate for one very important reason. It is not cartesian closed! There are algebraic cpo's D and E such that the cpo $[D \rightarrow E]$ is not algebraic. Therefore we restrict ourselves further to those algebraic cpo's which are *consistently complete*. These cpo's we call *Scott–Ershov domains* or simply *domains*. Domains do form a cartesian closed category.

In the first section we make precise all these notions and how they relate to continuity. Then, in Section 3.2, we prove a representation theorem which shows that a domain is completely determined by its compact elements in that it is *the completion* of its compact elements. In Section 3.3 we prove that the category of domains is cartesian closed and in the last section some further constructions on domains are briefly considered.

Section 3.1 Domains

We start by abstracting a notion of finite for elements in a cpo D. Recall that we consider directed sets $A \subseteq D$ as generalized sequences and that D is *complete* in the sense that each such sequence A "converges" to an element in D, namely $\sqcup A$.

To make matters concrete let $D = A \xrightarrow{p} B$ be the cpo of partial functions from the set A into the set B. A first property we observe for a finite element $f \in D$ is that it cannot be approximated by an increasing sequence of elements which are strictly smaller than f. Thus, in general, we should certainly require of a finite element a that if $a = \bigsqcup A$, where A is a directed set, then $a \in A$. However, we want a stronger requirement which certainly is true of finite elements in the function space $A \xrightarrow{p} B$, namely that if $a \in D$ is a "finite approximation" of an element x then it is a significant approximation in the sense that there is no way to approximate x which does not take a into account. Let us make this precise. Suppose $x = \bigsqcup A$ where A is directed. Then let $A' = \{y \in D : (\exists z \in A)(y \sqsubseteq z)\}$. that is we close A downwards to obtain A'. Clearly A' is also a directed set and we have $\bigsqcup A' = \bigsqcup A = x$. Thus we require that if a is to be a "finite" element then whenever $a \sqsubseteq \bigsqcup A$, where A is directed, we must have $a \in A'$. This leads us to the following abstraction of finiteness.

1.1 Definition Let D be a cpo. An element $a \in D$ is said to be *compact* or *finite* if whenever $A \subseteq D$ is a directed set and $a \sqsubseteq \bigsqcup A$ then there is $x \in A$ such that $a \sqsubseteq x$. The set of compact elements in D is denoted by D_c.

In order to easily distinguish between the compact elements and those elements which may not be compact, we use the notational convention that lower case letters from the beginning of the alphabet vary over D_c while lower case letters towards the end of the alphabet vary over D.

1.2 Examples

(i) The bottom element $\bot \in D$ is compact for each cpo D.

(ii) If D is a flat cpo or a finite cpo then $D_c = D$.

(iii) Let $\wp(\omega) = (\wp(\omega); \subseteq, \emptyset)$, where $\wp(\omega)$ is the power set of the natural numbers ω. Then $\wp(\omega)$ is a cpo and $\wp(\omega)_c = \wp_f(\omega) = \{K \subseteq \omega : K \text{ finite}\}$.

(iv) Consider the ordinal cpo's of Example 2.1.14. For $\omega + 1$, each $n \in \omega$ is compact. But $\omega = \bigsqcup \omega$ so ω is not compact, and hence $(\omega + 1)_c = \omega$. For an arbitrary successor ordinal α, $\alpha_c = \{\beta < \alpha : \beta \text{ a successor ordinal}\} \cup \{0\}$.

(v) Let $\mathbb{C}$ be the Cantor space of Example 2.1.12. Then $\mathbb{C}_c = \mathrm{SEQ}$.

(vi) Let $\mathcal{P}$ be the Baire space of Example 2.1.13. Then $\mathcal{P}_c = \{f \in \mathcal{P} : f \text{ finite}\}$.

(vii) Let $D = [A_\bot \rightarrow B_\bot]$ where A and B are sets. Then $f \in D$ is compact if and only if the set $\{x \in A_\bot : f(x) \neq \bot\}$ is finite or f is a constant function.

(viii) Let D be the following cpo.

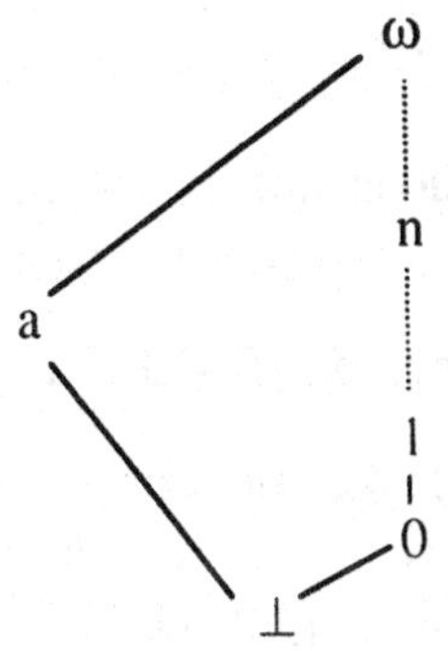

Referring to our preliminary discussion, note that a cannot be approximated strictly from below. Thus a satisfies the first requirement of being finite. However, a fails to satisfy the stronger requirement. We have that $a \sqsubseteq \omega$, but there is a way to approximate ω which does not take a into account at all, namely $\omega = \bigsqcup\{n : n \in \mathbb{N}\}$. Hence, by our definition, a is not a compact element.

Now we can make precise the algebraicity condition on cpo's.

1.3 Definition A cpo D is an *algebraic cpo* if for each $x \in D$, the set $\text{approx}(x) = \{a \in D_c : a \sqsubseteq x\}$ is directed and $x = \bigsqcup \text{approx}(x)$.

All examples in 1.2, except (viii), are algebraic cpo's. Example (viii) fails to be algebraic since $\text{approx}(a) = \{\bot\}$ and hence $a \neq \bigsqcup \text{approx}(a)$.

As will be made precise in the next section, a domain, and for that matter an algebraic cpo, is completely determined by its compact elements. A first observation in this direction is the following lemma.

1.4 Lemma Let D be an algebraic cpo.

(i) For $x, y \in D$, $x \sqsubseteq y$ if and only if $\text{approx}(x) \subseteq \text{approx}(y)$.

(ii) If $A \subseteq D$ is directed then $\text{approx}(\bigsqcup A) = \bigcup\{\text{approx}(x) : x \in A\}$.

Proof: The proof of (i) is left as an exercise. For (ii), by definition, if $a \in \text{approx}(\bigsqcup A)$ then $a \in D_c$ and $a \sqsubseteq \bigsqcup A$. Hence there is $x \in A$ such that $a \sqsubseteq x$, that is $a \in \text{approx}(x)$. □

We now give two useful propositions characterizing continuity of functions between algebraic cpo's in terms of how they act on compact elements.

1.5 Proposition Let D and E be cpo's and suppose D is algebraic. Then a function $f: D \to E$ is continuous if and only if for each $x \in D$,

$$f(x) = \bigsqcup\{f(a) : a \in \mathrm{approx}(x)\}.$$

Proof: Suppose first that f is continuous and let $x \in D$. Since D is algebraic, approx(x) is a directed set and $x = \bigsqcup \mathrm{approx}(x)$. By continuity it follows that

$$f(x) = f(\bigsqcup \mathrm{approx}(x)) = \bigsqcup f[\mathrm{approx}(x)] = \bigsqcup\{f(a) : a \in \mathrm{approx}(x)\}.$$

Conversely, suppose $f(x) = \bigsqcup\{f(a) : a \in \mathrm{approx}(x)\}$ for each $x \in D$. In particular, all such suprema exist. To show that f is monotone, suppose $x \sqsubseteq y$ in D. Then $\mathrm{approx}(x) \subseteq \mathrm{approx}(y)$ by Lemma 1.4. Thus for each $a \in \mathrm{approx}(x)$,

$$f(a) \sqsubseteq \bigsqcup\{f(b) : b \in \mathrm{approx}(y)\} = f(y)$$

and hence

$$f(x) = \bigsqcup\{f(a) : a \in \mathrm{approx}(x)\} \sqsubseteq f(y).$$

Having shown the monotonicity of f it only remains to show $f(\bigsqcup A) \sqsubseteq \bigsqcup f[A]$, whenever $A \subseteq D$ is directed. For such A, $\mathrm{approx}(\bigsqcup A) = \bigcup_{x \in A} \mathrm{approx}(x)$ by Lemma 1.4, and $f(\bigsqcup A) = \bigsqcup\{f(a) : a \in \mathrm{approx}(\bigsqcup A)\}$ by assumption. Let $a \in \mathrm{approx}(\bigsqcup A)$ and choose $x \in A$ such that $a \in \mathrm{approx}(x)$. Then

$$f(a) \sqsubseteq f(x) \sqsubseteq \bigsqcup\{f(y) : y \in A\} = \bigsqcup f[A].$$

It follows that $f(\bigsqcup A) = \bigsqcup\{f(a) : a \in \mathrm{approx}(\bigsqcup A)\} \sqsubseteq \bigsqcup f[A]$. □

We obtain the following important corollary.

1.6 Corollary Let D and E be cpo's and suppose D is algebraic. Then each monotone function $f: D_c \to E$ has a unique continuous extension $\bar{f}: D \to E$.

Proof: Assume that $f: D_c \to E$ is monotone and define $\bar{f}: D \to E$ by $\bar{f}(x) = \bigsqcup\{f(a) : a \in \mathrm{approx}(x)\}$. The function $\bar{f}$ is defined on all of D since, for $x \in D$, approx(x) is directed and hence $\{f(a) : a \in \mathrm{approx}(x)\}$ is directed by the monotonicity of f. The continuity and uniqueness follow immediately from Proposition 1.5. □

1.7 Proposition Let D and E be algebraic cpo's. Then $f: D \to E$ is continuous if and only if f is monotone and for each $x \in D$ and $b \in \mathrm{approx}(f(x))$ there is $a \in \mathrm{approx}(x)$ such that $b \sqsubseteq f(a)$.

Proof: First suppose that f is continuous and let $b \in \mathrm{approx}(f(x))$. Then $b \sqsubseteq f(x) = \bigsqcup\{f(a) : a \in \mathrm{approx}(x)\}$. The set $\{f(a) : a \in \mathrm{approx}(x)\}$ is directed since f is continuous and hence, by the compactness of b, there is $a \in approx(x)$ such that $b \sqsubseteq f(a)$.

Conversely suppose that the conditions on f hold and let $x \in D$. Again, by the monotonicity of f, the set $\{f(a): a \in approx(x)\}$ is directed and hence $\bigsqcup\{f(a): a \in approx(x)\}$ exists. For $b \in approx(f(x))$ there is $a \in approx(x)$ such that $b \sqsubseteq f(a)$. It follows that

$$f(x) = \bigsqcup approx(f(x)) \sqsubseteq \bigsqcup\{f(a): a \in approx(x)\}$$

and hence, by monotonicity, $f(x) = \bigsqcup\{f(a): a \in approx(x)\}$. □

In Section 3.3 we will give an example of an algebraic cpo D such that the cpo $[D \longrightarrow D]$ is not algebraic. To obtain a cartesian closed subcategory of the category of algebraic cpo's we therefore add one more requirement. A set $A \subseteq D$ is said to be *consistent* if there is $x \in D$ such that for each $y \in A$, $y \sqsubseteq x$, that is A has an upper bound in D. Expressed in terms of approximations, a set A is consistent if there is a common element x which each element of A approximates, or, in other words, A does not contain contradictory information.

Here we introduce the main concept of our text.

1.8 Definition A cpo D is a *Scott–Ershov domain*, or simply a *domain*, if
(i) D is an algebraic cpo, and
(ii) if the set $\{a, b\} \subseteq D_c$ is consistent then $a \sqcup b = \bigsqcup\{a, b\}$ exists in D.

All the examples of 1.2 are domains except, of course, example (viii) which is not even algebraic. Perhaps the simplest algebraic cpo which is not a domain is pictured by:

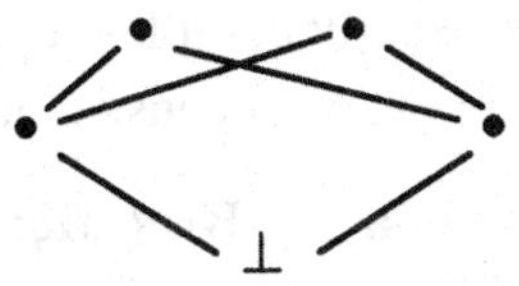

A cpo D is said to be *consistently complete* if $\bigsqcup A$ exists in D whenever $A \subseteq D$ is a consistent set. We shall show that condition (ii) in Definition 1.8, together with algebraicity, implies consistent completeness. Thus a domain is a *consistently complete algebraic cpo.*

1.9 Lemma Let D be a domain. If $K \subseteq D_c$ is a finite consistent set then $\bigsqcup K$ exists in D and is compact.

Proof: It suffices to show that $a \sqcup b$ is compact whenever $\{a,b\} \subseteq D_c$ is consistent, the general case being an easy induction on the size of K. Let $A \subseteq D$ be directed and suppose $a \sqcup b \sqsubseteq \bigsqcup A$. Then $a \sqsubseteq \bigsqcup A$ and $b \sqsubseteq \bigsqcup A$ and hence there are $x, y \in A$ such that $a \sqsubseteq x$ and $b \sqsubseteq y$. The set A is directed so there is $z \in A$ such that $x \sqsubseteq z$ and $y \sqsubseteq z$. But then $a \sqcup b \sqsubseteq z \in A$. □

1.10 Theorem Each domain is consistently complete.

Proof: Let D be a domain. We must show that $\bigsqcup A$ exists in D for each consistent set $A \subseteq D$. If $A = \emptyset$ then $\bigsqcup A = \bot \in D$. Suppose therefore that $A \neq \emptyset$ and that $x \in D$ is an upper bound of A. Let $B = \bigcup_{y \in A} \text{approx}(y)$. Then B is a consistent set of compact elements with x as an upper bound. Furthermore $\bigsqcup B = \bigsqcup A$ since D is algebraic, if indeed $\bigsqcup B$ exists. The set B need not be directed so in order to assert the existence of $\bigsqcup B$ we modify B to obtain a directed set C as follows. Let

$$C = \{\bigsqcup K : K \subseteq B \ \& \ K \text{ finite}\}.$$

Each finite $K \subseteq B$ is consistent and hence $\bigsqcup K \in D_c$ by Lemma 1.9. Furthermore, the set C is directed since $(\bigsqcup K_1) \sqcup (\bigsqcup K_2) = \bigsqcup (K_1 \cup K_2)$. Thus $\bigsqcup C$ exists in D. We show that $\bigsqcup C = \bigsqcup A$. If $y \in A$ then $\text{approx}(y) \subseteq C$ and hence $y = \bigsqcup \text{approx}(y) \sqsubseteq \bigsqcup C$, so $\bigsqcup C$ is an upper bound of A. Now suppose w is another upper bound of A and consider $\bigsqcup K \in C$ where $K \subseteq B$ is finite. Of course w is also an upper bound of B and hence of K. But then $\bigsqcup K \sqsubseteq w$ and hence $\bigsqcup C \sqsubseteq w$. □

We close this section with an observation giving a useful criterion for the consistency of a set $A \subseteq D$.

1.11 Proposition Let D be a consistently complete cpo. Then $A \subseteq D$ is consistent if and only if every finite subset of A is consistent.

Proof: To prove the non-trivial direction set $B = \{\bigsqcup K : K \subseteq A \ \& \ K \text{ finite}\}$. Then B is a directed set and hence $\bigsqcup B$ exists and is an upper bound of A. □

Section 3.2 The Representation Theorem

A domain or cpo D is complete in the sense that each directed set A, considered as a generalized sequence, has a limit in D, namely $\bigsqcup A$. In this section we will show that a domain D is completely determined by its compact elements D_c in the sense that D is *the completion* of D_c with respect to directed sets.

From Lemma 1.4 we see that a domain D is order isomorphic to a family of subsets of D_c, namely the family of sets approx(x) for $x \in D$. Each set approx(x) satisfies the following conditions: $\perp \in$ approx(x), if $a \in$ approx(x) and $b \sqsubseteq a$ where $b \in D_c$ then $b \in$ approx(x), and if $a, b \in$ approx(x) then $a \sqcup b \in$ approx(x). The last property is Lemma 1.9. Thus approx(x) is an ideal (to be defined below) and each domain is isomorphic to a family of ideals ordered by inclusion. Below we provide the details of this observation and its converse, that the family of all ideals over an appropriate set is a domain.

2.1 Definition A partial order $P = (P; \sqsubseteq, \perp)$ with least element $\perp$ is a *conditional upper semilattice with least element* (abbreviated *cusl*) if whenever $\{a, b\} \subseteq P$ is consistent in P, that is, has an upper bound in P, then $a \sqcup b$ exists in P.

Each domain D is a cusl. More interestingly, D_c is also a cusl. It is easy to think of natural examples of cusl's. Nonetheless, the example of the compact elements in a domain is completely general in that we shall show that given any cusl P there is a domain D such that $D_c \cong P$.

2.2 Definition Let P be a cusl. Then $I \subseteq P$ is an *ideal* if
(i) $\perp \in I$,
(ii) if $a \in I$ and $b \sqsubseteq a$ then $b \in I$, and
(iii) if $a, b \in I$ then $a \sqcup b$ exists in P and $a \sqcup b \in I$.

Let P be a cusl, let $a \in P$ and set $[a] = \{b \in P : b \sqsubseteq a\}$. It is easily verified that $[a]$ is an ideal, precisely because P is a cusl. The ideal $[a]$ is called the *principal ideal* generated by a. It is the smallest ideal containing a.

2.3 Theorem Let P be a cusl and let $\overline{P} = \{I \subseteq P : I \text{ an ideal}\}$. Then the structure $\overline{P} = (\overline{P}; \subseteq, [\perp])$ is a domain where the ordering $\subseteq$ is set inclusion. Furthermore, $\overline{P}_c = \{[a] : a \in P\}$. Finally, the map $\iota : P \to \overline{P}_c$ defined by $\iota(a) = [a]$ is order-preserving.

We say that $\overline{P}$ is *the completion of* P *by ideals*. Observe that the completion by ideals is *not* a closure operation in the usual sense since in general it is not the case that $\overline{\overline{P}} \cong \overline{P}$. Also observe that the map ι is injective since it is order-preserving and hence we may regard P as a substructure of $\overline{P}$ playing the role of the compact elements in $\overline{P}$.

Proof: Clearly $\overline{P}$ is a partial order with least element $[\perp]$. To show that $\overline{P}$ is a cpo suppose that $\mathcal{A} \subseteq \overline{P}$ is a directed set. It clearly suffices to show that $\bigcup \mathcal{A}$ is an ideal in P since then $\bigsqcup \mathcal{A} = \bigcup \mathcal{A}$ in $\overline{P}$. There is an $I \in \mathcal{A}$, since $\mathcal{A} \neq \emptyset$, so $\perp \in I \subseteq \bigcup \mathcal{A}$. Similarly one shows that $\bigcup \mathcal{A}$ is closed downwards. Now suppose that $a_1, a_2 \in \bigcup \mathcal{A}$. Choose ideals I_1 and I_2 in $\mathcal{A}$ such that $a_i \in I_i$ for $i=1,2$. Since $\mathcal{A}$ is directed there is an ideal $I_3 \in \mathcal{A}$ containing I_1 and I_2. In particular, $a_1, a_2 \in I_3$ and hence $a_1 \sqcup a_2 \in I_3 \subseteq \bigcup \mathcal{A}$, since I_3 is an ideal. This proves that $\bigcup \mathcal{A}$ is an ideal and that $\overline{P}$ is a cpo.

Next we show that the compact elements in $\overline{P}$ are exactly the principal ideals. Consider the principal ideal $[a]$ and suppose $\mathcal{A}$ is a directed set in $\overline{P}$ such that $[a] \subseteq \bigcup \mathcal{A}$. Then there is an ideal $I \in \mathcal{A}$ such that $a \in I$ and hence $[a] \subseteq I$ since ideals are closed downwards. Thus each principal ideal is compact. Now suppose the ideal $I \in \overline{P}$ is compact. Let $\mathcal{A} = \{[a] : a \in I\}$. We show that $\mathcal{A}$ is a directed set. It is clearly non-empty since I is non-empty. Furthermore, if $[a], [b] \in \mathcal{A}$ then $a, b \in I$ and hence $a \sqcup b \in I$. Thus $[a \sqcup b] \in \mathcal{A}$ and $\mathcal{A}$ is directed since $[a] \subseteq [a \sqcup b]$ and $[b] \subseteq [a \sqcup b]$. It follows that $\bigsqcup \mathcal{A} = \bigcup \mathcal{A}$ and, by the definition of $\mathcal{A}$, that $I \subseteq \bigcup \mathcal{A}$. By the compactness of I there is $a \in I$ such that $I \subseteq [a]$. But then $I = [a]$ and I is a principal ideal.

Let $I \in \overline{P}$. Then $\text{approx}(I) = \{[a] : a \in I\}$ is a directed set by the above argument and $I = \bigcup \text{approx}(I) = \bigsqcup \text{approx}(I)$. Thus $\overline{P}$ is an algebraic cpo.

To show that $\overline{P}$ is consistently complete suppose $[a]$ and $[b]$ are consistent in $\overline{P}$, say they have the ideal I as an upper bound. Then $a, b \in I$ and hence $a \sqcup b \in I$. In particular, $a \sqcup b$ exists in P. Clearly $[a \sqcup b]$ is an upper bound of $[a]$ and $[b]$. Suppose the ideal J is another upper bound of $[a]$ and $[b]$. Then $a, b \in J$ and hence $a \sqcup b \in J$, that is $[a \sqcup b] \subseteq J$. Thus $[a] \sqcup [b] = [a \sqcup b]$. This completes the proof that $\overline{P}$ is a domain.

Finally, it follows from its definition that the map $\iota : P \longrightarrow \overline{P}$ is order-preserving. □

In the above proof we used the fact that the supremum of a directed set in $\overline{P}$ is simply the union of that set. However, it is not true in general that the supremum of a *consistent* set in $\overline{P}$ is the union of that set. In fact, if I and J are consistent ideals then $I \cup J$ need not be an ideal. Of course, $I \sqcup J$ equals the least ideal containing I and J.

2.4 Examples

(i) Let $\omega = (\omega; \leq, 0)$ be the ordinal ω with the usual ordering. Then $\overline{\omega} \cong \omega + 1$, the ordinal domain of Example 2.1.14.

(ii) Let $\wp_f(\omega) = \{K \subseteq \omega : K \text{ finite}\}$. Then $\wp_f(\omega) = (\wp_f(\omega); \subseteq, \varnothing)$ is a cusl and $\overline{\wp_f(\omega)} \cong \wp(\omega)$ where $\wp(\omega)$ is the domain $\wp(\omega) = (\wp(\omega); \subseteq, \varnothing)$.

(iii) Consider Example 2.1.12 of the Cantor space as a domain. Then SEQ is a cusl and $\overline{\text{SEQ}} \cong \mathbb{C}$.

(iv) Consider your favourite cusl P. One of the authors' favourites is the upper semilattice of recursively enumerable Turing degrees. What is $\overline{P}$? It turns out that whatever $\overline{P}$ is, it is, up to isomorphism, a subdomain of the domain $\wp(\omega)$ provided P is countable. The upper semilattice of the recursively enumerable Turing degrees is countable.

Here is a proposition stating that the completion of P by ideals is the solution to a certain universal problem.

2.5 Proposition Let P be a cusl, $\overline{P}$ its completion by ideals, and let $\iota: P \to \overline{P}$ be the canonical embedding given by $\iota(a) = [a]$. Suppose D is a domain and $f: P \to D$ is monotone. Then there is a unique continuous function $\overline{f}: \overline{P} \to D$ such that the following diagram commutes.

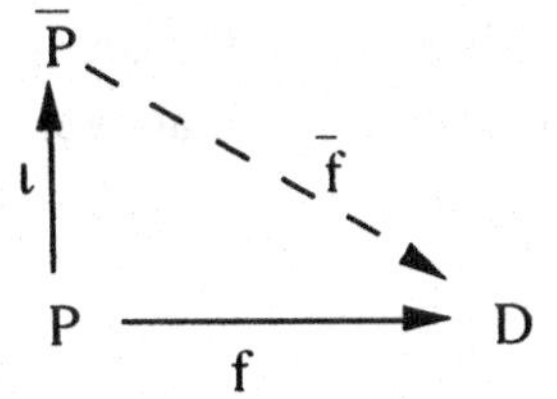

Proof: We first show that $\overline{f}$ is unique, assuming it exists. Let $I \in \overline{P}$ and recall that $I = \bigcup\{[a] : a \in I\} = \bigsqcup\{[a] : a \in I\}$ and $\text{approx}(I) = \{[a] : a \in I\}$. Then

$$\begin{aligned}\overline{f}(I) &= \bigsqcup\{\overline{f}([a]) : a \in I\} \\ &= \bigsqcup\{\overline{f} \circ \iota(a) : a \in I\} \\ &= \bigsqcup\{f(a) : a \in I\}\end{aligned}$$

where the first equality is due to the continuity of $\overline{f}$. This proves uniqueness.

To show existence we have no choice by the above but to define $\overline{f}$ by $\overline{f}(I) = \bigsqcup\{f(a) : a \in I\}$. Each ideal I is a directed set and f is monotone. It follows that $\{f(a) : a \in I\}$ is directed and hence that $\bigsqcup\{f(a) : a \in I\}$ exists in D. Thus $\overline{f}(I)$ is defined. To show that $\overline{f}$ is continuous note that for $a \in P$,

$$\overline{f}([a]) = \bigsqcup\{f(b) : b \in [a]\} = \bigsqcup\{f(b) : b \sqsubseteq a\} = f(a)$$

since f is monotone. Thus

$$\overline{f}(I) = \bigsqcup\{f(a) : a \in I\} = \bigsqcup\{\overline{f}([a]) : a \in I\}$$

so $\overline{f}$ is continuous by Proposition 1.5, and the diagram commutes. □

It remains to show that, up to isomorphism, each domain is uniquely determined by its set of compact elements. We prove this directly, but actually it is the essence of Proposition 2.5.

2.6 Representation theorem Let D be a domain. Then $\overline{D_c} \cong D$.

Proof: Let $\phi: \overline{D_c} \to D$ be defined by $\phi(I) = \sqcup I$. By Lemma 2.1.6 it suffices to show that ϕ is an order-preserving surjection. Note that an ideal I is a directed set, so $\phi(I)$ is defined. Clearly ϕ is monotone. Suppose $\sqcup I \sqsubseteq \sqcup J$ for $I, J \in \overline{D_c}$. Then, for $a \in I$, $a \sqsubseteq \sqcup J$ and hence $a \sqsubseteq b \in J$ for some b. But then $a \in J$ since J is closed downwards. Thus ϕ is order-preserving. It is also surjective since approx(x) is an ideal for each $x \in D$ and $\sqcup$approx(x)$=$x. □

As an illustration of a useful technique, we give another proof of Theorem 2.6, using Proposition 2.5, by giving the usual proof that a solution to a universal problem is unique up to isomorphism. Let $\iota: D_c \to \overline{D_c}$ be the canonical embedding and let $j: D_c \to D$ be the inclusion map. Recall from Corollary 1.6 that D with $j: D_c \to D$ also solves the universal problem of Proposition 2.5. Thus we obtain the following commutative diagram where $\bar{\iota}$ and $\bar{j}$ are the unique continuous functions given by Proposition 2.5 and the remark above.

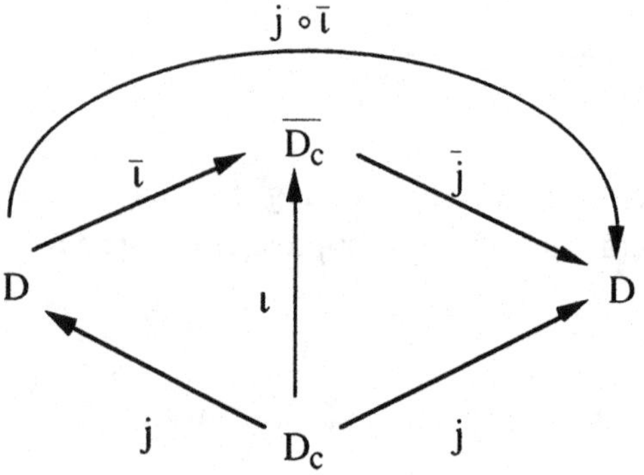

Consider the outer commuting diagram

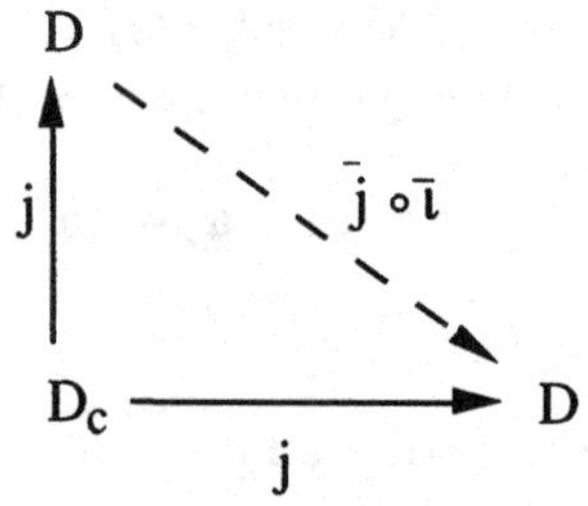

The function $\bar{j} \circ \bar{\iota}$ is the unique continuous function making the diagram commute, by Corollary 1.6. But clearly the identity mapping $id_D: D \to D$ also makes the diagram commute. We conclude that $\bar{j} \circ \bar{\iota} = id_D$. Reversing the roles of D and $\overline{D_c}$ in the above argument, and using Proposition 2.5, completes the proof.

Section 3.3 Cartesian Closure

In Chapter 2 we considered various constructions on cpo's and showed that the class of cpo's is closed under these. In this and the next section we re-examine these constructions for domains and show that the class of domains is also closed under them. In particular, we show that the category **Domain**, whose objects are domains and whose morphisms are the continuous functions between domains, is cartesian closed.

First we consider the cartesian product of two domains.

3.1 Theorem Let D and E be domains. Then the cpo $D \times E$ is a domain and $(D \times E)_c = D_c \times E_c$.

It then follows from the work already done in Section 2.2 that the projection functions are continuous and that $D \times E$ along with the projection functions is the product of D and E in the category **Domain**.

Proof: First we establish that $(D \times E)_c = D_c \times E_c$. Let $(a, b) \in D_c \times E_c$ and suppose $(a, b) \sqsubseteq \bigsqcup A$ where $A \subseteq D \times E$ is a directed set. Recall that by Lemma 2.2.2, each $\pi_i[A]$ is directed and $\bigsqcup A = (\bigsqcup \pi_0[A], \bigsqcup \pi_1[A])$. It follows that $a \sqsubseteq \bigsqcup \pi_0[A]$ and $b \sqsubseteq \bigsqcup \pi_1[A]$. Now a and b are compact in D and E, respectively, and hence there is $x \in \pi_0[A]$ and $y \in \pi_1[A]$ such that $a \sqsubseteq x$ and $b \sqsubseteq y$. But the set A is directed so there is $(z, w) \in A$ such that $x \sqsubseteq z$ and $y \sqsubseteq w$, and hence $(a, b) \sqsubseteq (z, w) \in A$. We have shown that $(a, b) \in (D \times E)_c$. For the converse inclusion let $(a, b) \in (D \times E)_c$ and suppose $a \sqsubseteq \bigsqcup A$ for some directed set $A \subseteq D$. Then $A \times \{b\} \subseteq D \times E$ is a directed set and

$$(a, b) \sqsubseteq (\bigsqcup A, b) = \bigsqcup (A \times \{b\}).$$

By the compactness of (a, b) in $D \times E$ there is $x \in A$ such that $(a, b) \sqsubseteq (x, b)$, that is $a \sqsubseteq x$. Thus $a \in D_c$ and, similarly, $b \in E_c$.

To show that $D \times E$ is algebraic note that for $(x, y) \in D \times E$,

$$\begin{aligned} \text{approx}((x, y)) &= \{(a, b) \in D_c \times E_c : a \sqsubseteq x \ \&\ b \sqsubseteq y\} \\ &= \text{approx}(x) \times \text{approx}(y). \end{aligned}$$

The sets approx(x) and approx(y) are both directed since D and E are algebraic and hence approx((x, y)) is directed. Furthermore,

$$(x,y) = (\bigsqcup \text{approx}(x), \bigsqcup \text{approx}(y)) = \bigsqcup \text{approx}((x,y))$$

again using the fact that D and E are algebraic and Lemma 2.2.2.

Finally suppose $\{(a,b),(c,d)\} \subseteq (D \times E)_c$ is a consistent set, say (x,y) is an upper bound. Then x is an upper bound of $\{a,c\}$ and y is an upper bound of $\{b,d\}$. It follows that $a \sqcup c$ exists in D and $b \sqcup d$ exists in E since D and E are assumed to be consistently complete. But clearly $(a,b) \sqcup (c,d) = (a \sqcup c, b \sqcup d)$ and hence $D \times E$ is consistently complete. □

Observe from the above proof that the cartesian product of algebraic cpo's is an algebraic cpo and that the cartesian product of consistently complete cpo's is a consistently complete cpo.

Now we turn to the most important and involved construction, that of the function space. At the end of this section, after establishing notation and some results, we give an example of an algebraic cpo D such that the cpo $[D \longrightarrow D]$ is not algebraic. That the class of algebraic cpo's is not closed under the function space operation is one reason we restrict ourselves to a subclass, namely the class of domains. We need to use the consistent completeness of domains in an essential way in order to show that the class of domains is closed under the function space construction.

Let D and E be domains. The first step in showing that the cpo $[D \longrightarrow E]$ is a domain is to characterize the set of compact elements $[D \longrightarrow E]_c$. For $a \in D_c$ and $y \in E$ let $<a;y>: D \longrightarrow E$ be the function defined by

$$<a;y>(x) = \begin{cases} y & \text{if } a \sqsubseteq x \\ \bot & \text{otherwise.} \end{cases}$$

3.2 Lemma Let $a \in D_c$ and $y \in E$. Then the function $<a;y>: D \longrightarrow E$ is continuous. Furthermore, if $f: D \longrightarrow E$ is continuous then $<a;y> \sqsubseteq f$ in $[D \longrightarrow E]$ if and only if $y \sqsubseteq f(a)$.

Proof: Clearly $<a;y>$ is monotone. Suppose $b \in \text{approx}(<a;y>(x))$. If $a \sqsubseteq x$ then $b \sqsubseteq y = <a;y>(a)$. Otherwise $b = \bot$ so $b \sqsubseteq <a;y>(\bot)$. Hence $<a;y>$ is continuous by Proposition 1.7, precisely because $a \in D_c$. Now let $f: D \longrightarrow E$ be continuous, $y \sqsubseteq f(a)$, and let $x \in D$. If $a \sqsubseteq x$ then

$$<a;y>(x) = y \sqsubseteq f(a) \sqsubseteq f(x)$$

by the monotonicity of f. Otherwise, trivially, $<a;y>(x) = \bot \sqsubseteq f(x)$. Thus $<a;y> \sqsubseteq f$ in $[D \longrightarrow E]$. The converse follows by definition. □

3.3 Lemma If $a \in D_c$ and $b \in E_c$ then $<a;b>$ is compact in $[D \longrightarrow E]$.

Proof: Let $\mathcal{F} \subseteq [D \longrightarrow E]$ be a directed set such that $<a; b> \sqsubseteq \bigsqcup \mathcal{F}$. Then

$$b = <a; b>(a) \sqsubseteq (\bigsqcup \mathcal{F})(a) = \bigsqcup \{f(a) : f \in \mathcal{F}\}.$$

But the set $\{f(a) : f \in \mathcal{F}\}$ is a directed subset of E and hence, by the compactness of b, there is $f \in \mathcal{F}$ such that $b \sqsubseteq f(a)$. But then $<a; b> \sqsubseteq f$ by Lemma 3.2. □

We say that the function $<a; b>$ is a *subbasic compact element* of $[D \longrightarrow E]$ provided $a \in D_c$ and $b \in E_c$. There is no reason to believe that all compact elements in $[D \longrightarrow E]$ are of the form $<a; b>$. For example, this is clearly not true in, say, $[\mathbb{N}_\perp \longrightarrow \mathbb{N}_\perp]$. In fact, the compact elements are the suprema of finite consistent sets of functions of the form $<a; b>$. To prove this we need the following technical lemma. It is an important result in that it reduces the consistency of finite sets of subbasic compact elements in $[D \longrightarrow E]$ to consistency in the domains D and E. Note that in its proof as well as in subsequent proofs we use consistent completeness in an essential way.

3.4 Lemma Let D and E be domains and suppose $a_1, \ldots, a_n \in D_c$ and $b_1, \ldots, b_n \in E_c$. Then the set $\{<a_1; b_1>, \ldots, <a_n; b_n>\} \subseteq [D \longrightarrow E]$ is consistent if and only if for each $I \subseteq \{1, \ldots, n\}$, $\{a_i : i \in I\}$ consistent $\Rightarrow$ $\{b_i : i \in I\}$ consistent.

Proof: Suppose for the only if direction that $\{<a_1; b_1>, \ldots, <a_n; b_n>\}$ is consistent and let $I \subseteq \{1, \ldots, n\}$ be such that $\{a_i : i \in I\}$ is consistent. Let f be an upper bound of $\{<a_1; b_1>, \ldots, <a_n; b_n>\}$ in $[D \longrightarrow E]$ and let $x \in D$ be an upper bound of $\{a_i : i \in I\}$. Then

$$i \in I \Rightarrow b_i = <a_i; b_i>(x) \sqsubseteq f(x)$$

and hence $f(x)$ is an upper bound of $\{b_i : i \in I\}$.

For the converse direction we assume the condition to be true, that is for each $I \subseteq \{1, \ldots, n\}$, if $\{a_i : i \in I\}$ is consistent then so is $\{b_i : i \in I\}$. We shall prove slightly more than is required, namely that $\{<a_1; b_1>, \ldots, <a_n; b_n>\}$ has a *least* upper bound in $[D \longrightarrow E]$. For each $d \in D_c$ let $I_d = \{i : a_i \sqsubseteq d\}$. Define $f : D_c \longrightarrow E$ by

$$f(d) = \bigsqcup \{b_i : i \in I_d\}.$$

For each $d \in D_c$, the set $\{a_i : i \in I_d\}$ is consistent in D and hence, by our condition, $\{b_i : i \in I_d\}$ is consistent in E. Thus $f(d)$ is defined by the consistent completeness of E. Furthermore, f is monotone. For if $d \sqsubseteq e$ then $I_d \subseteq I_e$ and hence $f(d) \sqsubseteq f(e)$. Extend f uniquely to a continuous function $f : D \longrightarrow E$ by Corollary 1.6. For each i we have $f(a_i) \sqsupseteq b_i$ and hence $<a_i; b_i> \sqsubseteq f$ by Lemma

3.2. Thus f is an upper bound of $\{<a_1;b_1>,\ldots,<a_n;b_n>\}$. Now suppose g is another upper bound. Let $d\in D_c$. For $i\in I_d$, we have

$$b_i=<a_i;b_i>(a_i)\sqsubseteq g(a_i)\sqsubseteq g(d)$$

and hence $f(d)\sqsubseteq g(d)$. Thus $f(d)\sqsubseteq g(d)$ for each $d\in D_c$ and hence, by continuity, $f(x)\sqsubseteq g(x)$ for each $x\in D$, that is $f\sqsubseteq g$. This completes the proof that $f=\bigsqcup\{<a_1;b_1>,\ldots,<a_n;b_n>\}$. □

The extra fact proved above is important enough to extract as a lemma.

3.5 Lemma If the set $\{<a_1;b_1>,\ldots,<a_n;b_n>\}\subseteq[D\longrightarrow E]$ is consistent then $\bigsqcup\{<a_1;b_1>,\ldots,<a_n;b_n>\}$ exists in $[D\longrightarrow E]$ and

$$(\bigsqcup\{<a_1;b_1>,\ldots,<a_n;b_n>\})(x)=\bigsqcup\{b_i:\ a_i\sqsubseteq x\}.$$

In the following lemma we give the first half of the characterization of the compact elements in $[D\longrightarrow E]$.

3.6 Lemma Let D and E be domains and suppose $a_1,\ldots,a_n\in D_c$ and $b_1,\ldots,b_n\in E_c$. If $\{<a_1;b_1>,\ldots,<a_n;b_n>\}\subseteq[D\longrightarrow E]$ is consistent then $\bigsqcup\{<a_1;b_1>,\ldots,<a_n;b_n>\}$ is compact in $[D\longrightarrow E]$.

Proof: Assume that $\{<a_1;b_1>,\ldots,<a_n;b_n>\}$ is consistent in $[D\longrightarrow E]$ and set $f=\bigsqcup\{<a_1;b_1>,\ldots,<a_n;b_n>\}$. For $x\in D$ let $I_x=\{i:\ a_i\sqsubseteq x\}$. Define a relation $\equiv$ on D by $x\equiv y\Leftrightarrow I_x=I_y$. Then $\equiv$ is an equivalence relation on D and, by Lemma 3.5, $x\equiv y\Rightarrow f(x)=f(y)$. There are at most 2^n distinct sets of the form I_x, say $I_1,\ldots,I_m$, and hence there are m equivalence classes of $\equiv$. Each equivalence class has a least element, namely $c_j=\bigsqcup\{a_i:\ i\in I_j\}$. The existence of c_j follows from the consistent completeness of D.

Suppose that $\mathcal{G}\subseteq[D\longrightarrow E]$ is a directed set and that $f\sqsubseteq\bigsqcup\mathcal{G}$. For fixed j, $1\leq j\leq m$, we have

$$\bigsqcup\{b_i:\ i\in I_j\}=f(c_j)\sqsubseteq(\bigsqcup\mathcal{G})(c_j)=\bigsqcup\{g(c_j):\ g\in\mathcal{G}\}.$$

Each $b_i\in E_c$ so $f(c_j)\in E_c$ by Lemma 1.9, and hence there is $g_j\in\mathcal{G}$ such that $f(c_j)\sqsubseteq g_j(c_j)$. But $\mathcal{G}$ is a directed set so there is $g\in\mathcal{G}$ such that $g_j\sqsubseteq g$ for each $j=1,\ldots,m$. To see that $f\sqsubseteq g$ let $x\in D$ and choose j such that $x\equiv c_j$. Then $c_j\sqsubseteq x$ and

$$f(x)=f(c_j)\sqsubseteq g_j(c_j)\sqsubseteq g(c_j)\sqsubseteq g(x).$$

This proves that f is compact. □

Observe that in the above proof we used the consistent completeness of both D and E.

3.7 Lemma Given $f \in [D \to E]$ let $\mathcal{F} \subseteq [D \to E]$ be the set

$$\mathcal{F} = \{\sqcup\{\langle a_1; b_1\rangle, \ldots, \langle a_n; b_n\rangle\} : a_i \in D_c,\ b_i \in E_c,\ \langle a_i; b_i\rangle \sqsubseteq f,\ i = 1, \ldots, n, \text{ and } n \geq 1\}.$$

Then $\mathcal{F}$ is directed and $f = \sqcup\mathcal{F}$.

Proof: The set $\mathcal{F}$ is directed by Lemma 3.5. Clearly $f \sqsupseteq \sqcup\mathcal{F}$ since f is an upper bound of $\mathcal{F}$. For the converse inequality, let $x \in D$. Then, by Proposition 1.7, given $b \in \text{approx}(f(x))$ there is $a \in \text{approx}(x)$ such that $b \sqsubseteq f(a)$. But then $\langle a; b\rangle \sqsubseteq f$, that is $\langle a; b\rangle \in \mathcal{F}$. It follows that

$$b \sqsubseteq (\sqcup\mathcal{F})(a) \sqsubseteq (\sqcup\mathcal{F})(x)$$

and hence $f(x) \sqsubseteq (\sqcup\mathcal{F})(x)$. The two inequalities imply $f = \sqcup\mathcal{F}$. □

Now we have all the ingredients needed to show that the function space of two domains is again a domain.

3.8 Theorem Let D and E be domains. Then the cpo $[D \to E]$ is a domain and $[D \to E]_c$ consists of all elements of the form $\sqcup\{\langle a_1; b_1\rangle, \ldots, \langle a_n; b_n\rangle\}$ where $a_i \in D_c$, $b_i \in E_c$, $n \geq 1$, and where the set $\{\langle a_1; b_1\rangle, \ldots, \langle a_n; b_n\rangle\}$ is consistent in $[D \to E]$.

Proof: If $\{\langle a_1; b_1\rangle, \ldots, \langle a_n; b_n\rangle\}$ is consistent then $\sqcup\{\langle a_1; b_1\rangle, \ldots, \langle a_n; b_n\rangle\}$ exists by Lemma 3.5 and is compact by Lemma 3.6. Suppose $f \in [D \to E]$ is compact. Let $\mathcal{F}$ be the set for f given in Lemma 3.7. Then $f = \sqcup\mathcal{F}$ and hence, since f is compact, $f = \sqcup\{\langle a_1; b_1\rangle, \ldots, \langle a_n; b_n\rangle\}$ for some element in $\mathcal{F}$. This characterizes the compact elements. Thus $[D \to E]$ is algebraic by Lemma 3.7 and consistently complete by Lemma 3.5. □

An important point to observe is the finitary character of the function space construction. More precisely, suppose that the compact elements in the domains D and E are finitary or concrete. Then the compact elements of $[D \to E]$ are also finitary since each such element is given by a finite collection of finitary objects in D and E. This is the crucial point in proving, as we do in Chapter 10, that if D and E are effective domains then $[D \to E]$ is also an effective domain.

Utilizing the work done in Section 2.3 we have that the function eval is continuous and that $[D \to E]$ along with eval is the exponentiation of the domains D and E in the category **Domain.** Recalling the remark following Theorem 3.1 we conclude that the category **Domain** is cartesian closed.

3.9 Example The partial continuous functionals.

Define inductively the following domains:

$$\begin{cases} C_0 = \mathbf{N}_\perp \\ C_{n+1} = [C_n \to \mathbf{N}_\perp]. \end{cases}$$

Then $\mathcal{C} = \{C_n\}_{n<\omega}$ is the domain version of the continuous functionals originally introduced by Kleene [1959] and Kreisel [1959]. The Kleene–Kreisel functionals are "total" objects and because of this they have a somewhat awkward topological characterization even though they have a natural characterization in terms of computations. Of course, the domain version of the continuous functionals contains many "partial" objects when we interpret $\perp$ as undefined. This is in analogy with recursive function theory, where it is more natural and easier to consider the class of *partial* recursive functions rather than the subclass of *total* recursive functions. In Section 8.4 we will show how to extract the Kleene–Kreisel continuous functionals from $\mathcal{C}$.

We close this section with an example showing that the class of algebraic cpo's is not closed under the function space construction.

3.10 Example Let D be the following cpo:

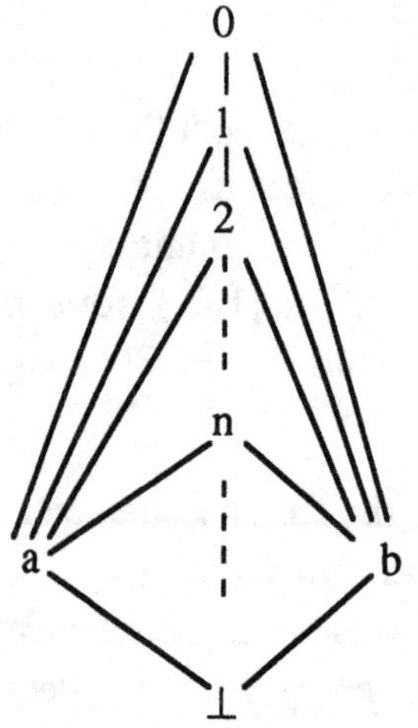

It is an easy exercise to see that D is algebraic and, in fact, $D_c = D$. Note that D is not a domain since the consistent set $\{a, b\}$ has no supremum in D. We will show that $\text{approx}(\text{id}_D) \subseteq [D \to D]$ is not a directed set and hence $[D \to D]$ is not algebraic.

By Lemmas 3.2 and 3.3, the functions $\langle a;a\rangle$ and $\langle b;b\rangle$ belong to $\mathrm{approx}(id_D)$. Thus it suffices to show that $\langle a;a\rangle$ and $\langle b;b\rangle$ have no upper bound in $\mathrm{approx}(id_D)$. Assume that $f\in[D\to D]$ is an upper bound of $\langle a;a\rangle$ and $\langle b;b\rangle$ such that $f\sqsubseteq id_D$. We show that f is not compact in $[D\to D]$ and hence $f\notin \mathrm{approx}(id_D)$. First note that f is the identity on $\{\bot,a,b\}$. Suppose $n\in\mathbb{N}$. Then $a\sqsubseteq n$ and $b\sqsubseteq n$ and hence $a=f(a)\sqsubseteq f(n)$ and $b=f(b)\sqsubseteq f(n)$. It follows that $f(n)\in\mathbb{N}$ and, by the monotonicity of f on D, we also have $n\leq m\Rightarrow f(n)\leq f(m)$, where $\leq$ is the usual ordering on $\mathbb{N}$.

For each $i\in\mathbb{N}$, define $f_i:\mathbb{N}\to\mathbb{N}$ by

$$f_i(n)=\begin{cases} f(n) & \text{if } n<i \\ f(n+1) & \text{if } n\geq i \end{cases}$$

and extend f_i to D by letting f_i be the identity on $\{\bot,a,b\}$. Then each f_i is monotone, since f is, and hence continuous. Furthermore, since $f(n+1)\sqsubseteq f(n)$ for each $n\in\mathbb{N}$ we have

(*) $\quad f_0\sqsubseteq f_1\sqsubseteq f_2\sqsubseteq\ldots\sqsubseteq f.$

On the other hand, $f_{n+1}(n)=f(n)$ for each $n\in\mathbb{N}$ and hence $f=\bigsqcup\{f_n: n\in\mathbb{N}\}$.

Suppose f were compact in $[D\to D]$. Then there is an n such that $f=f_n$ and moreover, by (*), $f=f_m$ for each $m\geq n$. By assumption $f\sqsubseteq id_D$ and hence $m\leq f(m)$ for each $m\in\mathbb{N}$. In particular, $f(m)<f(m+1)$ for some $m\geq n$. For such an m we have

$$f_m(m)=f(m+1)\neq f(m)$$

which contradicts $f=f_m$. The contradiction proves that f is not compact and hence that $\mathrm{approx}(id_D)$ is not directed. Thus $[D\to D]$ is not an algebraic cpo.

Section 3.4 Further Constructions

In this section we briefly reconsider the remaining cpo constructions described in Section 2.4. All proofs are straightforward and left to the reader.

4.1 Proposition If D and E are domains then $D+E$, the separated sum of D and E, is a domain and $(D+E)_c=in_0[D_c]\cup in_1[E_c]\cup\{\bot\}$.

4.2 Proposition If D and E are domains then $D\otimes E$, the smash product of D and E, is a domain and $(D\otimes E)_c=D_c\otimes E_c$.

In order to consider the strict function space we need to define strict basic functions corresponding to the subbasic compact elements of the ordinary function space. Let D and E be domains and suppose $a \in D_c$ and $b \in E_c$. Then define $\langle a; b\rangle_\perp : D \to E$ by

$$\langle a; b\rangle_\perp(x) = \begin{cases} b & \text{if } a \sqsubseteq x \ \&\ x \neq \perp \\ \perp & \text{otherwise.} \end{cases}$$

Clearly $\langle a; b\rangle_\perp$ is a strict function and it is continuous since $a \in D_c$. Repeating the proof for the full function space construction, with the obvious modifications, we obtain the following proposition.

4.3 Proposition Let D and E be domains. Then $[D \to_\perp E]$ is a domain and $[D \to_\perp E]_c$ consists of all elements of the form $\bigsqcup\{\langle a_1; b_1\rangle_\perp, \ldots. \langle a_n; b_n\rangle_\perp\}$, where $a_i \in D_c$, $b_i \in E_c$, $n \geq 1$ and where the set $\{\langle a_1; b_1\rangle_\perp, \ldots, \langle a_n; b_n\rangle_\perp\}$ is consistent.

4.4 Proposition If D and E are domains then $D \oplus E$, the smash sum of D and E, is a domain and $(D \oplus E)_c = in_0[D_c] \cup in_1[E_c]$.

Let **Domain**$_\perp$ be the category whose objects are domains and whose morphism sets consist of the strict continuous functions from one domain into another. Then, by the results in Section 2.4, the smash sum $D \oplus E$ together with the injections in_i is the coproduct of D and E in **Domain**$_\perp$.

4.5 Proposition If D is a domain then $D_\perp$, the lifting of D, is a domain and $(D_\perp)_c = (D_c)_\perp$.

As a final remark we note that *domain* could be replaced by *algebraic cpo* in all our constructions except the two function space constructions.

3.5 Exercises

1. Let P and Q be conditional upper semilattices with least elements (cusl's). Show that $\overline{P \times Q} \cong \overline{P} \times \overline{Q}$. What can be said for other constructions such as $\to$ and $+$?

2. Let P and Q be cusl's and suppose $f: P \to Q$ is an order-preserving surjection. Let $\iota_P: P \to \overline{P}$ and $\iota_Q: Q \to \overline{Q}$ be the canonical embeddings. Show that there is a unique continuous bijection $\overline{f}: \overline{P} \to \overline{Q}$, in fact an isomorphism, such that the following diagram commutes.

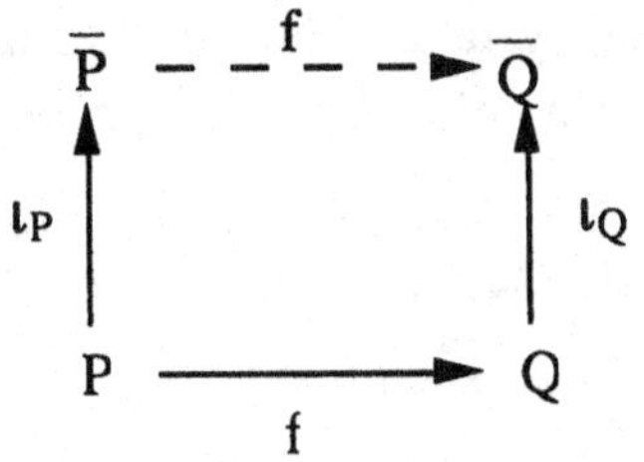

3. Let D be a cpo. A set $S \subseteq D$ is a *subbasis* if for any $x \in D$, we have $x = \bigsqcup\{a \in S : a \sqsubseteq x\}$. For example, if D is an algebraic cpo then D_c is a subbasis.
   (i) Show that if D is a consistently complete cpo with a subbasis of compact elements then D is a domain.
   (ii) Show that if D and E are domains then $S = \{\langle a; b\rangle : a \in D_c, b \in E_c\}$ is a subbasis of $[D \to E]$.

4. Let (f, g) be a projection pair for (D, E), where D and E are domains. Is it true that $g[E_c] \subseteq D_c$?

5. Let D be a domain and let D_m be the set of *maximal* elements in D, that is $D_m = \{x \in D : x \sqsubseteq y \Rightarrow x = y\}$. Show that if $x, y \in D_m$ and $x \neq y$ then there are $a \in \text{approx}(x)$ and $b \in \text{approx}(y)$ such that $\{a, b\}$ is inconsistent.

6. Show that if $x \in D$ then there is $y \in D_m$ (see Exercise 5) such that $x \sqsubseteq y$.

7. Let D be a domain. Show that if $A \subseteq D$, $A \neq \varnothing$, then $\sqcap A$ exists in D, where $\sqcap A$ is the greatest lower bound or infimum of A.

8. Show that if $f, g : D \to E$ are continuous then the function $h : D \to E$ defined by $h(x) = f(x) \sqcap g(x)$ is continuous. (See Exercise 7.)

9. Let D and E be domains and suppose there are projection pairs (f, g) for (D, E) and (f', g') for (E, D). Is it necessarily true that $D \cong E$? (Provide a proof or a counterexample.)

10. Let D be a domain and let I be an arbitrary set. Let $D^I = \{f \mid f : I \to D\}$, the set of *all* functions from I into D. Define a partial ordering $\sqsubseteq$ on D^I by

$$f \sqsubseteq g \Leftrightarrow (\forall i \in I)(f(i) \sqsubseteq g(i)).$$

Show that D^I is a domain under this ordering. Is D^I algebraic if D is only assumed to be algebraic, that is not necessarily consistently complete?

11. (Domains from neighbourhood systems.) Let Δ be a non-empty set. Then a family of subsets $\mathcal{D} \subseteq \wp(\Delta)$ is a *neighbourhood system* if

   (a) $\Delta \in \mathcal{D}$, and
   (b) if $X, Y, Z \in \mathcal{D}$ and $Z \subseteq X \cap Y$ then $X \cap Y \in \mathcal{D}$.

A *filter* over $\mathcal{D}$ is a subset $x \subseteq \mathcal{D}$ such that

   (a) $\Delta \in x$,
   (b) if $X \in x$ and $X \subseteq Y \in \mathcal{D}$ then $Y \in x$, and
   (c) if $X, Y \in x$ then $X \cap Y \in x$.

Thus a filter is the dual notion to that of an ideal. For each $X \in \mathcal{D}$ let $\uparrow X = \{Y \in \mathcal{D} : X \subseteq Y\}$. Then $\uparrow X$ is a filter, the *principal filter* determined by X. Finally, let $|\mathcal{D}| = \{x \subseteq \mathcal{D} : x \text{ a filter over } \mathcal{D}\}$.

(i) Let $\mathcal{D}$ be a neighbourhood system over Δ. Show that $|\mathcal{D}| = (|\mathcal{D}|; \subseteq, \{\Delta\})$ is a domain whose compact elements are $\uparrow X$ for $X \in \mathcal{D}$.
(ii) Let D be a domain. Show that there is a neighbourhood system $\mathcal{D}$ over D such that $D \cong |\mathcal{D}|$.
(iii) Let $\Delta = \mathbb{N}$ and let $\mathcal{D} = \{X \subseteq \mathbb{N} : \mathbb{N} - X \text{ is finite}\}$. Show that $|\mathcal{D}| \cong \wp(\omega) = (\wp(\omega); \subseteq, \varnothing)$.

Suppose $\mathcal{D}$ and $\mathcal{E}$ are neighbourhood systems. A binary relation $f \subseteq \mathcal{D} \times \mathcal{E}$ is an *approximable mapping* if

   (a) $\Delta_{\mathcal{D}} \, f \, \Delta_{\mathcal{E}}$,
   (b) if XfY and XfY' then $Xf(Y \cap Y')$, and
   (c) if XfY, $X' \subseteq X$ and $Y \subseteq Y'$ then $X'fY'$.

(iv) Try to motivate the definition of an approximable mapping (which, of course, is not a mapping) from a computational point of view.
(v) Suppose f is an approximable mapping from $\mathcal{D}$ to $\mathcal{E}$. Define $\bar{f} : |\mathcal{D}| \longrightarrow |\mathcal{E}|$ by $\bar{f}(x) = \{Y \in \mathcal{E} : (\exists X \in x)(XfY)\}$. Show that $\bar{f}$ is well-defined and continuous.
(vi) Now suppose $\bar{f} : |\mathcal{D}| \longrightarrow |\mathcal{E}|$ is continuous. Define a binary relation f on $\mathcal{D} \times \mathcal{E}$ by $XfY \Leftrightarrow Y \in \bar{f}(\uparrow X)$. Show that f is an approximable mapping. Show further that the operations in (v) and (vi) are inverses of each other.

Remark: This exercise shows that the theory of domains can be developed using the notion of neighbourhood systems. This is due to Scott [1982]. An advantage is that we can *prove* some properties of domains rather than axiomatize them. Nonetheless, we feel that the algebraic presentation is cleaner and easier to work with. In Chapter 6 we will discuss further the theory of neighbourhood systems. In addition we will describe information systems – also due to Scott [1982a] – which is yet another way to obtain domains.

12. (Berry [1978]) Let D be a domain. Then D is said to be a *dI-domain* if

    (a) y, z consistent $\Rightarrow$ $x \sqcap (y \sqcup z) = (x \sqcap y) \sqcup (x \sqcap z)$ for $x, y, z \in D$, and
    (b) approx(a) is finite for each $a \in D_C$.

    (i) Show that the class of dI-domains is closed under the formation of cartesian products, separated sums and liftings.

    Let D and E be dI-domains. A function $f: D \longrightarrow E$ is said to be *stable* if it is continuous and preserves consistent infima, that is for all $x, y \in D$

    $$x, y \text{ consistent} \Rightarrow f(x \sqcap y) = f(x) \sqcap f(y).$$

    Define a *stable ordering* $\sqsubseteq_S$ between stable functions $f, g: D \longrightarrow E$ by saying that $f \sqsubseteq_S g$ if

    (a) $f \sqsubseteq g$, that is $f(x) \sqsubseteq g(x)$ for each $x \in D$, and
    (b) $x \sqsubseteq y \Rightarrow f(x) = f(y) \sqcap f(x)$ for all $x, y \in D$.

    Let $[D \xrightarrow{s} E]$ denote the set of all stable functions from D into E.

    (ii) Let D and E be dI-domains. Show that $[D \xrightarrow{s} E]$, under the stable ordering $\sqsubseteq_S$, is a dI-domain.
    (iii) Let **DI** be the category whose objects are the dI-domains and whose morphism sets are the stable functions between dI-domains. Show that the category **DI** is cartesian closed.
    (iv) Let D and E be domains and suppose $f: D \longrightarrow E$ is a continuous function. Show that there is a continuous function $g: E \longrightarrow D$ such that $g \circ f = id_D$ and $f \circ g \sqsubseteq_S id_E$ if and only if there is a continuous function $g: E \longrightarrow D$ such that (f, g) is a projection pair for (D, E) and such that for each $x \in D$ and $y \in E$, $y \sqsubseteq f(x) \Rightarrow f \circ g(y) = y$.

CHAPTER 4

DOMAIN EQUATIONS

In Chapter 3 we defined binary operations $+$, $\times$, $\rightarrow$, $\oplus$, and $\otimes$ on domains and showed that the class of domains is closed under these. So we know that iterating these operations any number of times on any domains $D_1, \ldots, D_n$ yields a domain. In this chapter we shall investigate what happens when these operations are iterated transfinitely often. In particular, we want to determine whether the resulting object is a domain and whether there exist fixed points in this case. This leads us naturally to consider domain equations, that is, equations between terms built up from domains using these operations and possibly others. The question we want to address is whether such equations have solutions. In particular, if $D_1, \ldots, D_n$ are given (constant) domains and T is a term built up by the operations above from D and $D_1, \ldots, D_n$, we shall show that T has a fixed point, that is, there is a solution to the following domain equation

$$(*) \qquad D = T(D).$$

When datatypes are interpreted as domains, they are usually defined to be the least solution to certain domain equations. For example, the datatype of natural numbers is characterized by $\mathbb{N} = \{0\} + \mathbb{N}$, S-expressions by $S = A + (S \times S)$, where A is the set of atoms, and lists by $L = \{NIL\} + (S \times L)$. So it is important to know that such equations have solutions as domains. We shall establish the general result that each equation of the form $(*)$ has a solution and in fact a least such.

As running examples, the following two particular domain equations will be considered

$$(1) \qquad D = E + (D \times D)$$

$$(2) \qquad D = E + [D \rightarrow D]$$

where E is some constant domain and we want to find a solution D.

For our purposes it is enough to require that D be isomorphic to $T(D)$. In fact, for set-theoretic reasons, we cannot get equality in this setting. Note that the isomorphism equations $D \cong D \times D$ and $D \cong [D \rightarrow D]$ both have the trivial solution $D = \{\bot\}$. But when we add E to the equations, as was done above, it is no longer obvious how to solve the problem. The two equations are fundamentally different. Equation (1) corresponds to a positive inductive definition and can be solved within set theory by iteration (that is, by successively throwing in the pairs needed and stopping at stage ω). Equation (2) is much harder to solve since it involves functions from the whole space to itself. It is mainly for the purpose of solving equations of that type that the methods introduced below have been developed. It turns out that these methods are general enough to include solutions to equations of type (1) also.

We shall take up three methods for solving domain equations, all originally due to Scott. The first one is category-theoretic in nature, where we consider T as a functor and prove that it is continuous and hence has a least fixed point, essentially considering the category of domains as a cpo (albeit generalized, since this category is not small, that is, not a set). Here we use category theory as a convenient language but we do not use any deep results from the theory. Using the second approach, described in Chapter 6, where the class of domains is viewed as a large cpo, domain equations can be solved up to equality. However, in that case we study representations of domains rather than the domains themselves. The third method uses a universal domain $\mathcal{U}$ and will be described in Chapter 7.

Recall that a domain D is the completion by ideals of the cusl D_c. We first show how to solve cusl equations up to isomorphism and then we derive the corresponding result for domains. In fact, the categories **Cusl** and **Dom** introduced below are equivalent.

In the first section we study cusl's. In Section 4.2 we define suprema of ω-chains of cusl's, called direct limits. In Section 4.3 we introduce ω-continuous functors and show that such functors have fixed points. In Section 4.4 we define the concept of least fixed point category-theoretically and then we show that every ω-continuous functor has a least fixed point. Finally we define the subdomain relation and projection pairs and show how to obtain the corresponding results for domains.

The existence of solutions to domain equations was shown for domains in Scott's lectures on domain theory, Scott [1982], where he used category-theoretic methods to solve them. The category-theoretic methods were made more explicit in Smyth and Plotkin [1982].

Section 4.1 Cusl's

Recall that the set of compact elements of a domain is a conditional upper semilattice with least element (cusl). When solving domain equations category-theoretically, we shall first solve the corresponding problem for cusl's. Then we transfer these results to domains. Since every set can be made into a flat cusl by just adding a bottom element, the collection of all cusl's is not itself a set but a proper class. In order to view the class of cusl's as a cpo we need to introduce an ordering on it. In fact, two orderings between cusl's are introduced. The first, denoted by $\lhd$, is the subcusl relation and the second, $\trianglelefteq$, is defined in terms of cusl embeddings. Then $\lhd$ is a partial ordering, but there is no least element with respect to it, since two cusl's are comparable with respect to this ordering only if the set of elements of one of them is a subset of that of the other. For the same reason, $\lhd$ is not monotone with respect to the function space construction. In contrast to the above, we shall show that if P is a fixed cusl, then the *set* consisting of all subcusl's of P ordered by $\lhd$ is a domain.

By introducing cusl embeddings, we can compare cusl's that are disjoint or overlapping. For cusl's P and Q, $P \trianglelefteq Q$ if there exists a cusl embedding from P into Q. In contrast to $\lhd$, there is, up to isomorphism, a least element with respect to $\trianglelefteq$, namely the one-element cusl. The ordering $\trianglelefteq$ is reflexive and transitive but not antisymmetric even if we replace equality by isomorphism. We connect the two orderings by showing that $P \trianglelefteq Q$ if and only if P is isomorphic to a subcusl of Q.

We begin with the notion of a subcusl.

1.1 Definition Let $Q=(Q;\sqsubseteq,\bot)$ be a cusl. Then $P\subseteq Q$ is a *subcusl* of Q, denoted by $P \lhd Q$, if the following conditions hold.

(i) $\bot \in P$.

(ii) If $a,b\in P$ and $\{a,b\}$ is consistent in Q, then $a\sqcup_Q b\in P$.

The subcusl's of Q are exactly the substructures of $Q=(Q;\sqsubseteq,\sqcup,\bot)$. Furthermore, $\lhd$ is a partial ordering on cusl's. We shall prove that $\{P: P\lhd Q\}$ is a domain, for each cusl Q.

In verifying that a cpo is a domain when we have a candidate for the set of compact elements, the following lemma is useful.

1.2 Lemma Let D be a cpo, $C\subseteq D$ and let $C_x=\{y\in C:\ y\sqsubseteq x\}$, for $x\in D$. Assume that C satisfies the following conditions.

(i) $\bot_D\in C$.

(ii) $C\subseteq D_c$.

(iii) If $x\in D$, then for any $y, y'\in C_x$, $y\sqcup_D y'\in C_x$, and $x=\bigsqcup_D C_x$.

Then D is a domain with C as its set of compact elements.

Proof: To establish that D is a domain with $D_c=C$, it remains to verify the converse of (ii) and that D is algebraic and satisfies the consistency condition. So assume that $x\in D_c$. Since $\bot_D\in C$, $\bot_D\in C_x$. Then C_x is directed by (iii) and, since $x=\bigsqcup_D C_x$ and x is compact, we have that $x\sqsubseteq y\in C_x\subseteq C$, for some $y\in C$.

But $y \sqsubseteq x$ and so $x = y$. Hence $D_c \subseteq C$. Now the remaining properties trivially follow. □

1.3 Proposition Let Q be a cusl and let $\mathcal{S}(Q) = \{P: P \lhd Q\}$. Then $\mathcal{S}(Q) = (\mathcal{S}(Q); \subseteq, \{\perp\})$ is a domain.

Proof: First we note that, for $P_1, P_2 \in \mathcal{S}(Q)$, $P_1 \lhd P_2 \Leftrightarrow P_1 \subseteq P_2$. So $\mathcal{S}(Q)$ is a partially ordered set with a least element. Further, $\bigcup \mathcal{A} \in \mathcal{S}(Q)$ for any directed subset $\mathcal{A}$ and thus $\bigcup \mathcal{A} = \bigsqcup \mathcal{A}$, so $\mathcal{S}(Q)$ is a cpo.

Let $\mathcal{B} = \{P \in \mathcal{S}(Q): P \text{ finite}\}$. We show that $\mathcal{S}(Q)$ is a domain with $\mathcal{B}$ as its set of compact elements by verifying clause (iii) of Lemma 1.2 (clauses (i) and (ii) being trivial). For $P \in \mathcal{S}(Q)$, let $\mathcal{B}_P = \{P' \in \mathcal{B}: P' \subseteq P\}$. We claim that $\mathcal{B}_P$ is closed under binary suprema. Let $P_1, P_2 \in \mathcal{B}_P$ and let

$$P' = \{a \sqcup_Q b:\ a, b \in P_1 \cup P_2 \text{ and } \{a, b\} \text{ is consistent in } Q\}.$$

Note that $P_1, P_2 \subseteq P'$, since for any $a \in P_1 \cup P_2$, $\{a, \perp\}$ is consistent in Q. From the definition of P' it follows that $P' \lhd Q$ and also $P' = P_1 \sqcup P_2$. Clearly P' is finite and thus $P' \in \mathcal{B}_P$, establishing the claim. Further, for $x \in P$, we have that $\{\perp, x\} \in \mathcal{B}_P$. So $P \subseteq \bigcup \mathcal{B}_P \subseteq P$ and hence $P = \bigcup \mathcal{B}_P$. □

Note that Q is the top element in $\mathcal{S}(Q)$. It follows that *any* pair of elements from $\mathcal{S}(Q)$ has a supremum in the set, that is, $\mathcal{S}(Q)$ is an upper semilattice.

1.4 Definition Let $f: P \to Q$ where P and Q are cusl's. Then f is a *cusl embedding* if the following conditions hold.

(i) $f(\perp_P) = \perp_Q$.

(ii) f is order-preserving, that is, $a \sqsubseteq b \Leftrightarrow f(a) \sqsubseteq f(b)$.

(iii) If a, b are in P and if $\{f(a), f(b)\}$ is consistent in Q, then $\{a, b\}$ is consistent in P and $f(a \sqcup b) = f(a) \sqcup f(b)$.

Note that it follows from (ii) that each cusl embedding is injective.

1.5 Examples Let P and Q be cusl's. The following are cusl embeddings.

(a) $f: P \to P + Q$ defined by

$$f(a) = \begin{cases} (0, a) & \text{if } a \neq \perp_P \\ \perp & \text{otherwise.} \end{cases}$$

(b) $f: P \to P \times Q$ defined by

$$f(a) = (a, \perp_Q) \quad \text{for } a \in P.$$

The category **Cusl** has cusl's as objects and cusl embeddings as morphisms.

1.6 Definition Let P and Q be cusl's. Then $P \trianglelefteq Q$ if there exists a cusl embedding from P into Q.

1.7 Proposition Let P, Q and R be cusl's.
(a) $P \trianglelefteq P$.
(b) If $f: P \to Q$ and $g: Q \to R$ are cusl embeddings, then $g \circ f$ is a cusl embedding from P into R.

Proof: (a) Clearly, id_P is a cusl embedding from P into P. (b) is obvious.□

It follows from the proposition that $\trianglelefteq$ is a reflexive and transitive ordering on cusl's. However, it is not antisymmetric. Indeed, there are non-isomorphic cusl's for which there are cusl embeddings in both directions (see Exercise 4). Of course, there is a least element up to isomorphism with respect to the ordering $\trianglelefteq$, namely the one-point cusl. Also note that if $P \triangleleft Q$, then the inclusion mapping $\iota_P: P \to Q$ is a cusl embedding.

1.8 Theorem Let P and Q be cusl's. Then $P \trianglelefteq Q$ if and only if P is isomorphic to a subcusl of Q.

Proof: Assume that $f: P \to Q$ is a cusl embedding. Then $P \cong f[P]$, since f is order-preserving. Also, $\bot_Q = f(\bot_P) \in f[P]$. Condition (ii) of Definition 1.1 holds by virtue of condition (iii) of Definition 1.4. So $f[P] \triangleleft Q$.

For the converse, it is immediate that an isomorphism between P and P', where $P' \triangleleft Q$, is a cusl embedding. □

Section 4.2 Direct Limits in Cusl

In order to show that certain domain equations have solutions, we need to restrict ourselves to functors that are ω-continuous in analogy with the fixed point theorem 1.2.3. Recall that a function is ω-continuous if it preserves suprema of ω-chains. In this section we define what should be meant by an ω-chain of cusl's and then what the supremum of such a chain should be. We do this best in a category-theoretic framework.

2.1 Definition Let **K** be a category.
(a) An *ω-chain* $\Delta = (A_n, f_n)_{n<\omega}$ in **K** is a diagram

$$A_0 \xrightarrow{f_0} A_1 \xrightarrow{f_1} \cdots \longrightarrow A_n \xrightarrow{f_n} A_{n+1} \longrightarrow \cdots$$

where the A_n's are objects and the f_n's are morphisms in **K**.

(b) Let $\Delta=(A_n, f_n)_{n<\omega}$ be an ω-chain and let A be an object in $\mathbf{K}$. Then $\mu:\Delta\rightarrow A$ is a *cone* if $\mu=(\mu_n)_{n<\omega}$, where $\mu_n: A_n\rightarrow A$ is a morphism, and the following diagram commutes:

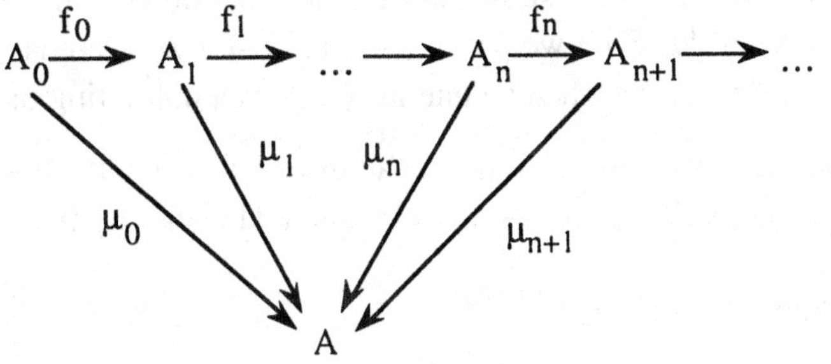

that is, $\mu_n=\mu_{n+1}\circ f_n$ for all n.

(c) A cone $\mu:\Delta\rightarrow A$ is *colimiting* if, for any cone $\nu:\Delta\rightarrow A'$, there exists a *unique* morphism $h: A\rightarrow A'$ such that $h\circ\mu_n=\nu_n$, for all n. Such a morphism h is called the *mediating* morphism between μ and ν. The diagram is as follows.

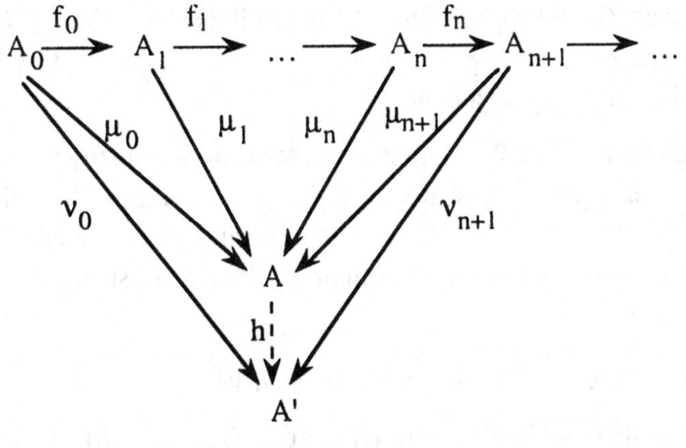

If $\mu:\Delta\rightarrow A$ is a colimiting cone, we say that (A,μ) is the *direct limit* of Δ. Usually, we omit explicit mention of the morphisms $(\mu_n)_{n<\omega}$ and write $A=\varinjlim A_n$ for the direct limit of the chain Δ.

Direct limits do not always exist. For example, consider the ω-chain consisting of $P_n=\{0,1,\ldots,n\}$, for $n\in\omega$, ordered linearly and where the embeddings are inclusion mappings ι_n. This ω-chain has no direct limit in the category **Fpo** having as objects finite partial orders with a least element and embeddings as morphisms. That is, there is no finite partial order P with embeddings $\mu_n: P_n\rightarrow P$ so that $(P,(\mu_n)_{n<\omega})$ is the direct limit of the chain $\Delta=(P_n, \iota_n)_{n<\omega}$. However, as we shall show below, Δ has a direct limit in the category **Cusl**, namely the cusl $\omega+1$ with inclusion mappings. (Cf. Exercise 11.4.11.)

In the remaining part of this section we consider the category **Cusl**. Recall that, for cusl's P and Q, $P \trianglelefteq Q$ if and only if there exists a cusl embedding from P into Q. Thus an ω-chain $\Delta=(P_n, f_n)_{n<\omega}$ in **Cusl** is an increasing sequence of cusl's, ordered by $\trianglelefteq$. We shall show later that a direct limit P of Δ is a least upper bound of the P_n's. First we prove that in **Cusl** every ω-chain has a direct limit and give a criterion for when a cone in **Cusl** is a colimiting one.

2.2 Definition Let $\Delta=(P_m, f_m)_{m<\omega}$ be an ω-chain in **Cusl**. For $m \leq n$, let $f_{mn}: P_m \to P_n$ be defined as follows: $f_{mm}=id_{P_m}$, and if $m<n$, then

$$f_{mn}=f_{n-1} \circ \ldots \circ f_{m+1} \circ f_m.$$

2.3 Proposition Let $\Delta=(P_m, f_m)_{m<\omega}$ be an ω-chain in **Cusl**.

(a) f_{mn} is a cusl embedding from P_m into P_n, for $m \leq n$.

(b) $f_{kn}=f_{mn} \circ f_{km}$, for $k \leq m \leq n$.

(c) If $i, j \geq \max(m, n)$, then $f_{mi}(x) \sqsubseteq_i f_{ni}(y) \Leftrightarrow f_{mj}(x) \sqsubseteq_j f_{nj}(y)$.

(d) For any cone $\mu: \Delta \to P$, $\mu_m=\mu_n \circ f_{mn}$, for $m \leq n$.

Proof: (a) follows from Proposition 1.7 and (b) is obvious. Using (b) and the fact that f_{ij} is order-preserving we get (c). Finally (d) is proved by induction using the defining property of a cone. □

Given an ω-chain $(P_n, f_n)_{n<\omega}$ in **Cusl** we want to construct a direct limit P. We do this in several steps. First we form the *disjoint union* Q of the P_n's. Explicitly, $Q=\bigcup_{n<\omega}(\{n\}\times P_n)$. Now Q contains infinitely many copies of the same element. For this reason we form a quotient to identify all such elements.

Define the relation ~ on Q by

$$(k, a) \sim (m, b) \text{ if } \exists n \geq k, m\ (f_{kn}(a)=f_{mn}(b)).$$

By Proposition 2.3(c), ~ is well-defined, that is $(k, a) \sim (m, b)$ if and only if $\forall n \geq k, m\ (f_{kn}(a)=f_{mn}(b))$. Then the quotient structure $Q/\sim$ formed in the standard way is a cusl.

2.4 Lemma The relation ~ is an equivalence relation on Q and $Q/\sim$ is a cusl.

Proof: Obviously, ~ is an equivalence relation. We order Q by the following relation $\sqsubseteq_Q$. For $(k, a), (m, b) \in Q$,

$$(k, a) \sqsubseteq_Q (m, b) \text{ if } \exists n \geq k, m\ (f_{kn}(a) \sqsubseteq_n f_{mn}(b)).$$

By Proposition 2.3(c), $\sqsubseteq_Q$ is well-defined and transitive. Then $\sqsubseteq_Q$ is a preordering, since it clearly also is reflexive. It is not antisymmetric, for $(0, \perp_0) \sqsubseteq_Q (n, \perp_n) \sqsubseteq_Q (0, \perp_0)$, since $f_{0n}(\perp_0)=\perp_n$, for all n.

Let $P_n=(P_n;\sqsubseteq_n,\bot_n)$ and let $\sqcup_n$ denote the partial supremum operation in P_n. We show that if the set $\{(k,a),(m,b)\}$ is consistent in Q, then it has a least upper bound in Q. Note that a least upper bound need not be unique, since $\sqsubseteq_Q$ is not antisymmetric. We shall show that, for $i=\max(k,m)$, $f_{ki}(a)\sqcup_i f_{mi}(b)$ exists and $(i,f_{ki}(a)\sqcup_i f_{mi}(b))$ is a least upper bound for the set. For if (n,d) is an upper bound for $\{(k,a),(m,b)\}$, let $j=\max(i,n)$. It follows that $(j,f_{nj}(d))$ is an upper bound for the set. Thus $\{f_{kj}(a),f_{mj}(b)\}$ is consistent and $f_{kj}(a)\sqcup f_{mj}(b)\in P_j$. Using Proposition 2.3 and the fact that cusl embeddings preserve suprema, we get that $e=f_{ki}(a)\sqcup f_{mi}(b)\in P_i$ and that

$$f_{kj}(a)\sqcup f_{mj}(b)=f_{ij}\circ f_{ki}(a)\sqcup f_{ij}\circ f_{mi}(b)=f_{ij}(f_{ki}(a)\sqcup f_{mi}(b)).$$

Thus $(i,e)\sqsubseteq_Q(n,d)$. Since (n,d) is arbitrary, it follows that (i,e) is a least upper bound for $\{(k,a),(m,b)\}$.

Note that $(k,a)\sim(m,b) \Leftrightarrow (k,a)\sqsubseteq_Q(m,b)$ and $(m,b)\sqsubseteq_Q(k,a)$. Hence if $(k,a)\sqsubseteq_Q(m,b)$, $(k,a)\sim(k',a')$ and $(m,b)\sim(m',b')$, then $(k',a')\sqsubseteq_Q(m',b')$. This means that $\sim$ is a congruence relation with respect to $\sqsubseteq_Q$. We use the notation $[(k,a)]$ for the equivalence class of (k,a) with respect to $\sim$. Let $R=Q/\sim$ $=\{[(k,a)]:(k,a)\in Q\}$. By the above, we can consistently define an induced partial ordering $\sqsubseteq_R$ on R as follows. For (k,a), $(m,b)\in Q$,

$$[(k,a)]\sqsubseteq_R[(m,b)] \Leftrightarrow (k,a)\sqsubseteq_Q(m,b).$$

The least element of R is $[(0,\bot_0)]=\{(n,\bot_n): n<\omega\}$. By the above, $\sqsubseteq_R$ is a preordering and since R is the quotient $Q/\sim$, the induced ordering is antisymmetric as well. Also, if $\{[(k,a)],[(m,b)]\}$ is consistent in R, then that set has a supremum in R by what we just proved. Hence R is a cusl. □

Next we define the cusl embedding $\mu_n:P_n\to Q/\sim$ by $\mu_n(a)=[(n,a)]$.

2.5 Lemma The function $\mu_n:P_n\to Q/\sim$ is a cusl embedding.

Proof: Since $\mu_n(\bot_n)=[(n,\bot_n)]=\bot$, (i) of Definition 1.4 holds. For (ii), $a\sqsubseteq_n b$ $\Leftrightarrow$ $(n,a)\sqsubseteq(n,b)$ $\Leftrightarrow$ $[(n,a)]\sqsubseteq[(n,b)]$ $\Leftrightarrow$ $\mu_n(a)\sqsubseteq\mu_n(b)$, by the definition of the orderings.

To show (iii), assume that $a,b\in P_n$ and that $\{\mu_n(a),\mu_n(b)\}$ is consistent, that is $\{[(n,a)],[(n,b)]\}$ is consistent. By the proof of Lemma 2.4, we have that $[(n,a)]\sqcup[(n,b)]=[(n,a\sqcup_n b)]$ and thus $\mu_n(a\sqcup_n b)=\mu_n(a)\sqcup\mu_n(b)$. □

Now we give a criterion for when a cone is colimiting. We prove one direction here and leave the converse for later (Theorem 2.8).

2.6 Lemma Let $\mu:\Delta\to P$ be a cone in **Cusl**, where $\Delta=(P_n, f_n)_{n<\omega}$. Then μ is a colimiting cone if for every $d\in P$ there is some $n<\omega$ and some $a\in P_n$ for which $\mu_n(a)=d$.

Proof: Assume the hypothesis of the lemma, and let $\nu:\Delta\to P'$ be any cone. Note that $P=\{\mu_n(a):\ a\in P_n, n<\omega\}$ by the assumption. Let $h:P\to P'$ be defined by $h(\mu_n(a))=\nu_n(a)$, for $a\in P_n$. We show that h is well-defined and, at the same time, order-preserving.

$$\begin{array}{llll} \mu_n(a)\sqsubseteq\mu_m(b) & \Leftrightarrow & \mu_i(f_{ni}(a))\sqsubseteq\mu_i(f_{mi}(b)) & \text{for } i=\max(n,m) \\ & \Leftrightarrow & f_{ni}(a)\sqsubseteq f_{mi}(b) & \text{since } \mu_i \text{ cusl embedding} \\ & \Leftrightarrow & \nu_i(f_{ni}(a))\sqsubseteq\nu_i(f_{mi}(b)) & \text{since } \nu_i \text{ cusl embedding} \\ & \Leftrightarrow & \nu_n(a)\sqsubseteq\nu_m(b) & \text{by Proposition 2.3(d).} \end{array}$$

It follows that $\mu_n(a)=\mu_m(b)\Leftrightarrow\nu_n(a)=\nu_m(b)$, and hence h is well-defined. To verify that h is a cusl embedding, it remains to show that h is strict and that condition (iii) of Definition 1.4 holds. We have that

$$h(\bot_P)=h(\mu_n(\bot_n))=\nu_n(\bot_n)=\bot_{P'},$$

since μ_n and ν_n are cusl embeddings. To show that (iii) holds, assume that the set $\{h(\mu_n(a)), h(\mu_m(b))\}$ is consistent in P' and let $i=\max(n,m)$. Then

$$h(\mu_n(a))\sqcup h(\mu_m(b))=\nu_n(a)\sqcup\nu_m(b)=\nu_i(f_{ni}(a))\sqcup\nu_i(f_{mi}(b)).$$

Since ν_i is a cusl embedding, $f_{ni}(a)\sqcup f_{mi}(b)$ exists and

$$\nu_i(f_{ni}(a)\sqcup f_{mi}(b))=\nu_i(f_{ni}(a))\sqcup\nu_i(f_{mi}(b)).$$

Also

$$\mu_i(f_{ni}(a)\sqcup f_{mi}(b))=\mu_i(f_{ni}(a))\sqcup\mu_i(f_{mi}(b))=\mu_n(a)\sqcup\mu_m(b).$$

Thus $\mu_n(a)\sqcup\mu_m(b)$ exists and

$$h(\mu_n(a)\sqcup\mu_m(b))=h(\mu_n(a))\sqcup h(\mu_m(b)),$$

which establishes (iii). □

Now it immediately follows that the cone $\mu:\Delta\to Q/{\sim}$ constructed above is a colimiting cone, which proves the following.

2.7 Theorem In **Cusl** every ω-chain has a direct limit.

In any category direct limits are unique up to isomorphism. We leave the proof of this as an exercise (Exercise 5). Now we give the promised converse to Lemma 2.6.

2.8 Theorem Let $\mu:\Delta\to P$ be a cone in **Cusl**, where $\Delta=(P_n,f_n)_{n<\omega}$ is an ω-chain. Then μ is a colimiting cone if and only if for every $d\in P$ there is some $n<\omega$ and some $a\in P_n$ for which $\mu_n(a)=d$.

Proof: To prove the remaining direction, let $\nu:\Delta\to Q/\sim$ be the direct limit constructed in the proof of Theorem 2.7. Then ν satisfies the condition in Lemma 2.6, that is, $Q/\sim=\{\nu_n(a):\ a\in P_n\}$. Let h be the mediating morphism between μ and ν. For $d\in P$, we have $h(d)=\nu_n(a)$ for some n and some $a\in P_n$. But $\nu_n(a)=h(\mu_n(a))$ and hence, by the injectivity of h, $d=\mu_n(a)$. □

Section 4.3 ω-continuous Functors and Fixed Points

In this section we consider functors that preserve direct limits, introduce our running examples T_+, $T_\times$ and $T_\rightarrow$ of functors and show that they are such. First we observe that all functors preserve ω-chains and cones.

3.1 Proposition Let T be a (covariant) functor from the category K into K', let $\Delta=(A_n,f_n)_{n<\omega}$ be an ω-chain and let $\mu:\Delta\to A$ be a cone in K.

(a) $T(\Delta)=(T(A_n),T(f_n))_{n<\omega}$ is an ω-chain in K'.

(b) $T(\mu)=(T(\mu_n))_{n<\omega}: T(\Delta)\to T(A)$ is a cone in K'.

Proof: (a) is obvious. For (b), we have that

$$T(\mu_{n+1})\circ T(f_n)=T(\mu_{n+1}\circ f_n)=T(\mu_n),$$

since μ is a cone and T preserves composition. □

If there is an embedding from an object A to an object B in a category, we interpret this as A being less than B. Note that by Proposition 3.1 functors preserve this order, that is they are monotone. In analogy with ω-continuous functions, a functor is ω-continuous if it preserves limits of ω-chains.

3.2 Definition Let T be a functor from the category K into K'. T is *ω-continuous* if T maps colimiting cones to colimiting cones, that is, if $\mu:\Delta\to A$ is a colimiting cone in K, then $T(\mu): T(\Delta)\to T(A)$ is a colimiting cone in K'.

Here are some trivial but useful examples.

3.3 Examples

(a) Let Q be a fixed cusl and let the *constant functor* T_Q: **Cusl** → **Cusl** be defined by

$$\begin{cases} \mathbf{T_Q}(P)=Q & \text{for every cusl } P \\ \mathbf{T_Q}(f)=id_Q & \text{for every cusl embedding } f:P\to P'. \end{cases}$$

Then $\mathbf{T_Q}$ is ω-continuous.

(b) Define the *identity functor* **id**: **Cusl** $\to$ **Cusl** as follows.

$$\begin{cases} \mathbf{id}(P)=P & \text{for every cusl } P \\ \mathbf{id}(f)=f & \text{for every cusl embedding } f:P\to Q. \end{cases}$$

Then **id** is ω-continuous.

Below we introduce our running examples of functors which will be used to solve the two domain equations mentioned in the introduction. Since the operations on domains take two arguments, we need to consider bifunctors. Recall the definition of $\mathbf{K}\times\mathbf{L}$ from Chapter 0.

3.4 Proposition Suppose that direct limits exist in the categories **K** and **L**. Then the same holds for the category $\mathbf{K}\times\mathbf{L}$ and

$$\varinjlim(A_n,B_n)\cong(\varinjlim A_n, \varinjlim B_n).$$

Proof: Let $\Delta=((A_n,B_n),(f_n,g_n))_{n<\omega}$ be an ω-chain in $\mathbf{K}\times\mathbf{L}$. Then we have that $\Delta_1=(A_n,f_n)_{n<\omega}$ and $\Delta_2=(B_n,g_n)_{n<\omega}$ are ω-chains in **K** and in **L**, respectively. Let $\mu:\Delta_1\to A$ and $\nu:\Delta_2\to B$ be colimiting cones in **K** and in **L**. Then $(\mu_n,\nu_n)_{n<\omega}:\Delta\to(A,B)$ is a cone in $\mathbf{K}\times\mathbf{L}$. If $(\mu'_n,\nu'_n)_{n<\omega}:\Delta\to(A',B')$ is any cone, let h be mediating between μ and μ' and let g be mediating between ν and ν'. Then (h,g) is mediating between $(\mu_n,\nu_n)_{n<\omega}$ and $(\mu'_n,\nu'_n)_{n<\omega}$. Further, if (h',g') is mediating between $(\mu_n,\nu_n)_{n<\omega}$ and $(\mu'_n,\nu'_n)_{n<\omega}$, then h' is mediating between μ and μ' and g' is mediating between ν and ν'. So $h=h'$ and $g=g'$. Thus (h,g) is unique and $(\mu_n,\nu_n)_{n<\omega}:\Delta\to(A,B)$ is a colimiting cone in $\mathbf{K}\times\mathbf{L}$. □

For each one of the constructions defined in Chapter 2, we introduce the corresponding functors on **Cusl**.

3.5 Separated sum Let $\mathbf{T_+}$: **Cusl** $\times$ **Cusl** $\to$ **Cusl** be defined as follows.

(a) $\mathbf{T_+}(P, Q)=P+Q$, where $P+Q$ is the separated sum of P and Q. (Cf. Definition 2.4.1.)

(b) For f_0 a cusl embedding from P into P' and f_1 a cusl embedding from Q into Q', let $\mathbf{T_+}(f_0,f_1):P+Q\to P'+Q'$ be defined by:

$$\mathbf{T_+}(f_0,f_1)(b)=\begin{cases}(i,f_i(a)) & \text{if } b=(i,a),\ i=0 \text{ or } 1 \\ \bot_{P'+Q'} & \text{otherwise.}\end{cases}$$

Clearly $T_+(P,Q)$ is a cusl and $T_+(f_0,f_1)$ is a cusl embedding. Also T_+ preserves identity maps. As for composition,

$$T_+(g_0,g_1) \circ T_+(f_0,f_1)(i,a) = T_+(g_0,g_1)(i,f_i(a)) = (i,g_i(f_i(a)))$$
$$= T_+(g_0 \circ f_0, g_1 \circ f_1)(i,a).$$

So T_+ is a functor from **Cusl** $\times$ **Cusl** into **Cusl**.

3.6 Product $T_\times$ is defined on **Cusl** $\times$ **Cusl** as follows.

(a) $T_\times(P,Q) = P \times Q$, where $P \times Q$ is ordered by: $(a,b) \sqsubseteq (d,e) \Leftrightarrow a \sqsubseteq d$ and $b \sqsubseteq e$.

(b) If $f: P \to P'$ and $g: Q \to Q'$ are cusl embeddings, then $f \times g: P \times Q \to P' \times Q'$ is defined by $(f \times g)(a,b) = (f(a), g(b))$. Let $T_\times(f,g) = f \times g$.

Clearly $T_\times$ is a functor from **Cusl** $\times$ **Cusl** into **Cusl**. (Cf. Section 2.2.)

3.7 Exponentiation We define $T_\to$: **Cusl** $\times$ **Cusl** $\to$ **Cusl** as follows.

(a) First we *define* consistency for sets $A \subseteq P \times Q$ and then we introduce an ordering on $((P \to Q))$, the set of finite non-empty consistent sets A.

We say that $A \subseteq P \times Q$ is *consistent* if, for each $I \subseteq A$,

$$\pi_0[I] \text{ is consistent in } P \Rightarrow \pi_1[I] \text{ is consistent in } Q,$$

where π_0 and π_1 are the projection functions for $P \times Q$ (see Definition 2.2.1). Put

$$((P \to Q)) = \{A \subseteq P \times Q: \ A \text{ is finite, non-empty and consistent}\}.$$

We order $((P \to Q))$ as follows. $A \sqsubseteq B$ if for each $I \subseteq A$, whenever $\pi_0[I]$ is consistent in P, then

$$\sqcup_Q \pi_1[I] \sqsubseteq \sqcup_Q \pi_1[\{(a,b) \in B: \ a \sqsubseteq \sqcup_P \pi_0[I]\}].$$

Then $\sqsubseteq$ is clearly reflexive and transitive. It is, however, not antisymmetric. (See Exercise 9.) In the usual way, this preorder induces an equivalence relation $\sim$ on $((P \to Q))$ defined by requiring the preorder to hold in both directions. In fact $\sim$ is a congruence relation with respect to $\sqsubseteq$.

Let $(P \to Q) = ((P \to Q))/\sim$ and let $(P \to Q)$ obtain the induced ordering:

$$[A] \sqsubseteq [B] \text{ if } A \sqsubseteq B,$$

where $[A]$ denotes the equivalence class of A with respect to $\sim$. If $\{A,B\}$ is consistent in $((P \to Q))$, then $A \cup B$ is a supremum of $\{A,B\}$. It follows that $(P \to Q) = ((P \to Q); \sqsubseteq, [\{(\bot,\bot)\}])$ is a cusl and we put $T_\to(P,Q) = (P \to Q)$.

The definitions have been chosen so that the equivalence class $[\{(a,b)\}]$ may be identified with the function $<a;b>$ in $[D\to E]$ and $[\{(a_i,b_i)\colon 1\le i\le n\}]$ may be identified with the function $\sqcup\{<a_i;b_i>\colon 1\le i\le n\}$. In other words, if D and E are domains, then $(D_c\to E_c)\cong[D\to E]_c$, the set of compact elements in the function space $[D\to E]$. (Cf. Section 3.3 and Corollary 6.9.)

(b) If $f\colon P\to P'$ and $g\colon Q\to Q'$ are cusl embeddings, let

$$T_\to(f,g)([\{(a_i,b_i)\colon\ 1\le i\le n\}])=[\{(f(a_i),g(b_i))\colon\ 1\le i\le n\}].$$

Clearly, $[\{(f(a_i),g(b_i))\colon\ 1\le i\le n\}]\in(P'\to Q')$. We show that $T_\to(f,g)$ is a cusl embedding.

(i) First, $T_\to(f,g)([\{(\perp,\perp)\}])=[\{(\perp,\perp)\}]$, since $f(\perp)=g(\perp)=\perp$, and thus $T_\to(f,g)$ is strict.

(ii) To show that $T_\to(f,g)$ is order-preserving, we first note that, for any set $I\subseteq\{1,2,\ldots,n\}$, $\{a_i\colon\ i\in I\}$ is consistent in P $\Leftrightarrow$ $\{f(a_i)\colon\ i\in I\}$ is consistent in P'. Now assume that

$$[\{(a_i,b_i)\colon\ 1\le i\le n\}]\sqsubseteq[\{(d_j,e_j)\colon\ 1\le j\le m\}].$$

Further assume that $I\subseteq\{1,2,\ldots,n\}$ and that $\{f(a_i)\colon i\in I\}$ is consistent in P'. Then we have that $\{a_i\colon\ i\in I\}$ is consistent in P and

$$\sqcup_Q\{b_i\colon i\in I\}\sqsubseteq\sqcup_Q\{e_j\colon\ d_j\sqsubseteq\sqcup_P\{a_i\colon i\in I\}\}.$$

Since g is order-preserving, it follows that

$$g(\sqcup_Q\{b_i\colon i\in I\})\sqsubseteq g(\sqcup_Q\{e_j\colon\ d_j\sqsubseteq\sqcup_P\{a_i\colon i\in I\}\}).$$

Since g preserves suprema of finite sets, we get that

$$\sqcup_{Q'}\{g(b_i)\colon i\in I\}\sqsubseteq\sqcup_{Q'}\{g(e_j)\colon\ d_j\sqsubseteq\sqcup_P\{a_i\colon i\in I\}\}.$$

Since f is a cusl embedding, we have that

$$\sqcup_{Q'}\{g(e_j)\colon d_j\sqsubseteq\sqcup_P\{a_i\colon i\in I\}\}=\sqcup_{Q'}\{g(e_j)\colon\ f(d_j)\sqsubseteq\sqcup_{P'}\{f(a_i)\colon i\in I\}\}.$$

It follows that

$$[\{(f(a_i),g(b_i))\colon\ 1\le i\le n\}]\sqsubseteq[\{(f(d_j),g(e_j))\colon\ 1\le j\le m\}]$$

that is, $T_\to(f,g)([\{(a_i,b_i)\colon\ 1\le i\le n\}])\sqsubseteq T_\to(f,g)([\{(e_j,d_j)\colon\ 1\le j\le m\}])$.

The converse is proved by reversing the implications in the above proof.

(iii) To verify that the condition on suprema is satisfied, let $A,B\in((P\to Q))$, and let $[A']=T_\to(f,g)([A])$ and let $[B']=T_\to(f,g)([B])$. Suppose that $\{[A'],[B']\}$

is consistent in $(P' \to Q')$. Then $A' \cup B'$ is a supremum of $\{A', B'\}$. We shall show that $\{A, B\}$ is consistent in $((P \to Q))$. We do this by showing that $A \cup B \in ((P \to Q))$, in other words that $A \cup B$ is consistent in $((P \to Q))$. So let K be a subset of $A \cup B$ such that $\pi_0[K]$ is consistent in P. Then $K = I \cup J$ for some $I \subseteq A$ and $J \subseteq B$ and $\pi_0[I]$ and $\pi_0[J]$ are consistent in P. It follows that $f[\pi_0[I]]$ and $f[\pi_0[J]]$ as well as $f[\pi_0[K]]$ are consistent in P'. Let

$$d = \sqcup_{Q'} \pi_1[\{(a, b) \in A' \cup B' : a \sqsubseteq \sqcup_{P'} f[\pi_0[K]]\}].$$

Then

$$\sqcup_{Q'} g[\pi_1[I]] \sqsubseteq d \text{ and } \sqcup_{Q'} g[\pi_1[J]] \sqsubseteq d.$$

Since g is a cusl embedding, we have that

$$g(\sqcup_Q \pi_1[I]) \sqsubseteq d \text{ and } g(\sqcup_Q \pi_1[J]) \sqsubseteq d.$$

It follows that $(\sqcup_Q \pi_1[I], \sqcup_Q \pi_1[J])$ is consistent in Q. Thus $\pi_1[K]$ is consistent in Q and hence $A \cup B \in ((P \to Q))$.

Finally, we have that

$$\begin{aligned} &\mathbf{T}_{\to}(f, g)([A] \sqcup [B]) = \mathbf{T}_{\to}(f, g)([A \cup B]) \\ &= [A' \cup B'] = [A'] \sqcup [B'] \\ &= \mathbf{T}_{\to}(f, g)([A]) \sqcup \mathbf{T}_{\to}(f, g)([B]). \end{aligned}$$

Hence $\mathbf{T}_{\to}$ is a cusl embedding. It follows that $\mathbf{T}_{\to}$ is a functor from **Cusl** × **Cusl** into **Cusl**.

3.8 Smash sum Let $\mathbf{T}_{\oplus}$ be defined on **Cusl** × **Cusl** as follows.

(a) $\mathbf{T}_{\oplus}(P, Q) = P \oplus Q$, where $P \oplus Q$ is the smash sum of P and Q. (Cf. Definition 2.4.4.)

(b) For cusl embeddings $f_0 : P \to P'$ and $f_1 : Q \to Q'$, let $\mathbf{T}_{\oplus}(f_0, f_1) : P \oplus Q \to P' \oplus Q'$ be defined by:

$$\mathbf{T}_{\oplus}(f_0, f_1)(b) = \begin{cases} (i, f_i(a)) & \text{if } b = (i, a),\ i = 0 \text{ or } 1 \\ \bot_{P' \oplus Q'} & \text{otherwise.} \end{cases}$$

Clearly $\mathbf{T}_{\oplus}(P, Q)$ is a cusl and $\mathbf{T}_{\oplus}(f_0, f_1)$ is a cusl embedding. Also $\mathbf{T}_{\oplus}$ preserves identity maps and composition. So $\mathbf{T}_{\oplus}$ is a functor from **Cusl** × **Cusl** into **Cusl**.

3.9 Smash product $\mathbf{T}_{\otimes}$ is defined on **Cusl** × **Cusl** by:

(a) $\mathbf{T}_{\otimes}(P, Q) = P \otimes Q$, the smash product of P and Q. (Cf. Definition 2.4.2.)

(b) If $f : P \to P'$ and $g : Q \to Q'$ are cusl embeddings, then $\mathbf{T}_{\otimes}(f, g) = f \times g$.

Clearly $\mathbf{T}_{\otimes}$ is a functor from **Cusl** × **Cusl** into **Cusl**.

3.10 Lifting $\mathbf{T}_\perp$ is defined on **Cusl** as follows.
(a) $\mathbf{T}_\perp(P)=P_\perp$, the lifting of P. (Cf. Definition 2.4.5.)
(b) If $f:P\to Q$ is a cusl embedding, then

$$\mathbf{T}_\perp(f)(x)=\begin{cases} f(x) & \text{if } x\in P \\ \perp & \text{if } x=\perp. \end{cases}$$

3.11 Strict exponentiation We define $\mathbf{T}_{\to\perp}$ as follows.
(a) We define consistency for sets $A\subseteq P\times Q$ in the same way as for exponentiation (see 3.7). Then put

$$((P\to_\perp Q))=\{A\subseteq P\times Q:\ A \text{ is finite, non-empty, consistent and } \forall x\in A(\pi_1(x)\neq\perp\Rightarrow\pi_0(x)\neq\perp)\}.$$

Then $((P\to_\perp Q))\subseteq((P\to Q))$ and the ordering on $((P\to_\perp Q))$ is the restriction of the ordering on $((P\to Q))$.

Let $(P\to_\perp Q)=((P\to_\perp Q))/\sim$ with the induced ordering. Put $\mathbf{T}_{\to\perp}(P,Q)=(P\to_\perp Q)$.

The definitions have been chosen so that the equivalence class $[\{(a,b)\}]$ may be identified with the function $\langle a;b\rangle_\perp$ in $[D\to_\perp E]$. In other words, if D and E are domains, then $(D_c\to_\perp E_c)\cong[D\to_\perp E]_c$, the set of compact elements in the strict function space $[D\to_\perp E]$. (Cf. Section 3.4.)

(b) If $f:P\to P'$ and $g:Q\to Q'$ are cusl embeddings, let

$$\mathbf{T}_{\to\perp}(f,g)([\{(a_i,b_i):\ 1\leq i\leq n\}])=[\{(f(a_i),g(b_i)):\ 1\leq i\leq n\}].$$

Then $\mathbf{T}_{\to\perp}(f,g)$ is a cusl embedding. It follows that $\mathbf{T}_{\to\perp}$ is a functor from **Cusl**$\times$**Cusl** into **Cusl**.

We shall show that $\mathbf{T}_+$, $\mathbf{T}_\times$ and $\mathbf{T}_\to$ are all ω-continuous, leaving the verification of the ω-continuity of the other functors as an exercise (see Exercise 13). But first we state a criterion for when a functor on **Cusl** or **Cusl**$\times$**Cusl** is ω-continuous.

3.12 Lemma (a) A functor **T**: **Cusl** $\to$ **Cusl** is ω-continuous if and only if whenever $\Delta=(P_n,f_n)_{n<\omega}$ is an ω-chain and $\mu:\Delta\to P$ is a colimiting cone in **Cusl**, then

$$\mathbf{T}(P)=\bigcup_{n<\omega}\mathbf{T}(\mu_n)[\mathbf{T}(P_n)].$$

(b) A bifunctor **T**: **Cusl**$\times$**Cusl** $\to$ **Cusl** is ω-continuous if and only if whenever $\Delta=((P_n,Q_n),(f_n,g_n))_{n<\omega}$ is an ω-chain and $(\mu_n,\nu_n)_{n<\omega}:\Delta\to(P,Q)$ is a colimiting cone in **Cusl**$\times$**Cusl**, then

$$T(P,Q) = \bigcup_{n<\omega} T(\mu_n, \nu_n)[T(P_n, Q_n)].$$

Proof: By Proposition 3.1 and Theorem 2.8. □

Note that the inclusions from left to right in the above equations follow from the definitions of a cone and of a functor. Thus in applying the lemma, we need only verify the other inclusions, as we do in the proof of the following propositions.

3.13 Proposition The bifunctors T_+ and $T_\times$ are ω-continuous.

Proof: Assume that $\Delta = ((P_n, Q_n), (f_n, g_n))_{n<\omega}$ is an ω-chain in **Cusl** × **Cusl** and that $(\mu_n, \nu_n)_{n<\omega} : \Delta \to (P,Q)$ is a colimiting cone. Then $\mu : (P_n, f_n)_{n<\omega} \to P$ and $\nu : (Q_n, g_n)_{n<\omega} \to Q$ are colimiting cones in **Cusl** and thus $P = \bigcup_{n<\omega} \mu_n[P_n]$ and $Q = \bigcup_{n<\omega} \nu_n[Q_n]$ by Theorem 2.8.

To see that T_+ is ω-continuous, using Lemma 3.12, note that

$$\begin{aligned} T_+(P,Q) &= P+Q = \{(0,a) : a \in P\} \cup \{(1,b) : b \in Q\} \cup \{\bot_{P+Q}\} \\ &= \bigcup_{n<\omega} \{(0,\mu_n(a)) : a \in P_n\} \cup \bigcup_{n<\omega} \{(1,\nu_n(b)) : b \in Q_n\} \cup \{\bot_{P+Q}\} \\ &= \bigcup_{n<\omega} (\{(0,\mu_n(a)) : a \in P_n\} \cup \{(1,\nu_n(b)) : b \in Q_n\} \cup \{\bot_{P+Q}\}) \\ &= \bigcup_{n<\omega} T_+(\mu_n, \nu_n)[T_+(P_n, Q_n)]. \end{aligned}$$

Similarly,

$$\begin{aligned} T_\times(P,Q) &= P \times Q = (\bigcup_{n<\omega} \mu_n[P_n]) \times (\bigcup_{n<\omega} \nu_n[Q_n]) \\ &= \{(\mu_n(a), \nu_m(b)) : a \in P_n,\ b \in Q_m\}. \end{aligned}$$

Let $(\mu_n(a), \nu_m(b)) \in T_\times(P,Q)$ and let $i = \max(n,m)$. Then $\mu_n(a) = \mu_i(f_{ni}(a))$ and $\nu_m(b) = \nu_i(g_{mi}(b))$, since μ and ν are cones. So

$$T_\times(\mu_i, \nu_i)(f_{ni}(a), g_{mi}(b)) = (\mu_i(f_{ni}(a)), \nu_i(g_{mi}(b))) = (\mu_n(a), \nu_m(b)),$$

and hence $(\mu_n(a), \nu_m(b)) \in \bigcup_{i<\omega} T_\times(\mu_i, \nu_i)[T_\times(P_i, Q_i)]$. Thus $(T_\times(\mu_n, \nu_n))_{n<\omega}$ is a colimiting cone and $T_\times$ is ω-continuous. □

3.14 Proposition The bifunctor $T_\to$ is ω-continuous.

Proof: Assume that $\Delta = ((P_n, Q_n), (f_n, g_n))_{n<\omega}$ is an ω-chain in **Cusl** × **Cusl** and that $(\mu_n, \nu_n)_{n<\omega} : \Delta \to (P,Q)$ is a colimiting cone. Then $\mu : (P_n, f_n)_{n<\omega} \to P$ and $\nu : (Q_n, g_n)_{n<\omega} \to Q$ are colimiting cones in **Cusl** and thus $P = \bigcup_{n<\omega} \mu_n[P_n]$ and $Q = \bigcup_{n<\omega} \nu_n[Q_n]$ by Theorem 2.8.

The structure of the proof of the ω-continuity of $T_\to$ is as follows. Assume that $[\{(d_i, e_i) : 1 \le i \le k\}] \in T_\to(P,Q)$. Then it is sufficient to find some n so that

$[\{(d_i, e_i): 1 \leq i \leq k\}] \in \mathbf{T}_{\to}(\mu_n, \nu_n)[\mathbf{T}_{\to}(P_n, Q_n)]$. Thus we need to find a consistent subset A of $P_n \times Q_n$ so that $\mathbf{T}_{\to}(\mu_n, \nu_n)([A]) = [\{(d_i, e_i): 1 \leq i \leq k\}]$. This in turn is achieved by finding n big enough so that $d_i = \mu_n(a_i')$ and $e_i = \nu_n(b_i')$, for $1 \leq i \leq k$, where $a_i' \in \pi_0[A]$ and $b_i' \in \pi_1[A]$.

The details of finding A and n as described above are as follows. Since $d_i \in P$, $d_i = \mu_{n_i}(a_i)$, for some $a_i \in P_{n_i}$, for $1 \leq i \leq k$. Similarly $e_i = \nu_{m_i}(b_i)$, for some $b_i \in Q_{m_i}$. Let $n = \max(\{n_i: 1 \leq i \leq k\} \cup \{m_i: 1 \leq i \leq k\})$. Then we have that $\mu_{n_i}(a_i) = \mu_n(f_{n_i n}(a_i))$ and $\nu_{m_i}(b_i) = \nu_n(g_{m_i n}(b_i))$, since μ and ν are cones. Let $a_i' = f_{n_i n}(a_i)$ and let $b_i' = g_{m_i n}(b_i)$, for $1 \leq i \leq k$. Then $a_i' \in P_n$ and $b_i' \in Q_n$. We want to show that $\{(a_i', b_i'): 1 \leq i \leq k\} \subseteq P_n \times Q_n$ is consistent in the sense of 3.7. Assume that $I \subseteq \{1,2,\ldots,k\}$ and that $\{a_i': i \in I\}$ is consistent in P_n. Then $\{\mu_n(a_i'): i \in I\}$ is consistent in P, since μ_n is monotone. Now

$$\{(\mu_n(a_1'), \nu_n(b_1')), \ldots, (\mu_n(a_k'), \nu_n(b_k'))\} = \{(d_i, e_i): 1 \leq i \leq k\},$$

which is consistent, and thus $\{\nu_n(b_i'): i \in I\}$ is consistent in Q. So $\{b_i': i \in I\}$ is consistent in Q_n, since ν_n is a cusl embedding. Hence it follows that the set $\{(a_i', b_i'): 1 \leq i \leq k\}$ is consistent in $((P_n \to Q_n))$ and thus it is an element of that set. We have that

$$\begin{aligned}\mathbf{T}_{\to}(\mu_n, \nu_n)([\{(a_i', b_i'): 1 \leq i \leq k\}]) &= [\{(\mu_n(a_i'), \nu_n(b_i')): 1 \leq i \leq k\}] \\ &= [\{(d_i, e_i): 1 \leq i \leq k\}].\end{aligned}$$

So $[\{(d_i, e_i): 1 \leq i \leq k\}] \in \bigcup_{n<\omega} \mathbf{T}_{\to}(\mu_n, \nu_n)[\mathbf{T}_{\to}(P_n, Q_n)]$ and thus $(\mathbf{T}_{\to}(\mu_n, \nu_n))_{n<\omega}$ is a colimiting cone. $\square$

Now we return to our original problem of showing that certain domain equations have solutions. First we show that any ω-continuous functor $\mathbf{T}$ on **Cusl** has a fixed point and then we prove that ω-continuity is preserved under composition of functors. First we define what a fixed point is in **Cusl**.

3.15 Definition Let $\mathbf{T}$ be a functor on **Cusl**. A cusl P is a *fixed point* for $\mathbf{T}$ if $P \cong \mathbf{T}(P)$.

The following theorem is analogous to the fixed point theorem (Theorem 1.2.3). The idea behind the proof is to start with the trivial cusl $\{\bot\}$. Then we iterate applications of the ω-continuous functor $\mathbf{T}$. A direct limit of the thus obtained ω-chain is then a fixed point for $\mathbf{T}$.

3.16 Theorem If $\mathbf{T}$ is an ω-continuous functor on **Cusl**, then $\mathbf{T}$ has a fixed point.

Proof: Let $\mathbf{T}$ be as stated and define $\Delta = (P_n, f_n)_{n<\omega}$ as follows. $P_0 = \{\bot_0\}$ and $P_{n+1} = \mathbf{T}(P_n)$, for $n < \omega$. Since $\mathbf{T}$ is a functor on **Cusl**, P_n is a cusl for each n.

Let $\perp_n$ denote the least element of P_n and let f_0 be the unique function mapping $\perp_0$ to $\perp_1$. Then f_0 is trivially a cusl embedding. Now we obtain cusl embeddings $f_n: P_n \to P_{n+1}$ by setting $f_{n+1} = T(f_n)$, for $n < \omega$. Hence Δ is the following ω-chain.

$$P_0 \xrightarrow{f_0} P_1 \xrightarrow{f_1 = T(f_0)} P_2 \longrightarrow \cdots \longrightarrow P_n \xrightarrow{f_n} P_{n+1} \xrightarrow{f_{n+1} = T(f_n)} P_{n+2} \longrightarrow \cdots$$

$$\{\perp_0\} \quad T(P_0) \qquad\qquad\qquad\qquad T^n(P_0) \quad T(P_n) \qquad T(P_{n+1})$$

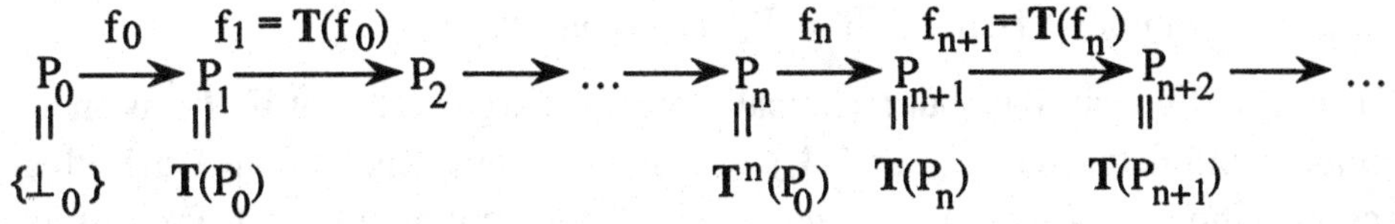

By Theorem 2.7, there is a colimiting cone $\mu: \Delta \to P$. We claim that P is a fixed point for T. Now $T(\mu): T(\Delta) \to T(P)$ is the following cone.

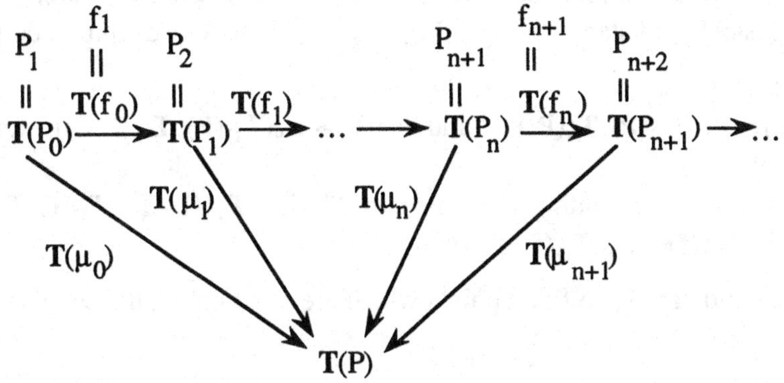

Since T is ω-continuous, $T(\mu)$ is a colimiting cone. But clearly it is the case that $(\mu_{n+1})_{n<\omega}: T(\Delta) \to P$ is a cone. By Theorem 2.8, it is colimiting since

$$P = \bigcup_{n<\omega} \mu_n[P_n] = \mu_0[P_0] \cup (\bigcup_{n<\omega} \mu_{n+1}[P_{n+1}]) = \bigcup_{n<\omega} \mu_{n+1}[P_{n+1}],$$

using the fact that $\mu_0(\perp_0) = \perp = \mu_1(\perp_1)$ and $P_0 = \{\perp_0\}$. It follows that $P \cong T(P)$ by the uniqueness of direct limits (see Exercise 5), so P is a fixed point for T. $\square$

3.17 Corollary Let T be an ω-continuous functor on **Cusl** and let P be the fixed point constructed in Theorem 3.16. Then the mediating morphism f between $T(\mu)$ and $(\mu_{n+1})_{n<\omega}$ is an isomorphism from $T(P)$ onto P.

Proof: By the proof of Theorem 3.16, both $T(\mu)$ and $(\mu_{n+1})_{n<\omega}$ are colimiting cones. If f is mediating between $T(P)$ and P and g is mediating between P and $T(P)$, then $g \circ f = id_{T(P)}$, $f \circ g = id_P$. Thus (f, g) is an isomorphism pair for $(T(P), P)$. $\square$

Next we show that ω-continuity is preserved under composition of functors.

3.18 Proposition If $\mathbf{T}_1$ and $\mathbf{T}_2$ are ω-continuous functors on **Cusl**, then so is $\mathbf{T}_1 \circ \mathbf{T}_2$.

Proof: Let $\mu: \Delta \to P$ be a colimiting cone. Then $\mathbf{T}_1(\mu): \mathbf{T}_1(\Delta) \to \mathbf{T}_1(P)$ is a colimiting cone, and so is $\mathbf{T}_2(\mathbf{T}_1(\mu)): \mathbf{T}_2(\mathbf{T}_1(\Delta)) \to \mathbf{T}_2(\mathbf{T}_1(P))$, since $\mathbf{T}_1$ and $\mathbf{T}_2$ are ω-continuous. Hence $\mathbf{T}_1 \circ \mathbf{T}_2$ is ω-continuous. □

It follows by a similar (but technically messier) argument that if $\mathbf{T}_1$ is an ω-continuous bifunctor and $\mathbf{T}_2$ and $\mathbf{T}_3$ are ω-continuous functors on **Cusl**, then the composition of $\mathbf{T}_1$ with $\mathbf{T}_2$ and $\mathbf{T}_3$ is also ω-continuous. (Cf. Proposition 2.2.4 and Exercise 8.)

By the results in this section, we can solve any cusl equation $P \cong \mathbf{T}(P)$, where $\mathbf{T}$ is a functor in one argument built up from $\mathbf{T}_+$, $\mathbf{T}_\times$, $\mathbf{T}_\to$, $\mathbf{T}_\oplus$, $\mathbf{T}_\otimes$, $\mathbf{T}_\perp$ and $\mathbf{T}_{\to\perp}$ and possibly constant functors $\mathbf{T}_{Q_1}, \mathbf{T}_{Q_2}, \ldots, \mathbf{T}_{Q_n}$. For example, define $\mathbf{T}_1$ and $\mathbf{T}_2$ by

(a) $\mathbf{T}_1(P) = \mathbf{T}_+(\mathbf{T}_Q(P), \mathbf{T}_\times(P,P))$ and $\mathbf{T}_2(P) = \mathbf{T}_+(\mathbf{T}_Q(P), \mathbf{T}_\to(P,P))$, for any cusl P.

(b) For f a cusl embedding from P into P', let $\mathbf{T}_1(f) = \mathbf{T}_+(\mathbf{T}_Q(f), \mathbf{T}_\times(f,f))$ and let $\mathbf{T}_2(f) = \mathbf{T}_+(\mathbf{T}_Q(f), \mathbf{T}_\to(f,f))$.

Then $\mathbf{T}_1$ and $\mathbf{T}_2$ have fixed points which are solutions to the equations:

(1) $$P \cong Q + (P \times P)$$

(2) $$P \cong Q + (P \to P)$$

considered in the introduction.

More generally, any cusl equation $P \cong \mathbf{T}(P)$ has a solution, if $\mathbf{T}$ is obtainable by composition from ω-continuous functors. We have shown that there are solutions to cusl equations but we have discussed neither the problem of finding the *least* solution up to isomorphism nor even the question what that should mean.

Section 4.4 Least Fixed Points

In this section we define the category-theoretic version of a *least* fixed point and then we show that every ω-continuous functor on **Cusl** has a least fixed point. The initial or least object in a category, if it exists, is such that there is a unique morphism from it to any object, which is reasonable since we use morphisms to express order. Hence our first attempt at defining a least fixed point in **Cusl** would be to require that it be a fixed point uniquely embeddable in any cusl which itself is a fixed point. As we shall see, however, we have to modify that definition in order to ensure that least fixed points exist. We first define the notion of a minimal fixed point.

4.1 Definition Let **T** be a functor on **Cusl**. A cusl P is a *minimal fixed point* of **T** if the following conditions hold.

(i) P is a fixed point of **T**.

(ii) For any fixed point Q of **T** there is a cusl embedding from P into Q.

By Exercise 4, there are cusl's P and Q for which there are cusl embeddings in both directions but where P is not isomorphic to Q. It follows by a similar argument that there exists an ω-continuous functor **T** on **Cusl** with non-isomorphic minimal fixed points. Hence if we strengthen condition (ii) above by requiring uniqueness of the cusl embedding, then there are ω-continuous functors on **Cusl** having no least fixed point. However by changing condition (ii) to require that there is a unique embedding from P into Q that respects the functor **T**, a **T**-embedding, we can prove that every ω-continuous functor on **Cusl** has a least fixed point. Indeed, the fixed point constructed in Theorem 3.16 is least in this sense as will be shown at the end of this section. Further, a fixed point (indeed a pre-fixed point) satisfying that condition is unique up to isomorphism.

In what follows, in talking about a fixed point P of **T**, we consider it as a pair (P, f), where f is an embedding of **T**(P) into P. The first results are quite general and can be stated for any category, although the terminology is adapted to the categories **Cusl** and **Dom**.

4.2 Definition Let **T** be a functor on the category **K**.

(a) A pair (A, f) is a *pre-fixed point* for **T** if f: **T**(A) → A. (A, f) is also called a **T**-*algebra.*

(b) Let (A, f) and (B, g) be pre-fixed points for **T**. A morphism h: A → B is a **T**-*morphism* if the following diagram commutes.

$$\begin{array}{ccc} T(A) & \xrightarrow{f} & A \\ {\scriptstyle T(h)}\downarrow & & \downarrow{\scriptstyle h} \\ T(B) & \xrightarrow{g} & B \end{array} \qquad \text{that is, } h \circ f = g \circ T(h).$$

(c) A pair (A, f) is a *least fixed point* for **T** if (A, f) is a pre-fixed point for **T** and for any pre-fixed point (B, g) for **T** there is a unique **T**-morphism from A into B.

4.3 Proposition For any category **K** and any functor **T** on **K**, the collection of **T**-algebras and **T**-morphisms is a category, called **T-K**.

Proof: We verify that for any T-algebra (A,f), id_A is a T-morphism, and that T-morphisms are closed under composition. Since T is a functor,

$$id_A \circ f = f = f \circ id_{T(A)} = f \circ T(id_A),$$

which shows that id_A is a T-morphism. Now let (A,f), (B,g) and (B',g') be T-algebras and let $h:A \to B$ and $h':B \to B'$ be T-morphisms. We have the following diagram.

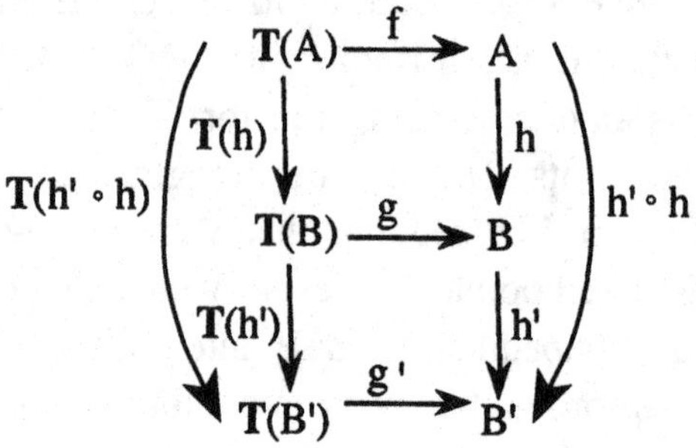

Then

$$(h' \circ h) \circ f = h' \circ (h \circ f) = h' \circ g \circ T(h) = g' \circ T(h') \circ T(h) = g' \circ T(h' \circ h),$$

showing that $h' \circ h$ is a T-morphism. □

It follows that least fixed points are unique up to isomorphism.

4.4 Corollary Let T be a functor on **K**.
(a) If (A,f) is a least fixed point of T, then the only T-morphism on A is id_A.
(b) If (A,f) and (B,g) are least fixed points of T, then A and B are isomorphic. In fact, the unique T-morphisms between them form an isomorphism pair.

Proof: (a) follows immediately. To show (b), we just observe that if $h:A \to B$ and $h':B \to A$ are T-morphisms, then $h' \circ h$ is a T-morphism from A into A and thus $h' \circ h = id_A$. Similarly $h \circ h' = id_B$, which shows that (h,h') is an isomorphism pair. □

Next we show that least fixed points are indeed fixed points.

4.5 Proposition Let T be a functor on **K**. If (A,f) is a least fixed point, then so is $(T(A),T(f))$, and f is an isomorphism.

Proof: Since $\mathbf{T}$ is a functor, $\mathbf{T}(f): \mathbf{T}^2(A) \to \mathbf{T}(A)$, showing that $(\mathbf{T}(A), \mathbf{T}(f))$ is a pre-fixed point. Let h be the unique $\mathbf{T}$-morphism from A into $\mathbf{T}(A)$ and consider the following diagram.

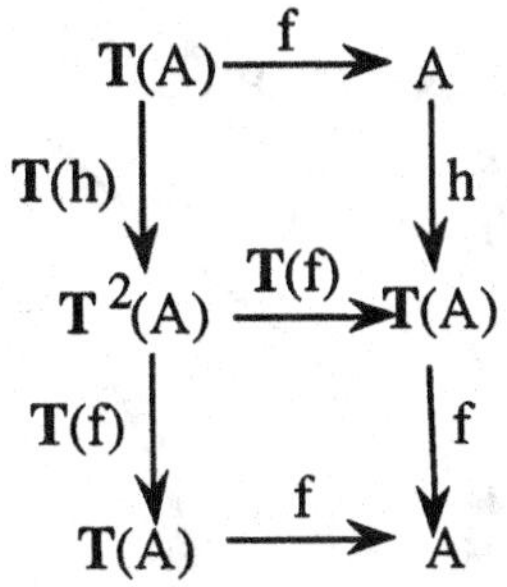

Since h is a $\mathbf{T}$-morphism, $h \circ f = \mathbf{T}(f) \circ \mathbf{T}(h) = \mathbf{T}(f \circ h)$. Also, f is a $\mathbf{T}$-morphism, since the trivial diagram on the bottom commutes. Thus $f \circ h$ is a $\mathbf{T}$-morphism on A and by Corollary 4.4 (a), $f \circ h = id_A$. By the above, $h \circ f = \mathbf{T}(f \circ h) = \mathbf{T}(id_A) = id_{\mathbf{T}(A)}$. Thus (f, h) is an isomorphism pair.

To show that $(\mathbf{T}(A), \mathbf{T}(f))$ is a least fixed point for $\mathbf{T}$, let (B, g) be a pre-fixed point for $\mathbf{T}$. Then there is a unique $\mathbf{T}$-morphism $k: A \to B$. It follows that $k \circ f: \mathbf{T}(A) \to B$ is also a $\mathbf{T}$-morphism, since

$$(k \circ f) \circ \mathbf{T}(f) = (g \circ \mathbf{T}(k)) \circ \mathbf{T}(f) = g \circ \mathbf{T}(k \circ f).$$

Further, the uniqueness of $k \circ f$ follows from the uniqueness of k. □

It follows that a least fixed point for $\mathbf{T}$ is a minimal fixed point for which there is a unique $\mathbf{T}$-morphism into any fixed point.

4.6 Corollary Let $\mathbf{T}$ be a functor on $\mathbf{K}$. If (A, f) is a least fixed point of $\mathbf{T}$, then (A, f) is a fixed point of $\mathbf{T}$ and for any fixed point (B, g) of $\mathbf{T}$ there is a unique $\mathbf{T}$-morphism from A into B. □

It just remains to show that the fixed point constructed in Theorem 3.16 for an ω-continuous functor $\mathbf{T}$ on **Cusl** is a least fixed point. First we note that there is a unique mediating morphism from that fixed point to any pre-fixed point.

For the following two results, let $\mathbf{T}$ be an ω-continuous functor on **Cusl**, and let (P, f) be the fixed point of $\mathbf{T}$ defined in Corollary 3.17. In particular, f is a mediating morphism between $\mathbf{T}(\mu)$ and $(\mu_{n+1})_{n<\omega}$.

4.7 Proposition For any pre-fixed point (Q, g) of $\mathbf{T}$, P is embeddable in Q, and the cusl embedding is unique if it is a mediating morphism.

Proof: Assume that (Q, g) is a pre-fixed point of $\mathbf{T}$, and let P_n, f_n, Δ and μ be as in the proof of Theorem 3.16. We want to define a cone $\nu: \Delta \to Q$ and we do this recursively. Let ν_0 be the unique embedding of $P_0=\{\bot_0\}$ into Q. Assume that $\nu_n: P_n \to Q$ is defined. Then $T(\nu_n): T(P_n) \to T(Q)$, so we let $\nu_{n+1} = g \circ T(\nu_n)$. We have the following diagram.

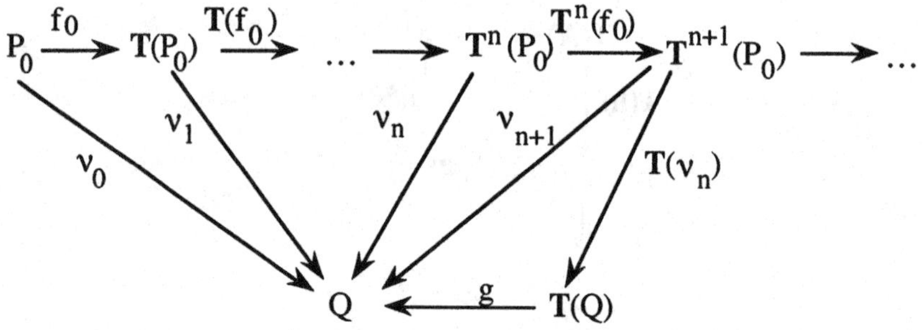

It remains to show that $(\nu_n)_{n<\omega}$ is indeed a cone, that is, that $\nu_n = \nu_{n+1} \circ T^n(f_0)$. This is done by induction on n. Since there is just one embedding from P_0 into Q, $\nu_0 = \nu_1 \circ f_0$. Now assume that $\nu_n = \nu_{n+1} \circ T^n(f_0)$. Then, by the definition of ν_{n+1} and ν_{n+2}, we get

$$\begin{aligned}\nu_{n+1} &= g \circ T(\nu_n) = g \circ T(\nu_{n+1} \circ T^n(f_0)) \\ &= g \circ T(\nu_{n+1}) \circ T^{n+1}(f_0) \\ &= \nu_{n+2} \circ T^{n+1}(f_0),\end{aligned}$$

as desired. Thus $\nu: \Delta \to Q$ is a cone and since $\mu: \Delta \to P$ is a colimiting cone there is a unique mediating morphism $h: P \to Q$. □

Finally we tie everything up by showing that the mediating morphism between the cones μ and ν above is a **T**-morphism, and conversely that any **T**-morphism from (P,f) into (Q,g) is a mediating morphism. Since P is a direct limit, mediating morphisms are unique and thus there is a unique **T**-morphism from P into Q. It follows that (P,f) is a least fixed point.

Let $\mu: \Delta \to P$, let (Q,g) be a pre-fixed point of **T** and let $\nu: \Delta \to Q$ be as in the proof of Proposition 4.7.

4.8 Lemma A cusl embedding h from P into Q is a mediating morphism from μ to ν if and only if it is a **T**-morphism.

Proof: Assume that h is mediating between μ and ν. We need to show that $h \circ f = g \circ T(h)$. We do this by showing that both $h \circ f$ and $g \circ T(h)$ are mediating morphisms between $T(\mu)$ and $\nu' = (\nu_{n+1})_{n<\omega}$ and hence equal. Now

$$h \circ f \circ T(\mu_n) = h \circ \mu_{n+1} = \nu_{n+1},$$

since f and h are mediating morphisms. Also

$$g \circ T(h) \circ T(\mu_n) = g \circ T(h \circ \mu_n) = g \circ T(\nu_n) = \nu_{n+1},$$

by the definition of $(\nu_n)_{n<\omega}$. Thus $h \circ f = g \circ T(h)$.

Conversely, assume that h is a T-morphism from (P,f) into (Q,g). We show by induction on n that $h \circ \mu_n = \nu_n$, for all n. This holds for $n=0$, since $P_0 = \{\bot_0\}$ and there is just one embedding from P_0 into Q. Now assume that $h \circ \mu_n = \nu_n$. Then, since f is mediating,

$$h \circ \mu_{n+1} = h \circ (f \circ T(\mu_n)) = h \circ f \circ T(\mu_n) = g \circ T(h) \circ T(\mu_n)$$
$$= g \circ T(h \circ \mu_n) = g \circ T(\nu_n) = \nu_{n+1},$$

using that h is a T-morphism. Thus h is mediating and we are done. □

4.9 Theorem Let T be an ω-continuous functor on **Cusl**. Then the fixed point (P,f) obtained in Corollary 3.17 is a least fixed point of T.

Proof: By Proposition 4.7 and Lemma 4.8. □

Section 4.5 Subdomains and Projection Pairs

In this section, we shall introduce domain-theoretic concepts that correspond to those of a subcusl and of a cusl embedding. Our main result in this chapter is that we can solve domain equations for domains. However, it is technically simpler to first solve the corresponding problem for cusl's and then derive the result for domains using the representation theorem and its converse to go back and forth between domains and cusl's.

We order domains by the subdomain relation, denoted $\lhd_c$, as well as the ordering $\trianglelefteq_c$ defined in terms of projection pairs. The orderings $\trianglelefteq$ and $\trianglelefteq_c$ are connected as follows. If P and Q are cusl's, then $P \trianglelefteq Q$ if and only if $\overline{P} \trianglelefteq_c \overline{Q}$, where $\overline{P}$ is the completion of P by ideals.

We begin with the notion of a subdomain. In the following definition, the subscript c stands for completion.

5.1 Definition Let $E = (E; \sqsubseteq_E, \bot_E)$ be a domain. Then $D \subseteq E$ is a *subdomain* of E, denoted by $D \lhd_c E$, if the following conditions hold.

(i) $\bot_E \in D$.

(ii) If $A \subseteq D$ is directed, then $\bigsqcup_E A \in D$.

(iii) If x is compact in D, then x is compact in E.

(iv) For any $a, b \in D_c$, if $\{a,b\}$ is consistent in E then $a \sqcup_E b \in D$.

(v) For any $x \in D$, $x = \bigsqcup_E(\mathrm{approx}_E(x) \cap D)$.

Note that conditions (i)–(ii) make D into a subcpo of E, where D is ordered by $\sqsubseteq_E$ restricted to D. Hence the set D_c of compact elements of D is well-defined. Condition (iv) implies that $\mathrm{approx}_E(x) \cap D$ is directed and thus it follows that $\bigsqcup_E(\mathrm{approx}_E(x) \cap D)$ exists. It is routine to see that the subdomains of E are exactly those substructures of $E = (E; \sqsubseteq_E, E_c, \sqcup_E, \bot_E)$ which are domains. Also, if $D \subseteq E$ with the ordering inherited from E is a *domain* that satisfies (i)–(iv), then D is a subdomain of E (that is, condition (v) also holds). Finally observe that if $D \triangleleft_c E$, then $D_c = D \cap E_c$, since the converse of (iii) is immediate.

To establish that $D \subseteq E$ is a subdomain of E with C as the set of compact elements, the following lemma is useful.

5.2 Lemma Let E be a domain. Then $D \subseteq E$ is a subdomain of E with $C \subseteq D$ as the set of compact elements if and only if the following conditions hold.

(i) $\bot_E \in C$.

(ii) If $A \subseteq C$ is directed, then $\bigsqcup_E A \in D$.

(iii) $C \subseteq E_c$.

(iv) For any $a, b \in C$, if $\{a, b\}$ is consistent in E, then $a \sqcup_E b \in C$.

(v) If $x \in D$ and $C_x = \{a \in C\colon a \sqsubseteq x\}$, then $x = \bigsqcup_E C_x$.

Proof: If A is a directed subset of D, then so is $\bigcup\{C_x\colon x \in A\}$ by condition (iv). From (v) we get that $\bigsqcup_E A = \bigsqcup_E(\bigcup\{C_x\colon x \in A\})$ and thus $\bigsqcup_E A \in D$ by (ii). This proves (ii) of Definition 5.1 and the remaining conditions follow from the observation that $C = D_c$. The other direction is trivial. □

In Proposition 1.3 we showed that $\mathcal{S}(Q) = \{P\colon P \triangleleft Q\}$ is a domain, for any cusl Q. Now we consider the corresponding result for $\mathcal{S}_c(E) = \{D\colon D \triangleleft_c E\}$, when E is a domain. One immediate obstacle is that $\mathcal{S}_c(E)$ is *not* closed under the union of directed sets. For this reason we introduce the following closure operation which does give us the supremum in $\mathcal{S}_c(E)$.

5.3 Definition Let E be a domain and let $\{D_i\colon i \in I\}$ be a directed family of subdomains of E. Then the *closure* of $\{D_i\colon i \in I\}$, $\mathrm{cl}(\{D_i\colon i \in I\})$, is the set

$$\{\bigsqcup_E A\colon A \subseteq \bigcup\{(D_i)_c\colon i \in I\},\ A \text{ directed}\}.$$

5.4 Lemma Let E be a domain and let $\mathcal{A} = \{D_i\colon i \in I\}$ be a directed family of subdomains of E. Then $\mathrm{cl}(\mathcal{A}) \triangleleft_c E$ and $\mathrm{cl}(\mathcal{A})$ is the supremum of $\{D_i\colon i \in I\}$ in $\mathcal{S}_c(E) = (\mathcal{S}_c(E); \subseteq, \{\bot\})$.

Proof: First we note that, for $D_1, D_2 \in \mathcal{S}_c(E)$, $D_1 \triangleleft_c D_2 \Leftrightarrow D_1 \subseteq D_2$. Let $D = \mathrm{cl}(\mathcal{A})$ and let $C = \bigcup\{(D_i)_c\colon i \in I\}$. For each $a \in C$, $a = \bigsqcup_E\{a\} \in D$, and thus $C \subseteq D$. We verify clauses (i)–(v) of Lemma 5.2 applied to C. Since $\mathcal{A}$ is directed, $\mathcal{A}$ is non-empty, and thus $\bot \in C$. Condition (ii) follows from the definition of D. Since $D_i \lhd_c E$ for $i \in I$, (iii) holds. To show (iv), let $a, b \in C$ and assume that $\{a,b\}$ is consistent in E. Then $a \in (D_i)_c$ and $b \in (D_j)_c$, for some $i, j \in I$. Since $\{D_i: i \in I\}$ is directed, $a, b \in D_k$ for some k. In fact, $a, b \in (D_k)_c$, since $a, b \in E_c$. Thus $a \sqcup_E b \in (D_k)_c \subseteq C$. For (v), let $x \in D$ and let $C_x = \{a \in C: a \sqsubseteq x\}$. Then $x = \bigsqcup_E A$, for some directed set $A \subseteq \bigcup\{(D_i)_c: i \in I\} = C$. So $x = \bigsqcup_E A \sqsubseteq \bigsqcup_E C_x \sqsubseteq x$ and hence $x = \bigsqcup_E C_x$. Thus $cl(\mathcal{A}) \lhd_c E$.

It remains to show that D is the supremum of $\{D_i: i \in I\}$ with respect to $\subseteq$ in $\mathcal{S}_c(E)$. Clearly $D_i \subseteq D$ so that D is an upper bound. If D' is an upper bound in $\mathcal{S}_c(E)$ for $\{D_i: i \in I\}$, then $D_c = \bigcup\{(D_i)_c: i \in I\} \subseteq D'_c$ and thus $D \subseteq D'$. □

We conclude this part with our main theorem.

5.5 Theorem Let E be a domain and let $\mathcal{S}_c(E) = \{D: D \lhd_c E\}$. Then $\mathcal{S}_c(E) = (\mathcal{S}_c(E); \subseteq, \{\bot\})$ is a domain.

Proof: By Lemma 5.4 we have that $\mathcal{S}_c(E)$ is a cpo. Let

$$\mathcal{B} = \{D \in \mathcal{S}_c(E): D \text{ finite}\}.$$

We show that $\mathcal{S}_c(E)$ is a domain with $\mathcal{B}$ as its set of compact elements by verifying clause (iii) of Lemma 1.2 (clauses (i) and (ii) being standard). Let $D \in \mathcal{S}_c(E)$ and let $\mathcal{B}_D = \{D' \in \mathcal{B}: D' \subseteq D\}$. Assume that $D_1, D_2 \in \mathcal{B}_D$ and set

$$D' = \{a \sqcup_E b: a, b \in D_1 \cup D_2 \text{ and } \{a, b\} \text{ consistent in } E\}.$$

Then $D_1, D_2 \subseteq D'$ and D' is finite. Clearly $D' \subseteq D$, since D is a domain. We claim that $D' \lhd_c E$ and that $D' = D_1 \sqcup D_2$. Since D' is finite, conditions (ii) and (v) of Definition 5.1 trivially hold. For (iii), let $x = a \sqcup_E b \in D'_c$. Then we have that $\{a,b\} \subseteq D_1 \cup D_2 = (D_1)_c \cup (D_2)_c \subseteq E_c$, and thus $a \sqcup_E b \in E_c$. Conditions (i) and (iv) follow from the definition of D'. Thus $D' \lhd_c E$ and $D' \in \mathcal{B}_D$. Clearly, also $D' = D_1 \sqcup_E D_2$.

It only remains to show that $D = cl(\mathcal{B}_D)$. Obviously, $cl(\mathcal{B}_D) \subseteq D$, since D is a domain. For the converse inclusion, assume that $x \in D$. Then $x = \bigsqcup_E approx_D(x)$. Now, for any $a \in D_c$, $\{\bot, a\} \in \mathcal{B}_D$. Thus $approx_D(x) \subseteq D_c \subseteq \bigcup\{D'_c: D' \in \mathcal{B}_D\}$ and hence $\bigsqcup_E approx_D(x) \in cl(\mathcal{B}_D)$, that is $x \in cl(\mathcal{B}_D)$. This completes the proof that $D = cl(\mathcal{B}_D)$. □

Note that E is the top element in $\mathcal{S}_c(E)$. It follows that *each* subset of $\mathcal{S}_c(E)$ has a supremum in the set, that is, $\mathcal{S}_c(E)$ is a complete upper semilattice.

Now we recall the notion of a projection pair between domains and study some of its properties. Then we introduce a relation $\trianglelefteq_c$ on domains, where $D \trianglelefteq_c E$ means that there exists a projection pair for (D, E). This relation will be shown to be a preorder, an appropriate relation to use when solving domain equations.

Finally, we make the connection with the first part by showing that $D \trianglelefteq_c E$ if and only if D is isomorphic to a subdomain of E.

The definition of a projection pair is quite general and was formulated for arbitrary cpo's in Definition 2.1.9. For convenience, we recall the definition here.

5.6 Definition Let D and E be cpo's. Then $(f, f^{\neg})$ is a *projection pair* for (D, E) if $f: D \to E$ and $f^{\neg}: E \to D$ are continuous functions such that $f \circ f^{\neg} \sqsubseteq id_E$ and $f^{\neg} \circ f = id_D$.

If $(f, f^{\neg})$ is a projection pair, then we call f an *embedding* and $f^{\neg}$ the corresponding *projection.*

We shall show later that f is indeed an embedding in the ordinary sense, that is, f is order-preserving. But first we consider some examples.

5.7 Examples Let D and E be domains.

(a) Let $f: D \to D+E$ and $f^{\neg}: D+E \to D$ be defined as follows.

$$f(x) = \begin{cases} (0,x) & \text{if } x \neq \bot_D \\ \bot & \text{otherwise} \end{cases} \qquad f^{\neg}(y) = \begin{cases} x & \text{if } y = (0,x) \\ \bot_D & \text{otherwise.} \end{cases}$$

Then $(f, f^{\neg})$ is a projection pair for $(D, D+E)$.

(b) The following is a projection pair for $(D, D \times E)$:

$$f(x) = (x, \bot_E) \text{ for } x \in D \qquad f^{\neg}(x,y) = x.$$

(c) Define $f: D \to [D \to D]$ and $f^{\neg}: [D \to D] \to D$ by

$$f(x) = \lambda y.x \text{ for } x \in D \qquad f^{\neg}(g) = g(\bot) \text{ for } g \in [D \to D].$$

Then $(f, f^{\neg})$ is a projection pair for $(D, [D \to D])$.

Here are some simple but important properties of projection pairs.

5.8 Proposition Let $(f, f^{\neg})$ be a projection pair for (D, E).

(a) If $(g, g^{\neg})$ is a projection pair for (D, E), then $f \sqsubseteq g \Leftrightarrow f^{\neg} \sqsupseteq g^{\neg}$.

(b) $f(\bot_D) = \bot_E$ and $f^{\neg}(\bot_E) = \bot_D$.

(c) For $x, y \in D$, $x \sqsubseteq y \Leftrightarrow f(x) \sqsubseteq f(y)$.

(d) For $x \in D$ and $y \in E$, $f(x) \sqsubseteq y \Leftrightarrow x \sqsubseteq f^{\neg}(y)$.

(e) $f[D_c] \subseteq E_c$.

Proof: (a) Assume that $f \sqsubseteq g$. Then

$$f^{\neg} = f^{\neg} \circ id_E \sqsupseteq f^{\neg} \circ (g \circ g^{\neg}) = (f^{\neg} \circ g) \circ g^{\neg} \sqsupseteq (f^{\neg} \circ f) \circ g^{\neg} = id_D \circ g^{\neg} = g^{\neg}.$$

Hence $f^{\neg} \sqsupseteq g^{\neg}$. For the converse, assume that $f^{\neg} \sqsupseteq g^{\neg}$. Then

$$f = f \circ (g^- \circ g) = (f \circ g^-) \circ g \sqsubseteq (f \circ f^-) \circ g \sqsubseteq g.$$

(b) We have that $\bot_D \sqsubseteq f^-(\bot_E)$. Since f is monotone,

$$f(\bot_D) \sqsubseteq f(f^-(\bot_E)) \sqsubseteq id_E(\bot_E) = \bot_E.$$

So $\bot_E = f(\bot_D)$. Also

$$f^-(\bot_E) = f^-(f(\bot_D)) = id_D(\bot_D) = \bot_D.$$

(c) The direction from left to right follows from the fact that f is monotone. Now assume that $f(x) \sqsubseteq f(y)$. Then

$$x = id_D(x) = f^- \circ f(x) \sqsubseteq f^- \circ f(y) = id_D(y) = y,$$

using the fact that f^- is also monotone.

(d) Let $x \in D$ and $y \in E$ and suppose that $f(x) \sqsubseteq y$. Then $x = f^-(f(x)) \sqsubseteq f^-(y)$, since f^- is monotone. Conversely, from $x \sqsubseteq f^-(y)$ we get that $f(x) \sqsubseteq f(f^-(y)) \sqsubseteq y$, by the monotonicity of f.

(e) Let $a \in D_c$ and assume that $f(a) \sqsubseteq \bigsqcup A$, where A is a directed subset of E. Then

$$a = f^-(f(a)) \sqsubseteq f^-(\bigsqcup A) = \bigsqcup \{f^-(y) : y \in A\}$$

by the continuity of f^-, where the latter set is directed. Since $a \in D_c$, $a \sqsubseteq f^-(y)$, for some $y \in A$. But then $f(a) \sqsubseteq f(f^-(y)) \sqsubseteq y$ and so $f(a)$ is compact in E. □

As a consequence of (a) in the above proposition, it is only necessary to specify one member of a projection pair, since one member of the pair uniquely determines the other. For if (f, f^-) and (g, g^-) are projection pairs for (D, E), then $f = g$ if and only if $f^- = g^-$. By (b), both f and f^- are strict, and by (c), f is order-preserving. Thus $f[D]$ is an isomorphic copy of D, while $f^-[E]$ is only a projection of E. In other words, we keep information when going up from D to E but we may lose information when projecting down.

5.9 Definition Let D and E be domains. Then $D \trianglelefteq_c E$ if there exists a projection pair for (D, E).

5.10 Proposition Let D, E and F be domains. Then
(a) $D \trianglelefteq_c D$.
(b) If (f, f^-) and (g, g^-) are projection pairs for (D, E) and (E, F), respectively, then $(g \circ f, f^- \circ g^-)$ is a projection pair for (D, F).

Proof: (a) Clearly (id_D, id_D) is a projection pair for (D, D).

(b) By Lemma 2.1.5, continuous functions are closed under composition. Further

$$g \circ f \circ f^- \circ g^- \sqsubseteq g \circ id_E \circ g^- = g \circ g^- \sqsubseteq id_F$$

and

$$f^- \circ g^- \circ g \circ f = f^- \circ id_E \circ f = f^- \circ f = id_D,$$

showing that $(g \circ f, f^- \circ g^-)$ is a projection pair. □

It follows from the proposition that $\trianglelefteq_c$ is a reflexive and transitive ordering on domains. However, it is not antisymmetric even when equality is replaced by isomorphism. Indeed, there are non-isomorphic domains for which there are projection pairs in both directions (see Exercise 4). Of course, there is a least element up to isomorphism with respect to the ordering $\trianglelefteq_c$, namely the one-element domain.

Next we show that a function from the compact elements in one domain to the compact elements in another can be extended to an embedding if and only if it is a cusl embedding.

5.11 Proposition Let $f: D \to E$ be a continuous function between domains. Then f is an embedding if and only if $f[D_c] \subseteq E_c$ and $f|_{D_c}$ is a cusl embedding.

Proof: Suppose that $f: D \to E$ is an embedding and let f^- be the corresponding projection. Then f maps compact elements of D to compact elements of E and f is order-preserving and strict by Proposition 5.8. To show that condition (iii) of Definition 1.4 holds, let $a, b \in D_c$ and assume that $\{f(a), f(b)\}$ is consistent in E. Since f^- is monotone, $a = f^-(f(a)) \sqsubseteq f^-(f(a) \sqcup f(b))$ and $b \sqsubseteq f^-(f(a) \sqcup f(b))$. Hence $\{a, b\}$ is consistent. Now, from the monotonicity of f, $f(a) \sqcup f(b) \sqsubseteq f(a \sqcup b)$. If y is an upper bound for $\{f(a), f(b)\}$ in E, then $f^-(y)$ is an upper bound for $\{a, b\}$ and hence $a \sqcup b \sqsubseteq f^-(y)$. So $f(a \sqcup b) \sqsubseteq f(f^-(y)) \sqsubseteq y$ and it follows that $f(a \sqcup b) = f(a) \sqcup f(b)$.

For the converse, assume that $f|_{D_c}: D_c \to E_c$ is a cusl embedding. Let B_y denote the set $\{a \in D_c : f(a) \sqsubseteq y\}$, for $y \in E$. By (i) of Definition 1.4, $\bot \in B_y$, so B_y is non-empty. We claim that B_y is directed. If $a, b \in B_y$, then y is an upper bound for $\{f(a), f(b)\}$. Then $a \sqcup b \in D$ and $f(a \sqcup b) = f(a) \sqcup f(b) \sqsubseteq y$, which proves the claim. Hence $\bigsqcup B_y$ exists in D and we thus define $g: E \to D$ by $g(y) = \bigsqcup B_y$.

We now show that g is continuous. If $y \sqsubseteq y'$, then $B_y \subseteq B_{y'}$ and hence $g(y) \sqsubseteq g(y')$, showing the monotonicity of g. Let $y \in E$ and let $b \in \text{approx}(g(y))$. Since $b \sqsubseteq \bigsqcup B_y = \bigsqcup \{a \in D_c : f(a) \sqsubseteq y\}$ and b is compact, we have that $b \sqsubseteq a$, for some $a \in B_y$. Then $b \in B_{f(a)}$ and thus $b \sqsubseteq \bigsqcup B_{f(a)} = g(f(a))$. Since $f(a) \in \text{approx}(y)$ it follows by Proposition 3.1.7 that g is continuous.

Next, to show that $f \circ g \sqsubseteq id_E$, let $y \in E$. Then

$$f(g(y)) = f(\bigsqcup_D B_y) = \bigsqcup_E \{f(a): a \in B_y\} \sqsubseteq y.$$

Finally we show that $g \circ f = id_D$. Since $g \circ f$ is continuous, we have that $g(f(x)) = \bigsqcup_D \{g(f(a)): a \in \text{approx}(x)\}$, for $x \in D$. Now, for $a \in \text{approx}(x)$,

$$\begin{aligned} g(f(a)) &= \bigsqcup_D B_{f(a)} \\ &= \bigsqcup_D \{b \in D_c: f(b) \sqsubseteq f(a)\} \\ &= \bigsqcup_D \{b \in D_c: b \sqsubseteq a\} \\ &= \bigsqcup_D \text{approx}(a) = a \end{aligned}$$

where the crucial equality follows from the fact that $f|_{D_c}$ is order-preserving. Thus $g \circ f = id_D$, and this concludes the proof that (f, g) is a projection pair for (D, E). □

5.12 Corollary Let D and E be domains. If $f: D_c \to E_c$ is a cusl embedding, then the unique continuous extension $\overline{f}: D \to E$ of f is an embedding.

From the proof we get the following corollary.

5.13 Corollary Let D and E be domains. If $f: D \to E$ is an embedding, then the associated projection is $f^{\urcorner}(y) = \bigsqcup_D \{a \in D_c: f(a) \sqsubseteq y\}$.

Note that if D is a subdomain of E, then the following is a projection pair for (D, E):

$$\begin{cases} f(x) = x & \text{for } x \in D \\ f^{\urcorner}(y) = \bigsqcup(\text{approx}_E(y) \cap D) & \text{for } y \in E. \end{cases}$$

Thus if $D \triangleleft_c E$, then $D \trianglelefteq_c E$ (see Exercise 27).

We have the following analogue of Theorem 1.8.

5.14 Theorem Let D and E be domains. Then $D \trianglelefteq_c E$ if and only if D is isomorphic to a subdomain of E.

Proof: Assume that D and E are domains and that $(f, f^{\urcorner})$ is a projection pair for (D, E). We show that $f[D] \triangleleft_c E$ and $D \cong f[D]$. Let $F = f[D]$ and $C = f[D_c]$. First note that $D \cong f[D]$, since f is order-preserving. By Proposition 2.1.10, F is a subcpo of E. It only remains to show that conditions (iii)–(v) of Lemma 5.2 hold as applied to C and F. Condition (iii) is satisfied by Proposition 5.8 (e) and (iv) follows from the fact that $f|_{D_c}$ is a cusl embedding by Proposition 5.11. Finally (v) holds by the definition of C since f is order-preserving and continuous.

For the converse, assume that g is an isomorphism between D and D' and that $D' \triangleleft_c E$. Let $(f, f^{\urcorner})$ be the projection pair for (D', E) given above. Then $(f \circ g, g^{-1} \circ f^{\urcorner})$ is a projection pair for (D, E). □

In Section 4.1 we introduced the subcusl ordering $\triangleleft$. Recall that by Theorem 3.2.3, if Q is a cusl, then $\overline{Q}$, the completion of Q by ideals, is a domain. We have the following connection between $\trianglelefteq$ and $\trianglelefteq_c$.

5.15 Theorem Let P and Q be cusl's and let $\overline{P}$ and $\overline{Q}$ be their completions by ideals. Then $P \trianglelefteq Q$ if and only if $\overline{P} \trianglelefteq_c \overline{Q}$.

Proof: Assume that $P \trianglelefteq Q$. By Theorem 1.8, there exists some $R \triangleleft Q$ such that $P \cong R$. By Theorem 3.2.3, $\overline{R}_c = \{[a]_R : a \in R\}$, where $[a]_R$ is the principal ideal determined by a in R. Define $f: \overline{R}_c \to \overline{Q}_c$ by $f([a]_R) = [a]_Q$. Then (i) of Definition 1.4 trivially holds. Condition (ii) follows from the fact that the inclusion map $\iota: R \to \overline{R}$ defined by $\iota(a) = [a]$ is order-preserving. Finally for (iii) we use that R is a subcusl of Q. Thus f is a cusl embedding and it follows by Corollary 5.12 that $\overline{R} \trianglelefteq_c \overline{Q}$. Since $\overline{P} \cong \overline{R}$, we get that $\overline{P} \trianglelefteq_c \overline{Q}$.

For the converse, assume that $\overline{P} \trianglelefteq_c \overline{Q}$. Then there is an embedding $f: \overline{P} \to \overline{Q}$. For $f' = f|_{\overline{P}_c}$, $f'[\overline{P}_c] \subseteq \overline{Q}_c$ and f' is a cusl embedding by Proposition 5.11. Hence $\overline{P}_c \trianglelefteq \overline{Q}_c$ and since, by Theorem 3.2.3, $P \cong \overline{P}_c$, it follows that $P \trianglelefteq Q$. □

Section 4.6 Domain Equations

In this section we show how to solve *domain* equations which have domains as solutions as promised in the introduction. We work over the category **Dom**. This category has domains as objects and projection pairs as morphisms. We consider ω-continuous functors on the category and solve domain equations $D \cong \mathbf{T}(D)$, when D is a domain and $\mathbf{T}$ is an ω-continuous functor on **Dom**. We use the facts established in the previous sections that we can solve *cusl* equations and that there is a correspondence between the ordering on cusl's and the ordering on their completions by ideals.

By Theorem 3.16, the *cusl* isomorphism $P \cong \mathbf{T}(P)$ has a solution when $\mathbf{T}$ is an ω-continuous functor on **Cusl**. To conclude the corresponding result for domains, we use the representation theorem (Theorem 3.2.6) and Theorem 3.2.3 to go back and forth between domains and cusl's. By Theorem 3.2.3, the completion by ideals $\overline{P}$ of a cusl P is a domain and $\overline{P}_c \cong P$. Conversely, if D is a domain, then D_c is a cusl and $\overline{D_c} \cong D$. We shall show that the operation of forming completions gives rise to a functor $\overline{\cdot}$ from **Cusl** into **Dom**, and the operation of restricting a domain to its set of compact elements defines a functor $(\cdot)_c$ from **Dom** into **Cusl**. Using these functors we can uniformly define a functor on **Cusl** from a functor on **Dom** and conversely. In fact, **Cusl** and **Dom** are equivalent categories as will be shown below.

6.1 Definition Let $\overline{\cdot}$: **Cusl** → **Dom** be defined as follows.

(a) $\overline{\cdot}(P)=\overline{P}$, for any cusl P.

(b) For $f:P\to Q$ a cusl embedding, let $\overline{f}:\overline{P}\to\overline{Q}$ be defined by

$$\overline{f}(I)=\{b\in Q:\ (\exists a\in I)(b\sqsubseteq f(a))\},$$

for $I\in\overline{P}$. It follows by Proposition 5.11 that $\overline{f}$ is an embedding. Let $\overline{f}^{-}:\overline{Q}\to\overline{P}$ be the corresponding projection and let $\overline{\cdot}(f)=(\overline{f},\overline{f}^{-})$.

Clearly $\overline{\cdot}$ is a functor.

6.2 Definition Let $(\cdot)_c$: **Dom** → **Cusl** be defined as follows.

(a) $(\cdot)_c(D)=D_c$, for any domain D.

(b) $(\cdot)_c(f,f^{-})=f|_{D_c}$.

By Proposition 5.11, $(\cdot)_c(f,f^{-})$ is a cusl embedding. Clearly $(\cdot)_c$ is a functor.

Since an embedding uniquely determines the corresponding projection in a projection pair, in what follows we just consider the embeddings and ignore the projections. However, this simplification is not possible when one is concerned with computability. In fact, f^{-} cannot in general be computed effectively from f and thus we need both members of the projection pair when solving domain equations effectively (see Chapter 10).

To fix notation, for the rest of this section, let $\iota_P:P\to\overline{P}_c$ be the isomorphism $\iota_P(a)=[a]$ and let $j_P:P\to\overline{P}$ be the embedding $j_P(a)=[a]$.

We will give a direct proof that the results previously proved for cusl's carry over to corresponding results for domains. However, an alternative method of showing this would be to use the fact established below that the categories **Cusl** and **Dom** are equivalent.

Recall that **Cusl** and **Dom** are equivalent categories if there are functors **F**: **Cusl** → **Dom** and **G**: **Dom** → **Cusl** together with natural isomorphisms $\mathbf{id}_{\mathbf{Cusl}}\cong\mathbf{G}\circ\mathbf{F}$ and $\mathbf{id}_{\mathbf{Dom}}\cong\mathbf{F}\circ\mathbf{G}$. We shall show that the functors $\overline{\cdot}$ and $(\cdot)_c$ above satisfy these conditions.

Let $\iota:\mathbf{id}_{\mathbf{Cusl}}\to(\cdot)_c\circ\overline{\cdot}$ be defined by $\iota(P)=\iota_P$. For $f:P\to Q$ consider the following diagram.

$$\begin{array}{ccc} P & \xrightarrow{\iota_P} & \overline{P}_c \\ {\scriptstyle \mathbf{id}(f)}\downarrow & & \downarrow{\scriptstyle \overline{f}\,|\,\overline{P}_c} \\ Q & \xrightarrow{\iota_Q} & \overline{Q}_c \end{array}$$

Then, for $a \in P$,

$$\overline{f}\,|\,\overline{P}_c([a]) = \overline{f}([a]) = [f(a)] = \iota_Q(f(a)).$$

Hence the diagram commutes which shows that ι is a natural transformation. In fact ι is an isomorphism since each ι_P is one.

Let $j: \mathbf{id}_{\mathbf{Dom}} \to \overline{\cdot} \circ (\cdot)_c$ be defined as follows. If D is a domain, let $j(D)$ be the unique continuous extension of j_{D_c} to D. For $f: D \to E$ consider the following diagram

$$\begin{array}{ccc} D & \xrightarrow{j(D)} & \overline{D}_c \\ {\scriptstyle \mathbf{id}(f)}\downarrow & & \downarrow{\scriptstyle \overline{f_c}} \\ E & \xrightarrow{j(E)} & \overline{E}_c \end{array}$$

For $x \in D$,

$$\begin{aligned} \overline{f_c}\,(j(D)(x)) &= \bigsqcup \{\overline{f_c}\,(j(D)(a)) :\ a \in \mathrm{approx}(x)\} \\ &= \bigsqcup \{[f(a)] :\ a \in \mathrm{approx}(x)\} = j(E)(f(x)). \end{aligned}$$

Hence the diagram commutes which shows that j is a natural transformation. In fact, j is an isomorphism since each $j(D)$ is one. This concludes the proof that **Dom** and **Cusl** are equivalent categories.

6.3 Lemma $\overline{\cdot}$ and $(\cdot)_c$ are ω-continuous functors.

Proof: Let $\Delta = (P_n, f_n)_{n<\omega}$ be an ω-chain and let $\mu: \Delta \to P$ be a colimiting cone in **Cusl**. Then $\overline{\Delta}$ is an ω-chain and $\overline{\mu}$ is a cone in **Dom** by Proposition 3.1. To show that $\overline{\mu}$ is colimiting, let $\nu: \overline{\Delta} \to D$ be a cone in **Dom**. It follows that $(\nu)_c: \overline{\Delta}_c \to D_c$ is a cone in **Cusl** and $\overline{\Delta}_c \cong \Delta$. For $\sigma_n = (\nu_n)_c \circ \iota_{P_n}$, $\sigma: \Delta \to D_c$ is a cone, where ι_{P_n} is the isomorphism defined above. There is a unique mediating morphism between μ and σ, since μ is colimiting. Then there is also a unique mediating morphism between $\overline{\mu}$ and ν, for a continuous function is completely determined by its behaviour on the compact elements. Thus $\overline{\mu}$ is colimiting.

The proof that $(\cdot)_c$ is ω-continuous is similar. □

For the rest of this section, we use the notation that if **T** is a functor on **Dom**, then **T'** is the functor on **Cusl** defined by

$$\mathbf{T}' = (\cdot)_c \circ \mathbf{T} \circ \bar{\cdot}.$$

In particular, $\mathbf{T}'(P) = \mathbf{T}(\bar{P})_c$ for each cusl P.

Similarly, if **T** is a bifunctor on **Dom**, then **T'** is the bifunctor on **Cusl** defined on objects as follows

$$\mathbf{T}'(P,Q) = \mathbf{T}(\bar{P},\bar{Q})_c \quad \text{for any cusl's } P \text{ and } Q.$$

On morphisms **T'** is defined so as to make the corresponding diagrams commute.

6.4 Corollary If **T** is an ω-continuous functor on **Dom**, then **T'** is an ω-continuous functor on **Cusl**.

Proof: By Proposition 3.18 and Lemma 6.3. □

We now give a criterion for when a cone in **Dom** is colimiting. We shall also show that in **Dom** every ω-chain has a direct limit. We do this by lifting the corresponding results for cusl's to their completions by ideals.

6.5 Theorem Let $\Delta = (D_n, f_n)_{n<\omega}$ be an ω-chain in **Dom**, and assume that $\mu: \Delta \to D$ is a cone in **Dom**. Then μ is a colimiting cone if and only if for every $d \in D_c$ there is some $n<\omega$ and some $a \in (D_n)_c$ for which $\mu_n(a) = d$.

Proof: By Theorem 2.8, μ_c is colimiting if and only if the above condition holds. Thus the theorem follows by Lemma 6.3. □

6.6 Corollary (a) A functor $\mathbf{T}: \mathbf{Dom} \to \mathbf{Dom}$ is ω-continuous if and only if whenever $\Delta = (D_n, f_n)_{n<\omega}$ is an ω-chain and $\mu: \Delta \to D$ is a colimiting cone in **Dom**, then

$$\mathbf{T}(D)_c = \bigcup_{n<\omega} \mathbf{T}(\mu_n)[\mathbf{T}(D_n)_c].$$

(b) A bifunctor $\mathbf{T}: \mathbf{Dom} \times \mathbf{Dom} \to \mathbf{Dom}$ is ω-continuous if and only if whenever $\Delta = ((D_n, E_n), (f_n, g_n))_{n<\omega}$ is an ω-chain and $(\mu_n, \nu_n)_{n<\omega} : \Delta \to (D,E)$ is a colimiting cone in $\mathbf{Dom} \times \mathbf{Dom}$, then

$$\mathbf{T}(D,E)_c = \bigcup_{n<\omega} \mathbf{T}(\mu_n, \nu_n)[\mathbf{T}(D_n, E_n)_c]. \quad \square$$

6.7 Theorem Every ω-chain in **Dom** has a direct limit.

Proof: Let Δ be an ω-chain in **Dom**. Then Δ_c is an ω-chain in **Cusl** and Δ_c has a direct limit P by Theorem 2.7. It follows by the proof of Lemma 6.3 that $\bar{P}$ is a direct limit of $\overline{\Delta_c} \cong \Delta$. □

Applying $\bar{\cdot}$ to both sides of the equation defining **T'** and using the representation theorem, we get the following lemma.

6.8 Lemma (a) If **T** is a functor on **Dom**, then $\bar{\cdot} \circ \mathbf{T}' \cong \mathbf{T} \circ \bar{\cdot}$.
(b) If **T** is a bifunctor from **Dom**×**Dom** into **Dom**, then

$$\overline{\mathbf{T}'(P,Q)} \cong \mathbf{T}(\bar{P},\bar{Q}).$$

Proof: (a) For any cusl P, $\mathbf{T}'(P) = \mathbf{T}(\bar{P})_c$ and hence $\overline{\mathbf{T}'(P)} = \overline{\mathbf{T}(\bar{P})_c}$. Since $\overline{D_c} \cong D$, for any domain D, by the representation theorem, we get that

$$\overline{\mathbf{T}'(P)} = \overline{\mathbf{T}(\bar{P})_c} \cong \mathbf{T}(\bar{P}).$$

The proof of (b) is similar. □

In particular, it follows that the completion operation distributes over the operations +, ×, →, ⊕, ⊗, and strict exponentiation.

6.9 Corollary Let P and Q be cusl's. Then

$$\overline{P+Q} \cong \bar{P}+\bar{Q}$$

$$\overline{P\times Q} \cong \bar{P}\times\bar{Q}$$

$$\overline{(P\to Q)} \cong [\bar{P}\to\bar{Q}].$$

$$\overline{P\oplus Q} \cong \bar{P}\oplus\bar{Q}$$

$$\overline{P\otimes Q} \cong \bar{P}\otimes\bar{Q}$$

$$\overline{(P\to_\perp Q)} \cong [\bar{P}\to_\perp\bar{Q}].$$

Proof: The corollary follows from Lemma 6.8, using the fact that **T'** corresponds to the same operation on **Cusl** as **T** on **Dom**. □

6.10 Theorem If **T** is an ω-continuous functor on **Dom**, then **T** has a fixed point.

Proof: Let **T** be an ω-continuous functor on **Dom**. Then **T'** is an ω-continuous functor on **Cusl** by Corollary 6.4 and thus **T'** has a fixed point P by Theorem 3.16. It follows that $\bar{P}$ is a fixed point for **T**, for if $P \cong \mathbf{T}'(P)$, then

$$\bar{P} \cong \overline{\mathbf{T}'(P)} = \overline{\mathbf{T}(\bar{P})_c} \cong \mathbf{T}(\bar{P}). \quad \square$$

By the results in this section and in Section 4.3, any domain isomorphism $D \cong \mathbf{T}(D)$ has a solution, if **T** is obtainable by composition from ω-continuous functors. In particular, consider such a domain equation, where **T** is built up from the operations $+$, $\times$, $\rightarrow$, $\oplus$, and $\otimes$, possibly using parameters. Then consider the corresponding cusl equation $P=T'(P)$, where T' is built up from the corresponding operations on **Cusl** and where any parameter E is replaced by the cusl E_c. This last equation has a solution by Theorem 3.16 and hence the corresponding domain equation has a solution by Corollary 6.9.

For example, let T_1 and T_2 be as defined at the end of Section 4.3. Then T_1' and T_2' have fixed points which are solutions (albeit only up to isomorphism) to the equations

(1) $$D=E+(D\times D)$$

(2) $$D=E+[D\rightarrow D]$$

considered in the introduction. This proves the following theorem.

6.11 Theorem Any domain equation built up by the operations $+, \times, \rightarrow, \oplus, \otimes$ and $\rightarrow_\perp$ and using domains as parameters has, up to isomorphism, a solution which is a domain.

Finally we show that every ω-continuous functor on **Dom** has a least fixed point in the sense of Section 4.4.

6.12 Proposition Let T be an ω-continuous functor on **Dom** and let D be the fixed point of T constructed in Theorem 6.10. Then for any pre-fixed point (E,g) of T, D is embeddable in E, and the embedding is unique if it is a mediating morphism.

Proof: Let j be defined as in the beginning of this section following Definition 6.2. If (E,g) is a pre-fixed point of T, then $(E_c,(g \circ T(j(E)^{-1}))_c)$ is a pre-fixed point of T' and the result follows by Proposition 4.7. □

6.13 Lemma Let T be an ω-continuous functor on **Dom** and let $\overline{P}$ be the fixed point of T constructed in Theorem 6.10. Further, let (E,g) be a pre-fixed point of T, let $\mu\colon\Delta\rightarrow P$ and $\nu\colon\Delta\rightarrow E_c$ be as in Proposition 4.7, and also let $\sigma_n=j(E)^{-1}\circ\overline{\nu_n}$. Then an embedding h from $\overline{P}$ into E is a mediating morphism from $\overline{\mu}$ to σ if and only if it is a T-morphism.

Proof: By Lemma 4.8, $h\colon P\rightarrow E_c$ is a mediating morphism from μ to ν if and only if h is a T'-morphism. Thus $\overline{h}\colon\overline{P}\rightarrow\overline{E_c}$ is mediating from $\overline{\mu}$ to $\overline{\nu}$ if and only if $\overline{h}$ is a T-morphism, and the desired result follows from this. □

6.14 Theorem If T is an ω-continuous functor on **Dom**, then T has a least fixed point.

Proof: Let (P,f) be the fixed point for $\mathbf{T}'$ defined in Corollary 3.17. By Proposition 6.12 and Lemma 6.13, it follows that $(\bar{P}, \bar{f} \circ j(\mathbf{T}(\bar{P})))$ is a least fixed point of $\mathbf{T}$. □

In Chapter 10 we shall discuss how to find effective solutions of domain equations.

4.7 Exercises

1. Give an example of cusl's P and Q such that $P \subseteq Q$ but where P is not a subcusl of Q.

2. Show that if $f: P \to Q$ is a surjective cusl embedding, then $P \cong Q$.

3. Let P and Q be cusl's and assume that $P \trianglelefteq Q$ and $Q \trianglelefteq P$.
   (a) Show that $|P| = |Q|$ (where $|P|$ denotes the cardinality of P).
   (b) Show that if P is finite then $P \cong Q$.

4. Give an example of cusl's P and Q such that $P \trianglelefteq Q$ and $Q \trianglelefteq P$ but where P is not isomorphic to Q.

5. Show that direct limits of ω-chains are unique up to isomorphism
   (a) for **Cusl**.
   (b) for any category having direct limits.

6. Show that the functors $\mathbf{T_Q}$ and **id** are ω-continuous.

7. Show that $\mathbf{K} \times \mathbf{L}$ is a category if $\mathbf{K}$ and $\mathbf{L}$ are categories.

8. Let $\mathbf{T}: \mathbf{K} \times \mathbf{L} \to \mathbf{M}$ be a functor. Determine whether any direction of the following holds: $\mathbf{T}$ is ω-continuous if and only if $\mathbf{T}$ is ω-continuous in each argument.

9. (a) Show that in the function space domain $[D \to E]$, where D and E are domains: $<a; b> \sqsubseteq <d; e> \;\Leftrightarrow\; b = \perp$ or $a \sqsupseteq d \;\&\; b \sqsubseteq e$.
   (b) Show that the ordering $\sqsubseteq$ on $((P \to Q))$ is not antisymmetric.
   (c) Show that $(P \to Q)$ has least element $[\{(\perp, \perp)\}]$. Further show that if A and B are consistent in $((P \to Q))$, then so is $A \cup B$ and

   $$[A] \sqcup [B] = [A \cup B].$$

   Conclude that $(P \to Q)$ is a cusl.

10. (a) Show that in the strict function space domain $[D\rightarrow_{\perp}E]$, where D and E are domains: $<a;b>_{\perp}\sqsubseteq<d;e>_{\perp} \Leftrightarrow b=\perp$ or $a=\perp$ & $b\sqsubseteq e$ or $a\sqsupseteq d$ & $b\sqsubseteq e$.
(b) Show that the ordering $\sqsubseteq$ on $((P\rightarrow_{\perp}Q))$ is not antisymmetric.
(c) Show that $(P\rightarrow_{\perp}Q)$ is a cusl.

11. Show that if P and Q are subcusl's of the cusl R, then $P+Q\lhd R+R$ and $P\times Q\lhd R\times R$.

12. Show that $\mathbf{T}_{+}$, $\mathbf{T}_{\times}$, $\mathbf{T}_{\rightarrow}$, $\mathbf{T}_{\oplus}$, $\mathbf{T}_{\otimes}$, $\mathbf{T}_{\perp}$ and $\mathbf{T}_{\rightarrow\perp}$ are functors from **Cusl**×**Cusl** into **Cusl**.

13. Show that the functors $\mathbf{T}_{\oplus}$, $\mathbf{T}_{\otimes}$, $\mathbf{T}_{\perp}$ and $\mathbf{T}_{\rightarrow\perp}$ are ω-continuous.

14. Let $\Delta=(P_n,f_n)_{n<\omega}$ be a chain in **Cusl** and let $\Delta'=(P_{n+1},f_{n+1})_{n<\omega}$. Show that if $\mu:\Delta\rightarrow P$ and $\nu:\Delta'\rightarrow Q$ are colimiting cones, then $P\cong Q$.

15. Let **K** be a category with an initial object in which every ω-chain has a direct limit. Show that if **T** is an ω-continuous functor on **K**, then **T** has a fixed point.

16. Show that there is an ω-continuous functor on **Cusl** with non-isomorphic minimal fixed points.

17. Give an example of domains D and E such that $D\subseteq E$ but where D is not a subdomain of E.

18. Let $E=\{[0,x]:\ 0\leq x\leq 1,\ x\in\mathbb{R}\}\cup\{[0,x):\ 0<x\leq 1,\ x\in\mathbb{R}\}$, where $[x,y]=\{z\in\mathbb{R}:\ x\leq z\leq y\}$ and $[x,y)=\{z\in\mathbb{R}:\ x\leq z<y\}$.
(a) Show that E ordered by $\subseteq$ is a domain.
(b) Find a subset D of E such that D satisfies conditions (i)–(iv) in Definition 5.1 but where D is not a subdomain of E.

19. Let E be a domain and let $\{D_i:\ i\in I\}$ be a directed family of subdomains of E. Let

$$\mathrm{clos}(\{D_i:\ i\in I\})=\{\sqcup_E A:\ A\subseteq\bigcup\{D_i:\ i\in I\},\ A \text{ directed}\}.$$

Show that $\mathrm{clos}(\{D_i:\ i\in I\})=\mathrm{cl}(\{D_i:\ i\in I\})$.

20. Show that there are domains $(D_i)_{i\in\omega}$ and E such that $D_i\lhd_c D_{i+1}\lhd_c E$, for all i, but where $\bigcup\{D_i:\ i\in\omega\}$ is not a subdomain of E.

21. Let E be a domain and suppose that $D \subseteq E$ is finite. Show that D is a subdomain of E if and only if D is a subcusl of E_c.

22. Show that there exists a projection pair (f, f^-) for domains (D, E) for which there is $y \in E_c$ but $f^-(y) \notin D_c$.

23. Show that if (f, f^-) is a projection pair for (D, E), then $f^-[E] = D$.

24. Show that if $f: D \to E$ is a surjective embedding, then $D \cong E$.

25. Let (f, f^-) be a projection pair for (D, E), where D and E are cpo's.
(a) Show that $(f \circ f^-) \circ (f \circ f^-) = f \circ f^-$.
(b) Show that $f \circ f^- \sqsubseteq_{[E \to E]} id_E$.
(c) Show that $D \cong \{x \in E : f \circ f^-(x) = x\}$.
A function like $f \circ f^-$ that satisfies (a)–(c) is called a *finitary projection* on the cpo E.

26. Let D and E be domains and assume that $D \trianglelefteq_c E$ and $E \trianglelefteq_c D$.
(a) Show that $|D| = |E|$.
(b) Show that if D is finite, then $D \cong E$.

27. Let D and E be domains. Show that if $D \triangleleft_c E$, then the following is a projection pair for (D, E).

$$\begin{cases} f(x) = x & \text{for } x \in D \\ f^-(y) = \bigsqcup(\mathrm{approx}_E(y) \cap D) & \text{for } y \in E. \end{cases}$$

28. Let P and Q be cusl's such that $P \triangleleft Q$. Give an explicit definition of a projection pair for $(\overline{P}, \overline{Q})$.

29. Let (f_D, f_D^-) be the projection pair for $(D, [D \to D])$ given in Example 5.7 (c). If D is a domain, let $\mathbf{T}(D) = [D \to D]$, and if $h: D \to E$ is an embedding, let $\mathbf{T}(h) = f_E \circ h \circ f_D^-$. Decide whether $\mathbf{T}$ is a functor on **Dom**.

30. Let $\Delta = (D_n, f_n)_{n<\omega}$ be a chain in **Dom** and let $\Delta' = (D_{n+1}, f_{n+1})_{n<\omega}$. Show that if $\mu: \Delta \to D$ and $\nu: \Delta' \to E$ are colimiting cones, then $D \cong E$.

31. If $f: P \to Q$ is a cusl embedding, let $P' = \{[a] : a \in P\}$, where $[a]$ is as in Theorem 3.2.3, and let $f': P' \to \overline{Q}$ be defined by $f'([a]) = [f(a)]$.
(a) Show that $\overline{f}$ as defined in Definition 6.1 is the unique continuous extension of f' to $\overline{P}$.
(b) Conclude that $\overline{f}: \overline{P} \to \overline{Q}$ is an embedding.

32. Give explicit definitions of functors $\mathbf{T}_+$, $\mathbf{T}_\times$, $\mathbf{T}_\to$, $\mathbf{T}_\oplus$, $\mathbf{T}_\otimes$, $\mathbf{T}_\bot$ and $\mathbf{T}_{\to\bot}$ from **Dom**×**Dom** into **Dom** and show that these functors are ω-continuous.

33. Show that Equation (1) from the introduction corresponds to a positive inductive definition and can be solved within set theory by iteration, that is, by successively throwing in the pairs needed and stopping at stage ω.

CHAPTER 5

TOPOLOGY

Topology, or the theory of topological spaces, is a thoroughly developed and established branch of mathematics. Its concepts and results are used in almost all areas. In the introduction to his famous treatise *General Topology* (Kelley [1955]), Kelley states that he almost labelled it: "What every young analyst should know". In fact, topology is useful in many areas not apparently related to analysis, such as logic and program semantics. As we shall see, Scott–Ershov domains viewed as topological spaces look quite different from the space of, say, real numbers.

The raison d'être of topological spaces is that the continuous functions live on them, that is continuity is a topological concept. More precisely, the topologies on spaces X and Y determine the continuous functions from X into Y. Conversely, given a class of functions from a set X into a set Y we may want to find topologies on X and on Y so that the functions that are continuous with respect to these make up the given class of functions. For example, we have already decided for good reasons which functions between domains are to be continuous. Scott has found a topology on domains for these functions, appropriately called the Scott topology. Ershov's concept of a domain was actually formalized as a topological notion, that is, a domain or, in his terminology, an f_0-space is a topological space with certain strong properties (see Exercise 10.7.4).

There are many connections and analogies between continuity and computability, some already observed in our presentation of the theory of domains. M. B. Smyth has noted the following analogy with topological spaces. He views a data type as a set together with a system of *finitely observable properties*. Here properties are meant as properties of elements of the set. A finitely observable property is then a property such that when it holds for an element we can find out that it does by a finite amount of observation. This does not imply that finitely observable properties are decidable, that is, we do not assert that the complement of a finitely observable property is finitely observable. Examples of finitely observable properties are the extreme ones, namely those which hold for all elements and those which hold for no element. Furthermore, finite conjunctions of finitely observable properties are finitely observable properties. One may also argue that disjunctions of finitely observable properties are again finitely observable properties (at least if the disjunction is presented in some effective way), since only one of the disjuncts needs to be verified. These observations concerning finitely observable properties are in exact analogy with the axioms for a topology. Note that an arbitrary conjunction of finitely observable properties should not in general be a finitely observable property since it may require making infinitely many observations.

The purpose of this chapter is to introduce some basic topological notions and results. When relevant we illustrate with the theory of domains. The reader with some background in topology should independently be able to find the Scott topology for domains and then go directly to Chapter 6. On the other hand, the reader with no background in topology may well benefit from also consulting a more complete treatment, for example Kelley [1955], Dugundji [1966], Engelking [1968] or Willard [1970]. Vickers [1989] is a treatment of topology from a computer science point of view.

Section 5.1 Open and Closed Sets

In this section we give the basic definitions of a topological space and illustrate with some examples.

1.1 Definition Let X be a non-empty set. A *topology* τ on X is a family $\tau \subseteq \wp(X)$ such that

(i) $X, \varnothing \in \tau$,

(ii) if $U, V \in \tau$ then $U \cap V \in \tau$, and

(iii) if $U_i \in \tau$ for $i \in I$ then $\bigcup_{i \in I} U_i \in \tau$. (I is an arbitrary index set.)

A *topological space* is a pair (X, τ) where X is a non-empty set and τ is a topology on X. Often we say that X is a topological space when the topology τ is understood. The elements of X are said to be the *points* of X while the elements of τ are the *open sets* in X.

1.2 Examples

(i) Let $X \neq \varnothing$ be a set. Then $\tau = \{\varnothing, X\}$ is a topology on X, called the *trivial* topology on X. At the other extreme, $\eta = \wp(X)$ is also a topology on X, called the *discrete* topology.

(ii) Let $X = \mathbb{R}$. Then $U \subseteq \mathbb{R}$ is open if $(\forall x \in U)(\exists \varepsilon > 0)((x-\varepsilon, x+\varepsilon) \subseteq U)$ where $(a, b) = \{x \in \mathbb{R} : a < x < b\}$. This gives the usual topology on the real line $\mathbb{R}$. Note that this topology is not closed under arbitrary intersections.

(iii) Let $X = (X; \leq)$ be a partially ordered set. Then say that $U \subseteq X$ is open precisely when it is upwardly closed, that is

$$x \in U \ \& \ x \leq y \Rightarrow y \in U.$$

This gives a topology on X called the *Alexandrov* topology.

(iv) Let $D = (D; \sqsubseteq, \perp)$ be a domain. The Alexandrov topology on D is not the one we want to consider since it does not give us the continuous functions that we have decided on. Instead we consider the *Scott* topology on D given by: $U \subseteq D$ is open if

(a) $x \in U \ \& \ x \sqsubseteq y \Rightarrow y \in U$
(b) $x \in U \Rightarrow (\exists a \in \text{approx}(x))(a \in U)$.

Recall that approx(x) is the set of compact approximations of x (Definition 3.1.3). Thus the Scott topology has, in general, fewer open sets than the Alexandrov topology. We call condition (a) the *Alexandrov condition* and condition (b) the *Scott condition.*

(v) The Scott topology for a cpo $D = (D; \sqsubseteq, \perp)$ is given by: $U \subseteq D$ is open if

(a) $x \in U \ \& \ x \sqsubseteq y \Rightarrow y \in U$
(b) $A \subseteq D$ directed & $\bigsqcup A \in U \Rightarrow (\exists x \in A)(x \in U)$.

It is an easy exercise to see that the two definitions of the Scott topology agree in case the cpo D happens to be a domain.

One immediate objection to the Smyth analogy between open sets and finitely observable properties, at least if some sort of effectivity is assumed in the verification of finitely observable properties, is that a topology is often uncountable; for example the usual topology on $\mathbb{R}$. It is not possible to compute directly on an uncountable set and hence the semidecidability requirement of the analogy has no meaning. This problem may be circumvented by considering a base for the topology, a subset of the topology generating it, which may be countable and computable. Disregarding computability, it is an established mathematical practice to present mathematical objects as simply as possible in terms of generators and construction principles.

1.3 Definition Let $X \neq \emptyset$ be a set. A family $\mathcal{B} \subseteq \wp(X)$ is a *topological base* on X if

(i) $\bigcup \mathcal{B} = X$, and
(ii) if $B_1, B_2 \in \mathcal{B}$ and $x \in B_1 \cap B_2$ then there is $B_3 \in \mathcal{B}$ such that $x \in B_3 \subseteq B_1 \cap B_2$.

A topological base $\mathcal{B}$ on X generates a topology on X by letting $U \subseteq X$ be open just in case U is a union of elements in $\mathcal{B}$. If $X = (X, \tau)$ is a topological space then $\mathcal{B}\subseteq\tau$ is said to be a *topological base for the space* X in case $\mathcal{B}$ is a topological base and the topology generated by $\mathcal{B}$ is τ.

1.4 Examples

(i) Consider the reals $\mathbb{R}$ with its usual topology. Then a base for this topology is $\mathcal{B}=\{(a,b): a,b\in\mathbb{Q}, a<b\}$. It is a countable base and, since its elements are determined by pairs of rational numbers, we may compute on $\mathcal{B}$.

(ii) Let $D=(D;\sqsubseteq,\perp)$ be a domain. For $a\in D_c$ let $B_a=\{x\in D: a\sqsubseteq x\}$. Clearly each B_a is open in the Scott topology and each open set is the union of such B_a's. To show that $\mathcal{B}=\{B_a: a\in D_c\}$ is a topological base consider $a,b\in D_c$. If $\{a,b\}$ is not consistent then $B_a\cap B_b=\varnothing$. On the other hand, if $\{a,b\}$ is consistent then $a\sqcup b\in D_c$ by Lemma 3.1.9 and $B_{a\sqcup b}=B_a\cap B_b$.

(iii) Recall the Cantor space 2^ω of Example 2.1.12. For $\sigma\in SEQ$, let $B_\sigma=\{f\in 2^\omega: \sigma\subseteq f\}$. Then the family $\{B_\sigma: \sigma\in SEQ\}$ is a base for a topology, the usual topology of the Cantor space. The Baire space ω^ω is made into a topological space similarly.

Suppose $\mathcal{S}$ is an arbitrary family of subsets of X. Then $\mathcal{S}$ generates a topology on X, the least topology containing $\mathcal{S}$. Of course, $\mathcal{S}$ need not be a topological base but it generates a base $\mathcal{B}$ consisting of all finite intersections of elements of $\mathcal{S}$ (adding X to $\mathcal{S}$ if necessary). The topology τ generated by $\mathcal{B}$ is the least topology containing $\mathcal{S}$ in the sense that if η is another topology such that $\mathcal{S}\subseteq\eta$ then $\tau\subseteq\eta$. We say that $\mathcal{S}$ is a *subbase* for the topology τ. Thus each family of subsets of a set forms a subbase for a topology on that set.

To exemplify, let D and E be domains and consider the function space $[D\to E]$. Then

$$\mathcal{S}=\{B_{<a;b>}: a\in D_c \text{ and } b\in E_c\}$$

is a subbase, but in general not a base, for the Scott topology on $[D\to E]$.

An important use of topology is to make mathematical sense of closeness or proximity between points and sets of points. Thus we are able to make precise for arbitrary topological spaces the intuitive notion of continuity. Continuity will be treated in the next section. Here we will introduce and study closed sets, in particular with regard to the notion of proximity between points and sets.

In the remainder of this section we let (X,τ) be a topological space.

1.5 Definition A set $F\subseteq X$ is *closed* in X if X–F is open in X.

De Morgan's laws applied to the definition of a topology immediately give us the following properties of closed sets.

1.6 Proposition (i) $\varnothing$, X are closed sets.
(ii) If F_1, F_2 are closed then $F_1 \cup F_2$ is closed.
(ii) If F_i is closed for each $i \in I$ then $\bigcap_{i \in I} F_i$ is closed.

Thus the family of closed sets is closed under finite unions and arbitrary intersections. Clearly, a topology on a set may equivalently be given by specifying a family of closed subsets satisfying Proposition 1.6.

Given a set $A \subseteq X$ we define the *closure* of A, denoted $\bar{A}$, by

$$\bar{A} = \bigcap \{F: A \subseteq F \text{ and } F \text{ closed}\}.$$

It follows that $\bar{A}$ is closed, in fact the least closed set containing A. The following proposition is an easy exercise.

1.7 Proposition (i) $\bar{\varnothing} = \varnothing$.
(ii) $A \subseteq \bar{A}$.
(iii) $\bar{\bar{A}} = \bar{A}$.
(iv) $\overline{A \cup B} = \bar{A} \cup \bar{B}$.

The conditions (i) to (iv) are known as the Kuratowski closure axioms. Suppose we have an operator $\bar{\ }: \wp(X) \longrightarrow \wp(X)$ satisfying the Kuratowski axioms. Then we obtain a topology on X by saying that the closed sets are precisely the sets $\bar{A}$ for $A \subseteq X$. This is yet another way of giving a topology on a set X.

Consider the space of reals $\mathbb{R}$ with its subset $\mathbb{Q}$ of rational numbers. Then $\bar{\mathbb{Q}} = \mathbb{R}$. We say that a set $A \subseteq X$ is *dense* in X if $\bar{A} = X$ and that a space X is *separable* if there is a countable dense subset of X. Thus $\mathbb{Q}$ is dense in $\mathbb{R}$ and $\mathbb{R}$ is separable. Equivalently, $A \subseteq X$ is dense in X if for each non-empty open set U, $A \cap U \neq \varnothing$.

Let D be a domain with the Scott topology. Then D_c is dense in D since each open set contains a compact element. It follows that a domain D is separable if and only if D_c is countable. When D_c is countable we say that D is *countably based.*

We shall establish another characterization of the closure $\bar{A}$ of a set A. Suppose $x \in X$ and $A \subseteq X$. Then x is said to be a *limit point* (*accumulation point* or *cluster point*) of A if for each open set U,

$$x \in U \Rightarrow U \cap (A - \{x\}) \neq \varnothing.$$

Thus x is a limit point of A if there is no way to separate x from A using an open set, disregarding x itself in case $x \in A$. Intuitively, x is a limit point of A just in case x is indistinguishably close to A. If $x \in A$ and x is not a limit point of A then x is said to be an *isolated point* of A. The set of limit points of A, called the *derived set* of A, is denoted by A^d. Here is the characterization.

1.8 Proposition $\bar{A} = A \cup A^d$.

Proof: If $x \notin \bar{A}$ then there is a closed set $F \supseteq A$ such that $x \notin F$. But then $x \in X-F$, where $X-F$ is open, and $(X-F) \cap A = \varnothing$. Conversely assume $x \notin A \cup A^d$. Then there is an open set U such that $x \in U$ and $U \cap A = \varnothing$. But then $X-U \supseteq A$ and is closed, that is $x \notin \bar{A}$. □

The proposition says that a closed set is closed in the sense that it contains all of its limit points.

A notion intimately related to that of the closure of a set, the dual notion, is the *interior* of a set. It is the largest open set contained in the set. More precisely, the *interior* of the set A, denoted A^o, is the set

$$A^o = \bigcup \{U \in \tau : U \subseteq A\}.$$

We leave the following proposition as an exercise.

1.9 Proposition $A^o = X - \overline{(X-A)}$.

Another related concept, to be used in Chapter 8, is that of the *boundary* of a set A, denoted ∂A. It is the set of points not in the interior of A nor in the interior of $X-A$. Thus $x \in \partial A$ if for each open set U such that $x \in U$, we have $U \cap A \neq \varnothing$ and $U \cap (X-A) \neq \varnothing$. An equivalent formulation is

$$\partial A = \bar{A} \cap \overline{(X-A)}.$$

Section 5.2 Continuity

Intuitively, a function $f: X \longrightarrow Y$ is continuous if for each $x \in X$ and $A \subseteq X$, whenever x is close to A then f(x) is close to f[A]. For topological spaces we have made precise what is meant by a point x being close to a set A, namely $x \in \bar{A}$. So for topological spaces X and Y we capture the intuitive notion of continuity by saying that f is continuous if for each $x \in X$ and $A \subseteq X$, $x \in \bar{A} \Rightarrow f(x) \in \overline{f[A]}$.

2.1 Proposition Let $f: X \longrightarrow Y$ where X and Y are topological spaces. Then the following are equivalent.

(i) For each $A \subseteq X$, $x \in \bar{A} \Rightarrow f(x) \in \overline{f[A]}$.
(ii) For each open $V \subseteq Y$, $f^{-1}[V]$ is open in X.

Proof: (i) ⇒ (ii). Suppose $V \subseteq Y$ is open while $f^{-1}[V]$ is not. Then $X - f^{-1}[V]$ is not closed and hence, by Proposition 1.8, there is $x \in f^{-1}[V]$ which is a limit point of $X - f^{-1}[V]$. But clearly,

$$f[X - f^{-1}[V]] \cap V = \varnothing$$

and hence

$$\overline{f[X - f^{-1}[V]]} \cap V = \varnothing$$

since V is open. Now, $f(x) \in V$ and hence $f(x) \notin \overline{f[X - f^{-1}[V]]}$, so that (i) fails for x and $X - f^{-1}[V]$.

(ii) ⇒ (i). Suppose $A \subseteq X$, $x \in \bar{A}$ and $f(x) \notin \overline{f[A]}$. Let $V = X - \overline{f[A]}$. Then V is an open set, $V \cap f[A] = \varnothing$ and hence $f^{-1}[V] \cap A = \varnothing$ and $x \in f^{-1}[V]$. But then $f^{-1}[V]$ cannot be an open set since x is a limit point of A. □

Here is the standard definition of continuity which according to the above proposition corresponds to our intuitive notion.

2.2 Definition Let (X, τ) and (Y, η) be topological spaces. Then a function $f: X \rightarrow Y$ is *continuous* if $f^{-1}[V] \in \tau$ whenever $V \in \eta$.

Since the inverse of a function preserves arbitrary unions and intersections it suffices to verify the condition for a base of η or in fact a subbase of η. An important observation is that the continuity of f is determined only by how f^{-1} operates on the open sets, that is there is no mention of points! This indicates that one should be able to develop topology by just considering the *algebra* of open sets and not requiring that these objects be sets of points. This is the theory of formal spaces, frames, or, as it is sometimes called, pointless topology. (One point of pointless topology is that the theory is more constructive than point set topology.) In Chapter 6 we will sketch the rudiments of this theory and show how it may be seen as a generalization of domain theory.

Let X and Y be topological spaces. If X has the discrete topology then each function from X into Y is continuous. The same is true if Y has the trivial topology. More interestingly, a function $f: \mathbb{R} \rightarrow \mathbb{R}$ is continuous in the sense above if and only if it is continuous in the usual "ε-δ sense".

The next proposition shows that the Scott topology is the correct one for domains.

2.3 Proposition Let D and E be domains. Then $f:D \to E$ is continuous with respect to the Scott topology if and only if f is continuous in the sense of Definition 2.1.3.

Proof: Suppose $f:D \to E$ is continuous in the sense of Definition 2.1.3 and consider the basic open set $B_b = \{z \in E: b \sqsubseteq z\}$ where $b \in E_c$. We must show that $f^{-1}[B_b]$ is open. Let $x \in f^{-1}[B_b]$ and suppose $x \sqsubseteq y$. Then $b \sqsubseteq f(x) \sqsubseteq f(y)$ by the monotonicity of f and hence $y \in f^{-1}[B_b]$. Furthermore, by Proposition 3.1.7, there is $a \in \text{approx}(x)$ such that $b \sqsubseteq f(a)$. But then $a \in f^{-1}[B_b]$ so that $f^{-1}[B_b]$ is indeed open.

Now suppose f is continuous with respect to the Scott topology. To show that f is monotone, suppose $x \sqsubseteq y$ and let $b \in \text{approx}(f(x))$. Then $x \in f^{-1}[B_b]$ and hence $y \in f^{-1}[B_b]$ by the Alexandrov condition of the Scott topology. But then $b \in \text{approx}(f(y))$. Thus $\text{approx}(f(x)) \subseteq \text{approx}(f(y))$ and hence $f(x) \sqsubseteq f(y)$. Finally, suppose again that $b \in \text{approx}(f(x))$. Then $x \in f^{-1}[B_b]$ and hence, by the Scott condition, there is $a \in \text{approx}(x)$ such that $a \in f^{-1}[B_b]$. But then $f(a) \in B_b$, that is $b \sqsubseteq f(a)$. This completes the proof, again using Proposition 3.1.7. □

Notice that the Alexandrov condition in the definition of the Scott topology corresponds to monotonicity of functions while the Scott condition corresponds to continuity or, more precisely, the requirement of Proposition 3.1.7.

The category of topological spaces, denoted **Top**, has as objects topological spaces and as morphisms the continuous functions between spaces. It is clear that **Top** is a category. In particular, it follows immediately from Definition 2.2 that the composition of two continuous functions is again continuous. The isomorphisms in **Top** are called homeomorphisms. Explicitly, a function $f:X \to Y$ is a *homeomorphism* if it is a continuous bijection and if $f^{-1}:Y \to X$ is continuous. The spaces X and Y are said to be *homeomorphic* if there is a homeomorphism $f:X \to Y$.

A function $f:X \to Y$ is said to be an *open mapping* if $f[U]$ is open in Y for each open $U \subseteq X$. Similarly, f is said to be a *closed mapping* if $f[F]$ is closed whenever $F \subseteq X$ is a closed set. The following characterization of a homeomorphism is an easy exercise.

2.4 Proposition Let $f:X \to Y$ be a continuous bijection. Then f is a homeomorphism if and only if f is an open mapping if and only if f is a closed mapping.

Thus for homeomorphic spaces X and Y there is a 1-1 correspondence not only between the points of the spaces but also between the open and closed sets.

Topology is the study of properties of topological spaces that are invariant under homeomorphisms.

Section 5.3 Topological Constructions

In this section we describe some important ways of constructing new topological spaces from given ones. First we consider the topology induced on a subset of a topological space.

3.1 Definition Let (X,τ) be a topological space and suppose $Y \subseteq X$. Then $\tau_Y = \{U \cap Y : U \in \tau\}$ is a topology on Y called the *subspace topology* or *relative topology* for Y.

A subset Y of a topological space X with the subspace topology is simply called a *subspace* of X. It is easy to see that τ_Y is indeed a topology. We also have the following proposition, the easy proof of which is left to the reader.

3.2 Proposition Let Y be a subspace of X.
(i) $F \subseteq Y$ is closed in $Y \Leftrightarrow F = H \cap Y$ for some H closed in X.
(ii) If $A \subseteq Y$ then $\overline{A} = Y \cap \overline{A}$ where the closure on the left-hand side is taken in Y and on the right-hand side in X.
(iii) If $\mathcal{B}$ is a base for X then $\{B \cap Y : B \in \mathcal{B}\}$ is a base for Y.

Consider the reals $\mathbb{R}$ with the usual topology. Then the irrational numbers $\mathbb{I}$ form a subspace of $\mathbb{R}$. One can show that $\mathbb{I}$ with the subspace topology is homeomorphic to the Baire space with the topology indicated in Example 1.4 (iii).

Suppose we want to study some topological structures, such as the Cantor or Baire spaces, using domain theory. As we shall see in the next section, for most interesting structures there is no hope of imposing an ordering on them such that the induced Scott topology coincides with the original one. In other words, we cannot construe these structures as domains. However, sometimes we can embed them into domains in such a way that the subspace topology induced by the Scott topology of the domain is the original one. In fact this has already been done in Examples 2.1.12 and 2.1.13 for the Cantor and Baire spaces. In Chapter 8 we will pursue this further by describing a general method for embedding ultrametric spaces into domains.

Let X be a topological space. Then X is said to have a *clopen base* if X has a topological base $\mathcal{B}$ such that each $B \in \mathcal{B}$ is closed.

3.3 Proposition Let $D=(D;\sqsubseteq,\bot)$ be a domain and consider the set of maximal elements $D_m=\{x\in D: x\sqsubseteq y \Rightarrow x=y\}$ in D. Then D_m, as a subspace of D, has a clopen base.

Proof: We consider the basic open sets $B_a=\{x\in D: a\sqsubseteq x\}$ in D, where $a\in D_c$, and show that $B_a\cap D_m$ is closed in D_m. For this it suffices to show that for each $x\in D_m-B_a$ there is $b\in \text{approx}(x)$ such that $B_a\cap B_b=\emptyset$. Let $x\notin B_a$. Suppose that for each $b\in\text{approx}(x)$, $B_a\cap B_b\neq\emptyset$. Then, for $b\in\text{approx}(x)$, $\{a,b\}$ is consistent and hence $a\sqcup b$ exists. Let

$$\mathcal{S}=\{a\sqcup b: b\in\text{approx}(x)\}.$$

Given $a\sqcup b_1$ and $a\sqcup b_2$ in $\mathcal{S}$, then $b_1\sqcup b_2\in\text{approx}(x)$ so $a\sqcup b_1\sqcup b_2\in\mathcal{S}$. Thus $\mathcal{S}$ is a directed set. Let $y=\bigsqcup\mathcal{S}$. Then $\text{approx}(x)\subseteq\text{approx}(y)$ so that $x\sqsubseteq y$. But $y\in B_a$ so $x\neq y$, that is $x\notin D_m$. □

Suppose we want to embed a topological space X into a domain D. A first attempt, regarding the non-maximal elements in D as proper approximations, is to embed X into D_m. Proposition 3.3 says that this is possible only for very special spaces. Fortunately, many spaces of interest in logic and computer science, such as the Cantor and Baire spaces and the free term algebra, are ultrametric spaces and all such spaces do have a clopen base.

Next we consider the cartesian product of a family of topological spaces. Let X_i be a set for each $i\in I$, where the index set I is non-empty and may be infinite. Then the *cartesian product* of the sets X_i is the set

$$\prod_{i\in I}X_i=\{f: I\longrightarrow \bigcup_{i\in I}X_i \mid f(i)\in X_i \text{ for each } i\in I\}.$$

For simplicity, when the index set I is understood we just write $\prod X_i$. In case I is finite, say $I=\{1,\ldots,n\}$, we obtain a set naturally equivalent to the finite cartesian product $X_1\times\ldots\times X_n$.

Along with the cartesian product we also have the associated projection functions $\pi_j:\prod X_i\longrightarrow X_j$ defined by $\pi_j(f)=f(j)$. We think of the cartesian product as the above set along with the associated projection functions.

Suppose we are given a family of topological spaces (X_i,τ_i) for $i\in I$ and we are to define a topology on $\prod X_i$. We certainly want the projection functions to be continuous since these form part of the cartesian product. It turns out that the least topology making the projection functions continuous is the most useful one to consider. Thus we choose as a subbase the family

$$\{\pi_j^{-1}[U]: j\in I \text{ and } U\in\tau_j\}.$$

A base for the desired topology is then obtained by taking all finite intersections of elements of this subbase.

3.4 Definition Let (X_i, τ_i) be topological spaces for $i \in I$. The *product topology* or *Tychonoff topology* on $\prod X_i$ is obtained from the topological base consisting of all sets $\prod U_i$ such that

(i) $U_i \in \tau_i$ for each $i \in I$, and
(ii) $U_i = X_i$ for all but finitely many i.

Observe that if $\mathcal{B}_i$ is a base for τ_i, then U_i may be taken from $\mathcal{B}_i$ for the finitely many i such that $U_i \neq X_i$. If the index set I is finite, then (ii) is vacuous.

A justification for the choice of the Tychonoff topology is the following characterization of continuity of a function into a cartesian product.

3.5 Proposition Let X and X_i for $i \in I$ be topological spaces. A function $f: X \longrightarrow \prod X_i$ is continuous if and only if $\pi_i \circ f$ is continuous for each $i \in I$.

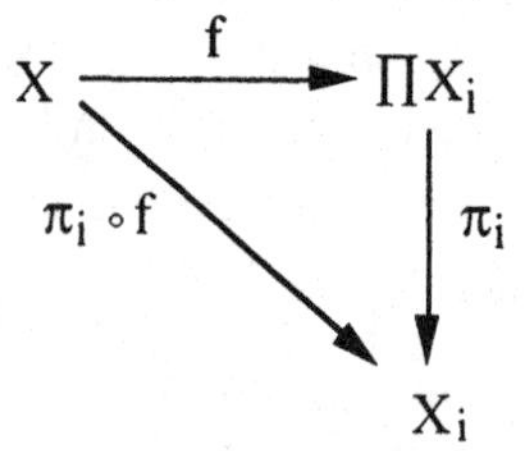

Proof: For the non-trivial direction assume $\pi_i \circ f$ is continuous for each $i \in I$. To prove that f is continuous it suffices to show that the inverse image under f of each element of the subbase given above is open. Let U_i be open in X_i. Then

$$f^{-1}[\pi_i^{-1}[U_i]] = (\pi_i \circ f)^{-1}[U_i]$$

which is open. □

The reader should verify that for domains $D_1, \ldots, D_n$, the Scott topology on the domain $D_1 \times \ldots \times D_n$ is the product topology of the Scott topologies for each D_i.

Let X be a set, X_i a topological space for each $i \in I$ and consider functions $f_i: X \longrightarrow X_i$. Then the *weak topology* on X induced by the functions f_i is the least topology making each f_i continuous. Thus the Tychonoff topology on $\prod X_i$ is the weak topology induced by the projection functions π_i. The dual notion is that of the *strong topology* induced on the set Y by the functions $f_i: Y_i \longrightarrow Y$ where

Y_i is a topological space for each $i \in I$. It is the largest topology on Y making each f_i continuous. Here we consider the simple case when I is a singleton.

3.6 Definition Let X be a topological space, Y a set, and suppose $f: X \longrightarrow Y$ is surjective. Then

$$\tau_f = \{V \subseteq Y : f^{-1}[V] \text{ is open in } X\}$$

is a topology, the *quotient topology* induced on Y by f.

It should be clear that τ_f is a topology and the largest one for which f is continuous.

We now connect the quotient topology with the usual way of obtaining a quotient structure. Let X be a topological space and suppose $\sim$ is an equivalence relation on X. Then $X/\sim$ denotes the set of equivalence classes of $\sim$. Furthermore we have the natural quotient map

$$v : X \longrightarrow X/\sim$$

given by $v(x) = [x]_\sim$, the equivalence class containing x. The quotient topology induced on $X/\sim$ by v is then the largest topology making v continuous. It is easily seen that $V \subseteq X/\sim$ is an open set in the quotient topology if and only if $\bigcup V$ is open in X.

Let D and E be domains and consider the smash product $D \otimes E$. As a set, $D \otimes E = D \times E/\sim$ where $\sim$ identifies all pairs containing $\bot$ in at least one component. The Scott topology of $D \otimes E$ is the quotient topology induced by $\sim$ on the Scott topology of $D \times E$.

Suppose X_i is a topological space for each $i \in I$ where, without loss of generality, we assume $i \neq j \Rightarrow X_i \cap X_j = \varnothing$. Let $X = \bigcup_{i \in I} X_i$ and say $U \subseteq X$ is open if and only if $U \cap X_i$ is open in X_i for each $i \in I$. The set X with this topology is the *sum* or *disjoint union* of the spaces X_i and is denoted $\oplus_{i \in I} X_i$.

Finally we briefly consider the function space construction. Suppose X and Y are topological spaces and let Y^X denote the set of all functions from X into Y. Then

$$Y^X = \prod_{i \in X} Y_i$$

where $Y_i = Y$ for each $i \in X$, so Y^X is a topological space using the Tychonoff topology.

3.7 Definition Let $\mathcal{F} \subseteq Y^X$. Then the subspace topology on $\mathcal{F}$ induced by the Tychonoff topology on Y^X is called the *topology of pointwise convergence*.

Note that the topology of pointwise convergence is independent of the topology on X.

To explain the choice of terminology we must deal with limits of sequences in topological spaces. Of course, ω-sequences do not suffice to describe convergence and completeness in arbitrary spaces, for the same reason we chose to consider cpo's rather than ω-cpo's. Nonetheless we will restrict ourselves to ω-sequences here.

Let X be a topological space and let $(x_n)_{n<\omega}$ (usually denoted simply by (x_n)) be a sequence of elements in X. Then (x_n) is said to *converge* to $x \in X$ or x is the *limit* of (x_n), denoted $x_n \longrightarrow x$ or $\lim_{n\to\infty} x_n = x$, if for each open set U such that $x \in U$ there is n_0 such that $n \geq n_0 \Rightarrow x_n \in U$. In other words, $x_n \longrightarrow x$ if each open set containing x also contains all but finitely many of the x_n.

A limit need not be unique. For example, $x_n \longrightarrow \bot$ for any sequence (x_n) in a domain. Limits are unique in case the space X has the Hausdorff property, described in the next section.

Now suppose $\mathcal{F} \subseteq Y^X$ is given the topology of pointwise convergence. Then a sequence (f_n) in $\mathcal{F}$ converges to f if and only if $(\pi_x(f_n))$ converges to $\pi_x(f)$ for each $x \in X$. But $\pi_x(f_n) = f_n(x)$ so this means that $(f_n(x)) \longrightarrow f(x)$ for each $x \in X$, that is the sequence converges pointwise.

Let D and E be domains. Then the Scott topology on the domain $[D \longrightarrow E]$ is the topology of pointwise convergence. This illuminates Theorem 2.3.2, recalling that directed sets in domains correspond to generalized sequences.

Section 5.4 Separation Axioms

As already mentioned, open sets are used to separate points or sets from other points or sets or, dually, to formalize proximity between points and sets of points in the sense that they cannot be separated. However, the definition of a topological space is very general and does not say much about separation. Consider, for example, a set X with the trivial topology. Then if $A \subseteq X$ is non-empty, $\bar{A}$ is the whole space. That is the topology is too weak to separate any point from A. To remedy this situation and to obtain non-trivial results one often assumes some additional axioms claiming certain separation properties.

In this section we give some of the usual separation axioms. These state to what degree points and closed sets can be separated.

4.1 Definition Let X be a topological space.

(i) X is a *T_0-space* if for each pair of distinct points $x, y \in X$ there is an open set containing one of the points but not the other.

(ii) X is a *T_1-space* if for each pair of distinct points $x, y \in X$ there is an open set U such that $x \in U$ and $y \notin U$.

(iii) X is a *T_2-space* or *Hausdorff space* if for each pair of distinct points $x, y \in X$ there are disjoint open sets U and V such that $x \in U$ and $y \in V$.

Clearly each T_i-space is a T_j-space for $j \leq i$. An example of a topological space which is not T_0 is a set X with the trivial topology, provided that X contains at least two points.

The importance of T_1-spaces is that they are exactly those spaces for which points are closed.

4.2 Proposition A topological space X is T_1 if and only if each singleton set is closed in X.

Proof: For the if direction suppose $x, y \in X$ are distinct points. By the hypothesis, $\{x\}$ is closed and $y \in X - \{x\}$, which is open. Conversely, suppose X is a T_1-space and let $x \in X$. For each $y \in X$ such that $y \neq x$ we choose an open set V_y such that $y \in V_y$ and $x \notin V_y$. Then $X - \{x\} = \bigcup_{y \neq x} V_y$ is open so $\{x\}$ is closed. □

It is straightforward to show that any non-trivial domain with the Scott topology is an example of a T_0-space which is not T_1. However, what is more interesting is that the partial order $\sqsubseteq$ of a domain D corresponds exactly to a natural order on D obtained when considering D as a topological space.

Let (X, τ) be a topological space and define a binary relation $\leq$ on X by

$$x \leq y \Leftrightarrow (\forall V \in \tau)(x \in V \Rightarrow y \in V).$$

It is immediate from its definition that the relation $\leq$ is reflexive and transitive, that is $\leq$ is a preorder. It is called the *specialization order* of X. Suppose $\leq$ is antisymmetric. Thus if $x \neq y$ then either $x \nleq y$ or $y \nleq x$. This means that either there is an open set U such that $x \in U$ and $y \notin U$ or there is an open set V such that $x \notin V$ and $y \in V$. In other words X is a T_0-space. Conversely, if X is a T_0-space then $\leq$ is antisymmetric. Thus $\leq$ being a partial order corresponds exactly to the space X being T_0. Suppose X is T_1. Then for distinct points $x, y \in X$ there are open sets U and V such that $x \in U$ and $y \notin U$ and $x \notin V$ and $y \in V$, so that x and y are not related by $\leq$. Thus the order $\leq$ is the discrete one (i.e. $\leq$ is $=$) for T_1-spaces. The converse also holds. To summarize, the preorder $\leq$ is a partial order if and only if the space X is T_0 and $\leq$ is the discrete order if and only if X is T_1.

4.3 Proposition Let $D = (D; \sqsubseteq, \perp)$ be a domain. Then the partial order $\sqsubseteq$ is the specialization order of D with respect to the Scott topology.

Proof: Let $\leq$ be the specialization order of D with respect to the Scott topology. Suppose $x \sqsubseteq y$ in D. Then for each open set V we have, by the Alexandrov condition of the Scott topology, $x \in V \Rightarrow y \in V$, that is $x \leq y$. Conversely, suppose $x \not\sqsubseteq y$. Then by Lemma 3.1.4 there is $a \in \text{approx}(x) - \text{approx}(y)$. But then for the basic open set $B_a = \{z \in D : a \sqsubseteq z\}$ we have $x \in B_a$ while $y \notin B_a$, that is $x \not\leq y$. $\square$

It follows immediately that any domain containing at least two points is a T_0-space which is not T_1.

To be concerned about spaces with weak separation properties, as we are here, is not that common. In fact, almost all spaces one meets in everyday mathematics are Hausdorff or have even stronger separation properties. (Another notable exception is that of the Zariski topology on the spectrum of a ring.) Each metric space (defined in Chapter 8) is clearly Hausdorff, for example the Cantor and Baire spaces, the real line $\mathbb{R}$ and the Euclidean spaces $\mathbb{R}^n$. Thus it is not possible to construe any of these spaces as a domain.

A characterization of Hausdorff spaces is the uniqueness of limits. More precisely, a space is Hausdorff if and only if (generalized) sequences converge to at most one point. Although an easy observation, we will not prove this fact here since we have not introduced generalized sequences such as nets or filters. However, suppose (x_n) is a sequence in a Hausdorff space and suppose that $x_n \longrightarrow x$. Let $y \neq x$ and choose disjoint open sets U and V such that $x \in U$ and $y \in V$. Then V contains only finitely many points of the sequence (x_n) since U must contain all but finitely many of the points by the fact that $x_n \longrightarrow x$. Thus the limit is unique.

The separation properties are preserved under most but not all of the topological constructions considered in Section 5.3, the notable exception being the quotient space construction.

4.4 Proposition Let $i = 0, 1, 2$.

(i) If X is a T_i-space and Y is a subspace of X then Y is a T_i-space.

(ii) If X_j is a T_i-space for each $j \in J$ then $\prod X_j$ and $\oplus X_j$ are T_i-spaces.

For completeness we mention some further axioms asserting separation between points and closed sets of points. A topological space X is *regular* if for each $x \in X$ and each closed set $F \subseteq X$ such that $x \notin F$, there are disjoint open sets U and V such that $x \in U$ and $F \subseteq V$. Of course, a set X with the trivial topology is regular. So to obtain a separation axiom fitting into the T_i-hierarchy one often assumes in addition that the space is T_1. Thus a space X is said to be a *T_3-space* if it is T_1 and regular. Since points in T_1-spaces are closed by Proposition 4.2, each T_3-space is T_2. Finally, we say that a space X is *normal* if whenever F_1

and F_2 are disjoint closed sets in X then there are disjoint open sets U and V such that $F_1 \subseteq U$ and $F_2 \subseteq V$. Just as for regularity one often makes the additional assumption that the space is T_1. Thus a normal T_1-space is said to be a *T_4-space*. Each metric space is T_4.

Section 5.5 Compactness

The classical Heine–Borel theorem states that any open cover of a closed finite interval of real numbers contains a finite subcover. The conclusion of this theorem has far-reaching consequences for general topological spaces and hence it has become a definition, that of compactness. The compact spaces form an extremely important class of topological spaces.

Let X be a topological space. A family $\{A_i\}_{i \in I}$ of sets is a *cover* of X if $A_i \subseteq X$ for each i and $X = \bigcup_{i \in I} A_i$. It is said to be an *open cover* if each A_i is an open set in X and it is a *finite cover* if the index set I is finite. A cover $\{B_j\}_{j \in J}$ is a *subcover* of $\{A_i\}_{i \in I}$ if for each $j \in J$ there is $i \in I$ such that $B_j = A_i$, that is the family $\{B_j\}_{j \in J}$ is a subfamily of $\{A_i\}_{i \in I}$.

5.1 Definition A topological space X is *compact* if each open cover of X has a finite subcover.

In the literature it is sometimes additionally required that the space X be Hausdorff, in which case the term for our notion would be *quasi-compact*.

5.2 Examples

(i) If X is a discrete space then X is compact if and only if X is finite.

(ii) A domain D with the Scott topology is compact. For suppose $\{U_i\}_{i \in I}$ is an open cover of D. Then $\bot \in U_i$ for some i and hence $U_i = D$. Thus each open cover of D has a subcover consisting of *one* element. This is an unusually strong form of compactness.

(iii) The space of real numbers $\mathbb{R}$ is not compact. The family $\{(-n, n) : n \in \mathbb{N}\}$ is an open cover which does not have a finite subcover.

(iv) A closed interval $[a, b] = \{x \in \mathbb{R} : a \leq x \leq b\}$ given the subspace topology inherited from $\mathbb{R}$ is compact. This is the Heine–Borel theorem (see Exercise 7).

(v) The Cantor space is a compact space while the Baire space is not.

The following Bolzano–Weierstrass type theorem is an illustration of the strength of compactness.

5.3 Proposition Let X be a compact space. Then each infinite set $A \subseteq X$ has a limit point in X.

Proof: Suppose X is compact. Let $A \subseteq X$ and suppose that A has no limit point in X. We show that A is finite. For each $x \in X$ there is an open set U_x such that $x \in U_x$ and $(A-\{x\}) \cap U_x = \emptyset$. Thus $\{U_x\}_{x \in X}$ is an open cover of X and, by compactness, has a finite subcover, say $X = U_{x_1} \cup \ldots \cup U_{x_n}$. Now let $y \in X - \{x_1, \ldots, x_n\}$. Then $y \in U_{x_i}$ for some i and hence $y \notin A$ since $(A - \{x_i\}) \cap U_{x_i} = \emptyset$. This shows that $A \subseteq \{x_1, \ldots, x_n\}$ so that A is finite. □

There is an equivalent and often useful formulation of compactness in terms of closed sets. Let X be a set. Then a non-empty family $\mathcal{F} \subseteq \wp(X)$ has the *finite intersection property* if $\bigcap \mathcal{F}' \neq \emptyset$ for each finite non-empty $\mathcal{F}' \subseteq \mathcal{F}$.

5.4 Proposition A topological space X is compact if and only if whenever $\mathcal{F} \subseteq \wp(X)$ is a non-empty family of closed sets with the finite intersection property then $\bigcap \mathcal{F} \neq \emptyset$.

Proof: To prove the only if direction suppose $\mathcal{F} = \{F_i\}_{i \in I}$ is a non-empty family of closed sets in X such that $\bigcap_{i \in I} F_i = \emptyset$. Let $U_i = X - F_i$. Then, by de Morgan's laws, $\{U_i\}_{i \in I}$ is an open cover of X. By compactness there is a finite set $J \subseteq I$ such that $\{U_j\}_{j \in J}$ covers X. But then, again by de Morgan's laws, $\bigcap_{j \in J} F_j = \emptyset$ so that $\mathcal{F}$ does not have the finite intersection property.

The converse is similar. Suppose X is not compact and consider an open cover $\{U_i\}_{i \in I}$ of X with no finite subcover. Then $\mathcal{F} = \{X - U_i\}_{i \in I}$ is a family of closed sets with the finite intersection property, but $\bigcap_{i \in I} F_i = \emptyset$. □

5.5 Corollary Let X be a compact topological space and suppose $\{F_i\}_{i \in \omega}$ is a family of closed sets in X such that $F_0 \supseteq F_1 \supseteq F_2 \supseteq \ldots$. If $F_i \neq \emptyset$ for each i then $\bigcap_{i \in \omega} F_i \neq \emptyset$.

Proof: The family has the finite intersection property since each $F_i \neq \emptyset$. □

We shall now briefly investigate compactness in relation to subspaces, continuous functions and products. Let X be a topological space. Then a set $A \subseteq X$ is said to be a *compact set* provided A is a compact space when given the subspace topology from X.

5.6 Proposition (i) Each closed subset of a compact space is compact.
(ii) Each compact subset of a Hausdorff space is closed.

Proof: (i) Let X be a compact space and suppose $F \subseteq X$ is a closed set. Let $\{U_i\}_{i \in I}$ be an open cover of F as a subspace of X. Choose sets V_i open in X such that $U_i = F \cap V_i$. Then $\{V_i\}_{i \in I}$ together with $X - F$ is an open cover of X.

By the compactness of X there is a finite subcover $\{V_{i_1},\dots,V_{i_n},X-F\}$ of X which in turn induces a finite subcover $\{U_{i_1},\dots,U_{i_n}\}$ of F.

(ii) Let X be a Hausdorff space and suppose $A\subseteq X$ is compact. To prove that A is closed it suffices, by Proposition 1.8, to show that A contains all of its limit points. So suppose $x\in X-A$. By the Hausdorff property of X we may choose for each $a\in A$ disjoint open sets U_a and V_a such that $a\in U_a$ and $x\in V_a$. Clearly, $\{U_a\cap A\}_{a\in A}$ is an open cover of A. By the compactness of A there are $a_1,\dots,a_n\in A$ such that $A\subseteq U_{a_1}\cup\dots\cup U_{a_n}$. But the set $V=V_{a_1}\cap\dots\cap V_{a_n}$ is open, $x\in V$ and $V\cap A=\varnothing$ since $V\cap U_{a_i}=\varnothing$ for each i. So x is not a limit point of A. □

5.7 Corollary Suppose X is a compact Hausdorff space. Then $F\subseteq X$ is compact if and only if F is closed.

The following proposition shows that the continuous image of a compact space is compact.

5.8 Proposition Let $f:X\longrightarrow Y$ be a continuous surjective function. If X is a compact space then so is Y.

Proof: Let $\{V_i\}_{i\in I}$ be an open cover of Y. Then, by the continuity of f, $\{f^{-1}[V_i]\}_{i\in I}$ is an open cover of X. By the compactness of X there is a finite subcover, say $\{f^{-1}[V_{i_1}],\dots,f^{-1}[V_{i_n}]\}$. But then $\{V_{i_1},\dots,V_{i_n}\}$ covers Y by the surjectivity of f. □

5.9 Corollary Let $f:X\longrightarrow Y$ be a continuous bijection. If X is compact and Y is Hausdorff then f is a homeomorphism.

Proof: By Proposition 2.4 it suffices to show that f is a closed mapping. Let $F\subseteq X$ be closed. Then F is compact by Proposition 5.6 and hence $f[F]$ is compact by Proposition 5.8. But then $f[F]$ is closed, again by Proposition 5.6. □

Finally we consider the cartesian product of topological spaces by proving the following classical theorem of Tychonoff. The theorem is one of the most fundamental results in topology. Its proof uses the axiom of choice, here given in the form of Zorn's lemma. This use of the axiom of choice is unavoidable since Kelley [1950] has shown that the Tychonoff theorem implies the axiom of choice. Thus the axiom of choice and the Tychonoff theorem are equivalent over, say, the usual Zermelo–Fraenkel set theory ZF. Recall our assumption that a topological space is non-empty.

5.10 Tychonoff's theorem Let $\{X_i\}_{i\in I}$ be a non-empty family of topological spaces. Then $\prod X_i$ is a compact space if and only if each X_i is compact.

Proof: For the easy direction suppose $\prod X_i$ is compact. Then $X_i = \pi_i[\prod X_i]$ is compact by Proposition 5.8, where π_i is the ith projection function.

The converse direction is where the axiom of choice is required. The problem is, as always with cartesian products, that complicated sets in the product may look nice along its projections. Furthermore, there may be no way of recovering the original set from its projections.

Suppose $\mathcal{F} = \{F_j\}_{j \in J}$ is a family of closed sets in $\prod X_i$ having the finite intersection property. Then for each i, the family $\{\pi_i[F_j]\}_{j \in J}$ has the finite intersection property in X_i. Assuming $\pi_i[F_j]$ would be closed in X_i (which it need not be, however this is not much of a problem since we may consider its closure) we would obtain a point $x_i \in \bigcap_{j \in J} \pi_i[F_j]$ by the compactness of X_i. Let $x \in \prod X_i$ be the point whose i'th component is x_i. Then one would like to say that $x \in \bigcap_{j \in J} F_j$. But this need not be the case even when J contains only two elements (why?). In order for this general strategy to work we must choose our points in the projections with great care, in fact only a choice function provided by the axiom of choice suffices in general. Equivalently, we may consider a larger family of sets than $\mathcal{F}$ to start with. Here we follow the latter approach.

Now we start the proof proper. Let $\mathcal{F} = \{F_j\}_{j \in J}$ be a family of closed sets in $\prod X_i$ having the finite intersection property. Consider the set

$$\mathcal{S} = \{\mathcal{D} \subseteq \wp(\prod X_i) : \mathcal{F} \subseteq \mathcal{D} \text{ and } \mathcal{D} \text{ has the finite intersection property}\}$$

and order $\mathcal{S}$ by inclusion. The original family $\mathcal{F}$ is in $\mathcal{S}$ and it is routine to verify that each chain in $\mathcal{S}$ has an upper bound in $\mathcal{S}$, namely the union of the chain. Thus Zorn's lemma provides us with a maximal element in $\mathcal{S}$, say this element is $\mathcal{E}$. (Observe that this argument would fail if we were in addition to require that each $\mathcal{D}$ in $\mathcal{S}$ should consist only of closed sets.) By the maximality of $\mathcal{E}$ it is clear that $\mathcal{E}$ is closed under finite intersections, that is if $E_1, \dots, E_n \in \mathcal{E}$ then $E_1 \cap \dots \cap E_n \in \mathcal{E}$. Furthermore, if $D \subseteq \prod X_i$ has non-empty intersection with each $E \in \mathcal{E}$, then $D \in \mathcal{E}$. For if not, then there would be $E_1, \dots, E_n \in \mathcal{E}$ such that $D \cap E_1 \cap \dots \cap E_n = \emptyset$. But $E = E_1 \cap \dots \cap E_n \in \mathcal{E}$ as already observed and hence $D \cap E = \emptyset$, which was not the case.

Denote the family $\mathcal{E}$ by $\mathcal{E} = \{E_k\}_{k \in K}$. For fixed $i \in I$ consider the collection $\{\overline{\pi_i[E_k]}\}_{k \in K}$. This is a family of closed sets in X_i having the finite intersection property since the latter is true of $\{\pi_i[E_k]\}_{k \in K}$. Using the compactness of X_i we choose a point $x_i \in \bigcap_{k \in K} \overline{\pi_i[E_k]}$. Let $x \in \prod X_i$ be the point defined by $x(i) = x_i$. We claim that $x \in \bigcap \mathcal{F}$, which proves the theorem. To prove this it suffices to show that x is an element of or a limit point of each F_j, since the sets F_j are closed. Thus it suffices to show that $U \cap F_j \neq \emptyset$ for each $j \in J$ whenever U is a basic open set in $\prod X_i$ containing x.

Recall that a basic open set U in $\prod X_i$ has the form $U=\prod V_i$ where V_i is open in X_i and only finitely many V_i differ from X_i, say $i=1,\dots,n$. So suppose $x\in U$ and fix $i\in I$ and $k\in K$. Now $x_i\in V_i\cap\overline{\pi_i[E_k]}$ so $V_i\cap\pi_i[E_k]\neq\varnothing$ since closed sets contain all their limit points. But then $\pi_i^{-1}[V_i]$ intersects each E_k and hence $\pi_i^{-1}[V_i]\in\mathcal{E}$ by the observation on $\mathcal{E}$ made above. Furthermore $U=\bigcap_{i=1}^{n}\pi_i^{-1}[V_i]\in\mathcal{E}$. The family $\mathcal{E}$ is in $\mathcal{S}$ and hence has the finite intersection property so, in particular, $U\cap F_j\neq\varnothing$ for each $j\in J$. The basic open set U was chosen arbitrarily, only with the proviso that $x\in U$, so x is a limit point of each F_j. Each F_j is closed so we have $x\in\bigcap_{j\in J}F_j$. □

The proof of the Tychonoff theorem is a good example of the often true and useful metamathematical slogan "the more ontology the simpler methodology" though in this case it should perhaps read "the more generality the simpler the proof". Rather than considering the original class of closed sets $\mathcal{F}$ we considered a much larger family of sets $\mathcal{E}$ with nice closure properties although we relaxed the requirement that the sets be closed, which turns out not to be so important. The essential property preserved from $\mathcal{F}$ was that $\mathcal{E}$ should have the finite intersection property.

Note that it is crucial for the proof that the product $\prod X_i$ is given the Tychonoff topology. In fact, the Tychonoff theorem is a sufficient reason to decide on a topology for product spaces.

5.11 Examples

(i) We say that $A\subseteq\mathbb{R}^n$ is bounded if $A\subseteq\prod_{i=1}^{n}[a_i,b_i]$ for some $a_i,b_i\in\mathbb{R}$. Clearly, if A is not bounded then A is not compact. Thus $A\subseteq\mathbb{R}$ is compact if and only if A is closed and bounded, by the Heine–Borel theorem and Corollary 5.7. This extends to $\mathbb{R}^n$ by the Tychonoff theorem.

(ii) Let $I_i=[0,1]\subseteq\mathbb{R}$ for each $i\in\omega$ and set $I^{\omega}=\prod_{i<\omega}I_i$. Then I^{ω} is compact by the Tychonoff theorem. This space is called the Hilbert cube.

(iii) Here is the usual construction of the Cantor space. Let

$$A_0=[0,1]$$
$$A_1=A_0-(1/3,2/3)$$
$$A_2=A_1-\big((1/9,2/9)\cup(7/9,8/9)\big)$$

and so on. At each stage one removes open intervals, a middle third of the corresponding closed intervals. Note that each A_n is closed and bounded and hence compact, $A_n\neq\varnothing$, and

$$A_0\supseteq A_1\supseteq A_2\supseteq A_3\supseteq\dots.$$

Let $C = \bigcap_{n<\omega} A_n$. Then $C \neq \varnothing$ by Corollary 5.5. Furthermore C is closed and hence compact.

Our previous formulation of the Cantor space was $2^\omega = \prod_{n<\omega}\{0,1\}$, that is the product of ω copies of $\{0,1\}$. The topology on 2^ω is the Tychonoff topology obtained from the discrete topology on $\{0,1\}$. Thus 2^ω in this formulation is compact by the Tychonoff theorem. The two versions of the Cantor space, C and 2^ω, are homeomorphic (see Exercise 8).

(iv) The Baire space ω^ω is a product of ω copies of $\mathbb{N}$ where $\mathbb{N}$ is given the discrete topology. Thus the Baire space is not compact since $\mathbb{N}$ is not compact.

5.6 Exercises

1. Suppose $\bar{\ }: \wp(X) \to \wp(X)$ satisfies the Kuratowski closure axioms of Proposition 1.7.
   (i) Show that the associated topology τ is indeed a topology on X and that $\bar{\ }$ is *the* closure operator with respect to τ.
   (ii) Is it always true that $\overline{A \cap B} = \bar{A} \cap \bar{B}$?

2. A subset G of a topological space is *regular open* (*regular closed*) if G is the interior of its closure (the closure of its interior).
   (i) Show that the complement of a regular open set is regular closed and vice versa.
   (ii) Show that $(\bar{A})^o$ is regular open for each $A \subseteq X$.
   (iii) Show that the intersection of regular open sets is regular open but that this need not be the case for the union.

3. Show that Proposition 2.2.4 does not hold for arbitrary topological spaces. That is, give examples of topological spaces X, Y, and Z and a function $f: X \times Y \to Z$ such that f is continuous in each argument but f is not continuous. What about the converse?

4. Let D and E be cpo's with the Scott topology (Example 1.2 (v)). Show that a function $f: D \to E$ is continuous in the topological sense if and only if f is continuous in the sense of Definition 2.1.3.

5. Let $B \subseteq X$ be fixed and define for each non-empty $A \subseteq X$, $\bar{A} = A \cup B$.
   (i) Show that this defines a topology on X.
   (ii) Under what conditions on B is the resulting topology T_0? T_1? T_2?

6. Let X be a topological space and define $\sim$ on X by $x \sim y$ if $\overline{\{x\}} = \overline{\{y\}}$.
   (i) Show that $\sim$ is an equivalence relation.
   (ii) Show that $X/\sim$ is a T_0-space.

7. Prove the Heine–Borel theorem stated in Example 5.2 (iv). [Given an open cover of $[a,b]$, let $c = \sup\{x \in [a,b]: [a,x]$ has a finite subcover$\}$.]

8. Let C be the Cantor space as presented in Example 5.11 (iii).
   (i) Show that C is precisely the set of points in the unit interval which have a ternary expansion without 1's. [That x has a ternary expansion means that $x = \sum x_i/3^i$ where $x_i \in \{0,1,2\}$.]
   (ii) Use (i) to show that C is homeomorphic to $2^\omega = \prod_{n<\omega}\{0,1\}$.

9. Give a direct proof, not using Tychonoff's theorem, that 2^ω is a compact space. [Use the topological base given in Example 1.4 (iii).]

CHAPTER 6

REPRESENTATION THEORY

In section two of chapter three we proved a representation theorem stating that a domain D is, up to isomorphism, the ideal completion of its compact elements, D_c. An ordered set having the properties derivable for D_c was christened a *cusl* or conditional upper semilattice with least element. It turns out that a somewhat weaker version of cusl's, namely *precusl's*, serves just as well as a representation of domains and is better suited for the purposes of the last section of this chapter, which deals with solutions of domain equations to identity. In this chapter we sketch, without detailed proof, the basic results known on the representation of domains in this sense.

We begin with two additional representations of domains, *information systems* and *formal spaces*. Both have their origins in the works of D. S. Scott, Scott [1982] and [1982a], where the latter were presented in a less general form as *neighbourhood systems*. The versions presented here differ at some points from those of Scott for reasons to be explained later. Each of these three representations has its own particular point of departure. Cusl's and precusl's, by virtue of their emphasis on an ordering, give an *algebraic* representation. Information systems, based upon a relation of entailment, give a *logical* representation in analogy with the corresponding notion in formal logical systems. Finally, formal spaces, through their emphasis upon a relation of (formal) inclusion between neighbourhoods, provide a *topological* representation. The latter has also been regarded, via the dual of a formal space known as a *locale*, as a means of understanding the *logic of domains* where domains are regarded as propositions and their elements as proofs or verifications of those proposition (see Abramsky [1991]).

In the third section of this chapter we make mathematically precise the relation between the categories corresponding to these three representations and the category of domains. Each of the three exhibits a fundamental mathematical point of view and their equivalence provides strong evidence for the generality of the notion of a domain. In the last section we develop the tools necessary for the solution of domain equations to identity using the representations of domains given by precusl's.

Section 6.1 Information Systems

Information systems were introduced in Scott [1982a]. The intention of the definition that follows is to formalize the properties of computations. The definitions presented here appeared first in Larsen and Winskel [1984].

1.1 Definition An *information system* is a triple $\mathbf{A}=(A;\mathrm{Con},\vdash)$ where A is a set, Con is a non-empty subset of $\wp_f(A)$ and $\vdash$ is a subset of $\mathrm{Con}\times A$ such that the following hold:

(i) $u\subseteq v\in\mathrm{Con} \Rightarrow u\in\mathrm{Con}$;

(ii) $a\in A \Rightarrow \{a\}\in\mathrm{Con}$;

(iii) $u\vdash a \Rightarrow u\cup\{a\}\in\mathrm{Con}$;

(iv) $u\in\mathrm{Con}$ and $a\in u \Rightarrow u\vdash a$;

(v) $(\forall a\in v)(u\vdash a)$ and $v\vdash b \Rightarrow u\vdash b$.

The set A is referred to as the set of *data objects* or *tokens*, each element of which should be thought of as a *bit of information* about the elements of the domain represented by $\mathbf{A}$. Tokens will be denoted by a, b and c with subscripts when necessary. Alternatively the elements of A can be thought of as *atomic propositions*. Con is the collection of finite *consistent* sets of tokens, that is, the predicate Con delineates finite sets of data objects that can be attributed to one and the same computation. Elements of Con will be denoted by u, v and w. Finally, $\vdash$ is the *entailment relation* of $\mathbf{A}$. An instance of the entailment relation, $u\vdash a$, means intuitively that the information in u about a potential computation is *at least as great as that contained in* a. Put otherwise, that the information in u is correctly attributed to some computation *has* a *as a consequence* or *entails* that the information in a can be correctly attributed to that computation.

The entailment relation is extended to a relation on Con as follows. Given $u,v\in\mathrm{Con}$, let $u\vdash v$ just in case $(\forall a\in v)(u\vdash a)$. Note that if we define $\le$ on Con by letting $v\le u$, if $u\vdash v$, then $\le$ is a preorder on Con with least element $\varnothing$.

1.2 Remark The above definition differs from that of Scott in that we omit the distinguished element Δ. In Scott's original definition he included Δ in the set of data objects and intended it as a *least informative* data object (or the *constant true* proposition). An additional axiom was included stating that $u\vdash\Delta$, for all $u\in\mathrm{Con}$. This omission has no substantial effect on the resulting structures (see Exercise 3). Note that the role of Δ on the level of $\le$ is played by $\varnothing$.

1.3 Examples

(1) $\perp = (\varnothing; \{\varnothing\}, \varnothing)$ is the *trivial* or *empty* information system.

(2) The *flat* information system given by an arbitrary set S is defined by letting $\text{flat}(S) = (S; \text{Con}, \vdash)$, where S is an arbitrary set and $\text{Con} = \{\varnothing\} \cup \{\{a\} : a \in S\}$. Its entailment relation is defined by letting $u \vdash a$ just in case $u = \{a\}$.

(3) $\text{Int} = (\mathbb{N}; \text{Con}, \vdash)$, where $\text{Con} = \wp_f(\mathbb{N})$ and $\{n_0, \ldots, n_{k-1}\} \vdash m$, if $m = 0$ or $m \leq n_i$ for some $i < k$.

(4) If A and B are arbitrary sets, then $A \longrightarrow_p B = (D; \text{Con}, \vdash)$, where $D = A \times B$ and $\{(a_0, b_0), \ldots, (a_{k-1}, b_{k-1})\} \in \text{Con}$ if, for all $i, j < k$, $a_i = a_j \Rightarrow b_i = b_j$, while $u \vdash c$ just in case $c \in u$, is the information system of *partial functions from* A *into* B.

Some consequences of the definition of $\vdash$ between elements of Con are the following.

1.4 Lemma
(i) $u \vdash v \Rightarrow u \cup v \in \text{Con}$;
(ii) $u \vdash u$;
(iii) $u \vdash v$ and $v \vdash w \Rightarrow u \vdash w$;
(iv) $u' \supseteq u$, $u \vdash v$ and $v \supseteq v' \Rightarrow u' \vdash v'$;
(v) $u \vdash v$ and $u \vdash v' \Rightarrow u \vdash v \cup v'$.

Proof: Exercise 4. □

Properties (i)–(v) have natural interpretations as conditions on $\leq$. (ii) and (iii) state that $\leq$ is reflexive and transitive. (i) states that the derivability relation is *sound.* (iv) states that $\subseteq$ and $\leq$ are compatible and, finally, (v) states that any two elements of Con with an upper bound with respect to $\leq$ have a *least upper bound* which is their union.

1.5 Definition Let $A = (A; \text{Con}, \vdash)$ be an information system. The *elements* or *points* of A are those subsets $\mathbf{m} \subseteq A$ such that:
(i) $u \subseteq \mathbf{m}$ and u finite $\Rightarrow u \in \text{Con}$; and
(ii) $u \subseteq \mathbf{m}$ and $u \vdash a \Rightarrow a \in \mathbf{m}$.

The points of an information system willl be denoted by boldface letters **m** and **n**. The collection of all elements of A will be denoted $|A|$.

1.6 Proposition Let $A = (A; \text{Con}, \vdash)$ be an information system. Then the structure $|A| = (|A|; \subseteq, \varnothing)$ is a domain. The set of compact elements of $|A|$ is $|A|_c = \{\bar{u} : u \in \text{Con}\}$ where $\bar{u} = \{a \in A : u \vdash a\}$.

Proof: To see that $|A|$ is complete, let $\mathcal{F} \subseteq |A|$ be directed. Let $\mathbf{m} = \bigcup \mathcal{F}$. Clearly, if $\mathbf{m}$ is a point, then $\mathbf{m} = \bigsqcup \mathcal{F}$ in $|A|$. To show that $\mathbf{m}$ is a point suppose $u = \{a_1, \ldots, a_k\} \subseteq \mathbf{m}$. Thus there are points $\mathbf{n}_1, \ldots, \mathbf{n}_k \in \mathcal{F}$ such that $a_i \in \mathbf{n}_i$ for $i = 1, \ldots, k$. $\mathcal{F}$ is directed so there is an $\mathbf{n} \in \mathcal{F}$ containing each $\mathbf{n}_i$. In particular, $u \subseteq \mathbf{n}$ so $u \in \mathrm{Con}$. In addition, if $u \vdash a$ then $a \in \mathbf{n} \subseteq \mathbf{m}$. This proves that $\mathbf{m} \in |A|$.

We leave as an easy exercise to show that $\bar{u} \in |A|$ for each $u \in \mathrm{Con}$. Let $\mathcal{F} \subseteq |A|$ be directed and suppose $u \in \mathrm{Con}$ and $\bar{u} \sqsubseteq \bigsqcup \mathcal{F} = \bigcup \mathcal{F}$. Then $u \subseteq \bigcup \mathcal{F}$ since $u \subseteq \bar{u}$, and hence, as above, there is an $\mathbf{n} \in \mathcal{F}$ such that $u \subseteq \mathbf{n}$. But $\mathbf{n}$ is closed under entailment so $\bar{u} \subseteq \mathbf{n} \in \mathcal{F}$. Thus $\bar{u}$ is compact. For the converse inclusion, assume $\mathbf{m} \in |A|$ is compact. Let $\mathcal{F} = \{\bar{u}\colon u \subseteq \mathbf{m}$ and u finite$\}$. Thus $\mathbf{m} = \bigcup \mathcal{F}$. Furthermore, $\mathcal{F}$ is directed. For suppose $\bar{u}, \bar{v} \in \mathcal{F}$. Then $u \cup v \subseteq \mathbf{m}$ and is finite so $u \cup v \in \mathrm{Con}$ and $\overline{u \cup v} \in \mathcal{F}$. By Lemma 1.4, $\overline{u \cup v}$ contains $\bar{u}$ and $\bar{v}$. Now, by compactness, there is $\bar{u} \in \mathcal{F}$ such that $\mathbf{m} = \bar{u}$.

The above also shows that $\mathrm{approx}(\mathbf{m}) = \{\bar{u}\colon u \subseteq \mathbf{m}$ and u finite$\}$ is directed and $\mathbf{m} = \bigsqcup \mathrm{approx}(\mathbf{m})$, that is $|A|$ is algebraic. Finally, suppose $\bar{u}, \bar{v} \in |A|_c$ are consistent. Then $\bar{u}, \bar{v} \subseteq \mathbf{m}$ for some point $\mathbf{m}$ and hence $u \cup v \in \mathrm{Con}$. We will show that $\overline{u \cup v} = \bar{u} \sqcup \bar{v}$, proving that $|A|$ is consistently complete. Clearly $\bar{u}, \bar{v} \subseteq \overline{u \cup v}$. Suppose $\bar{u}, \bar{v} \subseteq \mathbf{n} \in |A|$. Then $u \cup v \subseteq \mathbf{n}$. Thus $\bar{u} \sqcup \bar{v} = \overline{u \cup v}$. □

1.7 Examples Returning to each of the previously mentioned examples, we consider the domain of points for each of these.

(1') $|\bot| = \{\varnothing\}$, the one element domain.

(2') $|\mathrm{flat}(S)| = \{\{a\}\colon a \in S\} \cup \{\varnothing\}$, the flat domain over a set S.

(3') $|\mathrm{Int}| = \{\{n\colon n \leq m\}\colon m \in \mathbb{N}\} \cup \{\mathbb{N}\}$, corresponding to the domain obtained for the successor ordinal $\omega + 1$.

(4') $|A \to_p B|$ contains the graphs of all partial functions from A to B.

On the other hand, given a domain $D = (D; \sqsubseteq, \bot)$, define an information system $I(D) = (D_c; \mathrm{Con}, \vdash)$, where $u \in \mathrm{Con}$, if $u \subseteq D_c$ is finite and has an upper bound; and $u \vdash a$ if $a \sqsubseteq \bigsqcup u$.

1.8 Proposition If D is a domain, then $I(D)$ is an information system.

Proof: Exercise 5. □

In fact, D and $|I(D)|$ are isomorphic domains where the isomorphism pair is $\theta\colon D \to |I(D)|$ and $\phi\colon |I(D)| \to D$ given by:

$$\theta(x) = \{a \in D_c\colon a \sqsubseteq x\} = \mathrm{approx}(x) \quad \text{and} \quad \phi(\mathbf{m}) = \bigsqcup \mathbf{m}$$

(see Exercise 6). Thus information systems give a second representation of domains.

1.9 Second representation theorem Let D be a domain. Then $|I(D)| \cong D$.

A continuous mapping between domains cannot, in general, be expected to map compact elements to compact elements. Consider, for example, any mapping constantly equal to a non-compact element of its image domain. Thus to represent arbitrary continuous mappings between domains on the representations of those domains, we are forced to describe them as relations between approximations of a given argument and approximations of its value at that argument.

1.10 Definition Let $A=(A; Con, \vdash)$ and $A'=(A'; Con', \vdash')$ be information systems. Then a relation $f \subseteq Con \times Con'$ is an *approximable mapping* from A to A', if

(i) $\varnothing f \varnothing$;

(ii) $u f v$ and $u f v' \Rightarrow u f (v \cup v')$;

(iii) $u' \vdash u$ and $u f v$ and $v \vdash' v' \Rightarrow u' f v'$.

Implicitly, clause (ii) of the definition requires that $v \cup v' \in Con'$. In the formulation of the definition, the entailment relations $\vdash$ and $\vdash'$ denote their extensions to $Con \times Con$ and $Con' \times Con'$. Approximable mappings can be seen as generalizations of the entailment relation which itself gives the *identity approximable mapping*. Seen in this light the three clauses of the above definition state that the empty condition is always f-*derivable*, and that the conditions f-derivable from given u are pairwise compatible (and closed under union). Finally, clause (iii) of the definition states that the relation f is "transitive" with respect to the entailment relations of its domain and range. More concretely, if $u f v$ holds, then v is still f-derivable if we increase the information in u to u' and any decrease of the information in v to v' is f-derivable from u.

In order to see the precise connection between continuous mappings between domains and approximable mappings between the corresponding information systems, suppose that f is an approximable mapping from A to A' and define $|f|: |A| \to |A'|$ by $|f|(\mathbf{m}) = \bigcup \{v:\ u f v \text{ and } u \subseteq \mathbf{m}\}$. Then $|f|$ is continuous from the domain $|A|$ to the domain $|A'|$. Conversely, given domains D and D' and a continuous function $g: D \to D'$, define a relation $I(g) \subseteq Con \times Con'$ by $u\, I(g)\, v$, if $\bigsqcup v \sqsubseteq g(\bigsqcup u)$. Then $I(g)$ is an approximable mapping from the information system $I(D)$ to the information system $I(D')$.

Construction Principles

If $A_0 = (A_0; Con_0, \vdash_0)$ and $A_1 = (A_1; Con_1, \vdash_1)$ are information systems, then, corresponding to some of the construction principles we have considered on cpo's and domains, we have the following constructions on information systems:

$A_0 \times A_1$: the *product* of A_0 and A_1;
$A_0 \oplus A_1$: the *smash sum* of A_0 and A_1; and
$A_0 \to A_1$: the *function space* from A_0 to A_1.

The components of the respective information systems are given below while we leave as exercises (see Exercise 8) the verifications that they are, in fact, information systems.

Product: $A_0 \times A_1$ is $(Con_0 \times Con_1; Con_\times, \vdash_\times)$, where we define $Con_\times$ by letting $Con_\times = \{u \in \wp_f(Con_0 \times Con_1): \bigcup \pi_0[u] \in Con_0$ and $\bigcup \pi_1[u] \in Con_1\}$, and $u \vdash_\times (v, w)$ just in case $\bigcup \pi_0[u] \vdash_0 v$ and $\bigcup \pi_1[u] \vdash_1 w$.

Sum: $A_0 \oplus A_1$ is $(A_0 \oplus A_1; Con_\oplus, \vdash_\oplus)$, where $A_0 \oplus A_1 = \{0\} \times A_0 \cup \{1\} \times A_1$, with the usual embeddings $in_0: A_0 \to A_0 \oplus A_1$ and $in_1: A_1 \to A_0 \oplus A_1$. We define $Con_\oplus = \{\{0\} \times u : u \in Con_0\} \cup \{\{1\} \times v : v \in Con_1\}$ and let $\{i\} \times u \vdash_\oplus in_i(a)$ just in case $u \vdash_i a$.

Function Space: $A_0 \to A_1$ is the information system $(A_0 \to A_1; Con_\to, \vdash_\to)$, where $A_0 \to A_1 = Con_0 \times Con_1$, $w = \{(u_0, v_0), \ldots, (u_{n-1}, v_{n-1})\} \in Con_\to$ just in case for all $I \subseteq \{0, \ldots, n-1\}$:

$$\bigcup_{i \in I} u_i \in Con_0 \Rightarrow \bigcup_{i \in I} v_i \in Con_1, \text{ and}$$

$w \vdash_\to (u, v)$ if $\bigcup \{v_i : u \vdash_0 u_i \text{ and } i < n\} \vdash_1 v$, where w is as above.

We have, as usual, made use of the extension of the entailment relations to $Con \times Con$. It is now straightforward to show that the domains of points produced by these three constructs are isomorphic to the domains that result by applying the corresponding construction principle to the domains of points of the information systems we begin with. The proof of the first theorem below is left as an exercise for the reader.

1.11 Theorem Let A_0 and A_1 be information systems. Then the following isomorphisms hold: $|A_0 \times A_1| \cong |A_0| \times |A_1|$ and $|A_0 \oplus A_1| \cong |A_0| \oplus |A_1|$.

1.12 Theorem Let A_0 and A_1 be information systems. Then $|A_0 \rightarrow A_1|$ is precisely the set of approximable mappings from A_0 to A_1. Furthermore we have that $|A_0 \rightarrow A_1| \cong [|A_0| \rightarrow |A_1|]$.

Proof: For a given approximable mapping f from A_0 to A_1, we let $\mathbf{m}_f$ be the set $\mathbf{m}_f = \{(u, v) \in Con_0 \times Con_1 : u f v\}$. We shall show that $\mathbf{m}_f \in |A_0 \rightarrow A_1|$. Suppose that $w = \{(u_0, v_0), \ldots, (u_{n-1}, v_{n-1})\} \subseteq \mathbf{m}_f$. To show that $w \in Con_{\rightarrow}$, let $I \subseteq \{0, \ldots, n-1\}$ and suppose $u = \bigcup_{i \in I} u_i \in Con_0$. For each $i \in I$, $u \vdash_0 u_i$ and $u_i f v_i$ so $u f v_i$ by Definition 1.10 (iii). Using 1.10 (ii) we obtain $u f \bigcup_{i \in I} v_i$. In particular we have that $\bigcup_{i \in I} v_i \in Con_1$. Since I was arbitrary, we have that $w \in Con_{\rightarrow}$ as desired.

Suppose now that $w \vdash_{\rightarrow} (u, v)$, where $w \subseteq \mathbf{m}_f$ is as above. We want to show that $(u, v) \in \mathbf{m}_f$, that is that $u f v$. Let $I = \{i : u \vdash_0 u_i\}$. Thus we know that $\bigcup_{i \in I} v_i \vdash_1 v$ and $u \vdash_0 \bigcup_{i \in I} u_i$. In case $I = \emptyset$ then $u f v$, using 1.10 (i) and (iii). Suppose $I \neq \emptyset$. Then for each $i \in I$, $u_i f v_i$ and hence $u f v_i$ by 1.10 (iii). By 1.10 (ii) we have $u f \bigcup_{i \in I} v_i$ and hence, again by 1.10 (ii), $u f v$.

Conversely, given $\mathbf{m} \in |A_0 \rightarrow A_1|$, let $u f_{\mathbf{m}} v$ just in case $(u, v) \in \mathbf{m}$. Then $f_{\mathbf{m}}$ is an approximable mapping. We leave the proof of this and the existence of the asserted isomorphism as Exercise 9. □

Section 6.2 Formal Spaces

As indicated in the introduction to this chapter, a third representation of domains can be formulated in the language of *formal topology*. Here the notion of approximation or information is replaced by the topological notion of neighbourhood, essentially its *dual*. A formal space consists of two components, the first of which is a *formal calculus of neighbourhoods* while the second is a *covering relation* between neighbourhoods and families of neighbourhoods.

The structures of open sets which arise in this fashion are of course far more general than the topological structure of a domain. A natural restriction on the covering relation, corresponding to the fact that the Scott topology for domains is T_0, then yields essentially the notion of a *neighbourhood system* as originally defined in Scott [1982] (see Exercise 3.5.11). Conversely, the theory of formal spaces can be seen as a generalization of the theory of domains.

Formal spaces have been treated in a variety of ways in Fourman and Grayson [1982], Johnstone [1982], Sambin [1987] and Sigstam [1990]. Here we essentially follow the presentation in Sigstam.

First we introduce the formal analogue of the structure given by basic open sets ordered under inclusion in a topological space. Let $P = (P; \leq)$ be a preorder.

Then a subset $A \subseteq P$ is said to be *consistent*, denoted $\mathrm{Cons}(A)$, if there exists a $c \in P$ such that, for all $b \in A$, $c \leq b$, that is if A has a lower bound. We abbreviate $\mathrm{Cons}(\{a_0, \ldots, a_{n-1}\})$ by $\mathrm{Cons}(a_0, \ldots, a_{n-1})$.

2.1 Definition A structure $P = (P; \leq, \wedge)$ with partial binary operation $\wedge$ is a *neighbourhood system* if $(P; \leq)$ is a preorder and, for all $a, b \in P$, we have that $a \wedge b$ is defined iff $\mathrm{Cons}(a, b)$, and then $a \wedge b$ is some infimum of a and b.

The ordering $\leq$ is the formal analogue of inclusion while $\wedge$ is that of intersection. It is only a formal analogue, since it is not assumed to be antisymmetric (as in the case of inclusion on the sets of a topology) and, hence, the elements of P are better thought of as *names* for neighbourhoods in the topological sense.

Arbitrary unions of basic open sets are represented by *families of neighbourhoods* or arbitrary subsets $U \subseteq P$. We extend the binary infimum operation on P to subsets of P by setting, for $U, V \subseteq P$,

$$U \wedge V = \{u \wedge v:\ u \in U \text{ and } v \in V \text{ and } \mathrm{Cons}(u, v)\}.$$

2.2 Definition

(i) A *covering relation* on a neighbourhood system P is a relation $\mathrm{Cov} \subseteq P \times \wp(P)$ such that:
- (a) $a \in U \Rightarrow \mathrm{Cov}(a, U)$;
- (b) $a \leq b \Rightarrow \mathrm{Cov}(a, \{b\})$;
- (c) $\mathrm{Cov}(a, U)$ and $(\forall u \in U)\mathrm{Cov}(u, V) \Rightarrow \mathrm{Cov}(a, V)$;
- (d) $\mathrm{Cov}(a, U)$ and $\mathrm{Cov}(a, V) \Rightarrow \mathrm{Cov}(a, U \wedge V)$.

(ii) A *formal space* is a neighbourhood system $P = (P; \leq, \wedge)$ together with a covering relation Cov on P, written as a pair (P, Cov).

For $U, V \subseteq P$, let $U \leq V$, if for all $a \in U$ we have that $\mathrm{Cov}(a, V)$. Then the clauses of Definition 2.2 can be seen (see Exercise 10) to state of $\leq$ that:

(a') $U \leq U$ ($\leq$ is reflexive);

(b') $a \leq b$ (w.r.t. the ordering on P) $\Rightarrow \{a\} \leq \{b\}$ ($\leq$ on families *extends* formal inclusion between neighbourhoods);

(c') $U \leq V$ and $V \leq W \Rightarrow U \leq W$ ($\leq$ is transitive);

(d') $W \leq U$ and $W \leq V \Rightarrow W \leq U \wedge V$ ($\wedge$ between families is an everywhere defined infimum operation).

The covering relation as a component of a formal space should be thought of as a means of specifying an equivalence relation on families of neighbourhoods seen as names for (or constructions for) open sets.

To be precise, for $U,V \in \wp(P)$ we define $U \sim V$ if $U \leq V$ and $V \leq U$. Then $\sim$ is an equivalence relation on $\wp(P)$. Denote by $[U]$ the equivalence class containing U and define

$$[U] \leq [V] \Leftrightarrow U \leq V, \text{ and}$$
$$[U] \wedge [V] = [U \wedge V].$$

These are well-defined on the quotient structure $\wp(P)/\sim$ since $\sim$ is a congruence relation with respect to $\leq$ and $\wedge$. In Exercise 11 the reader is invited to verify the following proposition.

2.3 Proposition

(i) $[U] \wedge [V] =$ infimum of $[U]$ and $[V]$ w.r.t. $\leq$;

(ii) $[\bigcup_{i \in I} U_i] = \bigvee_{i \in I}[U_i]$, the supremum of the family $[U_i]$, $i \in I$, w.r.t. $\leq$;

(iii) $\bigvee_{i \in I}([U_i] \wedge [V]) = (\bigvee_{i \in I}[U_i]) \wedge [V]$.

For a formal space $F = (P, Cov)$ we let $O(P, Cov) = \wp(P)/\sim$, the collection of formal open sets of F. Proposition 2.3 shows that the structure

$$H(P, Cov) = (O(P, Cov); \leq, \wedge, \bigvee, [\emptyset], [P]),$$

the *algebra of formal open sets*, is a complete Heyting algebra. Abstract versions of the structure $H(P, Cov)$ have been studied in Johnstone [1982] and elsewhere. The following definition is included to indicate the abstract framework in which these structures can be studied.

2.4 Definition

(i) A structure $A = (A; \leq, \wedge, \bigvee, \perp, \top)$ is a *frame* if $(A; \leq)$ is a partially ordered set with least element $\perp$ and greatest element $\top$; $x \wedge y = \inf_{\leq}(x, y)$ exists for all x and y in A as does $\bigvee S = \sup_{\leq} S$, for all $S \subseteq A$; finally, we have the following *distributive law*: $\bigvee_{i \in I}(a_i \wedge b) = (\bigvee_{i \in I} a_i) \wedge b$.

(ii) A *frame homomorphism* is a function $f: A \rightarrow A'$, between frames, satisfying:

(a) $f(\top) = \top$;

(b) $f(a \wedge b) = f(a) \wedge f(b)$; and

(c) $f(\bigvee_{i \in I} a_i) = \bigvee_{i \in I} f(a_i)$.

2.5 Examples

(1) A simple example of a frame is $\mathbf{2} = (\{0, 1\}; \leq)$ where $0 \leq 1$.

(2) The definition of a frame was inspired by considering the algebra of open sets $(\tau; \subseteq, \cap, \cup, \emptyset, X)$ associated with a topological space (X, τ). The notion of a frame mapping arises by considering mappings between the algebras of open sets

(associated with two topological spaces) corresponding to taking the inverse image of an open set under a continuous mapping (see Definition 5.2.2). The reader is invited (see Exercise 13) to verify that the collection of frames forms a category, denoted **Frm**, taking frame homomorphisms as morphisms, and to verify that an isomorphism in **Frm** is just a bijective frame homomorphism.

2.6 Remarks We denote the element $[\{u\}]$, for $u \in P$, in $H(P, Cov)$ by $[u]$. Note that $[U] = \bigvee_{u \in U}[u]$. A greatest or least element of P (if it has one), corresponding to a neighbourhood approximating all or no points, respectively, is in some sense unnecessary since the resulting frame will contain $[P]$ and $[\varnothing]$. Compare this with the omission of a least informative data object in the definition of an information system in Section 6.1.

Next we define the analogue of an element or point of an information system. However, we should note that formal spaces are extremely general, as indicated by the example of algebras of open sets of a topological space, thus far beyond information systems.

2.7 Definition A *point* in a formal space $F = (P, Cov)$ is a subset $\mathbf{m} \subseteq P$ such that:

(i) $\mathbf{m} \neq \varnothing$;

(ii) if $a, b \in \mathbf{m}$, then $(\exists c \in \mathbf{m})(c \leq a$ and $c \leq b)$; and

(iii) if $a \in \mathbf{m}$ and $Cov(a, U)$, then $\mathbf{m} \cap U \neq \varnothing$.

The set of points of a formal space F will be denoted $Pt(F)$. Setting $U = \{b\}$ in clause (iii) of this definition we have that a point $\mathbf{m}$ is upwards closed. Clauses (ii) and (iii) together assert that a point $\mathbf{m}$ is closed under finite infima (see Exercise 14). Thus each point is a filter. However, not every filter is a point. In fact, the points are precisely those filters which are completely prime (see Remark 2.8 (3) below).

2.8 Remarks

(1) One can define a covering relation for an arbitrary frame by letting $Cov(a, U)$ iff $a \leq \bigvee U$ and, in so doing, define the *formal space of a frame* (see Exercise 15). Thus we obtain the set of points of an arbitrary frame A denoted $Pt(A)$.

(2) Let $F = (P, Cov)$ be a formal space. In order to see which *open set* an arbitrary $U \subseteq P$ corresponds to, let $U^* = \{\mathbf{m} \in Pt(F) : \mathbf{m} \cap U \neq \varnothing\}$. Writing a^* for $\{a\}^*$, one shows easily that $\tau = \{U^* : U \subseteq P\}$ is a topology on $Pt(F)$ with base $\{a^* : a \in P\}$ (Exercise 16).

(3) An equivalent (see Exercise 17) definition of a point over a frame A is that $\mathbf{m} \subseteq A$ satisfies:
(a) $\top \in \mathbf{m}$, $\bot \notin \mathbf{m}$;
(b) $a, b \in \mathbf{m} \Rightarrow a \wedge b \in \mathbf{m}$;
(c) $a \in \mathbf{m}$ and $a \leq b \Rightarrow b \in \mathbf{m}$; and
(d) $\bigvee S \in \mathbf{m} \Rightarrow (\exists s \in S)(s \in \mathbf{m})$.
This is just the definition of a *completely prime filter* on A, where condition (d) expresses complete primality.

(4) Seen as the image frame of a frame mapping, the frame **2** can also be used to define what is called the *spectrum of points* of a formal space (see Exercise 12). All three definitions of a point over a frame we have indicated thus far are equivalent in the sense that the resulting topological spaces are homeomorphic (see Exercise 18).

Generators and the Relation to Scott Domains

It is clear from Definition 2.2 that the set of possible covering relations on a given neighbourhood system is closed under arbitrary intersections. Consider a set $\mathcal{G} \subseteq P \times \wp(P)$, where P is a neighbourhood system. Thus there is a *least* covering relation R containing $\mathcal{G}$, namely

$$R = \bigcap \{\mathcal{H} : \mathcal{G} \subseteq \mathcal{H} \text{ and } \mathcal{H} \text{ is a covering relation}\}.$$

Note that $P \times \wp(P)$ is itself a covering relation so the considered family of covering relations is non-empty. The relation R is said to be the *covering relation generated by* $\mathcal{G}$ and $\mathcal{G}$ is said to be a *set of generators* for R.

There is a more constructive way to describe the covering relation generated by $\mathcal{G}$, namely, by viewing Definition 2.2 as inductively defining it.

2.9 Definition Let P be a neighbourhood system and let $\mathcal{G} \subseteq P \times \wp(P)$. Then the relation $Cov_{\mathcal{G}}$ generated by $\mathcal{G}$ is defined inductively by:
(i) $(a, U) \in \mathcal{G} \Rightarrow Cov_{\mathcal{G}}(a, U)$;
(ii) $a \in U \Rightarrow Cov_{\mathcal{G}}(a, U)$;
(iii) $a \leq b \Rightarrow Cov_{\mathcal{G}}(a, \{b\})$;
(iv) $Cov_{\mathcal{G}}(a, U)$ and $(\forall u \in U) Cov_{\mathcal{G}}(u, V) \Rightarrow Cov_{\mathcal{G}}(a, V)$; and
(v) $Cov_{\mathcal{G}}(a, U)$ and $Cov_{\mathcal{G}}(a, V) \Rightarrow Cov_{\mathcal{G}}(a, U \wedge V)$.

The formal space F which consists of the neighbourhood system P and the covering relation generated by $\mathcal{G}$ is denoted by $F = (P, \mathcal{G})$. It is a convenient way to present formal spaces, in particular when one is concerned with their effective content.

2.10 Example (Cantor space) We use the notation of 2.1.12. Let $P = SEQ$ and order P by

$$\sigma \leq \tau \Leftrightarrow \tau \subseteq \sigma.$$

Thus the empty sequence is the largest element in P. Define the set $\mathcal{G}$ of generators by

$$\mathcal{G} = \{(\sigma, \{\sigma * \langle 0 \rangle, \sigma * \langle 1 \rangle\}) : \sigma \in P\},$$

where $*$ is the concatenation operator, and let $F = (P, \mathcal{G})$. Then $Pt(F)$ is homeomorphic to 2^ω, the Cantor space. Note that both components of F have concrete or finitary descriptions. Of course, P is just the reverse ordering of a cusl whose domain completion contains 2^ω but by necessity also *all* approximations. Using formal spaces in this way we still have a finitary description of the Cantor space but when taking the completion, that is the points of the formal space, we obtain exactly what we want, namely 2^ω with the desired topology (Exercise 19).

The above example illustrates the generality and at the same time the constructive nature of formal spaces or rather the possibility of giving a constructive presentation. Now we will characterize those formal spaces which are representations of domains. First we make the following observation about the least covering relation associated with a neighbourhood system.

2.11 Proposition Let P be a neighbourhood system. Then for all $a \in P$ and $U \subseteq P$ we have that $Cov_\varnothing(a, U)$ if and only if $(\exists u \in U)(a \leq u)$.

Proof: The if direction follows from (i), (ii) and (iii) of Definition 2.9. The proof of the only if direction is by induction using Definition 2.9. For (i) this follows by the reflexivity of $\leq$ and for (ii) it is trivially true. For (iii) we have by the induction hypotheses that there is $u \in U$ such that $a \leq u$ and there is $v \in V$ such that $u \leq v$. But then $a \leq v$ by transitivity so $(\exists v \in V)(a \leq v)$. Finally for (iv), the induction hypotheses provide $u \in U$ and $v \in V$ such that $a \leq u$ and $a \leq v$. In particular, $Cons(u, v)$ and $a \leq u \wedge v \in U \wedge V$. □

2.12 Definition A formal space $F = (P, Cov)$ is a *Scott space* if for all $a \in P$ and $U \subseteq P$, $Cov(a, U) \Rightarrow (\exists u \in U)Cov(a, \{u\})$.

Noting that $Cov_\varnothing$ is contained in every covering relation on P, Proposition 2.11 shows that the Scott spaces are precisely those formal spaces whose covering relation can be generated by the empty set, in the following sense.

2.13 Theorem Let $F=(P,Cov)$ be a Scott space. Then there exists a neighbourhood system P' such that, for $F'=(P',Cov_{\emptyset})$, we have that $Pt(F)$ and $Pt(F')$ are homeomorphic spaces.

Proof: Let $P'=(P,\leq')$ be defined by $a\leq'_P b \Leftrightarrow Cov(a,\{b\})$. Then $\leq'$ is a preordering extending the given preordering on P. We leave the verification that $Pt(F)$ and $Pt(F')$ are homeomorphic as an exercise for the reader (see Exercise 20). □

In the remainder of this section we will restrict ourselves to Scott spaces of the form $F=(P,Cov_{\emptyset})$. By Theorem 2.13 this is no real restriction. We will also assume, without loss of generality, that the underlying neighbourhood system has a greatest element Δ (see Exercise 21).

First we observe that the points of a Scott space have a particularly simple form.

2.14 Proposition Let F be a Scott space (under the assumptions above). Then $Pt(F)$ is the set of filters over P.

Proof: We already know that each point is a filter. So assume $\mathbf{m}\subseteq P$ is a filter. Then (i) and (ii) of Definition 2.7 trivially hold. For (iii) assume that $a\in\mathbf{m}$ and that $Cov(a,U)$. Since F is a Scott space there is $u\in U$ such that $a\leq u$. But then $u\in\mathbf{m}$ by the fact that $\mathbf{m}$ is a filter and so $\mathbf{m}\cap U\neq\emptyset$. □

We can now prove that Scott spaces give rise to domains and that each domain can be obtained in this fashion from a Scott space. For P a neighbourhood system and $a\in P$ we let $\bar{a}$ denote the principal filter generated by a.

2.15 Third representation theorem

(i) Let $F=(P,Cov)$ be a Scott space. Then $\mathbf{Pt}(F)=(Pt(F);\subseteq,\bar{\Delta})$ is a domain. Furthermore, $Pt(F)_c=\{\bar{a}\in Pt(F): a\in P\}$.

(ii) Let $D=(D;\sqsubseteq,\bot)$ be a domain. Then $P=(D_c;\leq,\wedge)$ is a neighbourhood system with greatest element $\bot$, where $\leq$ is the reverse ordering of $\sqsubseteq$, that is $a\leq b \Leftrightarrow b\sqsubseteq a$, and if $Cons(a,b)$ then $a\wedge b=a\sqcup b$. Furthermore, $F=(P,Cov_{\emptyset})$ is a Scott space and $\mathbf{Pt}(F)\cong D$.

Proof: (i) Clearly $\bar{\Delta}$ is the least element in $Pt(F)$. If $\mathcal{H}\subseteq Pt(F)$ is directed then one easily sees that $\bigcup\mathcal{H}\in Pt(F)$ where the directedness is used to show closure under infima. Thus $\bigsqcup\mathcal{H}=\bigcup\mathcal{H}$ and $Pt(F)$ is a cpo. Let $a\in P$. Suppose $\bar{a}\subseteq\bigcup\mathcal{H}$ where $\mathcal{H}$ is a directed set. Then there is $\mathbf{m}\in\mathcal{H}$ such that $a\in\mathbf{m}$. But then $\bar{a}\subseteq\mathbf{m}$ so $\bar{a}$ is compact. Conversely, suppose $\mathbf{m}\in Pt(F)$ is compact. Then clearly $\mathbf{m}=\bigcup\{\bar{a}: a\in\mathbf{m}\}$ and the latter family is directed since $\mathbf{m}$ is a point.

Thus $\mathbf{m}=\bar{a}$ for some $a \in P$. It follows that $Pt(F)_c = \{\bar{a} : a \in P\}$ and that $Pt(F)$ is algebraic. For consistent completeness we note that $\bar{a} \sqcup \bar{b} = \overline{a \wedge b}$.
(ii) The filters over $(D_c; \leq)$ are precisely the ideals over $(D_c; \sqsubseteq)$. Thus (ii) follows from Theorem 3.2.6. □

We close this section with the definition of an approximable mapping between neighbourhood systems corresponding to approximable mappings between information systems. These represent the continuous functions between the corresponding domains.

2.16 Definition Let P_1 and P_2 be neighbourhood systems. Then an *approximable mapping* f from P_1 to P_2 is a relation from P_1 to P_2 satisfying:
(i) $\Delta_1 f \Delta_2$;
(ii) if afc and afd, then $afc \wedge d$;
(iii) if $b \leq_1 a$ and afc and $c \leq_2 d$, then bfd.

Given an approximable mapping f from P_1 to P_2 as in the definition, we obtain a continuous function between domains $\bar{f} : Pt(P_1) \longrightarrow Pt(P_2)$ by letting

$$\bar{f}(\mathbf{m}) = \{b \in P_2 : (\exists a \in \mathbf{m})(afb)\}.$$

Furthermore, each continuous function from $Pt(P_1)$ to $Pt(P_2)$ is obtained in this way.

Section 6.3 Relation between Representations

In this chapter we have discussed two additional representations of domains, namely, information systems and Scott spaces. In this section we introduce the notion of a precusl, a generalization of cusl appropriate for solving domain equations up to identity. We then give methods for transforming each of the representations of domains presented in this chapter into each of the others. It is a straightforward exercise to show that the domain represented by the representation and its transformation are isomorphic. These transformations can just as well be applied to the appropriate notion of mappings between two such representations, thus obtaining the transformations as functors.

3.1 Definition A *precusl* is a structure $P = (P; \sqsubseteq, \sqcup, \bot)$, where $\sqsubseteq$ is a preorder, $\bot$ is a distinguished least element and $\sqcup$ is a partial binary operation on P such that, for all $a, b \in P$: $a \sqcup b$ is defined if and only if the set $\{a, b\}$ is consistent in P (has an upper bound in P) and then $a \sqcup b$ is a supremum of a and b.

Since $\sqsubseteq$ is only assumed to be a preorder, there may be other least elements than $\perp$ as well as several suprema for given a and b for which $\{a, b\}$ is consistent. The definition of a precusl requires that a *distinguished* least element be given as part of the structure as well as an operation $\sqcup$ which, for consistent $\{a, b\}$, gives as its value a *distinguished* supremum $a \sqcup b$ of a and b. This will be important when solving domain equations to identity using precusl's in Section 6.4.

3.2 Definition Let $P = (P; \sqsubseteq, \sqcup, \perp)$ and $P' = (P'; \sqsubseteq', \sqcup', \perp')$ be precusl's. An *approximable mapping* from P to P' is a relation $f \subseteq P \times P'$ such that:

(i) $\perp f \perp'$;
(ii) afb and $afb' \Rightarrow afb \sqcup b'$;
(iii) afb, $a \sqsubseteq a'$ and $b' \sqsubseteq b \Rightarrow a'fb'$.

3.3 Remark The notion of an approximable mapping of cusl's is analogously defined. Notice that the category of cusl's with approximable mappings is a full subcategory of that of precusl's with approximable mappings, denoted **Precusl**. This *inclusion functor* has a left adjoint corresponding to a quotient of a precusl obtained by identifying a and b such that $a \sqsubseteq b$ and $b \sqsubseteq a$. It was this quotient operation which was implicit in the functorial solution of domain equations presented in Chapter 4 and it is also the source of difficulty in using cusl's to solve domain equations to identity.

If $P = (P; \sqsubseteq, \sqcup, \perp)$ is a precusl, then an *ideal* on P is a subset $I \subseteq P$ such that
(i) $\perp \in I$;
(ii) if $a, b \in I$, then $a \sqcup b \in I$ (notice that $\{a, b\}$ is then consistent in P);
(iii) if $a \in I$ and $b \sqsubseteq a$, then $b \in I$.

The *ideal completion* of P, denoted by $\overline{P}$, is the structure $(\mathrm{Id}(P); \subseteq, [\perp])$, where, for $a \in P$, $[a]$ denotes the *principal ideal* generated by a and Id(P) denotes the set of all ideals on P. Just as in the case of cusls, $\overline{P}$ is a domain. The extension of an approximable mapping of precusl's f, pointwise, to ideals is denoted $\overline{f}$ and is defined by

$$\overline{f}(I) = \{b \in P' : (\exists a \in I)(afb)\}.$$

The reader should verify that $\overline{\cdot}$ is a functor from **Precusl** to **Domain**.

Recall that, for an information system $(A; \mathrm{Con}, \vdash)$, we defined a relation $\leq$ on Con by letting $v \leq u$ if for all $a \in v$ we have $u \vdash a$. Note that $\varnothing \in \mathrm{Con}$ and, for all $u \in \mathrm{Con}$, $\varnothing \leq u$; hence $\varnothing$ is a least element with respect to $\leq$. Similarly one verifies that $\leq$ is reflexive and transitive on Con and is, therefore, a preordering on Con. We also showed that $u, v \in \mathrm{Con}$ have a least upper bound with respect to $\leq$ just in case $u \cup v \in \text{Con}$ (in which case $u \cup v$ is a least upper bound). Thus $(\text{Con}; \leq, \cup, \varnothing)$ is a precusl. We let $C(A)$ denote the precusl constructed in this way from A.

Conversely, suppose we are given a precusl $P = (P; \sqsubseteq, \sqcup, \perp)$. In order to describe its transformation into an information system we take as the set of *data objects* the entire underlying set of the precusl P and, for $u \subseteq P$ finite, we say that u is *consistent*, that is $u \in \text{Con}$, if u is consistent in P. Define the *entailment relation* of our information system, $\vdash$, between elements u in Con and a in P by $u \vdash a$ just in case $a \sqsubseteq \bigsqcup u$. We denote by $I(P)$ the structure $(P; \text{Con}, \vdash)$ so constructed from the precusl P.

3.4 Theorem Let $A = (A; \text{Con}, \vdash)$ be an information system and let $P = (P; \sqsubseteq, \sqcup, \perp)$ be a precusl. Then $I(P)$ is an information system and $C(A)$ is a precusl. Furthermore, $\overline{P} \cong |I(P)|$ and $|A| \cong \overline{C(A)}$.

Proof: We have already observed that $C(A)$ is a precusl. Thus we only verify the clauses in the definition of an information system for $I(P)$. Using the notation of the above construction, suppose that $u \subseteq v \in \text{Con}$ and that $a \in P$ is an upper bound of v in P. Then a is also an upper bound of u in P and, hence, $u \in \text{Con}$. If $a \in P$, then $a \sqsubseteq a$ and hence $\{a\} \in \text{Con}$. If $u \vdash a$, that is, $a \sqsubseteq \bigsqcup u$, then $\bigsqcup u$ is an upper bound for $u \cup \{a\}$ in P and we have that $u \cup \{a\} \in \text{Con}$. Let $u \in \text{Con}$ and $a \in u$. Clearly $a \sqsubseteq \bigsqcup u$ and hence $u \vdash a$. Finally, let $u, v \in \text{Con}$ and suppose that, for all $b \in v$, $u \vdash b$ and that $v \vdash c$, that is, for all $b \in v$ we have $b \sqsubseteq \bigsqcup u$ and $c \sqsubseteq \bigsqcup v$. But then $\bigsqcup v \sqsubseteq \bigsqcup u$ and, by the transitivity of $\sqsubseteq$, it follows that $c \sqsubseteq \bigsqcup u$, that is, $u \vdash c$.

The proof of the existence of the asserted isomorphisms is Exercise 23. □

Suppose that $A_1 = (A_1; \text{Con}_1, \vdash_1)$ and $A_2 = (A_2; \text{Con}_2, \vdash_2)$ are information systems and that f is an approximable mapping from A_1 to A_2. Define an approximable mapping of precusl's, from $C(A_1)$ to $C(A_2)$, by letting $u\,C(f)\,v$, just in case $u f v$. Then $C(f)$ is an approximable mapping of precusl's and f and $C(f)$ give rise to the "same" continuous functions $|f|$ and $\overline{C(f)}$ on their respective domain completions, modulo the isomorphisms.

Conversely, suppose that $P_1 = (P_1; \sqsubseteq_1, \sqcup_1, \perp_1)$ and $P_2 = (P_2; \sqsubseteq_2, \sqcup_2, \perp_2)$ are precusl's and that f is an approximable mapping of precusl's from P_1 to P_2. Define an approximable mapping of information systems from $I(P_1)$ to $I(P_2)$ by letting $u\,I(f)\,v$, just in case $\bigsqcup u\, f \bigsqcup v$. Then $I(f)$ is an approximable mapping of information systems and f and $I(f)$ give rise to the "same" continuous functions $\overline{f}$ and $|I(f)|$ on their respective domain completions, modulo the isomorphisms. Let **ISys** denote the category of information systems with approximable mappings of information systems as morphisms. Thus $C: \mathbf{ISys} \longrightarrow \mathbf{Precusl}$ and

$I:\mathbf{Precusl} \rightarrow \mathbf{ISys}$ are functors transforming representations of domains to representations of domains, equivalent in the sense that the respective domain completions are isomorphic, and similarly for the morphisms.

Turning to the comparison of Scott spaces and precusl's, let F be a Scott space. By Theorem 2.13, the covering relation in a Scott space can be taken to be the least covering relation on some neighbourhood system without affecting the space of points $Pt(F)$. For this choice of a presentation of a Scott space the covering relation can therefore be omitted. There are in general a variety of Scott spaces which, when transformed in the fashion outlined in Theorem 2.13, give rise to the same neighbourhood system. Hence, in terms of presentations, Scott spaces are more general than neighbourhood systems. In the discussion that follows we will restrict ourselves to neighbourhood systems.

Given a neighbourhood system $P=(P;\leq,\wedge,\Delta)$ with a greatest element Δ, define a precusl $PC(P)=(P;\sqsubseteq,\sqcup,\Delta)$, where, for $u,v\in P$, we let $u\sqsubseteq v$ just in case $v\leq u$ in P and we define $u\sqcup v=u\wedge v$. Conversely, given a precusl $P=(P;\sqsubseteq,\sqcup,\bot)$, define a neighbourhood system $Nbhd(P)=(P;\leq,\wedge,\bot)$, where, for $a,b\in P$, $a\leq b$ just in case $b\sqsubseteq a$ in P and $a\wedge b=a\sqcup b$. The reader will easily verify that $PC(P)$ and $Nbhd(D)$ are a precusl and a neighbourhood system, respectively (see Exercise 24). We define

$$u\,PC(f)\,v, \text{ if } u f v \quad \text{and} \quad a\,Nbhd(g)\,b, \text{ if } a g b,$$

where f is an approximable mapping of neighbourhood systems and g is an approximable mapping of precusl's. Letting **Nbhd** denote the category of neighbourhood systems with approximable mappings, one can show that we have defined functors $PC:\mathbf{Nbhd}\rightarrow\mathbf{Precusl}$ and $Scsp:\mathbf{Precusl}\rightarrow\mathbf{Nbhd}$ (see Exercise 24). In fact, the trivial natural isomorphisms $PC\circ Nbhd\cong\mathbf{I}_{\mathbf{Precusl}}$ and $Nbhd\circ PC\cong\mathbf{I}_{\mathbf{Nbhd}}$, together with these two functors, yield the following result.

3.5 Theorem The categories **Nbhd** and **Precusl** are equivalent.

Section 6.4 Solution of Domain Equations to Identity

As we pointed out in the discussion following Definition 4.6.2 the representation theorem for domains proved in Theorem 3.2.6 gives us in fact an equivalence of categories between the categories **Dom** and **Cusl**. This was exploited in Chapter 4 in order to facilitate the solution of domain equations up to isomorphism. One of the advantages of approaching this problem using one of the three other representations of domains given in this chapter is the possibility of solving domain equations *to identity*.

In Chapter 4 we considered in detail the solution of domain equations in the category **Dom**, where the equality symbol in the domain equation was read instead as isomorphism between the domains given on the left and right hand sides of the equation. There we could not expect equality in the true sense of the word. For example, a non-trivial solution to the equation $D=[D \longrightarrow D]$ to identity would imply that each element of D was also a continuous function from D to itself, thus having itself as an argument. This is easily seen to be impossible for set-theoretic reasons. A reasonable question to ask is whether these equations can *truly* be solved, that is, whether domains can be given such that the relevant equation holds reading the equality symbol as *identity*. The answer is yes if we use a somewhat weaker representation of domains than cusl's and was first pointed out by Scott (see Scott [1982a]). There Scott uses the original version of the information systems introduced in Section 6.1. Here we will give the necessary tools and results for solutions to identity in terms of the representation of domains in terms of precusl's.

4.1 Definition Let $P=(P; \sqsubseteq, \sqcup, \bot)$ and $P'=(P'; \sqsubseteq', \sqcup', \bot')$ be precusl's. We say that P is a *subprecusl* of P', denoted $P \leq P'$, if

(i) $P \subseteq P'$;

(ii) $\sqsubseteq = \sqsubseteq'|_P$;

(iii) $\bot = \bot'$; and

(iv) if $a, b \in P$ and $\{a, b\}$ is consistent in P', then $\{a, b\}$ is consistent in P and $a \sqcup b = a \sqcup' b$.

We would like to show that the class of precusl's ordered by $\leq$ is a *cpo-like structure*. Then we would aim to prove that the constructions corresponding to +, $\times$, $\longrightarrow$ and so on are continuous on this cpo, thus allowing us to use the existence of fixed points to solve domain equations to identity. One immediate difficulty is that the class of precusl's has no least element with respect to $\leq$. This can be remedied by fixing an element $\bot$ and considering only those precusl's having $\bot$ as a unique least element.

A *large cpo* is a structure $C=(C; \leq, \bot)$ where C is a (possibly proper) class, $\leq$ is a partial order on C such that the supremum of $\mathcal{A}$ exists in C for all directed subsets $\mathcal{A}$ of C, and $\bot$ is the least element in C. It is important that we only require suprema for directed *subsets* and not for directed subclasses. Note that if C is a large cpo and is itself a set then C is a cpo in the usual sense. A (class-)function $F: C \longrightarrow D$ between large cpo's is said to be *continuous*, if for all directed subsets $\mathcal{A}$ of C, $F[\mathcal{A}]$ is directed and $F(\bigsqcup \mathcal{A}) = \bigsqcup F[\mathcal{A}]$.

Let $\bot$ be a distinguished element and let $\text{Precusl}_\bot$ be the class of precusl's having $\bot$ as a unique least element. Clearly the precusl $\{\bot\}=(\{\bot\}; \sqsubseteq, \sqcup, \bot)$ is in $\text{Precusl}_\bot$. Define

$$\mathbf{Precusl}_{\perp} = (\text{Precusl}_{\perp}; \leq, \{\perp\})$$

where $\leq$ is the subprecusl relation of Definition 4.1.

4.2 Proposition $\mathbf{Precusl}_{\perp} = (\text{Precusl}_{\perp}; \leq, \{\perp\})$ is a large cpo.

Proof: It is easily verified that $\leq$ is a partial order on $\text{Precusl}_{\perp}$ and that $\{\perp\}$ is the least element. Let $(P_i)_{i\in I}$ be a directed family in $\mathbf{Precusl}_{\perp}$, where I is a set and $P_i = (P_i; \sqsubseteq_i, \sqcup_i, \perp)$. To construct the supremum of $(P_i)_{i\in I}$ let $P = \bigcup_{i\in I} P_i$ and define for $a, b \in P$

$$a \sqsubseteq b \text{ if } (\exists i \in I)(a \sqsubseteq_i b) \text{ and } a \sqcup b = c \text{ if } (\exists i \in I)(a \sqcup_i b = c).$$

The proof that $\sqsubseteq$ and $\sqcup$ are well-defined uses the fact that the family $(P_i)_{i\in I}$ is directed (see Exercise 26). Clearly $P = (P; \sqsubseteq, \sqcup, \perp) \in \text{Precusl}_{\perp}$ and P is the supremum in $\mathbf{Precusl}_{\perp}$ of $(P_i)_{i\in I}$. □

The functions on the large cpo $\mathbf{Precusl}_{\perp}$ we will now consider, namely *sum, product* and *function space*, all take two arguments. Just as with ordinary cpo's, a two-place function between large cpo's is *continuous*, just in case it is continuous in each of its arguments separately.

First we give a useful sufficient condition for continuity essentially stating that whenever a construction is monotone and finitary then it is continuous.

4.3 Proposition Let $F: \mathbf{Precusl}_{\perp} \to \mathbf{Precusl}_{\perp}$. Then F is continuous if
(i) F is monotone, and
(ii) If $\mathcal{A}$ is a directed subset of $\mathbf{Precusl}_{\perp}$ and $a \in F(\bigsqcup\mathcal{A})$, then there is a $P \in \mathcal{A}$ such that $a \in F(P)$.

Proof: Suppose that the conditions on F hold and let $\mathcal{A}$ be a directed subset of $\mathbf{Precusl}_{\perp}$. Since F is monotone the set $F[\mathcal{A}]$ is directed and $\bigsqcup F[\mathcal{A}] \leq F(\bigsqcup\mathcal{A})$. It remains to show that $F(\bigsqcup\mathcal{A}) \leq \bigsqcup F[\mathcal{A}]$.

Note that for $P \in \mathcal{A}$ we have that $F(P) \leq \bigsqcup F[\mathcal{A}] \leq F(\bigsqcup\mathcal{A})$. Let $a \in F(\bigsqcup\mathcal{A})$. By (ii) there is $P \in \mathcal{A}$ such that $a \in F(P) \subseteq \bigsqcup F[\mathcal{A}]$. Thus $F(\bigsqcup\mathcal{A}) \subseteq \bigsqcup F[\mathcal{A}]$. To prove that $F(\bigsqcup\mathcal{A}) \leq \bigsqcup F[\mathcal{A}]$ let $a, b \in F(\bigsqcup\mathcal{A})$. Using the fact that $\mathcal{A}$ is directed and F is monotone, there is $P \in \mathcal{A}$ such that $a, b \in F(P)$. But then

$$\begin{aligned} a \sqsubseteq b \text{ in } F(\textstyle\bigsqcup\mathcal{A}) &\Leftrightarrow a \sqsubseteq b \text{ in } F(P) \\ &\Leftrightarrow a \sqsubseteq b \text{ in } \textstyle\bigsqcup F[\mathcal{A}]. \end{aligned}$$

Similarly, the $\sqcup$ operations on $F(\bigsqcup\mathcal{A})$ and $\bigsqcup F[\mathcal{A}]$ agree, proving that $F(\bigsqcup\mathcal{A}) \leq \bigsqcup F[\mathcal{A}]$. □

For the second condition of this proposition to be satisfied, it clearly suffices that the construction of a new element in $F(P)$ only depend upon finitely many elements of P. Hence it is not surprising that the usual constructions, such as $\rightarrow$, $+$, and $\times$ are continuous.

In the following definitions we use the notation $P_i=(P_i;\sqsubseteq_i,\sqcup_i,\bot)\in \text{Precusl}_\bot$ for $i=0$ and 1.

4.4 Sum of Precusl's Let $F_+:\text{Precusl}_\bot\times\text{Precusl}_\bot\longrightarrow\text{Precusl}_\bot$ be given by

$$F_+(P_0,P_1)=P_0+P_1$$

where P_0+P_1 is the preordered set with unique least element $\bot$ as defined in Definition 2.4.1. The distinguished partial supremum operation on $F_+(P_0,P_1)$ is given by

$$\begin{array}{ll} \bot\sqcup x=x & \text{for } x\in P_0+P_1 \\ in_i(a)\sqcup in_i(b)=in_i(a\sqcup_i b) & \text{for consistent } a,b\in P_i. \end{array}$$

Clearly $F_+(P_0,P_1)\in\text{Precusl}_\bot$.

4.5 Product of Precusl's $F_\times:\text{Precusl}_\bot\times\text{Precusl}_\bot\longrightarrow\text{Precusl}_\bot$ is defined by setting

$$F_\times(P_0,P_1)=(P_0\times P_1)_\bot$$

where $(P_0\times P_1)_\bot$ is the lifting of the cartesian product as a preordered set as in Definitions 2.2.1 and 2.4.5. The distinguished partial supremum operation on $F_\times(P_0,P_1)$ is given by

$$\begin{array}{ll} \bot\sqcup x=x & \text{for } x\in (P_0\times P_1)_\bot \\ (a,b)\sqcup(c,d)=(a\sqcup_0 c,b\sqcup_1 d) & \text{for consistent } (a,b),(c,d)\in P_0\times P_1. \end{array}$$

Clearly $F_\times(P_0,P_1)\in\text{Precusl}_\bot$.

4.6 The function space $F_\rightarrow:\text{Precusl}_\bot\times\text{Precusl}_\bot\longrightarrow\text{Precusl}_\bot$ is given by setting

$$F_\rightarrow(P,Q)=((P\longrightarrow Q))_\bot$$

where $((P\longrightarrow Q))_\bot$ is the lifting of the preordered set $((P\longrightarrow Q))$ defined in Definition 4.3.7. Thus $F_\rightarrow(P,Q)$ is a preordered set with unique least element $\bot$. The distinguished partial supremum operation on $F_\rightarrow(P,Q)$ is given by

$$\begin{array}{ll} \bot\sqcup x=x & \text{for } x\in ((P\longrightarrow Q))_\bot \\ u\sqcup v=u\cup v & \text{for consistent } u,v\in ((P\longrightarrow Q)). \end{array}$$

Clearly $F_\rightarrow(P,Q)\in\text{Precusl}_\bot$.

It should now be straightforward to define functions on $\mathrm{Precusl}_\perp$ corresponding to other constructions, such as $\oplus$ and $\otimes$, and to verify that they are continuous.

4.7 Lemma The operations F_+, $F_\times$, $F_\rightarrow$, $F_\oplus$, and $F_\otimes$ on $\mathrm{Precusl}_\perp$ are continuous.

Proof: Since the case of the function space is usually the one which is critical we give the proof for $F_\rightarrow$ and leave the proof for the remaining constructions to the reader.

Recall that it suffices to show that $F_\rightarrow$ is continuous in each argument. We use Proposition 4.3 to show that $F_\rightarrow$ is continuous in the first argument, the case for the second argument being similar. That $F_\rightarrow$ is monotone is clear from its definition. Let $\mathcal{F}$ be a directed subset of $\mathrm{Precusl}_\perp$ and let Q be a fixed precusl. By Proposition 4.3 we need to show that if $u \in ((\sqcup\mathcal{F} \rightarrow Q))_\perp$ then for some $P \in \mathcal{F}$, $u \in ((P \rightarrow Q))_\perp$. If $u = \perp$ then this is trivial. So therefore suppose that $u = \{(a_1, b_1), \ldots, (a_n, b_n)\} \in ((P \rightarrow Q))$. Thus $a_i \in \bigcup\mathcal{F}$ and $b_i \in Q$, for $i = 1, \ldots, n$. Using the fact that $\mathcal{F}$ is directed, there is $P \in \mathcal{F}$ such that each $a_i \in P$. But then $u \in ((P \rightarrow Q))_\perp$, since $u \in ((\sqcup\mathcal{F} \rightarrow Q))_\perp$ and $P \leq \sqcup\mathcal{F}$. □

The preceding proof used, as mentioned earlier, the fact that continuity of F follows from the fact that an element of F(P) only depends upon (is constructed from) finitely many elements of P and this dependence is uniform, that is, the way in which F operates on those finitely many elements does not depend upon which argument P we consider.

To conclude that domain equations using the usual constructions can be solved to identity it remains to note that each continuous function on $\mathrm{Precusl}_\perp$ has a least fixed point. A result to this effect is necessary since $\mathrm{Precusl}_\perp$ is a class and not an ordinary cpo.

4.8 Theorem If $F: \mathrm{Precusl}_\perp \rightarrow \mathrm{Precusl}_\perp$ is continuous then F has a least fixed point.

Proof: We mimic the proof of Theorem 1.2.3. Recall that $\{\perp\}$ is the least element in $\mathrm{Precusl}_\perp$. Thus we define recursively

$$\begin{cases} P_0 = \{\perp\} \\ P_{n+1} = F(P_n). \end{cases}$$

Then $P_0 \leq P_1 \leq P_2 \leq \ldots$ is a chain of precusl's which is a *set* and hence $P = \sqcup\{P_n : n \in \mathbb{N}\}$ exists in $\mathrm{Precusl}_\perp$. The usual argument shows that P is the least fixed point of F. □

We have now arrived at the following result about the solution of domain equations.

4.9 Theorem Every domain equation, with parameters from $\mathrm{Precusl}_\perp$, formed using the usual operations such as $+$, $\times$, $\rightarrow$, $\oplus$, and $\otimes$ has a solution to identity in $\mathrm{Precusl}_\perp$.

Proof: By Lemma 4.7, each such equation gives rise to a continuous function $F:\mathrm{Precusl}_\perp \rightarrow \mathrm{Precusl}_\perp$. The least fixed point P of F gives the solution to identity, $P=F(P)$. □

Some remarks are in order. Theorem 4.9 states that each "domain equation" has a least solution *to identity*, that is the equality sign in the equation is interpreted as true (set-theoretic) equality. However, it is important to remember that the solution P is not a domain. It is only a *representation* of a domain. Consider, for example, the domain equation

(*) $\quad D=[D \rightarrow D]$.

What we have shown is that there is a precusl P with unique least element $\perp$ such that $P=F_{\rightarrow}(P)$, that is

$$P=((P \rightarrow P))_\perp.$$

Taking the completions on both sides we obtain

$$\bar{P} \cong [\bar{P} \rightarrow \bar{P}]$$

and, of necessity, we only have an isomorphism. Thus equality is only possible, in general, when we consider *representations* of domains.

A further observation is that the solution to a domain equation obtained in Theorem 4.9 does *not*, in general, correspond to the *least* domain solution obtained in Chapter 4. For example, the equation (*) has the trivial domain as a solution (up to isomorphism) whereas the completion of the precusl solution provided by Theorem 4.9 is infinite as is shown in the following example.

4.10 Example

To see how the first stages of the construction of a precusl solution to the equation $P=F_{\rightarrow}(P)$ develop, let $P_0=\{\perp\}$ and $P_{n+1}=F_{\rightarrow}(P_n)$ as in the proof of Theorem 4.8. Thus

$$P_1=F_{\rightarrow}(\{\perp\})=((\{\perp\} \rightarrow \{\perp\}))_\perp=\{\perp,\{(\perp,\perp)\}\}$$

with $\perp \sqsubseteq \{(\perp,\perp)\}$.

In order to visualize P_2 let $a = \{(\bot,\bot)\} = (\bot,\bot)$. Then P_2 seen as a directed graph is as follows.

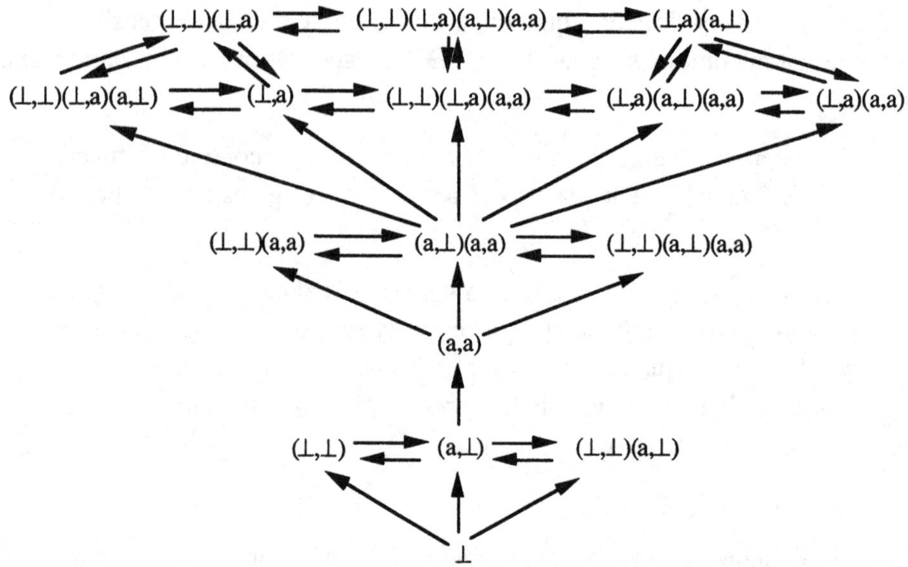

Some of the arrows corresponding to instances of the order relation have been deleted for the sake of readability.

6.5 Exercises

1. Show that **Cusl** is a full subcategory of **Precusl**.

2. Verify that taking the *ideal completion* of a precusl is a functor from **Precusl** to **Domain** and that taking the compact elements of a domain is a functor from **Domain** to **Precusl**.

3. Show that the definition of an information system which includes a *least informative data object* Δ is equivalent to the definition given in Section 6.1 in the sense that the corresponding cusl's are isomorphic.

4. Let A be an information system and define $\vdash$ between elements of Con as in Section 6.1. For $u, v, w \in \mathrm{Con}$, show that:
   (i) $u \vdash v \Rightarrow u \cup v \in \mathrm{Con}$;
   (ii) $u \vdash u$;
   (iii) $u \vdash v$ and $v \vdash w \Rightarrow u \vdash w$;
   (iv) $u' \supseteq u$, $u \vdash v$ and $v \supseteq v' \Rightarrow u' \vdash v'$;
   (v) $u \vdash v$ and $u \vdash v' \Rightarrow u \vdash v \cup v'$.

5. Let D be a domain and let I(D) be defined as in Section 6.1. Show that I(D) is an information system.

6. With D and I(D) as in the previous exercise, show that the *domain of elements* of I(D), that is, $(|I(D)|;\subseteq,\varnothing)$, is isomorphic to D (show that the mappings θ and ϕ given in Section 6.1 form an isomorphism pair).

7. Make as precise as you can the relationship between approximable mappings between information systems and the corresponding continuous functions between domains.

8. Let A and B be information systems and let $\oplus$, $\times$ and $\longrightarrow$ denote the construction principles for information systems described in Section 6.1. Show that $A\oplus B$, $A\times B$ and $A\longrightarrow B$ are also information systems.

9. Prove Theorem 1.11 and complete the proof of Theorem 1.12.

10. Show that the clauses of Definition 2.2 of Section 6.2 imply of the relation $\leq$ that:
(a') $U\leq U$ ($\leq$ is reflexive);
(b') $a\leq b$ (w.r.t. the ordering on P) $\Rightarrow$ $\{a\}\leq\{b\}$;
(c') $U\leq V$ and $V\leq W$ $\Rightarrow$ $U\leq W$ ($\leq$ is transitive); and
(d') $W\leq U$ and $W\leq V$ $\Rightarrow$ $W\leq U\wedge V$ ($\wedge$ between families is an everywhere defined infimum operation).

11. In the notation of Section 6.2, show that:
(i) $[U]\wedge[V]$ is well-defined and is the infimum (w.r.t. $\leq$ on equivalence classes of families of neighbourhoods) of $[U]$ and $[V]$;
(ii) $\bigvee_{i\in I}[U_i]$ is well-defined and is the supremum of $\{[U_i] : i\in I\}$; and
(iii) $\bigvee_{i\in I}([U_i]\wedge[V])=(\bigvee_{i\in I}[U_i])\wedge[V]$.

12. Recall the simple example of a frame: $\mathbf{2}=(\{0,1\},\leq)$ where $0\leq 1$. Show that by viewing $\mathbf{2}$ as the image frame of a frame mapping (that is, by considering all frame mappings $f: A\longrightarrow\mathbf{2}$, where A is a frame) one may give an alternative definition of the *spectrum of points* of a formal space.

13. Verify that the collection of frames forms a category, denoted **Frm**, where frame homomorphisms are taken as morphisms. Show that an isomorphism in **Frm** is just a bijective frame homomorphism.

14. Show that (ii) together with (iii) in Definition 2.7 asserts that a point **m** of a formal space (P, Cov) is closed under finite infima.

15. Given an arbitrary frame A, define a *covering relation* Cov(a, U) (between elements of A and subsets of A) to hold just in case $a \leq \bigvee U$. Use the relation Cov(a, U) to define the *formal space of the frame* A.

16. For $F=(P, Cov)$ a formal space, we denoted by Pt(F) its set of points. For $U \subseteq P$ we defined a topology on Pt(F) given by $\tau = \{U^* : U \subseteq P\}$, where $U^* = \{\mathbf{m} \in Pt(F) : \mathbf{m} \cap U \neq \emptyset\}$. Taking a^* to denote $\{a\}^*$, for $a \in P$, show that $\{a^* : a \in P\}$ is a base for the topology τ.

17. Show that an equivalent definition of a point over a frame A is a subset $\mathbf{m} \subseteq A$ such that:

    $\top \in \mathbf{m}, \ \bot \notin \mathbf{m}$
    $a, b \in \mathbf{m} \Rightarrow a \wedge b \in \mathbf{m}$
    $a \in \mathbf{m}$ and $a < b \Rightarrow b \in \mathbf{m}$; and
    $\bigvee S \in \mathbf{m} \Rightarrow (\exists s \in S)(s \in \mathbf{m})$;

    that is, $\mathbf{m}$ is a *completely prime filter* on A.

18. In Section 6.2 we mentioned three different definitions of the spectrum of points of a formal space (one by viewing it as a frame). Show that these three are equivalent in the sense that the resulting topological spaces are homeomorphic.

19. Let $F=(P, \mathcal{G})$ be the formal space of Example 2.10. Show that $Pt(F) \cong 2^{\omega}$ and that the topology on Pt(F) is the usual topology on the Cantor space (see Example 5.1.4 (iii)).

20. Complete the proof of Theorem 2.13.

21. Let $P=(P; \leq, \wedge)$ be a neighbourhood system and let Cov be any covering relation on P. Let P' denote P with the addition of a greatest element Δ. Show that the formal spaces (P, Cov) and (P', Cov'), where Cov' results from Cov by adding Cov'(a, $\{\Delta\}$) for all $a \in P$, give rise to isomorphic frames. Show also that given a Scott space $F=(P, Cov)$ there is a Scott space $F'=(P', Cov_{\emptyset})$ such that $\Delta \in P'$ is the greatest element and Pt(F) and Pt(F') are isomorphic domains.

22. Let f be an approximable mapping of neighbourhood systems from P_1 to P_2. Let $F_1=(P_1, Cov_{\emptyset})$ and $F_2=(P_2, Cov_{\emptyset})$. Show that the pointwise mapping $\bar{f}$, defined by $\bar{f}(\mathbf{m}) = \{c \in P_2 : a f c, \text{ for some } a \in \mathbf{m}\}$ maps $Pt(F_1)$ into $Pt(F_2)$ and is continuous.

23. Complete the proof of Theorem 3.4.

24. Verify that the operations PC(·) on Scott spaces and Scsp(·) on precusl's take Scott spaces to precusl's and precusl's to Scott spaces, respectively. Show further that they are, in fact, functors between the corresponding categories. Finally, give a complete proof of Theorem 3.5.

25. For $A \in \mathbf{ISys}$, show that id_A is simply the entailment relation of A. Similarly, show that, for $P \in \mathbf{Precusl}$, id_P is the relation on $P \times P$ given by $a\ id_P\ b$ if $b \sqsubseteq a$, and that, for $P = (P; \leq, \wedge, \Delta) \in \mathbf{Scsp}$, id_P is just $\leq$ on P.

26. Complete the proof of Proposition 4.2.

27. Show that the operations F_+ and $F_\times$ on precusl's are continuous mappings from $\mathrm{Precusl}_\perp \times \mathrm{Precusl}_\perp$ to $\mathrm{Precusl}_\perp$, where $\mathrm{Precusl}_\perp$ is the large cpo of Section 6.4. In addition, complete the proof that $F_\rightarrow$ is continuous in both of its arguments.

28. Let P be the solution to the domain equation $P = F_\rightarrow(P)$ discussed at the end of Section 6.4. Show that, for $D = \overline{P}$, we will have that $D \cong [D \longrightarrow D]$. [One way of doing this is to show that the cusl obtained from $F_\rightarrow(P)$ by taking the corresponding quotient is isomorphic to $[D \longrightarrow D]_c$.]

CHAPTER 7

A UNIVERSAL DOMAIN

A universal domain is a countably based domain such that every countably based domain can be embedded into it. We shall define such a universal domain $\mathcal{U}$. Every subdomain D of $\mathcal{U}$ will be assigned a mapping $\mathbf{c}_D$ from $\mathcal{U}$ into $\mathcal{U}$. We shall show that this assignment defines an embedding and that $\mathbf{c}_{D+E}$, $\mathbf{c}_{D\times E}$, and $\mathbf{c}_{[D\to E]}$ can be computed uniformly from $\mathbf{c}_D$ and $\mathbf{c}_E$. The functor **T** in the domain equation

$$(*) \qquad D = \mathbf{T}(D)$$

is then represented by a continuous function $F: \{\mathbf{c}_D\colon D \lhd_c \mathcal{U}\} \to \{\mathbf{c}_D\colon D \lhd_c \mathcal{U}\}$. In doing so we reduce the problem of solving domain equations to finding fixed points of continuous functions from a particular domain into itself, a problem whose solution we have already discussed in Chapter 1.

Further, $[\mathcal{U}\to\mathcal{U}]$ is embeddable into $\mathcal{U}$. By composing this embedding with the above-mentioned embedding of $\{D\colon D \lhd_c \mathcal{U}\}$ into $[\mathcal{U}\to\mathcal{U}]$, we get an embedding e of $\{D\colon D \lhd_c \mathcal{U}\}$ into $\mathcal{U}$, where every subdomain D of $\mathcal{U}$ is assigned an *element* e(D) of $\mathcal{U}$.

This method of solving domain equations is less general than the one described in Chapter 4, since in $\mathcal{U}$ we can only solve domain equations involving countably based domains. But if we are mainly concerned with studying effective domains, or domains which normally appear when doing semantics for programming languages, then this is no real limitation. However, the solution we obtain is just a code for a domain, which has to be decoded in order to obtain the domain itself.

In the first section, we define $\mathcal{U}$, following Scott in his lectures on domain theory, Scott [1982]. Then we show that every countably based domain can be embedded into it. In the second section it is shown that every subdomain D of $\mathcal{U}$ can be represented by a mapping $\mathbf{c}_D$ from $\mathcal{U}$ into $\mathcal{U}$. Then we show how to compute $\mathbf{c}_{D+E}$, $\mathbf{c}_{D\times E}$, and $\mathbf{c}_{[D\to E]}$ uniformly from $\mathbf{c}_D$ and $\mathbf{c}_E$.

Section 7.1 The Universal Domain $\mathcal{U}$

In this section we define the domain $\mathcal{U}$ and show that it is universal. There are several possibilities of defining such a domain; another example of a universal domain is $\wp(\omega)$.

We say that a domain is *countably based* (or *ω-algebraic*) if it has countably many compact elements.

1.1 Definition For $0 \leq r < s \leq 1$, let $[r,s)$ be the half-closed interval of rationals between r and s (including r but not s) and call an interval of this form *right-open*. Let

$$\mathcal{F} = \{I \subseteq [0,1) : I \neq \emptyset \text{ and } I \text{ is a finite union of right-open intervals with rational endpoints}\}.$$

Note that since the union of any two abutting or overlapping right-open intervals is an interval of the same form, any element I in $\mathcal{F}$ is equal to a *disjoint*, non-empty union of intervals. Thus, for some n, $I = \bigcup\{[r_{2i}, r_{2i+1}) : i \leq n\}$, where $0 \leq r_0 < r_1 < \ldots < r_n < \ldots < r_{2n} < r_{2n+1} \leq 1$. We illustrate I graphically as follows.

$\mathcal{F}$ will be the set of compact elements of the universal domain $\mathcal{U}$ to be defined.

In this chapter, we let $c(I)$ denote the complement of $I \in \mathcal{F}$ in $[0,1)$, that is $c(I) = [0,1) - I$.

We begin by stating some simple closure properties of $\mathcal{F}$.

1.2 Proposition

(i) If $I, I' \in \mathcal{F}$, then $I \cup I' \in \mathcal{F}$.

(ii) If $I \in \mathcal{F}$ and $I \neq [0,1)$, then $c(I) \in \mathcal{F}$.

(iii) If $I, I' \in \mathcal{F}$, then $I \cap I' \in \mathcal{F} \Leftrightarrow I \cap I' \neq \emptyset$.

Proof: Exercise 1. □

Next we show that $\mathcal{F}$ is a cusl (conditional upper semilattice with least element) when ordered by reverse inclusion. In fact, $\mathcal{F}$ is clearly a computable cusl (see Chapter 10).

1.3 Proposition $\mathcal{F} = (\mathcal{F}; \supseteq, [0,1))$ is a countable cusl.

Proof: $[0,1)$ is clearly the least element. Using Proposition 1.2, note that for I, $I' \in \mathcal{F}$, I and I' are consistent in $\mathcal{F}$ if and only if $I \cap I' \neq \varnothing$. Thus if $\{I, I'\}$ is consistent in $\mathcal{F}$, then $I \sqcup I' = I \cap I'$. Hence $\mathcal{F}$ is a cusl. $\mathcal{F}$ is countable, since every element I of $\mathcal{F}$ is determined by a finite sequence of rationals (as above) and the set of rationals is countable. □

The reverse inclusion ordering on $\mathcal{F}$ is quite natural, when we think of an element I of $\mathcal{F}$ as specifying the range of values that a number may assume. Then a shorter interval gives better information than a longer one and the best information is a single point. However, such maximal elements do not belong to $\mathcal{F}$ although they are represented by elements of the ideal completion $\bar{\mathcal{F}}$.

One way to prove universality is to consider $\mathcal{F}' = \mathcal{F} \cup \{\varnothing\}$. Then $[0,1)$ is the least element, $\varnothing$ the largest element and for every pair of elements $I, I' \in \mathcal{F}'$, $I \sqcup I' = I \cap I' \in \mathcal{F}'$ and $I \sqcap I' = I \cup I' \in \mathcal{F}'$. So $\mathcal{F}'$ is a lattice. Further, $\mathcal{F}'$ is distributive and, by Proposition 1.2, $\mathcal{F}'$ is complemented. Thus $\mathcal{F}'$ is a Boolean algebra. Also $\mathcal{F}'$ is countable and atomless, by the above. It is well-known that any two countable atomless Boolean algebras are isomorphic and this fact can be used to show that $\mathcal{U}$ is universal (see Exercise 2). Here we give a direct proof of this result, where we can actually *compute* the embedding f of D into $\mathcal{U}$, for any countably based domain D.

1.4 Definition Let $\mathcal{U} = \bar{\mathcal{F}}$, the completion of $\mathcal{F}$ by ideals.

Recall that the elements of $\mathcal{F}$ correspond to principal ideals in $\mathcal{U}$. However, $\mathcal{U}$ will contain many more ideals. In fact $\mathcal{U}$ is uncountable. We may also view $\mathcal{U}$ as containing the elements of $\mathcal{F}$ and, in addition, new elements. For example, if we have a chain of intervals $[r_n, s_n)$ in $\mathcal{F}$ such that $r_0 < r_1 < \ldots < r_n < \ldots < s_n < s_{n-1} < \ldots < s_0$ and the length of the interval $[r_n, s_n)$ approaches 0, as $n \to \infty$, then these intervals determine a single point in $\mathcal{U}$. The picture is as follows.

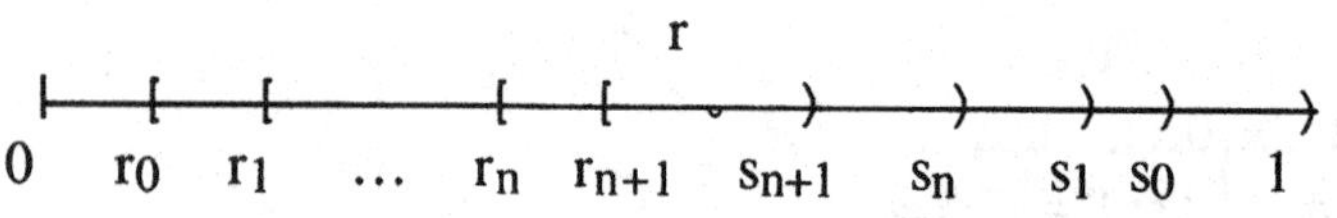

Let $[I_n]$ denote the principal ideal determined by $I_n = [r_n, s_n)$. We have that the set $J = \bigcup\{[I_n] : n < \omega\}$ is an ideal in $\mathcal{U}$, for it is the union of a directed set of ideals. This ideal is not principal and corresponds to the point r in the picture above. In fact, $J = \{I \in \mathcal{F} : r \in I\}$. But of course $\mathcal{U}$ also contains other non-principal ideals than those determined by a single point.

Now we come to our main result.

1.5 Theorem Let $P=(P;\sqsubseteq,\bot)$ be a countable cusl. Then there exists a cusl embedding $f:P\to\mathcal{F}$. Also, if P is computable, then f can be chosen to be a computable function.

Proof: Let $(a_n)_{n<\omega}$ be an enumeration of P with $a_0=\bot$. We define $f(a_n)$ by induction on n. The proof depends heavily on the fact that the rationals are dense. If $a\sqsubset b$, not only do we need that $f(b)\subset f(a)$ but we also need to leave room for $f(d)$ strictly between $f(b)$ and $f(a)$ for any d between a and b occurring later in the enumeration of P. For this purpose, we define the auxiliary function $g:\mathcal{F}\to\mathbb{Q}$ by:

$$g(I)=\text{the leftmost point in } I.$$

Since I is a non-empty finite union of right-open intervals, $g(I)$ is well-defined. Clearly, if $I\subseteq J$, then $g(I)\geq g(J)$. Also $g(\bigcup_{j<m} I_j)=\min\{g(I_j): j<m\}$ and if $\bigcap_{j<m} I_j\neq\varnothing$, then $g(\bigcap_{j<m} I_j)\geq\max\{g(I_j): j<m\}$.

Two elements $a,b\in P$ are *comparable* if $a\sqsubseteq b$ or $b\sqsubseteq a$ and *incomparable* otherwise. For any two elements $a,b\in P$ which are consistent but incomparable, we need to ensure that $f(a)\cap f(b)\neq\varnothing$, $f(a)\not\subseteq f(b)$ and $f(b)\not\subseteq f(a)$. More generally, for any finite consistent set $B\subseteq P$ and any finite set $C\subseteq P$ whose elements are incomparable with $\bigsqcup B$ or strictly above $\bigsqcup B$, we need to arrange matters so that

$$(\bigcap f[B])\cap c(\bigcup f[C])\neq\varnothing.$$

This is the motivation for condition (iv) in the following induction hypothesis, which is the crucial condition in carrying out the construction of the embedding.

We use the notation $\mathrm{Cons}(A)$ to denote that $A\subseteq P$ is a consistent set in P.

For $n<\omega$, let $A_n=\{a_0,a_1,\ldots,a_n\}$. Let $f(a_0)=[0,1)$. Assume inductively that f has been defined on A_n and that f satisfies conditions (i)–(viii) below. For any $B,C\subseteq A_n$ and for any $a,b\in A_n$:

(i) f is monotone, that is, if $a\sqsubseteq b$ then $f(a)\supseteq f(b)$.

(ii) $g(\bigcup f[A_n-\{a_0\}])>0$, for $n>0$.

(iii) $\mathrm{Cons}(B)\Leftrightarrow \bigcap f[B]\neq\varnothing$.

(iv) If $\mathrm{Cons}(B)$ and for every $a\in C$, $a\not\sqsubseteq\bigsqcup B$, then

$$(\bigcap f[B])\cap c(\bigcup f[C])\neq\varnothing \text{ and } g((\bigcap f[B])\cap c(\bigcup f[C]))=g(\bigcap f[B]).$$

(v) If $\mathrm{Cons}(B)$ and $\bigsqcup B\in A_n$, then $f(\bigsqcup B)=\bigcap f[B]$.

(vi) If $\mathrm{Cons}(B)$ and $a\sqsubset\bigsqcup B$, then

$$f(a)\supseteq\bigcap f[B] \text{ and } g(f(a))<g(\bigcap f[B]).$$

(vii) If Cons(B) and $a \sqsupset \sqcup B$, then $g(f(a)) > g(\bigcap f[B])$.
(viii) If Cons(B) and a and $\sqcup B$ are inconsistent, then

$$f(a) \cap (\bigcap f[B]) = \varnothing.$$

Note that the converse of (i) follows from (iv) by letting B and C be one-element sets. Thus f will in fact be order-preserving. Condition (ii) is needed to make room for any element which is inconsistent with all the previous elements in the enumeration. Conditions (vi)–(viii) ensure that we can consistently define $f(\sqcup B)$ by (v).

We shall define $f(a_{n+1})$ and leave it as an exercise to show that f satisfies conditions (i)–(viii) for any $B, C \subseteq A_{n+1}$ and for any $a, b \in A_{n+1}$. Let G be the directed graph of A_n, reflecting the ordering from P. Let B_1 be the set of all the predecessors of a_{n+1} in G. Since $\bot = a_0 \sqsubseteq a_{n+1}$, $B_1 \neq \varnothing$, while B_2–B_4 defined below may be empty. Let B_2 be the set of all the successors of a_{n+1} in G and let B_4 be all the elements in G which are consistent with a_{n+1} but not comparable with a_{n+1}. Finally, let B_3 be all the elements in G which are inconsistent with a_{n+1}. The picture is as follows.

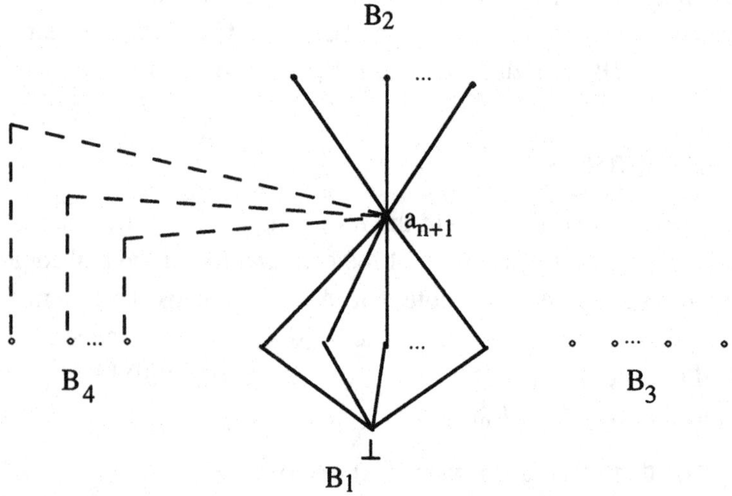

Note that the sets B_i are pairwise disjoint and that $A_{n+1} = \bigcup_{i=1}^{4} B_i \cup \{a_{n+1}\}$.

Let $I_1 = \bigcap f[B_1]$. Then $I_1 \neq \varnothing$ by condition (iii), for B_1 is consistent. In view of (vi), let

$$B_2' = \{\sqcup B : B \subseteq A_n, \text{ Cons}(B) \text{ and } a_{n+1} \sqsubset \sqcup B\}.$$

Then $B_2 \subseteq B_2'$ but B_2' may not be included in A_n. Let

$$I_2 = \bigcup \{\bigcap f[B] : \sqcup B \in B_2'\}.$$

Since A_n is finite, so is B_2'. In fact B_2' has at most 2^{n+1} elements. Thus $I_2 \in \mathcal{F}$, if $B_2' \neq \emptyset$. Also for every $b \in B_1$ and $\sqcup B \in B_2'$, $b \sqsubset \sqcup B$, since $b \sqsubseteq a_{n+1} \sqsubset \sqcup B$. Thus by (vi), $f(b) \supseteq \bigcap f[B]$ and $g(f(b)) < g(\bigcap f[B])$, for each $b \in B_1$, and hence $I_1 \supseteq \bigcap f[B]$. Also for any $\sqcup B \in B_2'$, $g(I_1) < g(\bigcap f[B])$. Thus it follows that $I_2 \subseteq I_1$ and $g(I_2) > g(I_1)$, if $I_2 \neq \emptyset$. So we may define $f(a_{n+1})$ as some subset of I_1 properly containing I_2.

Clearly $a_{n+1} \sqsupseteq \sqcup B_1$. We have two cases, depending on whether or not equality holds.

If $a_{n+1} = \sqcup B_1$, let $f(a_{n+1}) = I_1$.

For the remainder of the proof, we assume that $a_{n+1} \sqsupset \sqcup B_1$. To ensure that conditions (i), (vi) and (vii) will hold we define $f(a_{n+1})$ so that $I_2 \subset f(a_{n+1}) \subset I_1$ and $g(f(a_{n+1})) > g(I_1)$. Let

$$I_3 = \bigcup \{\bigcap f[B]:\ \sqcup B \in B_3\}.$$

We shall make sure that $f(a_{n+1}) \cap I_3 = \emptyset$. Note that $I_3 \in \mathcal{F}$ if $I_3 \neq \emptyset$, for B_3 is finite.

In order to ensure that $g(f(a_{n+1})) > g(I_1)$, we shall use the following function $h: \mathcal{F} \to \mathcal{F}$. For any $I = \bigcup \{[r_{2i}, r_{2i+1}):\ i \leq m\}$, where $0 \leq r_0 < r_1 < \ldots < r_n < \ldots < r_{2n} < r_{2n+1} \leq 1$, let

$$h(I) = \bigcup \{[r_{2i}, r_{2i+1}):\ 1 \leq i \leq m\} \cup [s_0, r_1),$$

where $s_0 = \frac{1}{2}(r_0 + r_1)$, that is, $h(I)$ is obtained from I by omitting the first half of the first interval in I. Clearly $h(I) \subseteq I$ and $g(h(I)) > g(I)$.

Let $\mathcal{A} = \{B \subseteq B_4:\ \mathrm{Cons}(B \cup \{a_{n+1}\})\}$ and let $B \in \mathcal{A}$. Then $\mathrm{Cons}(B \cup B_1)$. Let $C_B = \{a \in B_2 \cup B_4:\ a \not\sqsubseteq \sqcup(B \cup B_1)\}$. Clearly, for any $a \in B_3$, $a \not\sqsubseteq \sqcup(B \cup B_1)$, since $\sqcup(B \cup B_1)$ is consistent with a_{n+1} while a is not. We apply the induction hypothesis (iv) with $B \cup B_1$ and $B_3 \cup C_B$ and get:

$$(\bigcap f[B \cup B_1]) \cap c(\bigcup f[B_3 \cup C_B]) \neq \emptyset, \text{ that is,}$$
$$(\bigcap f[B]) \cap I_1 \cap c(\bigcup f[C_B]) \cap c(I_3) \neq \emptyset.$$

Let $J_B = (\bigcap f[B]) \cap I_1 \cap c(\bigcup f[C_B]) \cap c(I_3)$ and let $I_B = h(J_B)$, for $B \in \mathcal{A}$. Finally let $J = \bigcup \{I_B:\ B \in \mathcal{A}\}$.

Note that $\emptyset \in \mathcal{A}$, $C_\emptyset = B_2 \cup B_4$ and

$$J_\emptyset = I_1 \cap c(\bigcup f[B_2]) \cap c(\bigcup f[B_4]) \cap c(I_3).$$

Thus $\emptyset \neq I_\emptyset \subseteq J$ and so $J \neq \emptyset$ and $J \in \mathcal{F}$.

Now we define $f(a_{n+1})$ by:

$$f(a_{n+1}) = J \cup I_2.$$

In Exercises 3–6 you will be asked to show that f satisfies conditions (i)–(viii).

We have defined f so as to satisfy conditions (i)–(viii). To wrap up the proof, we need only show that f is a cusl embedding. Now $a_0 = \bot_P$ and $f(a_0) = [0,1)$. Further, f is order-preserving by conditions (i) and (iv) as remarked earlier. To show the condition on suprema, let $a_n, a_m \in P$ and assume that $f(a_n) \cap f(a_m) \in \mathcal{F}$, that is, $f(a_n) \cap f(a_m) \neq \varnothing$. By condition (iii), $\{a_n, a_m\}$ is consistent. It follows that $a_n \sqcup a_m \in P$ and, by (v), $f(a_n \sqcup a_m) = f(a_n) \cap f(a_m)$. □

It follows from the proof that the constructed embedding f is uniquely and computably determined from the cusl P and the given enumeration of P. In particular, if P is a computable cusl in the sense of Definition 10.2.1, then f is computable.

1.6 Corollary Every countably based domain is embeddable into $\mathcal{U}$.

Proof: By Corollary 4.5.12 and Theorem 1.5. □

Theorem 1.5 gives an explicit embedding of any countable cusl into $\mathcal{F}$ and hence of any countably based domain into $\mathcal{U}$. However, if we know more about the domain D to be embedded into $\mathcal{U}$, an embedding can be specified more simply as shown in some of the following examples.

1.7 The flat domain $\mathbb{N}_\bot$ Here all elements are compact. We enumerate them as follows: $\bot, 0, 1, 2, \ldots, n, \ldots$. By the theorem we then get:

$$f(\bot) = [0,1),$$
$$f(0) = [\tfrac{1}{2},1),$$
$$f(1) = \left[\tfrac{1}{4}, \tfrac{1}{2}\right),$$
$$\vdots$$
$$f(n) = \left[\frac{1}{2^{n+1}}, \frac{1}{2^n}\right).$$

1.8 $\omega+1$ We consider $\omega+1 = \omega \cup \{\omega\}$. Here $(\omega+1)_c = \omega$ and all elements are comparable. Enumerating ω in the natural way, we get by the theorem:

$$f(0) = [0,1),$$
$$f(n+1) = h(f(n)) = [1 - \tfrac{1}{2^n}, 1),$$

and the values are depicted as follows.

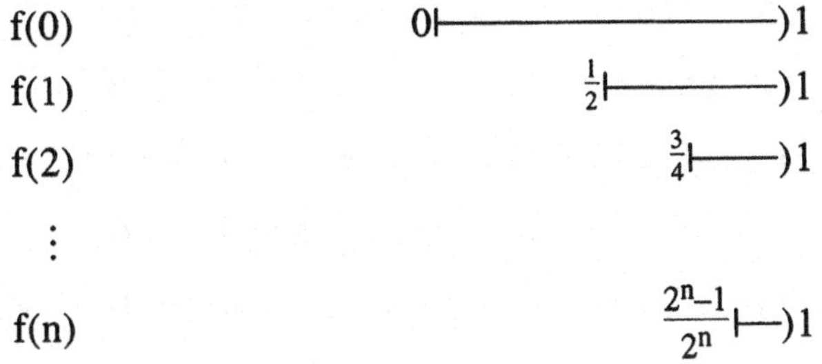

Let $[I_n]$ be the principal ideal determined by the interval $I_n = [1-\frac{1}{2^n}, 1)$. When we extend f to $\omega+1$ we get that

$$f(\omega) = \bigcup\{[I_n]:\ n<\omega\} = \{I \in \mathcal{F}:\ I \supseteq I_n,\ \text{for some}\ n<\omega\},$$

which is not an element of $\mathcal{F}$ or even determined by a point in $[0,1)$. In fact, $f(\omega)$ is determined by the missing right endpoint 1, that is,

$$f(\omega) = \{I \in \mathcal{F}:\ 1\ \text{is the right endpoint of the rightmost interval in}\ I\}.$$

In Exercise 7, you will be asked to show how to get an embedding $f':\omega+1 \to \mathcal{U}$ for which $f'(\omega)$ corresponds to a point in $[0,1)$.

1.9 $\omega\cdot 2+1$ All elements in $\omega\cdot 2+1$ except ω and $\omega\cdot 2$ are compact. We need to arrange them in an ω-sequence, so we fix the following enumeration:

$$0,\ 1,\ \omega+1,\ 2,\ \omega+2,\ \ldots,\ n,\ \omega+n,\ \ldots .$$

By the theorem, we then have

$$f(0) = [0,1),$$
$$f(1) = [\tfrac{1}{2}, 1),$$
$$f(\omega+1) = [\tfrac{3}{4}, 1),$$
$$f(2) = [\tfrac{3}{4}, 1) \cup h(f(1) \cap c(f(\omega+1))) = [\tfrac{3}{4}, 1) \cup \left[\tfrac{5}{8}, \tfrac{3}{4}\right) = [\tfrac{5}{8}, 1),$$
$$f(\omega+2) = h(f(\omega+1)),$$

etc.

Let $I_0 = [\frac{3}{4}, 1)$. We get that for the extended function $f:\omega\cdot 2+1 \to \mathcal{U}$,

$$f(\omega) = \{I \in \mathcal{F}:\ I_0 \subset I\} = [I_0] - \{I_0\}$$

and $f(\omega\cdot 2)$ is determined by 1 in a fashion similar to that of the previous example.

We have the following picture.

f(0)	$0 \vdash\!\!\text{———————})1$
f(1)	$\frac{1}{2}\vdash\!\!\text{————})1$
$f(\omega+1)$	$\frac{3}{4}\vdash\!\!\text{——})1$
f(2)	$\frac{5}{8}\vdash\!\!\text{—})\vdash\!\!\text{——})1$
$f(\omega+2)$	$\frac{7}{8}\vdash\!\!\text{—})1$
$\vdots$	
f(n)	$\vdash\!\!\text{—})\vdash\!\!\text{——})1$
$f(\omega+n)$	$\vdash\!\!\text{—})1$

1.10 Cantor space Here the compact elements are the finite sequences of 0's and 1's. If we enumerate them in order of length and, for sequences of the same length, count 0 as preceding 1, that is, as follows: <>, <0>, <1>, <00>, <01>, <10>, <11>, ... , we get by the theorem:

$f(<>)=[0,1)$	$0\vdash\!\!\text{———————})1$
$f(<0>)=h([0,1))=[\frac{1}{2},1)$	$\frac{1}{2}\vdash\!\!\text{————})1$
$f(<1>)=h([0,\frac{1}{2}))=\left[\frac{1}{4},\frac{1}{2}\right)$	$\frac{1}{4}\vdash\!\!\text{—})\frac{1}{2}\quad 1$
$f(<00>)=h(f(<0>))$	$\frac{3}{4}\vdash\!\!\text{——})1$
$\vdots$	
$f(\sigma*<0>)=h(f(\sigma))$	$\vdash\!\!\text{——})1$
$f(\sigma*<1>)=h(f(\sigma)\cap c(f(\sigma*<0>)))$	$\vdash\!\!\text{—})\quad 1$

Recalling the tree associated with the Cantor space as in 2.1.12, we know that each finite sequence σ has exactly two inconsistent extensions $\sigma*<0>$ and $\sigma*<1>$ at the next level in the tree. Thus we do not need to leave room for other elements inconsistent with $\sigma*<0>$ and $\sigma*<1>$ but we can simply split the interval in half as follows.

Let $f'(<>)=[0,1)$. Assume that $f'(\sigma)$ has been defined for every sequence σ of length n and that $f'(\sigma)$ is a single interval $[r_n, s_n)$. Then put

$$f'(\sigma*<0>)=[r_n,\frac{r_n+s_n}{2}) \qquad (=f'(\sigma)-h(f'(\sigma)))$$

$$f'(\sigma*<1>)=[\frac{r_n+s_n}{2},s_n) \qquad (=h(f'(\sigma))).$$

So we get:

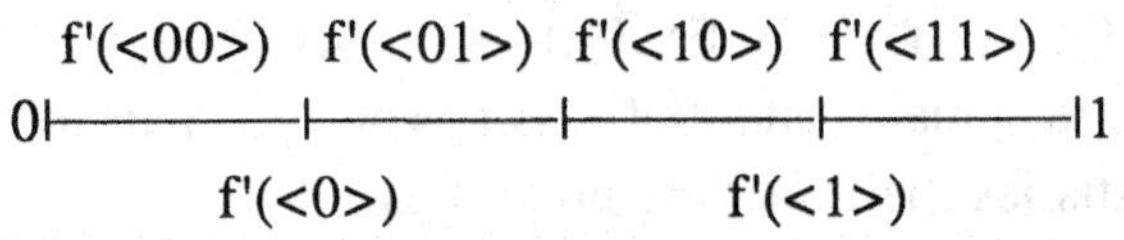

Note that ω-branches in the binary Cantor tree correspond to nested intervals, whose lengths approach 0 as $n \to \infty$, and thus an element of 2^ω is mapped by the extension of f' to the real determined by the intersection of the corresponding intervals.

1.11 $\wp(\omega)$ It is a fact that $\wp(\omega) = (\wp(\omega); \subseteq, \varnothing)$ (defined in Example 3.1.2) is another universal domain and $\wp(\omega)_c = \{A : A \subseteq \omega, A \text{ finite}\}$. Here we show how to embed $\wp(\omega)$ into $\mathcal{U}$. Now, for any $A \in \wp(\omega) - \{\varnothing\}$, $A = \bigcup_{a \in A} \{a\} = \bigsqcup_{a \in A} \{a\}$. Hence it is enough to define f on $\varnothing$ and on one-element sets and then we just put $f(A) = \bigcap_{a \in A} f(a)$, that is, for all other sets A the first case in the proof of Theorem 1.5 above applies.

Let $f(\varnothing) = [0,1)$, $f(\{0\}) = h(f(\varnothing))$, and let $A_n = \{\{0\}, \{1\}, \ldots, \{n\}\}$, for $n \in \mathbb{N}$. Note that $\{0\}, \{1\}, \ldots, \{n\}$ are all consistent and incomparable. In fact they are atoms of the Boolean algebra $\wp(\omega)$. Assume that f has been defined on A_n and that, for each $B \subseteq A_n$,

(∗) $$K_B = (\bigcap f[B]) \cap c(\bigcup f[A_n - B]) \neq \varnothing.$$

Then we define $f(\{n+1\})$ recursively by:

$$f(\{n+1\}) = \bigcup \{h(K_B) : B \subseteq A_n\}.$$

Then clearly f satisfies (∗) for A_{n+1}. The first few values of f are depicted below.

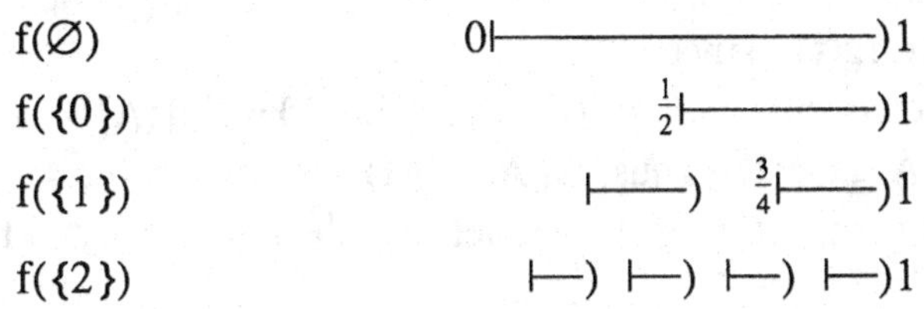

Section 7.2 Finitary Projections and Subdomains

In this section we show how to associate subdomains of a domain E with mappings from E to E in a one-one fashion.

For $f: E \to E$, let $\mathrm{Fix}(f) = \{x \in E: f(x) = x\}$. First note, by Exercise 4.7.25, that if D and E are domains and (f, f^{-}) is a projection pair for (D,E), then $f = f \circ f^{-}: E \to E$ satisfies the following properties:

(i) $f \circ f = f$
(ii) $f \sqsubseteq id_E$
(iii) rg(f) is a domain.

Below we show that if a continuous function $f: E \to E$ has these properties, then $rg(f) \triangleleft_c E$.

2.1 Definition

(a) A *retract* on a domain E is a continuous function $f: E \to E$ such that $f \circ f = f$.

(b) A retract f on a domain E is a *projection* if $f \sqsubseteq id_E$.

(c) A projection f on a domain E is *finitary* if rg(f) is a domain.

2.2 Lemma Let E be a domain. A continuous function $f: E \to E$ is a retract if and only if $rg(f) = \mathrm{Fix}(f)$.

Proof: If f is a retract, then $rg(f) \subseteq \mathrm{Fix}(f)$. Trivially $\mathrm{Fix}(f) \subseteq rg(f)$ and thus $rg(f) = \mathrm{Fix}(f)$. For the converse, assume that $rg(f) = \mathrm{Fix}(f)$ and let $y \in E$. Then $f(y) \in \mathrm{Fix}(f)$ and hence $f \circ f(y) = f(y)$. It follows that $f \circ f = f$. □

2.3 Proposition Let E be a domain. Then a projection f on E is finitary if and only if $rg(f) \triangleleft_c E$.

Proof: If f is a projection on E, then $rg(f) = \mathrm{Fix}(f)$, by Lemma 2.2. Now assume that f is finitary. Since rg(f) is a domain, it suffices to verify clauses (i)–(iv) of Definition 4.5.1.

(i) First $\bot = f(\bot) \in rg(f)$, since $f \sqsubseteq id_E$.

(ii) If A is a directed subset of rg(f), then $f(\bigsqcup_E A) = \bigsqcup_E f[A] = \bigsqcup_E A$, since f is continuous and $A \subseteq \mathrm{Fix}(f)$. Thus $\bigsqcup_E A \in rg(f)$.

(iii) Suppose x is compact in rg(f) and let $x \sqsubseteq \bigsqcup_E A$, where $A \subseteq E$ is directed. Then

$$x = f(x) \sqsubseteq f(\bigsqcup_E A) = \bigsqcup_E f[A].$$

Now $f[A] \subseteq rg(f)$ and $\bigsqcup_E f[A] \in rg(f)$ by (ii) and thus $x \sqsubseteq f(y)$, for some $y \in A$. Since $f \sqsubseteq id_E$, we have that $f(y) \sqsubseteq y$. So $x \sqsubseteq y$, for some $y \in A$, and hence x is compact in E.

(iv) Let a and b be compact elements in rg(f) and assume that $\{a, b\}$ is consistent in E. Then $a \sqcup b \in E$ and

$$a \sqcup b = f(a) \sqcup f(b) \sqsubseteq f(a \sqcup b) \sqsubseteq a \sqcup b$$

and so $f(a \sqcup b) = a \sqcup b$.

We have shown that if f is a finitary projection on E, then $rg(f) \lhd_c E$. The converse implication is trivial, since f is a projection. □

We also note that the domain $rg(f)$ associated with a finitary projection f is uniquely determined by it.

2.4 Lemma Let f and g be finitary projections on a domain E. Then

$$f \sqsubseteq g \text{ if and only if } rg(f) \lhd_c rg(g).$$

Proof: By Lemma 2.2, $rg(f) = Fix(f)$ and $rg(g) = Fix(g)$. Assume that $f \sqsubseteq g$. By the proof of Lemma 4.5.4, to show that $rg(f) \lhd_c rg(g)$, it is sufficient to show that $rg(f) \subseteq rg(g)$. If $x \in rg(f) = Fix(f)$, then $x = f(x) \sqsubseteq g(x) \sqsubseteq x$, and hence $g(x) = x$, that is, $x \in rg(g)$.

For the converse implication, assume that $rg(f) \lhd_c rg(g)$. For $x \in E$, we have that $f(x) \in rg(f) \subseteq rg(g) = Fix(g)$. Thus $g(f(x)) = f(x)$. Since $f(x) \sqsubseteq x$, it follows that $f(x) = g(f(x)) \sqsubseteq g(x)$, and so $f \sqsubseteq g$. □

Next we introduce a function sub_E from $\mathcal{S}_c(E) = \{D : D \lhd_c E\}$ into $[E \to E]$, for any domain E. For $D \in \mathcal{S}_c(E)$, let $(f_D, \mathfrak{f}_D)$ be the projection pair defined in the text following Corollary 4.5.13, that is as follows:

$$\begin{cases} f_D(x) = x & \text{for } x \in D \\ \mathfrak{f}_D(y) = \bigsqcup(approx_E(y) \cap D) & \text{for } y \in E. \end{cases}$$

2.5 Definition Let E be a domain. Define a function $sub_E : \mathcal{S}_c(E) \to [E \to E]$ by $sub_E(D) = f_D \circ \mathfrak{f}_D$.

By Exercise 4.7.25 and the above, $sub_E(D)$ is a finitary projection on E and $rg(sub_E(D)) = D$. It turns out that $sub_E(D)$ can be easily computed from D.

2.6 Lemma If D is a subdomain of E, then $sub_E(D) = \bigsqcup\{<a; a> : a \in D_c\}$.

Proof: Each $<a; a>$ for $a \in D_c$ is compact in $[E \to E]$, since $D_c \subseteq E_c$. Furthermore, $<a; a> \sqsubseteq id_E$ so that the set $\{<a; a> : a \in D_c\}$ is consistent and hence has a supremum in $[E \to E]$. For $y \in E$, we have

$$\begin{aligned} sub_E(D)(y) &= \bigsqcup(approx(y) \cap D) \\ &= \bigsqcup\{a \in D_c : a \sqsubseteq y\} \\ &= \bigsqcup\{<a; a>(y) : a \in D_c\} \\ &= (\bigsqcup\{<a; a> : a \in D_c\})(y). \end{aligned}$$ □

2.7 Lemma $\mathrm{sub}_E: \mathcal{S}_c(E) \to [E \to E]$ is an embedding.

Proof: It suffices by Proposition 4.5.11 to show that when sub_E is restricted to $\mathcal{S}_c(E)_c$, then its values are compact in $[E \to E]$ and that the restriction is a cusl embedding. Recall that the compact elements in $\mathcal{S}_c(E)$ are the finite subdomains of E. Furthermore, if D is compact in $\mathcal{S}_c(E)$, then $D_c = D$ by virtue of being finite and hence $D \subseteq E_c$, since $D \triangleleft_c E$. Thus $\mathrm{sub}_E(D) = \bigsqcup\{\langle a; a\rangle : a \in D\}$ is compact in $[E \to E]$, that is sub_E sends compact elements to compact elements.

By Lemma 2.6, $\mathrm{sub}_E(\{\bot\}) = \langle\bot; \bot\rangle = \bot_{[E\to E]}$, so (i) of Definition 4.1.4 holds. If $D \subseteq D'$ are finite subdomains of E, then

$$\mathrm{sub}_E(D) = \bigsqcup\{\langle a; a\rangle : a \in D\} \sqsubseteq \bigsqcup\{\langle a; a\rangle : a \in D'\} = \mathrm{sub}_E(D').$$

Conversely, assume that $\mathrm{sub}_E(D) \sqsubseteq \mathrm{sub}_E(D')$ and let $a \in D$. Then

$$a = \mathrm{sub}_E(D)(a) \sqsubseteq \mathrm{sub}_E(D')(a) \sqsubseteq a.$$

Thus $a = \mathrm{sub}_E(D')(a)$ and so $a \in D'$ which proves that $D \subseteq D'$. Hence sub_E is order preserving.

To prove that sub_E preserves suprema of compact elements, let D and D' be finite subdomains of E. Recall from the proof of Theorem 4.5.5 that D and D' are consistent and that $D \sqcup D' = F$, where

$$F = \{a \sqcup b : a \in D,\ b \in D' \text{ and } \{a, b\} \text{ consistent in } E\}.$$

By Lemma 2.6,

$$\mathrm{sub}_E(F) = \bigsqcup\{\langle a \sqcup b; a \sqcup b\rangle : a \in D,\ b \in D' \text{ and } \{a, b\} \text{ consistent in } E\}.$$

Thus clearly $\mathrm{sub}_E(D) \sqsubseteq \mathrm{sub}_E(F)$ and $\mathrm{sub}_E(D') \sqsubseteq \mathrm{sub}_E(F)$ and so we have that $\mathrm{sub}_E(D) \sqcup \mathrm{sub}_E(D') \sqsubseteq \mathrm{sub}_E(F)$. For the converse inequality, consider $a \sqcup b \in F$. Then for any $x \sqsupseteq a \sqcup b$, we have that $\mathrm{sub}_E(D)(x) \sqsupseteq a$ and $\mathrm{sub}_E(D')(x) \sqsupseteq b$ and thus

$$(\mathrm{sub}_E(D) \sqcup \mathrm{sub}_E(D'))(x) \sqsupseteq a \sqcup b.$$

It follows that for any x,

$$(\mathrm{sub}_E(D) \sqcup \mathrm{sub}_E(D'))(x) \sqsupseteq \bigsqcup\{a \sqcup b \in F : a \sqcup b \sqsubseteq x\} = \mathrm{sub}_E(F)(x). \qquad \square$$

We can also define a finitary projection SUB_E on $[E \to E]$ with the same range as sub_E. In other words, SUB_E singles out exactly those mappings that correspond to subdomains of E. (See Exercise 13.)

From the proof of Theorem 1.5, we see that the constructed cusl embedding $f: P \to \mathcal{F}$ is uniquely determined from an enumeration of P. Fix an enumeration

$\pi=(a_i)_{i<\omega}$ with $a_0=\bot$ of $\mathcal{U}_c$ and let π_+, $\pi_\times$, and $\pi_\to$ be the following enumerations of $(\mathcal{U}+\mathcal{U})_c$, $(\mathcal{U}\times\mathcal{U})_c$, and a subbase for $[\mathcal{U}\to\mathcal{U}]_c$, respectively:

$$\pi_+:\ \bot,\ (0,a_0),\ (1,a_0),\ \dots,\ (0,a_n),\ (1,a_n),\ \dots$$

$$\pi_\times:\ (a_0,a_0),\ (a_0,a_1),\ (a_1,a_0),\ \dots,\ (a_0,a_n),\ (a_1,a_{n-1}),\ \dots,\ (a_n,a_0),\ \dots$$

$$\pi_\to:\ \langle a_0;a_0\rangle,\ \langle a_0;a_1\rangle,\ \langle a_1;a_0\rangle,\ \dots,\ \langle a_0;a_n\rangle,\ \langle a_1;a_{n-1}\rangle,\ \dots,\ \langle a_n;a_0\rangle,\ \dots$$

Let $f_+:(\mathcal{U}+\mathcal{U})_c\to\mathcal{F}$ and $f_\times:(\mathcal{U}\times\mathcal{U})_c\to\mathcal{F}$ be the cusl embeddings uniquely determined by π_+ and $\pi_\times$, respectively. The embedding $f_\to:[\mathcal{U}\to\mathcal{U}]_c\to\mathcal{F}$ is uniquely determined by $\pi_\to$, since the remaining elements of $[\mathcal{U}\to\mathcal{U}]_c$ are suprema of elements from the subbase, and thus they are mapped by $f_\to$ to the supremum of the images of those elements.

Let (f_+,f_+^-), $(f_\times,f_\times^-)$, and $(f_\to,f_\to^-)$ be the projection pairs for $(\mathcal{U}+\mathcal{U},\mathcal{U})$, $(\mathcal{U}\times\mathcal{U},\mathcal{U})$, and $([\mathcal{U}\to\mathcal{U}],\mathcal{U})$ uniquely determined by the cusl embeddings f_+, $f_\times$, and $f_\to$, respectively.

By the above, every subdomain D of $\mathcal{U}$ can be represented by a finitary projection from $\mathcal{U}$ into $\mathcal{U}$, in fact by $sub_\mathcal{U}(D)$. For $D\triangleleft_c\mathcal{U}$, let

$$\mathbf{c}_D=sub_\mathcal{U}(D).$$

Next, for subdomains D, E of $\mathcal{U}$, we will define finitary projections $\mathbf{c}_{D+E}$, $\mathbf{c}_{D\times E}$, and $\mathbf{c}_{[D\to E]}$ from $\mathcal{U}$ into $\mathcal{U}$ in such a way that

$$rg(\mathbf{c}_{D+E})\cong D+E \text{ and } rg(\mathbf{c}_{D+E})\triangleleft_c\mathcal{U}$$

$$rg(\mathbf{c}_{D\times E})\cong D\times E \text{ and } rg(\mathbf{c}_{D\times E})\triangleleft_c\mathcal{U}$$

$$rg(\mathbf{c}_{[D\to E]})\cong[D\to E] \text{ and } rg(\mathbf{c}_{[D\to E]})\triangleleft_c\mathcal{U}.$$

It will follow from the work in Section 7.1 that $\mathbf{c}_{D+E}$, $\mathbf{c}_{D\times E}$, and $\mathbf{c}_{[D\to E]}$ can be computed uniformly from $\mathbf{c}_D$ and $\mathbf{c}_E$.

2.8 Definition

$$\mathbf{c}_{D+E}=f_+\circ sub_{\mathcal{U}+\mathcal{U}}(rg(\mathbf{c}_D)+rg(\mathbf{c}_E))\circ f_+^-$$

$$\mathbf{c}_{D\times E}=f_\times\circ sub_{\mathcal{U}\times\mathcal{U}}(rg(\mathbf{c}_D)\times rg(\mathbf{c}_E))\circ f_\times^-$$

$$\mathbf{c}_{[D\to E]}=f_\to\circ sub_{[\mathcal{U}\to\mathcal{U}]}(j[[rg(\mathbf{c}_D)\to rg(\mathbf{c}_E)]])\circ f_\to^-,$$

where j is the unique continuous function that lifts a compact element $\bigsqcup_{i=1}^{n}\langle a_i;b_i\rangle$ in $[D\to E]$ with $a_i\in D_c\subseteq\mathcal{U}$ and $b_i\in E_c\subseteq\mathcal{U}$ to the function $\bigsqcup_{i=1}^{n}\langle a_i;b_i\rangle$ in $[\mathcal{U}\to\mathcal{U}]$ that corresponds to it.

Finally, to every subdomain D of $\mathcal{U}$, we assign an *element* of $\mathcal{U}$ by

$$e(D)=f_\to(sub_\mathcal{U}(D)).$$

Then $e(D)$ is an element of $\mathcal{U}$ and $D \subseteq E \Leftrightarrow e(D) \sqsubseteq e(E)$.

2.9 Proposition $\mathbf{c}_{D+E}$, $\mathbf{c}_{D\times E}$, and $\mathbf{c}_{[D\to E]}$ are finitary projections from $\mathcal{U}$ into $\mathcal{U}$.

Proof: Since $\mathbf{c}_{D+E}$, $\mathbf{c}_{D\times E}$, and $\mathbf{c}_{[D\to E]}$ are composed of continuous functions, they are all continuous. To show that the functions are finitary projections, let $F = rg(\mathbf{c}_D) + rg(\mathbf{c}_E)$. Then

$$\begin{aligned}\mathbf{c}_{D+E} \circ \mathbf{c}_{D+E} &= f_+ \circ sub_{\mathcal{U}+\mathcal{U}}(F) \circ f_+^- \circ f_+ \circ sub_{\mathcal{U}+\mathcal{U}}(F) \circ f_+^- \\ &= f_+ \circ sub_{\mathcal{U}+\mathcal{U}}(F) \circ sub_{\mathcal{U}+\mathcal{U}}(F) \circ f_+^- \\ &= f_+ \circ sub_{\mathcal{U}+\mathcal{U}}(F) \circ f_+^- \\ &= \mathbf{c}_{D+E} \sqsubseteq id_{\mathcal{U}},\end{aligned}$$

since $sub_{\mathcal{U}+\mathcal{U}}(F)$ is a projection. The proof that $\mathbf{c}_{D\times E}$ and $\mathbf{c}_{[D\to E]}$ are projections is similar.

It remains to show that the projections are finitary. First we show that $rg(f_+|_F) = Fix(\mathbf{c}_{D+E})$. For $y \in F$,

$$y = sub_{\mathcal{U}+\mathcal{U}}(F)(y) = sub_{\mathcal{U}+\mathcal{U}}(F) \circ f_+^- \circ f_+(y).$$

It follows that

$$f_+(y) = f_+ \circ sub_{\mathcal{U}+\mathcal{U}}(F) \circ f_+^-(f_+(y)) = \mathbf{c}_{D+E}(f_+(y)),$$

that is, $f_+(y) \in Fix(\mathbf{c}_{D+E})$.

Conversely, for $x \in Fix(\mathbf{c}_{D+E})$,

$$x = \mathbf{c}_{D+E}(x) = f_+ \circ sub_{\mathcal{U}+\mathcal{U}}(F) \circ f_+^-(x) \in rg(f_+|_F).$$

Since f_+ is order-preserving, it follows that $Fix(\mathbf{c}_{D+E}) \cong F = D+E$. Thus $\mathbf{c}_{D+E}$ is finitary, for $rg(\mathbf{c}_{D+E}) = Fix(\mathbf{c}_{D+E})$.

The proof that $rg(\mathbf{c}_{D\times E}) \cong D\times E$ and $rg(\mathbf{c}_{[D\to E]}) \cong [D\to E]$ is similar. □

The set $rg(sub_{\mathcal{U}})$ consists of all finitary projections on $\mathcal{U}$. We denote this set by FIN. By Exercise 13, there is a finitary projection $SUB_{\mathcal{U}}$ on $[\mathcal{U}\to\mathcal{U}]$ with the same range as $sub_{\mathcal{U}}$. Thus $FIN = rg(sub_{\mathcal{U}}) = rg(SUB_{\mathcal{U}})$ is a domain.

2.10 Proposition The functions $F_+ : FIN \times FIN \to FIN$, $F_\times : FIN \times FIN \to FIN$, and $F_\to : FIN \times FIN \to FIN$ defined by $F_+(\mathbf{c}_D, \mathbf{c}_E) = \mathbf{c}_{D+E}$, $F_\times(\mathbf{c}_D, \mathbf{c}_E) = \mathbf{c}_{D\times E}$, and $F_\to(\mathbf{c}_D, \mathbf{c}_E) = \mathbf{c}_{[D\to E]}$ are continuous.

Proof: By Proposition 2.2.4, it is enough to show that the functions are continuous in each argument. The continuity follows from the fact that all the functions appearing in the definition of $\mathbf{c}_{D+E}$, $\mathbf{c}_{D\times E}$, and $\mathbf{c}_{[D\to E]}$, respectively, are continuous. □

By the results in this section, we can solve any domain equation $D=T(D)$, where T is a function on FIN obtainable by composition of continuous functions. For example, let us consider the domain equations

(1) $$D = E + (D \times D)$$

(2) $$D = E + [D \to D].$$

To solve (1), we look for a finitary projection $g:\mathcal{U}\to\mathcal{U}$ such that

(*) $$g=\mathbf{c}_{E+(rg(g)\times rg(g))}.$$

The function $F:FIN\to FIN$ defined by

$$F(g)=F_{+}(\mathbf{c}_{E}, F_{\times}(g,g))$$

is continuous by Proposition 2.10 and hence F has a least fixed point g which is a solution to (*). Then rg(g) is a domain, since g is finitary. By the proof of Proposition 2.9, it follows that

$$rg(g)=rg(\mathbf{c}_{E+(rg(g)\times rg(g))})\cong E+(rg(g)\times rg(g)).$$

Equation (2) is solved in a similar way.

7.3 Exercises

1. Prove Proposition 1.2.

2. Consider $\mathcal{F}'=\mathcal{F}\cup\{\varnothing\}$. Show that the following holds.
   (a) $\mathcal{F}'$ is a distributive lattice.
   (b) $\mathcal{F}'$ is a Boolean algebra.
   (c) Any two countable atomless Boolean algebras are isomorphic.
   (d) $\mathcal{U}$ is universal.

For Exercises 3–6 we use the notation introduced in the proof of Theorem 1.5.

3. Let $a_{n+1}=\sqcup B_1$.
   (a) Show that for any subset B of A_{n+1} there is a $B'\subseteq A_n$ such that $Cons(B) \Leftrightarrow Cons(B')$ and, if both B and B' are consistent, then $\sqcup B=\sqcup B'$.

(b) Show that f satisfies conditions (i)–(viii) for any $B, C \subseteq A_{n+1}$ and for any $a, b \in A_{n+1}$.

For Exercises 4–6, let $a_{n+1} \sqsupset \sqcup B_1$. We split the proof that f satisfies conditions (i)–(viii) for any $B, C \subseteq A_{n+1}$ and for any $a, b \in A_{n+1}$ as follows.

4. Let $B_3' = \{\sqcup B:\ B \subseteq A_n,\ \mathrm{Cons}(B)$ and a_{n+1} and $\sqcup B$ are inconsistent$\}$ and let $I_3' = \bigcup\{\bigcap f[B]:\ \sqcup B \in B_3'\}$. Show that the following holds.
   (a) f satisfies conditions (i)–(ii).
   (b) For any $D \in \mathcal{A}$, $I_3' \subseteq I_3 \cup (\bigcup f[C_D])$.
   (c) $f(a_{n+1}) \cap I_3' = \varnothing$.
   (d) f satisfies condition (iii).

5. For any consistent set B, show that the following holds.
   (a) For any $B' \in \mathcal{A}$: $(\bigcap f[B]) \cap J_{B'} \neq \varnothing$ if and only if $\sqcup B \sqsubseteq \sqcup(B' \cup B_1)$, and if $\sqcup B \sqsubseteq \sqcup(B' \cup B_1)$, then $J_{B'} \subseteq \bigcap f[B]$.
   (b) $$(\textstyle\bigcap f[B]) \cap f(a_{n+1}) = \bigcup\{I_{B'}:\ \sqcup B \sqsubseteq \sqcup(B' \cup B_1),\ B' \in \mathcal{A}\} \cup (\bigcup\{\bigcap f[B' \cup B]:\ \sqcup B' \in B_2',\ \mathrm{Cons}(B' \cup B)\}).$$
   (c) $(\bigcap f[B]) \cap (\bigcap\{c(I_{B'}):\ B' \in \mathcal{A}\}) \neq \varnothing$ and $$g((\textstyle\bigcap f[B]) \cap (\bigcap\{c(I_{B'}):\ B' \in \mathcal{A}\})) = g(\bigcap f[B]).$$
   (d) If $a_{n+1} \not\sqsubseteq \sqcup B$, then $(\bigcap f[B]) \cap c(f(a_{n+1})) \neq \varnothing$ and $$g((\textstyle\bigcap f[B]) \cap c(f(a_{n+1}))) = g(\bigcap f[B]).$$

6. Show that f satisfies conditions (iv)–(viii).

7. Define $h': \mathcal{F} \to \mathcal{F}$ as follows. For any $I = \bigcup\{[r_{2i}, r_{2i+1}):\ i \leq m\}$, $h'(I) = \bigcup\{[r_{2i}, r_{2i+1}):\ i < m\} \cup [r_{2m}, t_0)$, where $t_0 = \frac{1}{2}(r_{2m} + r_{2m+1})$, that is, $h'(I)$ is obtained from I by omitting the last half of the last interval in I. Show how to use h' to get an embedding $f': \omega+1 \to \mathcal{U}$ for which $f'(\omega)$ corresponds to a point in $[0,1)$. (Cf. Example 1.8.)

8. Give an explicit embedding of $\mathbf{N}_\perp \times \mathbf{N}_\perp$ into $\mathcal{U}$.

9. Give an explicit embedding of $[\mathbf{N}_\perp \to \mathbf{N}_\perp]$ into $\mathcal{U}$.

10. Give an example of a domain E and a continuous function $f: E \to E$ such that $\mathrm{rg}(f) = \mathrm{Fix}(f)$ but where f is not a projection.

11. Give an example of a projection that is not finitary.

12. Show that the function sub_E is not surjective in general.

13. Let the function $SUB_E : [E \to E] \to [E \to E]$ be the unique continuous extension of the function defined by:

$$SUB_E(\langle a; b \rangle) = \bigsqcup \{\langle d; d \rangle : a \sqsubseteq d \sqsubseteq b\}.$$

 (a) Show that $SUB_E : [E \to E] \to [E \to E]$ is a projection.

 (b) Show that $SUB_E[[E \to E]_c] = sub_E[\mathcal{S}_c(E)_c]$.

 (c) Show that $SUB_E : [E \to E] \to [E \to E]$ is a finitary projection.

14. Give an example of an enumeration $\pi = (a_i)_{i<\omega}$ of $\mathcal{U}_c$.

15. Show how to define $\mathbf{c}_{D \oplus E}$, $\mathbf{c}_{D \otimes E}$, and $\mathbf{c}_{[D \to_\perp E]}$ corresponding to the smash sum, smash product and strict function space constructions, respectively.

PART II

SPECIAL TOPICS

CHAPTER 8

REPRESENTABILITY IN DOMAINS

In this chapter we investigate some ways domains can be used in order to study other mathematical structures of interest. In Sections 8.1 and 8.2 we consider ultrametric spaces and algebras and show how these can be topologically embedded into domains in a simple way. In Section 8.3 we consider the problem of abstracting the "total" elements of a domain from the partial ones. Then, in Section 8.4, this is used to show how the Kleene–Kreisel continuous functionals are represented in the partial continuous functionals.

Section 8.1 Metric and Ultrametric Spaces

In a general topological space, open sets are used to separate points or sets of points from each other. In many concrete spaces of interest one can do much more in that there is a natural function or metric which to each pair of points assigns a distance between the points, a non-negative real number. It was Fréchet [1906] who abstracted the properties needed from natural metrics on concrete spaces, such as the Euclidean spaces, in order to develop an abstract theory of metric spaces. Chronologically, the theory of metric spaces preceded the general theory of topological spaces introduced by Hausdorff, so that the abstraction to metric spaces was a first important step in obtaining general topological spaces. On the other hand, the metric spaces form an important subclass of the topological spaces.

Metric spaces have been used with success by several authors in order to give semantics for certain programming language constructs. Some of the first references are de Bakker and Zucker [1982], Nivat [1975] and Arnold and Nivat [1980].

In this section we introduce metric spaces and discuss completions and fixed points. Of particular interest to us are the ultrametric spaces, which form a proper subclass of the metric spaces, since these are simpler and often sufficient for program semantics. In the next section it is shown that each ultrametric space can be topologically embedded into a domain, so that domain theory may be used to study them.

1.1 Definition Let $X \neq \emptyset$ be a set. A function $d: X \times X \longrightarrow \mathbb{R}$ is a *metric* on X if for each $x, y, z \in X$,

(i) $d(x,y) \geq 0$,

(ii) $d(x,y) = 0 \Leftrightarrow x = y$,

(iii) $d(x,y) = d(y,x)$, and

(iv) $d(x,y) \leq d(x,z) + d(z,y)$ (the triangle inequality).

A pair (X,d), where X is a non-empty set and d is a metric on X, is said to be a *metric space.* As usual we refer to the metric space X when the metric is understood. Each metric on X generates a topology via the topological base of all open "balls" or "spheres"

$$B(x;r) = \{y \in X : d(x,y) < r\}$$

for $x \in X$ and $r \in \mathbb{R}$. Actually it suffices to take $r \in \mathbb{Q}$ since $\mathbb{Q}$ is dense in $\mathbb{R}$. It is routine to verify that these sets do form a topological base and that a function between metric spaces is continuous in the usual ε-δ sense if and only if it is continuous with respect to the topologies induced by the metrics. Clearly, the metric inherited by a subset of a metric space induces the subspace topology. It is also easy to see that metric spaces have strong separation properties. Each metric space is normal, in fact a T_4-space.

1.2 Examples

(i) The real line $\mathbb{R}$ with the distance function $d(x,y) = |x-y|$ is a metric space. More generally, the usual metrics for the Euclidean spaces $\mathbb{R}^n$ are given by

$$d((x_1, \ldots, x_n), (y_1, \ldots, y_n)) = \sqrt{\sum_{i=1}^{n} (x_i - y_i)^2}\,.$$

(ii) Let X be a non-empty set and define a distance function d on X by

$$d(x,y) = \begin{cases} 0 & \text{if } x = y \\ 1 & \text{if } x \neq y. \end{cases}$$

This is a metric called the *discrete metric.* Note that it induces the discrete topology on X. Can one define a metric generating the trivial topology?

(iii) Let (X,d) be a metric space. Then define a new distance function d' by

$$d'(x,y) = \begin{cases} d(x,y) & \text{if } d(x,y) \leq 1 \\ 1 & \text{if } d(x,y) > 1. \end{cases}$$

Clearly d' is a metric on X. Furthermore the metrics d and d' induce the same topology on X. But d' is a *bounded* metric, that is the distance between any two points is less than a fixed number, while d may not be (e.g. the usual metric on

$\mathbb{R}$). Thus (X,d) and (X,d') are homeomorphic topological spaces but they need not be equivalent as metric spaces.

(iv) Consider the Cantor space in the form $2^\omega = \{f \mid f:\omega \to \{0,1\}\}$ or the Baire space $\omega^\omega = \{f \mid f:\omega \to \omega\}$ and define a distance function d by

$$d(f,g) = \begin{cases} 0 & \text{if } f = g \\ 2^{-n} & \text{if } f \neq g, \text{ where } n \text{ is least s.t. } f(n) \neq g(n). \end{cases}$$

It is easily verified that d is a metric. But note that d satisfies a strong form of the triangle inequality, namely

$$d(f,g) \le \max\{d(f,h), d(h,g)\}$$

where max gives the maximum element of the set.

As already observed, some information is lost when considering metric spaces as topological spaces. Metric spaces (X,d) and (Y,e) are said to be *isometric* if there is a bijection $f:X \to Y$ such that $d(x,y) = e(f(x), f(y))$ for each $x, y \in X$. The bijection f is called an *isometry.* Isometric spaces are clearly homeomorphic but homeomorphic metric spaces need not be isometric (Example 1.2 (iii)).

Recall from Proposition 5.5.3 that infinite subsets of compact spaces have limit points. For metric spaces we formulate another condition, weaker than compactness, which asserts the existence of limits.

Let (X,d) be a metric space and suppose (x_n) is a sequence in X converging to $x \in X$. Thus for each $\varepsilon > 0$ there is N such that $n \ge N \Rightarrow x_n \in B(x; \varepsilon/2)$. But then by the triangle inequality, $n, m \ge N \Rightarrow d(x_n, x_m) < \varepsilon$. A sequence (x_n) in X satisfying the condition

$$(\forall \varepsilon > 0)(\exists N)(\forall m, n \ge N)(d(x_m, x_n) < \varepsilon)$$

is said to be a *Cauchy sequence.* Thus each convergent sequence is a Cauchy sequence.

1.3 Definition A metric space (X,d) is *complete* if each Cauchy sequence in X converges in X.

The real numbers $\mathbb{R}$ with its usual metric is complete while the rationals $\mathbb{Q}$ is not. In fact $\mathbb{R}$ is constructed as *the completion* of $\mathbb{Q}$. This construction, for example using equivalence classes of Cauchy sequences of rational numbers, is sufficiently general to be carried out for an arbitrary metric space. To be precise, a metric space Y is *the completion* of the metric space X provided that Y is complete and there is an isometric embedding $f:X \to Y$ such that $f[X]$ is dense in Y. A function $f:X \to Y$ is an *isometric embedding* if f is injective and distance-preserving.

1.4 Theorem Each metric space X has a completion. The completion of X is unique up to an isometry leaving X fixed.

We omit the standard proof. Shortly we shall give another construction for the completion of ultrametric spaces which has the same topological strength. However, first we prove the classical Banach fixed point theorem, which is useful in program semantics.

Let (X,d) be a metric space. A function $f:X \rightarrow X$ is a *contraction mapping* if there is a real number $c<1$ such that $d(f(x),f(y)) \leq c \cdot d(x,y)$ for each $x,y \in X$. Note that each contraction mapping is continuous.

1.5 Theorem (Banach) Let (X,d) be a complete metric space. If $f:X \rightarrow X$ is a contraction mapping then f has a unique fixed point.

Proof: To show uniqueness suppose $f(x)=x$ and $f(y)=y$. Then

$$d(x,y)=d(f(x),f(y)) \leq c \cdot d(x,y).$$

This is only possible when $d(x,y)=0$, since $c<1$, which in turn implies that $x=y$.

To prove existence, we use the elementary fact from analysis that the series $\sum_{k=0}^{\infty} c^k$ converges whenever $|c|<1$. Define a sequence (x_n) in X by

$$\begin{cases} x_0 \in X & \text{(arbitrary)} \\ x_{n+1}=f(x_n). \end{cases}$$

Suppose we have shown that (x_n) is a Cauchy sequence so that $x_n \rightarrow x$ for some $x \in X$ by the completeness of X. We claim that $f(x)=x$. The function f is continuous so $f(x_n) \rightarrow f(x)$. But $x_{n+1}=f(x_n)$ so (x_n) and $(f(x_n))$ are essentially the same sequence. In particular, $f(x_n) \rightarrow x$ and hence $f(x)=x$ by the uniqueness of limits in Hausdorff spaces.

It remains to show that (x_n) is Cauchy. First of all, we claim that

$$d(x_{n+1},x_n) \leq c^n d(x_1,x_0).$$

This is certainly true for $n=0$. Assuming it is true for n, we have

$$\begin{aligned} d(x_{n+2},x_{n+1}) &= d(f(x_{n+1}),f(x_n)) \\ &\leq c \cdot d(x_{n+1},x_n) && \text{(contraction)} \\ &\leq c \cdot c^n d(x_1,x_0) && \text{(induction)} \\ &= c^{n+1} d(x_1,x_0). \end{aligned}$$

It follows that when $n>m$ then

$$d(x_n,x_m) \le \sum_{k=m}^{n-1} d(x_{k+1},x_k) \qquad \text{(triangle inequality)}$$
$$\le d(x_1,x_0) \sum_{k=m}^{n-1} c^k .$$

But $\sum_{k=m}^{n-1} c^k \to 0$ as $m,n \to \infty$ by the convergence of the series $\sum c^k$ so (x_n) is a Cauchy sequence. □

Observe that the notion of a contraction mapping ensures that the iteration of the map will yield the fixed point, provided the space is complete. This is analogous to the fixed point theorem for cpo's and domains and thus explains the interest of metric spaces and contraction mappings for program semantics. The analogy will be made explicit in Section 8.2 for ultrametric spaces.

Abstracting the observation in Example 1.2 (iv) for the Cantor and Baire spaces we obtain the ultrametric spaces.

1.6 Definition A metric space (X,d) is an *ultrametric space*, and d is an *ultrametric*, if d satisfies the following stronger form of (iv) in Definition 1.1:
(iv)' $d(x,y) \le \max\{d(x,z), d(z,y)\}$.

One should be aware that the geometric intuition from the Euclidean spaces $\mathbb{R}^n$ is not valid for ultrametric spaces, as the following proposition exemplifies.

1.7 Proposition Let (X,d) be an ultrametric space.
(i) If $y \in B(x;r)$ then $B(x;r) = B(y;r)$.
(ii) Each open ball $B(x;r)$ is closed.

Proof: (i) Follows immediately from the strong form of the triangle inequality.
(ii) Let $r>0$. If $y \notin B(x;r)$ then $B(y;r) \cap B(x;r) = \varnothing$ by (i) and hence

$$X - B(x;r) = \bigcup_{y \notin B(x;r)} B(y;r). \qquad \square$$

In the remaining part of this section we show how to topologically complete an ultrametric space. We shall do much more in that we consider algebras provided with a family of congruences satisfying some natural conditions. Such algebras can be construed as ultrametric spaces with continuous and even non-expansive operations (defined below), that is the algebra is a topological or ultrametric algebra. Then we complete the algebra using a projective limit construction, thus obtaining the ultrametric completion. The procedure is general in the following sense. Given an ultrametric space along with some non-expansive operations, we define a family of congruences such that the completion of the algebra with respect to this family is a complete ultrametric algebra into which the original algebra is topologically embedded, and the embedding is dense.

Let Σ be a signature and let $A=(A; \sigma_1,\dots,\sigma_k)$ be a Σ-algebra. A relation $\equiv$ is a *congruence relation* on A if it is an equivalence relation and if for each operation σ in A, say n-ary, if $x_i \equiv y_i$ for $i=1,\dots,n$ then $\sigma(x_1,\dots,x_n) \equiv \sigma(y_1,\dots,y_n)$.

1.8 Definition Let $A=(A; \sigma_1,\dots,\sigma_k)$ be a Σ-algebra. Then $\{\equiv_n\}_{n<\omega}$ is a family of *separating congruences* on A if

(i) each $\equiv_n$ is a congruence relation on A,

(ii) $x \equiv_{n+1} y \Rightarrow x \equiv_n y$, and

(iii) $\bigcap_{n<\omega} \equiv_n = \{(x,x): x \in A\}$.

Consider a Σ-algebra A together with a family $\{\equiv_n\}_{n<\omega}$ of separating congruences on A. Let (r_n) be a sequence of strictly decreasing positive real numbers such that $r_n \longrightarrow 0$. Then define an ultrametric d on A by

$$d(x,y)=\begin{cases} 0 & \text{if } x=y \\ r_n & \text{if } x \neq y, \text{ where } n \text{ is least s.t. } x \not\equiv_n y. \end{cases}$$

The distance function d is defined everywhere by (iii). It is easily seen to be an ultrametric, the ultrametric property (iv)' following from (ii).

The operations in A are continuous with respect to the ultrametric d. In fact, since $\equiv_m$ is a congruence relation for each operation σ in A and each $m<\omega$, the following stronger condition holds:

(*) $\qquad d(\sigma(x_1,\dots,x_n),\sigma(y_1,\dots,y_n)) \leq \max\{d(x_i,y_i): 1 \leq i \leq n\}.$

An operation σ satisfying (*) is said to be *non-expansive*.

To summarize, given a Σ-algebra A along with a family of separating congruences on A, we define an ultrametric on A making A into a topological algebra with non-expansive operations. The topological algebra A is independent of the choice of the sequence (r_n), since the spaces obtained using different sequences are homeomorphic. For purposes of computability, one therefore often chooses a recursive sequence of rational numbers, for example $r_n=2^{-n}$. In fact, this part of the theory need not refer to the real numbers $\mathbb{R}$ at all.

1.9 Examples

(i) Let $A=SEQ$ where SEQ is the set of finite sequences of 0's and 1's. Define $\equiv_n$ on SEQ by

$$\sigma \equiv_n \tau \Leftrightarrow (\forall i<n)(\sigma(i) \simeq \tau(i))$$

where $\simeq$ denotes strong equality meaning that either both sides are defined and equal or both sides are undefined. More generally, let Δ be a finite alphabet and let Δ^* be the set of all finite words over Δ. Define for each n, $\pi_n : \Delta^* \longrightarrow \Delta^*$ by $\pi_n(w) =$ first n symbols in w (or w if the number of symbols in w is less than or equal to n). Then define

$$w \equiv_n v \Leftrightarrow \pi_n(w) = \pi_n(v).$$

(ii) Let $\mathbb{Z}$ be the integers with addition and multiplication. Fix a prime number p and define

$$x \equiv_n y \Leftrightarrow x - y \in (p)^n$$

where (p) is the ideal generated by p.

(iii) Let R be a local commutative ring (local means that R has a unique maximal ideal $\mathbf{m}$). Define

$$x \equiv_n y \Leftrightarrow x - y \in \mathbf{m}^n.$$

By Krull's theorem, $\bigcap_{n<\omega} \mathbf{m}^n = \{0\}$, so $\{\equiv_n\}_{n<\omega}$ is a family of separating congruences.

(iv) Let A be an ultrametric space and let $\sigma_1, \ldots, \sigma_k$ be some non-expansive operations on A. Then there is a *bounded* ultrametric d on A, by Example 1.2 (iii), such that A with the two metrics are homeomorphic as topological spaces and such that the operations are non-expansive with respect to d. Let (r_n) be a sequence of strictly decreasing rational numbers such that $r_n \longrightarrow 0$. Sometimes it is convenient to choose r_0 to be at least as large as the bound of d. Define

$$x \equiv_n y \Leftrightarrow d(x, y) \leq r_n.$$

Then it is easily verified that $\{\equiv_n\}_{n<\omega}$ is a family of separating congruences on the algebra $A = (A; \sigma_1, \ldots, \sigma_k)$. Let d' be the ultrametric on A obtained as above from $\{\equiv_n\}_{n<\omega}$ and the sequence (r_n). Then the identity function is a homeomorphism between (A, d) and (A, d').

Now consider a fixed Σ-algebra $A = (A; \sigma_1, \ldots, \sigma_k)$ together with a family of separating congruences $\{\equiv_n\}_{n<\omega}$ on A. We shall construct *the completion* $\hat{A}$ of A.

Let $[x]_n$ denote the equivalence class of x with respect to $\equiv_n$. Then

$$A_n = A/\equiv_n = \{[x]_n : x \in A\}$$

is a Σ-algebra where the operations, for simplicity also denoted by σ_i, are defined by

$$\sigma_i([x_1]_n,\dots,[x_{n_i}]_n)=[\sigma_i(x_1,\dots,x_{n_i})]_n\,.$$

These operations are well-defined since $\equiv_n$ is a congruence relation. For $m\le n$, define $\phi^n_m : A_n \longrightarrow A_m$ by $\phi^n_m([x]_n)=[x]_m$. Then ϕ^n_m is well-defined by condition (ii) of Definition 1.8 and ϕ^n_m is a Σ-morphism, that is

$$\phi^n_m(\sigma_i([x_1]_n,\dots,[x_{n_i}]_n))=\sigma_i(\phi^n_m([x_1]_n),\dots,\phi^n_m([x_{n_i}]_n))$$

for each $i=1,\dots,k$. Furthermore $\phi^n_n=\mathrm{id}_{A_n}$ and $\phi^m_t\circ\phi^n_m=\phi^n_t$ whenever $t\le m\le n$. These observations say that $\{A_n : n<\omega\}$, $\{\phi^n_m : m\le n<\omega\}$ is an *inverse system* of Σ-algebras which is *surjective* in the sense that each ϕ^n_m is surjective. The *projective* or *inverse limit* of the inverse system is a Σ-algebra $\hat{A}=\varprojlim A_n$ together with a family of Σ-morphisms $\hat{\phi}_n : \hat{A}\longrightarrow A_n$ such that for each $m\le n$, $\hat{\phi}_m=\phi^n_m\circ\hat{\phi}_n$ and which is the solution to the following universal problem. If B is a Σ-algebra and $\psi_n : B\longrightarrow A_n$ is a family of Σ-morphisms such that for each $m\le n$, $\psi_m=\phi^n_m\circ\psi_n$, then there is a unique Σ-morphism θ making the diagrams below commute.

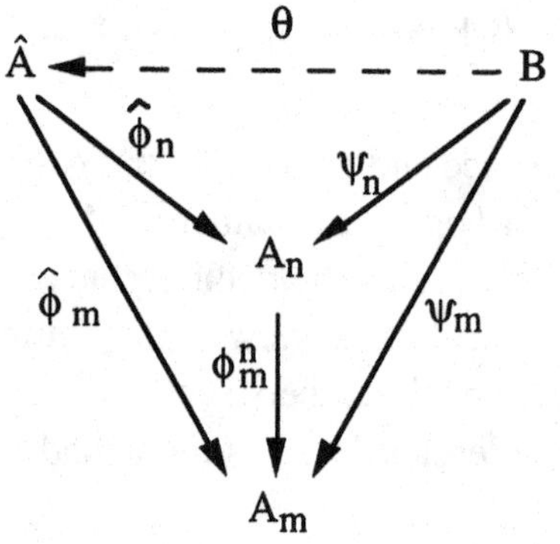

By Exercise 4, the projective limit $\hat{A}$ is unique up to a Σ-isomorphism. To show the existence let

$$\hat{A}=\Big\{(a_n)\in\prod_{n=0}^{\infty}A_n : \phi^{n+1}_n(a_{n+1})=a_n\Big\}$$

that is $\hat{A}$ consists of all sequences consistent with respect to the Σ-morphisms of the inverse system. To make $\hat{A}$ into a Σ-algebra define, for σ a t-ary operation,

$$\hat{\sigma}\big((a_{1,n})_n,\dots,(a_{t,n})_n\big)=\big(\sigma(a_{1,n},\dots,a_{t,n})\big)_n.$$

Furthermore, define $\hat{\phi}_m : \hat{A} \to A_m$ by $\hat{\phi}_m((a_n)_n) = a_m$. The reader is asked in Exercise 5 to verify that $\hat{\sigma}$ is well-defined on $\hat{A}$, and that each $\hat{\phi}_n$ is a Σ-morphism such that $\hat{\phi}_m = \phi_m^n \circ \hat{\phi}_n$ whenever $m \le n$.

To show that $\hat{A}$ together with the family of Σ-morphisms $\hat{\phi}_m$ is a solution to the universal problem above, suppose first that the Σ-morphism θ exists for B and ψ_n. Then, for each $b \in B$ and for each n, $\hat{\phi}_n(\theta(b)) = \psi_n(b)$ so that $\theta(b) = (\psi_n(b))_n$. This shows that θ is unique. To show the existence of θ we need to verify that $\theta : B \to \hat{A}$ defined by $\theta(b) = (\psi_n(b))_n$ is a well-defined Σ-morphism. First of all, for $m \le n$, $\phi_m^n(\psi_n(b)) = \psi_m(b)$ so $(\psi_n(b))_n \in \hat{A}$. Furthermore, for an m-ary operation σ,

$$\begin{aligned}\theta(\sigma_B(b_1, \ldots, b_m)) &= (\psi_n(\sigma_B(b_1, \ldots, b_m)))_n \\ &= (\sigma_{A_n}(\psi_n(b_1), \ldots, \psi_n(b_m)))_n \\ &= \hat{\sigma}((\psi_n(b_1))_n, \ldots, (\psi_n(b_m))_n) \\ &= \hat{\sigma}(\theta(b_1), \ldots, \theta(b_m))\end{aligned}$$

which says that θ is a Σ-morphism.

The Σ-algebra A can be embedded into $\hat{A}$ as follows. For each n let $v_n : A \to A_n$ be the canonical Σ-morphism defined by $v_n(x) = [x]_n$. Then $v_m = \phi_m^n \circ v_n$ for $m \le n$, so there is a unique Σ-morphism $\theta : A \to \hat{A}$ for which the diagrams below commute.

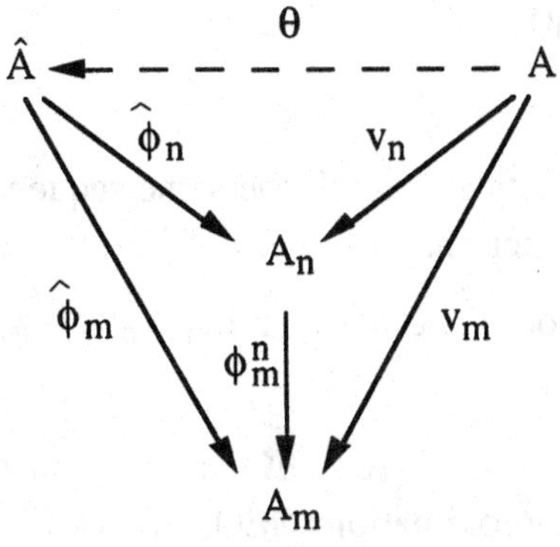

Suppose $\theta(a) = \theta(b)$. Then $\hat{\phi}_n(\theta(a)) = \hat{\phi}_n(\theta(b))$ and hence $v_n(a) = v_n(b)$ for each n. Expressed differently, $a \equiv_n b$ for each n. But then $a = b$ by (iii) of Definition 1.8. It follows that θ is injective so that θ is an embedding of A into $\hat{A}$.

Suppose we have made A into an ultrametric space as described above, using the sequence (r_n). Then we define a distance function $\hat{d}$ on $\hat{A}$ by

$$\hat{d}(x, y) = \begin{cases} 0 & \text{if } x = y \\ r_n & \text{if } x \ne y, \text{ where n is least s.t. } \hat{\phi}_n(x) \ne \hat{\phi}_n(y). \end{cases}$$

It is easily verified that $\hat{d}$ is an ultrametric on $\hat{A}$.

1.10 Theorem Suppose $A=(A;\sigma_1,\dots,\sigma_k)$ is a Σ-algebra together with a family of separating congruences $\{\equiv_n\}_{n<\omega}$ and let $\hat{A}=(\hat{A};\hat{\sigma}_1,\dots,\hat{\sigma}_k)=\varprojlim A/\equiv_n$. Let (r_n) be a sequence of strictly decreasing positive real numbers such that $r_n\longrightarrow 0$ and let d and $\hat{d}$ be the ultrametrics for A and $\hat{A}$ respectively, as defined above with respect to the sequence (r_n). Then the following hold.
(i) $\hat{A}$ is a complete ultrametric space.
(ii) The unique Σ-morphism $\theta: A\longrightarrow\hat{A}$ making the above diagrams commute is an isometry with respect to d and $\hat{d}$.
(iii) A is dense in $\hat{A}$.

Proof: (i) To show that $\hat{A}$ is complete, suppose (x_n) is a Cauchy sequence in $\hat{A}$. Then for each n there is some N_n such that $s,t\geq N_n \Rightarrow \hat{d}(x_s,x_t)<r_n$ or, in other words, $\hat{\phi}_n(x_s)=\hat{\phi}_n(x_t)$. Let $f:\omega\longrightarrow\omega$ be the increasing function which given n chooses the least such N_n. We claim that $x=(\hat{\phi}_n(x_{f(n)}))_n\in\hat{A}$. For, given $m\leq n$, we have that

$$\begin{aligned}\phi^n_m(\hat{\phi}_n(x_{f(n)})) &= \hat{\phi}_m(x_{f(n)})\\ &=\hat{\phi}_m(x_{f(m)})\end{aligned}$$

since f is increasing. To see that $x_n\longrightarrow x$ consider n and $t\geq f(n)$. Then

$$\hat{\phi}_n(x)=\hat{\phi}_n(x_{f(n)})=\hat{\phi}_n(x_t)$$

so that $\hat{d}(x,x_t)<r_n$.

(ii) The metrics are defined with respect to the same sequence (r_n) so θ is an isometry since $v_n=\hat{\phi}_n\circ\theta$ for each n.

(iii) Given $x\in\hat{A}$ and n, choose $a\in A$ such that $v_n(a)=\hat{\phi}_n(x)$. Then $\hat{d}(x,\theta(a))<r_n$ so $\theta[A]$ is dense in $\hat{A}$. □

Let us reconsider Examples 1.9. If $A=SEQ$ as in (i), then $\hat{A}$ is the Cantor space together with the finite approximations SEQ. If $A=\mathbb{Z}$ with the family of separating congruences as in (ii) then $\hat{A}$ is the ring of p-adic integers. Finally, the completion $\hat{R}$ of a local commutative ring R as in (iii) is again a local commutative ring whose unique maximal ideal is $\hat{\mathfrak{m}}=\{(a_n)\in\hat{R}: a_1=0\}$. (For a discussion of the effectiveness of the completion of local rings see Stoltenberg-Hansen and Tucker [1988].)

The construction of the completion given in Theorem 1.10 is completely general in topological terms.

1.11 Theorem Suppose $A=(A;\sigma_1,\dots,\sigma_k)$ is an ultrametric Σ-algebra with non-expansive operations. Then there is a complete ultrametric Σ-algebra $\hat{A}$ with non-expansive operations, $\hat{A}=(\hat{A};\hat{\sigma}_1,\dots,\hat{\sigma}_k)$, and a Σ-morphism $\theta:A\to\hat{A}$ such that

(i) θ is an embedding, and

(ii) each $x\in\hat{A}$ is the limit of some sequence $(\theta(a_n))$ where (a_n) is a Cauchy sequence in A. In particular, $\theta[A]$ is dense in $\hat{A}$.

Proof: As in Example 1.9 (iv) we may without loss of topological generality assume that the ultrametric d on A is bounded and then define a family of separating congruences $\{\equiv_n\}$ by

$$x\equiv_n y \Leftrightarrow d(x,y)\leq r_n$$

where (r_n) is a strictly decreasing sequence of positive real numbers such that $r_n\to 0$. Then we obtain $\hat{A}=(\hat{A};\hat{\sigma}_1,\dots,\hat{\sigma}_k)$ and the injective Σ-morphism $\theta:A\to\hat{A}$ by the construction of Theorem 1.10. To see that θ is continuous, just observe that the identity on A is a homeomorphism between (A,d) and (A,d') where d' is the ultrametric on A obtained from $\{\equiv_n\}$. This observation also suffices for (ii). □

Section 8.2 Ultrametric Algebras as Domains

In this section we describe how to embed an ultrametric algebra into a structured domain. The embedding will be done in such a way that the ultrametric completion of the algebra will correspond to the domain completion of the cusl of compact elements. As an illustration of the use of domain theory we give a simple proof of the Banach fixed point theorem for ultrametric spaces with no appeal to the theory of real numbers. Further applications, solving systems of *guarded equations*, are given in the exercises.

Throughout this section let $A=(A;\sigma_1,\dots,\sigma_k)$ be a fixed Σ-algebra and let $\{\equiv_n\}_{n<\omega}$ be a family of separating congruences on A. Let $\hat{A}=(\hat{A};\hat{\sigma}_1,\dots,\hat{\sigma}_k)$ be the completion of A obtained via the projective limit construction of Theorem 1.10. First we shall construct a domain $D(\hat{A})$, whose set of maximal elements $D(\hat{A})_m$ is $\hat{A}$, such that the ultrametric topology on $\hat{A}$ obtained from $\{\equiv_n\}_{n<\omega}$ is the subspace topology induced by the Scott topology on $D(\hat{A})$. Later we extend the construction so that the operations in A are also represented in $D(\hat{A})$ thus obtaining a *structured domain* or *Σ-domain*. Then, just as in Theorem 1.11, the construction is modified to embed an arbitrary ultrametric algebra with non-expansive operations.

In our construction we use the notation from Section 8.1. Without loss of generality we assume that $\equiv_0$ is the trivial congruence $A \times A$, that is $a \equiv_0 b$ for all $a, b \in A$. Let $D(\hat{A}) = \hat{A} \cup (\uplus_{n<\omega} A_n)$, where $\uplus$ denotes the *disjoint union*, and define a relation $\sqsubseteq$ on $D(\hat{A})$ by

$$\begin{aligned} x \sqsubseteq y \Leftrightarrow\ & (x \in A_m \ \&\ y \in A_n \ \&\ \phi^n_m(y) = x) \\ & \vee (x \in A_m \ \&\ y \in \hat{A} \ \&\ \phi_m(y) = x) \\ & \vee (x \in \hat{A} \ \&\ y \in \hat{A} \ \&\ x = y). \end{aligned}$$

Then put $\perp = [a]_0$, which is the unique element in A_0 by our assumption on $\equiv_0$.

2.1 Lemma $D(\hat{A}) = (D(\hat{A}); \sqsubseteq, \perp)$ is a domain and its set of compact elements is $D(\hat{A})_c = \uplus_{n<\omega} A_n$. Furthermore $D(\hat{A})_m = \hat{A}$ and $\widehat{\text{approx}(x)} = \{\phi_n(x) : n < \omega\}$ for each $x \in \hat{A}$. The subspace topology on $\hat{A}$ induced by the Scott topology on $D(\hat{A})$ is the ultrametric topology on $\hat{A}$ induced by $\{\equiv_n\}_{n<\omega}$.

Proof: Observe that $(\uplus_{n<\omega} A_n; \sqsubseteq)$ is an ω-tree (see Definition 11.1.2) with least element $\perp$ and that the infinite branches correspond exactly to the elements in $\hat{A}$. With this observation at hand, all statements but the last are easily verified. To see that the metric topology on $\hat{A}$ is the one induced by the Scott topology it suffices to note that for $x, y \in \hat{A}$,

$$\hat{d}(x, y) < r_n \Leftrightarrow \hat{\phi}_n(x) = \hat{\phi}_n(y) \Leftrightarrow \hat{\phi}_n(x) \sqsubseteq y. \qquad \square$$

Define a *rank function* $\rho : D(\hat{A}) \rightarrow \omega \cup \{\omega\}$ by

$$\rho(x) = \begin{cases} n & \text{if } x \in A_n \\ \omega & \text{if } x \in \hat{A}. \end{cases}$$

Considering $\omega \cup \{\omega\}$ as a domain of ordinals (Example 2.1.14) we have that ρ is continuous. A continuous function $\psi : D(\hat{A}) \rightarrow D(\hat{A})$ is said to be *rank-increasing* if $\rho(x) < \rho(\psi(x))$ whenever $x \in D(\hat{A})_c$.

Recall that fix is the least fixed point operator of Theorem 2.3.6.

2.2 Lemma Let $\psi : D(\hat{A}) \rightarrow D(\hat{A})$ be continuous and rank-increasing. Then $\text{fix}(\psi) \in \hat{A}$ and the fixed point of ψ is unique.

Proof: Recall that $\text{fix}(\psi) = \bigsqcup_{n<\omega} \psi^n(\perp)$. Clearly $\rho(\psi^n(\perp)) \geq n$ since ψ is rank-increasing so $\rho(\text{fix}(\psi)) = \omega$, that is $\text{fix}(\psi) \in \hat{A}$. The fixed point is unique since it is the least fixed point and since distinct elements in $\hat{A}$ are unrelated by $\sqsubseteq$. $\square$

Rank-increasing functions on $D(\hat{A})$ are essentially equivalent to contraction mappings on $\hat{A}$. A function $f : \hat{A} \rightarrow \hat{A}$ is said to be *contractive* if whenever

$x, y \in \hat{A}$ are distinct then $\hat{d}(f(x), f(y)) < \hat{d}(x, y)$. Of course, a contraction mapping on $\hat{A}$ is contractive.

2.3 Lemma (i) If $\psi: D(\hat{A}) \to D(\hat{A})$ is continuous and rank-increasing then $\psi|_{\hat{A}}: \hat{A} \to \hat{A}$ and is contractive.
(ii) If $f: \hat{A} \to \hat{A}$ is contractive then there is a continuous rank-increasing function $\psi_f: D(\hat{A}) \to D(\hat{A})$ such that $\psi_f|_{\hat{A}} = f$.

Proof: (i) To see that $\hat{A}$ is closed under ψ let $x \in \hat{A}$. By Proposition 3.1.5, $\psi(x) = \bigsqcup\{\psi(\hat{\phi}_n(x)) : n < \omega\}$. ψ is rank-increasing so $\rho(\psi(\hat{\phi}_n(x))) > n$ for each n. Thus $\rho(\psi(x)) = \omega$ by the monotonicity of ρ, that is $\psi(x) \in \hat{A}$.

Suppose that $x, y \in \hat{A}$ are distinct and $\hat{d}(x, y) = r_n$. Thus $\hat{\phi}_{n-1}(x) = \hat{\phi}_{n-1}(y)$, recalling our assumption on $\equiv_0$. But then $\psi(\hat{\phi}_{n-1}(x)) = \psi(\hat{\phi}_{n-1}(y))$ and, since ψ is rank-increasing, $\rho(\psi(\hat{\phi}_{n-1}(x))) = t \geq n$. If $t = \omega$ then

$$\psi(x) = \psi(\hat{\phi}_{n-1}(x)) = \psi(\hat{\phi}_{n-1}(y)) = \psi(y)$$

and hence $\hat{d}(\psi(x), \psi(y)) = 0$. Suppose $t < \omega$. Then, since $\psi(\hat{\phi}_{n-1}(z)) \sqsubseteq \psi(z)$ for each z,

$$\hat{\phi}_t(\psi(x)) = \psi(\hat{\phi}_{n-1}(x)) = \psi(\hat{\phi}_{n-1}(y)) = \hat{\phi}_t(\psi(y)).$$

But then $\hat{d}(\psi(x), \psi(y)) < r_t \leq r_n$ so that $\psi|_{\hat{A}}$ is contractive.

(ii) Each element in $D(\hat{A})_c$ is of the form $\hat{\phi}_n(x)$ for some $x \in \hat{A}$ and $n < \omega$. Given a contractive function $f: \hat{A} \to \hat{A}$ define $\psi_f: D(\hat{A})_c \to D(\hat{A})_c$ by

$$\psi_f(\hat{\phi}_n(x)) = \hat{\phi}_{n+1}(f(x)).$$

Then ψ_f is well-defined since f is contractive and ψ_f is rank-increasing by its definition. To see that ψ_f is monotone, let $\hat{\phi}_m(x) \sqsubseteq \hat{\phi}_n(y)$. Thus $m \leq n$ and

$$\hat{\phi}_m(x) = \phi_m^n(\hat{\phi}_n(y)) = \hat{\phi}_m(y).$$

It follows that $\hat{d}(x, y) < r_m$ and, since f is contractive, that $\hat{d}(f(x), f(y)) < r_{m+1}$. But then

$$\psi_f(\hat{\phi}_m(x)) = \hat{\phi}_{m+1}(f(x)) = \hat{\phi}_{m+1}(f(y)) \sqsubseteq \hat{\phi}_{n+1}(f(y)) = \psi_f(\hat{\phi}_n(y)).$$

Now we extend ψ_f continuously to $D(\hat{A})$ by Corollary 3.1.6. Let $x \in \hat{A}$. Then

$$\psi_f(x) = \bigsqcup_n \psi_f(\hat{\phi}_n(x)) = \bigsqcup_n \hat{\phi}_{n+1}(f(x)) = f(x)$$

so that $\psi_f|_{\hat{A}} = f$. □

2.4 Lemma Suppose $f: \hat{A} \to \hat{A}$ is contractive. Then f has a unique fixed point.

Proof: By Lemma 2.3 we choose a continuous rank-increasing function ψ_f on $D(\hat{A})$ such that $\psi_f|\hat{A}=f$. Then, by Lemma 2.2, $\text{fix}(\psi_f) \in \hat{A}$ and the fixed point is unique. □

Lemma 2.4 is a variant of the Banach fixed point theorem for *certain* complete ultrametric spaces. We use it to obtain the theorem for *all* ultrametric spaces. Note that the proof makes no appeal to the theory of real numbers.

2.5 Theorem Let (A,d) be a complete ultrametric space. If $f:A \longrightarrow A$ is a contraction mapping then f has a unique fixed point.

Proof: If f has a fixed point then it is unique by the easy argument of Theorem 1.5.

First we show that d may be assumed to be a bounded metric. Choose $x_0 \in A$ and suppose $d(x_0, f(x_0))=r$. If $r=0$ then x_0 is the fixed point of f and we are done. So suppose $r>0$. Let $B=\{y \in A: d(x_0,y) \leq r\}$ and let d' be the restriction of d to $B \times B$. Then (B,d') is an ultrametric space. Note that if $x,y \in B$ then

$$d(x,y) \leq \max\{d(x,x_0), d(x_0,y)\} \leq r$$

so d' is bounded by r. Furthermore, a sequence (b_n) in B is a Cauchy sequence in (B,d') if and only if it is a Cauchy sequence in (A,d). To see that (B,d') is complete, let (b_n) be a Cauchy sequence in B. Then $b_n \longrightarrow a$ in A since A is assumed to be complete. But then

$$d(x_0,a) \leq \max\{d(x_0,b_n), d(b_n,a)\} \leq r$$

for large n, so $a \in B$. Similarly, B is closed under f. For

$$\begin{aligned} d(x_0,f(x)) &\leq \max\{d(x_0,f(x_0)), d(f(x_0),f(x))\} \\ &\leq \max\{r, d(f(x_0),f(x))\}. \end{aligned}$$

If $x \in B$ then $d(f(x_0),f(x)) < d(x_0,x) \leq r$ since f is a contraction mapping, so $f(x) \in B$.

Thus we assume that (A,d) is a bounded ultrametric space and we may assume that the bound is 1. Suppose $c<1$ is a constant for the contraction mapping f. Then define as in Theorem 1.11 a family of separating equivalences $\{\equiv_n\}_{n<\omega}$ on A by

$$x \equiv_n y \Leftrightarrow d(x,y) \leq c^n.$$

Let $\hat{A}$ be the completion of A with respect to $\{\equiv_n\}_{n<\omega}$, let $\hat{d}$ be the associated ultrametric on $\hat{A}$, and let $\theta: A \longrightarrow \hat{A}$ be the associated embedding. Then θ is also surjective since A is complete. The contraction mapping f on A induces a function $\hat{f}:\hat{A}\to\hat{A}$ by, for $x\in A$,

$$\hat{f}(\theta(x))=\theta(f(x)).$$

If $\hat{d}(\theta(x),\theta(y))=c^n$ then $x\equiv_{n-1}y$ and hence $d(x,y)\le c^{n-1}$. Thus

$$d(f(x),f(y))\le c\cdot d(x,y)\le c^n$$

so that $f(x)\equiv_n f(y)$. This means that $\hat{d}(\hat{f}(\theta(x)),\hat{f}(\theta(y)))<c^n$ and hence $\hat{d}(\hat{f}(\theta(x)),\hat{f}(\theta(y)))\le c^{n+1}$. We have shown that $\hat{f}$ is contractive on $\hat{A}$. By Lemma 2.4, $\hat{f}$ has a fixed point $\theta(\bar{x})$ and then $\bar{x}$ is a fixed point of f by the injectivity of θ. □

We have yet to show how to embed the algebra $A=(A;\sigma_1,\dots,\sigma_k)$ into $D(\hat{A})$ as an algebra, that is how to interpret the operations $\sigma_1,\dots,\sigma_k$ on $D(\hat{A})$.

2.6 Definition A structure $D=(D;\sqsubseteq,\perp,\psi_1,\dots,\psi_k)$ is a *structured domain* or *Σ-domain* for a signature Σ if

(i) $(D;\sqsubseteq,\perp)$ is a domain, and

(ii) each ψ_i is a continuous n_i-ary operation on D, that is $\psi_i:D^{n_i}\to D$ is continuous, where the arity n_i is given by the signature Σ.

To complete the representation of the Σ-algebra A in $D(\hat{A})$ we need to find operations $\psi_1,\dots,\psi_k$ on $D(\hat{A})$ making $D(\hat{A})$ into a Σ-domain such that

$$\theta(\sigma_i(a_1,\dots,a_{n_i}))=\psi_i(\theta(a_1),\dots\theta(a_{n_i}))$$

for each $a_1,\dots,a_{n_i}\in A$. When this is accomplished we say that the Σ-domain $D(\hat{A})=(D(\hat{A});\sqsubseteq,\perp,\psi_1,\dots,\psi_k)$ *represents* A.

When making $D(\hat{A})$ into a Σ-domain we may have some choice in how to define the operations on the compact elements, which is crucial for arguments using fixed points. Let $\lambda:\omega\to\omega$ be a strictly monotone function. We say that $f:A^n\to A$ is *λ-congruent* if for each m,

$$a_1\equiv_m b_1,\dots,a_n\equiv_m b_n \Rightarrow f(a_1,\dots,a_n)\equiv_{\lambda(m)}f(b_1,\dots,b_n).$$

Note that each operation σ_i is id-congruent, where id is the identity function. Sometimes we can do better. For example, if σ_i is a constant, that is a 0-ary function, then σ_i is λ-congruent for each λ.

Let $f:A^n\to A$ be λ-congruent. Then define $\phi_f^\lambda:D(\hat{A})_c^n\to D(\hat{A})$ by

$$\phi_f^\lambda([a_1]_{m_1},\dots,[a_n]_{m_n})=[f(a_1,\dots,a_n)]_{\lambda(m)}$$

where $m=\min\{m_1,\dots,m_n\}$. By convention, if $n=0$ then $m=\omega$ and $\phi_a^\lambda=\theta(a)$, that is constants are interpreted appropriately.

2.7 Lemma Let $f: A^n \longrightarrow A$ be λ-congruent. Then $\overset{\lambda}{\phi}_f$ is well-defined and monotone.

Proof: That $\overset{\lambda}{\phi}_f$ is well-defined follows from the λ-congruence of f. Suppose $[a_1]_{m_1} \sqsubseteq [b_1]_{t_1}, \ldots, [a_n]_{m_n} \sqsubseteq [b_n]_{t_n}$. Then $m_i \le t_i$ and $[a_i]_{m_i} = [b_i]_{m_i}$ for $i=1,\ldots,n$. Let $m = \min\{m_1,\ldots,m_n\}$ and $t = \min\{t_1,\ldots,t_n\}$. Then $m \le t$ and

$$\begin{aligned}\overset{\lambda}{\phi}_f([a_1]_{m_1},\ldots,[a_n]_{m_n}) &= \overset{\lambda}{\phi}_f([a_1]_m,\ldots,[a_n]_m)\\ &= \overset{\lambda}{\phi}_f([b_1]_m,\ldots,[b_n]_m)\\ &= [f(b_1,\ldots,b_n)]_{\lambda(m)}\\ &\sqsubseteq [f(b_1,\ldots,b_n)]_{\lambda(t)} \qquad \text{since } m \le t\\ &= \overset{\lambda}{\phi}_f([b_1]_{t_1},\ldots,[b_n]_{t_n}). \ \square\end{aligned}$$

Now we may extend $\overset{\lambda}{\phi}_f$ to a continuous function $\overset{\lambda}{\phi}_f: D(\hat{A})^n \longrightarrow D(\hat{A})$. In fact, for $x_1,\ldots,x_n \in \hat{A}$,

$$\overset{\lambda}{\phi}_f(x_1,\ldots,x_n) = \bigsqcup_m \overset{\lambda}{\phi}_f(\hat{\phi}_m(x_1),\ldots,\hat{\phi}_m(x_n)).$$

2.8 Lemma Let $f: A^n \longrightarrow A$ be λ-congruent. Then for each $a_1,\ldots,a_n \in A$

$$\theta(f(a_1,\ldots,a_n)) = \overset{\lambda}{\phi}_f(\theta(a_1),\ldots,\theta(a_n)).$$

Proof: Let $a_1,\ldots,a_n \in A$. Then

$$\begin{aligned}\overset{\lambda}{\phi}_f(\theta(a_1),\ldots,\theta(a_n)) &= \bigsqcup_m \overset{\lambda}{\phi}_f(\hat{\phi}_m\theta(a_1),\ldots,\hat{\phi}_m\theta(a_n))\\ &= \bigsqcup_m \overset{\lambda}{\phi}_f([a_1]_m,\ldots,[a_n]_m)\\ &= \bigsqcup_m [f(a_1,\ldots,a_n)]_{\lambda(m)}.\end{aligned}$$

Since $[a]_t \sqsubseteq \theta(a)$, we have $\bigsqcup_m [f(a_1,\ldots,a_n)]_{\lambda(m)} \sqsubseteq \theta(f(a_1,\ldots,a_n))$ for each $a \in A$ and $t < \omega$. But $\lambda(m) \ge m$ since λ is strictly monotone, which implies that $\bigsqcup_m [f(a_1,\ldots,a_n)]_{\lambda(m)}$ is maximal in $D(\hat{A})$. It follows that equality must hold, that is $\bigsqcup_m [f(a_1,\ldots,a_n)]_{\lambda(m)} = \theta(f(a_1,\ldots,a_n))$. $\square$

We have shown that each λ-congruent function $f: A^n \longrightarrow A$ extends continuously to the whole domain $D(\hat{A})$ by $\overset{\lambda}{\phi}_f$. By similar arguments one easily proves

2.9 Lemma Let $\gamma: \omega \longrightarrow \omega$ and $\lambda: \omega \longrightarrow \omega$ be strictly monotone and suppose $\gamma(m) \le \lambda(m)$ for all $m < \omega$. If $f: A^n \longrightarrow A$ is λ-congruent then f is γ-congruent and, for all $x_1,\ldots,x_n \in \hat{A}$, $\overset{\lambda}{\phi}_f(x_1,\ldots,x_n) = \overset{\gamma}{\phi}_f(x_1,\ldots,x_n) \in \hat{A}$.

Thus $\hat{A} = D(\hat{A})_m$ is closed under $\overset{\lambda}{\phi}_f$ and the choice of λ plays no role on $\hat{A}$. However, the choice of λ does effect the behaviour of $\overset{\lambda}{\phi}_f$ on $D(\hat{A})_c$ and hence the process of taking fixed points of such functions. To summarize we have

2.10 Theorem Let $A=(A;\sigma_1,\ldots,\sigma_k)$ be a Σ-algebra along with a family of separating congruences $\{\equiv_n\}_{n<\omega}$ on A, and assume that each σ_i is λ_i-congruent. Then

$$D(\hat{A})=(D(\hat{A});\sqsubseteq,\perp,\phi_{\sigma_1}^{\lambda_1},\ldots,\phi_{\sigma_k}^{\lambda_k})$$

is a Σ-domain representing A.

The theorem is extended to an ultrametric algebra as follows.

2.11 Theorem Let $A=(A;\sigma_1,\ldots,\sigma_k)$ be an ultrametric Σ-algebra with non-expansive operations. Then there is a Σ-domain representing A.

Proof: This is analogous to Theorem 1.11. Note that we may, as there, assume that the metric d on A is bounded, since the operations remain non-expansive when replacing an unbounded ultrametric by a bounded one as in Example 1.9 (iv). Constructing $\{\equiv_n\}_{n<\omega}$ and then $\hat{A}$ as in the proof of Theorem 1.11, we see that each σ_i is id-congruent so that

$$D(\hat{A})=(D(\hat{A});\sqsubseteq,\perp,\phi_{\sigma_1}^{id},\ldots,\phi_{\sigma_k}^{id})$$

represents A. □

An n-ary operation σ on an ultrametric space (A,d) is said to be a *contraction operation* if there is $c<1$ such that

$$d(\sigma(a_1,\ldots,a_n),\sigma(b_1,\ldots,b_n))\leq c\cdot\max\{d(a_i,b_i): i=1,\ldots,n\}.$$

If σ is a contraction operation then, just as in the proof of Theorem 2.5, we may arrange the construction of $\{\equiv_n\}_{n<\omega}$ so that σ is s-congruent where $s:\omega\to\omega$ is the successor function and hence that σ is represented by ϕ_σ^s in $D(\hat{A})$.

Suppose $f:A\to A$ is a function obtained by composition of the operations on A and suppose the argument x of f(x) is within the scope of an s-congruent (or contraction) operation (x is then said to be *guarded*). Then by Lemma 2.4 the equation

$$x=f(x)$$

has a unique solution in $\hat{A}$. Furthermore, if in building f we had also allowed the fixed point operator fix but only for guarded scopes, then we would not obtain any new solutions. These assertions, made precise and extended to guarded *systems* of equations, make up Exercise 6. The theory of guarded systems of equations in this setting is further developed in Stoltenberg-Hansen and Tucker [1991].

Section 8.3 Total Elements of Domains

One reason for domain theory being a rather smooth theory is that the notion of partial element or approximation is included in the very concept of a domain. So even though continuous functions between domains are total in the sense that they have a value for each argument they nonetheless do describe partial behaviour. For example, when the value is $\perp$ for a certain argument, it should be interpreted as the function represented being undefined for that argument in the sense that no information about the value was computed.

Analogously, recursive function theory became a smooth mathematical theory when one began to consider partial functions rather than only total ones. After all, the concept of an algorithm naturally gives rise to partial functions since algorithmic computations often do not terminate. It is the undecidability of the halting problem which limits the effective treatment of the total recursive functions.

The notion of partiality in recursive function theory is usually external in the sense that we consider *partial* functions operating on, and taking values in, a domain of total objects, most often the natural numbers. In domain theory the converse is the case in that the functions we consider are *total* whereas the domains on which they operate always contain partial elements. The effect is however similar and a smooth theory is obtained.

In this section we shall briefly consider the problem of extracting the "total" elements of a domain, using an approach due to Berger [1993]. It will be used to prove a density theorem, the analogue of Kreisel's density theorem (Kreisel [1959]) for the continuous functionals.

Let us first consider a simple example, say the flat domain $\mathbb{N}_\perp$. Clearly the numbers in $\mathbb{N}_\perp$ should be considered as the total elements while $\perp$ should not be total. Similarly for any flat domain $A_\perp$, the set A should make up the total elements. Thus for flat domains, except possibly for the trivial domain $\emptyset_\perp$, it is reasonable to identify the set of total elements with the set of maximal elements. The same is true for the domains representing complete ultrametric algebras as in Section 8.2, such as the Cantor and Baire spaces. After all, these domains were constructed by adding approximations to the given complete ultrametric space.

When considering function spaces the situation is more complicated. It turns out that the natural notion of totality for function spaces is in general incomparable with that of maximality, as the examples below show. Suppose D and E are domains and suppose we have already decided that $M \subseteq D$ and $N \subseteq E$ are the sets of total elements. Then it is reasonable to say that the total elements of $[D \rightarrow E]$

are precisely those functions taking total elements in D to total elements in E. We introduce the following notation for that set:

$$\langle M,N\rangle=\{f\in[D\to E]:f[M]\subseteq N\}.$$

3.1 Example Consider the domain $[\mathbb{N}_\perp\to\mathbb{N}_\perp]$. As agreed above, the set of total elements of $[\mathbb{N}_\perp\to\mathbb{N}_\perp]$ should be $\langle\mathbb{N},\mathbb{N}\rangle$. Define $f\in[\mathbb{N}_\perp\to\mathbb{N}_\perp]$ by

$$f(x)=\begin{cases}0 & \text{if } x\neq\perp\\ \perp & \text{if } x=\perp.\end{cases}$$

Then $f\in\langle\mathbb{N},\mathbb{N}\rangle$, but f is not maximal in $[\mathbb{N}_\perp\to\mathbb{N}_\perp]$ since the constant 0 function is strictly larger. □

3.2 Example We shall construct $F\in[[\mathbb{N}_\perp\to\mathbb{N}_\perp]\to\mathbb{N}_\perp]$ which is maximal but not total. Let $f\in\langle\mathbb{N},\mathbb{N}\rangle$ be a fixed function which is not constant on $\mathbb{N}$. It follows that f is maximal in $[\mathbb{N}_\perp\to\mathbb{N}_\perp]$. Define $F:[\mathbb{N}_\perp\to\mathbb{N}_\perp]\to\mathbb{N}_\perp$ by

$$F(g)=\begin{cases}n & \text{if } \perp\neq g(n)\neq f(n)\ \&\ (\forall m<n)(g(m)=f(m))\\ \perp & \text{if no such } n\in\mathbb{N} \text{ exists.}\end{cases}$$

Note that F is not total since $F(f)=\perp$. We leave the easy verification that F is continuous to the reader. To obtain a contradiction, assume that F is not maximal. Let $G\in[[\mathbb{N}_\perp\to\mathbb{N}_\perp]\to\mathbb{N}_\perp]$ be such that $F\sqsubset G$. Then there is a compact g such that $\perp=F(g)\sqsubset G(g)\neq\perp$. Note that g cannot have a constant value in $\mathbb{N}$. Recall that then compactness of g in $[\mathbb{N}_\perp\to\mathbb{N}_\perp]$ means that the value of g differs from $\perp$ for only finitely many arguments. First suppose g is compatible with f, that is $g\sqsubseteq f$. Then, from the definition of F, we can easily find $g'\sqsupseteq g$ and $g''\sqsupseteq g$ such that $\perp\neq F(g')\neq F(g'')\neq\perp$. On the other hand we have

$$F(g')=G(g')=G(g)=G(g'')=F(g''),$$

the contradiction showing that g is not compatible with f. Thus there is a smallest $n\in\mathbb{N}$ such that $f(n)\neq g(n)\neq\perp$. But $F(g)=\perp$ so there is a smallest $m<n$ for which $g(m)=\perp$ for otherwise we would have $F(g)=n$. Let $g'\sqsupseteq g$ be such that $\perp\neq g'(m)\neq f(m)$ so that $F(g')=m$. Let $g''\sqsupseteq g$ be such that $(\forall k<n)(g''(k)=f(k))$. Then $F(g'')=n$ and we obtain

$$m=F(g')=G(g')=G(g)=G(g'')=F(g'')=n.$$

The contradiction shows that F is indeed maximal. □

These examples show that the maximality condition is inappropriate as a notion of totality. To find one such notion, which includes all examples given above, let us examine Example 3.1. Let $f\in[\mathbb{N}_\perp\to\mathbb{N}_\perp]$. We have agreed that f is total if $f(x)\neq\perp$ for each $x\in\mathbb{N}$. Fix $n\in\mathbb{N}$ and consider the question "is n the value of f(x)?"

The question has a *definite positive* answer if, in fact, $f(x)=n$. It has a *definite negative* answer if $f(x)=m\in\mathbb{N}$ for some $m\neq n$. If, on the other hand, $f(x)=\perp$ then no definite answer is available since $\perp\sqsubseteq m$ for each $m\in\mathbb{N}$.

Consider the basic open set in $[\mathbb{N}_\perp\to\mathbb{N}_\perp]$ determined by x and n,

$$B_{<x;n>}=\{f\in[\mathbb{N}_\perp\to\mathbb{N}_\perp]: <x;n>\sqsubseteq f\}.$$

Then

$$\begin{aligned} f(x)\neq\perp &\Leftrightarrow (\forall n\in\mathbb{N})\big(<x;n>\sqsubseteq f \text{ or } \neg\mathrm{Cons}(<x;n>,f)\big)\\ &\Leftrightarrow (\forall n\in\mathbb{N})\big(f\in B_{<x;n>} \text{ or } (\exists \text{ open } V)(f\in V\ \&\\ &\qquad\qquad\qquad\qquad V\cap B_{<x;n>}=\varnothing)\big)\\ &\Leftrightarrow (\forall n\in\mathbb{N})(f\notin\partial B_{<x;n>}) \end{aligned}$$

where ∂A is the topological boundary of the set A as defined in Section 5.1. We say that f *decides* an open set V if $f\notin\partial V$. The totality of f can then be expressed by saying that f decides $B_{<x;n>}$ for each $x,n\in\mathbb{N}$.

The connection with topological notions is natural. Recall that we may think of the open sets of a topological space as approximations or (semidecidable) propositions. Consider for some topological space assertions of the form $x\in U$ where U is open. Such an assertion is *definitely true* if, in fact, $x\in U$. It is *definitely false* if there is another definitely true assertion which contradicts it, that is if there is an open set V such that $x\in V$ and $V\cap U=\varnothing$. The assertion $x\in U$ is *decidable* if it is definitely true or definitely false, that is if $x\notin\partial U$.

To say that an element x in a domain D is total we require that the family of open sets which x decides is sufficiently rich. To say that a set $M\subseteq D$ is total we require that the family of open sets decided by *each* $x\in M$ is sufficiently rich. Thus we consider two notions: that of a total *element* and that of a total *set*. Of course, each element of a total set will be a total element. We now give the precise definitions.

3.3 Definitions Let D be a domain.

(i) A family $\mathcal{F}$ of open subsets of D is said to be *separating* if whenever $x_0,x_1,\dots,x_n\in D$ are topologically separated, that is there are open sets $U_0, U_1, \dots, U_n$ such that $x_i\in U_i$ and $U_0\cap U_1\cap\dots\cap U_n=\varnothing$, then $x_0, x_1, \dots, x_n$ can be topologically separated using elements of $\mathcal{F}$.

(ii) An element $x\in D$ *decides* an open set U if $x\notin\partial U$.

(iii) An element $x\in D$ *decides* a family $\mathcal{F}$ of open sets if x decides each $U\in\mathcal{F}$.

(iv) An element $x\in D$ is *total* if $\mathcal{F}(x)=\{U\subseteq D:\ U \text{ open } \&\ x\notin\partial U\}$ is a separating family of open sets.

(v) A set $M \subseteq D$ is *total* if $\mathcal{F}(M) = \{U \subseteq D\colon U \text{ open } \& (\forall x \in M)(x \notin \partial U)\}$ is a separating family of open sets.

Note that if $M \subseteq D$ is a total set and $x \in M$ then x is a total element. Of course, in order to verify that $M \subseteq D$ is a total set (or $x \in D$ is a total element) it suffices to find a family $\mathcal{F} \subseteq \mathcal{F}(M)$ (or $\mathcal{F} \subseteq \mathcal{F}(x)$) which is separating. Here are some further elementary observations.

3.4 Lemma Let D be a domain, $x \in D$, and let U be an open subset of D.
(i) If x decides U and $x \sqsubseteq y$ then y decides U.
(ii) If x decides U then there is $a \in \text{approx}(x)$ such that a decides U.
(iii) If $\mathcal{F}$ is a finite family of open sets and x decides $\mathcal{F}$ then there is $a \in \text{approx}(x)$ such that a decides $\mathcal{F}$.
(iv) If $x \sqsubseteq y$ and $y \in U$ then $x \in U \cup \partial U$.

Proof: (i) follows from the Alexandrov condition on open sets and (ii) from the Scott condition. Part (iii) follows from (i), (ii) and Lemma 3.1.9, and (iv) follows, again, from the Alexandrov condition. □

The following proposition shows that the set of maximal elements in a domain is a total set.

3.5 Proposition Let D be a domain. Then $x \in D_m$ if and only if x decides $\{B_a\colon a \in D_c\}$. In particular, D_m is a total set.

Proof: Suppose x is maximal and $x \notin B_a$ for some $a \in D_c$. Then by the proof of Proposition 5.3.3 there is $b \in D_c$ such that $x \in B_b$ and $B_a \cap B_b = \varnothing$, that is $x \notin \partial B_a$. Thus x decides $\{B_a\colon a \in D_c\}$. Conversely, suppose $x \sqsubset y$, so that x is not maximal, and let $b \in \text{approx}(y) - \text{approx}(x)$. Then $y \in B_b$, $x \notin B_b$ and hence $x \in \partial B_b$ by Lemma 3.4 (iv), that is x does not decide $\{B_a\colon a \in D_c\}$. The family $\{B_a\colon a \in D_c\}$ is clearly separating since it is a topological base, and hence D_m is a total set. □

Before we continue our development we note the following equivalence between topological separation and consistency in domains.

3.6 Lemma Let D be a domain and suppose $x_1, \ldots, x_n \in D$. Then $\text{Cons}(\{x_1, \ldots, x_n\})$ if and only if $x_1, \ldots, x_n$ are topologically inseparable.

Proof: The only if direction is immediate by the Alexandrov condition on open sets. Suppose $x_1, \ldots, x_n \in D$ are topologically inseparable. Thus, whenever $a_i \in \text{approx}(x_i)$ then $\{a_1, \ldots, a_n\}$ is consistent and hence $a_1 \sqcup \ldots \sqcup a_n$ exists by consistent completeness. Let

$$A=\{a_1 \sqcup \ldots \sqcup a_n : a_i \in \text{approx}(x_i),\ i=1,\ldots,n\}.$$

Clearly A is directed since

$$(a_1 \sqcup \ldots \sqcup a_n) \sqcup (b_1 \sqcup \ldots \sqcup b_n) = (a_1 \sqcup b_1) \sqcup \ldots \sqcup (a_n \sqcup b_n)$$

and hence $\bigsqcup A$ exists. Using $\perp$ we have $\text{approx}(x_i) \subseteq A$ for each i and hence $\bigsqcup A$ is an upper bound of $\{x_1,\ldots,x_n\}$. □

For later reference we mention a nice characterization of the total elements in a domain.

3.7 Proposition Let D be a domain. Then $x \in D$ is a total element if and only if for each $x_0,\ldots,x_k \in D$, if $x_0,\ldots,x_k$ are topologically separated then x and x_i are topologically separated for some i.

Proof: Let $x \in D$ be a total element and suppose $x_0,\ldots,x_k$ are topologically separated. Then for each i there is $V_i \in \mathcal{F}(x)$ such that $x_i \in V_i$ and $\bigcap_{i=0}^{k} V_i = \varnothing$. In particular, $x \notin V_i$ for some i. But $x \notin \partial V_i$ so x and x_i are topologically separated.

For the converse we assume that the condition holds and we prove that $\mathcal{F}(x)$ is a separating family of open sets. Let $x_0,\ldots,x_k \in D$ be topologically separated. Choose $a_0 \in \text{approx}(x_0), \ldots, a_k \in \text{approx}(x_k)$ so that $a_0,\ldots,a_k$ are topologically separated, that is $\bigcap_{i=0}^{k} B_{a_i} = \varnothing$. By our hypothesis there is i such that x and a_i are topologically separated. It follows that $x \notin \overline{B_{a_i}}$, the closure of B_{a_i}. Let

$$\begin{cases} V_i = B_{a_i} \\ V_j = B_{a_j} \cup (D - \overline{B_{a_i}}) & \text{for } j \neq i. \end{cases}$$

Then $x \in V_j$ for each $j \neq i$ and $x \notin \partial V_i$, so $x_j \in V_j \in \mathcal{F}(x)$ for $j=0,\ldots,k$. To show that $\bigcap_{j=0}^{k} V_j = \varnothing$ suppose $y \in \bigcap_{j=0}^{k} V_j$. In particular, $y \in B_{a_i}$ and hence $y \in B_{a_j}$ for each j, contradicting that $\bigcap_{j=0}^{k} B_{a_j} = \varnothing$. □

A further requirement one might reasonably place on a *set* M being a total set in a domain D is that elements in M should exist *essentially everywhere* in D. In the language of topology this means that M should be dense in D, that is $M \cap U \neq \varnothing$ for each open set U in D. In fact, the notion of total set can be seen as a tool for proving the density theorem, Theorem 3.9, where, as the name implies, the sets involved being dense is the main result. Of course, the set of maximal elements of a domain is dense.

We now turn to some domain constructions and show how to extend total sets in the given domains to a total set in the constructed domain. First we consider the simple case of the cartesian product. It is reasonable to want a pair to be total just in case each component is total.

3.8 Theorem Let D and E be domains. If $M \subseteq D$ and $N \subseteq E$ are total dense sets then $M \times N \subseteq D \times E$ is a total dense set.

Proof: Recall that the open sets in $D \times E$ are of the form $U \times V$, where U is open in D and V is open in E. So trivially, $M \times N$ is dense in $D \times E$. Let

$$\mathcal{G} = \{U \times V : U \in \mathcal{F}(M) \text{ and } V \in \mathcal{F}(N)\}.$$

Note that $D \in \mathcal{F}(M)$ and $E \in \mathcal{F}(N)$. To show that $\mathcal{G}$ is a separating family, suppose that $(x_0, y_0), \ldots, (x_n, y_n) \in D \times E$ are topologically separated. Thus there are basic open sets $B_{(a_i, b_i)}$ such that $(x_i, y_i) \in B_{(a_i, b_i)}$ and $\bigcap_{i=0}^{n} B_{(a_i, b_i)} = \varnothing$. The latter means that the set $\{(a_0, b_0), \ldots, (a_n, b_n)\}$ is not consistent and hence, by the proof of Theorem 3.3.1, that at least one of the sets $\{a_0, \ldots, a_n\}$ or $\{b_0, \ldots, b_n\}$ is not consistent in D or E respectively. Suppose the former is the case. Then there are $U_0, \ldots, U_n \in \mathcal{F}(M)$ such that $x_i \in U_i$ and $U_0 \cap \ldots \cap U_n = \varnothing$. But then we have that $(x_i, y_i) \in U_i \times E$ and $U_0 \times E \cap \ldots \cap U_n \times E = \varnothing$.

To complete the proof it suffices to show that $\mathcal{G} \subseteq \mathcal{F}(M \times N)$. So we let $(x, y) \in M \times N$ and $U \times V \in \mathcal{G}$. Thus x decides U and y decides V. We must show that (x, y) decides $U \times V$. If $(x, y) \in U \times V$ then we are done. If not, say $y \notin V$, then there is an open set V' such that $y \in V'$ and $V' \cap V = \varnothing$. But then $(x, y) \in D \times V'$ and $(D \times V') \cap (U \times V) = \varnothing$. We leave it as an exercise to show that in fact $\mathcal{G} = \mathcal{F}(M \times N)$. □

We now come to the most interesting construction, that of the function space.

3.9 Density theorem (Berger [1993]) Let D and E be domains. If $M \subseteq D$ and $N \subseteq E$ are total dense sets then $\langle M, N \rangle \subseteq [D \to E]$ is a total dense set.

Consider Example 3.3.9 of the partial continuous functionals. By Proposition 3.5, $\mathbb{N} \subseteq C_0$ is a total dense set. A function in C_{n+1} should be total precisely if it takes total elements in C_n to elements in $\mathbb{N}$. The density theorem shows that this set of total functions is dense in C_{n+1}, in particular it is non-empty. In the next section we will give a detailed analysis of the continuous functionals.

It is convenient to divide the theorem into two parts. Combining the following two lemmas gives the density theorem. In what follows we let D and E be given domains.

3.10 Lemma If $M \subseteq D$ is total and $N \subseteq E$ is dense then $\langle M, N \rangle$ is dense in $[D \to E]$.

Proof: Given a basic open set in $[D \to E]$ we must show that it contains an element of $<M,N>$. Equivalently, given $F = \sqcup_{i\leq n}<a_i; b_i> \in [D \to E]_c$ then we must find $g \in <M,N>$ such that $F \sqsubseteq g$.

Let $I = \{0,1,\dots,n\}$ and let $\mathcal{E} = \{J \subseteq I: \{b_j : j \in J\}$ is not consistent in $E\}$. For $J \in \mathcal{E}$, we know that $\{a_j : j \in J\}$ is not consistent in D by the nature of F and Lemma 3.3.4, which means that $\{a_j : j \in J\}$ can be topologically separated and hence separated using elements of $\mathcal{F}(M)$. For each $J \in \mathcal{E}$ and $i \in J$ we choose $U_{J,i} \in \mathcal{F}(M)$ such that $a_i \in U_{J,i}$ and $\bigcap_{i\in J} U_{J,i} = \emptyset$. If $J \subseteq I$ and $J \notin \mathcal{E}$ then $b_J = \sqcup\{b_j : j \in J\}$ exists in E_c. By the density of N we then choose some $z_J \in N$ such that $b_J \sqsubseteq z_J$.

For $x \in D$ consider the set

$$I_x = \{i \in I : (\forall J \in \mathcal{E})(i \in J \Rightarrow x \in U_{J,i})\},$$

that is I_x consists of those indices i for which x decides $U_{J,i}$ positively for all $J \in \mathcal{E}$. Note that $I_x \notin \mathcal{E}$, since if it were, then $x \in \bigcap_{i\in I_x} U_{I_x,i}$, contradicting the choice of the sets $U_{J,i}$. Finally we let $\mathcal{F}_0 = \{U_{J,i} : i \in J \in \mathcal{E}\}$. Now we define $g : D \to E$ by

$$g(x) = \begin{cases} z_{I_x} & \text{if } x \text{ decides } \mathcal{F}_0 \\ b_{I_x} & \text{otherwise.} \end{cases}$$

It remains to show that g has the required properties. First of all note that

$$a_i \sqsubseteq x \Rightarrow i \in I_x$$

simply because $U_{J,i}$ was chosen such that $a_i \in U_{J,i}$. It follows that $F \sqsubseteq g$. Furthermore $g \in <M,N>$, since if $x \in M$ then x decides $\mathcal{F}(M)$ and hence $\mathcal{F}_0$, so $g(x) = z_{I_x} \in N$.

The above statements are valid provided g is continuous, which we now prove. The crucial point here is the reduction of $\mathcal{F}(M)$ to the *finite* subset $\mathcal{F}_0$. First we consider the sets I_x. Clearly if $x \sqsubseteq x'$ then $I_x \subseteq I_{x'}$, by the Alexandrov condition on open sets. The Scott condition gives, for each $x \in D$, an element $c \in \text{approx}(x)$ such that $I_c = I_x$. For suppose $i \in I_x$ and $i \in J \in \mathcal{E}$. Then choose $c_{J,i} \in \text{approx}(x) \cap U_{J,i}$ and let

$$c = \sqcup\{c_{J,i} :\ i \in I_x \text{ and } i \in J \in \mathcal{E}\}.$$

Now suppose that x decides $\mathcal{F}_0$ and $x \sqsubseteq x'$. Suppose $i \in I_{x'}$ and let $i \in J \in \mathcal{E}$. Then $x' \in U_{J,i} \in \mathcal{F}_0$ and hence $x \in U_{J,i}$ since x decides $U_{J,i}$. It follows that $I_x = I_{x'}$.

To show that g is monotone suppose $x \sqsubseteq x'$ so that $I_x \subseteq I_{x'}$. If x decides $\mathcal{F}_0$ then $I_x = I_{x'}$ so $g(x) = z_{I_x} = z_{I_{x'}} = g(x')$. In case x does not decide $\mathcal{F}_0$ then $g(x) = b_{I_x} \sqsubseteq b_{I_{x'}} \sqsubseteq g(x')$.

Finally to show the continuity of g it suffices to show for each $x \in D$ that there is $e \in \mathrm{approx}(x)$ such that $g(e) = g(x)$. Choose $c \in \mathrm{approx}(x)$ such that $I_c = I_x$. If x decides $\mathcal{F}_0$ then, by Lemma 3.4 (iii), there is $d \in \mathrm{approx}(x)$ which decides $\mathcal{F}_0$. But then $e = c \sqcup d$ decides $\mathcal{F}_0$ and $I_e = I_x$ so that $g(e) = g(x)$. If, on the other hand, x does not decide $\mathcal{F}_0$, then neither does c. But in that case $g(x) = g(c)$. □

3.11 Lemma If $M \subseteq D$ is dense and $N \subseteq E$ is total then $\langle M, N\rangle$ is total in $[D \rightarrow E]$.

Proof: Let

$$\mathcal{G} = \{\langle x, U\rangle : x \in M \text{ and } U \in \mathcal{F}(N)\}$$

where $\langle x, U\rangle = \{f \in [D \rightarrow E] : f(x) \in U\}$. We shall show that $\mathcal{G}$ is a separating family of open sets in $[D \rightarrow E]$ and that $\langle M, N\rangle$ decides $\mathcal{G}$.

Suppose $U \subseteq E$ is open and $x \in D$. To show that $\langle x, U\rangle$ is an open set let $f \in \langle x, U\rangle$ and $f \sqsubseteq g$. Then $f(x) \sqsubseteq g(x)$ so $g \in \langle x, U\rangle$, since U is open, proving the Alexandrov condition. To verify the Scott condition let $f \in \langle x, U\rangle$ and choose $b \in \mathrm{approx}(f(x)) \cap U$. By continuity, choose $a \in \mathrm{approx}(x)$ such that $b \sqsubseteq f(a)$. Then $\langle a; b\rangle \sqsubseteq f$ and $\langle a; b\rangle(x) = b \in U$ so that $\langle a; b\rangle \in \langle x, U\rangle$.

To prove that $f \in \langle M, N\rangle$ decides $\mathcal{G}$ suppose $f \notin \langle x, U\rangle$, that is $f(x) \notin U$. But $f(x) \in N$ and hence decides U. Thus there is an open set V such that $f(x) \in V$ and $V \cap U = \emptyset$. But then $f \in \langle x, V\rangle$ and $\langle x, V\rangle \cap \langle x, U\rangle = \emptyset$.

It remains to show that $\mathcal{G}$ is a separating family. Let $f_0, \dots, f_n \in [D \rightarrow E]$ be topologically separated by basic open sets determined by $F_i = \bigsqcup_{j \in I_i} \langle a_{ij}; b_{ij}\rangle$. It follows that the set

$$\{\langle a_{ij}; b_{ij}\rangle : j \in I_i\,,\ i = 0, \dots, n\}$$

is not consistent in $[D \rightarrow E]$. By Lemma 3.3.4 there is a set $K \subseteq \bigcup_{i=0}^{n} \{i\} \times I_i$ such that $\{a_{ij} : (i,j) \in K\}$ is consistent in D while $\{b_{ij} : (i,j) \in K\}$ is not consistent in E. Set $K_i = \{j \in I_i : (i,j) \in K\}$. For each i, $c_i = \bigsqcup\{b_{ij} : j \in K_i\}$ exists in E, again by Lemma 3.3.4. The set $\{c_0, \dots, c_n\}$ is not consistent in E, that is $c_0, \dots, c_n$ can be separated topologically and hence by $U_0, \dots, U_n \in \mathcal{F}(N)$. On the other hand, since $\{a_{ij} : (i,j) \in K\}$ is consistent and M is dense, there is $x \in M$ such that $a_{ij} \sqsubseteq x$ for each $(i,j) \in K$. For such an x we have

$$f_i(x) \sqsupseteq f_i(\bigsqcup\{a_{ij} : j \in K_i\}) \sqsupseteq F_i(\bigsqcup\{a_{ij} : j \in K_i\}) \sqsupseteq \bigsqcup\{b_{ij} : j \in K_i\} = c_i.$$

But $c_i \in U_i$ and hence $f_i \in \langle x, U_i \rangle \in \mathcal{G}$. Furthermore, since $U_0 \cap \ldots \cap U_n = \emptyset$, we have $\langle x, U_0 \rangle \cap \ldots \cap \langle x, U_n \rangle = \emptyset$, which proves that $f_0, \ldots, f_n$ are separated by elements of $\mathcal{G}$. □

Consider the set $\langle M, N \rangle$ of total functions in $[D \rightarrow E]$ as in Theorem 3.9. If we were to extract the truly total functions then we should discard all partial information, that is we should consider the restrictions of the functions in $\langle M, N \rangle$ to M. Of course, there may be many distinct functions in $\langle M, N \rangle$ which when restricted to M become identical. Thus we are led to identify all such functions. This will be studied in detail in the next section for the continuous functionals. In the remaining part of this section we will describe a general method to obtain a set or space of total elements which has the construction just described as a special case.

Let D be a domain and let $M \subseteq D$ be a set of total elements (so *not* necessarily a total set). Define a binary relation $\sim$ on M by

$$x \sim y \Leftrightarrow \mathrm{Cons}(x, y).$$

It is this relation that is used to identify total elements as in the example of the function space.

3.12 Lemma The relation $\sim$ is an equivalence relation on M.

Proof: The relation $\sim$ is clearly reflexive and symmetric. To prove transitivity let $x, y, z \in M$ and suppose $x \not\sim z$. Then x and z are topologically separated by Lemma 3.6 and hence they are separated by elements of $\mathcal{F}(y)$. Thus we may choose $U, V \in \mathcal{F}(y)$ such that $x \in U$, $z \in V$ and $U \cap V = \emptyset$. Suppose $x \sim y$. Then $x \sqcup y$ exists and $x \sqcup y \in U$. But then, by Lemma 3.4 (iv), $y \in U$ so y and z are topologically separated by U and V, that is $y \not\sim z$. □

3.13 Definition Let D be a domain and let $M \subseteq D$ be a set of total elements. Let $\sim$ be the binary relation on M defined by $x \sim y \Leftrightarrow \mathrm{Cons}(x, y)$. We say that

$$\tilde{M} = M/{\sim} = \{[x]_{\sim} : x \in M\}$$

is the *space of total elements* obtained from $M \subseteq D$.

As usual, $[x]_{\sim}$ denotes the equivalence class with respect to $\sim$ containing x. In the sequel we shall simply write $[x]$ for $[x]_{\sim}$.

In the case the set M is upwards closed with respect to the domain ordering $\sqsubseteq$, we can define a canonical representative $\bar{x}$ of $[x]$. Of course, if x is total and $x \sqsubseteq y$ then y is also total by Lemma 3.4 (i).

3.14 Lemma If $M \subseteq D$ is a set of total elements which is upwards closed with respect to $\sqsubseteq$ in D then each equivalence class $[x]$ contains a unique element maximal in D.

Proof: We show that the set $[x]$ is directed. Suppose $y, z \in [x]$. Then $y \sim z$ and hence $y \sqcup z$ exists in M, $y \sim y \sqcup z$ and hence $x \sim y \sqcup z$, that is $y \sqcup z \in [x]$. Thus we may set $\tilde{x} = \bigsqcup[x]$. Clearly $\tilde{x} \in [x]$ and $\tilde{x}$ is maximal in D. □

We say that the element $\tilde{x}$ constructed in the proof is the *canonical* (*maximal*) representative of $[x]$. Unfortunately, there is in general no *continuous* function on D which given $x \in M$ has $\tilde{x}$ as value. This forces us to consider the quotient structure $\tilde{M}$ rather than the subspace $\{\tilde{x} : x \in M\}$.

In order to connect with the topological notion of continuity we briefly consider one possible topology on the space of total elements $\tilde{M}$. The domain D has the Scott topology and M inherits the subspace topology (5.3.1) from D. Then we give $\tilde{M}$ the quotient topology (5.3.6) from M. Thus $U \subseteq \tilde{M}$ is open precisely when $\bigcup U$ is open in M, that is if and only if $\bigcup U = V \cap M$ for some Scott open set $V \subseteq D$. We call this topology the *quotient topology* for $\tilde{M}$.

An important observation is that continuous functions between domains induce continuous functions between corresponding spaces of total elements.

3.15 Proposition Let D and E be domains and suppose $M \subseteq D$ and $N \subseteq E$ are sets of total elements. If $f: D \to E$ is a continuous function such that $f[M] \subseteq N$ then $\tilde{f}: \tilde{M} \to \tilde{N}$ defined by $\tilde{f}([x]) = [f(x)]$ is continuous with respect to the quotient topologies.

Proof: Exercise 10. □

Throughout the remaining part of this section we shall restrict ourselves to the situation where $M \subseteq D$ is a total *set* and not only a set of total elements.

3.16 Lemma Let D be a domain and let $M \subseteq D$ be a total set. Then, for each $V \in \mathcal{F}(M)$ and $x \in M$, $[x] \subseteq V$ if and only if $x \in V$.

Proof: For the non-trivial direction assume $x \in V$ and $x \sim y$. Then $x \sqcup y \in V$ since V is open and hence $y \in V$ since y decides V. □

For $V \in \mathcal{F}(M)$ define $\tilde{V} = \{[x] : x \in M \cap V\}$. By Lemma 3.16, $[x] \in \tilde{V}$ if and only if $[x] \subseteq V$, so

$$\bigcup \tilde{V} = \bigcup \{[x] : x \in M \cap V\} = \{x : x \in M \cap V\} = M \cap V.$$

Thus $\tilde{V}$ is open in $\tilde{M}$ for each $V \in \mathcal{F}(M)$, when $\tilde{M}$ is given the quotient topology.

3.17 Proposition If $M \subseteq D$ is a total set then $\tilde{M}$ is a Hausdorff space.

Proof: Let $[x], [y] \in \tilde{M}$ be distinct elements. Thus $x \not\sim y$ and hence x and y can be separated by $U, V \in \mathcal{F}(M)$. But then $\tilde{U}$ and $\tilde{V}$ are open sets in $\tilde{M}$ which separate $[x]$ and $[y]$. □

It turns out that the sets $\tilde{V}$ for $V \in \mathcal{F}(M)$ are also closed in $\tilde{M}$.

3.18 Lemma $V \cap M$ is closed in M for each $V \in \mathcal{F}(M)$.

Proof: By Proposition 5.1.8 it suffices to show that $V \cap M$ contains all its limit points. Suppose $y \in M$ and $y \notin V$. Since y decides V there is an open set W in D such that $y \in W$ and $W \cap V = \emptyset$. Thus $W \cap M$ is an open set in M witnessing that y is not a limit point of $V \cap M$. □

3.19 Corollary The set $\tilde{V}$ is open and closed in $\tilde{M}$ for each $V \in \mathcal{F}(M)$.

Proof: It remains to show that $\tilde{M} - \tilde{V}$ is open. But

$$\bigcup\{[x] : [x] \notin \tilde{V}\} = \{x \in M : x \notin V\} = M - (V \cap M)$$

which is open by Lemma 3.18. □

Section 8.4 The Continuous Functionals

The continuous functionals of finite type were introduced by Kleene [1959] (who called them the countable functionals) and Kreisel [1959]. An early example of their use was for obtaining constructive interpretations of classical mathematics. But they also have an independent interest and they have been studied extensively. A general reference for the theory of the continuous functionals is Normann [1980].

The Kleene–Kreisel continuous functionals, usually built up over the natural numbers $\mathbb{N}$, are *total* in that each functional is defined for all of its arguments. The *partial* continuous functionals of Example 3.3.9 are partial in the sense that $\perp$ is interpreted as undefined. Nonetheless they do contain the total continuous functionals in a very precise sense. In this section we use the results of Section 8.3 to show how to obtain total continuous functionals from given partial ones. Then we show that the type structure of the total continuous functionals obtained from the partial continuous functionals is naturally isomorphic to the Kleene–Kreisel continuous functionals.

First we define the set of finite type symbols. These serve as indices for finite type structures of various kinds.

4.1 Definition The set of *finite type symbols*, TS, is defined inductively by
(i) $o \in TS$,
(ii) if $\sigma, \tau \in TS$ then $(\sigma \to \tau), (\sigma \times \tau) \in TS$.

Often it is convenient to restrict oneself to the set of *pure type symbols*, P, obtained by replacing clause (ii) with

(ii') if $\sigma \in P$ then $(\sigma \to o) \in P$.

The set P is identified with $\mathbb{N}$ by identifying o with 0 and $(\sigma \to o)$ with $n+1$ when σ is identified with n.

For readability we omit parentheses in the type symbols when no confusion is possible.

Given a domain E there is a natural *type structure of domains* $\{D_\sigma\}_{\sigma \in TS}$ *over* E, defined inductively by

$$\begin{cases} D_o = E \\ D_{\sigma \to \tau} = [D_\sigma \to D_\tau] \\ D_{\sigma \times \tau} = D_\sigma \times D_\tau. \end{cases}$$

Restricting ourselves to the pure type symbols P we obtain the *pure type structure of domains* $\{D_n\}_{n \in P}$ *over* E. Thus the type structure consisting of the partial continuous functionals of Example 3.3.9 is the pure type structure of domains over $\mathbb{N}_\perp$.

Let us assume that we are given a type structure $\mathcal{D} = \{D_\sigma\}_{\sigma \in TS}$ of domains as defined above. We shall construct a type structure $\mathcal{G} = \{G_\sigma\}_{\sigma \in TS}$ such that the latter represents in a natural way the total elements of the former. Of course, it will be a total type structure in the sense that an element of $G_{\sigma \to \tau}$ is (identified with) a total function from G_σ into G_τ and $G_{\sigma \times \tau}$ is (identified with) $G_\sigma \times G_\tau$.

The first step is to obtain a type structure $\{\overline{G}_\sigma\}_{\sigma \in TS}$ such that each $\overline{G}_\sigma \subseteq D_\sigma$ is a dense total set in the sense of Section 8.3. Let $M \subseteq D_o$ be a dense total set. By induction on TS we define the type structure

$$\begin{cases} \overline{G}_o = M \\ \overline{G}_{\sigma \to \tau} = \langle \overline{G}_\sigma, \overline{G}_\tau \rangle = \{f \in [D_\sigma \to D_\tau] : f[\overline{G}_\sigma] \subseteq \overline{G}_\tau\} \\ \overline{G}_{\sigma \times \tau} = \overline{G}_\sigma \times \overline{G}_\tau. \end{cases}$$

Each $\overline{G}_\sigma \subseteq D_\sigma$ is a dense total set by Theorems 3.8 and 3.9.

Note that $\overline{G}_{\sigma \to \tau}$ is in general too large to faithfully represent the total objects in $D_{\sigma \to \tau}$. It may be the case for $f, g \in \overline{G}_{\sigma \to \tau}$ that $f(x) = g(x)$ for each $x \in \overline{G}_\sigma$ even though $f \neq g$, that is f and g behave differently on the approximations of an element of $\bar{G}_\sigma$ although they are identical on $\bar{G}_\sigma$. In order to identify all such functions we introduce the following equivalence relations.

4.2 Definition Let $\{D_\sigma\}_{\sigma\in TS}$ be a type structure of domains and let $\{\bar{G}_\sigma\}_{\sigma\in TS}$ be the type structure defined above over some dense total set $M\subseteq D_o$. For each $\sigma\in TS$ let $\sim_\sigma$ be the binary relation on $\bar{G}_\sigma$ defined by

$$x\sim_o y \Leftrightarrow x \text{ and } y \text{ are consistent in } D_o,$$
$$f\sim_{\sigma\to\tau} g \Leftrightarrow (\forall x\in\bar{G}_\sigma)(f(x)\sim_\tau g(x)),$$
$$(x,y)\sim_{\sigma\times\tau}(z,w) \Leftrightarrow x\sim_\sigma z \text{ and } y\sim_\tau w.$$

Thus $\sim_o$ is the equivalence relation $\sim$ introduced in Section 8.3.

4.3 Lemma The relation $\sim_\sigma$ is an equivalence relation on $\bar{G}_\sigma$.

Proof: The only non-trivial part is to show that $\sim_o$ is an equivalence relation and this is Lemma 3.12. □

The relation $\sim_\sigma$ is the consistency relation for each $\bar{G}_\sigma\subseteq D_\sigma$.

4.4 Lemma For each $\sigma\in TS$, $x\sim_\sigma y$ if and only if x and y are consistent in D_σ.

Proof: By induction on σ. It is true by definition for $\sigma=o$. The case $\sigma\times\tau$ is left to the reader. Let $f,g\in\bar{G}_{\sigma\to\tau}$ and suppose $f\not\sim_{\sigma\to\tau}g$. Choose $x\in\bar{G}_\sigma$ such that $f(x)\not\sim_\tau g(x)$. By the induction hypothesis there are open sets U and V in D_τ separating $f(x)$ and $g(x)$. But then, using the notation in the proof of Lemma 3.11, $<x,U>$ and $<x,V>$ are open sets in $D_{\sigma\to\tau}$ separating f and g.

Conversely, suppose f and g can be separated in $D_{\sigma\to\tau}$. Then, by the proof of Lemma 3.11, there is $x\in\bar{G}_\sigma$ and U in the separating family $\mathcal{F}(\bar{G}_\tau)$ such that $f(x)\in U$ and $g(x)\notin U$. But $g(x)$ decides U so there is an open set W in D_τ such that $g(x)\in W$ and $W\cap U=\emptyset$. By the induction hypothesis we then have $f(x)\not\sim_\tau g(x)$ and hence $f\not\sim_{\sigma\to\tau}g$. □

The desired set G_σ is obtained by taking the quotient of $\bar{G}_\sigma$ with respect to $\sim_\sigma$ as in Definition 3.13. For this to be well-defined in the sense that $G_{\sigma\to\tau}$ is (identifiable with) a set of functions from $\bar{G}_\sigma$ into $\bar{G}_\tau$, we need to show that $\sim_\sigma$ is a congruence relation with respect to all elements in $\bar{G}_{\sigma\to\tau}$.

4.5 Lemma Let $f\in\bar{G}_{\sigma\to\tau}$. If $x\sim_\sigma y$ then $f(x)\sim_\tau f(y)$.

Proof: If $x\sim_\sigma y$ then, by Lemma 4.4, $x\sqcup y$ exists and hence $f(x)\sim_\tau f(y)$ by the monotonicity of f. □

4.6 Corollary If $f\sim_{\sigma\to\tau}g$ and $x\sim_\sigma y$ then $f(x)\sim_\tau g(y)$.

Proof: By Lemma 4.5 and the definition of $\sim_{\sigma\to\tau}$, $f(x)\sim_\tau f(y)\sim_\tau g(y)$. □

For $\sigma\in TS$ and $x\in\bar{G}_\sigma$ let $[x]_\sigma$ denote the equivalence class with respect to $\sim_\sigma$ containing x. The quotient structure of $\bar{G}_\sigma$ with respect to $\sim_\sigma$ is the set

$$G_\sigma=\bar{G}_\sigma/{\sim_\sigma}=\{[x]_\sigma : x\in\bar{G}_\sigma\}.$$

4.7 Definition Let D be a domain and let $M\subseteq D$ be a dense total set. Then

$$\mathcal{G}=\{G_\sigma\}_{\sigma\in TS}$$

is the *total type structure over* $M\subseteq D$.

The total type structure $\mathcal{G}$ is natural in the following sense. The set $G_{\sigma\times\tau}$ is naturally identified with $G_\sigma\times G_\tau$ via the mapping

$$[(x,y)]_{\sigma\times\tau} \mapsto ([x]_\sigma,[y]_\tau).$$

Similarly, the set $G_{\sigma\to\tau}$ is naturally identified with a set of total functions from G_σ into G_τ by defining

$$[f]_{\sigma\to\tau}([x]_\sigma)=[f(x)]_\tau,$$

which is well-defined by Corollary 4.6.

Let us summarize what we have done. Given a domain E we easily obtain a type structure of domains $\mathcal{D}=\{D_\sigma\}_{\sigma\in TS}$ over E which we may think of as the *partial continuous functionals over* E. For a dense total set $M\subseteq E$ we have constructed a type structure $\mathcal{G}=\{G_\sigma\}_{\sigma\in TS}$ over $M\subseteq E$ where each G_σ may be seen as the total elements in D_σ over M. Thus we regard $\mathcal{G}$ as the *total continuous functionals over* $M\subseteq E$. In particular, if A is a set then the type structure of the *total continuous functionals over* A is obtained by setting $E=A_\perp$.

The rest of this section is devoted to proving that the type structure of the total continuous functionals over $\mathbb{N}$ is naturally isomorphic to the Kleene–Kreisel continuous functionals. First we need to give a precise definition of the latter. There are a number of essentially equivalent definitions in the literature. The one we choose, from Ershov [1974], is very close to Kreisel's original definition. For simplicity we restrict ourselves to pure type structures.

For each $n\in P$ we define a set of *formal neighbourhoods* Φ_n and a binary commutative operation $\cap$ on Φ_n denoting *formal intersection*:

$$\Phi_0=\{\{m\}: m\in\mathbb{N}\}\cup\{\varnothing\}.$$

$$\{m\}\cap\{n\}=\begin{cases}\{m\} & \text{if } m=n\\ \varnothing & \text{if } m\neq n.\end{cases}$$

$$U^0 \cap \varnothing = \varnothing \text{ for } U^0 \in \Phi_0.$$

Suppose we have defined Φ_n and the operation $\cap$ on Φ_n. Then let

$$\Phi_{n+1} = \{\{<U_i^n; n_i>: i=0,\ldots,k-1\}: n_i \in \mathbb{N}, k>0, \varnothing \neq U_i^n \in \Phi_n, \text{ and } U_i^n \cap U_j^n \neq \varnothing \Rightarrow n_i = n_j\} \cup \{\varnothing\}.$$

Suppose $U^{n+1} = \{<U_i^n; n_i>: i<k\}$ and $V^{n+1} = \{<V_j^n; m_j>: j<t\}$ belong to Φ_{n+1}. Then define

$$U^{n+1} \cap V^{n+1} = \begin{cases} \{<U_i^n; n_i>: i<k\} \cup \{<V_j^n; m_j>: j<t\} \\ \qquad\qquad \text{if } (\forall i<k)(\forall j<t)(U_i^n \cap V_j^n \neq \varnothing \Rightarrow n_i = m_j) \\ \varnothing \qquad\qquad \text{otherwise,} \end{cases}$$

and define $U^{n+1} \cap \varnothing = \varnothing$ for $U^{n+1} \in \Phi_{n+1}$. Finally we set $\Phi_n^+ = \Phi_n - \{\varnothing\}$.

Each element in Φ_n^+ should be thought of as a *consistent* neighbourhood. Two neighbourhoods $U^n, V^n \in \Phi_n$ are *consistent* when $U^n \cap V^n \neq \varnothing$.

Now we define a family $\{\overline{K}_n\}_{n \in P}$ and a relation $\in_n$ between $\overline{K}_n$ and Φ_n with the intuitive meaning that an element of $\overline{K}_n$ belongs to a formal neighbourhood in Φ_n. Each $\overline{K}_{n+1}$ will be a set of partial functions so the reader should recall the notation used in Section 1.1. Let $\overline{K}_0 = \mathbb{N}$ and define $\in_0$ by $m \in_0 U^0 \Leftrightarrow m \in U^0$. Suppose that $\overline{K}_n$ and $\in_n$ have been defined. Then let

$$\overline{K}_{n+1} = \{f \mid f: \Phi_n^+ \xrightarrow{p} \mathbb{N} \text{ such that (1) and (2)}\}$$

where

(1) $U^n \cap V^n \neq \varnothing \;\&\; f(U^n)\downarrow \;\Rightarrow\; f(U^n) \simeq f(U^n \cap V^n)$,

(2) $(\forall g \in \overline{K}_n)(\exists U^n \in \Phi_n^+)(g \in_n U^n \;\&\; f(U^n)\downarrow)$.

For $f \in \overline{K}_{n+1}$ and $U^{n+1} = \{<U_i^n; n_i>: i<k\} \in \Phi_{n+1}^+$ define

$$f \in_{n+1} U^{n+1} \Leftrightarrow (\forall i<k)(f(U_i^n) \simeq n_i).$$

Each neighbourhood U^n contains a finite amount of information and hence (1) is a notion of continuity, expressing that a value of f only depends on a finite amount of information. On the other hand we want to think of $f \in \overline{K}_{n+1}$ as taking arguments in $\overline{K}_n$. Condition (2), in connection with (1), assures us of a natural way of doing that.

4.8 Proposition If $f \in_n U^n$ and $f \in_n V^n$ then $U^n \cap V^n \neq \varnothing$ and $f \in_n U^n \cap V^n$.

Proof: The case $n=0$ is trivial. Let $f \in_{n+1} U^{n+1} = \{<U_i^n; n_i>: i<k\}$ and $f \in_{n+1} V^{n+1} = \{<V_j^n; m_j>: j<t\}$. If for some i,j, $U_i^n \cap V_j^n \neq \varnothing$ then, using (1),

$$n_i \simeq f(U_i^n) \simeq f(U_i^n \cap V_j^n) \simeq f(V_j^n) \simeq m_j$$

proving that $U^{n+1} \cap V^{n+1} \neq \varnothing$. Trivially $f \in_{n+1} U^{n+1} \cap V^{n+1}$. □

We can now view $f \in \bar{K}_{n+1}$ as being a total function defined on $\bar{K}_n$ as follows. Let $g \in \bar{K}_n$ and choose, by condition (2), $U^n \in \stackrel{+}{\Phi}_n$ such that $g \in_n U^n$ and $f(U^n)\downarrow$. Then set $f(g) = f(U^n)$. Proposition 4.8 and condition (1) imply that $f(g)$ is independent of the choice of U^n.

A crucial observation for defining the continuous functionals is Kreisel's density theorem, the analogue of Theorem 3.9. We state it here without proof, in view of having proved Theorem 3.9; the proof can be found in Kreisel [1959].

4.9 Kreisel's density theorem For each $U^n \in \stackrel{+}{\Phi}_n$ there is $f \in \bar{K}_n$ such that $f \in_n U^n$.

In analogy with the construction of $\mathcal{G}$ in Definition 4.7 we define an equivalence relation $\sim_n$ on $\bar{K}_n$ by

$$\begin{cases} m \sim_0 n \iff m = n \\ f \sim_{n+1} g \iff (\forall U^n \in \stackrel{+}{\Phi}_n)(f(U^n)\downarrow \;\&\; g(U^n)\downarrow \Rightarrow f(U^n) = g(U^n)). \end{cases}$$

4.10 Lemma Let $f, g \in \bar{K}_{n+1}$.

(i) $f \sim_{n+1} g \iff (\forall h \in \bar{K}_n)(f(h) = g(h))$.

(ii) $h \sim_n k \Rightarrow f(h) = f(k)$.

(iii) $f \sim_{n+1} g \;\&\; h \sim_n k \Rightarrow f(h) = g(k)$.

Proof: (i) Suppose $f \sim_{n+1} g$ and let $h \in \bar{K}_n$. Choose $U^n, V^n \in \stackrel{+}{\Phi}_n$ witnessing the values $f(h)$ and $g(h)$ respectively. By Proposition 4.8, $U^n \cap V^n \neq \varnothing$ and hence

$$f(h) \simeq f(U^n) \simeq f(U^n \cap V^n) \simeq g(U^n \cap V^n) \simeq g(V^n) \simeq g(h).$$

Conversely, suppose $f \not\sim_{n+1} g$ and let $U^n \in \stackrel{+}{\Phi}_n$ witness this. By the density theorem there is $h \in \bar{K}_n$ such that $h \in_n U^n$, so that $f(h) = f(U^n) \neq g(U^n) = g(h)$.

(ii) By condition (1) it suffices to show

$$h \sim_n k,\; h \in_n U^n,\; k \in_n V^n \Rightarrow U^n \cap V^n \neq \varnothing.$$

This is trivial for $n = 0$, so consider $n+1$. Say $U^{n+1} = \{\langle U_i^n; n_i\rangle : i < k\}$ and $V^{n+1} = \{\langle V_j^n; m_j\rangle : j < t\}$ and suppose $U_i^n \cap V_j^n \neq \varnothing$. Then

$$n_i \simeq h(U_i^n) \simeq h(U_i^n \cap V_j^n) \simeq k(U_i^n \cap V_j^n) \simeq k(V_j^n) \simeq m_j$$

proving that $U^{n+1} \cap V^{n+1} \neq \varnothing$.

(iii) Follows from (i) and (ii). □

4.11 Definition The (pure) type structure of the *Kleene–Kreisel continuous functionals* is the type structure $\mathcal{K}=\{K_n\}_{n\in P}$ where $K_n=\overline{K}_n/\sim_n$.

Of course, we identify K_0 with $\mathbb{N}$ and K_{n+1} with total functions from K_n into $\mathbb{N}$. That the latter is well-defined is the content of Lemma 4.10 (iii).

4.12 Theorem (Ershov [1974, 1977a]) Let $\mathcal{G}=\{G_n\}_{n\in P}$ be the pure total continuous functionals over $\mathbb{N}$ and let $\mathcal{K}=\{K_n\}_{n\in P}$ be the pure Kleene–Kreisel continuous functionals. Then $\mathcal{G}$ and $\mathcal{K}$ are naturally isomorphic.

In saying that $\mathcal{G}$ and $\mathcal{K}$ are *naturally isomorphic* we mean that, for each n, there are mappings $\phi_n:K_n\to G_n$ and $\theta_n:G_n\to K_n$ such that $\theta_n\circ\phi_n=id_{K_n}$ and $\phi_n\circ\theta_n=id_{G_n}$, and such that for $f\in K_{n+1}$ and $g\in K_n$,

$$f(g)=\phi_{n+1}(f)(\phi_n(g)),$$

and for $h\in G_{n+1}$ and $k\in G_n$,

$$h(k)=\theta_{n+1}(h)(\theta_n(k)).$$

The pure partial continuous functionals over $\mathbb{N}_\perp$, $\mathcal{C}=\{C_n\}_{n\in P}$, could be thought of as a more basic and natural object than $\mathcal{K}$, just as the partial recursive functions form a more natural class than the total recursive functions. Furthermore, many concepts for $\mathcal{K}$ have, via Ershov's theorem, natural counterparts for $\mathcal{C}$ where they may be much easier to study.

To prove Ershov's theorem we shall define mappings $^*:\overline{K}_n\to C_n$ and $^+:C_n\to\overline{K}_n$ such that when these are modified with the appropriate restrictions and quotients they will provide the desired isomorphism.

First we define mappings $\Psi_n:\overset{+}{\Phi}_n\to C_n$ by

$$\Psi_0(\{m\})=m\in\mathbb{N},$$
$$\Psi_{n+1}(\{<U_i^n;n_i>:i<k\})=\bigsqcup_{i<k}<\Psi_n(U_i^n);n_i>.$$

4.13 Proposition For each $U^n\in\overset{+}{\Phi}_n$, $\Psi_n(U^n)$ is defined and compact in C_n. Furthermore, for $U^n,V^n\in\overset{+}{\Phi}_n$,

$$U^n\cap V^n\neq\varnothing \Leftrightarrow \Psi_n(U^n) \text{ and } \Psi_n(V^n) \text{ are consistent in } C_n.$$

Proof: The case $n=0$ is clear. Let $U^{n+1}=\{<U_i^n;n_i>:i<k\}\in\overset{+}{\Phi}_{n+1}$. To show that $\Psi_{n+1}(U^{n+1})$ is well-defined and compact it suffices to show that the set

$$\{<\Psi_n(U_i^n);n_i>:i<k\}$$

is consistent in C_{n+1}. We use Lemma 3.3.4, but observe that we only need to consider pairs since the receiving domain C_0 is flat. So suppose $\Psi_n(U_i^n)$ and

$\Psi_n(U_j^n)$ are consistent in C_n. By the induction hypothesis, $U_i^n \cap U_j^n \neq \emptyset$ and hence $n_i = n_j$, since $U^{n+1} \in \overset{+}{\Phi}_{n+1}$.

Now let $V^{n+1} = \{<V_j^n; m_j>: j<t\} \in \overset{+}{\Phi}_{n+1}$ and suppose $U^{n+1} \cap V^{n+1} \neq \emptyset$. If $\Psi_n(U_i^n)$ and $\Psi_n(V_j^n)$ are consistent in C_n then, by induction, $U_i^n \cap V_j^n \neq \emptyset$ so $n_i = m_j$. This shows that $\Psi_{n+1}(U^{n+1})$ and $\Psi_{n+1}(V^{n+1})$ are consistent. Conversely, suppose the latter functions are consistent and suppose $U_i^n \cap V_j^n \neq \emptyset$. By induction, $\Psi_n(U_i^n)$ and $\Psi_n(V_j^n)$ are consistent and hence, again by Lemma 3.3.4, $n_i = m_j$. Thus $U^{n+1} \cap V^{n+1} \neq \emptyset$. □

The proposition states that there is an exact correspondence with regard to consistency between $\overset{+}{\Phi}_n$ and its image under Ψ_n. The problem is that this image does not make up all the compact elements in C_n. However the following consistency property suffices for our purposes. Suppose $\Psi_n(U^n)$ and $\Psi_n(V^n)$ are consistent in C_n. Then $U^n \cap V^n \neq \emptyset$ and hence

$$\Psi_n(U^n \cap V^n) = \Psi_n(U^n) \sqcup \Psi_n(V^n).$$

4.14 Lemma Let $f \in \overline{K}_{n+1}$. Then the set $\{\Psi_{n+1}(U^{n+1}) : f \in_{n+1} U^{n+1}\}$ is directed in C_{n+1}.

Proof: Each $\overline{K}_n$ is non-empty by the density theorem and hence the set is non-empty by condition (2) for f. The lemma now follows from Proposition 4.8 and the remark above. □

Given $f \in \overline{K}_{n+1}$ we set $f^* = \bigsqcup\{\Psi_{n+1}(U^{n+1}) : f \in_{n+1} U^{n+1}\}$. This gives us a mapping $^*: \overline{K}_{n+1} \longrightarrow C_{n+1}$ by Lemma 4.14. Note that each f^* is a strict function. Conversely, given $h \in C_{n+1}$ define a partial function $h^+ : \overset{+}{\Phi}_n \xrightarrow{p} \mathbb{N}$ by

$$h^+(U^n) = \begin{cases} h(\Psi_n(U^n)) & \text{if } h(\Psi_n(U^n)) \neq \bot \\ \uparrow & \text{if } h(\Psi_n(U^n)) = \bot. \end{cases}$$

Note that condition (1) holds for h^+ by the monotonicity of h, since if $U^n \cap V^n \neq \emptyset$ then $\Psi_n(U^n \cap V^n) = \Psi_n(U^n) \sqcup \Psi_n(V^n) \sqsupseteq \Psi_n(U^n)$.

4.15 Lemma (i) The image of $\overline{G}_{n+1}$ under the mapping $h \mapsto h^+$ is contained in $\overline{K}_{n+1}$.
(ii) The image of $\overline{K}_{n+1}$ under the mapping $f \mapsto f^*$ is contained in $\overline{G}_{n+1}$. Furthermore, for each $h \in \overline{G}_{n+1}$ there is $f \in \overline{K}_{n+1}$ such that $f^* \sqsubseteq h$.

Proof: By induction on n. The verification for $n=0$ is left to the reader. So assume that

$$^+: \overline{G}_n \longrightarrow \overline{K}_n \quad \text{and} \quad ^*: \overline{K}_n \longrightarrow \overline{G}_n$$

possess properties (i) and (ii) where $n>0$.

(i) Let $h \in \overline{G}_{n+1}$. It remains to show condition (2) for h^+. Let $g \in \overline{K}_n$. By the induction hypothesis, $g^* \in \overline{G}_n$ and hence $h(g^*) \in \mathbb{N}$. By continuity

$$h(g^*) = \sqcup\{h(\Psi_n(U^n)) : g \in_n U^n\} \in \mathbb{N}$$

so there is $U^n \in \Phi_n^+$ such that $g \in_n U^n$ and $h(\Psi_n(U^n)) = h(g^*)$. Thus $h^+(U^n)\downarrow$ and (2) holds.

(ii) First we show that if $f \in \overline{K}_{n+1}$ and $g \in \overline{K}_n$ then $f^*(g^*) \in \mathbb{N}$. We have

$$f^*(g^*) = f^*(\sqcup\{\Psi_n(U^n) : g \in_n U^n\}) = \sqcup\{f^*(\Psi_n(U^n)) : g \in_n U^n\}.$$

Choose $U^n \in \Phi_n^+$ such that $g \in_n U^n$ and $f(U^n)\downarrow$ by condition (2) for f, say $f(U^n) = m \in \mathbb{N}$. Let $V^{n+1} = \{<U^n; m>\}$. Then $f \in_{n+1} V^{n+1}$ and

$$f^*(g^*) \sqsupseteq f^*(\Psi_n(U^n)) \sqsupseteq \Psi_{n+1}(V^{n+1})(\Psi_n(U^n)) = <\Psi_n(U^n); m>(\Psi_n(U^n)) = m \in \mathbb{N}.$$

Now suppose $f \in \overline{K}_{n+1}$. Given $h \in \overline{G}_n$ there is by the induction hypothesis $g \in \overline{K}_n$ such that $g^* \sqsubseteq h$. But then $f^*(g^*) \sqsubseteq f^*(h)$ and hence, by the above, $f^*(h) \in \mathbb{N}$. This proves the first part of (ii).

For the second part, suppose $h \in \overline{G}_{n+1}$. From (i) we know $h^+ \in \overline{K}_{n+1}$. We claim $h^{+*} \sqsubseteq h$. Suppose $h^{+*}(x) = m \in \mathbb{N}$. Then there is $V^{n+1} = \{<V_i^n; n_i> : i < k\}$ such that $h^+ \in_{n+1} V^{n+1}$ and

$$m = \Psi_{n+1}(V^{n+1})(x) = \sqcup_{i<k} <\Psi_n(V_i^n); n_i>(x).$$

Hence there is $i<k$ such that $<\Psi_n(V_i^n); n_i>(x) = m$, i.e. $\Psi_n(V_i^n) \sqsubseteq x$ and $n_i = m$. But $h^+ \in_{n+1} V^{n+1}$ so $h^+(V_i^n) = n_i = m$ and hence $h(\Psi_n(V_i^n)) = m$. By monotonicity we then have $h(x) = m$. □

The proof contains some additional information, namely, if $h \in \overline{G}_{n+1}$ then $h^{+*} \in \overline{G}_{n+1}$ and $h^{+*} \sqsubseteq h$. In particular, $h^{+*} \sim_{n+1} h$. Furthermore, if $f \in \overline{K}_{n+1}$ then $f^{*+} \in \overline{K}_{n+1}$ and it is easily verified that $f \subseteq f^{*+}$, that is f is a subfunction of f^{*+}. It follows that $f \sim_{n+1} f^{*+}$.

In order to compose our mappings with the appropriate quotient maps we need the following lemma.

4.16 Lemma (i) $(\forall f, g \in \overline{K}_{n+1})(f \sim_{n+1} g \Rightarrow f^* \sim_{n+1} g^*)$.
(ii) $(\forall h, k \in \overline{G}_{n+1})(h \sim_{n+1} k \Rightarrow h^+ \sim_{n+1} k^+)$.

Proof: (i) Suppose $f, g \in \overline{K}_{n+1}$ and $f^* \not\sim_{n+1} g^*$. Then there is $x \in \overline{G}_n$ such that $f^*(x) \neq g^*(x)$. Hence there are $U^n, V^n \in \Phi_n^+$ such that

$$f(U^n) = f^*(x) = <\Psi_n(U^n); f^*(x)>(x) \text{ and } g(V^n) = g^*(x) = <\Psi_n(V^n); g^*(x)>(x).$$

In particular, $\Psi_n(U^n), \Psi_n(V^n) \sqsubseteq x$ so that $U^n \cap V^n \neq \emptyset$ by Proposition 4.13. By condition (1) for f and g we obtain $f(U^n \cap V^n) \neq g(U^n \cap V^n)$, that is $f \not\sim_{n+1} g$ in $\bar{K}_{n+1}$.

(ii) Suppose $h \sim_{n+1} k$ for $h, k \in \bar{G}_{n+1}$. Let $U^n \in \Phi_n^+$ be such that $h^+(U^n)\downarrow$ and $k^+(U^n)\downarrow$. Then $h^+(U^n) \simeq h(\Psi_n(U^n)) \in \mathbb{N}$ and $k^+(U^n) \simeq k(\Psi_n(U^n)) \in \mathbb{N}$. Since $\Psi_n(U^n)$ is compact in C_n and $\bar{G}_n$ is dense in C_n there is $x \in \bar{G}_n$ such that $\Psi_n(U^n) \sqsubseteq x$. But then $h^+(U^n) = h(x) = k(x) = k^+(U^n)$. □

Now we define, for each n, mappings $\phi_n : K_n \longrightarrow G_n$ and $\theta_n : G_n \longrightarrow K_n$ as follows:

$\phi_0 = \theta_0 =$ identity mapping on $\mathbb{N}$.

$\phi_{n+1} : K_{n+1} \longrightarrow G_{n+1}$ is defined by $[f]_{\sim_{n+1}} \mapsto [f^*]_{\sim_{n+1}}$.

$\theta_{n+1} : G_{n+1} \longrightarrow K_{n+1}$ is defined by $[h]_{\sim_{n+1}} \mapsto [h^+]_{\sim_{n+1}}$.

Then each ϕ_n and θ_n is well-defined by Lemmas 4.15 and 4.16. Furthermore we do have $\theta_n \circ \phi_n = \mathrm{id}_{K_n}$ and $\phi_n \circ \theta_n = \mathrm{id}_{G_n}$ since for $f \in \bar{K}_{n+1}$ and $h \in \bar{G}_{n+1}$, $f \sim_{n+1} f^{*+}$ and $h^{+*} \sim_{n+1} h$ as remarked above. Finally, for $f \in K_{n+1}$ and $g \in K_n$, we have $f(g) = \phi_{n+1}(f)(\phi_n(g))$, and for $h \in G_{n+1}$ and $k \in G_n$, we have $h(k) = \theta_{n+1}(h)(\theta_n(k))$.

This completes the proof of Theorem 4.12.

8.5 Exercises

1. Let (X,d) be an ultrametric space. Show that a sequence $(x_n)_{n \in \mathbb{N}}$ in X is Cauchy if and only if $\lim_{n \to \infty} d(x_n, x_{n+1}) = 0$. (This is clearly not true for the real numbers $\mathbb{R}$.)

2. Let (X,d) be a metric space. Show that if there is a set $Y \subseteq X$ such that Y is dense in X and d is an ultrametric on Y then d is an ultrametric on X.

3. Let X be an ultrametric space. For each $A \subseteq X$ and $r > 0$, define $B(A;r) = \bigcup \{B(x;r) : x \in A\}$.
   (i) Show that $B(A;r)$ is a clopen (closed and open) set.
   (ii) Show that $\bar{A} = \bigcap_{r>0} B(A;r) = \bigcap_{r>0} B(\bar{A};r)$.
   (iii) Let $\hat{X}$ be the completion of X. Show that for each $A \subseteq \hat{X}$, $B(A;r) = \overline{B(A;r) \cap X}$.

4. Show that the projective limit $\hat{A} = \varprojlim A_n$ of an inverse system of Σ-algebras A_n is unique up to a Σ-isomorphism.

5. Consider the construction of $\hat{A} = \varprojlim A_n$. Show that $\hat{\sigma}$ is well-defined on $\hat{A}$, that $\hat{\phi}_n : \hat{A} \longrightarrow A_n$ is a Σ-morphism and that $\hat{\phi}_m = \phi_m^n \circ \hat{\phi}_n$ whenever $m \leq n$.

6. Let $A = (A; \sigma_1, \ldots, \sigma_k, \tau_1, \ldots, \tau_s)$ be an ultrametric Σ-algebra where $\sigma_1, \ldots, \sigma_k$ are contraction operations and $\tau_1, \ldots, \tau_s$ are non-expansive operations. Consider a system of equations

$$E \begin{cases} X_1 = t_1 \\ \quad\vdots \\ X_n = t_n \end{cases}$$

where $X_1, \ldots, X_n$ are variables and $t_1, \ldots, t_n$ are terms built up from Σ and the variables $X_1, \ldots, X_n$. We say that a variable Y is *guarded* in t_i if Y is within the scope of some σ_j. Otherwise Y is *unguarded* in t_i, which we denote by $X_i \xrightarrow{u} Y$. We say that the system of equations E is *guarded* if the relation $\xrightarrow{u}$ is well-founded, that is the relation has no infinitely descending chain.
(i) Show that if E is a guarded system of equations then E has a unique solution $(a_1, \ldots, a_n)$ over the completion $\hat{A}$ of A.
(ii) Extend (i) to the case when E consists of infinitely many equations.
(iii) Give examples of ultrametric algebras with contraction operations.

7. Let $\mathcal{N}$ be the domain of lazy natural numbers:

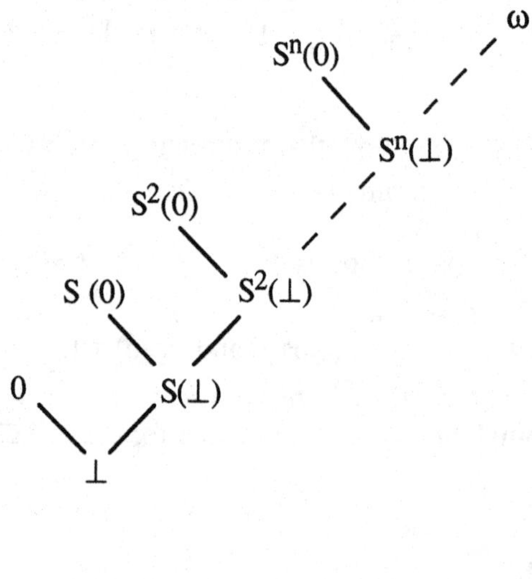

Let $N=\{S^n(0)\in\mathcal{N}: n\geq 0\}$. Show that N is a total set in $\mathcal{N}$ and determine $\mathcal{F}(N)$ explicitly.

8. Let E be a Σ-domain as in Definition 2.6. Define a type structure of Σ-domains $\{D_\sigma\}_{\sigma\in TS}$ over E and show that each D_σ is a Σ-domain.

9. (i) Prove Kreisel's density theorem 4.9.
(ii) What is the cardinality of $\overline{K}_{n+1}$ and K_{n+1}?

10. Let D and E be domains. Suppose that $M\subseteq D$ and $N\subseteq E$ are sets of total elements and that $f:D\longrightarrow E$ is a continuous function such that $f[M]\subseteq N$. Show that $\tilde{f}:\tilde{M}\longrightarrow\tilde{N}$ defined by $\tilde{f}([x])=[f(x)]$ is continuous. (This is really an easy topological result. What is required of f in general?)

11. Show that x is a total element of the domain D if and only if there is a unique $y\in D_m$ such that $x\sqsubseteq y$.

12. Let D be a domain and suppose $M\subseteq D$.
(i) M is a total set if and only if whenever N is a dense subset of a domain E then $<M,N>$ is a total set in $[D\longrightarrow E]$.
(ii) If M is closed upwards under $\sqsubseteq$ then M is dense in D if and only if whenever N is a total set in a domain E then $<M,N>$ is a total set in $[D\longrightarrow E]$.

13. (Berger [1990]) Let $\mathcal{R}=\{[a,b]: a,b\in\mathbb{Q}\text{ and } a\leq b\}\cup\{[-\infty,\infty]\}$, the set of non-empty closed intervals with rational endpoints. Define a partial order on $\mathcal{R}$ by

$$[a,b]\sqsubseteq[c,d] \Leftrightarrow a\leq c \text{ and } d\leq b,$$

that is $\sqsubseteq$ corresponds to set containment for the intervals. Then $\mathcal{R}=(\mathcal{R};\sqsubseteq,[-\infty,\infty])$ is a cusl. The domain which is the completion of $\mathcal{R}$ is denoted by $\overline{\mathcal{R}}$.
(i) Show that $\mathbf{m},\mathbf{n}\in\overline{\mathcal{R}}$ are topologically separated if and only if there are $[a,b]\in\mathbf{m}$ and $[c,d]\in\mathbf{n}$ such that $[a,b]\cap[c,d]=\varnothing$.
(ii) Show that $\mathbf{m}\in\overline{\mathcal{R}}$ is a total element if and only if $\inf\{b-a: [a,b]\in\mathbf{m}\}=0$.
(iii) Let R be the set of total elements in $\overline{\mathcal{R}}$ and let $\tilde{R}=R/\sim$ be the quotient of R, where $\sim$ is the consistency relation on R. Describe explicitly the elements in $\tilde{R}$. (You need to consider separately the cases when an equivalence class represents an irrational number and when it represents a rational number.)

(iv) Show that $\tilde{R}$ and $\mathbb{R}$ are homeomorphic topological spaces, where $\mathbb{R}$ is the space of real numbers.

14. Let $\mu \in [[\mathbb{N}_\perp \to \mathbb{N}_\perp] \to \mathbb{N}_\perp]$ be defined as follows:

$$\mu(g) = \begin{cases} n & \text{if } g(n) > 0 \ \& \ (\forall m < n)(g(m) = 0) \\ \perp & \text{if no such } n \in \mathbb{N} \text{ exists.} \end{cases}$$

Thus μ is a form of the usual μ-operator described in 9.1.3. Define $F : [\mathbb{N}_\perp \to \mathbb{N}_\perp] \to \mathbb{N}_\perp$ by

$$F(g) = \begin{cases} \perp & \text{if } g(\perp) = 0 \\ \mu(g) & \text{otherwise.} \end{cases}$$

(i) Show that F is continuous but not total.
(ii) Show that F is maximal in $[[\mathbb{N}_\perp \to \mathbb{N}_\perp] \to \mathbb{N}_\perp]$.

15. Let D be a domain and let $M \subseteq D$ be a total set. Let $\tilde{M}$ be the set of total elements obtained from $M \subseteq D$. Show that $\mathcal{B} = \{\tilde{V} : V \in \mathcal{F}(M)\}$ is a topological base for $\tilde{M}$. (Note that the topology generated by $\mathcal{B}$ is coarser, that is has possibly fewer open sets, than the quotient topology.)

16. Let D and E be domains and let $M \subseteq D$ and $N \subseteq E$ be total sets. Consider $\tilde{M}$ and $\tilde{N}$ with the topologies generated by $\mathcal{B}_M = \{\tilde{V} : V \in \mathcal{F}(M)\}$ and $\mathcal{B}_N = \{\tilde{V} : V \in \mathcal{F}(N)\}$ respectively.
(i) Show that $\tilde{M}$ is a Hausdorff space.
(ii) Let $f : D \to E$ be a continuous function such that $f[M] \subseteq N$. Show that $\tilde{f} : \tilde{M} \to \tilde{N}$ defined by $\tilde{f}([x]) = [f(x)]$ is continuous.
(iii) Is it true that every continuous function $\tilde{f} : \tilde{M} \to \tilde{N}$ is obtained as in (ii)?

17. Let D and E be domains and suppose $M \subseteq D$ and $N \subseteq E$ are total sets. Show that if $f \in \langle M, N \rangle$ then

$$V \in \mathcal{F}(N) \Rightarrow f^{-1}[V] \in \mathcal{F}(M).$$

18. Let D be a domain. For each open set V in D define $p_V : D \to \mathbb{B}_\perp$ by

$$p_V(x) = \begin{cases} tt & \text{if } x \in V \\ ff & \text{if } x \in \overline{V}^c \\ \perp & \text{otherwise.} \end{cases}$$

($\mathbb{B}_\perp$ is the domain for the Boolean set described in 2.1.11.)
(i) Show that p_V is continuous.
(ii) Show that for $x \in D$ and $M \subseteq D$, $V \in \mathcal{F}(x) \Leftrightarrow p_V(x) \neq \perp$ and $V \in \mathcal{F}(M) \Leftrightarrow \perp \notin p_V[M]$.

(iii) Let $p \in [D \longrightarrow \mathbb{B}_\perp]$ and let $V = p^{-1}(tt)$ and $W = p^{-1}(ff)$. Show that if $M \subseteq D$ is dense in D and $\perp \notin p[M]$ then $W \subseteq \overline{V}^c \subseteq \overline{W}$.

[This exercise indicates that one might as well use the Boolean-valued functions $[D \longrightarrow \mathbb{B}_\perp]$ to develop the theory of totality in Section 8.3. In fact, this may at times be advantageous since one may be able to use the fact that $[D \longrightarrow \mathbb{B}_\perp]$ is a domain.]

19. A domain D is said to be *coherent* if whenever $x_1, \dots, x_n$ are not consistent in D then there are $i, j \leq n$ such that x_i and x_j are not consistent.
(i) Show that each flat domain is coherent.
(ii) Let E be a coherent domain and let $\{D_\sigma\}_{\sigma \in TS}$ be the type structure of domains over E. Is each D_σ coherent?
(iii) Give an example of a domain which is not coherent.

20. Let D be a coherent domain and let $M \subseteq D$. Show that M is a total set if and only if whenever $a, b \in D_c$ are not consistent then there is $V \in \mathcal{F}(M)$ such that $a \in V$ and $b \notin \overline{V}$.

CHAPTER 9

BASIC RECURSION THEORY

The class of partial recursive functions is the mathematical abstraction of the class of partial functions computable by an algorithm. In this chapter we present them in the form of the μ-recursive functions. We then state some basic results, the main motivation being to set the stage for the theory of effective domains. Finally we show that the partial μ-recursive functions can be obtained from some simple initial functions using substitution and the fixed point theorem for computable functionals. This illuminates the central role of taking fixed points and supports the claim of Chapter 1 that the function computed by an algorithm or a program is the least fixed point of a computable functional.

Section 9.1 Partial Recursive Functions

An *algorithm for a class* $\mathcal{K}$ of problems is a method or procedure which can be described in a finite way (a finite set of instructions) and which can be followed by someone or something to yield a computation solving each problem in $\mathcal{K}$. The computation should proceed in discrete steps. For a given problem in $\mathcal{K}$ the procedure should say exactly how to perform each step in the computation. After performing a step, the procedure should prescribe how to do the next step. This next step must only depend on the problem and on the then existing situation, that is what has been done during previous steps. Finally, each problem should be solved in a finite number of steps, that is each computation should terminate with an instruction "do no more".

Let $f: A \rightarrow B$ be a function. An *algorithm for* f is an algorithm which computes f(a) for each $a \in A$, that is an algorithm for the class of problems {"What is f(a)?": $a \in A$}. The function f is said to be *computable* if there is an algorithm for f.

It is reasonable to assume, by the intended meaning of an algorithm explained above, that each problem in $\mathcal{K}$ should be a concrete or finite object. We say that an object is *finite* if it can be specified using finitely many symbols in some formal language. The canonical example of an infinite class of finite objects is the set $\mathbb{N}$ of natural numbers. Suppose we have another infinite class X of finite objects, where each object is described in the formal language L. Suppose further that there is an algorithm which decides the problem "is a an element of X?" for each finite object a describable in L, as well as an algorithm which decides when two descriptions in L denote the same element. Then it is not hard to construct a computable bijection between $\mathbb{N}$ and X. In other words, each infinite class of finite objects can be coded by a mapping onto the natural numbers in a computable way. Thus, in giving a mathematical abstraction of computability, we may as well restrict ourselves to $\mathbb{N}$.

The requirement that an algorithm should solve *each* problem in a class $\mathcal{K}$ is actually a requirement on the class $\mathcal{K}$ (to be algorithmically decidable) rather than on the concept of an algorithm. Indeed the *notion of an algorithm* is partial by its very nature. Regarding an algorithm as a finite set of instructions, there is certainly no a priori reason to expect the computation, obtained from applying the algorithm to a particular problem, to terminate. In fact, the negative answer to the halting problem says that there is no algorithm which, given an algorithm and a problem, decides whether or not the corresponding computation terminates. In particular, given an algorithm and the input data $a \in \mathbb{N}$ we obtain a computation which may terminate in a finite number of steps with a value $b \in \mathbb{N}$ or which may never terminate. Thus the class of algorithms operating on $\mathbb{N}$ naturally gives rise to a class of partial functions on $\mathbb{N}$, the class of partial (algorithmically) computable functions. It is this class of functions that we shall describe mathematically.

In the sequel we consider partial n-ary functions on $\mathbb{N}$. In this chapter, for simplicity, we will use the convention that *function* denotes an *n-ary partial function on the natural numbers.* When we want to emphasize that a function f is everywhere defined then we say that f is *total.* We will often use the notation $\mathbf{x} = x_1, \ldots, x_n$, that is $\mathbf{x}$ denotes the sequence $x_1, \ldots, x_n$.

First we need to consider certain operations on functions and determine precisely when the resulting function is defined.

1.1 Substitution Suppose that g is a k-ary function and that $h_1, \ldots, h_k$ are n-ary functions. Then

$$f(\mathbf{x}) \simeq g(h_1(\mathbf{x}), \ldots, h_k(\mathbf{x}))$$

is to be interpreted as follows: $f(\mathbf{x})\downarrow$ if and only if, for each i, $h_i(\mathbf{x})\downarrow$ and if $h_i(\mathbf{x}) = a_i$ then $g(a_1, \ldots, a_k)\downarrow$. Furthermore, in case that $f(\mathbf{x})\downarrow$ then $f(\mathbf{x}) = g(h_1(\mathbf{x}), \ldots, h_k(\mathbf{x}))$.

Clearly, if $g, h_1, \ldots, h_k$ are computable then so is f. For given $\mathbf{x} \in \mathbb{N}^n$, first compute $h_1(\mathbf{x})$. If $h_1(\mathbf{x})\downarrow$ then compute $h_2(\mathbf{x})$ and so on. If each $h_i(\mathbf{x})\downarrow$, say $h_i(\mathbf{x}) \simeq a_i$, then compute $g(a_1, \ldots, a_k)$. The given algorithm terminates if and only if $f(\mathbf{x})\downarrow$ and it does compute f.

1.2 Primitive recursion Let g be an n-ary function and h an (n+2)-ary function. Then

$$(*) \qquad f(\mathbf{x},y) \simeq \begin{cases} g(\mathbf{x}) & \text{if } y=0 \\ h(\mathbf{x},y-1,f(\mathbf{x},y-1)) & \text{if } y>0 \end{cases}$$

is defined inductively, or by primitive recursion, by

$$\begin{cases} f(\mathbf{x},0) \simeq g(\mathbf{x}) \\ f(\mathbf{x},y+1) \simeq h(\mathbf{x},y,f(\mathbf{x},y)). \end{cases}$$

Thus $f(\mathbf{x},y+1)\downarrow$, by the convention of 1.1, if and only if $f(\mathbf{x},z)\downarrow$ for each $z \le y$ and $h(\mathbf{x},y,f(\mathbf{x},y))\downarrow$. Note that the defined f is the unique function which satisfies the equation (*).

Suppose the functions g and h are computable. To compute $f(\mathbf{x},y)$ we first compute $f(\mathbf{x},0)$, that is $g(\mathbf{x})$. If this computation terminates then we compute $f(\mathbf{x},1)$ and so on until we obtain $f(\mathbf{x},y)$, if all computations involved terminate. This algorithm computes f.

1.3 The μ-operator Let g be an (n+1)-ary function. Then

$$f(\mathbf{x}) \simeq \mu y\,[g(\mathbf{x},y) \simeq 0]$$

is defined by

$$f(\mathbf{x}) \simeq y \;\Leftrightarrow\; (\forall z<y)(g(\mathbf{x},z)\downarrow \,\&\, g(\mathbf{x},z) \neq 0) \,\&\, g(\mathbf{x},y) \simeq 0.$$

Thus $\mu y\,[g(\mathbf{x},y) \simeq 0]$ computes the least y such that $g(\mathbf{x},y) \simeq 0$, *provided* $g(\mathbf{x},z)$ is defined for each $z<y$.

Suppose that g is computable. To compute $f(\mathbf{x})$ first compute $g(\mathbf{x},0)$. If this computation terminates then determine whether or not the result is 0. If yes, then $f(\mathbf{x}) \simeq 0$. If no, then compute $g(\mathbf{x},1)$ and so on. This computation procedure motivates the definition of the μ-operator and shows that f is computable. Note that if, for example, $g(\mathbf{x},0)\uparrow$ and $g(\mathbf{x},1) \simeq 0$ then $f(\mathbf{x})\uparrow$. This is reasonable since we will not in general be able to find out in a finite number of steps that it is *not* the case that $g(\mathbf{x},0) \simeq 0$.

All of 1.1 to 1.3 are means of defining new functions given previously defined ones. In order to define the μ-recursive functions we need to introduce some simple *initial functions* on $\mathbb{N}$. These are total and clearly computable.

1.4 Definition Some initial functions:
(i) $Z(x)=0$, the constant zero function.
(ii) $S(x)=x+1$, the successor function.
(iii) $\pi_i^n(x_1,\dots,x_n)=x_i$, $1\le i\le n$, the projection functions.

1.5 Definition The class $\mu\text{-}\mathcal{R}$ of *(partial) μ-recursive functions* is defined inductively by:

(i) $Z, S, \pi_i^n \in \mu\text{-}\mathcal{R}$ where $1\le i\le n$ and $n\ge 1$.

(ii) If $g, h_1,\dots,h_k \in \mu\text{-}\mathcal{R}$, where g is k-ary and each h_i is n-ary, and

$$f(\mathbf{x}) \simeq g(h_1(\mathbf{x}),\dots,h_k(\mathbf{x}))$$

then $f\in\mu\text{-}\mathcal{R}$.

(iii) If $g, h \in \mu\text{-}\mathcal{R}$, where g is n-ary and h is (n+2)-ary, and

$$f(\mathbf{x},y) \simeq \begin{cases} g(\mathbf{x}) & \text{if } y=0 \\ h(\mathbf{x},y-1,f(\mathbf{x},y-1)) & \text{if } y>0 \end{cases}$$

then $f\in\mu\text{-}\mathcal{R}$.

(iv) If $g\in\mu\text{-}\mathcal{R}$, where g is (n+1)-ary, and $f(\mathbf{x})\simeq \mu y\,[g(\mathbf{x},y)\simeq 0]$ then $f\in\mu\text{-}\mathcal{R}$.

Thus $\mu\text{-}\mathcal{R}$ is the smallest class of functions containing the initial functions (i), and closed under substitution (ii), primitive recursion (iii) and the μ-operator (iv).

1.6 Church–Turing thesis: The class of (partial) functions on the natural numbers $\mathbb{N}$ computable by algorithms is identical to the class $\mu\text{-}\mathcal{R}$ of μ-recursive functions.

Should the thesis be true, and there is rather general agreement that it is, it means that we have not only captured the notion of computability in precise mathematical terms, but we have also managed to give a non-trivial inductive definition of this extremely important class of functions.

1.7 Definition The class $\mathcal{PRIM}$ of the *primitive recursive functions* is defined inductively by:

(i) $Z, S, \pi_i^n \in \mathcal{PRIM}$ where $1\le i\le n$ and $n\ge 1$.

(ii) If $g, h_1,\dots,h_k \in \mathcal{PRIM}$, where g is k-ary and each h_i is n-ary, and

$$f(\mathbf{x}) = g(h_1(\mathbf{x}),\dots,h_k(\mathbf{x}))$$

then $f\in\mathcal{PRIM}$.

(iii) If $g, h \in \mathcal{PRIM}$ where g is n-ary and h is (n+2)-ary and

$$f(\mathbf{x}, y) = \begin{cases} g(\mathbf{x}) & \text{if } y = 0 \\ h(\mathbf{x}, y-1, f(\mathbf{x}, y-1)) & \text{if } y > 0 \end{cases}$$

then $f \in \mathcal{PRIM}$.

Note that $\mathcal{PRIM}$ contains only total functions. Thus it is appropriate to use $=$ in (ii) and (iii) of Definition 1.7 rather than $\simeq$. Most of the computable functions we ordinarily meet in mathematics, such as polynomial functions or the gcd function discussed in Chapter 1, are primitive recursive. The Ackermann function of Exercise 1.3.4 is an example of a total μ-recursive function which is not primitive recursive. However, the point of the Ackermann function is precisely that it "diagonalizes" itself out of the class $\mathcal{PRIM}$ thus demonstrating that all recursions cannot be formulated as primitive recursion.

An n-ary relation $R \subseteq \mathbb{N}^n$ is *μ-recursive (primitive recursive)* if its *characteristic function* c_R is μ-recursive (primitive recursive), where

$$c_R(\mathbf{x}) = \begin{cases} 0 & \text{if } R(\mathbf{x}) \\ 1 & \text{if } \neg R(\mathbf{x}). \end{cases}$$

The relation R and its characteristic function c_R are usually identified. For example, we will often write $f(\mathbf{x}) \simeq \mu y\, R(\mathbf{x}, y)$ for the function which provides the least y such that $R(\mathbf{x}, y)$, if such y exists, and is undefined otherwise. To see that f is recursive in case R is recursive, note that $f(\mathbf{x}) \simeq \mu y\, [c_R(\mathbf{x}, y) \simeq 0]$.

We close this section by showing that the *predecessor* function $P: \mathbb{N} \to \mathbb{N}$, defined by $P(0) = 0$ and $P(x+1) = x$, is primitive recursive. First define $\tilde{P}(x, y)$ by

$$\tilde{P}(x, y) = \begin{cases} Z(x) & \text{if } y = 0 \\ \pi_2^3(x, y-1, \tilde{P}(x, y-1)) & \text{if } y > 0. \end{cases}$$

Then $P(x) = \tilde{P}(\pi_1^1(x), \pi_1^1(x))$ showing that $P \in \mathcal{PRIM}$.

Observe that a function in $\mathcal{PRIM}$ has arity ≥ 1. It follows that a function defined by the primitive recursive scheme (iii) must have at least arity 2. This is the reason for the need to introduce the auxiliary function $\tilde{P}$ above. An alternative is to allow 0-ary functions, that is constants, and assert that 0 is primitive recursive and hence that all constants are primitive recursive.

Section 9.2 Some Basic Results

In this section we review some of the basic results about partial recursive functions and recursively enumerable sets. The purpose is not to give a comprehensive account of this very extensive and rich theory but only to remind the reader of some key concepts and results and, primarily, to establish notation. There are numerous texts containing various parts of recursion theory. The standard text is still Rogers [1967]. A good elementary account is Cutland [1980]. A recent book containing a wealth of information about basic recursion theory is Odifreddi [1989].

The starting point is the following fundamental result. Recall that, in this chapter, by a *function* we mean a *partial function on the natural numbers*. Furthermore, we simply write *recursive* for μ-recursive.

2.1 Normal form theorem (Kleene) There is a primitive recursive function U and, for each $n \geq 1$, primitive recursive $(n+2)$-ary relations T_n such that for each n-ary recursive function f there is an $e \in \mathbb{N}$ satisfying

(i) $f(x_1, \ldots, x_n)\downarrow \Leftrightarrow \exists y T_n(e, x_1, \ldots, x_n, y)$, and

(ii) $f(x_1, \ldots, x_n) \simeq U(\mu y T_n(e, x_1, \ldots, x_n, y))$.

The relations or predicates T_n are known as Kleene's T-predicates. The number e in the normal form theorem is called an *index* of f. So each recursive function has an index. Conversely, every number e is an index for an n-ary recursive function $\phi_e^{(n)}$, namely

$$\phi_e^{(n)}(x_1, \ldots, x_n) \simeq U(\mu y T_n(e, x_1, \ldots, x_n, y)).$$

Thus $\{\phi_e^{(n)} : e \in \mathbb{N}\}$ is the set of *all* n-ary recursive functions. We often write ϕ_e for $\phi_e^{(1)}$ or even for $\phi_e^{(n)}$, when the arity is clear from the context.

In order to prove the theorem we must first agree on a method for coding a finite sequence of natural numbers as one number. An easy way to do this, though computationally not the most efficient, is to use the unique factorization theorem for numbers. So let $p_0, p_1, p_2, \ldots$ be an enumeration of the prime numbers in strictly increasing order. Define

$$(*) \qquad \langle x_1, \ldots, x_n \rangle = p_0^n \cdot p_1^{x_1} \cdot \ldots \cdot p_n^{x_n}.$$

Thus the exponent of p_0 tells us how long the coded sequence is and the exponents of $p_1, \ldots, p_n$ give us $x_1, \ldots, x_n$ respectively. For each number $x \geq 2$ we define

$(x)_n$ = the exponent of p_n in the unique factorization of x,
$lh(x) = (x)_0$, and
$Seq(x) \Leftrightarrow x \neq 0 \ \& \ (\forall n \leq x)(n > 0 \ \& \ (x)_n \neq 0 \Rightarrow n \leq lh(x))$.

We say that x is a *sequence number* if Seq(x); lh(x) is the *length* of x; and $(x)_n$ is the n'th component of x. Clearly x is a sequence number if and only if it has the form (*). It is standard to show that $(\cdot)_n$, lh and Seq are primitive recursive.

The next step is to assign an index to each function in μ-$\mathcal{R}$. This is done by recursion on the inductive Definition 1.5. We assign <0> to Z, <1> to S and <2, n, i> to π_i^n. Having assigned e to g and $e_1, \ldots, e_k$ to $h_1, \ldots, h_k$ respectively, we assign $\langle 3, e, e_1, \ldots, e_k \rangle$ to $f(\mathbf{x}) \simeq g(h_1(\mathbf{x}), \ldots, h_k(\mathbf{x}))$. Having assigned e and e' to g and h respectively, we assign <4, e, e'> to the function f defined by primitive recursion from g and h as in clause (iii). Finally, having assigned e to g we assign <5, e> to $f(\mathbf{x}) \simeq \mu y\,[g(\mathbf{x}, y) \simeq 0]$.

It should be clear that given an index e for a recursive function f we can algorithmically from e determine the arity of f. Furthermore, given an argument $\mathbf{x} = x_1, \ldots, x_n$ of that arity we can algorithmically perform the computation $f(\mathbf{x})$ coded by e using the method of computing described in 1.1 to 1.4 and the correspondence between codes and the schemes of Definition 1.5 outlined above. The point is that if this computation terminates then the whole computation can be coded as a number in a primitive recursive way. This is encoded into Kleene's famous T-predicates, which express the following: $T_n(e, \mathbf{x}, y)$ if and only if the computation determined by the algorithm given by e and the arguments $\mathbf{x}$ terminates, is coded by w, has z as value and y = <z, w>.

We refer to any basic text on recursion theory, e.g. Kleene [1952], for a description of how computations are coded and a proof that T_n is indeed a primitive recursive predicate.

2.2 Enumeration theorem There is an (n + 1)-ary recursive function ϕ such that for all e and $\mathbf{x}$,

$$\phi(e, \mathbf{x}) \simeq \phi_e^{(n)}(\mathbf{x}).$$

Proof: Set $\phi(e, \mathbf{x}) \simeq U(\mu y T_n(e, x_1, \ldots, x_n, y))$, which is recursive. □

The enumeration theorem corresponds to the existence of a universal Turing machine. Thus the number e can be seen as a program and $\mathbf{x}$ as the input arguments. This illustrates the nowadays well-known observation that programs and data may be viewed as the same sort of objects though they are given different meanings.

2.3 S-m-n theorem For each $m, n \geq 1$ there is an $(m+1)$-ary primitive recursive function S_n^m such that

$$\phi^{(n)}_{S^m_n(e,x_1,\ldots,x_m)}(y_1,\ldots,y_n) \simeq \phi^{(m+n)}_e(x_1,\ldots,x_m,y_1,\ldots,y_n).$$

Proof: We consider for simplicity the case $m=n=1$. Suppose we are given e and x. Recalling the indexing of the μ-recursive functions given above, we define a function t by

$$\begin{cases} t(0) = \langle 0 \rangle \\ t(x+1) = \langle 3, \langle 1 \rangle, t(x) \rangle. \end{cases}$$

Thus t is primitive recursive and $\phi_{t(x)}$ is the constant function with value x. Note that

$$\phi_e(x,y) \simeq \phi_e(\phi_{t(x)}(y), \pi^1_1(y)) \simeq \phi_e(\phi_{t(x)}(y), \phi_{\langle 2,1,1 \rangle}(y)).$$

So we set $S^1_1(e,x) = \langle 3, e, t(x), \langle 2,1,1 \rangle \rangle$, which is primitive recursive. □

The enumeration theorem and the s-m-n theorem are inverses of each other in the sense that the former says that an index can be seen as an argument while the latter says that an argument can be incorporated into an index.

The s-m-n theorem has the important, almost magical consequence that the recursive functions are closed under recursions.

2.4 Second recursion theorem (Kleene) For each (n+1)-ary recursive function f there is an index e such that for all $\mathbf{x}$

$$\phi^{(n)}_e(\mathbf{x}) \simeq f(e, \mathbf{x}).$$

Proof: Let $g(y) = S^1_n(y,y) = S^1_n(\pi^1_1(y), \pi^1_1(y))$. Thus g is primitive recursive and hence $h(y,\mathbf{x}) \simeq f(S^1_n(y,y), \mathbf{x})$ is recursive with, say, index e. By the s-m-n theorem

$$f(S^1_n(y,y),\mathbf{x}) \simeq h(y,\mathbf{x}) \simeq \phi_e(y,\mathbf{x}) \simeq \phi_{S^1_n(e,y)}(\mathbf{x}).$$

Setting $y=e$, we obtain

$$f(S^1_n(e,e),\mathbf{x}) \simeq \phi_{S^1_n(e,e)}(\mathbf{x}). \qquad \square$$

When defining a recursive function g, the second recursion theorem allows us to use g (in terms of an index of g) in its own algorithmic definition. Of course, the second recursion theorem is closely related to the fixed point theorem, which in this setting is called the first recursion theorem.

An important observation, which will be used in Lemma 2.13, is the *uniformity* of the second recursion theorem. This means that there is a recursive, in fact primitive recursive, function r such that, from an index of f, r computes the index e of the theorem, that is for each d

$$\phi^{(n)}_{r(d)}(\mathbf{x}) \simeq \phi^{(n+1)}_{d}(r(d), \mathbf{x}).$$

This follows immediately since an index of h in the proof is obtained uniformly from an index of f.

Recall that a recursive relation is a relation whose characteristic function is recursive. Thus we may use the indices for recursive functions to index recursive relations. We define a *characteristic index* of a recursive relation to be an index of its characteristic function. Of course, not every number is a characteristic index. On the other hand a recursive relation will have infinitely many characteristic indices.

It is routine to prove that recursive relations are closed, uniformly, under the logical connectives &, $\vee$ and $\neg$. Here we identify as usual relations and predicates. Thus the connectives &, $\vee$ and $\neg$ correspond to set-theoretic intersection, union and complement respectively. Recursive relations are also closed under bounded quantification, when the bound is given by a recursive function or, more generally, bounded quantification over finite sets given by canonical indices as described below. However, the recursive relations are *not* closed under unbounded quantification. Recursive functions are closed under definition by cases, when the conditions are recursive relations.

We now consider those relations which are *effectively generated.* A relation is effectively generated if there is an algorithm which computes indefinitely, now and then producing an output, such that the relation is precisely the set of outputs. For a set A this can be shown to be equivalent to saying that $A = \emptyset$ or A is the range of a total recursive function. The effectively generated relations correspond exactly to the *semicomputable* relations. A relation is semicomputable if there is an algorithm which given **x** terminates with the answer that "**x** belongs to the relation" just in case **x** does belong to the relation and does not provide an answer in case **x** does not belong to the relation. Thus the algorithm *verifies* membership but does not decide membership. The notion of semicomputable is made precise as follows.

2.5 Definition An n-ary relation is *recursively enumerable* (*r.e.*) if it is the domain of an n-ary (partial) recursive function.

An indexing of the n-ary r.e. relations is obtained by setting

$$W_e^{(n)} = \text{domain of } \phi_e^{(n)} = \{\mathbf{x} : \phi_e^{(n)}(\mathbf{x})\downarrow\}.$$

We call e an *r.e. index* of the relation $W_e^{(n)}$. Since each number e is an index of an n-ary recursive function, each number is also an r.e. index of an n-ary r.e. relation. We simply write W_e for the r.e. *set* with index e.

2.6 Proposition Let $A \subseteq \mathbb{N}$. Then the following are equivalent:
(i) A is r.e.
(ii) There is a recursive binary relation R such that $x \in A \Leftrightarrow \exists y R(x,y)$.
(iii) $A = \varnothing$ or A is the range of a total recursive function.

Proof: (i) $\Rightarrow$ (ii). Assume $A = W_e$. If we set $R(x,y) \Leftrightarrow T_1(e,x,y)$ then (ii) holds by the normal form theorem.

(ii) $\Rightarrow$ (iii). Let R be the given recursive relation and let $a \in A$. Define

$$f(x) = \begin{cases} (x)_1 & \text{if } (\exists y<(x)_2) R((x)_1,y) \\ a & \text{otherwise.} \end{cases}$$

Then f is a total recursive function with range A.

(iii) $\Rightarrow$ (i). The everywhere undefined function is clearly recursive and hence $\varnothing$ is r.e. Suppose A is the range of a total recursive function f. Then define

$$g(x) \simeq \mu y[f(y) = x].$$

It follows that g is recursive with domain A. □

The analogue of the halting problem for Turing machines shows that there are r.e. sets which are not recursive. In fact, the structure of the r.e. sets is extremely complicated and has been extensively studied (see Soare [1987]).

2.7 Proposition Let $K_0 = \{<x,y> : \phi_x(y)\downarrow\}$. Then K_0 is an r.e. set which is not recursive.

Proof: Let ϕ be the function from the enumeration theorem. Define

$$f(x) \simeq \begin{cases} \phi((x)_1,(x)_2) & \text{if Seq}(x) \ \& \ \text{lh}(x)=2 \\ \uparrow & \text{otherwise.} \end{cases}$$

Then f is recursive with domain K_0.

To show that K_0 is not recursive we use a *diagonalization argument.* Define

$$g(x) \simeq \begin{cases} \phi(x,x)+1 & \text{if } <x,x> \in K_0 \\ 0 & \text{if } <x,x> \notin K_0. \end{cases}$$

If K_0 were recursive then g would be a total recursive function, say with index e. Thus, by the totality of g, $<e,e> \in K_0$ and hence

$$\phi_e(e) = g(e) = \phi(e,e) + 1 = \phi_e(e) + 1,$$

which is impossible. □

The r.e. relations are closed under the logical connectives & and $\vee$, that is under intersection and union. They are also closed under quantification over finite sets and under unbounded existential quantification. However, the r.e. relations are *not* closed under $\neg$, that is under the taking of complements. In fact it is easy to show that an n-ary relation R is recursive if and only if R and its complement $\mathbb{N}^n - R$ are both r.e.

We can also define r.e. sets with the help of the second recursion theorem. Suppose f is a total recursive function. Then, for each e, using the enumeration theorem,

$$\phi_{f(e)}(x) \simeq \phi(f(e),x) \simeq \psi(e,x)$$

where ψ is recursive. By the second recursion theorem there is e such that for each x, $\phi_e(x) \simeq \psi(e,x) \simeq \phi_{f(e)}(x)$. This says that $W_e = W_{f(e)}$. As an example, it is easy to define a total recursive function f such that $W_{f(n)} = \{n\}$. It then follows that there is an e such that $W_e = \{e\}$.

We now remind ourselves how to code or index finite sets of natural numbers. Let $A = \{x_1, x_2, \ldots, x_n\}$ where the listed elements are distinct. Then we say that $e = 2^{x_1} + 2^{x_2} + \ldots + 2^{x_n}$ is the *canonical index* of the finite set A. By convention we let 0 be the canonical index of $\varnothing$. Note that each number e is the canonical index of a finite set D_e. To see which set D_e is, write e in binary notation. Then a number x is in D_e precisely when the x'th position in the binary expansion contains a 1. For example, $D_5 = \{0,2\}$ and $D_{13} = \{0,2,3\}$.

It is clear that we can go *effectively* (or *uniformly*) from a canonical index of a finite set to a characteristic index of the same set, and from a characteristic index of a recursive set to an r.e. index of that set. To be precise, this means that there is a total recursive function f and a partial recursive function g such that f(e) is a characteristic index for D_e and if e is a characteristic index for a recursive set A then $g(e)\downarrow$ and $A = W_{g(e)}$.

2.8 Proposition It is not possible to pass effectively from an r.e. index of a recursive set to a characteristic index. Neither is it possible to pass effectively from a characteristic index of a finite set to a canonical index.

Proof: For the first part, suppose it were possible. This means that there is a recursive function f such that if W_e is recursive then $f(e)\downarrow$ and $f(e)$ is a characteristic index for W_e. Define, using the second recursion theorem, an r.e. set W_e by

$$W_e = \begin{cases} \{0\} & \text{if } f(e)\downarrow \ \& \ \phi_{f(e)}(0) \simeq 1 \\ \varnothing & \text{otherwise.} \end{cases}$$

Then W_e is finite so it is clearly recursive. In particular $f(e)\downarrow$. But $\phi_{f(e)}$ cannot be the characteristic function of W_e.

For the second part, assume there is a recursive function f such that if ϕ_e is a characteristic function of a finite set D then $f(e)\downarrow$ and $D = D_{f(e)}$. Let W be an r.e., non-recursive set. By an easy extension of Proposition 2.6 there is an injective total recursive function g whose range is W. Using the s-m-n theorem there is a total recursive function h such that

$$\phi_{h(e)}(x) \simeq \begin{cases} 0 & \text{if } e = g(x) \\ 1 & \text{otherwise.} \end{cases}$$

Note that $\phi_{h(e)}$ is a characteristic function of a finite set for each e, since g is recursive and injective. Thus $f(h(e))\downarrow$ for each e and

$$D_{f(h(e))} = \begin{cases} \{e\} & \text{if } e \in W \\ \varnothing & \text{if } e \notin W. \end{cases}$$

But then $e \notin W \Leftrightarrow D_{f(h(e))} = \varnothing$ and hence $\mathbb{N} - W$ is recursive. Thus W is recursive, contradicting the choice of W. □

Clearly there are algorithms which given a canonical index e provide us with the elements of D_e and, conversely, given a finite set of numbers compute a canonical index for it. Thus we may informally talk about recursive functions whose values are finite sets though what we mean is that the values are canonical indices of finite sets.

The intersection of a finite set D with an arbitrary set A is of course always finite but we cannot in general compute an index for it. However, in the case that A is recursive, then we can compute a canonical index of $D \cap A$ from a canonical index of D and a characteristic index of A. Appealing to the Church–Turing thesis we simply check each element of D to see whether or not it belongs to A. Note that this algorithm will not work when A is r.e. In fact, it is *not* in general possible to compute a canonical index of $D \cap A$ from a canonical index of D and an r.e. index of A. If it were possible then we could compute a canonical index of $\{x\} \cap A$ from x and an r.e. index of A, which would imply that A was recursive.

Proposition 2.6 provides an enumeration of each non-empty r.e. set in terms of a total recursive function. Often it is more convenient to give effective enumerations of r.e. sets in terms of (canonical indices of) finite sets in such a way that we obtain progressively better finite approximations of the r.e. set.

2.9 Definition A total recursive function $\lambda n.W^n$ (where W^n is a finite set identified with its canonical index) is an *enumeration* of the set W if

(i) $m \leq n \Rightarrow W^m \subseteq W^n$, and

(ii) $W = \bigcup_{n \in \mathbf{N}} W^n$.

2.10 Proposition (i) Each r.e. set W has an enumeration $\lambda n.W^n$.

(ii) If $\lambda n.W^n$ is an enumeration of the set W, then W is r.e.

Proof: (i) Let $W = W_e$ and set

$$W_e^n = \{x < n : (\exists m < n) T_1(e, x, m)\}.$$

Then W_e^n is the intersection of a finite set and a recursive set and hence, by the remarks above, a canonical index of W_e^n is computed uniformly from e and n. Thus $\lambda n.W_e^n$ is an enumeration of W_e by the normal form theorem 2.1.

(ii) Suppose $\lambda n.W^n$ is an enumeration of W. Then

$$x \in W \Leftrightarrow \exists n (x \in W^n)$$

which is r.e. by Proposition 2.6. □

From the proof we see that $\lambda en.W_e^n$ is a total recursive function of two arguments. We call the enumeration $\lambda n.W_e^n$ the *standard enumeration* of W_e.

An effective version of the axiom of choice holds for r.e. relations. The choice function obtained is called a *selection operator*.

2.11 Proposition Let R be an $(n+1)$-ary r.e. relation. Then there is an n-ary recursive function f, obtained uniformly from an r.e. index of R, such that

(i) $f(\mathbf{x})\downarrow \Leftrightarrow \exists y R(\mathbf{x}, y)$, and

(ii) $f(\mathbf{x})\downarrow \Rightarrow R(\mathbf{x}, f(\mathbf{x}))$.

Proof: Let e be an r.e. index of R. By the s-m-n theorem there is a primitive recursive function s such that $W_{s(e,\mathbf{x})} = \{y : R(\mathbf{x}, y)\}$.
Let

$$g(\mathbf{x}) \simeq \mu n [W^n_{s(e,\mathbf{x})} \neq \emptyset]$$

and then define

$$f(\mathbf{x}) \simeq \mu y [y \in W^{g(\mathbf{x})}_{s(e,\mathbf{x})}]. \qquad \square$$

We conclude this section with a non-standard result due to Berger [1993], which is a key recursion-theoretic fact used in the generalization of the Kreisel–Lacombe–Shoenfield theorem to effective domains. It is a clever application of the second recursion theorem.

2.12 Branching lemma Let V and W be r.e. sets such that W contains all r.e. indices of V. Let $\lambda p.V^p$ be an enumeration of V and let r be a total recursive function. Then there is $e \in W$ and $p \in \mathbb{N}$ such that

$$W_e = V^p \cup W_{r(p)}.$$

Furthermore, such e and p are computed uniformly from an r.e. index of W and recursive indices of the functions $\lambda p.V^p$ and r.

Proof: Let $\lambda p.W^p$ be an enumeration of W such that $W^0 = \varnothing$ and define W_e, using the second recursion theorem, by

$$x \in W_e \Leftrightarrow \exists p((x \in V^p \,\&\, e \notin W^p) \vee (x \in W_{r(p)} \,\&\, e \in W^{p+1} - W^p)).$$

If $e \notin W$ then $W_e = V$ by the definition of W_e, so $e \in W$ by the assumption on W. It follows that $e \in W$. Let p be the unique number such that $e \in W^{p+1} - W^p$. Then

$$W_e = V^p \cup W_{r(p)}.$$

The claimed uniformities follow from the uniformity of the second recursion theorem. □

The branching lemma says that if W contains all r.e. indices of V then, for some p, it also contains an r.e. index of $W_{r(p)}$ modulo a finite part of V. That is we branch along $W_{r(p)}$ for some p and still stay within W.

When applying the branching lemma to the generalization of the Kreisel–Lacombe–Shoenfield theorem in Chapter 10 we need to relativize to an arbitrary subset $M \subseteq \mathbb{N}$.

2.13 Relativized branching lemma Let $s, t : \mathbb{N} \to \mathbb{N}$ and $r : \mathbb{N}^2 \to \mathbb{N}$ be total recursive functions. Suppose $M \subseteq \mathbb{N}$ has the property that if $n \in M$ then $W_{s(n)}$ contains all r.e. indices of $W_{t(n)}$. Then there is a total recursive function $b : \mathbb{N} \to \mathbb{N}$ and a partial recursive function $p : \mathbb{N} \to \mathbb{N}$ such that $M \subseteq \mathrm{dom}(p)$ and for each $n \in \mathrm{dom}(p)$

$$W_{b(n)} = W_{t(n)}^{p(n)} \cup W_{r(n,p(n))}.$$

Proof: Define by the uniform version of the second recursion theorem a total recursive function b such that

$$(*)\qquad x \in W_{b(n)} \Leftrightarrow \exists m\,((x \in W^m_{t(n)} \,\&\, b(n) \notin W^m_{s(n)}) \vee (x \in W_{r(n,m)} \,\&\, b(n) \in W^{m+1}_{s(n)} - W^m_{s(n)})).$$

Let p be the partial recursive function defined by

$$p(n) \simeq \mu m\,[b(n) \in W^{m+1}_{s(n)} - W^m_{s(n)}].$$

From (*) it then follows that if $n \in \mathrm{dom}(p)$ then

$$W_{b(n)} = W^{p(n)}_{t(n)} \cup W_{r(n,p(n))}.$$

To show that $M \subseteq \mathrm{dom}(p)$, let $n \in M$. If $b(n) \notin W_{s(n)}$ then, again by (*), $W_{b(n)} = W_{t(n)}$ and hence, by the assumption on M, $b(n) \in W_{s(n)}$. Thus $b(n) \in W_{s(n)}$, that is $n \in \mathrm{dom}(p)$. □

Section 9.3 Fixed Points

In this section we consider a class $\mathcal{FR}$ of partial functions on $\mathbb{N}$ obtained from some simple initial functions by closing under substitution and taking least fixed points. We then prove that $\mu\text{-}\mathcal{R} \subseteq \mathcal{FR}$. The proof of the converse inclusion,which we sketch, is the content of Kleene's first recursion theorem.

We already observed that the partial function defined by primitive recursion is the least and in fact the only solution of equation (*) in 1.2. Primitive recursion may easily be defined using a functional, as was done in Section 1.1 for the greatest common divisor, in such a way that the least fixed point of the functional is the solution of the equation for primitive recursion. By allowing arbitrary functionals of the kind described below we obtain more general kinds of recursion than just primitive recursion. In particular we obtain the μ-operator, thus giving us all computable functions.

The class of functionals in question is built up from the following initial functionals, application and definition by cases. We write $\mathbf{g}$ for the function arguments $g_1, \dots, g_m$ and $\mathbf{x}$ for the number arguments $x_1, \dots, x_n$, and we use semicolon to indicate their separation:

$$\mathrm{Ap}_j(\mathbf{g};\mathbf{x}) \simeq g_j(\mathbf{x}), \quad 1 \le j \le m, \quad \text{and}$$

$$\mathrm{DC}(g_1, g_2, g_3; \mathbf{x}) \simeq \begin{cases} g_1(\mathbf{x}) & \text{if } g_3(\mathbf{x}) \simeq 0 \\ g_2(\mathbf{x}) & \text{if } g_3(\mathbf{x})\downarrow \,\&\, g_3(\mathbf{x}) > 0 \\ \uparrow & \text{if } g_3(\mathbf{x})\uparrow. \end{cases}$$

3.1 Definition The class $\mathcal{EF}$ of *explicit functionals* is defined inductively by:
(i) $\mathrm{Ap}_j(\mathbf{g};\mathbf{x}) \in \mathcal{EF}$ and $\mathrm{DC}(g_1, g_2, g_3; \mathbf{x}) \in \mathcal{EF}$.

(ii) If $G(\mathbf{g};\mathbf{x}) \in \mathcal{EF}$ and if each g_i occurs in the list of function arguments $\mathbf{h}$ and if each x_j occurs in the list of number arguments $\mathbf{y}$ and $F(\mathbf{h};\mathbf{y}) \simeq G(\mathbf{g};\mathbf{x})$ then $F(\mathbf{h};\mathbf{y}) \in \mathcal{EF}$.

(iii) If $G, H_1, \dots, H_k \in \mathcal{EF}$ and $F(\mathbf{g};\mathbf{x}) \simeq G(\mathbf{g}; H_1(\mathbf{g};\mathbf{x}), \dots, H_k(\mathbf{g};\mathbf{x}))$ then $F(\mathbf{g};\mathbf{x}) \in \mathcal{EF}$.

Clause (ii) allows us to permute the order of the arguments as well as to introduce new (dummy) arguments. Clause (iii), when combined with (ii) and the use of projection functions, allows for a general form of substitution or composition.

Our notation is an extension to several arguments of the notation used in Section 1.1. Thus if $F(g_1, \dots, g_m; x_1, \dots, x_n) \in \mathcal{EF}$, we assume that g_i varies over $(\mathbf{N}^{n_i} \xrightarrow{p} \mathbf{N})$ and that x_j ranges over $\mathbf{N}$. To be precise, the functional $F(g_1, \dots, g_m; x_1, \dots, x_n)$ is a function

$$F: (\mathbf{N}^{n_1} \xrightarrow{p} \mathbf{N}) \times \dots \times (\mathbf{N}^{n_m} \xrightarrow{p} \mathbf{N}) \longrightarrow (\mathbf{N}^{n} \xrightarrow{p} \mathbf{N}),$$

so that $F(\mathbf{g};\mathbf{x})$ is just another way of writing $F(\mathbf{g})(\mathbf{x})$. We say that the functional F just described has *arity* $(n_1, \dots, n_m; n)$.

3.2 Definition Let $F = F(\mathbf{g};\mathbf{x})$ be a functional of arity $(n_1, \dots, n_m; n)$.

(i) F is *monotone* if whenever $g_i \subseteq h_i$, $i = 1, \dots, m$, and $F(\mathbf{g};\mathbf{x}) \simeq a$ then $F(\mathbf{h};\mathbf{x}) \simeq a$.

(ii) A monotone functional F is *continuous* if whenever $F(\mathbf{g};\mathbf{x}) \simeq a$ then there are finite partial functions $h_i \subseteq g_i$, $i = 1, \dots, m$, such that $F(\mathbf{h};\mathbf{x}) \simeq a$.

Thus a functional F is monotone if it is monotone in each argument with respect to the ordering $\subseteq$, and it is continuous if it is continuous in each argument, as defined in Section 1.1. That is, F is monotone and continuous if, for each i, the functional in one argument $\lambda g_i.F(g_1, \dots, g_i, \dots, g_m)$ is monotone and continuous for each choice of parameters $g_j \in (\mathbf{N}^{n_j} \xrightarrow{p} \mathbf{N})$, $j \neq i$.

Suppose that each g_i is a computable partial function (in the informal sense). Then it is clear, by induction on $\mathcal{EF}$, that the partial function $F(\mathbf{g})$ is also computable for each $F \in \mathcal{EF}$.

3.3 Lemma Every explicit functional is monotone and continuous.

Proof: By induction on $\mathcal{EF}$. □

3.4 Definition Let $\mathbf{g} = g_1, \dots, g_m$ where $g_i \in (\mathbf{N}^{n_i} \xrightarrow{p} \mathbf{N})$. Then $f \in (\mathbf{N}^{n} \xrightarrow{p} \mathbf{N})$ *is defined by recursion from* $\mathbf{g}$ if there is an explicit functional F of arity $(n_1, \dots, n_m, n; n)$ such that f is the least fixed point of $\lambda f.F(\mathbf{g}, f)$.

3.5 Lemma Let F be an explicit functional of arity $(n_1,\ldots,n_m,n;n)$ and let $g_i \in (\mathbb{N}^{n_i} \xrightarrow{p} \mathbb{N})$ for $i=1,\ldots,m$. Then $\lambda f.F(\mathbf{g},f)$ has a least fixed point.

Proof: By Lemma 3.3 and the first recursion theorem 1.1.3. □

Recall from the proof of Theorem 1.1.3 that the least fixed point f of $\lambda f.F(\mathbf{g},f)$ is $f=\bigcup\{f^n : n\in\mathbb{N}\}$ where

$$\begin{cases} f^0=\varnothing \\ f^{n+1}=F(\mathbf{g},f^n). \end{cases}$$

It follows that the least fixed point f is computable whenever each g_i is computable. We denote the least fixed point of $\lambda f.F(\mathbf{g},f)$ by $F^\infty(\mathbf{g})$.

Definition 3.6 The class $\mathcal{FR}$ of *partial fixed-point recursive functions* is defined inductively by:

(i) The functions Z,S,P,π_i^n for $1\le i\le n$ and $n\ge 1$, are in $\mathcal{FR}$.

(ii) If $g,h_1,\ldots,h_k\in\mathcal{FR}$ then $f(\mathbf{x})\simeq g(h_1(\mathbf{x}),\ldots,h_k(\mathbf{x}))\in\mathcal{FR}$.

(iii) If $g_1,\ldots,g_m\in\mathcal{FR}$ and f is defined by recursion from $g_1,\ldots,g_m$ then $f\in\mathcal{FR}$.

Thus $\mathcal{FR}$ is the smallest class of partial functions containing the elementary initial functions (i) and closed under substitution (ii) and recursion (iii). Note that, contrary to the case of μ-$\mathcal{R}$, we have included the predecessor function P as an initial function.

Before continuing our main development it is convenient to establish that explicit functionals can be defined by explicit definitions using the variables appearing in the definition of the functional and using projection functions as parameters.

Let $\mathbf{g}=g_1,\ldots,g_m$ and $\mathbf{x}=x_1,\ldots,x_n$ be lists of syntactic objects, where each g_i has an arity $n_i>0$. Then the class of *terms* obtained from $\mathbf{g}$ and $\mathbf{x}$ is defined inductively by:

(i) x_i is a term, for $i=1,\ldots,n$.

(ii) If $t_1,\ldots,t_k$ are terms and g_j is k-ary, then $g_j(t_1,\ldots,t_k)$ is a term.

We consider g_i as a variable over $(\mathbb{N}^{n_i}\xrightarrow{p}\mathbb{N})$ and x_j as a variable over $\mathbb{N}$. However, if we let each g_i be a particular element $\tilde{g}_i\in(\mathbb{N}^{n_i}\xrightarrow{p}\mathbb{N})$, that is we give an *instantiation* $\tilde{\mathbf{g}}$ of $\mathbf{g}$, then each term t obtained from $\mathbf{g}$ and $\mathbf{x}$ may be viewed as a partial function $\phi_t:\mathbb{N}^n\xrightarrow{p}\mathbb{N}$ in the obvious way. Namely, $\phi_{x_i}=\pi_i^n$ and if $t=g_j(t_1,\ldots,t_k)$ then $\phi_t(\mathbf{x})\simeq\tilde{g}_i(\phi_{t_1}(\mathbf{x}),\ldots,\phi_{t_k}(\mathbf{x}))$.

3.7 Lemma If t is a term obtained from $\mathbf{g}=g_1,\ldots,g_m$ and $\mathbf{x}=x_1,\ldots,x_n$ then there is an explicit functional F such that for each instantiation $\tilde{\mathbf{g}}$ of $\mathbf{g}$,

$$\phi_t(\mathbf{x})\simeq F(\pi_1^n,\ldots,\pi_n^n,\tilde{\mathbf{g}};\mathbf{x}).$$

Proof: By induction on terms. If $t = x_i$ then $\phi_t(\mathbf{x}) \simeq Ap_i(\pi_1^n, \ldots, \pi_n^n, \mathbf{g}; \mathbf{x})$. Now suppose that $t = g_j(t_1, \ldots, t_k)$. Inductively we assume there are explicit functionals F_i such that $\phi_{t_i}(\mathbf{x}) \simeq F_i(\pi_1^n, \ldots, \pi_n^n, \mathbf{g}; \mathbf{x})$, for $i = 1, \ldots, k$. Using the notation $\pi = \pi_1^n, \ldots, \pi_n^n$, we define F by

$$F(\pi, \mathbf{g}; \mathbf{x}) \simeq Ap_{n+j}(\pi, \mathbf{g}; F_1(\pi, \mathbf{g}; \mathbf{x}), \ldots, F_k(\pi, \mathbf{g}; \mathbf{x})).$$

Then $F \in \mathcal{EF}$ by clause (iii) of Definition 3.1 and $\phi_t(\mathbf{x}) \simeq F(\pi, \mathbf{g}; \mathbf{x})$. □

We show by an example how the lemma, in combination with clause (ii) of Definition 3.1, allows us to define explicit functionals by explicit definitions using a finite list of projection functions π as parameters. Assume that g is a partial n-ary function and that h is a partial (n+2)-ary function. Define

$$F(\pi, P, g, h, f; \mathbf{x}, y) \simeq DC(g(\mathbf{x}), h(\mathbf{x}, P(y), f(\mathbf{x}, P(y))), y; \mathbf{x}, y),$$

where π includes $\pi_1^3, \pi_2^3, \pi_3^3$. We claim that F is an explicit functional. To verify this, let

$$G(\pi, P, g, h, f; u, v, w) \simeq DC(\pi_1^3, \pi_2^3, \pi_3^3; u, v, w).$$

Then $G(\pi, P, g, h, f; u, v, w) \in \mathcal{EF}$ by clause (ii) of Definition 3.1. Let

$$H_1(\pi, P, g, h, f; \mathbf{x}, y) \simeq g(\mathbf{x}),$$
$$H_2(\pi, P, g, h, f; \mathbf{x}, y) \simeq h(\mathbf{x}, P(y), f(\mathbf{x}, P(y))), \quad \text{and}$$
$$H_3(\pi, P, g, h, f; \mathbf{x}, y) \simeq y,$$

where each H_i exists by Lemma 3.7. Then define

$$F(\pi, P, g, h, f; \mathbf{x}, y) \simeq$$
$$G(\pi, P, g, h, f; H_1(\pi, P, g, h, f; \mathbf{x}, y), H_2(\pi, P, g, h, f; \mathbf{x}, y), H_3(\pi, P, g, h, f; \mathbf{x}, y)).$$

Thus F is an explicit functional by clause (iii) of Definition 3.1 and, in fact,

$$F(\pi, P, g, h, f; \mathbf{x}, y) \simeq \begin{cases} g(\mathbf{x}) & \text{if } y = 0 \\ h(\mathbf{x}, P(y), f(\mathbf{x}, P(y))) & \text{if } y > 0. \end{cases}$$

3.8 Lemma $\mathcal{FR}$ is closed under primitive recursion.

Proof: Let $g, h \in \mathcal{FR}$ where g is n-ary and h is (n+2)-ary and let F be the explicit functional defined above. Then $f = F^\infty(\pi, P, g, h)$ is the partial function obtained by primitive recursion from g and h. Since $\pi, P, g, h \in \mathcal{FR}$, we have that $f \in \mathcal{FR}$. □

3.9 Lemma $\mathcal{FR}$ is closed under μ-recursion.

Proof: Let $g \in \mathcal{FR}$ be an (n+1)-ary partial function and suppose that $h(\mathbf{x}) \simeq \mu y[g(\mathbf{x}, y) \simeq 0]$. We must show that $h \in \mathcal{FR}$. Define an explicit functional F by

$$F(\pi, S, g, f; \mathbf{x}, y) \simeq DC(y, f(\mathbf{x}, S(y)), g(\mathbf{x}, y); \mathbf{x}, y)$$

and let $f = F^{\infty}(\pi, S, g)$. Thus $f \in \mathcal{FR}$ and f satisfies

$$(*) \qquad f(\mathbf{x}, y) \simeq \begin{cases} y & \text{if } g(\mathbf{x}, y) \simeq 0 \\ f(\mathbf{x}, S(y)) & \text{if } g(\mathbf{x}, y)\downarrow \ \& \ g(\mathbf{x}, y) \neq 0 \\ \uparrow & \text{if } g(\mathbf{x}, y)\uparrow. \end{cases}$$

Suppose that $g(\mathbf{x}, y) \simeq 0$ and, for each $z < y$, $g(\mathbf{x}, z)\downarrow$ and $g(\mathbf{x}, z) \neq 0$. Then we see from (*) that

$$f(\mathbf{x}, 0) \simeq f(\mathbf{x}, 1) \simeq \ldots \simeq f(\mathbf{x}, P(y)) \simeq f(\mathbf{x}, y) \simeq y.$$

Suppose on the other hand that $g(\mathbf{x}, z)$ is defined but greater than 0 for each z. Then, letting the least fixed point $f = \bigcup\{f^n : n \in \mathbb{N}\}$ as in the proof of Lemma 3.5, we see that for each n,

$$f^n(\mathbf{x}, 0) \simeq f^{n-1}(\mathbf{x}, 1) \simeq \ldots \simeq f^0(\mathbf{x}, n).$$

But $f^0(\mathbf{x}, n)$ is undefined so $f(\mathbf{x}, 0)$ is undefined. Similarly, if y is the least number such that $g(\mathbf{x}, y)\uparrow$ and $g(\mathbf{x}, z) > 0$ for each $z < y$, then $f(\mathbf{x}, 0)\uparrow$. Thus we have shown that $f(\mathbf{x}, 0) \simeq \mu y[g(\mathbf{x}, y) \simeq 0]$. It follows that

$$h(\mathbf{x}) \simeq \mu y[g(\mathbf{x}, y) \simeq 0] \simeq f(\mathbf{x}, Z(\pi_1^n(\mathbf{x})))$$

and hence $h \in \mathcal{FR}$. □

3.10 Theorem $\mu\text{-}\mathcal{R} = \mathcal{FR}$.

Proof: That $\mu\text{-}\mathcal{R} \subseteq \mathcal{FR}$ follows from Lemma 3.8 and Lemma 3.9. The converse inclusion is Kleene's *first recursion theorem*. Here we only sketch the argument.

From the definition of $\mathcal{FR}$ it clearly suffices to show that if f is defined by recursion from **g**, where $\mathbf{g} = g_1, \ldots, g_m \in \mu\text{-}\mathcal{R}$, then $f \in \mu\text{-}\mathcal{R}$. The first step is to prove, by induction on $\mathcal{EF}$, that for each explicit functional F and each choice of (partial) functions $\mathbf{g} = g_1, \ldots, g_m \in \mu\text{-}\mathcal{R}$, the (partial) function $F(\mathbf{g})$ is μ-recursive. Furthermore, an index of $F(\mathbf{g})$ as a μ-recursive function is obtained *uniformly* from indices of **g** using a primitive recursive and hence μ-recursive function. Here we assume that we have some acceptable numbering of the recursive functions such as the one sketched in Section 9.2.

Now suppose f is defined by recursion from $\mathbf{g} \in \mu\text{-}\mathcal{R}$, that is $f = F^{\infty}(\mathbf{g})$ for some $F \in \mathcal{EF}$. Then, as already observed,

$$f(\mathbf{x}) \simeq y \Leftrightarrow \exists n\,(f^n(\mathbf{x}) \simeq y)$$

where

$$\begin{cases} f^0 = \varnothing \\ f^{n+1} = F(\mathbf{g}, f^n). \end{cases}$$

By the above, there is a primitive recursive function s such that $s(n)$ is a μ-recursive index of f^n. But then the relation

$$\exists n\,(f^n(\mathbf{x}) \simeq y)$$

is r.e. in the sense of μ-$\mathcal{R}$, that is the graph of f is an r.e. relation, and hence $f \in \mu$-$\mathcal{R}$. □

CHAPTER 10

EFFECTIVE DOMAINS

To make precise the notion of effectivity on domains we use recursion theory and the *theory of numerations*. The first section recalls some basic concepts from the theory of numerations and computable structures. Then the effectivity of cusl's and domains is studied. A main result is that the solutions of domain equations obtained in Chapter 4 are effective. The latter part of the chapter considers constructive domains. In particular, generalizations to domains of the Myhill–Shepherdson and the Kreisel–Lacombe–Shoenfield theorems are proved.

Section 10.1 Numerations of Abstract Structures

Recursive function theory has been used by many authors to make precise the notion of effectivity for algebraic structures. A fundamental paper is Fröhlich and Shepherdson [1956]. Here we choose to use the basic definitions from Mal'cev [1960]; see also Rabin [1960]. For an extensive survey of the theory of numerations see Ershov ([1973], [1975], [1977]).

Recall that a (finitary) *structure* A is a tuple $A=(A;R_1,\dots,R_t,\sigma_1,\dots,\sigma_k)$ where

(i) A is a non-empty set,
(ii) $\sigma_i: A^{n_i} \to A$ is an n_i-ary operation on A (constants are 0-ary operations),
(iii) $R_j \subseteq A^{n_j}$ is an n_j-ary relation on A.

A *numbering* or *numeration* of the algebraic structure A is a surjective function $\alpha:\Omega_\alpha \to A$ where $\Omega_\alpha \subseteq \omega$. As usual we identify ω with the natural numbers. Thus each element $a \in A$ is coded by one or more numbers in Ω_α via the function α, viz. those $n \in \Omega_\alpha$ such that $\alpha(n)=a$. Identifying all numbers coding the same element induces an equivalence relation $\equiv_\alpha$ on Ω_α by

$$m \equiv_\alpha n \Leftrightarrow \alpha(m)=\alpha(n).$$

In this way *equality* between elements in A is translated to *equivalence* between codes for those elements.

1.1 Definition Let $\alpha:\Omega_\alpha \to A$ be a numbering of the finitary structure $A=(A;R_1,\dots,R_t,\sigma_1,\dots,\sigma_k)$. Then α is an *effective numbering* of A and the pair (A,α) is an *effective structure* if Ω_α is a recursive set and (i) and (ii) below hold.

(i) For each $i=1,\dots,k$ there is an n_i-ary partial recursive function $\hat{\sigma}_i$ such that for each $m_1,\dots,m_{n_i}\in\Omega_\alpha$,

$$\hat{\sigma}_i(m_1,\dots,m_{n_i})\downarrow \text{ and}$$
$$\sigma_i(\alpha(m_1),\dots,\alpha(m_{n_i}))=\alpha(\hat{\sigma}_i(m_1,\dots,m_{n_i}));$$

that is, given codes for elements $a_1,\dots,a_{n_i}$ then $\hat{\sigma}_i$ computes a code for $\sigma_i(a_1,\dots,a_{n_i})$. So the following diagrams commute.

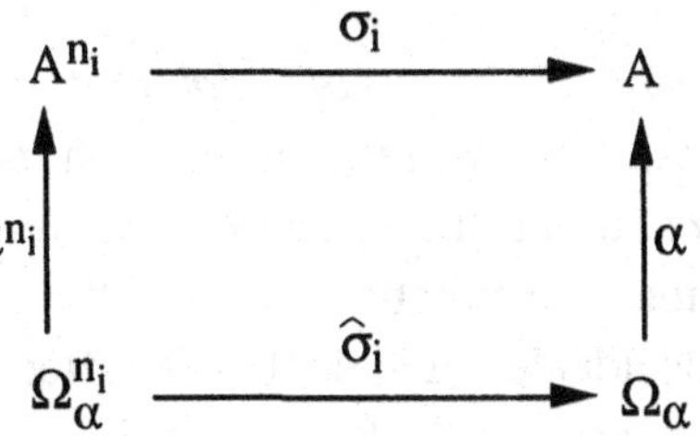

(ii) For each $j=1,\dots,t$ there is an n_j-ary recursive relation $\hat{R}_j$ such that for each $m_1,\dots,m_{n_j}\in\Omega_\alpha$, $\hat{R}_j(m_1,\dots,m_{n_j}) \Leftrightarrow R_j(\alpha(m_1),\dots,\alpha(m_{n_j}))$.

We say that $\hat{\sigma}_i$ and $\hat{R}_j$ *track* σ_i and R_j respectively. Note that an effective numbering makes no demands on the relation $\equiv_\alpha$.

In order to compare effective numberings of a given structure A we define a preorder $\leq_A$ on the set of all effective numberings of A by $\alpha\leq_A\beta$ if there is a partial recursive function f such that for each $n\in\Omega_\alpha$, $f(n)\downarrow$ and $\beta f(n)=\alpha(n)$. The effective numberings α and β of A are said to be *recursively equivalent* if $\alpha\leq_A\beta$ and $\beta\leq_A\alpha$.

1.2 Definition (i) An effective numbering α of a structure A is *computable* if $\equiv_\alpha$ is a recursive relation.

(ii) The pair (A,α) is a *computable* structure if α is a computable numbering of the structure A.

We say that the structure A is *computable* if there is an α such that (A,α) is computable. However, it is important to remember that it is the structure (A,α) with which we deal when considering computability. There are natural structures A with computable numberings α and β such that (A,α) and (A,β) are not computably isomorphic, a notion we introduce shortly.

Let A and B be structures with effective numberings α and β respectively. A function $f: A \to B$ is said to be *(α, β)-computable* if there is a partial recursive function $\hat{f}$ such that for each $m \in \Omega_\alpha$, $\hat{f}(m)\downarrow$ and $f(\alpha(m)) = \beta(\hat{f}(m))$, that is $\hat{f}$ *tracks* f in the sense that the following diagram commutes.

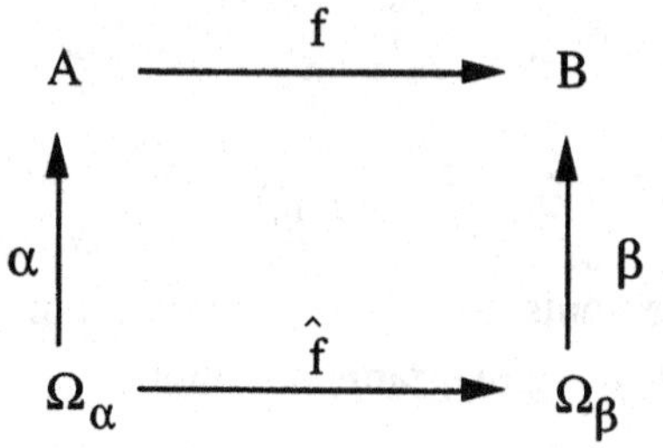

A set $C \subseteq A$ is said to be *α-decidable* (*α-semidecidable*) if $\alpha^{-1}[C]$ is recursive (r.e.). An index for $\alpha^{-1}[C]$ will often be referred to as an α-index. A set $C \subseteq A$ is said to be *weakly α-semidecidable* if there is an r.e. set $W \subseteq \Omega_\alpha$ such that $C = \alpha[W]$. Of course, for computable structures (A, α) the notions of α-semidecidable and weakly α-semidecidable coincide, but for effective structures they may be distinct as should be apparent from Theorem 5.2.

Suppose we have a category **K** whose objects are algebraic structures of the same similarity type and whose morphisms are certain functions between the structures, often the homomorphisms. For example, we may take the category of groups or rings, or, as we shall do in the next section, the category **Cusl**. Then we can form a new category ***CK*** from **K** as follows. The objects in ***CK*** are all (A, α) where A is an object in **K** and α is a computable numbering of A. The morphisms from (A, α) to (B, β) are the (α, β)-computable morphisms from A to B, that is

$$\mathrm{Hom}_{\boldsymbol{CK}}\big((A, \alpha), (B, \beta)\big) = \{f \in \mathrm{Hom}_{\mathbf{K}}(A, B): \ f \text{ is } (\alpha, \beta)\text{-computable}\}.$$

It is an easy exercise to show that ***CK*** is a category. By, for example, (A, α) and (B, β) being *computably isomorphic* we mean that they are isomorphic in the sense of ***CK*** for the appropriate category **K**.

Let α be an effective numbering of A. Then the relation $\equiv_\alpha$ is a congruence relation with respect to each tracking function $\hat{\sigma}$ and each tracking relation $\hat{R}$. To see this let σ be an n-ary operation and suppose that for each $i = 1, \ldots, n$ we have $m_i \equiv_\alpha t_i$. Then

$$\begin{aligned} \alpha(\hat{\sigma}(m_1, \ldots, m_n)) &= \sigma(\alpha(m_1), \ldots, \alpha(m_n)) \\ &= \sigma(\alpha(t_1), \ldots, \alpha(t_n)) \\ &= \alpha(\hat{\sigma}(t_1, \ldots, t_n)) \end{aligned}$$

that is $\hat{\sigma}(m_1,\ldots,m_n)\equiv_\alpha\hat{\sigma}(t_1,\ldots,t_n)$. The argument for $\hat{R}$ is similar. Thus the operations $\hat{\sigma}$ and the relations $\hat{R}$ are well-defined on the equivalence classes of $\equiv_\alpha$ and we may form the quotient structure

$$\Omega_\alpha/{\equiv_\alpha}=(\Omega_\alpha/{\equiv_\alpha};\hat{R}_1,\ldots,\hat{R}_t,\hat{\sigma}_1,\ldots,\hat{\sigma}_k).$$

The mapping $[m]\mapsto\alpha(m)$ gives an isomorphism $\Omega_\alpha/{\equiv_\alpha}\cong A$, where $[m]$ denotes the equivalence class containing m.

In this way we have a presentation of a computable structure (A,α) on the natural numbers such that each operation and relation of the structure, *including equality*, is recursive. This presentation can itself be coded as one number. Here is one way it can be done. Consider the operation σ of A which is, say, m-ary. Then $\hat{\sigma}$ is an m-ary recursive function. Let e be a recursive index for $\hat{\sigma}$, that is $\hat{\sigma}=\phi_e^{(m)}$. In order to include the arity of $\hat{\sigma}$ into its code we choose $\langle e,m\rangle$ as a code for $\hat{\sigma}$. Similarly we choose a code for a relation $\hat{R}$ from its characteristic index. Let $s_1,\ldots,s_k$ and $r_1,\ldots,r_t$ be such codes for $\hat{\sigma}_1,\ldots,\hat{\sigma}_k$ and $\hat{R}_1,\ldots,\hat{R}_t$ respectively, and let a be a characteristic index for Ω_α and b a characteristic index for $\equiv_\alpha$. Then the number $\langle\langle a,b\rangle,\langle r_1,\ldots,r_t\rangle,\langle s_1,\ldots,s_k\rangle\rangle$ is an index for $\Omega_\alpha/{\equiv_\alpha}$. It is said to be a *presentation* of the computable structure (A,α).

Let A and B be structures of the same similarity type and suppose that $\phi: A\longrightarrow B$ is a surjective homomorphism. For an effective numbering α of A we define a numbering $\alpha':\Omega_\alpha\longrightarrow B$ by $\alpha'(m)=\phi(\alpha(m))$.

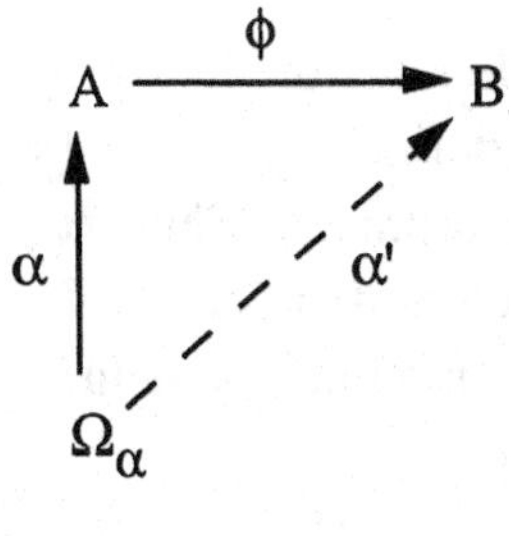

Then α' is an effective numbering of B. To see this, suppose σ_A is an n-ary operation in A and σ_B is the corresponding operation in B. Then

$$\begin{aligned}\sigma_B(\alpha'(m_1),\ldots,\alpha'(m_n))&=\sigma_B(\phi(\alpha(m_1)),\ldots,\phi(\alpha(m_n)))\\&=\phi(\sigma_A(\alpha(m_1),\ldots,\alpha(m_n)))\\&=\phi(\alpha(\hat{\sigma}_A(m_1,\ldots,m_n)))\\&=\alpha'(\hat{\sigma}_A(m_1,\ldots,m_n)).\end{aligned}$$

Thus we see that the recursive tracking function $\hat{\sigma}_A$ also tracks σ_B via α'. Similarly, the recursive tracking relation $\hat{R}_A$ also tracks R_B via α' since we do require our homomorphisms to satisfy

$$R_A(x_1,\ldots,x_n) \Leftrightarrow R_B(\phi(x_1),\ldots,\phi(x_n)).$$

We say that α' is the *effective numbering obtained from* α *via* ϕ.

1.3 Proposition Let $\phi: A \longrightarrow B$ be a surjective homomorphism. If $\alpha: \Omega_\alpha \longrightarrow A$ is an effective numbering of A then $\alpha': \Omega_\alpha \longrightarrow B$ defined by $\alpha' = \phi \circ \alpha$ is an effective numbering of B.

1.4 Corollary If $\phi: A \longrightarrow B$ is an isomorphism and (A, α) is computable then so is (B, α'), where α' is the effective numbering obtained from α via ϕ. In addition, (A, α) and (B, α') have identical presentations.

Proof: Assume first, more generally, that ϕ is a surjective homomorphism. Define the binary relation $\sim$ on A by

$$x \sim y \Leftrightarrow \phi(x) = \phi(y)$$

so that $B \cong A/\sim$, the quotient of A with respect to $\sim$. Then

$$\begin{aligned} m \equiv_{\alpha'} n &\Leftrightarrow \alpha'(m) = \alpha'(n) \\ &\Leftrightarrow \phi(\alpha(m)) = \phi(\alpha(n)) \\ &\Leftrightarrow \alpha(m) \sim \alpha(n). \end{aligned}$$

Thus (B, α') is computable just in case $\sim$ is α-decidable. In particular, when ϕ is injective we have $m \equiv_{\alpha'} n \Leftrightarrow \alpha(m) = \alpha(n) \Leftrightarrow m \equiv_\alpha n$ so (B, α') is computable and each presentation of (A, α) is also a presentation of (B, α'). □

Again let (A, α) be a computable structure and suppose $\sim$ is a congruence relation on A. Then $\phi: A \longrightarrow A/\sim$ defined by $\phi(x) = [x]$, the equivalence class containing x, is a surjective homomorphism. Thus α', the effective numbering obtained from α via ϕ, is an effective numbering of $A/\sim$. Furthermore, if $\sim$ is α-decidable then $(A/\sim, \alpha')$ is a computable structure. We call α' the *quotient numbering* of (A, α) with respect to $\sim$.

1.5 Proposition Suppose (A, α) is a computable structure and $\sim$ is a congruence relation on A. Let α' be the quotient numbering of (A, α) with respect to $\sim$. If $\sim$ is α-decidable then $(A/\sim, \alpha')$ is computable with a presentation obtained uniformly from a presentation of (A, α) and an α-index of $\sim$.

1.6 Examples

(i) The structure $\mathbb{N} = (\mathbb{N}; 0, S, +, \cdot, \leq)$ of natural numbers is computable by letting α = identity. (As usual we identify the natural numbers $\mathbb{N}$ with ω.)

(ii) The ring of integers $\mathbb{Z} = (\mathbb{Z}; 0, S, +, \cdot, \leq)$ is computable. For example we may define $\alpha: \omega \longrightarrow \mathbb{Z}$ by $\alpha(\langle 0, n\rangle) = n$, $\alpha(\langle 1, n\rangle) = -n$ and $\alpha(x) = 0$ when x is not of the form $<0,n>$ or $<1,n>$. It is routine to define the required tracking functions.

(iii) The field of rational numbers $\mathbf{Q}=(\mathbb{Q};0,1,+,\cdot,^{-1};\leq)$ is computable. Let β be a computable numbering of $\mathbb{Z}$. Define $\alpha:\omega\to\mathbb{Q}$ by $\alpha(<m,n>)=\beta(m)/\beta(n)$ when $\beta(n)\neq 0$ and set $\alpha(x)=0$ otherwise. Recall that $p/q=r/s$ if and only if $p\cdot s=r\cdot q$. It follows that the problem of deciding $\equiv_\alpha$ is effectively or recursively reduced to the problem of deciding $\equiv_\beta$, which is recursive.

Here we have to deal with the problem that one of the operations, namely the multiplicative inverse $^{-1}$, is not a total operation. However, a partial operation is not problematic with regard to computations as long as its domain is decidable. For given an argument x we first decide if the operation is defined for x. If it is, we then, and only then, compute its value for that argument.

(iv) The field of algebraic numbers is computable. In fact, every countable algebraically closed field is computable (Rabin [1960]). The universal field of a given characteristic, that is the algebraically closed field of countably infinite transcendence degree over its prime subfield, is an example of a structure which has many inequivalent computable numberings.

(v) Let Σ be a finite alphabet and let Σ^* be the set of all (finite) words over Σ. Then the structure $\Sigma^*=(\Sigma^*;\text{conc},\varepsilon)$ is computable, where conc is the binary operation of concatenation and ε is the empty word. For example, if we let $\Sigma=\{a_1,\dots,a_n\}$ then we may define $\alpha:\omega\to\Sigma^*$ by

$$\alpha(<i_1,\dots,i_k>)=a_{i_1}\dots a_{i_k}$$

when $i_1,\dots,i_k\in\{1,\dots,n\}$ and $\alpha(x)=\varepsilon$ otherwise. As indicated in Chapter 9, one may in fact develop recursion theory directly on Σ^* rather than on $\mathbb{N}$ (see Machtey and Young [1978]).

Finally we shall give a notion of effective functors on categories of the kind we have considered in this section. Our notion is ad hoc, but it is sufficient for our purposes and hopefully easily understood.

We restrict ourselves to categories **K** and **L** for which we can form $\mathcal{C}\mathbf{K}$ and $\mathcal{C}\mathbf{L}$ respectively. It is convenient to first consider the notion of an effective functor $\mathbf{F}:\mathcal{C}\mathbf{K}\to\mathcal{C}\mathbf{L}$. Clearly this should be analogous to a computable function. However, we have to take into account that there is in general no way of coding (isomorphism classes of) computable structures as a recursive set.

1.7 Definition Let $\mathbf{F}:\mathcal{C}\mathbf{K}\to\mathcal{C}\mathbf{L}$ be a functor. Then $\mathbf{F}$ is an *effective* functor if there are partial recursive functions $\hat{F}:\omega\to\omega$ and $\tilde{F}:\omega^3\to\omega$ such that

(i) if $n\in\omega$ is a presentation of the computable structure (A,α) then $\hat{F}(n)$ is a presentation of the computable structure $\mathbf{F}(A,\alpha)$, and

(ii) if f is an (α,β)-computable morphism from A into B and $\hat{f}$ is an index of a tracking function for f with respect to α and β, m is a presentation of (A,α) and n is a presentation of (B,β), then $\tilde{F}(m,n,\hat{f})$ is an index of a tracking function for $\mathbf{F}(f):\mathbf{F}(A,\alpha)\to\mathbf{F}(B,\beta)$.

We say that $\langle\hat{e},\tilde{e}\rangle$ is an *index* of an effective functor $\mathbf{F}:\mathcal{C}\mathbf{K}\to\mathcal{C}\mathbf{L}$ if $\hat{e}$ is an index of $\hat{F}$ and $\tilde{e}$ is an index of $\tilde{F}$.

Now we extend the notion of effectivity to functors from $\mathbf{K}$ to $\mathbf{L}$.

1.8 Definition A functor $\mathbf{F}:\mathbf{K}\to\mathbf{L}$ is *effective* if there is an effective functor $\bar{\mathbf{F}}:\mathcal{C}\mathbf{K}\to\mathcal{C}\mathbf{L}$ such that

(i) for each object (A,α) in $\mathcal{C}\mathbf{K}$, $\bar{\mathbf{F}}(A,\alpha)=(\mathbf{F}(A),\gamma)$ for some γ, and

(ii) for each morphism $f:(A,\alpha)\to(B,\beta)$, $\bar{\mathbf{F}}(f)=\mathbf{F}(f)$.

We say that e is an *index* of an effective functor $\mathbf{F}:\mathbf{K}\to\mathbf{L}$ if e is an index of a corresponding effective functor $\bar{\mathbf{F}}:\mathcal{C}\mathbf{K}\to\mathcal{C}\mathbf{L}$.

Clearly the identity functor on a category $\mathbf{K}$ is effective. Also a constant functor from $\mathbf{K}$ to $\mathbf{L}$ is effective as long as the constant value is a computable structure in $\mathbf{L}$. Finally it is easily verified that effective functors are closed under composition and that an index for the composition is computed uniformly from indices of the given effective functors.

Section 10.2 Computable Cusl's

Each element of a domain is the limit of its compact approximations. Suppose we can effectively compute on the compact elements of a domain. Then these computations may be extended to the whole domain by saying that the result of a computation is the limit of the results of the computation on each compact approximation. Recall that a compact element a has the property that any sequence converging to a must also include a, in the way described in Section 3.1. For this reason we are forced to be able to compute on the cusl of compact elements of a domain in the sense of Section 10.1, in order to have a computation theory on the domain. We will now develop the theory of computable cusl's.

Let P be a cusl. Normally we view P as a structure of the form $(P;\sqsubseteq,\bot)$, while axiomatizing the required properties of $\sqsubseteq$ and $\bot$. However, when considering the computability of a cusl P it is reasonable to require these properties to be computable. Therefore it is convenient to make them explicit in the structure. From Definition 3.2.1 we see that the operations and relations relevant for a cusl are the constant $\perp$, the partial binary operation $\sqcup$, the ordering $\sqsubseteq$, and the consistency relation Cons defined by

$$\mathrm{Cons}(a,b) \Leftrightarrow \exists c(a \sqsubseteq c \;\&\; b \sqsubseteq c).$$

Thus, when considering computability, we view a cusl P as a structure of the form $P=(P;\sqsubseteq,\mathrm{Cons},\sqcup,\perp)$, although later we write $P=(P;\sqsubseteq,\perp)$ as usual.

2.1 Definition Let P be a cusl. Then (P,α) is a *computable cusl* if α is a computable numbering of the structure $P=(P;\sqsubseteq,\mathrm{Cons},\sqcup,\perp)$.

Note that the ordering $\sqsubseteq$ is definable from Cons and $\sqcup$ by

$$a \sqsubseteq b \Leftrightarrow \mathrm{Cons}(a,b) \;\&\; a \sqcup b = b.$$

It follows that if α is a numbering of P for which Cons and $=$ are α-decidable and $\sqcup$ is α-computable, then $\sqsubseteq$ is also α-decidable.

2.2 Proposition Let (P,α) be a computable cusl and let K vary over finite subsets of P.

(i) The relation $\mathrm{Cons}(K) \Leftrightarrow \exists b(\forall a \in K)(a \sqsubseteq b)$ is α-decidable.

(ii) The partial function $K \mapsto \bigsqcup K$ is α-computable.

Let us describe precisely how the statements of the proposition are to be interpreted. Recall from Section 9.2 the notion of a canonical index e for the finite set of numbers D_e. To say that the relation Cons(K) is α-decidable when K varies over finite subsets of P we mean that the set

$$\overline{\mathrm{Cons}} = \{e \in \omega : \mathrm{Cons}(\alpha[D_e \cap \Omega_\alpha])\}$$

is recursive. Similarly, to say that $K \mapsto \bigsqcup K$ is α-computable we mean that there is a recursive function $\widehat{\bigsqcup}$ such that for each e, if $\overline{\mathrm{Cons}}(e)$ (that is $e \in \overline{\mathrm{Cons}}$) then $\alpha(\widehat{\bigsqcup}(e)) = \bigsqcup \alpha[D_e \cap \Omega_\alpha]$.

Although all computations take place within the natural numbers ω in terms of the chosen numbering α, we will, for clarity and brevity, sometimes suppress the numberings in our arguments and informally manipulate elements in the structure, as above, rather than their codes.

Proof: From a canonical index for a finite set $K \subseteq P$ we can compute $|K|$, the cardinality of K. If $|K|=0$ or 1 then Cons(K) is true and $\bigsqcup K$ is trivially computed. Suppose $|K| \geq 2$. Then we can α-computably partition K as $K = K' \cup \{a\}$, for some $a \in K$, and inductively decide Cons(K') and, in case Cons(K'), compute $\bigsqcup K'$. Now, $\mathrm{Cons}(K) \Leftrightarrow \mathrm{Cons}(K') \;\&\; \mathrm{Cons}(\bigsqcup K', a)$, and

Cons is therefore α-decidable. Furthermore, in case Cons(K) we have $\bigsqcup K = (\bigsqcup K') \sqcup a$ which is α-computable by the computability of $\sqcup$. $\square$

The argument just given is an informal one. This is a common method in recursion theory, often called an *argument by Church's thesis.* It means that when presenting an algorithm informally as above one trusts the thesis that the algorithm can be translated into a function belonging to, for example, the μ-recursive functions. The induction involved in arguments like the one above translates into some kind of recursion, in this case a simple primitive recursion.

2.3 Examples

(i) Every finite cusl is clearly computable.

(ii) Whenever A is a countable set then $A_\perp$ is a computable cusl.

(iii) Let $\wp_f(\omega) = (\wp_f(\omega); \subseteq, \emptyset)$ be the cusl of finite subsets of ω ordered by inclusion. Define $\alpha : \omega \to \wp_f(\omega)$ by $\alpha(e) = D_e$, the finite set with canonical index e. Then $(\wp_f(\omega), \alpha)$ is a computable cusl.

(iv) Consider the cusl SEQ defined in 2.1.12 with the ordering $\sqsubseteq$ defined there. Let

$$\Omega_\alpha = \{n \in \omega : \text{Seq}(n) \ \& \ (\forall i < \text{lh}(n))((n)_{i+1} = 0 \text{ or } (n)_{i+1} = 1)\}.$$

Thus Ω_α is a recursive set. Define $\alpha : \Omega_\alpha \to \text{SEQ}$ by $\alpha(n) = \sigma$, where $\sigma(i) = (n)_{i+1}$ for $i < \text{lh}(n)$. Then (SEQ, α) is a computable cusl.

(v) Let $\mathcal{P}_c = \{f \in \mathbb{N} \xrightarrow{p} \mathbb{N} : f \text{ is finite}\}$ be the cusl of the compact elements in the domain $\mathcal{P}$ of partial functions on $\mathbb{N}$ defined in 2.1.13. Let Ω_α be the recursive set defined by

$$\Omega_\alpha = \{e \in \omega : (\forall x \in D_e)(\text{Seq}(x) \ \& \ \text{lh}(x) = 2) \ \& \\ (\forall x \in D_e)(\forall y \in D_e)((x)_1 = (y)_1 \Rightarrow (x)_2 = (y)_2)\}.$$

Define $\alpha : \Omega_\alpha \to \mathcal{P}_c$ by $\alpha(e) = f$, where $\text{graph}(f) = \{((x)_1, (x)_2) : x \in D_e\}$. Then $(\mathcal{P}_c, \alpha)$ is a computable cusl.

(vi) Let $\mathcal{F}$ be the cusl of Definition 7.1.1 whose completion defines the universal domain $\mathcal{U}$. Using the computability of the rational numbers (Example 1.6 (iii)) it is routine to verify that $\mathcal{F}$ is a computable cusl.

Consider the category **Cusl** introduced in Chapter 4. Recall that its objects are cusl's and the set of morphisms between cusl's P and Q is the set of cusl embeddings from P into Q. Now form the category ***C*Cusl** as in Section 10.1. Thus the objects of ***C*Cusl** are the computable cusl's (P, α) and the morphisms from (P,α) to (Q,β) are the (α,β)-computable cusl embeddings from P into Q. By the fact that ***CCusl*** is a category we do have the concepts of ω-chain, cone and colimiting cone for ***CCusl*** (cf. 4.2.1). However, these concepts are not satisfactory in our setting. Just as we have added computability or effectivity requirements on the objects and morphisms in **Cusl** we must also put effectivity requirements on the various concepts used when studying ***CCusl***. Thus, for example, we want an ω-chain to be a computable object, that is it should be given by a recursive function which for each n computes a presentation for the n'th object and a recursive index for a tracking function for the n'th morphism. Of course, these remarks also apply to ***CK*** for an arbitrary concrete category **K**.

2.4 Definition (i) An ω-chain $\Delta=((P_n,\alpha_n),f_n)$ in ***CCusl*** is a *computable ω-chain* if there are total recursive functions $\rho,\tau:\omega\longrightarrow\omega$ such that for each n, $\rho(n)$ is a presentation of (P_n,α_n) and $\tau(n)$ is a recursive index of a tracking function for f_n with respect to α_n and α_{n+1}, that is $\phi_{\tau(n)}:\Omega_{\alpha_n}\longrightarrow\Omega_{\alpha_{n+1}}$ tracks f_n with respect to α_n and α_{n+1}.
(ii) Let $\Delta=((P_n,\alpha_n),f_n)$ be a computable ω-chain and let (P,α) be a computable cusl. A cone $\mu=(\mu_n)_{n<\omega}:\Delta\longrightarrow(P,\alpha)$ in ***CCusl*** is a *computable cone* if there is a total recursive function η such that $\phi_{\eta(n)}:\Omega_{\alpha_n}\longrightarrow\Omega_\alpha$ tracks μ_n.
(iii) Let $\mu:\Delta\longrightarrow(P,\alpha)$ be a computable cone and suppose it is a colimiting cone in ***CCusl***. Then $\mu:\Delta\longrightarrow(P,\alpha)$ is a *computable colimiting cone* if given any other computable cone $\mu':\Delta\longrightarrow(P',\alpha')$, the unique mediating embedding $h:P\longrightarrow P'$ is (α,α')-computable uniformly in (ρ',τ',η'), the computing machinery for μ'.

What we have required is that there are effective procedures which give us (indices for) the ω-chain and the various embeddings. So we do not *only* require that the embeddings exist and are computable but that we must be able to compute them uniformly from the given data.

Here is the computable version of Theorem 4.2.7.

2.5 Theorem Let $\Delta=((P_n,\alpha_n),f_n)$ be a computable ω-chain of cusl's. Then $P=\varinjlim P_n$ is computable with a numbering α obtained uniformly from Δ. Furthermore there is a computable colimiting cone $\mu:\Delta\longrightarrow(P,\alpha)$, obtained uniformly from Δ.

Proof: Let ρ and τ be the recursive functions associated with the computable ω-chain Δ. We verify that the proof of Theorem 4.2.7 is effective. Recall that P may be taken as $Q/\sim$ where $Q=\bigcup_{n<\omega}(\{n\}\times P_n)$, the disjoint union of the P_n, and the equivalence $\sim$ is defined by

$$(k,a)\sim(m,b)\ \Leftrightarrow\ (\exists n\geq k,m)(f_{kn}(a)=f_{mn}(b)).$$

First we define a numbering $\beta:\Omega_\beta \longrightarrow Q$. Let $\Omega_\beta = \{<n,k>: k \in \Omega_n\}$. Then Ω_β is a recursive set since

$$x \in \Omega_\beta \Leftrightarrow \mathrm{Seq}(x) \ \&\ \mathrm{lh}(x)=2 \ \&\ (x)_2 \in \Omega_{(x)_1}$$

where the last conjunct is recursive using ρ. Define $\beta:\Omega_\beta \longrightarrow Q$ by

$$\beta(<n,k>) = (n, \alpha_n(k)).$$

To decide the ordering $\sqsubseteq_Q$ β-computably, consider (k,a) and (m,b). Compute $n=\max(k,m)$ and then, using τ, compute $f_{kn}(a)$ and $f_{mn}(b)$ and decide $f_{kn}(a) \sqsubseteq f_{mn}(b)$ α_n-computably in P_n. Thus $\sqsubseteq_Q$ is β-computable using ρ and τ. Implicit in the proof of Lemma 4.2.4 we have that (k,a) and (m,b) are consistent in Q if and only if $f_{kn}(a)$ and $f_{mn}(b)$ are consistent in P_n. It follows that the Cons relation on Q is β-decidable. Similarly, the least upper bound operation is β-computable and $\sim$ is β-decidable. But then, by Proposition 1.5, the quotient structure $P=Q/\sim$ is computable using the quotient numbering α of $Q/\sim$ obtained from β.

To see that the cone $\mu=(\mu_n)_{n<\omega}:\Delta \longrightarrow (P,\alpha)$ is computable we note that a tracking function for μ_n is given by

$$k \mapsto <n,k>$$

which is recursive, uniformly in n. This uniformity provides us with the desired function η.

Suppose $\mu':\Delta \longrightarrow (P',\alpha')$ is a computable cone. Then, by Lemma 4.2.6, there is a unique mediating embedding $h:P \longrightarrow P'$ defined by $h(\mu_n(a)) = \mu'_n(a)$ for $a \in P_n$. This embedding is (α,α')-computable, for given $<n,k> \in \Omega_\alpha$,

$$h(\alpha(<n,k>)) = h(\mu_n(\alpha_n(k))) = \mu'_n(\alpha_n(k)) = \alpha'(\hat{\mu}'_n(k)).$$

Thus the function

$$<n,k> \mapsto \hat{\mu}'_n(k) = \phi_{\eta'(n)}(k)$$

tracks h with respect to α and α' and it is recursive uniformly in the computable cone μ', that is in η'. This completes the proof that $\mu:\Delta \longrightarrow (P,\alpha)$ is a computable colimiting cone, obtained uniformly from Δ. □

The following effective version of Theorem 4.3.16 is the key to providing effective solutions to domain equations.

2.6 Theorem Let $\mathbf{F}:\mathbf{Cusl} \longrightarrow \mathbf{Cusl}$ be an ω-continuous effective functor. Then the least fixed point of $\mathbf{F}$ is computable with a presentation obtained uniformly from an index of $\mathbf{F}$.

Proof: Let $\overline{F}:\mathcal{C}\mathbf{Cusl}\longrightarrow\mathcal{C}\mathbf{Cusl}$ be an effective functor associated with $\mathbf{F}$ and let $\Delta=(P_n,f_n)$ be the ω-chain constructed in the proof of Theorem 4.3.16. Fix some canonical presentation a_0 of the trivial cusl $P_0=\{\bot_0\}$ with respect to a numbering α_0. Then we obtain an ω-chain $\overline{\Delta}=((P_n,\alpha_n),f_n)$ in $\mathcal{C}\mathbf{Cusl}$ where $(P_{n+1},\alpha_{n+1})=\overline{\mathbf{F}}(P_n,\alpha_n)=(\mathbf{F}(P_n),\alpha_{n+1})$ and $f_{n+1}=\overline{\mathbf{F}}(f_n)=\mathbf{F}(f_n)$. By Theorem 2.5 it suffices to show that $\overline{\Delta}$ is computable. Using the notation for effective functors we shall construct the required recursive functions ρ and τ.

Define $\rho:\omega\longrightarrow\omega$ by

$$\rho(n)=\begin{cases} a_0 & \text{if } n=0\\ \widehat{F}(\rho(n-1)) & \text{if } n>0\end{cases}$$

which is recursive uniformly in $\widehat{F}$. The unique embedding $f_0:P_0\longrightarrow P_1$ is clearly computable with respect to the numberings α_0 and α_1. Furthermore we obtain an index $\widehat{f}_0$ for a tracking function uniformly in $\widehat{F}$, since a code for $\bot_1$ is recursively obtained from $\widehat{F}(a_0)$.

Now define $\tau:\omega\longrightarrow\omega$ by

$$\tau(n)=\begin{cases} \widehat{f}_0 & \text{if } n=0\\ \widetilde{F}(\rho(n-1),\rho(n),\tau(n-1)) & \text{if } n>0.\end{cases}$$

Then τ is recursive uniformly in $\widetilde{F}$ and $\widehat{F}$, and $\tau(n)$ is an index of a tracking function for f_n with respect to α_n and α_{n+1}.

The functions ρ and τ make $\overline{\Delta}=((P_n,\alpha_n),f_n)$ into a computable ω-chain, uniformly in (an index for) $\mathbf{F}$. Thus, by Theorem 2.5, the least fixed point $P=\underrightarrow{\lim}\,P_n$ of $\mathbf{F}$ is computable uniformly in $\mathbf{F}$. □

To be precise, recall that a *least* fixed point of $\mathbf{F}$ is a pair (P,f) where f is the mediating morphism between $\mathbf{F}(\mu)$ and $(\mu_{n+1})_{n<\omega}$ as given in Corollary 4.3.17. We leave it as an exercise to show that f is computable uniformly in $\mathbf{F}$, that is an index for a tracking function of f can be computed from an index of $\mathbf{F}$.

The notion of an effective functor from **Cusl** to **Cusl** extends readily to functors $\mathbf{F}:\mathbf{Cusl}^n\longrightarrow\mathbf{Cusl}$. Thus a bifunctor $\mathbf{F}:\mathbf{Cusl}\times\mathbf{Cusl}\longrightarrow\mathbf{Cusl}$ is *effective* if there is an effective functor $\overline{\mathbf{F}}:\mathcal{C}\mathbf{Cusl}\times\mathcal{C}\mathbf{Cusl}\longrightarrow\mathcal{C}\mathbf{Cusl}$ such that

(i) $\overline{\mathbf{F}}((P,\alpha),(Q,\beta))=(\mathbf{F}(P,Q),\gamma)$ for some γ, and

(ii) if $(f,g):((P,\alpha),(Q,\beta))\longrightarrow((P',\alpha'),(Q',\beta'))$ is a morphism in $\mathcal{C}\mathbf{Cusl}\times\mathcal{C}\mathbf{Cusl}$ then $\overline{\mathbf{F}}(f,g)=\mathbf{F}(f,g)$.

To say that $\overline{\mathbf{F}}:\mathcal{C}\mathbf{Cusl}\times\mathcal{C}\mathbf{Cusl}\longrightarrow\mathcal{C}\mathbf{Cusl}$ is *effective* means that there are partial recursive functions $\widehat{F}:\omega^2\longrightarrow\omega$ and $\widetilde{F}:\omega^6\longrightarrow\omega$ such that

(i) if m and n are presentations of (P,α) and (Q,β) respectively, then $\widehat{F}(m,n)$ is a presentation of $\overline{\mathbf{F}}((P,\alpha),(Q,\beta))$, and

(ii) if $\hat{f}$ and $\hat{g}$ are indices of tracking functions for $f:(P,\alpha)\longrightarrow(P',\alpha')$ and $g:(Q,\beta)\longrightarrow(Q',\beta')$ respectively and m and m' are presentations of (P,α) and (P',α') and n and n' are presentations of (Q,α) and (Q',α') respectively, then $\tilde{F}(m,m',\hat{f},n,n',\hat{g})$ is an index of $\bar{\mathbf{F}}(f,g)$.

It remains to show that the functors on **Cusl** corresponding to the usual domain constructions are effective. Recall the functors defined in 4.3.5 to 4.3.11.

2.7 Proposition The bifunctor $\mathbf{T}_\times:\mathbf{Cusl}\times\mathbf{Cusl}\longrightarrow\mathbf{Cusl}$ is effective.

Proof: We argue somewhat informally when defining the functor $\bar{\mathbf{T}}_\times$ on $\mathcal{C}\mathbf{Cusl}\times\mathcal{C}\mathbf{Cusl}$ and the required recursive functions $\hat{T}_\times$ and $\tilde{T}_\times$. Suppose we are given presentations of (P,α) and (Q,β). Then let

$$\Omega_\gamma=\{<x,y>: x\in\Omega_\alpha, y\in\Omega_\beta\}$$

and define $\gamma:\Omega_\gamma\longrightarrow P\times Q$ by

$$\gamma(<x,y>)=(\alpha(x),\beta(y)).$$

We set $\bar{\mathbf{T}}_\times((P,\alpha),(Q,\beta))=(P\times Q,\gamma)$.

Note that Ω_γ is a recursive set with a characteristic index obtained effectively from the given presentations. Let x_0 and y_0 be the designated codes in the presentations for $\bot_P$ and $\bot_Q$ respectively. Then we set $<x_0,y_0>$ as the designated γ-code for $\bot_{P\times Q}$ in the presentation we are constructing.

Next suppose $\widehat{Cons}_\alpha$ and $\widehat{Cons}_\beta$ are the recursive tracking relations for consistency in P and Q respectively, given in the presentations. Then $\widehat{Cons}_\gamma$ defined by

$$\widehat{Cons}_\gamma(x,y) \Leftrightarrow \widehat{Cons}_\alpha((x)_1,(y)_1) \,\&\, \widehat{Cons}_\beta((x)_2,(y)_2)$$

tracks the consistency relation in $P\times Q$ for γ, and a characteristic index for $\widehat{Cons}_\gamma$ can be computed uniformly from characteristic indices of $\widehat{Cons}_\alpha$ and $\widehat{Cons}_\beta$ and hence from the given presentations. Similarly we can compute a characteristic index of the tracking relation for $\sqsubseteq_{P\times Q}$.

A recursive function tracking the supremum operation on $P\times Q$ is given by

$$\widehat{\sqcup}_\gamma(x,y)=<\widehat{\sqcup}_\alpha((x)_1,(y)_1),\widehat{\sqcup}_\beta((x)_2,(y)_2)>$$

and a recursive index of $\widehat{\sqcup}_\gamma$ can be computed uniformly from the given presentations.

Finally, for $x,y\in\Omega_\gamma$,

$$\begin{aligned} x\equiv_\gamma y &\Leftrightarrow \gamma(x)=\gamma(y)\\ &\Leftrightarrow (\alpha((x)_1),\beta((x)_2))=(\alpha((y)_1),\beta((y)_2)) \end{aligned}$$

$$\Leftrightarrow \alpha((x)_1)=\alpha((y)_1) \;\&\; \beta((x)_2)=\beta((y)_2)$$
$$\Leftrightarrow (x)_1 \equiv_\alpha (y)_1 \;\&\; (x)_2 \equiv_\beta (y)_2$$

which is recursive uniformly in $\equiv_\alpha$ and $\equiv_\beta$.

We have shown that $\overline{T}_\times((P,\alpha),(Q,\beta))=(P\times Q,\gamma)$ is a computable cusl. Furthermore, the algorithm implicit in the above discussion provides us with our desired recursive function $\hat{T}_\times$.

It remains to define $\tilde{T}_\times$. Consider embeddings $f:P\to P'$ and $g:Q\to Q'$ which are (α,α')-computable and (β,β')-computable with indices $\hat{f}$ and $\hat{g}$ respectively. A tracking function for $<f,g>:P\times Q\to P'\times Q'$ with respect to the numberings given by $\overline{T}_\times$ should be a function h which for $x\in\Omega_\alpha$ and $y\in\Omega_\beta$ satisfies

$$h(<x,y>)=<\phi_{\hat{f}}(x),\phi_{\hat{g}}(y)>.$$

Using the enumeration theorem 9.2.2 define a recursive function $k:\omega^3\to\omega$ by

$$k(x,y,z)\simeq<\phi_x((z)_1),\phi_y((z)_2)>.$$

Then, using the s-m-n theorem 9.2.3, there is a primitive recursive function $t:\omega^2\to\omega$ such that

$$\phi_{t(x,y)}(z)\simeq k(x,y,z)\simeq<\phi_x((z)_1),\phi_y((z)_2)>.$$

Clearly, $t(\hat{f},\hat{g})$ is an index of a tracking function for $<f,g>$ respecting $\overline{T}_\times$, so we define $\tilde{T}_\times$ by $\tilde{T}_\times(m,m',\hat{f},n,n',\hat{g})=t(\hat{f},\hat{g})$. □

In the proof we were quite explicit when defining $\tilde{T}_\times$ which enabled us to see that $\tilde{T}_\times$ is a total function and, in fact, primitive recursive. The same is true for $\hat{T}_\times$. It turns out that each construction we consider uses only simple primitive recursive operations such as pairing and unpairing, functions representing propositional logical connectives and quantification over finite sets. In addition we utilize uniformities, as above, with the primitive recursive functions stemming from the s-m-n theorem as the main ingredients. However, even though the tracking functions $\hat{T}_\times$ and $\tilde{T}_\times$ are total they only perform meaningful work on meaningful data.

2.8 Proposition The bifunctor $T_\to$: **Cusl** $\times$ **Cusl** $\to$ **Cusl** is effective.

Proof: Again we argue rather informally. Suppose we are given presentations of (P,α) and (Q,β). Recall that $((P\to Q))$ consists of finite consistent subsets of $P\times Q$, and that $(P\to Q)=((P\to Q))/\sim$. We give a numbering of $((P\to Q))$ and then we take the quotient numbering.

Let Ω_γ be the set of $e\in\omega$ such that

(a) $(\forall x \in D_e)(Seq(x) \,\&\, lh(x)=2 \,\&\, (x)_1 \in \Omega_\alpha \,\&\, (x)_2 \in \Omega_\beta)$, and
(b) $(\forall I \subseteq D_e)(\widehat{Cons}_\alpha(\{(x)_1 : x \in I\}) \Rightarrow \widehat{Cons}_\beta(\{(x)_2 : x \in I\}))$

where the $\widehat{Cons}$ relations are extensions as in Proposition 2.2 of the binary relations given in the presentations. Since all quantifiers range over given finite sets, Ω_γ is a recursive set and it is obtained uniformly from the given presentations of (P,α) and (Q,β). Now define $\gamma:\Omega_\gamma \longrightarrow ((P \longrightarrow Q))$ by

$$\gamma(e)=\{(\alpha((x)_1),\beta((x)_2)): x \in D_e\}.$$

The relation $\sqsubseteq$ on $((P \longrightarrow Q))$ is tracked by

$$e \mathrel{\widehat{\sqsubseteq}}_\gamma e' \Leftrightarrow ((\forall I \subseteq D_e)[\widehat{Cons}_\alpha(\{(x)_1 : x \in I\}) \Rightarrow$$
$$\widehat{\bigsqcup}_\beta\{(x)_2 : x \in I\} \mathrel{\widehat{\sqsubseteq}}_\beta \widehat{\bigsqcup}_\beta\{(y)_2 : y \in D_{e'} \,\&\, (y)_1 \mathrel{\widehat{\sqsubseteq}}_\alpha \widehat{\bigsqcup}_\alpha\{(x)_1 : x \in I\}\}]).$$

Again, this is clearly a recursive relation obtained uniformly from the given presentations. Furthermore, the relation $\sim$ is γ-decidable, uniformly from $\widehat{\sqsubseteq}_\gamma$.

Let $\delta:\Omega_\delta=\Omega_\gamma \longrightarrow (P \longrightarrow Q)=((P \longrightarrow Q))/\sim$ be the quotient numbering obtained from γ as in Proposition 1.5. It follows that $\equiv_\delta$ is recursive. We leave it as an exercise to verify that the consistency relation is δ-decidable and that the supremum operation is δ-computable with a tracking relation and tracking operation obtained uniformly from the given presentations. Note that $\bot_{(P\to Q)}=[\{(\bot_P,\bot_Q)\}]$ so that a designated δ-code for $\bot_{(P\to Q)}$ is also obtained from the presentations.

We set $\overline{T}_\to((P,\alpha),(Q,\beta))=((P \longrightarrow Q),\delta)$. The described uniformities provide us with the desired recursive function $\overline{T}_\to$.

It remains to define $\widetilde{T}_\to$. Let h and k be primitive recursive functions such that $h(e)=|D_e|$, the cardinality of D_e, and $k(i,e)=$ the i'th element in a one-one enumeration of D_e for $1 \leq i \leq h(e)$. First define the partial recursive function $t:\omega^3 \longrightarrow \omega$ by

$$t(x,y,z) \simeq \sum_{i=1}^{h(e)} 2^{<\phi_x((k(i,e))_1),\phi_y((k(i,e))_2)>}.$$

Thus whenever the right hand side is defined, its value is a canonical index of the finite set

$$\{<\phi_x((z)_1),\phi_y((z)_2)>: z \in D_e\}.$$

By the s-m-n theorem there is a primitive recursive function s such that

$$\phi_{s(x,y)}(e) \simeq t(x,y,e).$$

We define $\widetilde{T}_\to$ by $\widetilde{T}_\to(m,m',x,n,n',y)=s(x,y)$. It easily follows that if $f:P \longrightarrow P'$ and $g:Q \longrightarrow Q'$ are (α,α')-computable and (β,β')-computable embed-

dings with indices $\hat{f}$ and $\hat{g}$ respectively then $\tilde{T}_{\rightarrow}(m, m', \hat{f}, n, n', \hat{g})$ is an index of a tracking function for the (δ, δ')-computable embedding
$\mathbf{T}_{\rightarrow}(f, g) : (P \longrightarrow Q) \longrightarrow (P' \longrightarrow Q')$. □

2.9 Proposition The functors $\mathbf{T}_{+}$, $\mathbf{T}_{\otimes}$, $\mathbf{T}_{\oplus}$, $\mathbf{T}_{\rightarrow\bot}$ and $\mathbf{T}_{\bot}$ on **Cusl** are effective.

Proof: Exercise 1. □

Recall our observation that effective functors are closed under composition and that a constant functor is effective whenever its value is a computable cusl. Thus any "domain equation" using computable cusl's as parameters and using the cusl constructions discussed here gives rise to an ω-continuous effective functor $\mathbf{T} : \mathbf{Cusl} \longrightarrow \mathbf{Cusl}$. Furthermore, there is an effective procedure which given a domain equation, including presentations of the cusl's appearing as parameters, computes an index for the corresponding functor **T**. It follows by Theorem 2.6 that the least solution of the domain equation exists and is a computable cusl with a presentation obtained effectively from the given equation.

2.10 Theorem The least solution of a domain equation built up by $\rightarrow$, $\times$, $+$, $\otimes$, $\oplus$, $\rightarrow_{\bot}$ and $\bot$ and using computable cusl's as parameters is a computable cusl. A presentation of this solution is obtained effectively from the given equation.

Section 10.3 Effective Domains

The notion of computability from the previous sections is not the correct one to use for domains. A trivial reason is that many domains of interest are uncountable and therefore cannot support the standard theory of computability outlined in Section 10.1. More fundamentally, domains are conceived as the *completion* of a set of concrete elements, viz. the compact elements, and computations on an element in the completion are determined by the way the computations act on its approximations. The theory of computability on domains reflects this in the sense that a domain is effective when the cusl of compact elements of the domain is computable. In this section we study the theory of effective domains. In particular we relate this notion to the work in the previous sections to show that least solutions to domain equations, with effective domains as parameters, are effective.

3.1 Definition Let D be a domain. Then (D,α) is an *effective domain* if (D_c,α) is a computable cusl, where D_c is the structure $D_c=(D_c;\sqsubseteq,\mathrm{Cons},\sqcup,\bot)$ of compact elements.

By a *presentation* of the effective domain (D,α) we mean a presentation of the computable cusl (D_c,α). We say that a domain D is *effective* if (D,α) is an effective domain for some α.

Let (P,α) be a computable cusl and let $\overline{P}$ be the completion of P by ideals. Define $\overline{\alpha}:\Omega_\alpha\to\overline{P}_c$ by $\overline{\alpha}(n)=[\alpha(n)]$, the principal ideal generated by $\alpha(n)$. From the proof of Theorem 3.2.3 it follows directly that $\overline{\alpha}$ is a computable numbering of $\overline{P}_c$ and, in fact, that a presentation of (P,α) is also a presentation of $(\overline{P}_c,\overline{\alpha})$ and hence of the effective domain $(\overline{P},\overline{\alpha})$. We make this observation explicit.

3.2 Proposition If (P,α) is a computable cusl then $(\overline{P},\overline{\alpha})$ is an effective domain. Furthermore, each presentation of (P,α) is also a presentation of $(\overline{P},\overline{\alpha})$.

Suppose that D and E are isomorphic domains via, say, the isomorphism $\psi:D\to E$, and suppose (D,α) is effective. Then $\psi|_{D_c}:D_c\to E_c$ is a cusl isomorphism and hence (E_c,α') is computable by Corollary 1.4, where $\alpha'=\psi\circ\alpha$. Furthermore, each presentation of (D_c,α) is also a presentation of (E_c,α') and hence of (E,α'). Thus, using the representation theorem 3.2.6, we can recursively construct the effective domain (D,α) up to isomorphism from its representation.

We now have a host of examples of effective domains. The completion of each cusl in Examples 2.3 is effective. In particular, every finite domain is effective, $\mathbb{N}_\bot$ is effective, the domain $\wp(\omega)$ is effective, the Baire and Cantor domains are effective and the universal domain $\mathcal{U}$ is effective. In addition, effective domains are closed under the domain constructions of Chapter 3, as will be shown shortly.

Let (D,α) be an effective domain. We know that each element of D is obtained as the limit of a sequence of compact elements. Of course, such a sequence need not be computable. In fact, since there are only countably many computable sequences, most elements in an uncountable domain do not have effective approximations. Let $x\in D$ and consider an α-computable sequence $f:\omega\to D_c$ such that $x=\bigsqcup\{f(n):n<\omega\}$, and let $\hat{f}:\omega\to\Omega_\alpha$ be a recursive tracking function of f. We have

$$a\in\mathrm{approx}(x)\ \Leftrightarrow\ \exists n\,(a\sqsubseteq f(n))$$

and hence

$$m\in\alpha^{-1}[\mathrm{approx}(x)]\ \Leftrightarrow\ \exists n\,(m\ \widehat{\sqsubseteq}\ \hat{f}(n))$$

which shows that $\alpha^{-1}[\text{approx}(x)]$ is r.e., that is approx(x) is α-semidecidable. Conversely, if approx(x) is α-semidecidable let $\hat{f}:\omega \to \Omega_\alpha$ be a total recursive function enumerating $\alpha^{-1}[\text{approx}(x)]$. Then the function $f:\omega \to D_c$ tracked by $\hat{f}$ is a computable sequence whose limit is x. The uniformities implicit in the above constructions motivate the following definition.

3.3 Definition Let (D,α) be an effective domain. Then $x \in D$ is an *(α-)computable element* if $\alpha^{-1}[\text{approx}(x)]$ is r.e. An r.e. index of $\alpha^{-1}[\text{approx}(x)]$ is an *(α-)index* of the computable element x.

Other terms for computable in the literature are *recursive* or *effective.* Note that each compact element in an effective domain is computable.

A continuous function between domains should be effective if its values on computable elements can be effectively approximated. To capture this, recall from Definition 6.3.2 the way continuous functions between domains are represented by approximable mappings between their respective cusl's of compact elements.

3.4 Definition Let (D,α) and (E,β) be effective domains. A continuous function $f:D \to E$ is *(α,β)-effective* if the relation $R \subseteq D_c \times E_c$ defined by

$$R(a,b) \Leftrightarrow b \sqsubseteq f(a)$$

is (α,β)-semidecidable, that is the relation

$$\hat{R}(m,n) \Leftrightarrow R(\alpha(m),\beta(n))$$

is r.e. An r.e. index for $\hat{R}$ is an *effective index for* f with respect to α and β.

3.5 Proposition Let (D,α), (E,β) and (F,γ) be effective domains and let $f:D \to E$ and $g:E \to F$ be continuous and (α,β)-effective and (β,γ)-effective respectively.

(i) If $x \in D$ is α-computable then $f(x) \in E$ is β-computable.

(ii) The composition $h = g \circ f: D \to F$ is (α,γ)-effective.

Proof: (i) Let $\hat{R}$ be the r.e. tracking relation for f. Suppose $x \in D$ is computable. Then $V = \alpha^{-1}[\text{approx}(x)]$ is r.e. and hence

$$W = \{n \in \omega : (\exists m \in V)\hat{R}(m,n)\}$$

is r.e. We claim that $W = \beta^{-1}[\text{approx}(f(x))]$. Let $n \in W$ and choose $m \in V$ such that $\hat{R}(m,n)$, that is $\beta(n) \sqsubseteq f(\alpha(m))$. But $f(\alpha(m)) \sqsubseteq f(x)$ by the monotonicity of f so $\beta(n) \in \text{approx}(f(x))$. For the converse inclusion assume $\beta(n) \in \text{approx}(f(x))$. Then

$$\beta(n) \sqsubseteq f(x) = \bigsqcup\{f(a) : a \in \text{approx}(x)\}$$

by the continuity of f and hence there is an $a \in \text{approx}(x)$ such that $\beta(n) \sqsubseteq f(a)$. But then there is $m \in V$ such that $\hat{R}(m,n)$ so $n \in W$.

(ii) Suppressing the numberings and letting a, b and d vary over D_c, E_c and F_c respectively we have by the continuity of g,

$$d \sqsubseteq g(f(a)) \iff (\exists b \sqsubseteq f(a))(d \sqsubseteq g(b)).$$

The right hand side is semidecidable by the effectivity of f and g. □

We observe that the above proof is uniform. Thus an r.e. index of W is obtained uniformly from r.e. indices of V and $\hat{R}$. Similarly an index of h is obtained uniformly from indices of f and g.

Before giving examples of effective continuous functions we observe that the effectivity of domains is preserved under all our usual domain constructions.

3.6 Theorem Let (D,α) and (E,β) be effective domains. Then $D\times E$, $[D\to E]$, $D+E$, $D\otimes E$, $D\oplus E$, $[D\to_\perp E]$ and $D_\perp$ are effective domains with presentations obtained uniformly from presentations of (D,α) and (E,β).

Proof: We consider the case of $D\times E$, the others being completely analogous. That (D,α) and (E,β) are effective domains means that (D_c,α) and (E_c,β) are computable cusl's. By the proof of Proposition 2.7, $(D_c\times E_c,\gamma)$ is a computable cusl with a presentation obtained uniformly from the given ones. Using Proposition 3.2 we obtain the effective domain $(\overline{D_c\times E_c},\overline{\gamma})$ with the presentation unchanged. From the distributivity of the completion operator (Corollary 4.6.9) and the representation theorem 3.2.6 we get

$$\overline{D_c\times E_c} \cong \overline{D_c}\times\overline{E_c} \cong D\times E.$$

This isomorphism gives rise to the effective domain $(D\times E,\gamma')$, by Corollary 1.4, again with the same presentation. □

To minimize notation we will always assume that the numbering of the effective domain $D\times E$ we consider is the one obtained from the given effective domains (D,α) and (E,β) as above, and similarly for the other domain constructions.

The following is an important conceptual observation.

3.7 Proposition Let (D,α) and (E,β) be effective domains. Then a continuous function $f:D\to E$ is effective if and only if f is a computable element in $[D\to E]$.

Proof: We suppress the numberings in the argument. For an arbitrary compact element $\bigsqcup_{i<n}\langle a_i; b_i\rangle$ in $[D\to E]$ we have

$$\bigsqcup_{i<n}\langle a_i; b_i\rangle \sqsubseteq f \Leftrightarrow (\forall i<n)(\langle a_i; b_i\rangle \sqsubseteq f) \Leftrightarrow (\forall i<n)(b_i \sqsubseteq f(a_i))$$

and the latter is semidecidable whenever f is effective. Thus f is a computable element in $[D \longrightarrow E]$ if f is effective. For the converse we need only note that for $a \in D_c$, $b \in E_c$,

$$b \sqsubseteq f(a) \Leftrightarrow \langle a; b\rangle \in \text{approx}(f). \qquad \square$$

Recall the partial continuous functionals of Example 3.3.9. Clearly $C_0 = \mathbb{N}_\bot$ is an effective domain and hence each C_n is effective with a presentation obtained uniformly from n. Proposition 3.7 tells us that we may restrict ourselves to the effective continuous functions from C_n into C_0 for these are precisely the computable elements in C_{n+1}.

All the functions associated with our domain constructions, such as eval, curry, the projection functions and so on, are effective. We verify this for eval, leaving the remaining ones as easy exercises. Suppressing numberings we assume that D and E are effective domains and consider $\text{eval}: [D \longrightarrow E] \times D \longrightarrow E$. We have

$$\begin{aligned} b \sqsubseteq \text{eval}(\bigsqcup_{i<n}\langle a_i; b_i\rangle, a) &\Leftrightarrow b \sqsubseteq (\bigsqcup_{i<n}\langle a_i; b_i\rangle)(a) \\ &\Leftrightarrow b \sqsubseteq \bigsqcup\{b_i : a_i \sqsubseteq a\} \end{aligned}$$

which is even decidable.

3.8 Proposition Let (D, α) be an effective domain. Then $\text{fix}: [D \longrightarrow D] \longrightarrow D$ is effective.

Proof: Using the notation in the proof of Theorem 2.3.6, $\text{fix} = \bigsqcup\{h_n : n < \omega\}$. Thus, by Exercise 2, it suffices to show that each h_n is effective uniformly in n. But this follows immediately by Proposition 3.5 since

$$h_{n+1}(f) = \text{eval}(f, h_n(f)). \qquad \square$$

3.9 Corollary Let (D, α) be an effective domain. If $f: D \longrightarrow D$ is effective then fix(f) is a computable element in D.

Proof: By Propositions 3.8, 3.7 and 3.5. $\square$

In the remaining part of this section we consider domain equations and their effective solutions. Most of the work has already been done in Section 10.2 in the apparently simpler setting of cusl's. Here we only need to transfer those results to effective domains, in a manner analogous to the treatment in Section 4.6.

Recall that the category **Dom** has domains as objects and projection pairs as morphisms. In non-effective considerations of **Dom** one could just as well choose embeddings as the morphisms since each embedding determines its corresponding projection uniquely by Corollary 4.5.13. However, this correspondence is in general not effective.

Given effective domains (D,α) and (E,β) we say that a projection pair $(f,f^-):(D,\alpha)\longrightarrow(E,\beta)$ is *(α,β)-effective* if f is (α,β)-effective and f^- is (β,α)-effective. The number $<e,e'>$ is an *index* of (f,f^-) if e is an index of f and e' is an index of f^-.

First we need to make precise what it means for a functor on **Dom** to be effective. For this we modify Definitions 1.7 and 1.8 to take into account that an effective domain is not in general a computable structure and that morphisms are pairs of functions.

Let $\mathcal{E}$**Dom** be the category whose objects are the effective domains and whose set of morphisms from (D,α) to (E,β) consists of all (α,β)-effective projection pairs.

3.10 Definition (i) A functor $\overline{\mathbf{F}}:\mathcal{E}\mathbf{Dom}\longrightarrow\mathcal{E}\mathbf{Dom}$ is *effective* if there are recursive functions $\hat{F}:\omega\longrightarrow\omega$ and $\tilde{F}:\omega^3\longrightarrow\omega$ such that:

(a) if $n\in\omega$ is a presentation of (D,α) then $\hat{F}(n)$ is a presentation of $\overline{\mathbf{F}}(D,\alpha)$, and

(b) if (f,f^-) is an (α,β)-effective projection pair from (D,α) into (E,β) and e is an index of (f,f^-) with respect to α and β, m is a presentation of (D,α) and n is a presentation of (E,β), then $\tilde{F}(m,n,e)$ is an index of the effective projection pair $\overline{\mathbf{F}}(f,f^-):\overline{\mathbf{F}}(D,\alpha)\longrightarrow\overline{\mathbf{F}}(E,\beta)$.

(ii) A functor $\mathbf{F}:\mathbf{Dom}\longrightarrow\mathbf{Dom}$ is *effective* if there is an effective functor $\overline{\mathbf{F}}:\mathcal{E}\mathbf{Dom}\longrightarrow\mathcal{E}\mathbf{Dom}$ such that:

(a) for each object (D,α) in $\mathcal{E}$**Dom**, $\overline{\mathbf{F}}(D,\alpha)=(\mathbf{F}(D),\gamma)$ for some γ, and

(b) for each morphism $(f,f^-):(D,\alpha)\longrightarrow(E,\beta)$, $\overline{\mathbf{F}}(f,f^-)=\mathbf{F}(f,f^-)$.

As was the case for computable structures, this notion of effectivity is easily extended to functors $\mathbf{F}:\mathbf{Dom}^n\longrightarrow\mathbf{Dom}$.

Next we consider the functors $\bar{\cdot}:\mathbf{Cusl}\longrightarrow\mathbf{Dom}$ and $(\cdot)_c:\mathbf{Dom}\longrightarrow\mathbf{Cusl}$ introduced in 4.6.1 and 4.6.2. To say that these are *effective* we mean that there are functors $\mathbf{F}^+:\mathcal{C}\mathbf{Cusl}\longrightarrow\mathcal{E}\mathbf{Dom}$ and $\mathbf{F}^-:\mathcal{E}\mathbf{Dom}\longrightarrow\mathcal{C}\mathbf{Cusl}$ such that

(a) $\mathbf{F}^+(P,\alpha)=(\overline{P},\gamma)$ for some γ and $\mathbf{F}^-(D,\beta)=(D_c,\delta)$ for some δ,

(b) $\mathbf{F}^+(f)=(\overline{f},\overline{f}^-)$ and $\mathbf{F}^-(f,f^-)=f|_{D_c}$,

and which are effective in the following usual sense. There are recursive functions $\hat{F}^+,\hat{F}^-:\omega\longrightarrow\omega$ and $\tilde{F}^+,\tilde{F}^-:\omega^3\longrightarrow\omega$ such that $\hat{F}$ takes presentations to presentations and $\tilde{F}$ takes indices (along with relevant presentations) of morphisms to indices of morphisms, analogously to Definition 3.10.

3.11 Proposition The functors $\bar{\cdot}:\mathbf{Cusl}\rightarrow\mathbf{Dom}$ and $(\cdot)_c:\mathbf{Dom}\rightarrow\mathbf{Cusl}$ are effective.

Proof: Let $\mathbf{F}^+(P,\alpha)=(\bar{P},\bar{\alpha})$. Then, by Proposition 3.2, $(\bar{P},\bar{\alpha})$ is an effective domain and we may take $\hat{F}^+=$ identity. Similarly, we let $\mathbf{F}^-(D,\alpha)=(D_c,\alpha)$ and, by the definition of a presentation, we may also set $\hat{F}^-=$ identity.

It remains to define $\tilde{F}^+$ and $\tilde{F}^-$. Let $f:P\rightarrow Q$ be an (α,β)-computable cusl embedding. We need to show that $\mathbf{F}^+(f)=(\bar{f},\bar{f}^-):\bar{P}\rightarrow\bar{Q}$ is an (α,β)-effective projection pair and we must be able to compute an index for $\mathbf{F}^+(f)$ uniformly from presentations of P and Q and an index of f. We argue informally, letting a vary over P and b vary over Q. Note that $\bar{f}([a])=[f(a)]$ and hence

$$[b]\subseteq\bar{f}([a]) \Leftrightarrow b\sqsubseteq f(a).$$

It follows that the tracking relation for $\bar{f}$ is even $(\bar{\alpha},\bar{\beta})$-decidable. Since we deal with a projection pair we also have

$$[a]\subseteq\bar{f}^-([b]) \Leftrightarrow \bar{f}([a])\subseteq[b] \Leftrightarrow f(a)\sqsubseteq b$$

and hence the tracking relation for $\bar{f}^-$ is $(\bar{\beta},\bar{\alpha})$-decidable. Characteristic indices, and hence r.e. indices, are obtained uniformly from an (α,β)-index of f and a characteristic index of $\widehat{\sqsubseteq}_\beta$, and the latter is obtained effectively from a presentation of (Q,β). We let $\tilde{F}^+:\omega^3\rightarrow\omega$ be the recursive function implicit in this uniformity.

To define $\tilde{F}^-:\omega^3\rightarrow\omega$ suppose $(f^+,f^-):(D,\alpha)\rightarrow(E,\beta)$ is an (α,β)-effective projection pair. First observe that $f^+(a)=b$ is (α,β)-semidecidable for $a\in D_c$ and $b\in E_c$. This holds since $b\sqsubseteq f^+(a)$ is semidecidable by the effectivity of f^+, and $f^+(a)\sqsubseteq b\Leftrightarrow a\sqsubseteq f^-(b)$ is semidecidable by the effectivity of f^-. Define $f:D_c\rightarrow E_c$ by

$$f(a)=\text{some } b\,[f^+(a)=b].$$

Then $f=f^+|_{D_c}=\mathbf{F}^-(f^+,f^-)$. The relation within the bracket is (α,β)-semidecidable so f is indeed (α,β)-computable by Proposition 9.2.11. Furthermore an index of the (α,β)-computable function f is obtained uniformly from an (α,β)-r.e. index of the relation within the brackets and hence uniformly from an (α,β)-index of (f^+,f^-). We let $\tilde{F}^-$ be the recursive function implicit in this uniformity. □

Using the functors $\bar{\cdot}$ and $(\cdot)_c$ we may effectively move between the categories **Cusl** and **Dom**.

3.12 Lemma (i) If the functor $\mathbf{F}:\mathbf{Dom}\rightarrow\mathbf{Dom}$ is effective then

$$\mathbf{F}'=(\cdot)_c\circ\mathbf{F}\circ\bar{\cdot}:\mathbf{Cusl}\rightarrow\mathbf{Cusl}$$

is effective with an index obtained uniformly from an index of **F**.

(ii) If the functor $\mathbf{G}:\mathbf{Cusl}\longrightarrow\mathbf{Cusl}$ is effective then

$$\mathbf{G}'=\overline{\cdot}\circ\mathbf{G}\circ(\cdot)_c:\mathbf{Dom}\longrightarrow\mathbf{Dom}$$

is effective with an index obtained uniformly from an index of **G**.

Proof: We prove (i), (ii) being analogous. The functor $\overline{\mathbf{F}}':\mathcal{C}\mathbf{Cusl}\longrightarrow\mathcal{C}\mathbf{Cusl}$ is just the composition $\overline{\mathbf{F}}'=\mathbf{F}^{-}\circ\overline{\mathbf{F}}\circ\mathbf{F}^{+}$. By Proposition 3.11, recursive tracking functions $\widehat{\mathbf{F}'}:\omega\longrightarrow\omega$ and $\widetilde{\mathbf{F}}':\omega^3\longrightarrow\omega$ are given by $\widehat{\mathbf{F}'}=\widehat{\mathbf{F}}$ and

$$\widetilde{\mathbf{F}}'(m,n,e)=\widetilde{\mathbf{F}}^{-}(\widehat{\mathbf{F}}(m),\widehat{\mathbf{F}}(n),\widetilde{\mathbf{F}}(m,n,\widetilde{\mathbf{F}}^{+}(m,n,e))).$$

The claimed uniformity is immediate. □

3.13 Corollary The functors $\mathbf{T}_\times$, $\mathbf{T}_\rightarrow$, $\mathbf{T}_+$, $\mathbf{T}_\otimes$, $\mathbf{T}_\oplus$, $\mathbf{T}_{\rightarrow\perp}$ and $\mathbf{T}_\perp$ on **Dom** are effective.

Proof: This follows from the easy generalization of Lemma 3.12 to bifunctors using the corresponding results for cusl's in Propositions 2.7, 2.8 and 2.9. □

Here is our main theorem.

3.14 Theorem Let $\mathbf{F}:\mathbf{Dom}\longrightarrow\mathbf{Dom}$ be an ω-continuous effective functor. Then the least fixed point of **F** is effective with a presentation obtained uniformly from an index of **F**.

Proof: The functor $\mathbf{F}'=(\cdot)_c\circ\mathbf{F}\circ\overline{\cdot}:\mathbf{Cusl}\longrightarrow\mathbf{Cusl}$ is effective by Lemma 3.12 and hence, by Theorem 2.6, the least fixed point P of $\mathbf{F}'$ is a computable cusl. Thus $P\cong(\mathbf{F}(\overline{P}))_c$ and hence

$$\overline{P}\cong\overline{(\mathbf{F}(\overline{P}))_c}\cong\mathbf{F}(\overline{P}).$$

A presentation of P and hence of $\overline{P}$ is obtained uniformly from an index of **F** by the uniformities established in Lemma 3.12 and Theorem 2.6. □

Again we should have been precise in that a least fixed point of **F** is a pair $(D,(f,f^{-}))$ as in the proof of Theorem 4.6.14. We leave it as an exercise to show that the mediating projection pair (f,f^{-}) making $(\overline{P},(f,f^{-}))$ into a least fixed point is effective with an index obtained uniformly from an index of **F**.

It is easily verified that effective functors on **Dom** are closed under composition and that each constant functor whose value is an effective domain is effective. It follows that any domain equation built up by $\rightarrow$, $\times$, $+$, $\otimes$, $\oplus$, $\rightarrow_\perp$ and $\perp$ and using effective domains as parameters gives rise to an ω-continuous effective functor $\mathbf{F}:\mathbf{Dom}\longrightarrow\mathbf{Dom}$. Furthermore there is an effective procedure which given a domain equation, including presentations of the domains appearing as parameters, computes an index of the corresponding functor **F**. We summarize these observations.

3.15 Theorem The least solution of a domain equation built up by $\rightarrow$, $\times$, $+$, $\otimes$, $\oplus$, $\rightarrow_\perp$ and $\perp$ and using effective domains as parameters is an effective domain. A presentation of this solution is obtained effectively from the given equation.

Section 10.4 Constructive Subdomains

In this section we study subsets of an effective domain containing only computable elements and having a numbering amenable to the numbering of the domain. In particular, we study the subset of all computable elements, which has nice effective closure properties.

4.1 Definition Let (D,α) be an effective domain and suppose $D_c \subseteq B \subseteq D$. Then (B,γ) is a *constructive subdomain* of (D,α) if $\gamma:\Omega_\gamma \rightarrow B$ is a surjective numbering such that $\Omega_\gamma \subseteq \omega$ is recursive, and

(i) the inclusion mapping $\iota: D_c \rightarrow B$ is (α,γ)-computable, and

(ii) the relation $R(n,m) \Leftrightarrow \alpha(n) \sqsubseteq \gamma(m)$ is r.e., that is $\mathrm{approx}(\gamma(m))$ is α-semidecidable uniformly in m.

We say that γ is a *constructive numbering* of B if (B,γ) is a constructive subdomain. Trivially, (D_c,α) is a constructive subdomain of (D,α).

In the literature one often considers constructive domains (B,γ,α) outright without reference to containment in a domain D. These are also called *constructive f0-spaces*, following Ershov. However, using the ideal completion of (B,γ,α) one can easily construct an effective domain (D,α) such that (B,γ) is a constructive subdomain of (D,α). Thus our situation is completely general. (See Exercises 4 and 5.)

The γ-equality relation is not decidable in general. The following observation is the best possible. Recall that an n-ary relation R on $\mathbb{N}$ is Π_2^0 if it is definable by

$$R(\mathbf{x}) \Leftrightarrow \forall y \exists z S(\mathbf{x},y,z)$$

where S is a recursive relation.

4.2 Proposition Let (B,γ) be a constructive subdomain of (D,α). Then the equality relation $\equiv_\gamma$ is a Π_2^0 relation.

Proof: We have

$$\begin{aligned} n \equiv_\gamma m &\Leftrightarrow \gamma(n) = \gamma(m) \\ &\Leftrightarrow \text{approx}(\gamma(n)) = \text{approx}(\gamma(m)) \\ &\Leftrightarrow \alpha^{-1}[\text{approx}(\gamma(n))] = \alpha^{-1}[\text{approx}(\gamma(m))] \\ &\Leftrightarrow \forall k(\alpha(k) \sqsubseteq \gamma(n) \Leftrightarrow \alpha(k) \sqsubseteq \gamma(m)) \end{aligned}$$

which is easily seen to be Π^0_2 using Definition 4.1 (ii). □

The most interesting constructive subdomain is the one consisting of *all* computable elements.

4.3 Definition Let (D, α) be an effective domain. Then $D_k = \{x \in D : x$ is α-computable$\}$.

4.4 Theorem Let (D, α) be an effective domain. Then there is a numbering $\bar{\alpha} : \omega \to D_k$ such that $(D_k, \bar{\alpha})$ is a constructive subdomain of (D, α).

Proof: Consider some fixed standard enumeration $\{W_e : e < \omega\}$ of the r.e. sets where W^n_e denotes (a canonical index for) the finite part of W_e generated by stage n in the standard enumeration. Define a function $f : \wp_f(\omega) \to \omega$ by

$$f(K) = \begin{cases} \mu n[\alpha(n) = \bigsqcup \alpha[K]] & \text{if } \alpha[K] \text{ consistent} \\ 0 & \text{otherwise.} \end{cases}$$

Then f is recursive since (D, α) is an effective domain. Next we effectively define finite sets V^n_e by

$$V^0_e = \{n_0\} \text{ where } \alpha(n_0) = \bot, \text{ and}$$

$$V^{n+1}_e = \begin{cases} V^n_e \cup W^n_e \cup \{f(V^n_e \cup W^n_e)\} & \text{if } \alpha[V^n_e \cup W^n_e] \text{ consistent} \\ V^n_e & \text{otherwise.} \end{cases}$$

Let $V_e = \bigcup \{V^n_e : n < \omega\}$. Then V_e is an r.e. set since a canonical index of V^n_e is obtained recursively from e and n. Note that $\alpha[V^n_e]$ is a directed set for each n and hence $\alpha[V_e]$ is directed. Thus we may define $\bar{\alpha}(e) = \bigsqcup \alpha[V_e]$.

Suppose $x \in D_k$ and let $W_e = \alpha^{-1}[\text{approx}(x)]$. Clearly $V^0_e \subseteq W_e$ since $\bot \in \text{approx}(x)$. Assume inductively that $V^n_e \subseteq W_e$. Then $\alpha[V^n_e \cup W^n_e]$ is consistent since it is bounded by x. But then $\alpha(f(V^n_e \cup W^n_e)) \in \text{approx}(x)$ and hence $V^{n+1}_e \subseteq W_e$. Thus $V_e \subseteq W_e$. But then $V^n_e \cup W^n_e \subseteq W_e$ for each n and hence $\alpha[V^n_e \cup W^n_e]$ is consistent, again since it is bounded by x. It follows that $V_e = W_e$. In particular, $\bar{\alpha}(e) = x$.

On the other hand, for $e \in \omega$ we have

(*) $\quad \alpha(n) \in \text{approx}(\bar{\alpha}(e)) \Leftrightarrow (\exists m \in V_e)(\alpha(n) \sqsubseteq \alpha(m))$

since $\text{approx}(\sqcup A) = \cup\{\text{approx}(y) : y \in A\}$ for each directed set A. Thus $\bar{\alpha}(e) \in D_k$. We have shown that $\bar{\alpha} : \omega \longrightarrow D_k$ is a surjective numbering.

To show that $(D_k, \bar{\alpha})$ is a constructive subdomain consider first condition (ii) of Definition 4.1. We have

$$\alpha(n) \sqsubseteq \bar{\alpha}(e) \Leftrightarrow \alpha(n) \in \text{approx}(\bar{\alpha}(e))$$

since $\alpha(n)$ is compact, and this is an r.e. relation by (*) and the uniform construction of V_e. Finally, to see that the inclusion $\iota : D_c \longrightarrow D_k$ is $(\alpha, \bar{\alpha})$-computable it suffices to note that the set $\{n : \alpha(n) \sqsubseteq \alpha(m)\}$ is r.e. with an index e obtained uniformly from m. That is there is a total recursive function $\hat{\iota}$ such that $W_{\hat{\iota}(m)} = \{n : \alpha(n) \sqsubseteq \alpha(m)\}$. But then we have $V_{\hat{\iota}(m)} = W_{\hat{\iota}(m)}$ and $\alpha(m) = \sqcup\alpha[V_{\hat{\iota}(m)}] = \bar{\alpha}(\hat{\iota}(m))$ so that $\iota : D_c \longrightarrow D_k$ is tracked by $\hat{\iota}$. □

We refer to $\bar{\alpha}$, the numbering obtained in Theorem 4.4, as the *canonical numbering* of D_k. We shall see in Corollary 4.12 that all recursively complete numberings of D_k are recursively equivalent to $\bar{\alpha}$. Thus, when studying D_k, we may without loss of generality work with $\bar{\alpha}$. Here we isolate some simple but useful properties of $\bar{\alpha}$ from the proof of Theorem 4.4.

4.5 Lemma Let (D, α) be an effective domain and let $\bar{\alpha}$ be the canonical numbering of D_k.

(i) There is a total recursive function $t : \omega \longrightarrow \omega$ such that for each $e \in \omega$, $W_{t(e)} = \alpha^{-1}[\text{approx}(\bar{\alpha}(e))]$ and $\bar{\alpha}(t(e)) = \bar{\alpha}(e)$.
(ii) $W_e = \alpha^{-1}[\text{approx}(x)] \Rightarrow \bar{\alpha}(e) = x$.
(iii) If $\alpha[W_e]$ is directed then $\bar{\alpha}(e) = \sqcup\alpha[W_e]$.

The following lemma describes a useful way to effectively approximate $\bar{\alpha}(e)$.

4.6 Lemma Let (D, α) be an effective domain. Then there is a function $\tilde{\alpha} : \omega^2 \longrightarrow D_c$ and a total recursive function $s : \omega^2 \longrightarrow \omega$ such that for each $e \in \omega$:
(i) $m \leq n \Rightarrow \tilde{\alpha}(e, m) \sqsubseteq \tilde{\alpha}(e, n)$,
(ii) $\bar{\alpha}(e) = \sqcup_{n<\omega}\tilde{\alpha}(e, n)$, and
(iii) $\tilde{\alpha}(e, n) = \alpha(s(e, n))$.

Proof: Using the notation in the proof of Theorem 4.4 we set $\tilde{\alpha}(e, n) = \sqcup\alpha[V_e^n]$ and $s(e, n) = \mu k[\alpha(k) = \sqcup\alpha[V_e^n]]$. □

4.7 Proposition Suppose (B, γ) is a constructive subdomain of (D, α). Then $B \subseteq D_k$ and the inclusion $\iota : B \longrightarrow D_k$ is $(\gamma, \bar{\alpha})$-computable.

Proof: For each $e \in \Omega_\gamma$ the set $W = \{n \in \omega : \alpha(n) \sqsubseteq \gamma(e)\}$ is r.e. uniformly in e, since γ is a constructive numbering. Thus there is a total recursive function h

such that $\alpha^{-1}[\text{approx}(\gamma(e))] = W_{h(e)}$. But then, by Lemma 4.5, $\bar{\alpha}(h(e)) = \gamma(e)$. Thus $\gamma(e) \in D_k$ and h tracks the inclusion $\iota : B \longrightarrow D_k$. □

The constructive subdomain D_k of (D, α) is of central interest in our study. It is of course in general not a domain since it may not be complete. However, D_k is the unique constructive subdomain which is recursively complete.

4.8 Definition A constructive subdomain (B, γ) of an effective domain (D, α) is *recursively complete* if $\bigsqcup A \in B$ whenever $A \subseteq B$ is a weakly γ-semidecidable directed set.

4.9 Proposition Let (D, α) be an effective domain.
(i) If the constructive subdomain (B, γ) is recursively complete then $B = D_k$.
(ii) If γ is a constructive numbering of D_k then (D_k, γ) is recursively complete.

Proof: To prove (i) let $x \in D_k$. Then $\alpha^{-1}[\text{approx}(x)]$ is an r.e. set and hence, since the inclusion $\iota : D_c \longrightarrow B$ is (α, γ)-computable, approx(x) is weakly γ-semidecidable. But then $x = \bigsqcup \text{approx}(x) \in B$, since B is recursively complete.

To prove (ii) assume that γ is a constructive numbering of D_k. As previously remarked, $\text{approx}(\bigsqcup A) = \bigcup \{\text{approx}(x) : x \in A\}$ for directed sets A. Suppose $A = \gamma[W]$ is a directed set, where W is an r.e. set. Then

$$\alpha^{-1}[\text{approx}(\bigsqcup A)] = \{n \in \omega : (\exists m \in W)(\alpha(n) \sqsubseteq \gamma(m))\}$$

and hence $\alpha^{-1}[\text{approx}(\bigsqcup A)]$ is r.e. In particular, $\bigsqcup A \in D_k$. □

4.10 Definition Let γ be a constructive numbering of D_k. Then γ is a *recursively complete numbering* if there is a total recursive function h such that if $\gamma[W_e]$ is a directed set then $\gamma(h(e)) = \bigsqcup \gamma[W_e]$.

4.11 Theorem Let (D, α) be an effective domain and let $\bar{\alpha}$ be the canonical numbering of D_k. Then $\bar{\alpha}$ is a recursively complete numbering. Furthermore, if γ is a recursively complete numbering of D_k then the identity $\text{id} : D_k \longrightarrow D_k$ is $(\bar{\alpha}, \gamma)$-computable.

Proof: Let h be a total recursive function such that

$$W_{h(e)} = \{n \in \omega : (\exists m \in W_e)(\alpha(n) \sqsubseteq \bar{\alpha}(m))\}.$$

Then $W_{h(e)} = \alpha^{-1}[\text{approx}(\bigsqcup \bar{\alpha}[W_e])]$ whenever $\bar{\alpha}[W_e]$ is a directed set, and $\bar{\alpha}(h(e)) = \bigsqcup \bar{\alpha}[W_e]$ by Lemma 4.5 (ii).

Now suppose that γ is a recursively complete numbering of D_k and h is the associated total recursive function. Since γ is a constructive numbering there is a recursive function g such that $\gamma[W_{g(e)}]=\text{approx}(\bar{\alpha}(e))$ for each e. But then $\bar{\alpha}(e)=\bigsqcup\gamma[W_{g(e)}]=\gamma(h(g(e)))$ so that $h\circ g$ tracks the identity. □

4.12 Corollary D_k is *stable* with respect to recursively complete numberings in the sense that all recursively complete numberings are recursively equivalent.

Proof: Given recursively complete numberings β and γ of D_k we must show that there exists a recursive function $h:\Omega_\beta\longrightarrow\Omega_\gamma$ such that for each $n\in\Omega_\beta$, $\beta(n)=\gamma(h(n))$. But this follows from Proposition 4.7 and Theorem 4.11. □

The results above state that up to recursive equivalence there is one and only one recursively complete subdomain of an effective domain as long as we require the numberings to be recursively complete. Therefore, given an effective domain (D,α), we will in the sequel without loss of generality consider the recursively complete subdomain $(D_k,\bar{\alpha})$.

4.13 Examples

(i) Let (D,α) be an effective flat domain. Then $D_k=D$.

(ii) Let $\mathbb{C}$ be the Cantor space as a domain described in 2.1.12 and consider $\mathbb{C}$ as an effective domain using the numbering described in Example 2.3 (iv). Then $\mathbb{C}_k=\text{SEQ}\cup\{f:\omega\longrightarrow\{0,1\}\mid f \text{ is recursive}\}$.

(iii) Let $\mathcal{P}$ be the effective domain of partial functions on $\mathbb{N}$ with the numbering given in Example 2.3 (v). Then $\mathcal{P}_k$ is the set of partial recursive functions, usually denoted $\mathcal{PR}$.

(iv) Let $\wp(\omega)$ be the effective domain given in Example 2.3 (iii). Then $\wp(\omega)_k$ is the family of r.e. sets.

Finally we note that continuous effective functions, when restricted to the constructive or computable elements, are computable with respect to the canonical numberings.

4.14 Proposition Let (D,α) and (E,β) be effective domains. If $f:D\longrightarrow E$ is a continuous (α,β)-effective function then $f|_{D_k}:D_k\longrightarrow E_k$ is $(\bar{\alpha},\bar{\beta})$-computable.

Proof: That $f|_{D_k}$ takes its values in E_k is the content of Proposition 3.5 (i). Using the approximations of Lemma 4.6 and the continuity of f we have

$$f(\bar{\alpha}(e))=f(\textstyle\bigsqcup_{n<\omega}\tilde{\alpha}(e,n))=\bigsqcup_{n<\omega}f(\tilde{\alpha}(e,n))$$

and hence

$$\beta^{-1}[\text{approx}(f(\bar{\alpha}(e)))]=\{m\in\omega:\exists n\,(\beta(m)\sqsubseteq f(\alpha(s(e,n))))\}.$$

It follows from the effectivity of f that there is a total recursive function h such that $W_{h(e)} = \beta^{-1}[\text{approx}(f(\bar{\alpha}(e)))]$. But then $\bar{\beta}h(e) = f(\bar{\alpha}(e))$ by Lemma 4.5, so that h tracks $f|_{D_k}$ with respect to $(\bar{\alpha}, \bar{\beta})$. □

The converse of Proposition 4.14 is the content of a generalized version of the Myhill–Shepherdson theorem.

Section 10.5 The Myhill–Shepherdson Theorem

The Myhill–Shepherdson theorem states that the effective operators on $\mathcal{PR}$, the partial recursive functions on $\mathbb{N}$, are exactly the restrictions of the effectively continuous operators on $\mathcal{P}$, the partial functions on $\mathbb{N}$. Let $\mathcal{P} = (\mathcal{P}, \alpha)$ be the effective domain of partial functions where α is the numbering given in Example 2.3 (v). Then $\mathcal{PR} = \mathcal{P}_k$ and the Myhill–Shepherdson theorem translated into our language reads that the $(\bar{\alpha}, \bar{\alpha})$-computable functions $f: \mathcal{P}_k \to \mathcal{P}_k$ are exactly the restrictions to $\mathcal{P}_k$ of the effective continuous functions from $\mathcal{P}$ into $\mathcal{P}$, that is the restrictions to $\mathcal{P}_k$ of the elements in $[\mathcal{P} \to \mathcal{P}]_k$.

The Rice–Shapiro theorem is closely related to that of Myhill–Shepherdson. It states that a class $\mathcal{A}$ of r.e. sets is completely r.e. if and only if there is an r.e. set V such that for each r.e. set W,

$$W \in \mathcal{A} \Leftrightarrow (\exists e \in V)(D_e \subseteq W).$$

That $\mathcal{A}$ is *completely r.e.* means that the set $\{e \in \omega : W_e \in \mathcal{A}\}$ is r.e. Thus the Rice–Shapiro theorem in our setting reads as follows. Let $\wp(\omega) = (\wp(\omega), \alpha)$ be the effective domain obtained from Example 2.3 (iii). Then $\mathcal{A} \subseteq \wp(\omega)_k$ is $\bar{\alpha}$-semidecidable if and only if there is an r.e. set V such that

$$\bar{\alpha}(n) \in \mathcal{A} \Leftrightarrow (\exists e \in V)(\alpha(e) \sqsubseteq \bar{\alpha}(n)).$$

In this section we extend the Rice–Shapiro theorem to an arbitrary effective domain. Then we show that this theorem also is a generalization of the Myhill–Shepherdson theorem.

Recall that the Scott topology on a domain D is generated by the basic open sets $B_a = \{x \in D : a \sqsubseteq x\}$ for $a \in D_c$.

5.1 Definition Let (D, α) be an effective domain.

(i) A set $U \subseteq D$ is *effectively open* if there is an r.e. set W such that

$$U = \bigcup_{e \in W} B_{\alpha(e)}.$$

An r.e. index of W is an *index* of the effectively open set U.

(ii) If $B \subseteq D$ then $U \subseteq B$ is *effectively open in* B if there is an effectively open set $V \subseteq D$ such that $U = V \cap B$. An index of V is also an *index* of U.

In particular, an effective open set is open in the (relativized) Scott topology. Here is the main theorem.

5.2 Theorem (Ershov [1977a]) Let (D, α) be an effective domain. Then $U \subseteq D_k$ is $\bar{\alpha}$-semidecidable if and only if U is effectively open in D_k.

Proof: First assume that U is effectively open in D_k. Let W be an r.e. set such that $U = \bigcup_{e \in W}(B_{\alpha(e)} \cap D_k)$. Then

$$\bar{\alpha}(n) \in U \Leftrightarrow (\exists e \in W)(\alpha(e) \sqsubseteq \bar{\alpha}(n))$$

which is an r.e. relation since $\bar{\alpha}$ is a constructive numbering. Thus U is $\bar{\alpha}$-semidecidable.

For the converse, assume $U \subseteq D_k$ is $\bar{\alpha}$-semidecidable. Then the set $W = \{e \in \omega : \alpha(e) \in U\}$ is r.e. since the inclusion $\iota : D_c \longrightarrow D_k$ is $(\alpha, \bar{\alpha})$-computable. Suppose we have shown that U is an open set. Then, by the Alexandrov and Scott conditions on open sets,

$$U = \bigcup_{e \in W}(B_{\alpha(e)} \cap D_k)$$

so that U is effectively open.

It thus remains to prove that U is open, that is, that it satisfies the Alexandrov and Scott conditions. We first consider the former. Let $x = \bar{\alpha}(m)$ and $y = \bar{\alpha}(n)$ and suppose that $x \in U$ and $x \sqsubseteq y$. We shall show $y \in U$, using the simple version of the branching lemma 9.2.12. Let $W = \bar{\alpha}^{-1}[U]$ and let t be the total recursive function of Lemma 4.5. If $W_e = W_{t(m)}$ then, by Lemma 4.5,

$$\bar{\alpha}(e) = \bar{\alpha}(t(m)) = \bar{\alpha}(m) = x \in U$$

so that W contains all r.e. indices of $W_{t(m)}$. By the branching lemma, letting r be the constant function with value $t(n)$, there is $p \in \omega$ and $e \in W$ such that

$$W_e = W^p_{t(m)} \cup W_{t(n)}.$$

But $W_{t(m)} = \alpha^{-1}[\text{approx}(x)] \subseteq \alpha^{-1}[\text{approx}(y)] = W_{t(n)}$ and hence $W_e = W_{t(n)}$. Thus, again by Lemma 4.5, $y = \bar{\alpha}(n) = \bar{\alpha}t(n) = \bar{\alpha}(e) \in U$.

To verify the Scott condition let x, m and W be as above. Using Proposition 2.2 we can define a total recursive function r such that $W_{r(p)}$ is a singleton set consisting of an α-index for $\bigsqcup \alpha[W^p_{t(m)}]$. Again by the branching lemma there is $p \in \omega$ and $e \in W$ such that $W_e = W^p_{t(m)} \cup W_{r(p)}$. Thus $\alpha[W_e]$ is directed and hence, by Lemma 4.5,

$$\bar{\alpha}(e) = \sqcup\alpha[W_e] = \sqcup\alpha[W^{p}_{t(m)} \cup W_{r(p)}] \sqsubseteq \bar{\alpha}t(m) = x.$$

Furthermore, $\bar{\alpha}(e)$ is compact since $\sqcup\alpha[W^{p}_{t(m)} \cup W_{r(p)}]$ is the supremum of a finite set of compact elements. □

The theorem is uniform in the sense that there are total recursive functions which given an $\bar{\alpha}$-semidecidable index of U compute an index of U as an effectively open set and conversely.

To say that a class $\mathcal{A}$ of r.e. sets is completely r.e. means precisely that $\mathcal{A}$ is an $\bar{\alpha}$-semidecidable subset of $\wp(\omega)_k$. And to say that $\mathcal{A}$ is effectively open in $\wp(\omega)_k$ means that there is an r.e. set V such that

$$W \in \mathcal{A} \Leftrightarrow (\exists e \in V)(\alpha(e) \sqsubseteq_{\wp(\omega)} W)$$

that is

$$W \in \mathcal{A} \Leftrightarrow (\exists e \in V)(D_e \subseteq W).$$

Thus Ershov's theorem applied to $\wp(\omega)$ gives the Rice–Shapiro result.

Ershov's theorem also provides a generalization of Rice's theorem, the latter stating that a class of r.e. sets $\mathcal{A}$ is *completely recursive* (in our language $\bar{\alpha}$-decidable in $\wp(\omega)_k$) if and only if $\mathcal{A} = \varnothing$ or $\mathcal{A}$ contains all r.e. sets.

5.3 Corollary Let (D, α) be an effective domain and suppose $\mathcal{A} \subseteq D_k$. Then $\mathcal{A}$ is $\bar{\alpha}$-decidable if and only if $\mathcal{A} = \varnothing$ or $\mathcal{A} = D_k$.

Proof: For the nontrivial direction suppose $\mathcal{A}$ is $\bar{\alpha}$-decidable. Then $\mathcal{A}$ and $D_k - \mathcal{A}$ are $\bar{\alpha}$-semidecidable and hence, by Ershov's theorem, open. Using the Alexandrov condition on open sets we see that if $\bot \in \mathcal{A}$ then $\mathcal{A} = D_k$ and if $\bot \notin \mathcal{A}$ then $D_k - \mathcal{A} = D_k$, that is $\mathcal{A} = \varnothing$. □

We now turn to the Myhill–Shepherdson theorem.

5.4 Definition Let (D, α) and (E, β) be effective domains and suppose $B \subseteq D$ and $C \subseteq E$. Then $f: B \to C$ is *effectively continuous* if there is a total recursive function g such that $f^{-1}[B_{\beta(e)} \cap C] = \bigcup_{m \in W_{g(e)}} (B_{\alpha(m)} \cap B)$.

Thus a function $f: D \to E$ is effectively continuous if f is continuous with respect to the Scott topologies and the inverse image of an effectively open set is effectively open uniformly in an index for the effectively open set.

5.5 Proposition Let (D, α) and (E, β) be effective domains and suppose $D_c \subseteq B \subseteq D$ and $E_c \subseteq C \subseteq E$.

(i) A continuous function $f: B \to C$ is effectively continuous if and only if the relation $b \sqsubseteq f(a)$ on $D_c \times E_c$ is (α, β)-semidecidable.

(ii) A continuous function $f:B \to C$ has a unique continuous extension $\bar{f}:D \to E$ and $\bar{f}$ is effective if and only if f is effectively continuous.

Proof: Exercise 3. □

Here is the generalization of the Myhill–Shepherdson theorem.

5.6 Theorem Let (D,α) and (E,β) be effective domains. Then a function $f:D_k \to E_k$ is $(\bar{\alpha},\bar{\beta})$-computable if and only if there is a continuous (α,β)-effective function $\bar{f}:D \to E$ such that $\bar{f}|_{D_k}=f$.

Proof: The if direction is Proposition 4.14. For the only if direction suppose that $f:D_k \to E_k$ is $(\bar{\alpha},\bar{\beta})$-computable and let $\hat{f}$ be a tracking function of f. Consider a basic open set $B_{\beta(e)} \cap E_k$. Then

$$\bar{\alpha}(n) \in f^{-1}[B_{\beta(e)} \cap E_k] \Leftrightarrow \beta(e) \sqsubseteq f\bar{\alpha}(n) \Leftrightarrow \beta(e) \sqsubseteq \bar{\beta}\hat{f}(n)$$

and the latter relation is r.e. since $(E_k,\bar{\beta})$ is a constructive subdomain. It follows that $f^{-1}[B_{\beta(e)} \cap E_k]$ is $\bar{\alpha}$-semidecidable with an index obtained uniformly from e. Then, by Theorem 5.2 and its uniformity, $f^{-1}[B_{\beta(e)} \cap E_k]$ is effectively open with an index obtained uniformly from e, that is f is effectively continuous. By Proposition 5.5, f has an extension $\bar{f}:D \to E$ which is (α,β)-effective and continuous. □

Section 10.6 The Kreisel–Lacombe–Shoenfield Theorem

In this section we prove a generalization of the Kreisel–Lacombe–Shoenfield theorem to effective domains. In analogy with the Myhill–Shepherdson theorem, the Kreisel–Lacombe–Shoenfield theorem also concerns the extension of effective operators to effectively continuous functions. An important difference, which makes the proof more complicated, and interesting, is that in the Kreisel–Lacombe–Shoenfield theorem the set on which the effective operator is defined is not even semidecidable. Instead the sets have other properties which are abstracted in the generalization to domains. Our exposition builds on Berger [1993].

Let $\mathcal{R}$ be the class of total recursive functions on $\mathbb{N}$, let $\mathcal{PR}$ be the class of partial recursive functions and let $\mathcal{P}$ be the class of partial functions on $\mathbb{N}$. So $\mathcal{R} \subseteq \mathcal{PR} \subseteq \mathcal{P}$.

6.1 Theorem (Kreisel–Lacombe–Shoenfield [1959]) The effective operations on $\mathcal{R}$ are precisely the restrictions of the effectively continuous functionals on $\mathcal{P}$ mapping $\mathcal{R}$ into $\mathcal{R}$.

Let $\mathcal{P}=(\mathcal{P},\alpha)$ be the effective domain of partial functions on $\mathbb{N}$. A first difficulty, as already remarked, is that $\mathcal{R}$ is not $\bar{\alpha}$-semidecidable. In fact, $\bar{\alpha}^{-1}[\mathcal{R}]$ is a complete Π^0_2-set. This leads us to the following definition.

6.2 Definition Let A and B be structures with numerations α and β respectively, and suppose $M \subseteq A$. Then $f: M \longrightarrow B$ is said to be *(α,β)-computable* if there is a partial recursive function $\hat{f}$ such that $\alpha^{-1}[M] \subseteq \mathrm{dom}(\hat{f})$ and such that for each $n \in \alpha^{-1}[M]$, $f(\alpha(n)) = \beta(\hat{f}(n))$.

The significant properties of $\mathcal{R}$ in the Kreisel–Lacombe–Shoenfield theorem are that each element in $\mathcal{R}$ is maximal and hence total in $\mathcal{P}$ (in the sense of 8.3.3 (iv)), and that $\mathcal{R}$ is dense in $\mathcal{P}$ in an effective way. The latter is made precise as follows.

6.3 Definition Let (D,α) be an effective domain. Then $M \subseteq D_k$ is *effectively dense in* D if there is a total recursive function d such that for each $n \in \omega$,

$$\bar{\alpha}d(n) \in B_{\alpha(n)} \cap M,$$

that is $\alpha(n) \sqsubseteq \bar{\alpha}d(n) \in M$.

We now state the generalization of the Kreisel–Lacombe–Shoenfield theorem to effective domains. Another generalization of a more topological nature, to countable T_0-spaces satisfying certain effectivity requirements, is given in Spreen and Young [1984].

6.4 Theorem (Berger [1993]) Let (D,α) and (E,β) be effective domains and let $M \subseteq D_k$ be effectively dense in D. If $F: M \longrightarrow E_k$ is an $(\bar{\alpha},\bar{\beta})$-computable function such that $F(x)$ is total in E for each $x \in M$ then there is an $(\bar{\alpha},\bar{\beta})$-computable function $G: D_k \longrightarrow E_k$ such that $F(x) \sqsubseteq G(x)$ for each $x \in M$.

6.5 Remarks

(i) If $F(x)$ is maximal in E for each $x \in M$ then we obtain equality between F and G on M, that is G is an extension of F.

(ii) The classical Kreisel–Lacombe–Shoenfield theorem is obtained by letting $D=E=\mathcal{P}$ and $M=\mathcal{R}$ using a standard numbering.

(iii) The function G can be extended to a continuous effective function $\bar{G}: D \longrightarrow E$ by the Myhill–Shepherdson theorem.

(iv) Berger actually proved a slightly stronger result in that D_k need only be a constructive qf-space. The proof below does not require D to be consistently complete.

Proof: Let $\hat{F}$ be a partial recursive function tracking F with respect to $(\bar{\alpha}, \bar{\beta})$ and let d be a total recursive function witnessing that M is effectively dense in D with respect to α.

Recall our approximation functions of Lemma 4.6. We have for each $n \in \bar{\alpha}^{-1}[M]$,

$$F(\bar{\alpha}(n)) = \bigsqcup_{i \in \omega} \tilde{\beta}(\hat{F}(n), i).$$

Given $x \in D_k$ we want to define a set

$$A_x = \{\tilde{\beta}(\hat{F}(n), i) : \langle n, i\rangle \in V_x\}$$

where V_x is an r.e. set with an index obtained uniformly from an $\bar{\alpha}$-index of x. The intention is to set $G(x) = \bigsqcup A_x$. Thus we need to have that A_x is a consistent set and that V_x is sufficiently large to ensure $F(x) \sqsubseteq G(x)$ whenever $x \in M$. The latter is achieved by putting $\langle n, i\rangle \in V_x$ whenever $\bar{\alpha}(n) = x \in M$. To show the consistency of A_x it suffices by Proposition 3.1.11 to consider finite subsets of A_x. And for this, by Proposition 8.3.7, it will suffice to show that $\tilde{\beta}(\hat{F}(n), i)$ and $F(\bar{\alpha}d(r))$ are consistent whenever $\tilde{\alpha}(n, q) \sqsubseteq \alpha(r)$ for certain q depending on n and i. It is here that the totality of $F(\bar{\alpha}d(r))$ is used. The strategy is, given n, i and q, to attempt to find an r such that $\tilde{\alpha}(n, q) \sqsubseteq \alpha(r)$ and such that $\tilde{\beta}(\hat{F}(n), i)$ and $F(\bar{\alpha}d(r))$ are *inconsistent*. By a rather ingenious use of the branching lemma 9.2.13 we obtain a partial recursive function p such that if $\tilde{\alpha}(n, p(n, i)) \sqsubseteq \alpha(r)$ then $\tilde{\beta}(\hat{F}(n), i)$ and $F(\bar{\alpha}d(r))$ are *consistent*. Thus p lifts us to a level where we fail to find inconsistent $\tilde{\beta}(\hat{F}(n), i)$ and $F(\bar{\alpha}d(r))$ provided $\tilde{\alpha}(n, p(n, i)) \sqsubseteq \alpha(r)$.

To start the technical construction we define a relation R on $\mathbb{N}$ by

$$R(n, q, i, r) \Leftrightarrow \tilde{\alpha}(n, q) \sqsubseteq \alpha(r) \ \&\ n \in \mathrm{dom}(\hat{F}) \ \&\ \neg\mathrm{Cons}\big(\tilde{\beta}(\hat{F}(n), i), F(\bar{\alpha}d(r))\big).$$

Then R is an r.e. relation since

$$\neg\mathrm{Cons}\big(\tilde{\beta}(\hat{F}(n), i), F(\bar{\alpha}d(r))\big) \Leftrightarrow \big(\exists b \in \mathrm{approx}(F(\bar{\alpha}d(r)))\big)\neg\mathrm{Cons}(\tilde{\beta}(\hat{F}(n), i), b).$$

Let $f : \omega^3 \longrightarrow \omega$ be the partial recursive function defined using a selection operator by

$$f(n, q, i) \simeq (\text{some } r) R(n, q, i, r).$$

Thus there is a total recursive function $s : \omega^3 \longrightarrow \omega$ such that

$$W_{s(n,q,i)} = \begin{cases} \{r\} & \text{if } f(n, q, i) \simeq r \\ \varnothing & \text{if } f(n, q, i)\uparrow. \end{cases}$$

Let $h : \omega^3 \longrightarrow \omega$ be a total recursive function such that

$$W_{h(n,q,i)} = \alpha^{-1}[\text{approx}(\tilde{\alpha}(n,q))] \cup \{k \in \omega : (\exists r \in W_{s(n,q,i)})(\alpha(k) \sqsubseteq \bar{\alpha}d(r))\}.$$

By Lemma 4.5 we then have

$$\bar{\alpha}h(n,q,i) = \begin{cases} \bar{\alpha}d(r) & \text{if } W_{s(n,q,i)} = \{r\} \\ \tilde{\alpha}(n,q) & \text{if } W_{s(n,q,i)} = \varnothing. \end{cases}$$

Finally, let $v : \omega^2 \longrightarrow \omega$ be a total recursive function such that

$$W_{v(n,i)} = \{e \in \omega : \ e \in \text{dom}(\hat{F}) \ \& \ \tilde{\beta}(\hat{F}(n), i) \sqsubseteq \bar{\beta}\hat{F}(e)\}.$$

Suppose $n \in \bar{\alpha}^{-1}[M]$, $i \in \omega$, and suppose further that $W_e = W_{t(n)}$ where t is the total recursive function of Lemma 4.5. Then

$$\bar{\alpha}(e) = \bar{\alpha}t(n) = \bar{\alpha}(n).$$

In particular, $e \in \bar{\alpha}^{-1}[M]$ so $e \in \text{dom}(\hat{F})$. Furthermore,

$$\tilde{\beta}(\hat{F}(n), i) \sqsubseteq \bar{\beta}\hat{F}(n) = F(\bar{\alpha}(n)) = F(\bar{\alpha}(e)) = \bar{\beta}\hat{F}(e).$$

Thus whenever $\bar{\alpha}(n) \in M$ then each r.e. index of $W_{t(n)}$ belongs to $W_{v(n,i)}$.

By the branching lemma 9.2.13 there is a total recursive function $b : \omega^2 \longrightarrow \omega$ and a partial recursive function $p : \omega^2 \longrightarrow \omega$ such that for each $n, i \in \omega$, if $\bar{\alpha}(n) \in M$ then $p(n,i)\downarrow$ and whenever $p(n,i)\downarrow$ then $b(n,i) \in W_{v(n,i)}$ and

$$W_{b(n,i)} = W^{p(n,i)}_{t(n)} \cup W_{h(n,p(n,i),i)}.$$

It is convenient to have chosen the effective enumeration of $W_{t(n)}$ appearing above given by

$$W^m_{t(n)} = \{k \leq m : \alpha(k) \sqsubseteq \tilde{\alpha}(n,m)\}.$$

For each $x \in D_k$ let

$$V_x = \{\langle n,i\rangle : \ (n,i) \in \text{dom}(p), \ \ n \in \text{dom}(\hat{F}) \ \text{and} \ \tilde{\alpha}(n, p(n,i)) \sqsubseteq x\}.$$

Then V_x is r.e. with an index obtained uniformly from an $\bar{\alpha}$-index of x. Finally put

$$A_x = \{\tilde{\beta}(\hat{F}(n), i) : \langle n,i\rangle \in V_x\}.$$

Suppose we have shown that A_x is consistent. Then we define $G : D_k \longrightarrow E_k$ by

$$G(x) = \bigsqcup A_x.$$

Clearly,

$$\beta(m) \in \text{approx}(G(x)) \Leftrightarrow$$
$$(\exists k)(\exists \langle n_1, i_1\rangle, \ldots, \langle n_k, i_k\rangle \in V_x)\big(\beta(m) \sqsubseteq \sqcup_{j=1}^{k} \tilde{\beta}(\hat{F}(n_j), i_j)\big).$$

It follows that an r.e. index for $\beta^{-1}[\text{approx}(G(x))]$ is obtained uniformly from an $\bar{\alpha}$-index for x. Thus, by Lemma 4.5, there is a total recursive function $\hat{G}$ which given an $\bar{\alpha}$-index for x computes a $\bar{\beta}$-index for $G(x)$. In other words, G is $(\bar{\alpha}, \bar{\beta})$-computable.

Now suppose $\bar{\alpha}(n) = x \in M$. Then $\langle n, i\rangle \in V_x$ and hence $\tilde{\beta}(\hat{F}(n), i) \in A_x$. Furthermore

$$F(x) = F(\bar{\alpha}(n)) = \bar{\beta}\hat{F}(n) = \sqcup_{i \in \omega} \tilde{\beta}(\hat{F}(n), i)$$

so $F(x) \sqsubseteq G(x)$.

It remains to show that A_x is consistent. A first observation is

$$(*) \qquad p(n,i)\downarrow \;\Rightarrow\; \bar{\alpha}b(n,i) = \bar{\alpha}h(n, p(n,i), i).$$

For in case the premise holds then, by our choice of enumeration of $W_{t(n)}$, $W^{p(n,i)}_{t(n)} \subseteq W_{h(n,p(n,i),i)}$, so $W_{b(n,i)} = W_{h(n,p(n,i),i)}$ and hence by Lemma 4.5, $\bar{\alpha}b(n,i) = \bar{\alpha}h(n, p(n,i), i)$.

Let $\langle n, i\rangle \in V_x$ and suppose $\tilde{\alpha}(n, p(n,i)) \sqsubseteq \alpha(r)$. We shall show that $\tilde{\beta}(\hat{F}(n), i)$ and $F(\bar{\alpha}d(r))$ are consistent. Suppose not. Then $R(n, p(n,i), i, r)$ so $W_{s(n,p(n,i),i)} = \{r'\}$ for some r' such that $R(n, p(n,i), i, r')$. By (*) and the definition of h,

$$\bar{\alpha}b(n,i) = \bar{\alpha}h(n, p(n,i), i) = \bar{\alpha}d(r').$$

Furthermore $b(n,i) \in W_{v(n,i)}$ since $\langle n, i\rangle \in V_x$. But then

$$\tilde{\beta}(\hat{F}(n), i) \sqsubseteq \bar{\beta}\hat{F}b(n,i) = F(\bar{\alpha}b(n,i)) = F(\bar{\alpha}d(r'))$$

showing that $\tilde{\beta}(\hat{F}(n), i)$ and $F(\bar{\alpha}d(r'))$ are indeed consistent, contradicting $R(n, p(n,i), i, r')$.

To establish the consistency of A_x it suffices by Proposition 3.1.11 to consider all its finite subsets. So suppose we are given

$$\tilde{\beta}(\hat{F}(n_1), i_1), \ldots, \tilde{\beta}(\hat{F}(n_k), i_k) \in A_x.$$

Then $\tilde{\alpha}(n_1, p(n_1, i_1)), \ldots, \tilde{\alpha}(n_k, p(n_k, i_k))$ are consistent since they are bounded by x. Furthermore their supremum is compact, so there is an r such that $\tilde{\alpha}(n_j, p(n_j, i_j)) \sqsubseteq \alpha(r)$ for $j = 1, \ldots, k$. By the above, $\tilde{\beta}(\hat{F}(n_j), i_j)$ and $F(\bar{\alpha}d(r))$ are consistent for each j. But then $\tilde{\beta}(\hat{F}(n_1), i_1), \ldots, \tilde{\beta}(\hat{F}(n_k), i_k)$ are consistent by Proposition 8.3.7 since $F(\bar{\alpha}d(r))$ is total in E by assumption. □

The following corollaries use the assumptions of Theorem 6.4.

6.6 Corollary If $F:M \longrightarrow E_k$ is $(\bar{\alpha},\bar{\beta})$-computable and $F(x) \in E_m$ for each $x \in M$ then F is effectively continuous.

Proof: F extends to $(\bar{\alpha},\bar{\beta})$-computable $\tilde{F}:D_k \longrightarrow E_k$ which in turn, by the generalized Myhill–Shepherdson theorem 5.6, extends to a continuous effective function $\bar{F}:D \longrightarrow E$. Then $F=\bar{F}|_M$ is effectively continuous. □

In general it is not possible to obtain G in the theorem which is equal to F on M. However, if $N \subseteq E_k$ contains only total elements then we are often interested in the quotient structure of total objects $\tilde{N}=N/\sim$, with, say, the quotient topology.

6.7 Corollary Suppose $F:M \longrightarrow N$ is $(\bar{\alpha},\bar{\beta})$-computable where $M \subseteq D_k$ is effectively dense and $N \subseteq E_k$ contains only total elements. Then $\tilde{F}:M \longrightarrow \tilde{N}$ defined by $\tilde{F}(x)=[F(x)]$ is continuous.

Proof: Let $N'=\{z \in E: (\exists y \in N)(y \sqsubseteq z)\}$. Then N' contains only total elements by Lemma 8.3.4. Furthermore $\tilde{N}'$ and $\tilde{N}$ are homeomorphic spaces. By Theorem 6.4 there is an $(\bar{\alpha},\bar{\beta})$-computable function $G:D_k \longrightarrow E_k$ such that $F(x) \sqsubseteq G(x)$ for $x \in M$. By the generalized Myhill–Shepherdson theorem, $G:M \longrightarrow N'$ is continuous and hence $\tilde{G}:M \longrightarrow \tilde{N}'$ is continuous, being a composition of G and the factoring map. Using a homeomorphism $h:\tilde{N}' \longrightarrow \tilde{N}$ we have $\tilde{F}=h \circ \tilde{G}$. □

10.7 Exercises

1. Show that the functors $\mathbf{T}_+$, $\mathbf{T}_\otimes$, $\mathbf{T}_\oplus$, $\mathbf{T}_{\to\perp}$ and $\mathbf{T}_\perp$ on **Cusl** are effective.

2. Let (D,α) be an effective domain. Suppose $f:\omega \longrightarrow \omega$ is a total recursive function such that the set $A=\{\bar{\alpha}(f(n)): n \in \omega\}$ is consistent, where $\bar{\alpha}$ is the canonical numbering of D_k. Show that $\sqcup A$ is computable with an $\bar{\alpha}$-index obtained uniformly from an index of f.

3. Prove Proposition 5.5.

4. Let X be a T_0-space. An element $a \in X$ is said to be *finite* if there is an open set U_a, $a \in U_a$, such that if V is open and $a \in V$ then $U_a \subseteq V$ (that is the open set U_a generates the filter of open sets containing a). Let $X_0=\{a \in X: a \text{ is finite}\}$. Then X is said to be an f_0-space if the following hold:

(a) $\{U_a : a \in X_0\}$ is a base for the topology on X.
(b) $(\forall a, b \in X_0)(U_a \cap U_b \neq \emptyset \Rightarrow (\exists c \in X_0)(U_a \cap U_b = U_c))$.
(c) There is $a \in X_0$ such that $X = U_a$.
Finally, let $\sqsubseteq$ be the specialization ordering on X defined immediately preceding Proposition 5.4.3.

(i) Show that $U_a = U_b$ if and only if $a = b$.
(ii) Show that $X_0 = (X_0; \sqsubseteq, \perp)$ is a cusl where $U_\perp = X$.
(iii) Let $x \in X$. Show that the set $\{a \in X_0 : a \sqsubseteq x\}$ is directed and that $x = \bigsqcup\{a \in X_0 : a \sqsubseteq x\}$.
(iv) Show that there is a continuous order-preserving embedding $f : X \rightarrow \overline{X_0}$ taking X_0 onto the compact elements in $\overline{X_0}$, where $\overline{X_0}$ is the completion by ideals of the cusl X_0. (Thus we may consider X as a subspace of the domain $\overline{X_0}$.)

5. Let X be an f_0-space as defined in Exercise 4. Then (X, α_0) is said to be an *effective f_0-space* if (X_0, α_0) is a computable cusl. A surjective numbering $\alpha : \omega \rightarrow X$ is a *constructive numbering* with respect to (X, α_0) if
(a) the inclusion mapping $\iota : X_0 \rightarrow X$ is (α_0, α)-computable, and
(b) the relation $R(n,m) \Leftrightarrow \alpha_0(n) \sqsubseteq \alpha(m)$ is r.e.
We say that (X, α_0, α) as above is a *constructive f_0-space*. Show that (the embedding of) (X, α) is a constructive subdomain of the effective domain $(\overline{X_0}, \alpha_0)$.

6. Let $\mathbf{F} : \mathbf{K} \rightarrow \mathbf{L}$ and $\mathbf{G} : \mathbf{L} \rightarrow \mathbf{M}$ be effective functors as in Definition 1.8. Show that $\mathbf{G} \circ \mathbf{F} : \mathbf{K} \rightarrow \mathbf{M}$ is an effective functor whose index can be computed uniformly from indices for $\mathbf{F}$ and $\mathbf{G}$.

7. Consider the solutions of domain equations up to identity in Precusl as described in Section 6.4. Show that the solution to any domain equation, containing the usual constructs and computable precusl's as parameters, is computable.

8. Use Exercise 13 in Chapter 8 to prove that every effective operator on the constructive reals is continuous (Ceitin [1967], Moschovakis [1964]).

9. Let (D, α) be an effective domain. Let $V_e = \bigcup_{n \in W_e} B_{\alpha(n)}$ be the effectively open set with index e (see Definition 5.1). A family $\mathcal{F}$ of open sets is said to be *effectively separating* if there is an algorithm which given α-indices for $a_1, \ldots, a_n \in D_c$ such that the set $\{a_1, \ldots, a_n\}$ is inconsistent, computes $e_1, \ldots, e_n$ such that $V_{e_i} \in \mathcal{F}$ and the V_{e_i} separate the a_i. A set $M \subseteq D$ is *effectively total* if $\mathcal{F}(M)$ is effectively separating.

(i) Let (D,α) and (E,β) be effective domains and suppose that $M \subseteq D$ and $N \subseteq E$ are effectively dense and effectively total sets. Show that $M \times N \subseteq D \times E$ and $<M,N> \subseteq [D \longrightarrow E]$ are effectively dense and effectively total sets.
(ii) Conclude that the total sets in the type structure of domains over $\mathbf{N}_\perp$ are effectively dense and effectively total.

10. Let (D,α) be an effective domain and let $M \subseteq D$ be an effectively dense set. Show that there is an effective continuous function $\mathrm{select}_M : [D \longrightarrow \mathbb{B}_\perp] \longrightarrow D$ such that for each $p \in [D \longrightarrow \mathbb{B}_\perp]$,

$$\varnothing \neq p^{-1}(tt) \in \mathcal{F}(M) \Rightarrow \mathrm{select}_M(p) \in p^{-1}(tt) \cap M.$$

[Recall Exercise 8.5.18.]

11. Let $\mathcal{G} = \{G_\sigma\}_{\sigma \in TS}$ be the total type structure over $\{tt, ff\} \subseteq \mathbb{B}_\perp$ (see Definition 8.4.7). To say that $f \in G_\sigma$ is *effective* means that there is an effective $\overline{f} \in D_\sigma$ such that $f = [\overline{f}]_\sigma$. Suppose that $f \in G_{\sigma \times \tau \to o}$ is effective and satisfies

$$(\forall x \in G_\sigma)(\exists y \in G_\tau)(f(x,y) = tt).$$

Show that there is an effective functional $\mathrm{select}_f \in G_{\sigma \to \tau}$ such that

$$(\forall x \in G_\sigma)(f(x, \mathrm{select}_f(x)) = tt).$$

CHAPTER 11

POWER DOMAINS

Power domains were introduced by Plotkin [1976] in order to give a semantics for non-deterministic or parallel programs. Assume that each run or possible outcome of a class of non-deterministic programs has an interpretation in a fixed domain D. Then an interpretation of a non-deterministic program in this class would be the *set* of interpretations of all possible outcomes of the program. Thus an appropriate domain to interpret this class of non-deterministic programs should be something analogous to the power set of D, let us call it a power domain of D. In this chapter we shall introduce three concepts of power domains, due to Smyth [1978], Hoare and Plotkin [1976], respectively. It turns out that Scott–Ershov domains are closed under Smyth's and Hoare's power domain operations but unfortunately not under Plotkin's. The class of countably based algebraic cpo's (we call these *quasidomains*) *is* closed under Plotkin's power domain construction. However, as we observed in Chapter 3, this class is not satisfactory for semantics, since it is *not* closed under the formation of function space. Therefore we introduce the class of SFP-objects, a subclass of the quasidomains, which is closed under all three power domain constructions as well as under the formation of function space. In fact the category of SFP-objects is the largest full subcategory of the category of quasidomains which is cartesian closed. Thus every countably based Scott–Ershov domain is an SFP-object but there are SFP-objects that are not domains.

In the first section we give the three concepts of power domains. We also show that the class of quasidomains is closed under the formation of power domains, whichever definition of power domain we choose. In Section 2 we show that Scott–Ershov domains are closed under Smyth's and Hoare's power domain operations. Then we introduce SFP-objects as limits of finite partial orders and prove that the category of SFP-objects and embeddings is closed under Plotkin's power domain construction as well as being cartesian closed. Finally, in Section 3, we provide a useful algebraic characterization of SFP-objects.

Section 11.1 Definition of the Power Domains

As indicated in the introduction, we want the interpretation of a non-deterministic program to be a subset of a domain D, where D contains interpretations of all possible runs or outcomes of the program. It should be intuitively clear that a particular run or computation of a non-deterministic program is modelled by a tree, where branching in the tree corresponds to non-deterministic choice. Thus the subsets of D that we are interested in are those generated by a tree.

1.1 Example Consider the following flow chart:

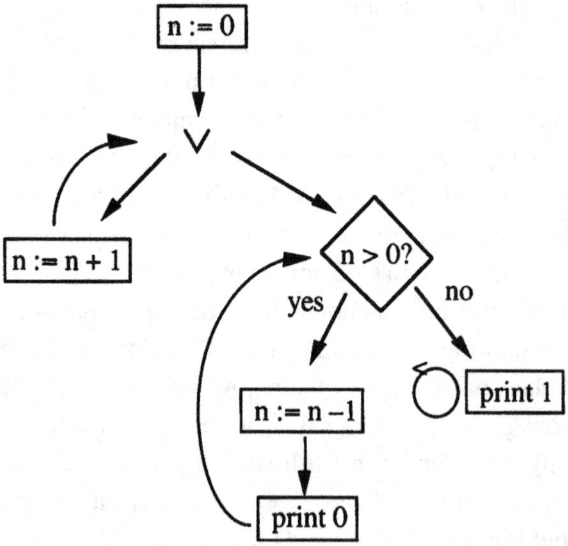

Here $\vee$ represents non-deterministic choice.

Let $\Sigma = \{0,1\}$ and consider the Cantor space domain $\mathbb{C} = \Sigma^* \cup 2^\omega$. We have that $\mathbb{C}_c = \Sigma^*$ with the empty sequence $\langle\rangle$ as its least element. (See 2.1.12 and Exercise 2.5.11.) The possible outputs (that is printouts) of the above program are strings in $\mathbb{C}$ and the successive computations of the program may be illustrated by a finitary branching tree as follows. The branching points correspond to the non-deterministic choices made in the course of a run of the program and there are only finitely many alternatives at each such point.

Since $\mathbb{C}$ is a domain, $\bigsqcup\gamma$ exists in $\mathbb{C}$ for every branch γ in the tree. The interpretation of the program is then defined as the set

$$\{\bigsqcup\gamma:\ \gamma \text{ is an } \omega\text{-branch in the tree}\},$$

that is, $\{<>\}\cup\{0^n1^\omega:\ n\geq 0\}$. The elements of the power domains will be sets of this kind.

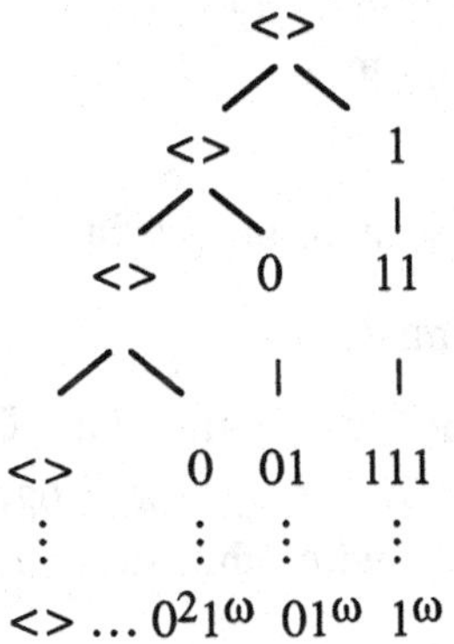

Before giving the formal definition of the elements of the power domains, we need to introduce some terminology for trees.

A *tree* $T=(T,\leq_T)$ is a partially ordered set with a least element (the *root*) such that, for every $x\in T$, the set of predecessors of x is well-ordered. In fact, we are only going to consider trees such that the set of predecessors of each element is finite. For such trees the following definitions suffice.

1.2 Definition Let T be a tree such that the set of predecessors of each element in T is finite.

(a) For $x\in T$, $\sigma(x)=$ the number of predecessors of x. $\sigma(x)$ is called the *height* of x.

(b) T is *finitary branching* if, for all $x\in T$, the set of immediate successors of x is finite.

(c) T is an *ω-tree* if T contains elements of height n for each $n\in\omega$.

(d) A *branch* γ in T is a chain in T which is closed downwards, that is if $y\leq_T x$ and $x\in\gamma$, then $y\in\gamma$. A *maximal branch* in T is a branch in T with no proper extension in T.

Each branch γ of T is assigned a height, namely the supremum of the heights of its elements. If T is an ω-tree, any branch of height ω (*ω-branch*) is maximal, but the converse is not true in general. However, given any finitely branching ω-tree, it is possible to "prune" it to obtain an ω-tree where all maximal branches are ω-branches.

In this section we shall consider *countably based algebraic cpo's*, which we call *quasidomains*. They are not Scott–Ershov domains in general, since they are not necessarily consistently complete.

1.3 Definition Let $D=(D;\sqsubseteq,\bot)$ be a quasidomain and let $T=(T;\leq_T)$ be a finitary branching ω-tree such that all maximal branches in T are ω-branches. Let $\zeta: T\to D$ be monotone and put

$$T^{\zeta}_{\omega}=\{\bigsqcup\{\zeta(t):\ t\in\gamma\}:\ \gamma \text{ an } \omega\text{-branch in } T\}.$$

T^{ζ}_{ω} is the set *generated by* T using ζ.

ζ is called a *labelling of* T and T together with ζ is a *labelled tree*. T is also called a *generating tree over* D. Strictly speaking, a labelled tree T is a pair (T,ζ) of a tree and a labelling. As with other structures, however, we often denote it simply by T.

Notice that T^{ζ}_{ω} is well-defined, since D is a cpo and $\{\zeta(t): t\in\gamma\}$ is a chain in D, by monotonicity. For $n<\omega$, let

$$T^{\zeta}_{n}=\{\zeta(x):\ \sigma(x)=n\}.$$

T^{ζ}_{n} is called the n'th *level* of the tree T. For T^{ζ}_{ω} as well as for T^{ζ}_{n} we omit the superscript ζ in case only one labelling is involved.

1.4 Definition If D is a quasidomain, let

$$\mathcal{F}(D)=\{T^{\zeta}_{\omega}:\ (T,\zeta) \text{ is a generating tree over } D\}.$$

The elements of $\mathcal{F}(D)$ will be the *objects of the power domain* of D. For example, the set $\{<>\}\cup\{0^n1^{\omega}: n\geq 0\}$ considered in the motivating example is T_{ω} for the tree T of successive outputs of the program described. Thus $\mathcal{F}(D)$ will consist of all sets representing the final outcomes of programs where the successive outputs of the program form a tree which is labelled by elements of D.

Note that $\mathcal{F}(D)\subseteq\wp(D)-\{\emptyset\}$, where $\wp(D)$ is the power set of D. We first show that $\mathcal{F}(D)$ contains all finite non-empty subsets of D and is closed under union.

1.5 Lemma Let D be a quasidomain. Then
(a) $\{\bot\}\in\mathcal{F}(D)$.
(b) If A is a finite non-empty subset of D, then $A\in\mathcal{F}(D)$.
(c) If $A, B\in\mathcal{F}(D)$, then $A\cup B\in\mathcal{F}(D)$.

Proof: (a) The following figure describes a generating tree for $\{\bot\}$:

(b) Let $A=\{a_0, a_1, \ldots, a_n\}$. A generating tree for A is:

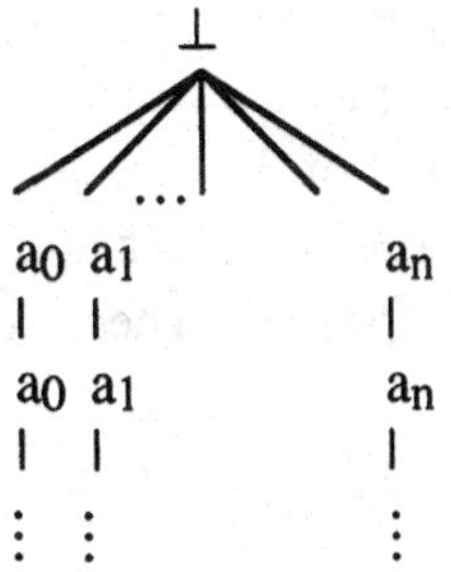

(c) Let T and T' be generating trees for A and B, respectively. Then the following figure describes a generating tree for $A \cup B$:

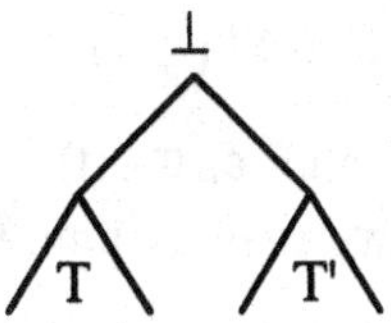

□

1.6 Lemma Let $f: D \to D'$ be continuous. If $A \in \mathcal{F}(D)$, then $f[A] \in \mathcal{F}(D')$.

Proof: If $A = T_\omega^\zeta$ under the labelling $\zeta: T \to D$, then $f \circ \zeta: T \to D'$ is also a labelling of T, by monotonicity. Further $f[A] = T_\omega^{f \circ \zeta}$, by continuity. □

Next we show that it is always possible to label the generating trees by compact elements in the quasidomain D.

1.7 Proposition For any generating tree T over the quasidomain D, there is a generating tree $T' = (T, \zeta')$ such that $\zeta'[T] \subseteq D_c$ and $T_\omega = T'_\omega$.

Proof: Let $a_0, a_1, \ldots, a_n, \ldots$ be an enumeration of the countably many compact elements of D (allowing repetitions, say, when D_c is finite) and let $T = (T, \zeta)$ be the given labelled ω-tree. We are going to construct a labelled tree $T' = (T, \zeta')$ with the required properties, that is we shall construct a new labelling $\zeta': T \to D_c$ such that $T_\omega = T'_\omega$. The intuitive and simple idea is that since each maximal branch is an ω-branch and each element in D is the supremum of a countable chain of compact elements, we should be able to relabel each ω-branch with the corresponding chain of compact elements. Let

$$A^t = \{a_i : a_i \sqsubseteq \zeta(t) \text{ and } i \leq \sigma(t)\},$$

for $t \in T$. We shall define $\zeta' : T \to D_c$ by induction on $\sigma(t)$.

For $\sigma(t) = 0$, that is t is the root of T, let $\zeta'(t) = \bot$.

For $\sigma(t) > 0$, we inductively assume that $\zeta'(s)$ is defined and compact for all nodes $s \in T$ with height strictly less than $\sigma(t)$ and that $\zeta'(s) \sqsubseteq \zeta(s)$ for all such nodes. Let t' be the immediate predecessor of t. Thus $\zeta'(t') \sqsubseteq \zeta(t') \sqsubseteq \zeta(t)$ so that $A^t \cup \{\zeta'(t')\}$ is a finite subset of the directed set $\text{approx}(\zeta(t))$ and hence has an upper bound in that set. Choose some $a \in \text{approx}(\zeta(t))$ which is an upper bound of $A^t \cup \{\zeta'(t')\}$ and put $\zeta'(t) = a$. Then clearly the induction hypothesis holds for t.

It remains to show that $T_\omega = T'_\omega$. Let γ be an ω-branch in T. Then, clearly,

$$\bigsqcup\{\zeta'(t) : t \in \gamma\} \sqsubseteq \bigsqcup\{\zeta(t) : t \in \gamma\}.$$

To show the converse direction, it suffices to show that for each a_n in the enumeration of D_c:

$$a_n \sqsubseteq \bigsqcup\{\zeta(t) : t \in \gamma\} \Rightarrow a_n \sqsubseteq \bigsqcup\{\zeta'(t) : t \in \gamma\}.$$

So suppose $a_n \sqsubseteq \bigsqcup\{\zeta(t) : t \in \gamma\}$. Thus $a_n \sqsubseteq \zeta(t)$, for some t, by compactness, where, by the monotonicity of ζ, we may assume that $\sigma(t) \geq n$. But then $a_n \in A^t$ and hence $a_n \sqsubseteq \zeta'(t)$ by the construction. □

Later on we shall show that a power domain is a *prequasidomain*, that is, it satisfies the conditions for being a quasidomain except for antisymmetry. We first define what will turn out to be the compact elements of $\mathcal{F}(D)$ as well as an ordering on $\mathcal{F}(D)$. Intuitively, whatever ordering we choose, T_ω should be a supremum of $\{T_n : n < \omega\}$. By Proposition 1.7, T_n can be chosen as a finite subset of D_c and by Lemma 1.5, $T_n \in \mathcal{F}(D)$. This motivates the following definition.

1.8 Definition If D is a quasidomain, then

$$\mathcal{M}(D) = \{A \subseteq D_c : A \text{ finite and } A \neq \varnothing\}.$$

Now we define what it means for an element in $\mathcal{M}(D)$ to approximate an element of $\mathcal{F}(D)$. Three orderings on $\mathcal{M}(D) \times \mathcal{F}(D)$ have been proposed, giving rise to three different notions of a power domain. Note that $\mathcal{M}(D) \subseteq \mathcal{F}(D)$ by the above.

1.9 Definition Let D be a quasidomain. The orderings $\sqsubseteq_0$, $\sqsubseteq_1$ and $\sqsubseteq_2$ are defined on $\mathcal{M}(D)\times\mathcal{F}(D)$ as follows. For $A \in \mathcal{M}(D)$, $S \in \mathcal{F}(D)$:

$A \sqsubseteq_0 S$	$\Leftrightarrow$	$(\forall x \in S)(\exists a \in A)(a \sqsubseteq x)$	(Smyth)
$A \sqsubseteq_1 S$	$\Leftrightarrow$	$(\forall a \in A)(\exists x \in S)(a \sqsubseteq x)$	(Hoare)
$A \sqsubseteq_2 S$	$\Leftrightarrow$	$A \sqsubseteq_0 S$ and $A \sqsubseteq_1 S$	(Plotkin).

The elements of A could be thought of as giving finite pieces of information about a non-deterministic computation and the elements of S as giving total information about the computation. Then $A \sqsubseteq_0 S$ holds if every piece of total information is approximated by a finite piece in A, and $A \sqsubseteq_1 S$ holds if every element of A has a total extension. All three orderings seem reasonable. The ordering $\sqsubseteq_2$, which gives rise to the Plotkin power domain, is called the *Egli–Milner* ordering. It might seem the most plausible, but the other two are technically simpler to work with. Here we investigate all three orderings, leaving the choice of which one to use in a particular application to the reader.

For the rest of this section, i stands for 0, 1 or 2.

We start with the following interesting but simple observations.

1.10 Lemma Let T be a generating tree over a quasidomain D.
(a) If $m \leq n$, then $T_m \sqsubseteq_i T_n$.
(b) For each $n \in \omega$, $T_n \sqsubseteq_i T_\omega$. □

Now we extend $\sqsubseteq_i$ to $\mathcal{F}(D)\times\mathcal{F}(D)$. Note that this extension is defined in the same way as the *specialization order* of a topological space in Section 4 of Chapter 5. In fact, the three different orderings correspond to three different topologies, where the basic open sets are of the form $\{S \in \mathcal{F}(D): A \sqsubseteq_i S\}$, for $A \in \mathcal{M}(D)$, when $i = 0, 1, 2$.

1.11 Definition Let $S, S' \in \mathcal{F}(D)$. Then
(a) $S \sqsubseteq_i S' \Leftrightarrow (\forall A \in \mathcal{M}(D))(A \sqsubseteq_i S \Rightarrow A \sqsubseteq_i S')$.
(b) $S \equiv_i S' \Leftrightarrow S \sqsubseteq_i S'$ & $S' \sqsubseteq_i S$.

Here are some further immediate observations about the extended orderings.

1.12 Lemma
(a) $\sqsubseteq_i$ is a preorder.
(b) $\sqsubseteq_i$ on $\mathcal{F}(D)\times\mathcal{F}(D)$ is an extension of $\sqsubseteq_i$ on $\mathcal{M}(D)\times\mathcal{F}(D)$.
(c) For $S, S' \in \mathcal{F}(D)$, if $S' \subseteq S$, then $S \sqsubseteq_0 S'$ and $S' \sqsubseteq_1 S$. □

1.13 Remark
None of the relations $\sqsubseteq_i$ is antisymmetric as shown by the following examples.

1. The relation $\sqsubseteq_0$ is not antisymmetric, for let $S \in \mathcal{F}(D)$ be such that $\bot \in S$. Then $S \equiv_0 \{\bot\}$.

2. The relation $\sqsubseteq_1$ is not antisymmetric on $\mathcal{M}(\mathbb{C})$, for let $A = \{0, 011\}$, $B = \{01, 011\}$. Then $A \equiv_1 B$.

3. The relation $\sqsubseteq_2$ is not antisymmetric on $\mathcal{M}(\mathbb{C})$, for let $A = \{0, 011\}$, $B = \{0, 01, 011\}$. Then $A \equiv_2 B$.

The main result of this section is that, for $i = 0, 1, 2$, the quotient structure $\mathcal{F}_i(D) = \mathcal{F}(D)/\equiv_i$ is a quasidomain. That theorem will follow from the following lemmas. As an intermediate step we have the proposition that T_ω is a supremum of $\{T_n : n < \omega\}$ as a consequence of the following technical lemma.

1.14 Lemma Let D be a quasidomain, let T be a finitary branching ω-tree, let $\zeta : T \to D$ be monotone and let $A \in \mathcal{M}(D)$. If $A \not\sqsubseteq_0 T_m$, for all m, then there is an ω-branch $\{t_n : n < \omega\}$ in T such that for all $a \in A$: $a \not\sqsubseteq \bigsqcup\{\zeta(t_n) : n < \omega\}$.

Proof: Say that a point t in T avoids A if $\zeta(t)$ does not extend any point in A, that is $(\forall a \in A)(a \not\sqsubseteq \zeta(t))$. Consider the following property $P(s)$ for $s \in T$:

$$P(s) \Leftrightarrow (\forall m)(\exists t \geq s)(\sigma(t) \geq m \text{ and } t \text{ avoids } A).$$

Note that if $P(s)$, then s avoids A.

Assume that $A \not\sqsubseteq_0 T_m$, for all m. We are going to define an ω-branch $t_0 < t_1 < \ldots < t_{n-1} < t_n < \ldots$ in T of points such that $P(t_n)$ holds for each n. Let t_0 be the root of T. Since $A \not\sqsubseteq_0 T_m$, for each m, there certainly are points arbitrarily high up in the tree that avoid A, that is, $P(t_0)$ holds.

Now suppose that we have defined $t_0 < t_1 < \ldots < t_{n-1} < t_n$ so that $\sigma(t_i) = i$ and $P(t_i)$ holds. We shall define t_{n+1}. Let $s_1, s_2, \ldots, s_k$ be the immediate successors of t_n. If $P(s_i)$ does not hold, then there is a bound m_i such that all points in the subtree determined by s_i that avoid A have height $< m_i$. Should $P(s_i)$ fail for all i, $1 \leq i \leq k$, let $m = \max\{m_i : 1 \leq i \leq k\}$. Then each point in the subtree above t_n that avoids A has height at most m, contradicting the induction hypothesis. Thus there is some s_i for which $P(s_i)$ holds. Let t_{n+1} be one such. The picture is:

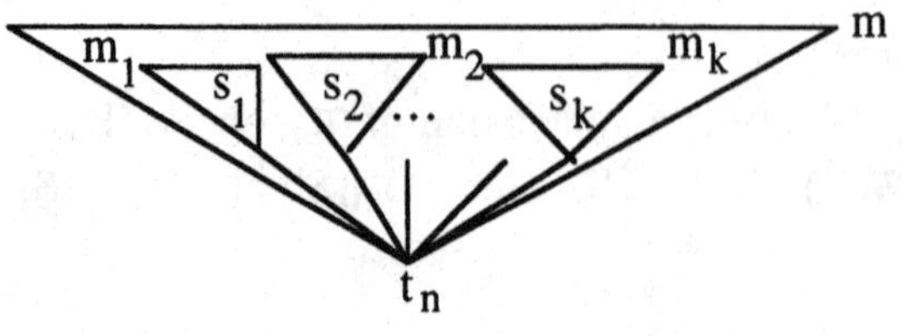

Consider the defined ω-branch $\{t_n: n<\omega\}$. Suppose that $a \sqsubseteq \bigsqcup\{\zeta(t_n): n<\omega\}$, for some $a \in A$. Since a is compact, this would mean that $a \sqsubseteq \zeta(t_n)$ for some $n<\omega$. But this is not the case since t_n avoids A. □

1.15 Lemma Let D be a quasidomain, T a generating tree over D, and let $A \in \mathcal{M}(D)$. If $A \sqsubseteq_i T_\omega$, then $A \sqsubseteq_i T_m$, for some m.

Proof: $\underline{i=0}$. Since $\bigsqcup\{\zeta(t_n): n<\omega\} \in T_\omega$ it follows by Lemma 1.14 that if $A \not\sqsubseteq_0 T_m$, for all m, then $A \not\sqsubseteq_0 T_\omega$. The claim in the lemma is the contrapositive of this statement.

$\underline{i=1}$. Now assume that $A \sqsubseteq_1 T_\omega$. Thus, for each $a \in A$, by compactness, there is some $t_a \in T$ such that $a \sqsubseteq \zeta(t_a)$. Since A is finite, let $k = \max\{\sigma(t_a): a \in A\}$. Every t_a has some extension at level k, since T has no finite maximal branches, and thus a has an extension at level k, for each $a \in A$. From this it follows that $A \sqsubseteq_1 T_k$.

$\underline{i=2}$. Finally assume that $A \sqsubseteq_2 T_\omega$. Then $A \sqsubseteq_0 T_\omega$ and $A \sqsubseteq_1 T_\omega$. It follows by the above that $A \sqsubseteq_0 T_m$, for some m, and $A \sqsubseteq_1 T_k$, for some k. Then, by Lemma 1.10 (a), $A \sqsubseteq_2 T_p$, for all $p \geq m, k$. □

1.16 Proposition If T is a generating tree over the quasidomain D, then T_ω is a supremum of $\{T_n: n<\omega\}$ with respect to each one of the preorders $\sqsubseteq_i$.

Proof: By Lemma 1.10 (b), $T_n \sqsubseteq_i T_\omega$. Now assume that Y is an upper bound of the T_n's for $n<\omega$. Then, by Lemma 1.15, for any $A \in \mathcal{M}(D)$, if $A \sqsubseteq_i T_\omega$, then $A \sqsubseteq_i T_n$, for some n. Thus $A \sqsubseteq_i Y$ and hence, by definition, $T_\omega \sqsubseteq_i Y$. □

The following is a technical lemma used to replace a directed subset of a countable set by an ω-chain having the same supremum. (Cf. Exercise 2.5.18.)

1.17 Lemma If C is a countable preordered set and B is a directed subset of C, then there is an ω-chain $A \subseteq B$ such that

$$(\forall b \in B)(\exists a \in A)(b \sqsubseteq a).$$

Proof: Choose an enumeration of B, say $B = \{b_n: n<\omega\}$, and let B_n denote the initial segment $\{b_0, b_1, \ldots, b_n\}$. We define the ω-chain $A = \{a_n: n<\omega\}$ recursively as follows.

Let $a_0 = b_0$. Assume that $a_0, a_1, \ldots, a_n$ have been defined so that $a_0 \sqsubseteq a_1 \sqsubseteq \ldots \sqsubseteq a_n$. Since $B_n \cup \{a_n\}$ is a finite subset of the directed set B, there is some element of B which extends all elements of that set. Let a_{n+1} be one such. Then the ω-chain $A = \{a_n: n<\omega\}$ has the required property. □

Before proceeding to our main theorem, we give an equivalent characterization of prequasidomains, which will be used to establish that $\mathcal{F}(D)$ is a prequasidomain.

If D is a set preordered by $\sqsubseteq$, and $x, y \in D$, we say that x and y are *equivalent* if $x \sqsubseteq y$ & $y \sqsubseteq x$ and we write $x \equiv y$ for this equivalence relation. We say, as usual, that $a \in D$ is *compact* in D if whenever $A \subseteq D$ is directed and has a supremum y and $a \sqsubseteq y$, then $a \sqsubseteq x$, for some $x \in A$. A set $C \subseteq D$ is a set of compact elements of D *up to equivalence* if each element in C is compact and if for each compact element $a \in D$ there is some $b \in C$ so that $a \equiv b$. That is, C will contain a representative for each compact element in D and in the quotient structure $(D/\equiv; \sqsubseteq)$, $C/\equiv$ will be the set of compact elements.

1.18 Lemma Let D be a set preordered by $\sqsubseteq$ and let C be a countable subset of D. Then D is a prequasidomain with C a set of compact elements up to equivalence if and only if

(i) D has a least element.

(ii) If $A \subseteq C$ is a chain, then A has a supremum in D.

(iii) If $x \in D$, then there is a non-empty chain $A \subseteq C$ such that x is a supremum of A.

(iv) If $a \in C$ and $a \sqsubseteq x \in D$, where x is a supremum of some ω-chain A in C, then $a \sqsubseteq b$, for some $b \in A$.

Proof: To show the non-trivial direction, assume that D with C satisfies conditions (i)–(iv). By Lemma 1.17, for any directed subset B of C, there is an ω-chain A included in B so that, for any $x \in D$:

$$x \text{ is a supremum of } A \Leftrightarrow x \text{ is a supremum of } B.$$

Further, by (ii), any such chain A has a supremum in D and thus any directed subset of C has a supremum in D. In particular, it follows that for any chain included in C there is an ω-subchain having the same suprema. In what follows we can thus without loss of generality assume that all chains considered that are included in C are actually ω-chains.

Now we prove the lemma.

For $x \in D$, let $C_X = \{a \in C : a \sqsubseteq x\}$ and, by (iii) and the above, let A_X be a non-empty ω-chain included in C such that x is a supremum of A_X. Trivially, $A_X \subseteq C_X$. We show that each C_X is directed. For $a, a' \in C_X$, there are, by (iv), $b, b' \in A_X$ for which $a \sqsubseteq b$, $a' \sqsubseteq b'$. Since A_X is a chain, $b \sqsubseteq b'$ or $b' \sqsubseteq b$, say that $b' \sqsubseteq b$. It follows that $a, a' \sqsubseteq b \in C_X$. This shows that C_X is directed and that $(\forall a \in C_X)(\exists b \in A_X)(a \sqsubseteq b)$. It follows that x is a supremum of C_X.

To show that every directed subset of D has a supremum, let B be a directed subset of D. By the above, C_x is directed and x is a supremum of C_x, for every $x \in B$. Then $B' = \bigcup\{C_x : x \in B\}$ is directed. Since $B' \subseteq C$, by the above, B' has a supremum y in D. We show that y is a supremum of B. Let $x \in B$. Then x is a supremum of C_x. It follows that $x \sqsubseteq y$, since y is an upper bound of C_x. Thus y is an upper bound of B. Now, for any upper bound z of B, we have that for each $x \in B$ and each $a \in C_x$, $a \sqsubseteq x \sqsubseteq z$. Thus $y \sqsubseteq z$, since y is a supremum of B'. It follows that y is a supremum of B and hence D is closed under suprema of directed subsets.

It just remains to show that C is a set of compact elements of D up to equivalence. Let $a \in C$ and assume that $a \sqsubseteq x$, where x is a supremum of some directed set $B \subseteq D$. By the above, x is then a supremum of some ω-chain $A \subseteq B \cap C$. By (iv) we get that $a \sqsubseteq b$, for some $b \in A \subseteq B$. Thus a is compact in D.

To prove the second part, let $a \in D$ be compact. Then a is a supremum of C_a and C_a is directed. Since a is compact, $a \sqsubseteq b$, for some $b \in C_a$. Thus $a \sqsubseteq b \sqsubseteq a$ and hence $a \equiv b$, for some $b \in C$.

We have thus shown that C is a set of compact elements of D up to equivalence. Further, for every $x \in D$, $C_x \subseteq \text{approx}(x)$, C_x is directed and x is a supremum of C_x. Thus D is a prequasidomain. □

1.19 Theorem Let D be a quasidomain. Then $\mathcal{F}(D)$ is a prequasidomain with $\mathcal{M}(D)$ as its set of compact elements up to equivalence, for each one of the preorderings $\sqsubseteq_i$.

Proof: We verify clauses (i)–(iv) of Lemma 1.18.

(i) $\{\bot\}$ is a least element.

(ii) Since $\mathcal{M}(D)$ is countable, we need only consider ω-chains. So let $(A_n)_{n<\omega}$ be an ω-chain in $\mathcal{M}(D)$ with respect to $\sqsubseteq_i$. We construct a tree T with levels labelled by the points in $\bigcup\{A_n : n<\omega\} \cup \{\bot\}$. The root is labelled by $\bot$. We shall arrange matters so that all points at level $n+1$ are labelled by elements of $A_n \cup \{\bot\}$. For every $a \in A_n$ and $b \in A_{n+1}$ for which $a \sqsubseteq_i b$ add an arc in the tree, disjoint arcs for different a's so that T will be a *tree*.

<u>i=2</u>. Let $(A_n)_{n<\omega}$ be an ω-chain with respect to $\sqsubseteq_2$. The above construction ensures that we get a generating tree for which $T_{n+1} = A_n$, since every point in A_n has an extension in A_{n+1} and every point in A_{n+1} extends some point in A_n. Hence $T_\omega \in \mathcal{F}(D)$ is a supremum of $\{A_n : n<\omega\}$.

<u>i=0</u>. Since $A_n \sqsubseteq_0 A_{n+1}$, every point in A_{n+1} extends some point in A_n. Hence we get a tree by the above construction. Now T may contain finite maximal bran-

ches, but at least one branch is infinite, for T has height ω and each level is finite. "Prune" T to obtain a tree T' for which all maximal branches are ω-branches. We claim that T'_ω is a supremum of $\{A_n : n<\omega\}$. Since $T'_{n+1} \subseteq A_n$, we get that $A_n \sqsubseteq_0 T'_{n+1}$, by Lemma 1.12 (c). Thus T'_ω is an upper bound of the A_n's. Note that it follows by Lemma 1.14 that for each n there is some m such that $T'_n \sqsubseteq_0 A_m$. If not, then there would have been an infinite branch in the part of the tree that was pruned, which contradicts the fact that we only pruned off finite maximal branches. Now suppose that Y is an upper bound of $\{A_n : n<\omega\}$ and let $A \in \mathcal{M}(D)$ be such that $A \sqsubseteq_0 T'_\omega$. Then, by Lemma 1.15, $A \sqsubseteq_0 T'_n$, for some n. By the above, it follows that, for some m,

$$A \sqsubseteq_0 T'_n \sqsubseteq_0 A_m \sqsubseteq_0 Y.$$

Hence $T'_\omega \sqsubseteq_0 Y$ is a supremum of $\{A_n : n<\omega\}$. Further, $T'_\omega \in \mathcal{F}(D)$. This establishes (ii) when $i=0$.

<u>$i=1$</u>. Let level $n+1$ of the tree consist of points labelled by the points in A_n and a new point labelled by $\bot$ (independently of whether $\bot$ is in A_n or not). For any point in A_{n+1} that is not an extension of a point in A_n, connect it with the point labelled by $\bot$ at the previous level. We need $\bot$ at each level to make T into a labelled tree. Then T is a generating tree over D and T_ω is a supremum of $\{A_n \cup \{\bot\} : n<\omega\}$, by Proposition 1.16. Thus (ii) holds since

$$x \text{ is a supremum of } \{A_n \cup \{\bot\} : n<\omega\} \Leftrightarrow x \text{ is a supremum of } \{A_n : n<\omega\}.$$

(iii) By Proposition 1.7 we need only consider generating trees labelled by compact elements. For such trees T, each $T_n \in \mathcal{M}(D)$. Hence (iii) follows from Proposition 1.16.

(iv) Let $A \in \mathcal{M}(D)$ and assume that $A \sqsubseteq_i S$, where S is a supremum of some ω-chain $(A_n)_{n<\omega}$ in $\mathcal{M}(D)$. Let T_ω be the supremum of $(A_n)_{n<\omega}$ constructed in (ii). Then $S \equiv_i T_\omega$ and thus $A \sqsubseteq_i T_\omega$. Then, by Lemma 1.15, $A \sqsubseteq_i T_n$, for some n. But then by the proof of (ii), $A \sqsubseteq_i A_j$, for some j, which establishes (iv). □

Now we form the quotient $\mathcal{F}_i(D) = \mathcal{F}(D)/\equiv_i$ of $\mathcal{F}(D)$ by identifying elements S and S' such that $S \equiv_i S'$. Let $[S]_i$ denote the equivalence class of S with respect to $\equiv_i$. Since $\equiv_i$ is a congruence relation on $\mathcal{F}(D)$ with respect to $\sqsubseteq_i$, the relation $\sqsubseteq_i$ defined on $\mathcal{F}_i(D)$ by $[S]_i \sqsubseteq_i [S']_i \Leftrightarrow S \sqsubseteq_i S'$ is a partial ordering on $\mathcal{F}_i(D)$. Using the fact that $(\mathcal{F}(D); \sqsubseteq_i)$ with a countable subset C satisfies the conditions (i)–(iv) of Lemma 1.18 if and only if $(\mathcal{F}(D)/\equiv_i; \sqsubseteq_i)$ with $C/\equiv_i$ does (see Exercise 3), we obtain our main theorem.

1.20 Theorem If D a quasidomain, then $\mathcal{F}_i(D) = (\mathcal{F}_i(D); \sqsubseteq_i, [\{\perp\}]_i)$ is a quasidomain, for $i = 0, 1, 2$.

Section 11.2 Closure under the Power Domain Constructions

First we show that domains are preserved under Smyth's and Hoare's power domain operations, that is under $\mathcal{F}_0$ and $\mathcal{F}_1$.

2.1 Proposition If D is a domain, then $\mathcal{F}_0(D)$ and $\mathcal{F}_1(D)$ are domains.

Proof: In view of Theorem 1.20, we only need to show that $\mathcal{F}_i(D)$ is consistently complete, for $i = 0, 1$.

Let $[A]_i$ denote the equivalence class of A with respect to $\equiv_i$.

$\underline{i=0}$. Assume that $A, B \in \mathcal{M}(D)$ are consistent with respect to $\sqsubseteq_0$. Let

$$C = \{a \sqcup b:\ a \in A,\ b \in B \text{ and } \{a, b\} \text{ is consistent in } D\}.$$

Then C is non-empty and finite and hence in $\mathcal{M}(D)$ and $[C]_0 = [A]_0 \sqcup [B]_0$.

$\underline{i=1}$. If $A, B \in \mathcal{M}(D)$, then $[A \cup B]_1 = [A]_1 \sqcup [B]_1$. □

So domains are closed under all the usual operations such as $+, \times, \rightarrow$ and also under the power domain operations $\mathcal{F}_0$ and $\mathcal{F}_1$. However, $\mathcal{F}_2$ does not preserve consistent completeness as shown by the following example.

2.2 Example Let D be the following domain (cusl):

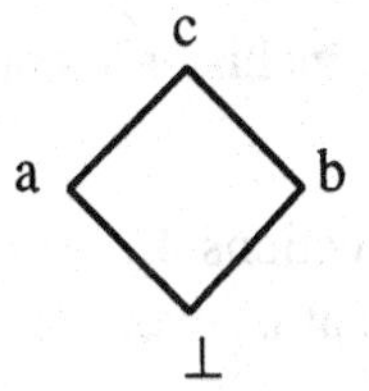

Let $E = D \times D$, $A = \{(a, \perp), (b, \perp)\}$ and let $B = \{(\perp, a), (\perp, b)\}$. Then we have that $A, B \in \mathcal{M}(E)$ and $\{A, B\}$ is consistent under the $\sqsubseteq_2$-ordering but has no least upper bound. In fact $C = \{(a, a), (b, b)\}$ and $D = \{(a, b), (b, a)\}$ are incomparable minimal upper bounds of $\{A, B\}$.

Thus if we want to solve domain equations involving $\mathcal{F}_2$, we need to consider some other type of objects. By Theorem 1.20, quasidomains are closed under $\mathcal{F}_2$, but unfortunately the category of quasidomains is not cartesian closed (see Example

3.3.10). Therefore, we introduce the following category, which is the largest cartesian closed full subcategory of quasidomains containing all countably based domains. It is also closed under each power domain construction.

Let **QDom** be the category of quasidomains with embeddings as morphisms. Recall that embeddings are the first components of projection pairs (see Definitions 2.1.9 and 4.5.6). Note that a finite partial order D with a least element is a cpo and in fact an algebraic cpo, since $D = D_c$. Let **Fpo** be the category having as objects finite partial orders with a least element and embeddings as morphisms. Then **Fpo** is a subcategory of **QDom**. SFP-objects are obtained by completing ω-chains in **Fpo**. We shall show later that such completions always exist (see Theorem 2.13). As observed earlier (see the discussion in Section 4.2 and also Exercise 11), however, the completions do not in general belong to **Fpo**.

2.3 Definition D is an *SFP-object* (sequence of finite partial orders) if there is a colimiting cone in **QDom** of an ω-chain in **Fpo** with direct limit D.

The category **SFP** consists of SFP-objects and embeddings.

2.4 Examples

1. Every finite partial order with a least element is an SFP-object. In particular, the following figure describes an SFP-object which is not a domain.

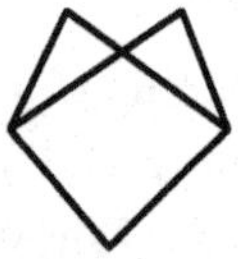

2. $\omega+1$ is an SFP-object, for $\omega+1 = \varinjlim D_n$, where $D_n = \{0, 1, \ldots, n\}$ ordered linearly and where the inclusion mappings $\iota_n : D_n \to D_{n+1}$ are the embeddings.

Analogously to the results in Sections 4.2 and 4.3, we establish that *every* ω-chain in **Fpo** has a direct limit, that is, every ω-chain in **Fpo** gives rise to an SFP-object.

2.5 Definition Let $\Delta = (D_n, f_n)_{n<\omega}$ be an ω-chain in the category **Fpo**. Let $f_{mn} : D_m \to D_n$ be defined as follows:

$$f_{mn} = \begin{cases} f_{n-1} \circ \ldots \circ f_{m+1} \circ f_m & \text{if } m < n \\ id_{D_m} & \text{if } m = n \\ f_n^- \circ f_{n+1}^- \circ \ldots \circ f_{m-1}^- & \text{if } n < m, \end{cases}$$

where $f_n^- : D_{n+1} \to D_n$ is the projection corresponding to f_n.

2.6 Proposition Let $\Delta=(D_n,f_n)_{n<\omega}$ be an ω-chain in **Fpo**.

(a) If $m\leq n$, then (f_{mn},f_{nm}) is a projection pair for (D_m,D_n).

(b) $f_{kn}=f_{mn}\circ f_{km}$ and $f_{nk}=f_{mk}\circ f_{nm}$, for $k\leq m\leq n$.

(c) If $i,j\geq \max(m,n)$, then $f_{mi}(x)\sqsubseteq_i f_{ni}(y) \Leftrightarrow f_{mj}(x)\sqsubseteq_j f_{nj}(y)$.

(d) For any cone $\mu:\Delta\rightarrow D$ in **QDom**, $\mu_m=\mu_n\circ f_{mn}$ and $f_{mn}=\mu_n^-\circ\mu_m$.

Proof: (a) follows from Proposition 4.5.10 and (b) is obvious. Using (b) and the fact that f_{ij} is order-preserving when $j\geq i$ we get (c). Finally the first part of (d) is proved by induction using the defining property of a cone. The second part follows from the first by applying μ_n^- to both sides, using that (μ_n,μ_n^-) is a projection pair. □

2.7 Definition Let $\Delta=(D_n,f_n)_{n<\omega}$ be an ω-chain in the category **Fpo**, where the ordering on D_n is denoted by $\sqsubseteq_n$. Then define D_ω by:

$$D_\omega=\{(x_n)_{n<\omega}:\ x_n\in D_n \text{ and } f_n^-(x_{n+1})=x_n \text{ for all } n\}.$$

D_ω is ordered by $\sqsubseteq_\omega$ defined by, for $(x_n)_{n<\omega},(y_n)_{n<\omega}\in D_\omega$:

$$(x_n)_{n<\omega}\sqsubseteq_\omega (y_n)_{n<\omega} \text{ if } x_n\sqsubseteq_n y_n \text{ for all } n.$$

D_ω is called the *inverse limit* of $(D_n,f_n^-)_{n<\omega}$ and we write $D_\omega=\varprojlim D_n$ (cf. Section 8.1).

Next we define $\mu_m:D_m\rightarrow D_\omega$ by

$$\mu_m(x)=(f_{mn}(x))_{n<\omega}.$$

Let π_m be the m'th projection, that is $\pi_m:D_\omega\rightarrow D_m$ is defined by

$$\pi_m((x_n)_{n<\omega})=x_m.$$

We shall show that (μ_m,π_m) is a projection pair for (D_m,D_ω) and also that the cone $\mu:\Delta\rightarrow D_\omega$ is colimiting in **QDom**.

2.8 Lemma Let C be a directed subset of D_ω and let $C_m=\pi_m[C]$. Then C_m is directed in D_m and $\sqcup C=(\sqcup C_m)_{m<\omega}$. In particular, D_ω is a cpo.

Proof: π_m is trivially monotone. The lemma is proved using the same argument as that used in the proof of Lemma 2.2.2. □

2.9 Lemma If $x\in D_\omega$, then $f_{mn}(x_m)\sqsubseteq x_n$.

Proof: If $n\leq m$, then $f_{mn}(x_m)=x_n$, for D_ω is the inverse limit of $(D_n,f_n^-)_{n<\omega}$. If $m<n$, then, by Proposition 2.6 (a), (f_{mn},f_{nm}) is a projection pair for (D_m,D_n). It follows that

$$f_{mn}(x_m) = f_{mn}(f_{nm}(x_n)) \sqsubseteq x_n. \square$$

2.10 Proposition The pair (μ_m, π_m) is a projection pair for (D_m, D_ω).

Proof: To show that μ_m is continuous it suffices to establish monotonicity, since D_m is finite. This in turn follows from the monotonicity of f_{mn}. By Lemma 2.8, π_m is monotone and

$$\pi_m(\sqcup C) = \sqcup C_m = \sqcup \pi_m[C].$$

Thus π_m is continuous. Also, by Lemma 2.9,

$$\mu_m \circ \pi_m((x_n)_{n<\omega}) = \mu_m(x_m) = (f_{mn}(x_m))_{n<\omega} \sqsubseteq (x_n)_{n<\omega}$$

which shows that $\mu_m \circ \pi_m \sqsubseteq id_{D_\omega}$. Further

$$\pi_m \circ \mu_m(x) = \pi_m((f_{mn}(x))_{n<\omega}) = f_{mm}(x) = x.$$

We have thus shown that (μ_m, π_m) is a projection pair for (D_m, D_ω). $\square$

2.11 Proposition If $\Delta = (D_n, f_n)_{n<\omega}$ is an ω-chain in **Fpo**, then $D_\omega \in$ **QDom** and $(D_\omega)_c = \bigcup \{\mu_n[D_n] : n<\omega\}$.

Proof: We verify the conditions in Lemma 1.18 with $C = \bigcup \{\mu_n[D_n] : n<\omega\}$. D_ω is partially ordered since each D_n is. Clearly C is countable, since each D_n is finite. (i) holds, since $(\perp_n)_{n<\omega}$ is the least element of D_ω. (ii) follows from Lemma 2.8. For (iii), if $x = (x_m)_{m<\omega} \in D_\omega$, let

$$A = \{\mu_m(x_m) : m<\omega\} = \{(f_{mn}(x_m))_{n<\omega} : m<\omega\}.$$

Then A is a non-empty subset of C and if $\mu_m(x_m)$, $\mu_n(x_n) \in A$ and $m<n$, then

$$\mu_m(x_m) = \mu_n(f_{mn}(x_m)) \sqsubseteq \mu_n(x_n)$$

by Proposition 2.6 and Lemma 2.9. Hence A is a chain and $\sqcup A \in D_\omega$. Clearly x is an upper bound for A and thus $\sqcup A \sqsubseteq x$. If y is an upper bound for A, then $f_{mm}(x_m) = x_m \sqsubseteq y_m$, for all m, and hence $x \sqsubseteq y$. Thus $x = \sqcup A$.

To show (iv), let $a = \mu_m(b)$, for some m and some $b \in D_m$, and assume that $a \sqsubseteq \sqcup B$, where B is a chain in C. By Lemma 2.8, then $\sqcup B = (\sqcup B_n)_{n<\omega}$. Now $b_n = \sqcup B_n \in B_n$, for B_n is finite. From the definition of μ_m, $a = \mu_m(b) \sqsubseteq (b_n)_{n<\omega}$ entails that $b \sqsubseteq b_m$. Since $b_m \in B_m = \pi_m[B]$, there exists some $x \in B$ for which $x_m = b_m$. Using Lemma 2.9 and the monotonicity of f_{mn}, we get

$$f_{mn}(b) \sqsubseteq f_{mn}(b_m) = f_{mn}(x_m) \sqsubseteq x_n \quad \text{for all } n,$$

which shows that $a = \mu_m(b) = (f_{mn}(b))_{n<\omega} \sqsubseteq x$. Since $x \in B$, (iv) holds. $\square$

Now we give a criterion for when a cone is colimiting. We prove one direction here and leave the converse for later (Theorem 2.14).

2.12 Lemma Let $\mu:\Delta\to D$ be a cone in **QDom**, where $\Delta=(D_n, f_n)_{n<\omega}$ is an ω-chain in **Fpo**. Then μ is a colimiting cone if $D_c=\bigcup\{\mu_n[D_n]: n<\omega\}$.

Proof: Assume the hypothesis of the lemma, and let $\nu:\Delta\to D'$ be any cone. Let $h: D_c\to D'$ be defined by $h(\mu_n(a))=\nu_n(a)$, for $a\in D_n$. Then h is well-defined and order-preserving (see the proof of Lemma 4.2.6). Clearly h is also unique.

Notice that the sequence $(\mu_n \circ \nu_n^-)_{n<\omega}$ is increasing, since, by (d) of Proposition 2.6,

$$\begin{aligned}\mu_n \circ \nu_n^- &= \mu_{n+1} \circ f_n \circ \nu_n^- \\ &= \mu_{n+1} \circ \nu_{n+1}^- \circ \nu_n \circ \nu_n^- \\ &\sqsubseteq \mu_{n+1} \circ \nu_{n+1}^-.\end{aligned}$$

Thus we may define $g: D'\to D$ by

$$g=\bigsqcup\{\mu_n \circ \nu_n^-: n<\omega\}.$$

Then g is continuous, since each μ_n and ν_n^- is. Let $\bar{h}$ be the unique continuous extension of h to D. We have that

$$\begin{aligned}\bar{h} \circ g(x) &= \bar{h}(\bigsqcup\{\mu_n \circ \nu_n^-(x): n<\omega\}) \\ &= \bigsqcup\{h \circ \mu_n \circ \nu_n^-(x): n<\omega\} \\ &= \bigsqcup\{\nu_n \circ \nu_n^-(x): n<\omega\}\sqsubseteq x.\end{aligned}$$

Similarly,

$$\begin{aligned}g \circ h(\mu_m(a)) &= g(\nu_m(a)) \\ &= \bigsqcup\{\mu_n \circ \nu_n^-(\nu_m(a)): m\le n<\omega\} \\ &= \bigsqcup\{\mu_n \circ \nu_n^- \circ \nu_n \circ f_{mn}(a): m\le n<\omega\} \\ &= \bigsqcup\{\mu_n \circ f_{mn}(a): m\le n<\omega\} \\ &= \bigsqcup\{\mu_m(a)\}=\mu_m(a).\end{aligned}$$

Thus $(\bar{h}, g)$ is a projection pair for (D, D'). It follows that $\bar{h}$ is the mediating morphism between μ and ν. □

Now it immediately follows that the cone $\mu:\Delta\to D_\omega$ defined above is a colimiting cone, which proves the following.

2.13 Theorem Every ω-chain in **Fpo** has a direct limit in **QDom**.

Here is the promised converse to Lemma 2.12.

2.14 Theorem Let $\mu:\Delta\to D$ be a cone in **QDom**, where $\Delta=(D_n, f_n)_{n<\omega}$ is an ω-chain in **Fpo**. Then μ is colimiting if and only if $D_c=\bigcup\{\mu_n[D_n]: n<\omega\}$.

Proof: To prove the remaining direction, let $\nu:\Delta\to D_\omega$ be the direct limit obtained in Theorem 2.13. Then ν satisfies the condition in Lemma 2.12, that is, $(D_\omega)_c=\{\nu_n(a): a\in D_n, n<\omega\}$. Let h be the mediating morphism between μ and ν. For $d\in D_c$, we have $h(d)=\nu_n(a)$ for some n and some $a\in D_n$. But $\nu_n(a)=h(\mu_n(a))$ and hence, by the injectivity of h, $d=\mu_n(a)$. □

2.15 Definition Let $\mathbf{F_i}$: **QDom** → **QDom** be defined as follows, for $i=0,1,2$.

(a) $\mathbf{F_i}(D)=\mathcal{F}_i(D)$, for any quasidomain D.

(b) Let $f:D\to E$ be an embedding. For any generating tree (T,ζ) over D, $f\circ\zeta:T\to E$ is a labelling of T over E. Let $\mathbf{F_i}(f):\mathcal{F}_i(D)\to\mathcal{F}_i(E)$ be defined by

$$\mathbf{F_i}(f)([T^\zeta_\omega]_i)=[T^{f\circ\zeta}_\omega]_i,$$

for every $[T^\zeta_\omega]_i\in\mathcal{F}_i(D)$.

Note that for an embedding $f:D\to E$ in **QDom** and for $[S]_i\in\mathcal{F}_i(D)$, we have that

$$\mathbf{F_i}(f)([S]_i)=[\{f(x):\ x\in S\}]_i=[f[S]]_i.$$

For any quasidomain C and any generating tree (T,ζ) over C, let $\overline{(T,\zeta)}$ denote the labelled tree extended with the level T^ζ_ω. If (T,ζ) is a generating tree over D, let $D'=\overline{(T,\zeta)}$ and let $E'=\overline{(T,f\circ\zeta)}$. It follows from the above equation that if $f^-:E\to D$ is the projection corresponding to f, then $(f|_{D'},f^-|_{E'})$ is an isomorphism pair for (D',E').

We show that $\mathbf{F_i}(f)$ is an embedding with the corresponding projection $\mathbf{F_i}(f)^-:\mathcal{F}_i(E)\to\mathcal{F}_i(D)$ defined by

$$\mathbf{F_i}(f)^-([T^\zeta_\omega]_i)=[T^{f^-\circ\zeta}_\omega]_i,$$

for every $[T^\zeta_\omega]_i\in\mathcal{F}_i(E)$.

To show that $\mathbf{F_i}(f)$ is monotone, assume that $[S]_i\sqsubseteq_i[S']_i$ in $\mathcal{F}_i(D)$. To establish that $\mathbf{F_i}(f)([S]_i)\sqsubseteq_i\mathbf{F_i}(f)([S']_i)$ in $\mathcal{F}_i(E)$, it is sufficient to show that for every $B\in\mathcal{M}(E)$, if $B\sqsubseteq_i f[S]$, then $B\sqsubseteq_i f[S']$. This in turn follows from the assumption using the above-mentioned isomorphism.

To establish the continuity of $\mathbf{F_i}(f)$, let $[S]_i$ be an element of $\mathcal{F}_i(D)$ and let $[B]_i\in\text{approx}(\mathbf{F_i}(f)([S]_i))$. By Proposition 3.1.7, it suffices to show that there is some $[A]_i\in\text{approx}([S]_i)$ such that $[B]_i\sqsubseteq_i\mathbf{F_i}(f)([A]_i)$. By Theorem 1.19, we may assume that $B\in\mathcal{M}(E)$. By the isomorphism, for $A=f^-[B]$, the above condition is satisfied.

The proof that $\mathbf{F_i}(f)^-$ is continuous is similar.

By computation,

$$\mathbf{F_i}(f) \circ \mathbf{F_i}(f)^{-}([S]_i) = [\{f \circ f^{-}(x):\ x \in S\}]_i$$
$$\sqsubseteq_i [\{x:\ x \in S\}]_i = [S]_i.$$

Similarly,

$$\mathbf{F_i}(f)^{-} \circ \mathbf{F_i}(f)([S]_i) = [\{f^{-} \circ f(x):\ x \in S\}]_i$$
$$= [\{x:\ x \in S\}]_i = [S]_i.$$

We have thus shown that $(\mathbf{F_i}(f), \mathbf{F_i}(f)^{-})$ is a projection pair for $(\mathcal{F}_i(D), \mathcal{F}_i(E))$. It follows that $\mathbf{F_i}$ is a well-defined functor on **QDom**.

In particular the restriction of $\mathbf{F_i}$ to **Fpo** is a functor on **Fpo**. Hence any ω-chain Δ in **Fpo** is mapped by $\mathbf{F_i}$ to an ω-chain of power domains in **Fpo**. Also, by Proposition 4.3.1, any cone $\mu:\Delta \to D$ in **QDom** is mapped by $\mathbf{F_i}$ to a cone of power domains in **QDom**. Analogously to the results in Sections 4.2 and 4.3, we establish that $\mathbf{F_i}$ preserves direct limits of ω-chains in **Fpo**.

2.16 Theorem If $\Delta = (D_n, f_n)_{n<\omega}$ is an ω-chain in **Fpo** and $D = \varinjlim \Delta$, then $\mathbf{F_i}(D) = \varinjlim \mathbf{F_i}(\Delta)$.

Proof: Let $\mu:\Delta \to D$ be a colimiting cone in **QDom**. In view of Theorem 2.14 we need to show that

$$\mathbf{F_i}(D)_c \subseteq \bigcup \{\mathbf{F_i}(\mu_n)[\mathbf{F_i}(D_n)]:\ n<\omega\},$$

the reverse inclusion being trivial. Let $[A]_i \in \mathbf{F_i}(D)_c$. By Theorem 1.19, then $A \equiv_i B$ for some $B \in \mathcal{M}(D)$, and thus B is a finite non-empty subset of

$$D_c = \bigcup \{\mu_n[D_n]:\ n<\omega\}.$$

Let $B_n' = \{a \in D_n:\ \mu_n(a) \in B\}$, for $n<\omega$. If B contains an element $\mu_m(b)$ where $m<n$ and $b \in D_m$, then

$$\mu_m(b) = \mu_n(f_{mn}(b))$$

by Proposition 2.6. Since B is finite, it follows that $B = \mu_n[B_n']$ for some n. Since B_n' is a finite non-empty subset of D_n, $B_n' \in \mathcal{M}(D_n)$ and $[B_n']_i \in \mathbf{F_i}(D_n)_c$. Then $[A]_i = [B]_i = \mathbf{F_i}(\mu_n)([B_n']_i)$ and thus $[A]_i \in \mathbf{F_i}(\mu_n)[\mathbf{F_i}(D_n)]$. □

From this it follows that SFP-objects are closed under $\mathbf{F_i}$. They are also closed under all the usual operations, such as $+$, $\times$, and $\to$. Thus we can solve SFP-equations involving all the usual operations by the method described in Chapter 4.

The functors $\mathbf{T}_+$ and $\mathbf{T}_\times$ on **QDom** are defined in the same way as the corresponding functors on **Cusl** in Chapter 4.3. (See Definitions 4.3.5 and 4.3.6.)

When defining $T_{\rightarrow}$ we consider the category $\mathbf{Cpo_E}$, having cpo's as objects and embeddings as morphisms, since **QDom** is not closed under exponentiation.

2.17 Exponentiation Let $T_{\rightarrow}$ be defined on $\mathbf{Cpo_E} \times \mathbf{Cpo_E}$ as follows.

(a) $T_{\rightarrow}(D, E) = [D \rightarrow E]$, where $[D \rightarrow E]$ is the function space of D and E.

(b) If $f: D \rightarrow D'$ and $g: E \rightarrow E'$ are embeddings, then $T_{\rightarrow}(f, g)$ is defined by:

$$T_{\rightarrow}(f, g)(h) = g \circ h \circ f^{-},$$

where f^{-} is the projection corresponding to f.

Then $T_{\rightarrow}(f, g): [D \rightarrow E] \rightarrow [D' \rightarrow E']$ is an embedding with the corresponding projection

$$T_{\rightarrow}^{-}(f, g)(h) = g^{-} \circ h \circ f.$$

It follows that $T_{\rightarrow}$ is a functor from $\mathbf{Cpo_E} \times \mathbf{Cpo_E}$ into $\mathbf{Cpo_E}$.

2.18 Theorem If D and E are SFP-objects, then so are $D + E$ and $D \times E$.

Proof: Suppose that D and E are SFP-objects. Then there exist ω-chains $\Delta = (D_n, f_n)_{n<\omega}$ and $\Delta' = (E_n, g_n)_{n<\omega}$ in **Fpo** and colimiting cones $\mu: \Delta \rightarrow D$ and $\nu: \Delta' \rightarrow E$. Let

$$T_+(\Delta, \Delta') = (T_+(D_n, E_n), T_+(f_n, g_n))_{n<\omega}$$

and

$$T_\times(\Delta, \Delta') = (T_\times(D_n, E_n), T_\times(f_n, g_n))_{n<\omega}.$$

Then $T_+(\Delta, \Delta')$ and $T_\times(\Delta, \Delta')$ are ω-chains in **Fpo**.

Let the *separated sum* of μ and ν, $\mu + \nu$, be the cone from $T_+(\Delta, \Delta')$ to $D + E$ with the embeddings given by

$$(\mu + \nu)_n = T_+(\mu_n, \nu_n).$$

Let the *product* of μ and ν, $\mu \times \nu$, be the cone from $T_\times(\Delta, \Delta')$ to $D \times E$ with the embeddings given by

$$(\mu \times \nu)_n = T_\times(\mu_n, \nu_n).$$

Then, by Theorem 2.14, $D_c = \bigcup_{n<\omega} \mu_n[D_n]$ and $E_c = \bigcup_{n<\omega} \nu_n[E_n]$. We omit the proof that $\mu + \nu: T_+(\Delta, \Delta') \rightarrow D + E$ and $\mu \times \nu: T_\times(\Delta, \Delta') \rightarrow D \times E$ are colimiting cones, since it is entirely similar to the proof of the corresponding result in Chapter 4 (see Theorem 4.3.13). It follows that:

$$D + E = \varinjlim T_+(\Delta, \Delta') \text{ and } D \times E = \varinjlim T_\times(\Delta, \Delta'). \qquad \square$$

2.19 Theorem If D and E are SFP-objects, then so is $[D\to E]$.

Proof: Suppose that D and E are SFP-objects. Then there exist ω-chains $\Delta=(D_n,f_n)_{n<\omega}$ and $\Delta'=(E_n,g_n)_{n<\omega}$ in **Fpo** and colimiting cones $\mu:\Delta\to D$ and $\nu:\Delta'\to E$. Let

$$\mathbf{T}_{\to}(\Delta,\Delta')=(\mathbf{T}_{\to}(D_n,E_n),\ \mathbf{T}_{\to}(f_n,g_n))_{n<\omega}.$$

Then $\mathbf{T}_{\to}(\Delta,\Delta')$ is an ω-chain in **Fpo**.

Let the *exponentiation* of μ and ν, $[\mu\to\nu]$, be the cone from $\mathbf{T}_{\to}(\Delta,\Delta')$ to $[D\to E]$ with the embeddings given by

$$[\mu\to\nu]_n=\mathbf{T}_{\to}(\mu_n,\nu_n).$$

We need to show that $[\mu\to\nu]:\mathbf{T}_{\to}(\Delta,\Delta')\to[D\to E]$ is a colimiting cone. Using Lemma 2.12, it suffices to prove that $[D\to E]$ is a quasidomain with the countable set $\bigcup\{\mathbf{T}_{\to}(\mu_n,\nu_n)[\mathbf{T}_{\to}(D_n,E_n)]:n<\omega\}$ as its set of compact elements. We do this by verifying conditions (i)–(iv) of Lemma 1.18.

For ease of notation, we set $F_n=\mathbf{T}_{\to}(f_n,g_n)$ and $\sigma_n=\mathbf{T}_{\to}(\mu_n,\nu_n)$, for $n<\omega$.

(i) Clearly, $[D\to E]$ has $<\perp;\perp>$ as its least element.

(ii) holds since $[D\to E]$ is a cpo.

(iii) Assume that $k\in[D\to E]$ and let

$$A=\{\sigma_n(h):\ h\in[D_n\to E_n],\ \sigma_n(h)\sqsubseteq k,\ n<\omega\}.$$

Clearly $\sigma_n(<\perp;\perp>)=<\perp;\perp>\sqsubseteq k$ and thus $A\neq\emptyset$. To show that A is directed, let $h\in[D_n\to E_n]$ and $h'\in[D_m\to E_m]$ be such that $\sigma_n(h)$, $\sigma_m(h')\sqsubseteq k$, and assume that $n\leq m$. Note that $\sigma_m(\sigma_m^-(k))\sqsubseteq k$ and hence $\sigma_m(\sigma_m^-(k))\in A$. But clearly,

$$\sigma_n(h)=\sigma_m(F_{nm}(h))=\sigma_m(\sigma_m^-(\sigma_n(h)))\sqsubseteq\sigma_m(\sigma_m^-(k)),\ \text{and}$$
$$\sigma_m(h')\sqsubseteq\sigma_m(\sigma_m^-(k))$$

proving that A is directed. By Lemma 1.17, A can then be replaced by an ω-subchain having the same supremum.

It thus remains to show that $k=\bigsqcup A$. For the non-trivial direction $k\sqsubseteq\bigsqcup A$, fix $x\in D$ and let $b\in\text{approx}(k(x))$. It suffices to find $a\in\text{approx}(x)$ such that $b\sqsubseteq(\bigsqcup A)(a)$.

By the continuity of k there is $a\in\text{approx}(x)$ for which $b\sqsubseteq k(a)$. Choose m and $a''\in D_m$ such that $\mu_m(a'')=a$. Then choose $n\geq m$ and $b'\in E_n$ such that $\nu_n(b')=b$ and let $a'=f_{mn}(a'')$. Consider the function $<a';b'>\in[D_n\to E_n]$. An easy calculation shows that

$$\sigma_n(<a'; b'>) = <a; b>$$

where the crucial observation is that

$$a \sqsubseteq \mu_n(\mu_n^-(y)) \Leftrightarrow a \sqsubseteq y$$

for each $y \in D$. But

$$<a; b>(a) = b \sqsubseteq k(a)$$

and hence $<a; b> \in A$ by Lemma 3.3.2, so $b \sqsubseteq (\bigsqcup A)(a)$.

(iv) Now let k be an element of $\bigcup\{\sigma_n[T_{\rightarrow}(D_n, E_n)] : n < \omega\}$ and suppose that $k \sqsubseteq \bigsqcup\{k_m : m < \omega\}$, where $(k_m)_{m<\omega}$ is a chain in $[D \rightarrow E]$. Choose n and $k' \in [D_n \rightarrow E_n]$ such that $\sigma_n(k') = k$. Thus

$$\begin{aligned} k' = \sigma_n^-(k) &\sqsubseteq \sigma_n^-(\bigsqcup\{k_m : m < \omega\}) \\ &= \bigsqcup\{\sigma_n^-(k_m) : m < \omega\}. \end{aligned}$$

But k' is compact, since $[D_n \rightarrow E_n]$ is finite, so there is some m such that $k' \sqsubseteq \sigma_n^-(k_m)$. But then

$$k = \sigma_n(k') \sqsubseteq \sigma_n(\sigma_n^-(k_m)) \sqsubseteq k_m$$

which proves (iv). □

Section 11.3 An Alternative Definition of SFP-objects

In this section, we give an alternative definition of SFP-objects, a definition that is more analogous to that of a Scott–Ershov domain. Then we show the equivalence between the two definitions.

3.1 Definition Let $D = (D; \sqsubseteq, \perp)$ be a cpo and let $A \subseteq D$. An element $x \in D$ is a *minimal upper bound* (*mub*) for A if
(i) x is an upper bound for A and
(ii) x is not strictly greater than any other upper bound for A.

For $A \subseteq D$, we denote the set of upper bounds of A in D by $UB_D(A)$ and the set of minimal upper bounds of A in D by $MUB_D(A)$.

For $A \subseteq D$, we successively throw in the minimal upper bounds of its finite subsets using the following recursive definition:

$$U_D^0(A) = A$$

$$U_D^{n+1}(A) = \bigcup\{MUB_D(B) : B \text{ is a finite subset of } U_D^n(A)\}.$$

Then we collect the minimal upper bounds thus obtained as follows.

$$U_D^*(A) = \bigcup \{U_D^n(A) : n < \omega\}.$$

As usual we omit the subscript D when this can be done without ambiguity. Now we have all the concepts needed to define sfp-domains, where we replace the requirement of bounded completeness for domains by the following weaker requirement.

3.2 Definition D is an *sfp-domain* if D is a quasidomain that satisfies the following. For every finite subset A of D_c,

(i) MUB(A) is *complete*, that is, every upper bound of A is above some element of MUB(A), and

(ii) $U^*(A)$ is finite.

It follows that, for any finite set A of compact elements of an sfp-domain D, MUB(A) is finite. Below we establish that D_c is closed under mub's of finite subsets and that U^* is monotone and closed under minimal upper bounds.

3.3 Lemma Let $D = (D; \sqsubseteq, \bot)$ be a quasidomain and let $A, B \subseteq D$.

(a) If x is a mub of a finite subset A of D_c, then $x \in D_c$.

(b) $A \subseteq B \Rightarrow U^*(A) \subseteq U^*(B)$.

(c) If $B \subseteq U^*(A)$ and B is finite, then $MUB(B) \subseteq U^*(A)$.

Proof: (a) Let x be a mub of a finite subset A of D_c and let

$$B = \{a \in D_c : a \sqsubseteq x\}.$$

Since A is a finite subset of the directed set B, A has an upper bound $y \in B$. Then $y \sqsubseteq x$ and hence $x = y$, since x is minimal.

(b) is obvious.

(c) If B is a finite subset of $U^*(A)$, then $B \subseteq U^n(A)$, for some n. Hence $MUB(B) \subseteq U^{n+1}(A) \subseteq U^*(A)$. □

Before proving our main result, we need the following general observation that an embedding commutes with the operation of forming the set of minimal upper bounds.

3.4 Lemma Let $D = (D; \sqsubseteq)$ and $E = (E; \sqsubseteq)$ be partial orderings and suppose that $\mu : D \to E$ and $\pi : E \to D$ are monotone functions such that $\mu \circ \pi \sqsubseteq id_E$ and $\pi \circ \mu = id_D$. Then, for $A \subseteq D$,

(a) $MUB_E(\mu[A]) = \mu[MUB_D(A)]$, and

(b) $MUB_E(\mu[A])$ is complete if and only if $MUB_D(A)$ is complete.

Proof: (a) Assume that x is a mub of $\mu[A]$ in E. Then, by monotonicity, $\pi(x)$ is an upper bound of $\pi \circ \mu[A]=A$ in D. To show that $\pi(x)$ is a mub of A, suppose that $a \sqsubseteq \pi(x)$ is an upper bound of A. Then $\mu(a)$ is an upper bound of $\mu[A]$ and $\mu(a) \sqsubseteq \mu(\pi(x)) \sqsubseteq x$. By the minimality of x, we have that equality must hold, and hence $a=\pi(\mu(a))=\pi(x)$. It follows that $\pi(x)$ is a mub of A in D and that $x \in \mu[MUB_D(A)]$.

Conversely, assume that $x \in \mu[MUB_D(A)]$ and let $a \in MUB_D(A)$ be such that $x=\mu(a)$. Clearly, by monotonicity, x is an upper bound of $\mu[A]$. Suppose y is an upper bound of $\mu[A]$ and $y \sqsubseteq x$. Then $\pi(y)$ is an upper bound of A and $\pi(y) \sqsubseteq \pi(x) = a$. By the minimality of a, equality must hold. It follows that $x=y$, that is, $x \in MUB_E(\mu[A])$.
(b) It follows from the proof of (a) that $\pi[MUB_E(\mu[A])]=MUB_D(A)$. Hence it is easily verified that $MUB_E(\mu[A])$ is complete if and only if $MUB_D(A)$ is complete. □

3.5 Theorem D is an sfp-domain if and only if D is an SFP-object.

Proof: Let D be an sfp-domain and let $(a_n)_{n<\omega}$ be an enumeration of D_c. Further, let $A_n=\{a_0, a_1, \ldots, a_n\}$ and let

$$D_n=U^*(A_n),$$

for $n<\omega$. D_n is finite, since D is an sfp-domain. By Lemma 3.3 (a), $D_n \subseteq D_c$.

Each D_n is thus a finite cpo and $D_n \subseteq D_{n+1}$, by Lemma 3.3 (b). For each n, define a projection pair (f_n, f_n^-) for (D_n, D_{n+1}) as follows. Let $f_n: D_n \to D_{n+1}$ be the inclusion mapping and let $f_n^-: D_{n+1} \to D_n$ be defined by:

$$f_n^-(a)=\bigsqcup\{b \in D_n:\ b \sqsubseteq a\}.$$

To show that f_n^- is well-defined, note that $a \in D_{n+1}$ is an upper bound of the finite set $A=\{b \in D_n:\ b \sqsubseteq a\}$. Since $MUB(A)$ is complete, then there is some $a' \in MUB(A)$ such that $a' \sqsubseteq a$. By Lemma 3.3 (c), $MUB(A) \subseteq U^*(A_n)=D_n$, and thus $a' \in D_n$. It follows that A is directed and hence has a supremum in D_n. Thus f_n^- is well-defined and $f_n^-(a) \sqsubseteq a$. Clearly f_n^- is monotone, hence continuous. It follows that (f_n, f_n^-) is a projection pair for each n.

Let $\Delta=(D_n, f_n)_{n<\omega}$. Then Δ is an ω-chain in **Fpo**. Let $\mu:\Delta \to D$ be the cone defined by letting $\mu_n: D_n \to D$ be the inclusion mapping. By definition and Lemma 3.3 (a), $D_c=\bigcup\{D_n:\ n<\omega\}$. Hence, by Theorem 2.14, μ is a colimiting cone with direct limit D. So D is an SFP-object.

To establish the converse, let D be an SFP-object. Then there exist an ω-chain $\Delta=(D_n, f_n)_{n<\omega}$ in **Fpo** and a colimiting cone $\mu:\Delta \to D$ in **QDom** with direct limit D. Since D is a quasidomain, we need only show that D satisfies conditions (i)–(ii) in Definition 3.2. Clearly each D_n satisfies these conditions.

By Theorem 2.14, $D_c = \bigcup\{\mu_n[D_n] : n < \omega\}$. It follows that any finite subset B of D_c is of the form $\mu_n[A]$, for some n and some $A \subseteq D_n$. Thus it is sufficient to show that $MUB_D(\mu_n[A])$ is complete and that $U^*(\mu_n[A])$ is finite, for any finite $A \subseteq D_n$. The fact that $MUB_D(\mu_n[A])$ is complete follows from $MUB_{D_n}(A)$ being complete by Lemma 3.4 (b). To show that $U_D{}^*(\mu_n[A])$ is finite, it suffices to show that $MUB_D(\mu_n[B]) \subseteq \mu_n[D_n]$ for each $B \subseteq D_n$. But this is immediate from Lemma 3.4 (a). □

In particular, it follows that the class of SFP-objects extends the class of countably based domains.

3.6 Corollary Every countably based domain is an SFP-object. □

Finally we mention, without proof, a nice characterization of **SFP**, due to Smyth [1983].

3.7 Theorem **SFP** is the largest full subcategory of **QDom** that is cartesian closed.

The problem of studying cartesian closed subcategories of the category of algebraic cpo's, that is, when the condition of being countably based is dropped, has been considered by Jung [1989].

11.4 Exercises

1. Show that if D is a finite partial order, then $\mathcal{M}(D) = \mathcal{F}(D) = \wp(D) - \{\varnothing\}$.

2. Show that given any finitely branching ω-tree, it is possible to prune it to obtain an ω-tree where all maximal branches are ω-branches.

3. Show that if $P = (P; \sqsubseteq)$ is a preordered set and C is a countable subset of P, then P with C satisfies the conditions (i)–(iv) of Lemma 1.18 if and only if $P/\!\equiv$ with $C/\!\equiv$ does, where, for $a, b \in P$: $a \equiv b \Leftrightarrow a \sqsubseteq b$ and $b \sqsubseteq a$.

4. (a) Show that if D is a quasidomain, then $\mathcal{F}_1(D)$ is a domain.
(b) Show that if D is an SFP-object, then $\mathcal{F}_0(D)$ is a domain.
(c) Give an example of a quasidomain D for which $\mathcal{F}_0(D)$ is not a domain.

5. Let A, B, C and D be as in Example 2.2. Show that $[A]_0 \sqcup [B]_0 = [C \cup D]_0$.

6. Let T be the tree in Example 1.1 and let T' be the following tree:

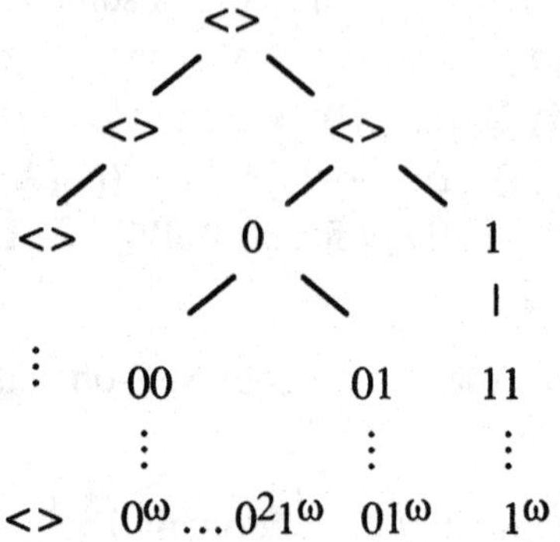

Show that $T_\omega \equiv_2 T'_\omega$.
This example shows that the two apparently distinct underlying programs cannot be distinguished even by the relation $\sqsubseteq_2$.

7. (a) Describe $\mathcal{F}(\mathbb{N}_\perp)$.
(b) Describe $\mathcal{F}(D)$ for the lazy domain D of natural numbers:

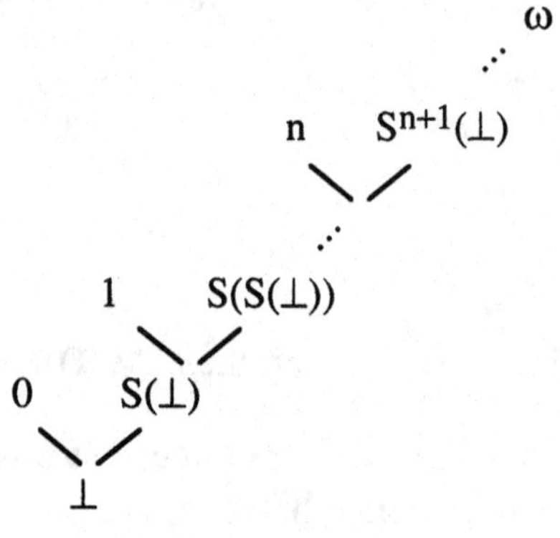

8. Let D be the following domain (cusl):

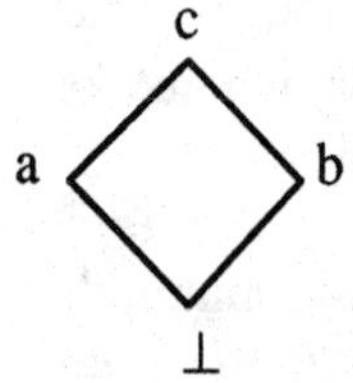

Determine $\mathcal{F}_i(D)$ for $i = 0, 1, 2$.

9. Let D be a quasidomain. For $A \subseteq D$, define

$$\mathrm{Con}(A) = \{y \in D : (\exists x, z \in A)(x \sqsubseteq y \sqsubseteq z)\}.$$

(a) Show that $A \equiv_2 \mathrm{Con}(A)$, for $A \subseteq D$.
(b) Show that for $A, B \subseteq D$ we have:

$$A \equiv_2 B \Leftrightarrow \mathrm{Con}(A) = \mathrm{Con}(B).$$

(c) Show that if D is finite, then

$$\mathcal{F}_2(D) \cong \{\mathrm{Con}(A) : A \subseteq D \text{ and } A \neq \varnothing\},$$

where the set on the right is ordered by inclusion.

10. Show that $\mathbf{F_i}$ is a functor on **QDom** and that the restriction of $\mathbf{F_i}$ to **Fpo** is a functor on **Fpo**.

11. Construct the inverse limit D_ω of $\Delta = (D_n, \iota_n)_{n<\omega}$ defined in Example 2.4 (2). Show that $D_\omega = \{\mu_n(n) : n < \omega\} \cup \{(0, 1, \ldots, n, \ldots)\}$, where μ_n is as defined in the text. This shows that $\omega + 1$ is isomorphic to D_ω.

12. Consider the following three conditions on an algebraic cpo D.
(i) D is countably based.
(ii) For every finite subset A of D_c, $\mathrm{MUB}(A)$ is complete.
(iii) For every finite subset A of D_c, $U^*(A)$ is finite.
Find algebraic cpo's D and E satisfying two of the conditions but not all three for which the function space $[D \to E]$ is *not* an algebraic cpo satisfying the same two conditions.

There are three cases to consider, one for each one of the conditions. This exercise illustrates that no two of the conditions suffice to get a cartesian closed category.

CHAPTER 12

DOMAINS AS MODELS OF FORMAL THEORIES

The λ-calculus was originally introduced as a tool for the study of functionality and higher order logic. Later it was shown that the number-theoretic functions representable in the λ-calculus were precisely those represented in radically different approaches to the notion of computability such as Turing machines or the schemes defining the partial recursive functions we have seen previously. Thus as a tool for studying computability, the λ-calculus is completely general. It also inspired early work on the programming language LISP and can itself be viewed as a high level programming language. Though entirely too cumbersome for everyday programming needs there are well known methods for representing programs, written in standard imperative programming languages like FORTRAN, as λ-terms (see Tennant [1981]). One reason for doing so is in order to understand these programs as functions in the standard mathematical sense of the word. Once these terms are then modelled or interpreted in a mathematical structure like a Scott–Ershov domain one can claim to have understood them in terms of the functions they are names for or denote, hence the terminology *denotational semantics*. Although the study of the denotational semantics for programming languages falls outside the scope of this book, we will summarize in this chapter the results showing that the λ-calculus itself can be modelled using domains. In doing so we hope that we will have provided at least the basic material needed to make the transition from the mathematical theory of domains to the topic of program semantics.

We begin this chapter with a brief survey of the λ-calculus. Here we review only those notions and results which are necessary for an understanding of the discussions of models of the λ-calculus that follow. This comprises the first section. In the second we present the definition of a model of the λ-calculus. Most results on the λ-calculus are presented without proof (or only a brief sketch). The interested reader is directed to the texts by Barendregt [1984] and Hindley and Seldin [1986] for a detailed presentation. Domain theoretic models of the λ-calculus are discussed in Section 3. In Section 4 we introduce the *simply typed λ-calculus* and give an interpretation of its types as domains and its terms as elements of domains. This is achieved using the constructions of product and function space on domains introduced in Chapter 3. In the final section of this chapter we introduce *parametrizations* or continuous families of domains indexed by a domain and give two infinitary operations of *disjoint sum* and *product* which have been used to interpret the terms and types of various *constructive* logics with bounded existential and universal quantifiers.

Section 12.1 The λ-calculus

The λ-calculus is the result of work in two areas: combinatory logic (due to Schönfinkel and Curry) and the λI-calculus (due to Church). Both are studies of (i) a term language and its substitution operator and (ii) an equivalence relation between terms. The fundamental operations in the λ-calculus are *application* and *abstraction* on terms built formally from symbols for variables:

$$(ab) \quad (\text{or } \mathrm{App}(a, b)) \quad \text{and} \quad (\lambda x.a),$$

where a and b are similarly constructed terms and x is a variable.

The relation of equality between λ-terms is given in terms of axioms and rules for an equivalence relation which, in addition, is a congruence with respect to the above two operations. In addition, and most importantly, we have an axiom scheme known as *β-conversion.* The latter is the paradigm of what are called *rewrite rules* in the theory of functional programming languages.

We assume that we have an infinite list of variable symbols $x_0, x_1, x_2, \ldots$. The symbols x, y, and z will be used as syntactic variables for elements of this list.

1.1 Definition The set of *lambda terms*, denoted Λ, is given inductively by
(i) $x \in \Lambda$, for all variables x;
(ii) if $M \in \Lambda$ and x is a variable, then $(\lambda x.M) \in \Lambda$;
(iii) if $M, N \in \Lambda$, then $(MN) \in \Lambda$.

Uppercase roman letters will be used as syntactic variables over the collection of λ-terms. We use boldface variable symbols $\mathbf{x}$ to denote a string of variables $x_1, \ldots, x_n$ and write $\lambda\mathbf{x}.M$ instead of $(\lambda x_1.(\lambda x_2.(\ldots(\lambda x_n.M)\ldots)))$. When parentheses are omitted here we use the notational convention that association is to the right. Boldface uppercase letters $\mathbf{N}$ are used to denote a string of λ-terms $N_1, \ldots, N_n$, and we write $M\mathbf{N}$ instead of $(\ldots((MN_1)N_2)\ldots N_n)$ for a given a λ-term M. When parentheses are omitted here the convention is association to the left. In terms like $\lambda xy.xx$ where the parentheses for both application and abstraction are omitted, the convention is that those for application take precedence over those for abstraction. This term is then shorthand for $(\lambda x.(\lambda y.(xx)))$.

Some examples of λ-terms are $\lambda x.x$, $\lambda x.xx$ and $\lambda xy.x$. The intended interpretations of these three examples are the *identity function, application of an operation to itself* and the *projection of a pair of inputs in its first coordinate.* Two further examples which directly relate to the topic of this text are the *fixed point* terms $\lambda x.(\lambda y.x(yy))(\lambda y.x(yy))$ and $(\lambda zx.x(zzx))(\lambda zx.x(zzx))$ which are commonly associated with the names Curry and Turing, respectively. The reason for calling them such will become clearer when we have seen the axioms for the equality relation between λ-terms.

A *subterm* of a term M is a substring which is a lambda term. An occurrence of a variable x in a λ-term M is said to be *bound* if that occurrence is in a subterm of M of the form $\lambda x.N$, otherwise it is *free.* The set of *free variables of a λ-term* M, denoted FV(M), is the collection of variables which have free occurrences in M.

One of the central purposes of the *λ-calculus* is to provide a formal tool for the study of functions and their evaluation at arguments, that is, a theory of functionality. The operations of abstraction and application can be seen as formalizing components of the standard mathematical treatment of, for example, polynomial functions. There, no formal symbol like λ of the λ-calculus is introduced. But one distinguishes between a real *polynomial* in one variable $a_n x^n + a_{n-1} x^{n-1} + ... + a_1 + a_0$ and the *polynomial function* taking a real number α to the evaluation of that polynomial at α, $a_n \alpha^n + a_{n-1} \alpha^{n-1} + ... + a_1 \alpha + a_0$. Two things can be learned from this example from mathematical practice. The first of these is that there are a multitude of *polynomial expressions* which are normally regarded as the same polynomial, for example, $a_n x^n + a_{n-1} x^{n-1} + ... + a_1 + a_0$ and $a_0 + a_1 x + ... + a_{n-1} x^{n-1} + a_n x^n$. In fact there is a simple set of rules which can be used to decide whether two polynomial expressions are the same polynomial. Secondly the intuition used in viewing a polynomial as a function is simple, namely, substitute a proposed argument for the function for all occurrences of the variable (and compute according to the laws governing addition and multiplication). By the first observation, there are many polynomial expressions which give rise to one and the same polynomial function. What is more, the rules for identifying these expressions as polynomials are intended to reflect that identification.

As defined earlier, the set of lambda terms is a set of syntactic expressions without any additional structure. Abstraction and application are two operations on λ-terms, the first unary and the second binary, which can be applied to arbitrary λ-terms yielding new ones. The distinction between function and functional expression or form is made explicit through the use of λ-abstraction. What remains then is to explain appropriate grounds for identifying two λ-terms in a way compatible with their behaviour as functions, that is, to formalize the process of substitution and evaluation. The presence of the abstraction operator complicates somewhat the explanation of substitution and hence of evaluation. Symbols for variables x play two distinct roles, one as *place holders*, like the case of polynomials, and the other as a component of the abstraction operation or the operation of building names for functions. The former correspond precisely to the free occurrences of x. Accordingly we define the operation of substituting a λ-term N for a variable x in another λ-term M, denoted by M[N/x], as the result of replacing all *free* occurrences of x in M by N. Then we formalize the intuition behind the evaluation of a function by identifying the application of a function to an argument $((\lambda x.M)N)$ with M[N/x]. This identification is usually written as $((\lambda x.M)N)=M[N/x]$ and is called the *convertibility* or *conversion* relation between λ-terms.

There is, however, an additional difficulty here as the following example illustrates. Consider the λ-term $((\lambda y.(\lambda x.y))x)$. By the above this is convertible with $(\lambda x.y)[x/y]$ which, by the definition of substitution is the same as $\lambda x.x$, that is, we have that $((\lambda y.(\lambda x.y))x)=(\lambda x.y)[x/y]=\lambda x.x$. The intention of $(\lambda y.(\lambda x.y))$ is, however, the function which takes an argument and returns the function which is constantly equal to that argument. The latter is intended to represent the identity function, clearly a different function from the former. This situation can be remedied by adding to the above definition of substitution the requirement that no free occurrence of a variable in N becomes bound in M[N/x]. When we write M[N/x] it is assumed that this requirement is satisfied. Finally we include an axiom scheme known as α-*conversion* among the axioms for the convertibility relation. This asserts that two λ-terms which differ only in the names some of their bound variables are convertible.

Having formalized the essential components of functionality and function application mentioned earlier, we introduce a theory λ for deriving instances of the convertibility relation between λ-terms. We use M[N/x] to denote the operation of substitution and we use the usual symbol for equality = to denote the relation of convertibility. $M[N_1,\dots,N_n/x_1,\dots,x_n]$ will denote the result of *simultaneously* substituting N_i for x_i in M, for $i=1,\dots,n$, with a requirement on the binding of free occurrences of variables analogous to that for M[N/x].

1.2 Definition The equational theory consisting of the following axioms and rules is called the *theory* λ. Its formulae have the form $M = N$, where $M,N \in \Lambda$. The theory λ consists of the following axioms

(λ0) $(\lambda x.M)=\lambda y.(M[y/x])$, if $y \notin FV(M)$ (α-conversion)

(λ1) $((\lambda x.M)N)=M[N/x]$ (β-conversion)

(λ2) $M=M$

(λ3) $M=N \Rightarrow N=M$

(λ4) $M=N, N=L \Rightarrow M=L$
(λ5) $M=N \Rightarrow ML=NL$
(λ6) $M=N \Rightarrow LM=LN$
(λ7) $M=N \Rightarrow \lambda x.M=\lambda x.N$ (ξ-rule).

Recall that an instance of an equation of the form (λ0) or (λ1) is an axiom only if the requirement on the substitution is satisfied.

1.3 Remarks

(1) (λ2)–(λ4) state that convertibility is an equivalence relation. (λ5)–(λ7) state that it is a congruence relation with respect to abstraction and application.
(2) An alternative approach is to study λ-terms under an asymmetric relation of *reduction*, denoted $\underset{\beta}{\Rightarrow}$, which is generated by a *rewrite rule* corresponding to β-conversion (see Exercise 1). This rule states that a term M *reduces* to N, denoted by $M \underset{\beta}{\Rightarrow} N$, if N results from M by replacing an occurrence of a sub-term of the form $((\lambda x.S)T)$ by $S[T/x]$.
(3) The theory λ is sometimes strengthened to include an *η-rule*. It states that if $x \notin FV(M)$, then $\lambda x.Mx=M$. The resulting theory is denoted λη. The η-rule together with the ξ-rule yield what is called an *extensional* theory. From the formula $Mx=Nx$ we derive by the ξ-rule the equation $\lambda x.Mx=\lambda x.Nx$. Then, assuming that x has no free occurrence in either M or N, we derive $M=N$, by the η-rule and the transitivity of convertibility. Hence from the fact that the *graphs* of M and N are the same up to convertibility, that is, $Mx=Nx$ is derivable in λη, it follows that M and N are themselves convertible.
(4) Notice that the term $\lambda x.xx$ has the property that the result of applying it to itself is a λ-term which is convertible with itself. More precisely, by (λ1) we have that $(\lambda x.xx)(\lambda x.xx)=(\lambda x.xx)(\lambda x.xx)$. In terms of the reduction relation mentioned in (2) the term $(\lambda x.xx)(\lambda x.xx)$ produces an infinite sequence of β-reductions all producing the term $(\lambda x.xx)(\lambda x.xx)$.

If $M=N$ is derivable using (λ0)–(λ7), then we write $\lambda \vdash M=N$ and say that M and N are *convertible.* A *combinator* or a *closed* λ-term is a term $M \in \Lambda$ such that $FV(M)=\varnothing$ (in theories containing atoms, to be a combinator also requires that the term in question contains no atoms). We have already seen a number of examples of combinators, e.g. the term $\lambda x.xx$ mentioned above. Others are $\lambda x.(\lambda y.x(yy))(\lambda y.x(yy))$ and $(\lambda zx.x(zzx))(\lambda zx.x(zzx))$, the fixed point combinators of Curry and Turing respectively. The subset of Λ consisting of all combinators is denoted Λ^o. Three additional combinators of special interest are $\mathbf{I} \equiv \lambda x.x$, $\mathbf{K} \equiv \lambda xy.x$ and $\mathbf{S} \equiv \lambda xyz.xz(yz)$, which in λ satisfy, for all terms M, N and L,

$$\mathbf{IM}=\mathrm{M},\ \mathbf{KMN}=\mathrm{M} \text{ and } \mathbf{SMNL}=\mathrm{ML(NL)}.$$

Combinatory Logic

In closing this section we mention the closely related theory of *combinatory logic* or CL. This is a theory of combinatorial terms constructed with the help of constants **k** and **s** related to the λ-terms **K** and **S** above. The terms of CL are then constructed from **k** and **s** together with variables by means of application. Constants and variables are called the atoms of the theory. A *combinator* is a CL-term whose only atoms are **k** and **s**.

CL is also an equational theory and the two most important axioms assert the equalities noted above for **K** and **S**. Because CL does not contain any variable binding operations one completely avoids bound variables, which are the primary difficulty involved in defining the substitution operator in the λ-calculus.

It turns out that the combinators **k** and **s** are *combinatorially complete*. This means that **k** and **s** with the operation of application alone are enough to represent the action of any term. This is usually shown by *defining* λ-abstraction with the help of **k** and **s** roughly as follows. A term λ*x.M is defined by induction on the complexity of M:

$$\begin{aligned}&\lambda^*x.M=\mathbf{k}M, \text{ if } x\notin FV(M)\\&\lambda^*x.x=\mathbf{skk}\\&\lambda^*x.Mx=M, \text{ if } x\notin FV(M) \text{ and}\\&\lambda^*x.MM'=\mathbf{s}(\lambda^*x.M)(\lambda^*x.M'), \text{ if } x\in FV(M) \text{ or } x\in FV(M') \text{ and}\\&\qquad\qquad M'\neq x.\end{aligned}$$

Thus, for every term M(**x**), there is a combinator F such that F**x**=M(**x**) is derivable and, in fact, for all **N** we have a derivation of F**N**=M[**N**/**x**]. The F here can be taken to be the combinator λ***x**.M. The ξ-rule fails in CL as a straightforward example shows (take M=sxyz and N=xz(yz) and compare λ*x.M with λ*x.N). However the η-rule holds by the definition of λ*. Thus there are difficulties in comparing the two theories λ and CL whose solution goes beyond the scope of this text. Nonetheless a familiarity with the basic notions mentioned above will help the reader in understanding the discussion of models for the λ-calculus in the next section.

Section 12.2 Models of the λ-calculus

A primary obstacle to finding a mathematical structure which models the theory λ is the possibility, in λ, of applying any λ-term to itself. Thus we must, at one and the same time, be able to interpret any closed term as an object of such a structure and as an operation on that structure taking elements to elements. However, if a set has more than one element, then the set of all functions from that set to itself cannot possibly be represented uniquely by the elements of that set. The solution then to the problem of finding some subset of the set of all functions on a set which can non-trivially model λ-terms (that is, not interpret all of them as the same object) is due to Scott [1972] and is to restrict oneself to the continuous functions on a domain. It marked the beginnings of domain theory. In this section we present the definition of a model of the λ-calculus. Of the two operations generating λ-terms, the one most easily interpreted as an operation on a structure is application.

2.1 Definition

(i) An *applicative structure* is a pair $A=(A;\cdot)$ where $\cdot$ is a binary operation on the set A. Such an A is said to be *extensional*, if for all $a, b \in A$ we have that $(\forall x \in A)(a\cdot x = b\cdot x) \Rightarrow a=b$. To simplify notation we will write ab instead of $a\cdot b$. We say that A is *combinatorially complete*, if for every function f constructed from variables $x_1, \ldots, x_n$ (varying over A) and A's operation there is $a \in A$ such that

$$(\forall d_1, \ldots, d_n \in A)(ad_1 \ldots d_n = f(d_1, \ldots, d_n)),$$

where $f(d_1, \ldots, d_n)$ denotes the value of f obtained by substituting d_i for x_i in f for $i=1, \ldots, n$.

(ii) A *combinatory algebra* $C=(C;\cdot)$ is an applicative structure with at least two distinct elements **k** and **s** satisfying, for all $a, b, c \in C$, **k**ab = a and **s**abc = ac(bc).

2.2 Proposition An applicative structure $A=(A;\cdot)$ is combinatorially complete if and only if A is a combinatory algebra.

Proof: To obtain elements **k** and **s** in a combinatorially complete A apply combinatorial completeness to the instances of functions f_1 and f_2 given by $f_1(x_1,x_2)=x_1$ and $f_2(x_1,x_2,x_3)=x_1x_3(x_2x_3)$. To show the combinatorial completeness of a combinatory algebra C use induction on the construction of f. For f of the form of a variable x take the element of C to be **skk**. For f of the form f'f" and elements a and b of C already obtained for f' and f", respectively, take the element of C to be **s**ab. □

Any function ρ from the set of variables of the λ-calculus into A will be called an A-*valuation* or simply a *valuation*, if the structure A is clear from the context. Given a valuation ρ, a variable x and some $d \in A$, then $\rho[d/x]$ will denote the valuation which agrees with ρ on all variables $y \neq x$ and takes the value d at x. We begin with the definition of a model of λ which most closely parallels the definition of a model of a first-order theory.

2.3 Definition A *λ-model* (or a *model of* λ) is a triple $L = (L; \cdot, [\![\,]\!])$ where $(L; \cdot)$ is an applicative structure and $[\![\,]\!]$ is a mapping which, to each λ-term M and *valuation* ρ, associates an element $[\![M]\!]_\rho \in L$ in such a way that:

(M1) $[\![x]\!]_\rho = \rho(x)$

(M2) $[\![MN]\!]_\rho = [\![M]\!]_\rho \cdot [\![N]\!]_\rho$

(M3) $[\![\lambda x.M]\!]_\rho \cdot d = [\![M]\!]_{\rho[d/x]}$, for all $d \in L$

(M4) $[\![M]\!]_\rho = [\![M]\!]_\sigma$, if $\rho(x) = \sigma(x)$ for all $x \in FV(M)$

(M5) $[\![\lambda x.M]\!]_\rho = [\![\lambda y.(M[y/x])]\!]_\rho$, if $y \notin FV(M)$ and

(M6) $(\forall d \in L)([\![M]\!]_{\rho[d/x]} = [\![N]\!]_{\rho[d/x]}) \Rightarrow [\![\lambda x.M]\!]_\rho = [\![\lambda x.N]\!]_\rho$.

2.4 Remark The first two clauses follow the inductive definition of λ-terms, while (M3) is intended to capture the nature of λ-abstraction whose character is tied to the substitution operator used in formulating the axiom of β-conversion. (M4) is standard for the treatment of valuations in models of first-order theories, while (M5) and (M6) correspond to the axiom scheme for *α–conversion* and the *ξ-rule*, respectively. Notice that if $(L; \cdot, [\![\ ]\!])$ is a λ-model, then $(L; \cdot)$ is a combinatory algebra, and hence is combinatorially complete (choose $[\![\lambda xy.x]\!]_\rho = \mathbf{k}$ and $[\![\lambda xyz.xz(yz)]\!]_\rho = \mathbf{s}$; see Exercise 2).

2.5 Remark Before continuing we should point our that there is a class of λ-models for which little effort is required to verify their being λ-models. These models for λ, as well as its various extensions, are known as *term models* and are familiar objects to the student of mathematical logic. In the case of the theory λ, the term model is defined as follows. For each term M, define the *equivalence class of* M *in* λ to be $[M]_\lambda = \{N : \lambda \vdash M = N\}$. Then the term model of λ, denoted $A(\lambda) = (A(\lambda); \cdot, [\![\,]\!])$, is defined as follows:

$$A(\lambda) = \{[M]_\lambda : M \text{ is a } \lambda\text{-term}\},$$
$$[M]_\lambda \cdot [N]_\lambda = [MN]_\lambda, \text{ and}$$
$$[\![M]\!]_\rho = [M[N_1/x_1, \ldots, N_n/x_n]]_\lambda,$$

where $x_1, \ldots, x_n$ are the free variables of M and $\rho(x_i) = [N_i]_\lambda$, for $i = 1, \ldots, n$. For M without free variables, it follows that $[\![M]\!]_\rho = [M]_\lambda$. The verification that $A(\lambda)$ is a model of λ is routine (Exercise 3). Since term models are a reflection of syntax, many regard them as *mathematically uninformative*. Nonetheless, the conditions of any *reasonable* definition of a model should be satisfied by the term model.

For $a, b \in A$, where A is an applicative structure, we say that a and b are *extensionally equivalent*, denoted $a \sim b$, if $ac = bc$, for all $c \in A$. The relation $\sim$ is clearly an equivalence relation so let $[a]$ denote the equivalence class of a with respect to $\sim$. We are now in a position to introduce an equivalent definition of λ-model which, in practice, is easier to use. It is formulated in terms of a function Λ on A whose role is, for $a \in A$, to choose a representative of $[a]$.

2.6 Definition A *syntax-free λ-model* is a triple $(A; \cdot, \Lambda)$ such that $(A; \cdot)$ is an applicative structure, $\Lambda : A \longrightarrow A$, and

(i) $(A; \cdot)$ is combinatorially complete,
(ii) $\Lambda(a) \sim a$,
(iii) $a \sim b \Rightarrow \Lambda(a) = \Lambda(b)$,
(iv) $(\exists e \in A)(\forall a \in A)(e \cdot a = \Lambda(a))$.

If $(A; \cdot, \Lambda)$ is a syntax-free λ-model, then $[\![\,]\!]$ can be defined by recursion on λ-terms in terms of Λ by:

(a) $[\![x]\!]_\rho = \rho(x)$,
(b) $[\![MN]\!]_\rho = [\![M]\!]_\rho \cdot [\![N]\!]_\rho$,
(c) $[\![\lambda x.M]\!]_\rho = \Lambda(a)$, where $(\forall b \in A)(a \cdot b = [\![M]\!]_{\rho[b/x]})$.

Clause (c) in this definition states that in order to interpret a term in abstraction form $\lambda x.M$ we use the function Λ to choose an element of the extensional equivalence class of M seen as a function in x. The resulting structure $(A; \cdot, [\![\,]\!])$ is then a λ-model. Conversely, if $(A; \cdot, [\![\,]\!])$ is a λ-model, then $(A; \cdot, \Lambda)$ is a syntax-free λ-model, where Λ can be defined by

$$\Lambda(a) = [\![\lambda x.rx]\!]_{\sigma[a/r]}, \quad \text{for any } \sigma \text{ (see Exercise 4).}$$

2.7 Theorem Using the above definitions of Λ and $[\![\,]\!]$ we have that $(A; \cdot, \Lambda)$ is a syntax-free λ-model if and only if $(A; \cdot, [\![\,]\!])$ is a λ-model.

This theorem justifies our now referring to both of the structures in Definitions 2.3 and 2.6 as λ-models. The latter definition is just a finite set of *first order axioms* and is independent of the syntax of the theory λ. Its only defect is the mention of the function Λ. It can be shown that Λ is *representable* in the combinatory algebra underlying any λ-model. Hence one solution is to replace Λ in the definition by a representative for Λ. This is the tack taken in a further refinement of these definitions known as a *Scott–Meyer λ-model* (the interested reader is referred to Hindley and Seldin [1986]).

2.8 Theorem If $(A;\cdot)$ is an extensional combinatory algebra and we let $\Lambda(a)=a$, then $(A;\cdot,\Lambda)$ is an extensional λ-model. Further, if $(A;\cdot,\Lambda')$ is a λ-model for some Λ', then $\Lambda'=\Lambda$.

In fact the λ-model of the theorem is a model of the extensional theory $\lambda\eta$. If a combinatory algebra is extensional, then Theorem 2.8 gives a method of producing an extensional λ-model. Alternatively, we can use the distinguished elements $\mathbf{k}, \mathbf{s} \in A$ to define $[\![\,]\!]$ on *combinatory terms,* that is, terms built up from variables, the constants **k, s** and application. For general λ-terms, one can simulate λ-abstraction on combinatory terms using **k** and **s** as described at the end of Section 12.1.

Section 12.3 Domain-like λ-models

In this section we discuss a λ-model, denoted by D_∞, which is produced using methods related to those introduced in Chapter 4. It is due to Scott [1972] and was the first non-trivial model of λ. This model was originally intended as a model of a theory of computable functions of higher type.

The essence of Scott's idea can be described as follows. The solution proceeds by constructing the desired domain as the *limit* of a sequence of domains obtained by iterating the function space construction. The elements of this limit should then be infinite sequences $f=(f_0,f_1,f_2,...)$ of functions on the respective iterates. We could then define the application of one such sequence $(f_0,f_1,f_2,...)$ to another $(g_0,g_1,g_2,...)$ by taking it to be the sequence $(f_1(g_0),f_2(g_1),f_3(g_2),...)$. The application of $(f_0,f_1,f_2,...)$ to itself would then make sense and simply be the sequence $(f_1(f_0),f_2(f_1),f_3(f_2),...)$. Although this is the idea behind Scott's solution, this simple definition of application does not suffice to obtain a λ-model.

Recall the construction of an inverse limit described in Section 1 of Chapter 8. D_∞ is also the inverse limit of a projective or inverse system constructed by starting with the flat domain for the natural numbers $\mathbb{N}_\perp$ and iterating the function space construction. Define inductively D_n for each n by

$$D_0=\mathbb{N}_\perp$$
$$D_{n+1}=[D_n\rightarrow D_n].$$

The order relation on D_n will be denoted by $\sqsubseteq_n$ and its least element by $\perp_n$. The sets D_n will be the objects of our *projective system.* The morphisms between these objects are the projections f_n^- in projection pairs (f_n,f_n^-) which are defined as follows. We begin with (f_0,f_0^-) where $f_0:D_0\rightarrow D_1$ and $f_0^-:D_1\rightarrow D_0$ are given by:

$f_0(d) = (\lambda\, x \in D_0)\, d$
$f_0^-(g) = g(\bot_0).$

The notation λ on the right hand side of the definition of f_0 should be read as *that function taking* $d \in D_0$ *to the function on* D_0 *which is constant with value* d. Proceeding inductively we let $f_n : D_n \to D_{n+1}$ and $f_n^- : D_{n+1} \to D_n$, for $n \geq 1$, be given by

$f_n(d) = f_{n-1} \circ d \circ f_{n-1}^-$
$f_n^-(e) = f_{n-1}^- \circ e \circ f_{n-1}$,

where $d \in D_n$ and $e \in D_{n+1}$. That these last two equations hold is equivalent to the assertion that the following diagrams are commutative.

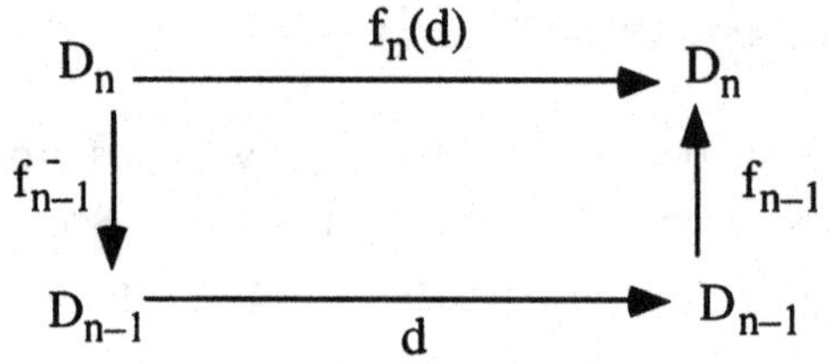

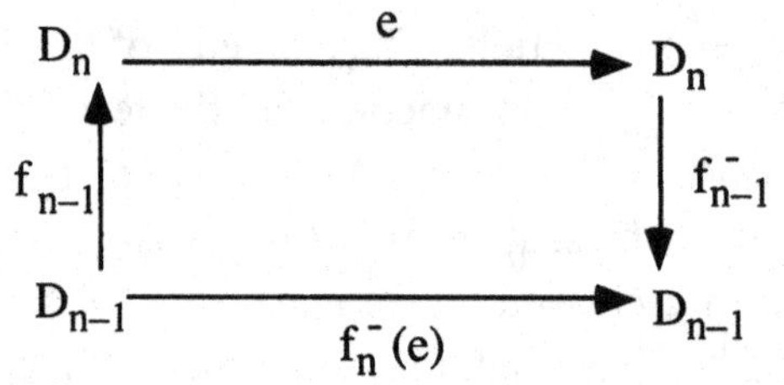

3.1 Proposition For all $n \geq 0$, (f_n, f_n^-) is a projection pair.

Proof: Exercise 7. □

The sequence (f_n, f_n^-) is used as in Chapter 4 to define the morphisms $f_{n,m} : D_n \to D_m$ for all $n, m \in \mathbb{N}$ by letting

$$f_{n,m} = \begin{cases} f_m^- \circ f_{m+1}^- \circ \ldots \circ f_{n-1}^- & \text{when } n > m \\ id_{D_n} & \text{when } n = m \\ f_{m-1} \circ f_{m-2} \circ \ldots \circ f_n & \text{when } n < m. \end{cases}$$

The reader should verify that $f_{n,m} \in [D_n \to D_m]$ and that the pairs $(f_{n,m}, f_{m,n})$, for $n \leq m$, are projection pairs (see Exercise 8).

Now we let $D_\infty = \varprojlim(D_n, f_{n,m})_{n\geq m}$. The elements of D_∞ can be viewed as infinite sequences $d=(d_0,d_1,d_2,\ldots)$ such that $d_n \in D_n$ and $f_n^-(d_{n+1})=d_n$, for all $n\geq 0$. This identification is exploited systematically, for example, when defining application on D_∞. Associated with the limit structure D_∞ is the family of mappings, $f_{\infty,n}: D_\infty \to D_n$, given by

$$f_{\infty,n}(d)=d_n \quad \text{(i.e., the } n^{th} \text{ coordinate of } d).$$

In our special case, we also have mappings $f_{n,\infty}: D_n \to D_\infty$ defined by

$$f_{n,\infty}(a)=(f_{n,0}(a), f_{n,1}(a), f_{n,2}(a), \ldots).$$

The ordering on D_∞ is defined coordinatewise. It follows then that

$$\bot=(\bot_0,\bot_1,\bot_2,\ldots),$$

and, if $X\subseteq D_\infty$ is directed, then each of the X_n is directed and

$$\sqcup X=(\sqcup X_0, \sqcup X_1, \sqcup X_2, \ldots),$$

where $X_n=\{a_n : a\in X\}=\{f_{\infty,n}(a): a\in X\}$. Thus we have

3.2 Proposition $D_\infty=(D_\infty; \sqsubseteq, \bot)$ is a cpo.

The pairs $(f_{n,\infty}, f_{\infty,n})$ are projection pairs, for each $n\in\mathbb{N}$ and, for $d\in D_\infty$, $d=\sqcup_{n\geq 0} f_{n,\infty}(d_n)$. The latter can be used to show that $D_\infty=(D_\infty;\sqsubseteq,\bot)$ is a domain (Exercise 9).

One defines *application on* D_∞, by letting

$$a\cdot b=\sqcup f_{n,\infty}(a_{n+1}(b_n))_{n\geq 0}, \quad \text{for } a,b\in D_\infty.$$

To see that this application gives a value in D_∞, notice that the family $\{f_{n,\infty}(a_{n+1}(b_n)) : n\geq 0\}$ is increasing and hence directed:

$$\begin{aligned}
f_{n,\infty}(a_{n+1}(b_n)) &= f_{n,\infty}((f_{n+1}^-(a_{n+2}))(f_n^-(b_{n+1}))) \\
&= f_{n,\infty}(f_n^- \circ a_{n+2} \circ f_n(f_n^-(b_{n+1}))) \\
&= f_{n,\infty}(f_n^-(a_{n+2}(f_n(f_n^-(b_{n+1}))))) \\
&\sqsubseteq f_{n,\infty}(f_n^-(a_{n+2}(b_{n+1}))) \\
&= f_{n+1,\infty}(a_{n+2}(b_{n+1})).
\end{aligned}$$

Thus D_∞ is an applicative structure. The easiest way of showing that D_∞ is a λ-model, is to show that it is an extensional combinatory algebra. To this end we introduce *stratified* analogues of the combinators **k** and **s**. For $n\geq 2$, we define $\mathbf{k}_n \in D_n$ by

$$\mathbf{k}_n=(\lambda x\in D_{n-1})(\lambda y\in D_{n-2}).f_{n-2}^-(x)$$

and, for $n \geq 3$, we define $s_n \in D_n$ by

$$s_n = (\lambda x \in D_{n-1})(\lambda y \in D_{n-2})(\lambda z \in D_{n-3}).x(f_{n-3}(z))(y(z)).$$

Then we let

$$\mathbf{k} = (\bot_0, Id_{D_0}, k_2, k_3, \ldots) \text{ and } \mathbf{s} = (\bot_0, Id_{D_0}, f_2^-(s_3), s_3, s_4, \ldots).$$

3.3 Proposition Both $\mathbf{k}$ and $\mathbf{s}$ are elements of D_∞ and, on D_∞, we have that $\mathbf{k} \cdot a \cdot b = a$ and $\mathbf{s} \cdot a \cdot b \cdot c = a \cdot c \cdot (b \cdot c)$.

Proof: Exercise 11. □

Thus D_∞ is a combinatory algebra. If we can show that D_∞ is extensional then, by Theorem 2.8, we will have shown that D_∞ is an extensional λ-model.

3.4 Lemma $D_\infty = (D_\infty; \cdot)$ is an extensional combinatory algebra.

Proof: It remains to show that D_∞ is extensional. Suppose that $a \cdot c = b \cdot c$ for all $c \in D_\infty$. We need to show that $a = b$, that is $a_n = b_n$ for each n. For the latter it suffices to consider $n \geq 1$. Suppose that $c \in D_n$. Then $a \cdot f_{n,\infty}(c) = b \cdot f_{n,\infty}(c)$, that is

$$(a_{m+1}(f_{\infty,m}(f_{n,\infty}(c))))_{m\geq 0} = (b_m(f_{\infty,m}(f_{n,\infty}(c))))_{m\geq 0}.$$

In particular

$$a_{n+1}(c) = a_{n+1}(f_{\infty,n}(f_{n,\infty}(c))) = b_{n+1}(f_{\infty,n}(f_{n,\infty}(c))) = b_{n+1}(c).$$

But then $a_{n+1} = b_{n+1}$. □

3.5 Theorem Letting $\Lambda(a) = a$, we have that $(D_\infty; \cdot, \Lambda)$ is an extensional λ-model.

Proof: Apply Theorem 2.8 and Lemma 3.4. □

It is often mentioned in the presentation of the foregoing results that D_∞ is not only the inverse limit of the above mentioned inverse system, but also a *direct* (or *inductive*) *limit* of a directed system based on the same D_n's. In fact, we have already defined embeddings $f_{n,m} : D_n \to D_m$ for $n \leq m$. Thus

$$\Delta = (D_n, f_{n,m})_{n \leq m < \omega}$$

is an ω-chain in the category **Dom**. By Theorem 4.6.7, the ω-chain Δ has a direct limit D_ω in **Dom** with the associated embeddings $f_{n,\omega} : D_n \to D_\omega$. In Exercise 10, the reader is asked to prove that D_∞ and D_ω are isomorphic domains.

Section 12.4 Simply Typed λ-calculus

Another equational theory, closely related to λ, is that of the *simply typed λ-calculus*. The theory of functionality embodied by the λ-calculus is based upon the two complementary operations of abstraction and application. The first takes a term M which may or may not depend on a variable x and produces a term λx.M which is best regarded as a *name* for "that operation which on input x produces output M". The second allows for *unrestricted application* of any term M to any other term N, App(M, N) or, simply, MN. It is the latter which poses an insurmountable obstacle to a *set-theoretic* model of the λ-calculus, that is, a model where the terms are interpreted both as elements of a set and as comprising the set of all functions from that set to itself. The reason is simple, a function $f: S \longrightarrow S$, for example, cannot meaningfully be applied to itself f(f), for this would require that $f \in S$ and hence that the set of functions interpreting the terms of the λ-calculus L have the property that $L \longrightarrow L$ (all functions from L to L) is a subset of L itself. Such a set is forced then to consist of at most one element by an easy cardinality argument. In this case all the terms of the λ-calculus would be interpreted as one and the same object, hardly an interesting model of the theory λ. The previous section presented Scott's solution to this problem.

Along different lines, one may object to the treatment of functionality implicit in the λ-calculus. In everyday mathematical practice the information involved in giving a function consists in part of a rule describing how one computes the function and in part of the *sort* or *type* of its arguments as well as that of its values, e.g., taking the determinant of a square matrix with real number components. These types arise from a number of fixed *fundamental* or *atomic types* (natural numbers, real numbers, etc.) by forming the cartesian product of given types and the type of functions from one type to another. In fact we will specify a simple way of generating the set of *simple type symbols* using for the closure operations symbols reminiscent of those for the cartesian product and function space. These then give the collection of *simple types* once we have specified the atomic types and an interpretation of the closure operation symbols. In the simply typed λ-calculus each term will have a type symbol associated with it, its type, and application will be restricted in such a way that the application MN is well-formed just in case the type symbols associated with M and N are of the appropriate forms (we would in general not consider taking the determinant of anything other than a matrix!). In analogy with Definition 8.4.1 we introduce a simplified version of finite type symbols. For the sake of this discussion we consider only a single atomic type symbol, although, in general, there may be more than one.

4.1 Definition The collection of *simple or finite type symbols*, denoted by Typ, is defined inductively by:

(i) the *atomic* type symbol o is an element of Typ;

(ii) if $\sigma, \tau \in$ Typ, then $(\sigma \rightarrow \tau)$ is an element of Typ.

The symbols generated in the above definition can be interpreted as *mathematical objects* by specifying a set corresponding to o and, given sets corresponding to symbols σ and τ, by specifying the binary operation on them corresponding to the symbol $\rightarrow$. For example, take an arbitrary set to correspond to o and interpret $\sigma \rightarrow \tau$ as the set of all functions from the set interpreting σ to the set interpreting τ.

We let λ^{Typ} denote the *theory of simply typed lambda terms*. For each type symbol σ, we have an infinite collection of *variables of type* σ, denoted by $x^\sigma, y^\sigma, z^\sigma, \ldots$.

4.2 Definition Let $\sigma \in$ Typ and define the *terms of* λ^{Typ} *of type* σ, denoted Λ_σ, by:

(i) each variable of type σ is an element of Λ_σ;

(ii) if $M \in \Lambda_{\sigma\rightarrow\tau}$ and $N \in \Lambda_\sigma$, then $(MN) \in \Lambda_\tau$;

(iii) if $M \in \Lambda_\tau$ and $x^\sigma \in \Lambda_\sigma$, then $(\lambda x^\sigma.M) \in \Lambda_{\sigma\rightarrow\tau}$.

The set of simply typed λ-terms, denoted by Λ^{Typ}, is the union of all Λ_σ over all type symbols σ. The formulae of the theory λ^{Typ} are equations $M=N$ where $M, N \in \Lambda_\sigma$, for some type symbol σ. The set of closed terms of type σ is denoted $\Lambda_{0,\sigma}$. We say that L *has type* σ if $L \in \Lambda_\sigma$. Some examples are $\lambda x^\sigma.x^\sigma \in \Lambda_{\sigma\rightarrow\sigma}$, $\lambda x^{\sigma\rightarrow\tau}.(x^{\sigma\rightarrow\tau}y^\sigma) \in \Lambda_{(\sigma\rightarrow\tau)\rightarrow\tau}$ and $\lambda x^\sigma.\lambda y^\tau.y^\tau \in \Lambda_{\sigma\rightarrow(\tau\rightarrow\tau)}$.

In analogy with the theory λ, the theory λ^{Typ} has as axioms and rules the *typed versions* of the equality axioms and rules as well as *β-conversion* which, for $N \in \Lambda_\sigma$ and $M \in \Lambda_\tau$, takes the form

$$(\lambda x^\sigma.M)N = M[N/x^\sigma], \text{ both elements of } \Lambda_\tau.$$

4.3 Remarks

(1) As with the λ-calculus, it suffices for combinatorial completeness to have the operation of application together with all the closed terms

$$\mathbf{K}_{\sigma\tau} = \lambda x^\sigma.\lambda x^\tau.x^\sigma \text{ of type } \sigma \rightarrow (\tau \rightarrow \sigma) \text{ and}$$

$$\mathbf{S}_{\sigma\tau\mu} = \lambda x^{\sigma\rightarrow(\tau\rightarrow\mu)}.\lambda y^{\sigma\rightarrow\tau}.\lambda z^\sigma.x^{\sigma\rightarrow(\tau\rightarrow\mu)}z^\sigma(y^{\sigma\rightarrow\tau}z^\sigma) \text{ of type}$$
$$(\sigma \rightarrow (\tau \rightarrow \mu)) \rightarrow ((\sigma \rightarrow \tau) \rightarrow (\sigma \rightarrow \mu)),$$

for all type symbols σ, τ and μ.
(2) Just as with λ, provable equations between typed terms can be generated from a notion of reduction.
(3) All $M \in \Lambda^{Typ}$ are strongly normalizable (for a discussion of this result see Gandy [1980] or Girard [1989]), that is, given a typed λ-term M, all chains of reductions starting with M are finite in length. Some consequences are that there are no global *fixed point operators* in λ^{Typ} and that the set of provable equalities in λ^{Typ} is decidable.

We turn now to the question of models for λ^{Typ}. There are two different sorts of things to be interpreted as mathematical objects. On the one hand each type symbol in Typ is to be interpreted as a set and, on the other hand, each term in $\Lambda_{0,\sigma}$ is to be interpreted as an element of the set interpreting σ.

4.4 Definition A *combinatory type structure* is a structure of the form $\mathbf{A} = (\{A_\sigma : \sigma \in Typ\}, \{\cdot_{\sigma\tau} : \sigma,\tau \in Typ\})$ such that A_σ is a set for each $\sigma \in Typ$ with A_0 having more than one element and such that for each $\sigma,\tau \in Typ$, $\cdot_{\sigma\tau} : A_{\sigma\to\tau} \times A_\sigma \to A_\tau$ is a *typed application operator*. Furthermore, for all $\sigma,\tau,\mu \in Typ$, there are $\mathbf{k}_{\sigma\tau} \in A_{\sigma\to(\tau\to\sigma)}$ and $\mathbf{s}_{\sigma\tau\mu} \in A_{(\sigma\to(\tau\to\mu))\to((\sigma\to\tau)\to(\sigma\to\mu))}$ satisfying

$$\mathbf{k}_{\sigma\tau}xy = x \text{ and } \mathbf{s}_{\sigma\tau\mu}xyz = xz(yz).$$

The combinatory type structure $\mathbf{A}$ is said to be *extensional*, if for all M, $N \in A_{\sigma\to\tau}$ we have that:

$$(\forall z \in A_\sigma)(Mz = Nz \Rightarrow M = N).$$

For $M,N \in \Lambda_{0,\sigma}$, the relation $\mathbf{A} \models M = N$ (stating that *the equation* $M = N$ *is true in* $\mathbf{A}$) holds just in case the interpretations of M and N as elements of A_σ are the same. The combinatory completeness of the typed λ-terms corresponding to $\mathbf{k}_{\sigma\tau}$ and $\mathbf{s}_{\sigma\tau\mu}$ has as a consequence that any combinatory type structure yields interpretations of all typed λ-terms.

It turns out to be considerably easier to find models of λ^{Typ} than it is for λ, in particular, there are set-theoretic models.

4.5 Definition If X is any set with more than one element, then the *full type structure over* X is $\mathbf{A}_X = (\{X_\sigma : \sigma \in Typ\}, \{\cdot_{\sigma\tau} : \sigma,\tau \in Typ\})$, where X_σ is defined by the following induction on $\sigma \in T$:

$$X_0 = X$$
$$X_{\sigma\to\tau} = X_\sigma \to X_\tau \quad \text{(i.e., the set of } \textit{all} \text{ functions from } X_\sigma \text{ to } X_\tau\text{)}$$

and, for $f \in X_{\sigma\to\tau}$ and $a \in X_\sigma$, we let $f \cdot_{\sigma\tau} a = f(a)$.

The structure $\mathbf{A}_X$ is clearly an extensional combinatory type structure.

4.6 Remarks

(1) In sharp contrast with structures for interpreting the untyped λ-calculus, any combinatory type structure can be *collapsed* onto an extensional type structure. More precisely, if $\mathbf{A}$ is a combinatory type structure, then (uniformly in $\mathbf{A}$) we can construct an extensional type structure $\mathbf{A}^e$, the *extensional collapse* of $\mathbf{A}$, such that $\mathbf{A} \models M=N$ implies $\mathbf{A}^e \models M=N$. For $x, y \in A_\sigma$, define a relation $=_\sigma$ by induction on σ:

$$x =_o y \text{ if } x = y$$
$$x =_{\sigma\to\tau} y \text{ if } (\forall z, z' \in A_\sigma)(z =_\sigma z' \Rightarrow xz =_\tau yz').$$

Letting $A^e_\sigma = A_\sigma/{=_\sigma}$, we have the desired extensional type structure.

(2) An important example of a combinatory type structure is the collection of *hereditarily recursive operations*, denoted by HRO. For $m, n \in \mathbb{N}$, let $m \cdot n$ denote $\phi_m(n)$ (that is, *the* m'th *partial recursive function applied to* n). Define

$$A_o = \mathbb{N}$$
$$A_{\sigma\to\tau} = \{n \in \mathbb{N} : (\forall m \in A_\sigma)(n \cdot m \text{ is defined and } n \cdot m \in A_\tau)\}.$$

Then $\text{HRO} = (\{A_\sigma\}, \{\cdot_{\sigma\tau}\})$, where $\cdot_{\sigma\tau}$ is $\cdot$ for all $\sigma, \tau \in \text{Typ}$. By using the s-m-n theorem one can show that elements $\mathbf{k}_{\sigma\tau}$ and $\mathbf{s}_{\sigma\tau\mu}$ can be found independently of σ, τ and μ and, therefore, that HRO is a combinatory type structure. Since equality on HRO is the identity relation on natural numbers, it is not an extensional structure. An example of an *extensional* combinatory type structure, known as the *hereditarily effective operations*, is obtained in a similar fashion though we must *hereditarily* identify elements of a given level if their graphs are equal as functions on the previous level. Explicitly, we define simultaneously the levels of the type structure and an equality relation on that level

$$A_o = \mathbb{N}$$
$$A_{\sigma\to\tau} = \{n \in \mathbb{N} : (\forall m, m' \in A_\sigma)(n \cdot m\downarrow \wedge\, n \cdot m \in A_\tau \wedge (m =_\sigma m' \Rightarrow n \cdot m =_\tau n \cdot m'))\}$$

where $x =_o y$ if $m = n$, and $n =_{\sigma\to\tau} n'$ if $(\forall m \in A_\sigma)(n \cdot m =_\tau n' \cdot m)$. Then $\text{HEO} = (\{A_\sigma\}, \{\cdot_{\sigma\tau}\})$, where $\cdot_{\sigma\tau}$ is $\cdot$ for all $\sigma, \tau \in \text{Typ}$. It is known that HRO^e and HEO are distinct, in fact, they are already incomparable for all pure type levels "above" $(((o\to o)\to o)\to o)$ (see Troelstra [1973]).

The type structure of domains $\{D_\sigma : \sigma \in \text{Typ}\}$ over $\mathbb{N}_\perp$, as introduced in Section 8.4, provides a combinatory type structure which is extensional. Recall that

$$D_0 = \mathbb{N}_\perp$$
$$D_{\sigma\to\tau} = [D_\sigma \to D_\tau].$$

We simply take $\cdot_{\sigma\tau}$ to be application. Then we obtain continuous $\mathbf{k}_{\sigma\tau}$ and $\mathbf{s}_{\sigma\tau\mu}$ using the continuity of application and verify that the resulting data give a combinatory type structure and, hence, a model of the simply typed λ-calculus (see Exercise 12).

Section 12.5 Parametrizations

In this last section we briefly consider two additional constructions on domains. Both build on the notion of a continuous family of domains also called a *parametrization*. These constructions were initially introduced in order to interpret type expression constructions in theories of typed λ-terms which extend the simply typed λ-calculus by adding symbols whose intended interpretations are those of possibly *infinite products* and *infinite disjoint unions* of *dependent* families of types. Two examples are the *second-order typed λ-calculus* and Martin-Löf's *intuitionistic theory of types*. The presentation of these theories themselves is beyond the scope of this text. The reader interested in a discussion of them is directed to Girard [1989] for the former and to Martin-Löf [1984] for the latter. For a more detailed presentation of the material in this section we refer to Palmgren and Stoltenberg-Hansen [1992].

These two new constructions on domains are presented here using one of our representations of domains, namely precusl's. The version we consider here will correspond to sums and products of monotone families of precusl's indexed or parametrized by a precusl. Recall from Section 6.4 that $\mathrm{Precusl}_\perp$ denotes the class of precusl's with a fixed symbol $\perp$ for their least element.

5.1 Definition A *parametrization* (of precusl's) is a pair (P, F), where $P \in \mathrm{Precusl}_\perp$ and $F: P \to \mathrm{Precusl}_\perp$ is a monotone function, that is, if $u \sqsubseteq v \in P$ then $F(u) \leq F(v)$.

Given two parametrizations, (P, F) and (Q, G), we let $(P, F) \leq (Q, G)$ if $P \leq Q$ and, for all $u \in P$, $F(u) \leq G(u)$. Let PAR denote the class of all parametrizations and consider the (large) structure $\mathbf{PAR} = (\mathrm{PAR}; \leq, (\{\perp\}, F_\perp))$, where $F_\perp(\{\perp\}) = \{\perp\}$.

5.2 Theorem $\mathbf{PAR}$ is a large cpo.

A *family of types indexed by a type* is interpreted by a parametrization. The key to being able to interpret the disjoint union and general product constructions of these theories is the following constructions on parametrizations which in the formulation here yield precusl's.

Disjoint Unions or Sums

Let (P,F) be a parametrization and define the *disjoint union or sum* $\Sigma(P,F) = (\Sigma(P,F); \sqsubseteq, \sqcup, \bot)$, where

$$\Sigma(P,F) = \{(u,t) : u \in P \text{ and } t \in F(u)\} \cup \{\bot\}$$

and

$$(u,t) \sqsubseteq (u',t') \Leftrightarrow u \sqsubseteq_P u' \text{ and } t \sqsubseteq_{F(u')} t', \text{ and } \bot \sqsubseteq v, \text{ for all } v \in \Sigma(P,F).$$

If (u_0,t_0) and (u_1,t_1) have an upper bound (u,t), then $u_0 \sqcup u_1$ exists in P and $t_0 \sqcup t_1$ exists in $F(u_0 \sqcup u_1)$. Define $(u_0,t_0) \sqcup (u_1,t_1) = (u_0 \sqcup u_1, t_0 \sqcup t_1)$. This provides a designated supremum in $\Sigma(P,F)$. Note that $\bot$ is the distinguished least element in $\Sigma(P,F)$ so $\Sigma(P,F) \in \text{Precusl}_\bot$.

5.3 Theorem If $(P,F) \in \text{PAR}$, then $\Sigma(P,F) \in \text{Precusl}_\bot$.

Products

Let $(P,F) \in \text{PAR}$. A finite subset $A \subseteq_f \{(u,t) : u \in P \text{ and } t \in F(u)\}$ is *consistent* if for each $B \subseteq A$,

$$\pi_0[B] \text{ consistent in } P \Rightarrow \pi_1[B] \text{ consistent in } F(\bigsqcup \pi_0[B]),$$

where π_i are the usual projection functions. Define the *product* of the family (P,F), denoted $\prod(P,F)$, by letting $\prod(P,F) = (\prod(P,F); \sqsubseteq, \sqcup, \bot)$ where

$$\prod(P,F) = \{A \subseteq_f \{(u,t) : u \in P \text{ and } t \in F(u)\} : A \text{ consistent}\} \cup \{\bot\}$$

and where $\sqsubseteq$ is defined as follows. The element $\bot$ will be the distinguished least element. For finite consistent sets $A, B \subseteq_f \{(u,t) : u \in P \text{ and } t \in F(u)\}$ set $A \sqsubseteq B$ if for each $C \subseteq A$, if $\pi_0[C]$ is consistent then

$$\bigsqcup \pi_1[C] \sqsubseteq \bigsqcup \{s : \exists v((v,s) \in B \;\&\; v \sqsubseteq \bigsqcup \pi_0[C])\},$$

where the suprema are taken in $F(\bigsqcup \pi_0[C])$. Clearly the above is well-defined. To see that $\prod(P,F) \in \text{Precusl}_\bot$, we note that if sets A and B are consistent in $\prod(P,F)$ then $A \cup B$ is a supremum. Thus we define $A \sqcup B$ to be $A \cup B$.

5.4 Theorem If $(P,F) \in \text{PAR}$, then $\prod(P,F) \in \text{Precusl}_\bot$.

Continuous families of domains were used first by Girard [1986] and Coquand, Gunter and Winskel [1989] for the sake of modelling dependent types in the second-order or *polymorphic* typed λ-calculus. By introducing the notion of a *continuous functor* from a domain, viewed as a category, to the category **Dom** of domains with projection pairs as morphisms, the constructions of this section can be defined on domains (cf. Palmgren and Stoltenberg-Hansen [1990]; see also Exercise 15). The representations of domains presented in Chapter 6 (in particular information systems) were later used by Palmgren [1993] to give an interpretation of dependent types and *universes* for intuitionistic type theory exploiting the induced representation of continuous families of domains as parametrizations.

12.6 Exercises

1. A *redex* (β-redex) is a λ-term of the form $(\lambda x.M)N$ and its *contractum* is $M[N/x]$. Define a binary relation on λ-terms by letting $M \underset{\beta}{\Rightarrow}^1 N$, if N results from M by replacing some subterm of M which is a redex by its contractum. Let $\underset{\beta}{\Rightarrow}$ denote the reflexive, transitive closure of $\underset{\beta}{\Rightarrow}^1$ and define $M \equiv N$, if there exists L such that $M \underset{\beta}{\Rightarrow} L$ and $N \underset{\beta}{\Rightarrow} L$. A *reduction relation* $\Rightarrow$ is said to be *Church–Rosser*, if for all λ-terms M, N and L: $M \Rightarrow N$ and $M \Rightarrow L$ implies that there exists a λ-term P such that $N \Rightarrow P$ and $L \Rightarrow P$. Assuming that $\underset{\beta}{\Rightarrow}$ is Church–Rosser (which it is), show that $\equiv$ is an equivalence relation on the set of λ-terms.

2. Show that if $(L; \cdot, [\![\ ]\!])$ is a λ-model in the sense of Definition 2.3, then $(L; \cdot)$ is a combinatory algebra.

3. Show that the term model of λ described in Remark 2.5, $A(\lambda) = (A; \cdot, [\![\ ]\!])$, is a λ-model.

4. For $\Lambda(a) = [\![\lambda x.rx]\!]_{\rho[a/r]}$, for any ρ, in a λ-model $A = (A, \cdot, [\![\ ]\!])$, verify the following properties of Λ:
   (i) $\Lambda(a) \sim a$,
   (ii) $\Lambda(a) \sim \Lambda(b) \Rightarrow \Lambda(a) = \Lambda(b)$,
   (iii) $a \sim b \Rightarrow \Lambda(a) = \Lambda(b)$, and
   (iv) $\Lambda(\Lambda(a)) = \Lambda(a)$.

   In addition, show that Λ is represented by the interpretation of the Church numeral $\bar{1}$:

   $$e = [\![\bar{1}]\!] = [\![\lambda xy.xy]\!]_\rho.$$

5. Give a proof of Theorem 2.8.

6. In the notation of Theorem 2.8, show that $(A;\cdot,\Lambda)$ is extensional if and only if A is the image of Λ.

7. Taking (f_n, f_n^-), for $n \geq 0$, as in the construction of D_∞, show that each of the (f_n, f_n^-) is a projection pair.

8. If $f_{n,m} \in [D_n \to D_m]$ are the composite mappings based on the (f_n, f_n^-) as in the previous exercise, show that the pairs $(f_{n,m}, f_{m,n})$ are projection pairs for $n \leq m$.

9. Using the property that, for $d \in D_\infty$, $d = \bigsqcup_{n \geq 0} f_{n,\infty}(f_{\infty,n}(d))$, show that $(D_\infty; \sqsubseteq, \bot)$ is a domain.

10. Let D_∞ and D_ω be the domains defined in Section 12.3. Show that $D_\infty \cong D_\omega$.

11. Show that $\mathbf{k}$ and $\mathbf{s}$ defined immediately preceding Proposition 3.3 are in fact elements of D_∞ and that they satisfy the equalities $\mathbf{k} \cdot a \cdot b = a$ and $\mathbf{s} \cdot a \cdot b \cdot c = a \cdot c \cdot (b \cdot c)$.

12. Define $\mathbf{k}_{\sigma\tau}$ and $\mathbf{s}_{\sigma\tau\mu}$ for the type structure of domains $\{D_\sigma : \sigma \in \mathrm{Typ}\}$ over $\mathbf{N}_\bot$ given at the end of Section 12.4. Verify that the resulting structure is a combinatory type structure and, hence, a model of the simply typed λ-calculus.

13. Show that the ordering $\leq$, defined on PAR by letting $(P,F) \leq (Q,G)$ if $P \leq Q$ and, for all $u \in P$, $F(u) \leq G(u)$, is a partial ordering and that suprema of directed *sets* exist for that ordering. Conclude that PAR is a *large cpo*.

14. Show that the ordering $\sqsubseteq_{\Pi(P,F)}$, defined on $\Pi(P,F)$ in Section 12.5, is a preorder.

15. A functor from a domain D (seen as a category; see Chapter 0) to the category **Dom** which preserves direct limits is said to be *continuous*. Let $F: D \to$ **Dom** be a continuous functor. Define ordered structures $\Sigma(D,F)$ and $\Pi(D,F)$ corresponding to the Σ and Π constructions of Section 12.5 and prove that they are domains.

16. Let $F: D \to$ **Dom** and $G: \Sigma(D,F) \to$ **Dom** be continuous functors as described in Exercise 15. Define $\Sigma(F,G): D \to$ **Dom** and $\Pi(F,G): D \to$ **Dom** by

$$\Sigma(F,G)(x) = \Sigma(F(x), \lambda y.G(x,y))$$

and

$$\Pi(F,G)(x) = \Pi(F(x), \lambda y.G(x,y)).$$

(i) Make $\Sigma(F,G)$ and $\Pi(F,G)$ into functors by extending the above definitions to morphisms.
(ii) Prove that $\Sigma(F,G)$ and $\Pi(F,G)$ are continuous.

17. A *universal type* or a *universe* in the context of typed versions of the λ-calculus is an important tool for the purpose of typing programs or algorithms possessing varying degrees of *polymorphism* (as well as for metamathematical investigations). These are algorithms which are defined in the same way or by the same term on a variety of domains of definition, e.g. the *identity function* given by the untyped λ-term $\lambda x.x$. Having introduced a collection of type construction principles, the notion of an algorithm uniformly defined for all types given by these can be made meaningful by introducing a new type U. *Terms of type* U can be taken to be codes for all types constructed by previously defined constructions. There should also be a decoding function T, that is, T(a) should denote the type coded by $a \in U$.

    Thus an algorithm can be said to be *polymorphic relative to* U, if it has the form $\lambda x^U.M^{T(x)\to T(x)}$. Having discussed the question of modelling a typed version of the λ-calculus, it is natural to ask how one would model a universal type. One way of proceeding is to define, as before, a continuous construction which, given a collection of constant domains, constructs codes for the previously defined type constructions in question. A model for our universal type could then be taken to be a fixed point for the resulting construction.

    Define a *universe operator* (U,T) on PAR which, given an element (P,F) of PAR, produces a new element (U(P,F),T(P,F)) of PAR. U(P,F) should satisfy: for all $u \in U(P,F)$, if $F' : T(P,F)(u) \to rg(T(P,F))$ and $(T(P,F)(u), F')$ is a parametrization, then there exist $v, w \in U(P,F)$ such that $v = \Pi(T(P,F)(u), F')$ and $w = \Sigma(T(P,F)(u), F')$.
    (i) Make U(P,F) into a functor by extending the above definition to morphisms.
    (ii) Prove that U(P,F) is continuous and conclude that (U,T) has a fixed point.
    This fixed point can reasonably be called a family or *universe of precusl's closed under* Π and Σ. The reader interested in a detailed account of this and related results is referred to Palmgren [1993] and Palmgren and Stoltenberg-Hansen [1992].

REFERENCES

S. Abramsky

[1991] Domain theory in logical form, *Ann. Pure Appl. Logic* **51** (1991), 1–77.

M. A. Arbib and E. G. Manes

[1975] *Arrows, Structures and Functors*, Academic Press, New York, 1975.

A. Arnold and M. Nivat

[1980] Metric interpretations of infinite trees and semantics of nondeterministic recursive programs, *Theor. Comp. Sci* **11** (1980), 181–205.

H. P. Barendregt

[1984] *The Lambda Calculus, its Syntax and Semantics*, Studies in Logic 103, North-Holland, Amsterdam, 1984.

U. Berger

[1990] Totale Objekte und Mengen in der Bereichstheorie, *Doktorgrad thesis*, Ludwig-Maximilians-Universität München, 1990.

[1993] Total sets and objects in domain theory, *Ann. Pure Appl. Logic* **60** (1993), 91–117.

G. Berry

[1978] Stable models of typed λ-calculi, in: *Fifth International Colloquium on Automata, Languages and Programs* (G. Ausiello and C. Böhm eds.), Lecture Notes in Computer Science 62, Springer-Verlag, Berlin, 1978, 72–89.

G. S. Ceitin

[1967] Algorithmic operators in constructive metric spaces, *Trudy Mat. Inst. Steklov* **67** (English translation, *Amer. Math. Soc. Trans.*) **64** (1967), 1–80.

T. Coquand, C. Gunter and G. Winskel

[1989] Domain theoretic models of polymorphism, *Infor. and Comp.* **76** (1989), 123–167.

N. J. Cutland

[1980] *Computability: an introduction to recursive function theory*, Cambridge University Press, Cambridge, 1980.

J. W. de Bakker and J. I. Zucker

[1982] Processes and the denotational semantics of concurrency, *Infor. and Control* **54** (1982), 70–120.

J. Dugundji

[1966] *Topology*, Allyn and Bacon, Boston, 1966.

R. Engelking

[1968] *Outline of General Topology*, North-Holland, Amsterdam, 1968.

Y. L. Ershov

[1973] Theorie der Numerierungen I, *Z. Math. Logik Grundlagen Math.* **19** (1973), 289–388.

[1974] Maximal and everywhere defined functionals, *Algebra and Logic* **13** (1974), 374–397.

[1975] Theorie der Numerierungen II, *Z. Math. Logik Grundlagen Math.* **21** (1975), 473–584.

[1976] Hereditarily effective operations, *Algebra and Logic* **15** (1976), 642-654.

[1977] Theorie der Numerierungen III, *Z. Math. Logik Grundlagen Math.* **23** (1977), 289–371.

[1977a] The model C of the partial continuous functionals, in: *Logic Colloquium 76*, (R. O. Gandy and J. M. E. Hyland eds.), Studies in Logic 87, North-Holland, Amsterdam, 1977, 455–467.

M. P. Fourman and R. J. Grayson

[1982] Formal Spaces, in: *Heyting Symposium* (A. Troelstra and D. van Dalen eds.), North-Holland, Amsterdam, 1982, 455–467.

M. Fréchet

[1906] Sur Quelques Points du Calcul Fonctionnel, *Rendiconti di Palermo* **22** (1906), 1–74.

A. Fröhlich and J. C. Shepherdson

[1956] Effective procedures in field theory, *Phil. Trans. Royal Soc. London* **(A)** **248** (1956), 407–432.

R. O. Gandy

[1980] An early proof of normalisation by A.M. Turing, in: *To H.B. Curry: Essays on Combinatory Logic, Lambda-Calculus and Formalism* (J. R. Hindley and J. P. Seldin eds.), Academic Press, New York and London, 1980, 453–456.

G. Gierz, K. H. Hofmann, K. Keimel, J. D. Lawson, M. Mislove and D. S. Scott

[1980] *A Compendium of Continuous Lattices*, Springer-Verlag, Berlin, 1980.

J. Y. Girard

[1986] System F: fifteen years later, *Theor. Comp. Sci.* **45** (1986), 159–192.

[1989] *Proofs and Types*, Cambridge Tracts in Computer Science 7, Cambridge University Press, Cambridge, 1989.

M. J. C. Gordon

[1979] *The Denotational Description of Programming Languages, An Introduction*, Springer-Verlag, Berlin, 1979.

C. A. Gunter

[1987] Universal Profinite Domains, *Infor. and Comp.* **72** (1987), 1–30.

J. R. Hindley and J. P. Seldin

[1986] *Introduction to Combinators and λ-calculus*, London Mathematical Society Student Texts 1, Cambridge University Press, Cambridge, 1986.

P. T. Johnstone

[1982] *Stone Spaces*, Cambridge Studies in Advanced Mathematics 3, Cambridge University Press, Cambridge, 1982.

A. Jung

[1989] *Cartesian Closed Categories of Domains*, CWI Tracts 66, Centrum voor Wiskunde en Informatica, Amsterdam, 1989.

J. L. Kelley

[1950] The Tychonoff product theorem implies the axiom of choice, *Fund. Math.* **37** (1950), 75–76.

[1955] *General Topology*, Van Nostrand, Princeton, 1955.

S. C. Kleene

[1952] *Introduction to Metamathematics*, North-Holland, Amsterdam, 1952.

[1959] Countable functionals, in: *Constructivity in Mathematics* (A. Heyting ed.), Studies in Logic, North-Holland, Amsterdam, 1959, 81–100.

G. Kreisel

[1959] Interpretation of analysis by means of constructive functionals of finite types, in: *Constructivity in Mathematics* (A. Heyting ed.), Studies in Logic, North-Holland, Amsterdam, 1959, 101–128.

G. Kreisel, D. Lacombe and J. R. Shoenfield

[1959] Partial recursive functionals and effective operations, in: *Constructivity in Mathematics* (A. Heyting ed.), Studies in Logic, North-Holland, Amsterdam, 1959, 195–207.

K. G. Larsen and G. Winskel

[1984] Using information systems to solve domain equations effectively, in: *Semantics of Data Types* (G. Kahn, D. B. MacQueen and G. Plotkin eds.), Springer Lecture Notes in Computer Science 173, Springer-Verlag, Berlin, 1984, 109–129.

M. Machtey and P. Young

[1978] *An Introduction to the General Theory of Algorithms*, North-Holland, Amsterdam, 1978.

S. Maclane

[1971] *Categories for the Working Mathematician*, Graduate Texts in Mathematics 5, Springer-Verlag, Berlin, 1971.

A. I. Mal'cev

[1960] Constructive algebras I, in: *The Metamathematics of Algebraic Systems. Collected Papers: 1936–1967* (B. F. Wells III ed.), North-Holland, Amsterdam, 1960, 148–212.

P. Martin-Löf

[1984] *Intuitionistic Type Theory*, Studies in Proof Theory 1, Bibliopolis, Napoli, 1984.

A. R. Meyer

[1982] What is a model of the λ-calculus?, *Infor. and Control* **52** (1982), 87–122.

Y. N. Moschovakis

[1964] Recursive metric spaces, *Fund. Math.* **55** (1964), 215–238.

M. Nivat

[1975] On the interpretation of polyadic recursive program schemes, *Sympos. Math.* **15** (1975), 255–281.

D. Normann

[1980] *Recursion on the Countable Functionals*, Lecture Notes in Mathematics 811, Springer-Verlag, 1980.

P. Odifreddi

[1989] *Classical Recursion Theory*, North-Holland, Amsterdam, 1989.

E. Palmgren

[1993] An information system interpretation of Martin-Löf's partial type theory with universes, *Infor. and Comp.* **106** (1993), 26–60.

E. Palmgren and V. Stoltenberg-Hansen

[1990] Domain interpretations of Martin-Löf's partial type theory, *Ann. Pure App. Logic* **48** (1990), 135–196.

[1992] Remarks on Martin-Löf's partial type theory, *BIT* **32** (1992), 70–83.

G. Plotkin

[1976] A powerdomain construction, *SIAM J. Comput.* **5** (1976), 452–488.

[1981] *Post-Graduate Lecture Notes in Advanced Domain Theory* (incorporating the "Pisa Notes"), Department of Computer Science, University of Edinburgh, 1981.

M. O. Rabin

[1960] Computable algebra, general theory and theory of computable fields, *Trans. Am. Math. Soc.* **95** (1960), 341–360.

H. Rogers

[1967] *Theory of Recursive Functions and Effective Computability*, McGraw-Hill, New York, 1967.

G. Sambin

[1987] Intuitionistic formal spaces, in: *Mathematical Logic and its Applications* (D. Skordev ed.), Plenum Press, New York, 1987, 187–204.

D. S. Scott

[1972] Continuous lattices, in: *Toposes, Algebraic Geometry and Logic* (F. W. Lawvere ed.), Springer Lecture Notes in Mathematics 274, Springer-Verlag, Berlin, 1972, 97–136.

[1976] Data types as lattices, *SIAM Jour. Comp.* **5** (1976), 522–587.

[1980] Relating theories of the λ-calculus, in: *To H. B. Curry, Essays on Combinatory Logic, Lambda Calculus and Formalism* (J. R. Hindley and J. P. Seldin eds.), Academic Press, New York, 1980, 403–450.

[1982] Lecture notes on a mathematical theory of computation, in: *Theoretical Foundations of Programming Methodology* (M. Broy and G. Schmidt eds.), Reidel, Dordrecht, 1982, 145–292.

[1982a] Domains for denotational semantics, in: *Proceedings ICALP 1982* (M. Nielsen and E. M. Schmidt eds.), Springer Lecture Notes in Computer Science 140, Springer-Verlag, Berlin, 1982, 577–613.

I. Sigstam

[1990] On formal spaces and their effective presentations, *Ph.D. thesis*, Uppsala University, 1990.

M. B. Smyth

[1978] Power domains, *J. Comp. Syst. Sci.* **16** (1978), 23–36.

[1983] The largest cartesian closed category of domains, *Theor. Comp. Sci.* **27** (1983), 109–119.

[1983] Powerdomains and predicate transformers: a topological view, in: *Automata, Languages and Programming* (J. Diaz ed.), Lecture Notes in Computer Science 154, Springer-Verlag, Berlin, 1983, 662–675.

[1988] Quasi uniformities: reconciling domains with metric spaces, in: *Mathematical Foundations of Programming Language Semantics* (A. M. Main, A. Melton, M. Mislove and D. Schmidt eds.), Lecture Notes in Computer Science 298, Springer-Verlag, Berlin, 1988, 236–253.

M. B. Smyth and G. D. Plotkin

[1982] The category-theoretic solution of recursive domain equations, *SIAM J. Comput.* **11** (1982), 761–783.

R. I. Soare

[1987] *Recursively Enumerable Sets and Degrees*, Perspectives in Mathematical Logic, Springer-Verlag, Berlin, 1987.

D. Spreen and P. Young

[1984] Effective operators in a topological setting, in: *Computation and Proof Theory: Proceedings of the Logic Colloquium '83* (M. M. Richter et al. eds.), Springer Lecture Notes in Mathematics 1104, Springer-Verlag, 1984, 437–451.

V. Stoltenberg-Hansen and J. V. Tucker

[1988] Complete local rings as domains, *J. Symbolic Logic* **53** (1988), 603–624.

[1991] Algebraic and fixed point equations over inverse limits of algebras, *Theor. Comp. Sci.* **87** (1991), 1–24.

J. E. Stoy

[1977] *Denotational semantics: the Scott-Strachey approach to programming languages*, MIT Press, Cambridge, Mass., 1977.

R. D. Tennant

[1981] *Principles of Programming Languages*, Prentice-Hall International Series in Computer Science, Prentice-Hall International, Englewood Cliffs, 1981.

A. S. Troelstra

[1973] *Metamathematical Investigation of Intuitionistic Arithmetic and Analysis*, Lecture Notes in Mathematics 344, Springer-Verlag, Berlin, 1973.

S. Vickers

[1989] *Topology via Logic*, Cambridge Tracts in Theoretical Computer Science 5, Cambridge University Press, Cambridge, 1989.

S. Willard

[1970] *General Topology*, Addison-Wesley Series in Mathematics, Addison-Wesley, 1970.

INDEX OF SYMBOLS

INDEX